The Reception of Virginia Woolf in Europe

The Athlone Critical Traditions Series:
The Reception of British Authors in Europe

Series Editor: Elinor Shaffer,
School of Advanced Study, University of London

Forthcoming volumes in the series include:

The Reception of James Joyce in Europe
Edited by Geert Lernout

The Reception of William Beckford in Europe
Edited by John Wilton-Ely and Elinor Shaffer

The Reception of Laurence Sterne in Europe
Edited by Peter De Voogd and John Neubauer

The Athlone Critical Traditions Series:
The Reception of British Authors in Europe

Series Editor: Elinor Shaffer
School of Advanced Study, University of London

The Reception of Virginia Woolf in Europe

Edited by Mary Ann Caws
and Nicola Luckhurst

continuum
LONDON • NEW YORK

Continuum
The Tower Building, 11 York Road, London, SE1 7NX
370 Lexington Avenue, New York, NY 10017-6503

First published 2002

British Library Cataloguing-in-Publication Data
A catalogue record for this book is available from the British Library.

ISBN 0-8264-5588-3 (hardback)

Library of Congress Cataloging-in-Publication Data
The reception of Virginia Woolf in Europe/edited by Mary Ann Caws and Nicola Luckhurst.
p. cm. — (The Athlone critical traditions series: the reception of British authors in Europe)
Includes bibliographical references and index.
ISBN 0–8264–5588–3
1. Woolf, Virginia, 1882–1941—Criticism and interpretation—History. 2. Woolf, Virginia, 1882–1941—Appreciation—Europe. 3. English fiction—Appreciation—Europe. I. Caws, Mary Ann. II. Luckhurst, Nicola. III. Series.

PR6045.O72 Z8644 2001
823′.912—dc21 2001028836

Typeset by BookEns Ltd., Royston, Herts.
Printed and bound in Great Britain by
MPG Books Ltd, Bodmin, Cornwall

Contents

Series Editor's Preface

The reception of British authors in Britain has in good part been studied; indeed, it forms our literary history. By contrast, the reception of British authors in Europe has not been examined in any systematic, long-term or large-scale way.

It is the aim of this Series to initiate and forward the study of the reception of British authors in Continental Europe, or, as we would now say, the rest of Europe. This is part of the grander task of considering the history and culture of Europe as a whole, rather than as isolated national histories with a narrow national perspective. The perspectives of other nations greatly add to our understanding of individual contributors to that history. The history of the reception of British authors extends our knowledge of their capacity to stimulate and to call forth new responses, not only in their own disciplines but in wider fields and to diverse publics in a variety of historical circumstances. Often these responses provide quite unexpected and enriching insights into our own history, politics and culture. Individual works and personalities take on new dimensions and facets. They may also be subject to enlightening critiques. Our knowledge of British writers is simply incomplete and inadequate without these reception studies.

By 'authors' we intend writers in any field whose works have been recognized as making a contribution to the intellectual and cultural history of our society. Thus the Series includes literary figures, such as Byron and Virginia Woolf, philosophers such as Francis Bacon and David Hume, historians and political figures such as Edmund Burke, and scientists such as Charles Darwin, whose works have had a broad impact on thinking in every field. In some cases individual works of the same author have dealt with different subjects, each with virtually its own reception history; so Burke's *Reflections on the French Revolution* (1790) was instantaneously translated and moulded thinking on the power struggles in the Europe of his own day; his youthful 'Essay on the Feeling of the Beautiful and Sublime' exerted a powerful influence on aesthetic thought and the practice of writing and remains a seminal work for certain genres of fiction; his only just collected parliamentary speeches on, for example, the Indian question will now be re-examined in the light of the subsequent history of the European presence overseas and of current attitudes towards it.

The research project examines the ways in which selected authors have been translated, published, distributed, read, reviewed and discussed on the continent of Europe. In doing so it throws light not only on specific strands of intellectual and cultural history but also on the processes involved in the dissemination of ideas and of texts. The project brings to bear the theoretical and critical approaches that have characterized the growing fields of reader response theory and reception studies in the last quarter of a century. These critical approaches have illuminated the activity of the reader in bringing the text to life and stressed the changing horizons of the reading public or community of which the reader is a part. The project also takes cognizance of the material studies of the history of the book that have begun to explore the production, publication and distribution of manuscripts and books. Increasingly, other media too are playing a role in these processes. The Series as published by Continuum Books is open-ended and multi-volumed, each volume based upon a particular author. The authors may be regarded according to their discipline, or looked at across disciplines within their period. Thus the philosophers Bacon and Hume may be compared; or Hume may be considered as belonging to an eighteenth-century group that includes writers like Swift and Sterne, historians and political figures such as Gibbon and Burke. In period terms one may discern a Romantic group; a Victorian group; a *fin-de-siècle* and early Modernist group. Period designations differ from discipline to discipline, and are shifting even within a discipline: Blake, who was a 'Pre-Romantic' poet a generation ago, is now considered a fully fledged Romantic; Virginia Woolf may be regarded as a *fin-de-siècle* aesthete whose affinities are with Walter Pater or as an epoch-making Modernist like Eliot or Joyce. Terms referring to period and style often vary from country to country. What happens to a 'Victorian' author transplanted to 'Wilhelmine' Germany? Are the English Metaphysical poets to be regarded as 'baroque' in continental terms? It is most straightforward to classify them simply according to century, for the calendar is for the most part shared. But the various possible groupings will provide a context for reception and enrich our knowledge of each author.

Division of each volume by country or by linguistic region is dictated by the historical development of Europe; each volume necessarily adopts a different selection of countries and regions, depending on period and on the specific reception of any given author. Countries or regions are treated either substantially, in several chapters or sections where this is warranted, for example, the French reception of Woolf, or on a moderate scale, or simply as a brief section. In some cases, where a rich reception is located that has not been reported or of which the critical community is not aware, more detailed coverage may be justified, for example, the reception of Woolf in the different linguistic communities of the Iberian peninsula. In general, comparative studies have neglected Spain in favour of France, Germany and Italy, and this imbalance needs to be righted. Where separate coverage of any particular country or region is not justified by the extent of the reception, relevant material is incorporated into the bibliography and the Timeline. Thus an early translation may be noted, although there was subsequently a minimal response to the author or work, or a very long gap in the reception in that region.

This kind of material will be fully described in the database (see below). It is, of course, always possible, and indeed to be hoped and expected, that further aspects of reception will later be uncovered, and the long-term research project forwarded, through this initial information. Reception studies often display an author's intellectual and political impact and reveal effects abroad that are unfamiliar to the authors' compatriots. Thus, Byron, for example, had the power of carrying and incarnating liberal political thought to regimes and institutions to whom it was anathema; and Virginia Woolf came to be an icon for women writers in countries where there was little tradition of women's writing. By the same token the study of censorship, or more broadly impediments to dissemination, and of modes of circumventing control, becomes an important aspect of reception studies. In Bacon studies, the process of dissemination of his ideas through the private correspondence of organized circles was vital. Certain presses and publishers also play a role, and the study of modes of secret distribution under severe penalty is a particularly fascinating subject, whether in Catholic Europe or Soviet Russia. Irony and aesopian devices are highly developed under controlling regimes. A surprising number of authors live more dangerously abroad than at home.

New electronic technology makes it possible to undertake reception studies on this scale. An extensive database stores information about editions, translations, accompanying critical prefaces or afterwords, illustrations, biographies and correspondence, early reviews, important essays and book-length studies of the authors, and comments, citations and imitations or reworkings, including satire and pastiche by other writers. Some authors achieve the status of fictional characters in other writers' works. The recording of full details of translations and translators is a particular concern, since often the names of translators are not supplied, or their identity is concealed behind pseudonyms or false attributions. The nature of the translation is often a determining factor in the reception of a work or an author. The database also records the character and location of rare works. Selected texts and passages are included, together with English translations. The database can be searched for a variety of further purposes, potentially yielding a more complete picture of the interactions of writers, translators, critics, publishers and public across Europe in different periods from the Renaissance to the present.

Dr Elinor Shaffer, FBA
Director, Research Project
Reception of British Authors in Europe

Acknowledgements

The Research Project on the Reception of British Authors in Europe is happy to acknowledge the support of the British Academy, the Leverhulme Foundation, the Arts and Humanities Research Board and the European Science Foundation. We are also greatly indebted to the School of Advanced Study, University of London, where the project is based; and in particular to the Dean, Terence Daintith, for his unfailing support and his acute advice, and to the Institute of English Studies, Institute of Germanic Studies and Institute of Romance Studies, which collaborated with us in the colloquium on 'Virginia Woolf: Her Reception in Europe', held at the School of Advanced Study in October 1998, that first brought the contributors together. We also acknowledge gratefully the good counsel of the Advisory Board of the project, which has met twice a year since its inception. We would also like to acknowledge the invaluable services of Dr Paul Barnaby, Research Fellow to the project, who carried out additional research into Woolf's European presence, and extended the bibliographies of the volume, as well as constructing the Timeline. The editors of this volume owe a great debt to Dr Barnaby. We would also like to thank the assistants on the project, Charlotte Pattison and Benedetta Bassetti, whose administrative, linguistic and technological skills have been indispensable to the establishment of the project and its efficient running.

List of Contributors

Graça Abranches is a researcher in the Centre for Social Studies, University of Coimbra, Portugal. From 1975 to 2000 she was lecturer in English Literature and Feminist Studies in the Faculty of Arts, University of Coimbra. She has published numerous articles and essays on nineteenth-century and modernist women's fiction, feminist theory and criticism, discourse and power, gender and education. She edited a bilingual anthology of Portuguese women poets *Escrever do avesso/Writing in Reverse* (1997) and has two books in print *Já Garrett dizia que os sexos eram três . . .* and *O lugar do avesso: ensaios de critica feminista*.

Mary Ann Caws is Distinguished Professor of English, French and Comparative Literature, Graduate Center, City University of New York; Past President of the Modern Language Association of America; Guggenheim Fellow, Fulbright Fellow, Rockefeller Foundation (Bellagio); National Endowment for the Humanities Senior Fellow, Getty Scholar, life member of Clare Hall, Cambridge University; author, editor, translator: *Surrealism and the Literary Imagination, The Poetry of Dada and Surrealism, The Inner Theatre of Recent French Poetry, The Eye in the Text: Essays on Perception, Mannerist to Modern, A Metapoetics of the Passage: Architextures Surrealist and After, Reading Frames in Modern Fiction, The Art of Interference: Stressed Readings in Visual and Verbal Texts, Women of Bloomsbury: Virginia, Vanessa, and Carrington, The Surrealist Look: An Erotics of Encounter, Surrealism and the Art of Display, Picasso's Weeping Woman: The Life and Art of Dora Maar*; monographs on André Breton, René Char, Pierre Reverdy, Robert Desnos, Edmond Jabes, Robert Motherwell, Yves Bonnefoy, Virginia Woolf, Marcel Proust; editor of *Surrealist Painters and Poets, Manifesto: A Century of Isms, Vita Sackville-West: Selected Writings, Surrealist Love Poems.*

María José Gámez Fuentes is a Lecturer in the Department of English and Romance Philology at the Universitat Jaume I, Castellón. She graduated from the University of Valencia and did both her MA and PhD in Critical Theory and Cultural Studies at the University of Nottingham (UK). She has published widely in the field of cultural and gender studies.

Jacqueline A. Hurtley is a Professor of English Literature at the University of Barcelona, where she has worked since 1971. She has degrees in Spanish with Italian and English. She published *Josep Janés. El combat per la cultura* in 1986 and *Josep Janés: editor de literatura inglesa* in 1992, which was awarded the Enrique García y Díez Research Prize by the Spanish Association for Anglo-American Studies (AEDEAN). She contributed to *Ireland in Writing: Interviews with Writers and Academics* (1998). She is currently working on a biography of the founder of the British Council in Spain, Walter Starkie.

Katerina K. Kitsi-Mitakou is a Lecturer in the Department of English at the Aristotle University of Thessaloniki, Greece. Her PhD thesis on Virginia Woolf has been published as a book under the title *Feminist Readings of the Body in Virginia Woolf's Novels* (Thessaloniki 1997). She has published in the fields of modernism, feminist theory and criticism, nineteenth-century English fiction and theories of the body.

Ida Klitgård is an External Lecturer in English at the Department of English, University of Copenhagen. She holds a degree in English and Translation Studies and finished her doctoral studies in English Literature at the University of Copenhagen, Denmark, in 2000. She has also studied American literary history in the USA, received an MPhil in Modernist Studies at Glasgow University, and taught English at two Danish universities. Her thesis explores a modernist poetics of the sublime in Virginia Woolf's *The Waves*, with emphasis on the construction of figurative language and leitmotifs. She has published articles on James Joyce and Virginia Woolf, including critiques of Danish translations of *Ulysses* and *The Waves*. She is also the co-author of a major English-Danish dictionary, translator of a book on James Joyce, and reviewer of translated prose for the national journal *Information*.

Alberto Lázaro is a Senior Lecturer in English Literature at the University of Alcalá (Madrid), where he has been teaching twentieth-century English literature since 1987. He holds a PhD in English philology from the University of Valladolid (1985) and has done extensive research on twentieth-century British fiction. His publications include books on *The Thought and Work of George Orwell* (1987), *New Myths in Contemporary English Literature* (1992), *Colonialism and Post-colonialism in English Literature* (1994) and numerous articles and essays on various writers including H. G. Wells, T. S. Eliot, James Joyce, John Braine, John Wain, Tom Sharpe, Rose Tremain and William Boyd. He is currently a national contributor for the *Annotated Bibliography for English Studies*, writing reviews of Spanish scholarship on twentieth-century English poetry and fiction.

Laura María Lojo Rodríguez is a Lecturer in English literature at the Department of English, University of Santiago de Compostela (Spain), where she has taught for four years. Her PhD thesis was on Virginia Woolf's short fiction, and she has published several articles on the same topic, as well as on Milton, T. S. Eliot, Elizabeth Bowen, Frank O'Connor and short fiction theory. At present, she is working on a critical edition which compiles translations from

English into Galician from Irish short fiction writers, such as Lady Gregory, W. B. Yeats, James Joyce, Frank O'Connor and Elizabeth Bowen.

Nicola Luckhurst is a Lecturer in Literature at Goldsmiths College, London. A graduate of St John's College, Oxford, where she also completed her DPhil (1996), she has published on Marcel Proust (*Science and Structure in Proust's 'À la recherche du temps perdu'* (2000); 'Proust's Beard', in *Dying Words: The Last Moments of Writers and Philosophers* (2000)) and Virginia Woolf (*Bloomsbury in 'Vogue'* (1998); '"To quote my quotation from Montaigne"', in *Virginia Woolf: Reading the Renaissance* (1999); *Virginia Woolf in Camera*, co-authored with Martine Ravache (2000)), and co-edited a collection of the letters of Stéphane Mallarmé (1998). She has translated Freud's *Studies in Hysteria* and is completing a study of the photographer and writer, Gisèle Freund.

Laura Marcus is Reader in English at the University of Sussex. Her publications include *Auto/biographical Discourses: Theory, Criticism, Practice* (1994), *Virginia Woolf: Writers and Their Work* (1997) and, as editor, *Culture, Modernity and 'the Jew'* (1998), *Close Up: Cinema and Modernism* (1998) and Sigmund Freud's *The Interpretation of Dreams: New Interdisciplinary Essays* (1999). She is a contributor to *The Cambridge Companion to Virginia Woolf*, author of numerous essays on nineteenth- and twentieth-century literature and culture, and co-editor of the journal *Women: a Cultural Review*. She is currently writing a book on cinema, modernism and early film aesthetics, entitled *The Tenth Muse: Cinema and Modernism*.

Ansgar Nünning has been Professor of English and American Literary and Cultural Studies at the Justus-Liebig-University of Giessen since 1996, following a ten-year period as lecturer and assistant professor at the University of Cologne. He is the author of books on the functions of the narrator in George Eliot's novels (1989), on Virginia Woolf's nonfictional prose (1991, co-authored with Vera Nünning), on historical fiction and historiographic metafiction (1995), on eighteenth-century English literature (1998, co-authored with Vera Nünning), on the twentieth-century English novel (1998) and of an introduction to English studies for German students (1999). He has edited an introductory volume on literary theories, models and methods (1995), a history of English literature, a collection of essays on unreliable narration (1998), a volume entitled *Intercultural Studies: Fictions of Empire* (1996), an encyclopedia of literary and cultural theory (1998, 2nd rev. edn 2001), and an issue on Postmodern Parody of *EJES: European Journal of English Studies* 3.2 (1999). He is also one of the advisory editors of the volume *German Studies in English* of the Annotated Bibliography for English Studies, a member of the editorial committee of *Orbis Litterarum*, and one of the editors of *EJES: European Journal of English Studies*. His articles on narrative theory, historiographic metafiction, the street ballad, the eighteenth- and twentieth-century English novel, poetry of the Nineties, Virginia Woolf, Peter Ackroyd, Julian Barnes, Peter Carey, J. G. Farrell, John Fowles, Ian McEwan, Peter Shaffer, Stevie Smith, Graham Swift and literary and cultural theory have appeared in numerous scholarly journals and collections of essays.

Vera Nünning has been Professor of English Literary and Cultural Studies at the University of Brunswick since 2000, following a ten-year period as lecturer and assistant professor at the University of Cologne. She is the author of books on Virginia Woolf's aesthetics (1990), on Virginia Woolf's nonfictional prose (1991), on eighteenth-century English literature (1998), on Catharine Macaulay and the political culture of English radicalism (1998), on the nineteenth-century English novel (2000) and of an introduction to American history for German students (1998). Together with Ansgar Nünning she has edited German editions of the letters of Junius (1989) and of Aphra Behn's *Oroonoko* (1990) as well as a volume entitled *Intercultural Studies: Fictions of Empire* (1996) and collections of essays on the twentieth-century English novel (1998) and on multiperspectivism in the English novel (2000). Other publications include articles on Elizabeth I, Aphra Behn, Henry Fielding, Oliver Goldsmith, eighteenth-century historiography, the culture of sensibility, eighteenth-century British cultural history, literature and imperialism, the aesthetics of the Nineties and Virginia Woolf.

Manuela Palacios is a Professor of English Literature at the University of Santiago de Compostela (Spain). She has published her PhD dissertation on the visual imagery in Woolf's writing (*Virginia Woolf y la pintura*, Santiago 1992) and translated Woolf's *To the Lighthouse* into Galician. In addition she has written various articles on the intertextuality of literature and painting or film, as well as on translation studies. She is currently working on a book about modernist women poets in Britain.

Françoise Pellan is a Professor of Modern English Literature at the University of Burgundy (Dijon). Her publications include: a critical study of Virginia Woolf's works (essays and fiction): *Virginia Woolf. L'ancrage et le voyage* (1994), and a translation and critical edition of *To the Lighthouse: Vers le Phare* (1996).

Sergio Perosa is a Professor of Anglo-American Literature and Chair of the Department of Anglo-American and Latin-American Studies at the University of Venice, where he also served as Dean of the Faculty of Modern Languages. A former President of the European Association for American Studies, he has published: in the USA, *The Art of F. S. Fitzgerald* (1965), *Henry James and the Experimental Novel* (1978), *American Theories of the Novel, 1793-1903* (1984); in Italy, *Vie della narrativa americana* (1980), *Storia del teatro americano* (1982), *Le isole Aran* (1987), *Bagliori dal Commonwealth* (1991), *L'isola la donna il ritratto* (1996) (*From Islands to Portraits*, 2000), translations and/or editions of Shakespeare, Virginia Woolf, Henry James, Herman Melville, John Berryman and others.

Carole Rodier holds a doctorate on Woolf (*L'Imaginaire woolfien*, Editions du Temps, Paris, 2001, with a preface by J. Guiget). She teaches at Brasenose College, Oxford. She is the treasurer of the Société d'Études Woolfiennes, a member of the École de Grenoble and of a team (SEMA) at the ENS-Lyon. She has published several articles on Woolf, as well as on Katherine Mansfield, Paul Auster, Walter Scott, Shakespeare (as part of the Agrégation syllabus), Arthur Miller and Beckett, and a review of Juan Marsé. She is the editor of the magazine *Théâtre du Monde*. She has co-organized two symposia on Woolf and has worked as a literary adviser on behalf of the Woolf Estate.

Catherine Sandbach-Dahlström is a graduate of Somerville College, Oxford, and Reader in English Literature at Stockholm University. She is the author of *Be Good Sweet Maid: Charlotte Yonge's Domestic Fiction* and of a number of articles on feminist criticism and on historicism, as well as on Virginia Woolf's work. She is in the process of completing a book entitled *Conversing about Collusion: Virginia Woolf and the Sexual Politics of Criticism.*

Urszula Terentowicz-Fotyga is a Lecturer in English Literature at Maria Curie-Sklodowska University in Lublin. Currently, she is finishing her doctoral thesis on spatial models of inner and outer worlds in Virginia Woolf's novels. She publishes on Woolf and Beckett. Her other area of interest is the motif of madness in contemporary literature.

Pierre-Éric Villeneuve obtained a PhD in Semiotics from the University of Quebec at Montreal, and has taught at the University of Toronto and Brock University. He has published several articles on Virginia Woolf in various periodicals, in both French and English, and recently completed a book manuscript on Woolf and her letter-writing practice entitled *Everyday Woolf: The Invention of Life in Letters.*

Wolfgang Wicht studied English and Russian at the universities of Greifswald and Rostock. He was a lecturer at Rostock and in 1984 was appointed Professor of English Literature at the University of Potsdam, specializing in Shakespeare (doctoral dissertation) and twentieth-century English literature. He has published papers on Shakespeare, Yeats, Eliot, Woolf, Joyce, Heaney and others. Since his early retirement in 1993 he has written *Utopianism in James Joyce's* Ulysses (2000).

Preface: Virginia Woolf's Crossings

Where shall we go? How happy I am.

Virginia Woolf, *Diary*, 11 March 1935

These essays, prepared by a wide range of scholars from different countries in Europe, attempt to address both the general question of how Virginia Woolf is received, translated and evaluated in the various parts of Europe, and the differing local questions, problems and solutions. Many issues arise here, both personal and political: censorship and adaptation, publicity and image, style of writing and style of translation. Upon these and other elements depend the acceptance in the various countries concerned of Woolf the person and Woolf the author, over the years. It is the evolution of that acceptance that all of us in our separate studies are tracing here, with its ramifications in the field loosely known as European modernism, of which Woolf is one of the principal icons.

Very often, the reception of such a larger-than-life, globally important figure depends on the possible resemblance with a like figure on the local scene. To take a very few examples: in Spain, Woolf is sometimes compared to Azorín, sometimes to T. S. Eliot, to Katherine Mansfield and sometimes to the romantics, and especially Wordsworth, whereas in America, she is compared to Emily Dickinson – a very different comparison indeed. Of course, the reception of James Joyce often runs parallel to that of Woolf, as being the two leading high modernist writers, and several of these essays deal with that parallel.

As, in non-English speaking countries, translation sometimes precedes reception, and the translating style itself greatly influences the way in which Woolf's works are read, many of these essays deal with the pragmatic and ideological aspects of both translation and message, or style and content. How do we translate modernism? That question could be inscribed over any particular attempt at rendering the work of Virginia Woolf intelligible in a tongue not its own, and yet not losing its sting, its irony or its style. It is clearly the case that the political climate controls what texts can be and are translated in what moment, and thus it is to be expected that the more 'modernist' works will be later in coming to lands like Denmark and Poland, where modernism arrives with a certain delay, and earlier in lands like France. For example, in a country with deeply rooted religious traditions and where political pressures are strongest, such manifesto-type works as *A Room of One's Own* meet more resistance, and Woolf's more modernist works, such as *Mrs Dalloway*, *To the*

Lighthouse, and *The Waves* are slower to be accepted into the canon. The issue of realist and anti-realist aesthetics goes past the realm of the simple aesthetic, into that of the general politico-literary climate.

In the 1990s, with its emphasis on the personal, Woolf was taken as a spokeswoman for the woman writer: representative, admired and loved. In every country, the climate of receptiveness or refusal of feminism has always been the primary component of the reception of Virginia Woolf, known above all as its spokesperson. But by now the climate permits greater subtleties of interpretation and reinterpretation, even with the received wisdom about such opposed approaches to life as that of Mrs Ramsay and Lily Briscoe, in *To the Lighthouse*. In more recent years, Woolf's particular brand of feminism has met with less distrust, and – despite the occasional resistance to her 'upperclassness' and her very 'Englishness' – her work and what in it was once silenced, or muted, from Galicia to Greece, is now welcomed. The birds of *The Waves* start to sing in all the tongues in which Woolf has been translated, and all over Europe.

About the difficulties of translating many of Woolf's works, some of these essays speak feelingly. In many cases, it is the translators themselves who have written the essays, so we are privileged to see the matter at minimal distance. The central and general issue of how we translate modernist texts in their varied techniques has definite implications for the more local discussions of fidelity to sound and rhythm of a specific language, to the concreteness of its images and to its particular brand of wit. Clearly, the translation of such experimental texts is already an issue, especially in the case of *Orlando*, for its revolutionary illustration of gender change, and *Flush* for its doglife-writing. Woolf's characteristic style can be stressed and exaggerated, as was the case in Italy, with the translations of the celebrated Giulia Celenza, translator of Shakespeare and Swinburne, or played down, as was later done, muting her revolutionary experimentalism. This is again a case of dumbing down the birds. When one superb translation appears, the text can be retranslated, as often happens, but there is a single rendering that sticks in the mind. As a model case of two opposite translations, we might take Cecile Wajsbrot's French translation of *The Waves*, which has none of the seductive infidelities of Marguerite Yourcenar's rendering, and which captures much of Woolf's own subtlety. Well-known writers translating may take, wrongly or rightly, liberties that others may not feel fitting. The task of the translator, to invoke Walter Benjamin only in passing, is not the same as that of a writer; the privilege and the duty of one and the other are distinct.

All of us gathered in these pages have felt it both our duty and our privilege to present the widest range possible of the various reactions of translators, interpreters, critics and readers to the reception of the writer who for us best makes concrete, represents and exalts not only modernism and feminism, but that joy in and vigour of living manifest in the epigraph, both in its question that we might all ask: 'where shall we go?' and its possible and positive sequel.

Mary Ann Caws
City University of New York

Timeline: European Reception of Virginia Woolf

Year	Translations	Criticism	Other
1923–25			**France**: Participation of Bloomsbury Group in 'Entretiens de Pontigny'
1926	**France:** First Woolf translation – 'Time Passes' by Charles Mauron in *Commerce*		
1926–27	**Switzerland:** Extracts from *Jacob's Room* in the *Bibliothèque universelle et Revue de Genève*		
1927	**First Swedish translation:** *Jacob's Room* **France:** extracts from *Jacob's Room* in the *Revue Nouvelle* and the *Revue Bleue*	**France:** Jacques Émile Blanche's 'Entretien avec Virginia Woolf' in *Nouvelles littéraires* **Italy:** Carlo Linati's essay on Woolf in the *Corriere della Sera*	
1928	**First German translation:** *Mrs Dalloway*	**Spain:** Antonio Marichalar introduces Woolf in an article on Lytton Strachey in the *Revista de Occidente*	**France:** Woolf awarded Prix Fémina-Vie-Heureuse-Anglais for *To the Lighthouse*
1929	**First Czech translation:** *Orlando* **France:** *Mrs Dalloway* and *To the Lighthouse* **Germany:** *Orlando*	**France:** Louis Gillet's review of *Orlando* in the *Revue des deux mondes*	
1930	**First Catalan translation:** *Mrs Dalloway* (by Cèsar-August Jordana)	**France:** Jean Jacques Mayoux's 'Le Roman de l'espace et du temps: Virginia Woolf', in the *Revue anglo-américaine* **Italy:** Mario Praz's review of *A Room of One's Own* in *La Stampa*	

Year	Translations	Criticism	Other
1931	**First Spanish translation:** 'Time Passes' in the *Revista de Occidente* (anon.) **France:** Charles Mauron's *Orlando* **Germany:** *To the Lighthouse*		
1932		**France:** Floris Delattre's *Le Roman psychologique de Virginia Woolf* **Germany:** Ingeborg Badenhasen's *Die Sprache Virginia Woolfs*	
1933	**First Italian translation:** *Orlando* **France:** *Night and Day*		
1934	**First Latvian translation:**'Time Passes' in journal *Daugava* **Germany:** *Flush* **Italy:** *To the Lighthouse* (introd. Emilio Cecchi)	**Spain:** Victoria Ocampo's *Carta a Virginia Woolf* in the *Revista de Occidente*	**London:** Meeting of Woolf and Victoria Ocampo
1935	**France:** Charles Mauron's *Flush*	**Germany:** Ruth Gruber's *Virginia Woolf: A Study*	**London:** Woolf participates in the 'Congrès des Écrivains' **Spain:** Intertextual presence of Woolf in Ramón Otero Pedrayo's Galician novel *Devalar*
1935–36	**Argentina:** Jorge Luis Borges's translation of *A Room of One's Own*, in Victoria Ocampo's journal *Sur*		
1936	**First Greek translation:** 'Moments of Being: *Slater's Pins Have No Points*' (trans. Yiorgos Delios) in *Makedonikes Imeres* **Argentina:** Borges's *A Room of One's Own* published in volume form		
1937	**Argentina:** Borges's translation of *Orlando* **France:** Marguerite Yourcenar's translation of *The Waves*	**France:** Maurice Blanchot reviews Yourcenar's *The Waves* in *L'Insurgé* **Germany:** Gertrud Lohmüller's *Die Frau im Werk von Virginia Woolf*	**London:** Marguerite Yourcenar's visit to Woolf

Year	Translations	Criticism	Other
1937–39		**Greece:** Articles by Yiorgos Delios **Poland:** Reviews of Woolf's novels by 'Quidam'	
1938	**Argentina:** Antonio Marichalar's *To the Lighthouse* **Czechoslovakia:** *Flush* **France:** *The Years* **Spain:** Catalan *Flush*	**Argentina:** Victoria Ocampo's *Virginia Woolf, Orlando y cía* **Portugal:** Paulo Quintela's review of *The Years*	
1939	**Argentina:** *Mrs Dalloway*		**London:** Accompanied by Victoria Ocampo, Gisèle Freund photographs Woolf **Poland:** Wanda Melcer gives a lecture on Woolf to the Polish Academy of Literature
1940	**First Hungarian translation:** *The Years* **Chile:** *The Waves*		
1941	**First Danish translation:** *The Years* **Argentina:** *Three Guineas*		
1942	**France:** *Jacob's Room* **Sweden:** *The Years*		Woolf banned by the Nazis as an enemy author
1943	**Chile:** *Between the Acts*		
1944	**Spain:** *Flush*		
1945	**First Polish translation:** 'The Patron and the Crocus' in Katowice journal *Odra* **France:** *Between the Acts* **Denmark:** *Mrs Dalloway* **Hungary:** *Orlando*	**Spain:** Ricardo Gullón's study of Woolf in *Novelistas ingleses contemporáneos*	
1946	**First Croatian translation:** *The Years* **First Portuguese (Brazilian) translations:** *Mrs Dalloway* and *The Waves* **Italy:** *Mrs Dalloway* and *Flush* **Spain:** *Jacob's Room* and *The Years*	**Switzerland:** Erich Auerbach's *Mimesis* (concluding chapter on *To the Lighthouse)* **Italy:** Emilio Cecchi's essays on Woolf collected in *Scrittori inglesi e americani*	

Year	Translations	Criticism	Other
1947	**France:** new translation of *Between the Acts* **Hungary:** *Flush* **Spain:** *Night and Day*	**Italy:** Mario Praz's *Prospettive della letteratura inglese da Chaucer a Virginia Woolf* **Portugal:** Manuela Porto's *Virginia Woolf: o problema da mulher nas letras*	
1948	**First Dutch translation:** *Mrs Dalloway* **First Norwegian translation:** *To the Lighthouse* **Brazil:** *Orlando* (trans. Cecília Meireles) **France:** *The Voyage Out* **Hungary**: *Mrs Dalloway*		
1949	**Denmark:** *Letter to a Young Poet*	**France:** Simone de Beauvoir's discussion of *The Waves* in *The Second Sex*	
1950	**Italy:** *Jacob's Room* (by Anna Banti) and *A Haunted House*		
1951	**First translation in Portugal:** short stories translated by Manuela Porto **France:** *A Room of One's Own* **Italy:** *The Voyage Out*	**France:** Maxime Chastaing's *La philosophie de Virginia Woolf* **Italy:** Vittoria Sanna's *Il romanzo di Virginia Woolf*; Giorgio Melchiori's 'The Moment as a Time Unit in Fiction'	
1952	**France:** new translation of *The Voyage Out* **Sweden:** selected essays	**Italy:** Anna Banti's 'Umanità della Woolf'	
1953	**Denmark:** *Flush*; selected essays **Sweden:** *To the Lighthouse*	**West Germany:** Hilde Spiel's 'Virginia Woolf: Bildnis einer genialen Frau'	
1954	**Argentina:** *A Writer's Diary* **West Germany:** *The Years* **Portugal:** reprint of 1946 Brazilian *Mrs Dalloway*	**Argentina:** Victoria Ocampo's *Virginia Woolf en su diario* **West Germany:** Franz Stanzel's article on the narrative situation in *Jacob's Room*, *Mrs Dalloway* and *To the Lighthouse*	
1955	**First Serbian translations:** *Mrs Dalloway* and *To the Lighthouse* **Italy:** *The Years*		

Year	Translations	Criticism	Other
1956	**First Finnish translation:** *Mrs Dalloway* **West Germany:** *To the Lighthouse* **Italy:** *The Waves*; new translation of *The Voyage Out* **Serbia:** selected essays **Spain:** Janés publish a selection of Woolf novels as a 'Collected Works'	**France:** Monique Nathan's *Virginia Woolf par elle-même*	**Italy:** translation of Auerbach's *Mimesis*
1957	**West Germany:** selected essays **Italy:** *Night and Day*	**Spain:** José García Lora's comparative study of Woolf and Azorín in journal *Ínsula*	**Spain:** translation of *The Waves* forbidden by Francoist censors
1958	**France:** *A Writer's Diary* **Netherlands:** *A Room of One's Own* **Poland:** *The Years* **Sweden:** *A Room of One's Own*	**France:** Maurice Blanchot's review of *A Writer's Diary* in the *Nouvelle Revue Française* (subsequently in *Le Livre à venir*) **West Germany:** Adorno's 'The Position of the Narrator in the Contemporary Novel'	
1959	**Italy:** *A Writer's Diary* **West Germany:** *The Waves* **Norway:** selected essays		
1960	**West Germany:** *Granite and Rainbow*; selected stories **Serbia:** *The Waves*	**Portugal:** Jorge de Sena's entry on Woolf in *História da Literatura Inglesa*	
1961	**West Germany:** *Orlando* **Poland:** *Mrs Dalloway*	**France:** Nathalie Sarraute's interview with Ann Villelaur, 'Virginia Woolf ou la visionnaire du maintenant'	
1962	**Denmark:** *Orlando* **Poland:** *To the Lighthouse* **Portugal:** reprint of 1948 Brazilian *Orlando*	**France:** Jean Guiguet's *Virginia Woolf et son œuvre*	**Italy:** translation of Monique Nathan's *Virginia Woolf par elle-même*
1963	**France:** Woolf's essays on fiction **West Germany:** *Between the Acts* **Italy:** selected essays	**Greece:** Yiorgos Delios's *Dio Anglides pezografi: Virgina Woolf & Katherine Mansfield*	
1965	**First Macedonian translation:** *To the Lighthouse*	**Argentina:** *Orlando* acclaimed as one of the greatest English novels	**Denmark:** translation of Auerbach's *Mimesis*

Year	Translations	Criticism	Other
1965 (cont.)	**First Slovenian translation:** *Mrs Dalloway* **Czechoslovakia:** Czech *To the Lighthouse* **West Germany:** selected short stories	in Borges's *Introducción a la literatura inglesa*	**Italy:** translation of Bernard Blackstone's *Virginia Woolf*
1966	**First Bosnian translation:** *Mrs Dalloway* **Hungary:** *Orlando*		
1967	**Greece:** *Mrs Dalloway* **Macedonia:** *Mrs Dalloway* **Spain:** new translation of *A Room of One's Own*		
1968	**First Lithuanian translation:** 'Modern Fiction' in journal *Pergale* **First Romanian translations:** *Mrs Dalloway* and *Orlando* **Czechoslovakia:** Czech *Between the Acts* **France:** selected short stories	**Italy:** Vita Amoruso's *Virginia Woolf*	**France:** translation of Auerbach's *Mimesis* **Poland:** translation of Auerbach's *Mimesis*
1970	**Spain:** reprint of 1930 Catalan *Mrs Dalloway*		
1971	**Hungary:** *To the Lighthouse*; new translation of *Mrs Dalloway*		
1972	**Romania:** *To the Lighthouse* and selected essays **Spain:** *The Waves*		**Spain:** censors lift ban on translation of *The Waves*
1973	**First Icelandic translation:** *A Room of One's Own* **Denmark:** *A Room of One's Own* (by Elsa Gress) **Greece:** new translation of *Mrs Dalloway* **Romania:** *The Waves* **Spain:** Catalan *The Years*, trans. Maria-Antònia Oliver, introd. Maria-Aurèlia Capmany	**France:** Viviane Forrester's *Virginia Woolf*	
1973-74			**France:** translation of Quentin Bell's biography
1973-79	**France:** Woolf's collected novels published by Stock (in previously published translations)		

Year	Translations	Criticism	Other
1974	**Croatia:** *To the Lighthouse* **Italy:** *A Room of One's Own* **Slovenia:** *Orlando* **Spain:** *Mrs Dalloway's Party*	**West Germany:** Ingeborg Weber-Brandies's *Virginia Woolf – 'The Waves'* **Italy:** Giovanni Luciani's study of Woolf's literary criticism: *La polvere della lettura* **Spain:** two articles by philosopher José Luis Aranguren in journal *Triunfo*; first Spanish doctoral thesis on Woolf by Manuel Míguez	**France:** Cerisy Colloquium on 'Woolf and the Bloomsbury Group' co-ordinated by Jean Guiguet **Italy:** Italian translation of Quentin Bell's biography; writer Lalla Romano presents TV programme on Woolf
1975	**First Estonian translation:** 'Kew Gardens' in journal *Looming* **Czechoslovakia:** Czech *Mrs Dalloway* **Italy:** *Three Guineas* **Spain:** new translation of *Mrs Dalloway*	**Italy:** Mirella Billi's *Virginia Woolf*	**Spain:** Marta Pessarrodona's translation of extracts from Leonard Woolf's autobiography as: *La muerte de Virginia*
1976	**First Slovak translation:** *Mrs Dalloway* **Brazil:** *To the Lighthouse* **France:** selected essays **Netherlands:** *Orlando* **Spain:** *The Voyage Out*; new translation of *Between the Acts*		
1977	**East Germany:** Insel-Verlag begin publishing Woolf's works with reprint of 1928 translation of *Mrs Dalloway* **Finland:** *To the Lighthouse* **France:** *Moments of Being* and *Three Guineas* **Italy:** *Moments of Being* **Netherlands:** *A Writer's Diary* **Poland:** selected essays **Spain:** selected essays; new translations of *Jacob's Room* and *Three Guineas* **Sweden:** *Moments of Being* and *Mrs Dalloway*	**France:** *Virginia Woolf et le groupe de Bloomsbury*, Proceedings of the 1974 Cerisy Colloquium	**West Germany:** translation of Quentin Bell's biography **Italy:** Foundation of Virginia Woolf University in Rome

Year	Translations	Criticism	Other
1978	**First Russian translation:** selected essays in journal *Pamir* **West Germany:** *A Room of One's Own* and *Three Guineas* **Hungary:** *The Waves* **Italy:** *Between the Acts*: Mondadori bring out 'Meridiani' edition of Woolf's novels **Netherlands:** *Flush* **Portugal:** *A Room of One's Own* (introd. Maria Isabel Barreno) and *Three Guineas* **Romania:** *Between the Acts* **Spain:** new translation of *To the Lighthouse* (by Carmen Martín Gaite)		
1979	**Brazil:** *Night and Day* **East Germany:** reprint of 1931 *To the Lighthouse* **Finland:** *The Waves* **Italy:** two selections of essays **Spain:** *Moments of Being* and *A Haunted House*		**Spain:** translation of Herbert Marder's *Feminism and Art*; Dolores Padín's painting *Vida, muerte y resurrección de Virginia Woolf* **Sweden:** Kerstin Elert's *Portraits of Women in Selected Novels by Virginia Woolf and E. M. Forster*
1979-80			**Spain:** Marta Pessarrodona's translation of Quentin Bell's biography
1980	**Brazil:** *Jacob's Room* **Finland:** *A Room of One's Own* **Greece:** *A Room of One's Own* **Hungary:** *The Death of the Moth* **Netherlands:** *Mrs Dalloway* and *Three Guineas* **Norway:** *Mrs Dalloway* **Romania:** *A Writer's Diary*	**France:** Deleuze's and Guattari's interpretation of Woolf in *Mille Plateaux*; Marie-Paule Vigne's *Le Thème de l'eau dans l'œuvre de Virginia Woolf* **Italy:** Paola Zaccaria's *Virginia Woolf: trama e ordito di una scrittura* **Portugal:** Maria Ondina Braga's entry on Woolf in *Mulheres escritoras*.	**Denmark:** performance of Edna O'Brien's *Virginia* **West Germany:** translation of Spater's and Parsons's *A Marriage of True Minds* **Italy:** translation of Phyllis Rose's *Woman of Letters*

Year	Translations	Criticism	Other
1980 (cont.)	**Spain:** *Freshwater* **Sweden:** *The Waves*	**Spain:** Catalina Montes's *En torno a 'Mrs Dalloway' de Virginia Woolf*	
1980-85	**Italy:** *The Collected Letters*		
1981	**Brazil:** *Between the Acts*; new translation of *The Waves* **Croatia:** *Mrs Dalloway* **France:** *Freshwater* **West Germany:** Fischer begin publication of Woolf's *Collected Works* in translation with *Jacob's Room* and *Moments of Being* **Greece:** *To the Lighthouse* and Olympia Karagiorga's anthology of Woolf passages *Virginia Woolf: mia megali agnosti* **Italy:** *The Pargiters* and *Women and Writing* **Netherlands:** *A Haunted House*, *To the Lighthouse* and *Women and Writing* **Spain:** *Women and Writing*; new translation of *A Writer's Diary*	**East Germany:** Wolfgang Wicht's *Woolf, Joyce, Eliot: Kunstkonzeptionen und Künstlergestalten* **Poland:** Zbigniew Juszczak's *Zasłona w rajskie ptaki*	
1981-90	**France:** *The Diary of Virginia Woolf*		
1982	**Brazil:** *The Years*; new translation of *To the Lighthouse* **Denmark:** *To the Lighthouse* **Greece:** *Three Guineas* and new translation of *To the Lighthouse* **Italy:** *The London Scene*; new translation of *Night and Day* **Netherlands:** *Jacob's Room* and *Moments of Being* **Portugal:** *Mrs Dalloway* **Sweden:** *Orlando* and *Flush*	**West Germany:** Willi Erzgräber's *Virginia Woolf: eine Einführung*; Gisela von Wysocki's *Weiblichkeit und Modernität: Über Virginia Woolf*	
1983	**First Bulgarian translation:** *The Death of the Moth*		

Year	Translations	Criticism	Other
1983 (cont.)	**Czechoslovakia:** Czech *A Haunted House*; Slovak *To the Lighthouse* and *The Waves* **Denmark:** *Three Guineas* (trans. Inger Christensen) **Estonia:** *To the Lighthouse* **Finland:** *Flush* **France:** *Women and Writing* **West Germany:** *Night and Day* **East Germany:** reprint of 1929 *Orlando* **Italy:** *Freshwater* **Netherlands:** *The London Scene* **Poland:** *The Waves* **Portugal:** new translation of *The Years* **Romania:** *The Years* **Spain:** new translation of *The Years*		
1983-87			**West Germany:** four biographies of Woolf
1984	**Denmark:** new translation of *Mrs Dalloway* (by Jørgen Christian Hansen) **Finland:** *Orlando* **France:** *The London Scene* **Greece:** *Orlando* and two translations of *The Waves* **Spain:** *Roger Fry* and Catalan *To the Lighthouse* **Sweden:** *Three Guineas*	**France:** Paul Ricoeur's analysis of *Mrs Dalloway* in *Time and Narrative*; Anne Bragance's *Virginia Woolf, ou, La Dame sur le piédestal*	**Portugal:** translation of Monique Nathan's *Virginia Woolf par elle-même*
1985	**France:** *The Pargiters*, selected essays, correspondence with Vita Sackville-West; new translation of *Night and Day* **Netherlands:** *The Waves* **Portugal:** selected essays; new translations of *A Room of One's Own* and *To the Lighthouse* **Spain:** Catalan *Orlando* (trans. Maria-Antònia Oliver) and *A Room of One's Own*	**Denmark:** Tania Ørum's *Pamelas døtre* **France:** Françoise Defromont's *Virginia Woolf: vers la maison de lumière*	**Spain:** Intertextual presence of Woolf in award-winning Catalan novel: Olga Xirinacs's *Al meu cap una llosa*

Year	Translations	Criticism	Other
1985-87	**Portugal:** *The Diary of Virginia Woolf*		
1986	**Brazil:** *Moments of Being* **Finland:** *Moments of Being* **East Germany:** selected essays **Greece:** new translation of *The Waves* **Hungary:** *A Room of One's Own* **Netherlands:** selected letters **Russia:** two translations of *Flush* **Slovenia:** *The Waves* **Spain:** *The London Scene*		**Greece:** translation of Monique Nathan's *Virginia Woolf par elle-même* **Spain:** Barcelona exhibition on Bloomsbury
1987	**Finland:** selected short stories **Greece:** *A Haunted House, Jacob's Room* and a selection of letters and diary entries from Woolf's 1932 visit to Greece **Portugal:** *Flush* **Romania:** *Night and Day*	**France:** Daniel Ferrer's *V. Woolf and the Madness of Language*	**Denmark:** Jette Lundbo Levy's fictional dialogue between Woolf and Italian politician and writer Rossana Rossanda in *Modstandens figure* **West Germany:** translation of Lyndall Gordon's biography of Woolf
1988	**East Germany:** reprint of 1959 translation of *The Waves* **Georgia:** selected essays **Greece:** *Books and Portraits*; new translation of *Jacob's Room* **Italy:** *Collected Shorter Fiction* **Portugal:** *A Haunted House*; new translation of *The Waves* **Slovenia:** *To the Lighthouse* **Spain:** Catalan *Flush*		**West Germany:** selections from Leonard Woolf's autobiography translated as *Mein Leben mit Virginia*
1989	**Brazil:** extracts from *The Diary of Virginia Woolf* **Bulgaria:** *Mrs Dalloway* **West Germany:** *The Common Reader. First Series, Collected Shorter Fiction, The Voyage Out, Women and Writing* **East Germany:** *A Room of One's Own* and *Three Guineas*		**Italy:** translation of extracts of Leonard Woolf's autobiography as: *La mia vita con Virginia*

Year	Translations	Criticism	Other
1989 (cont.)	**Portugal:** new translation of *Jacob's Room* **Russia:** selected writings **Spain:** Catalan *The Waves* (trans. Maria-Antònia Oliver) and *Between the Acts*		
1990	**France:** essays on English and Russian literature **Germany:** *The Common Reader. Second Series*, *A Haunted House*, two volumes of selected short stories **Greece:** new translation of *Mrs Dalloway* **Portugal:** *Mrs Dalloway's Party* **Romania:** *Jacob's Room* **Sweden:** *Collected Shorter Fiction*	**Germany:** Sabine Hotho-Jackson's *Zwischen Tradition und Moderne: Geschichte bei Virginia Woolf*; Vera Nünning's *Die Ästhetik Virginia Woolfs*	**France:** Edward Dalloway appears in Julia Kristeva's novel *Les Samouraïs* **Germany:** translation of Louise DeSalvo's *Virginia Woolf: The Impact of Childhood*
1991	**Germany:** selected short stories; new translations of *The Waves* and *To the Lighthouse* **Greece:** *The Years* **Italy:** selected essays **Portugal:** new translations of *Between the Acts* and *Orlando* **Serbia:** *Between the Acts*, *Orlando* and selected short stories **Spain:** selected letters	**Italy:** Armanda Guiducci's biography *Virginia e l'Angelo*	**Denmark:** extracts from Leonard Woolf's autobiography translated into Danish as *Virginia* **Spain:** international conference on Woolf's influence, at the University of Alcalá de Henares, to mark fiftieth anniversary of her death; Ana María Navales's short stories *Cuentos de Bloomsbury* **Sweden:** translation of Quentin Bell's biography
1992	**France:** *Paper Darts* **Germany:** *The London Scene*, selected short stories; new translations of *Between the Acts* and *Orlando* **Greece:** *Flush* **Italy:** selected essays; new translations of *Mrs Dalloway*, *To the Lighthouse*, *The Waves* and *Freshwater*.	**Spain:** Proceedings of University of Alcalá de Henares conference published as *La huella de Virginia Woolf*; Manuela Palacios's study of Woolf and painting: *Virginia Woolf y la pintura*	European release of Sally Potter's film *Orlando* **Spain:** intertextual presence of Woolf in Maria-Antònia Oliver's Catalan novel *Joana E*

Year	Translations	Criticism	Other
	Portugal: new translations of *Jacob's Room*, *To the Lighthouse*, *The Waves* and *Between the Acts* **Russia:** selected writings **Sweden:** *Paper Darts*		
1993	**First Basque translation:** *To the Lighthouse* **First Galician translation:** *To the Lighthouse* by Manuela Palacios and Xavier Castro **Bulgaria:** *Orlando* **France:** *A Passionate Apprentice*, selected letters; new translations of *Jacob's Room*, *Mrs Dalloway*, *Orlando*, *To the Lighthouse* and *The Waves* **Germany:** new translation of *Flush* **Italy:** correspondence with Vita Sackville-West; new translations of *Mrs Dalloway*, *Orlando* and *A Room of One's Own* **Norway:** *Orlando* **Russia:** *Mrs Dalloway* **Spain:** selections from *The Diary of Virginia Woolf*; new translations of *Orlando*, *Mrs Dalloway* and *To the Lighthouse* **Sweden:** *Between the Acts*	**Spain:** Dámaso López's *La crítica literaria del grupo de Bloomsbury*; Aránzazu Usandizaga's *Amor y literatura: la búsqueda literaria de la identidad femenina*	
1993-94	**Spain:** *A Moment's Liberty*		
1994	**Czech Republic:** *Orlando*; new translation of *Flush* **Denmark:** *The Waves* **Estonia:** *A Room of One's Own* **France:** Gallimard begin publication of 'Pléiade' edition of Woolf's works with new translation of *Mrs Dalloway* **Germany:** selected essays	**France:** Françoise Pellan's *L'Ancrage et le voyage* **Spain:** Woolf prominent in Carmen Blanco's Galician history of feminism: *O contradiscurso das mulleres*	

Year	Translations	Criticism	Other
1994 (cont.)	**Italy:** Mondadori publish one-volume Selected Fiction; new translations of *Jacob's Room*, *The Years* and *Orlando* **Lithuania:** *Mrs Dalloway* **Poland:** *Flush*, two translations of *Orlando* **Portugal:** correspondence with Vita Sackville-West; new translations of *A Haunted House* and *Orlando* **Romania:** *The Voyage Out* **Serbia:** *A Room of One's Own* **Spain:** *Collected Shorter Fiction, The Waves* and *Paper Darts*; new translation of *Mrs Dalloway*		
1995	**France:** 'Four Hidden Letters' **Italy:** *Books and Portraits*; new translation of *The Waves*; two new translations of *A Room of One's Own* (one bilingual) **Norway:** new translation of *To the Lighthouse* **Portugal:** *A Voyage Out*		**France:** Didier-érudition produce a critical edition of *The Waves* in original English. **Italy:** translation of Jane Dunn's *A Very Close Conspiracy: Vanessa Bell and Virginia Woolf* **Spain:** intertextual presence of Woolf in Ana María Navales's *Tres mujeres*
1995-96	**Italy:** *The Common Reader*		
1996	**France:** *Letter to a Young Poet*; new translation of *To the Lighthouse* **Greece:** selected short stories; new translation of *A Haunted House* **Italy:** new translation of *Night and Day* **Netherlands:** selected letters **Portugal:** selected short stories; new translation of *Mrs Dalloway* **Russia:** selected writings	**Spain:** Carlos Herrero Quirós's *Virginia Woolf: proceso creativo y evolución literaria*	**France:** Formation of the Société d'Études Woolfiennes (SEW)

Year	Translations	Criticism	Other
1997	**Czech Republic:** *The Waves* **Estonia:** *Orlando* and selected essays **Greece:** *Letter to a Young Poet* **Poland:** *A Room of One's Own*	**Greece:** Katerina K. Kitsi-Mitakou's *Feminist Readings of the Body in Virginia Woolf's Novels*	**France:** international symposium of the SEW ('Metamorphosis in Woolf's Works'); educational TV channel 'Arte' broadcast programme on Virginia Woolf
1998	**Czech Republic:** *A Room of One's Own* **Estonia**: *Mrs Dalloway* **France:** new translation of *Letter to a Young Poet* **Germany:** *Moments of Being*; new translation of *Jacob's Room* **Greece:** selected essays **Italy:** Mondadori bring out 'Meridiani' edition of Woolf's works **Lithuania:** *Flush* and *A Room of One's Own* **Macedonia:** *A Room of One's Own* **Slovenia:** *A Room of One's Own*		**France:** radio channel 'France Culture' broadcast programme on Virginia Woolf **Sweden:** translation of Auerbach's *Mimesis*
1999	**Estonia:** *The Waves* **France:** *Roger Fry* **Germany:** new translation of *Mrs Dalloway* **Greece:** selected essays **Hungary:** selected essays **Romania:** *A Room of One's Own* **Spain:** new translation of *To the Lighthouse* (by Dámaso López); Catalan translation of literary criticism	**Germany:** Gudrun Rogge-Wiest's *Wahrnehmung und Perspektivik in ausgewählten Romanen Virginia Woolfs*	**France:** second international symposium of the SEW ('Things in Woolf's Works') **Germany:** translation of Hermione Lee's biography **Greece:** performances of Edna O'Brien's play *Virginia* and Robert Wilson's and Darryl Pinckney's stage adaptation of *Orlando*; Argiro Mantoglou's novel *Virginia Woolf Café*
2000	**Croatia:** *Orlando* **Germany:** new translation of *The Years* **Netherlands:** new translation of *The London Scene* **Slovakia:** *A Room of One's Own*		**France:** translation of Hermione Lee's biography **Portugal:** intertextual presence of Woolf in Maria Velho Costa's *Irene ou o contrato social* **Spain:** Nora Catelli's exhibition on Woolf at the *Centre de Cultura Contemporània*, Barcelona

This timeline has been prepared from bibliographical material provided by the contributors to the volume and from the following bibliographical sources: B. J. Kirkpatrick and Stuart N. Clarke, *A Bibliography of Virginia Woolf*, 4th edn (1997), the *Index Translationum*, 1932–2000, and the national library and/or national union catalogues of Bulgaria, Croatia, Czechoslovakia, the Czech Republic, Denmark, Estonia, Finland, France, Germany, Greece, Hungary, Iceland, Italy, Latvia, Lithuania, Macedonia, the Netherlands, Norway, Poland, Portugal, Romania, Russia, Serbia, Slovakia, Slovenia, the Former Soviet Union, Spain (and Catalonia) and Sweden.

Abbreviations

The following abbreviations of titles of works by and about Virginia Woolf are used throughout the book.

BP	*Books and Portraits*
BTA	*Between the Acts*
CDB	*Captain's Death Bed*
CDML	*The Crowded Dance of Modern Life*
CE	*Collected Essays*
CR 1	*The Common Reader: 1st Series*
CR 2	*The Common Reader: 2nd Series*
CSF	*The Complete Shorter Fiction*
CW	*Contemporary Writers*
D	*The Diary of Virginia Woolf (vols 1–5)*
DM	*The Death of the Moth and Other Essays*
E	*The Essays of Virginia Woolf*
FB	*Flush: A Biography*
FC	*Freshwater: A Comedy*
GR	*Granite and Rainbow*
HH	*A Haunted House and Other Stories*
JR	*Jacob's Room*
L	*The Collected Letters of Virginia Woolf (vols 1–6)*
LS	*The London Scene*
LYP	*Letter to a Young Poet*
MB	*Moments of Being*
MD	*Mrs Dalloway*
MDP	*Mrs Dalloway's Party*
MT	*Monday or Tuesday*
ND	*Night and Day*
O	*Orlando*
PA	*A Passionate Apprentice: The Early Journals 1897–1909*
R	*Reviewing*
RF	*Roger Fry*
ROO	*A Room of One's Own*
SSS	*Selected Short Stories*
TG	*Three Guineas*
TL	*To the Lighthouse*
TM	*The Moment*
TP	*The Pargiters*
TW	*The Waves*
TY	*The Years*
VO	*The Voyage Out*
VW	Quentin Bell, *Virginia Woolf: A Biography*
WD	*A Writer's Diary*
WE	*A Woman's Essays*
W&W	*Women and Writing*

Introduction

Nicola Luckhurst

> One of the very great writers of our times . . . one of the spiritual lights of Europe.
> Edmond Jaloux[1]

Virginia Woolf was first read in translation in the 1920s. In the 1930s, with the proliferation of translations, reviews and the first book-length studies of her writing, one can begin to talk about a 'European reception'. But by the end of that decade, Europe was at war. With the rise of fascism, writers such as Woolf, a feminist who was married to a Jew and whose polemical essay *TG* attacked patriarchy, were censored. And even in those countries where censorship was not enforced, the dynamic of cultural exchange was significantly diminished. Yet in 1940, at a time when national boundaries were shifting, when it had become difficult to envisage what Europe would become, Woolf wrote 'The Leaning Tower', an essay whose conclusion makes 'a Utopian gesture towards a future where the constraints of class and nation would cease to determine literary value' (Sandbach-Dahlström, 148).

> Literature is no one's private ground [Woolf states]; literature is common ground. It is not cut up into nations; there are no wars there. Let us trespass freely and fearlessly and find our way for ourselves. It is thus that English literature will survive this war and cross the gulf (1947, 125).

This volume both documents the first moments of encounter and dissemination of the pre-war years and maps, narrates and analyses Woolf's reception in that new unimaginable Europe. The contributors include both scholars and translators of Woolf. Their esssays examine some of the most resonant and vital areas of her European reception in Catalonia, Denmark, France, Galicia, Germany (and the former East Germany), Greece, Italy, Poland, Portugal, Spain and Sweden. The timeline provides a comprehensive overview of Woolf's reception throughout Europe.

Early reception

For Woolf reaching new readers in Europe was a source of anxiety and delight – 'Two books on Virginia Woolf have just appeared in France and

[1] 'Un des très grands écrivains de ce temps . . . une des lumières spirituelles de l'Europe.'

Germany. This is a danger signal. I must not settle into a figure', she notes in 1932 (*D* 4, 85). Her delight at the thought of her texts made new by their passage into another language is tempered by the fear that a hardening into one sort of profile (that of the canonical writer) would impede her flexibility towards the world and writing. The comment is characteristic – ironically so for this volume – of Woolf's mistrust of what happens when reading becomes the reception of 'professional scholarship', [2] and the mistrust is heightened here by the loss of control that is involved in the passage into another language and culture. Yet the newness afforded by translation also allowed Woolf a release from the responsibilities of authorship – from the intense and literal involvement with the production of her books at the Hogarth Press, from her concerns about the dissemination of her image as an author. Letting her texts loose in another language gave them life, vigour, newness. When Ocampo proposed the translation into Spanish of *O* and *TL*, Woolf accepted because translation would 'on the one hand, preserve this "remoteness" ... but ... also make them appear "brand new" to a somehow "remote" readership' (Lojo Rodríguez, 233). The degree of otherness, of exoticism sets aside notions of competition and control. As the boxes of requests from would-be translators and the boxes of Leonard Woolf's replies – all politely declining the requests – indicate,[3] Woolf seems on the whole to have been protected from the practicalities of translation. Nothing indicates that she knew of the competition to translate her books, or of the unofficial or 'pirated' translations of them.

If distanced from the translation of her own texts, Woolf was otherwise engaged in and concerned with the translation process, both specifically, through her own involvement in the translation of Russian literature, and more generally, through the publication of key translations – Rilke and Freud, among others – by the Hogarth Press. Laura Marcus's analysis of the Press as 'an important site and conduit for the European and international dimensions of modernist culture' (Marcus, 328) reveals that 'despite her seeming indifference to foreign-language versions of her own texts, [Woolf] was fascinated by the historical, philosophical, cultural and literary questions raised by translation' (Marcus, 330).

Two meetings: France and Spain

Woolf did, however, meet two of her French translators, and the patron and mediator of her work into Spanish. I would like briefly to evoke these

---

[2] See Susan Stanford Friedman's article, 'Uncommon Readings: Seeking the Geopolitical Woolf': 'screening her uncommonness behind the mask of the "common reader", Woolf anchored her oppositional consciousness in the position of the outsider, including preeminently, being outside the academy .... And yet the very internationality of Virginia Woolf locates her firmly in the center of an institution she scorned' (1996, 24).

[3] These materials, held at the Reading archive, are examined in Laura Marcus's contribution to this volume.

encounters of the 1920s and the late 1930s as representing key moments of reception from the beginning and end of the period sketched in the opening paragraph, that is the period of reception during Woolf's lifetime. In the first, in 1927, Woolf travels to France. In the second, in 1939, she is visited for the last time by the Argentinian, Victoria Ocampo, accompanied by the German photographer, Gisèle Freund. In both instances Woolf is present as a figure.

France – 1927

> If we don't abuse the Americans we abuse the French.
>
> Letter to Jacques Émile Blanche, 22 December 1931 (*L* 6, 529)

> This is very near the end of the London season. I go to Ethel [Sand]'s at Dieppe (I'm rather proud of crossing the channel again) on Wednesday, then back to Newhaven, where I may be met by my own car. . . . the World gave me this for writing The Lighthouse, I reflect.
>
> 23 July 1927 (*D* 3, 147)

Woolf's success meant that both she and her books could travel. 'The World gave me this for writing The Lighthouse,' she notes, referring to the car which is the first stage of a journey to France where she will be interviewed and translated.

The translation of Woolf is embedded in what could be described as an exemplary scene of reception. The year is 1927. Woolf is visiting Ethel Sands and Nan Hudson, American painters who live in France, in Auppegard near Dieppe.[4] Jacques Émile Blanche, portrait painter and writer, lives nearby, and comes to interview Woolf for the literary periodical, *Les Nouvelles littéraires*. But the text which results not only reports Woolf's words, it also depicts vividly her person, her manner of speaking, the staging of the meeting. Woolf is visibly and literally received in France – a double reception which, as this volume documents, is present throughout her reception in Europe. Characteristic, too, is the co-presence in this interview of another exemplary modernist – Proust. Blanche asks Woolf about her writing; Woolf asks Blanche about Proust. In fact, the insistence with which she interrogates the painter, whose portrait of Proust is the image by which the writer is perhaps best known, tends to obscure discussion of her own work.

Proust haunted Woolf, and haunts this volume – as, together with Joyce, they are repeatedly received as leading exponents of the modernist novel. Often the trinity of Joyce, Proust and Woolf is rearranged in a pecking order that is invariably to Woolf's disadvantage, whether she is perceived to be slighter, more genteel and less experimental than Joyce, or simply as writing in the wake of Proust – in Nathalie Sarraute's words, 'une seconde Proust'. Invariably underlying both value judgements is gender, the 'disadvantage' of writing as a woman. Woolf's own pecking order was somewhat different. Joyce she was able to dismiss; Proust she could not.

---

4 On Ethel Sands and Nan Hudson, see Caws and Wright (2000, 123–29).

> What remains to be written after that? I'm only in the first volume, and there are, I suppose, faults to be found, but I am in a state of amazement; as if a miracle were being done before my eyes. How, at last, has someone solidified what has always escaped – … One has to put the book down and gasp … Far otherwise is it with Ulysses; to which I bind myself like a martyr to a stake (Letter to Roger Fry, 3 October 1922; *L* 2, 565).

In conversation with Blanche, Woolf pre-empts the comparison with Proust, as if perhaps to aid her passage into French literary culture, a passage which is performed by Blanche's accompanying translations of the opening pages of *TL* and 'Kew Gardens' (the first translation of a complete text by Woolf into French).[5]

The Hogarth Press had in fact republished 'Kew Gardens' (first pub. 1917) in 1927, the year of Woolf and Blanche's meeting. As Alice Staveley (2000, 241) argues,

> this return to Kew was bigger and bolder, a more materially confident assertion of Woolf's original, and originary, vision … The 'new' *Kew Gardens* appeared at a time when Woolf was becoming an increasingly well-recognized writer: that is both an award-winning novelist – *To the Lighthouse* won the 1927 Femina Vie Heureuse prize … and a writer aware of the material awards that accrued from her growing popularity and increased reading public.

Blanche's article notes with some regret the rise of Woolf's international readership, referring to 'the curiosity of a public that fashion causes to increase every year as much in America as in England',[6] the suggestion being that Woolf has become too 'à la mode' ('Vous êtes trop "fashionable" Madame, aurait-on envie d'ajouter'), has outgrown her image as an avant-garde and côterie writer which the staging of this interview seeks to preserve (Blanche 1927, 2).

The intimacy of this meeting, the privileged conversation which takes place between, one might say, Woolf, Blanche and Proust, could be described as characteristic of Woolf's reception in France. Pierre-Éric Villeneuve's chapter in this volume takes three exemplary readers of Woolf – Simone de Beauvoir, Nathalie Sarraute and Maurice Blanchot – to examine her 'cultural impact … on the French intellectual scene, particularly on the thinking and works of writers of the generation that emerged following her death' (Villeneuve, 23). The theoretical and philosophical approaches of scholars working on Woolf in France in recent years might in turn be said to spring from these privileged encounters, as is suggested by Carole Rodier's analysis of the *état présent* of French scholarship on Woolf.

But the reception of Woolf in France is privileged not only because of this

---

5 Charles Mauron had translated the middle section of *To the Lighthouse*, as 'Le Temps passe', for the journal *Commerce*, no. 10 (Winter 1926), 89–113. See 'Literary Translations', Caws and Wright (2000, 351–69); and in this volume Marcus, 333–7.

6 'La curiosité d'un public que la mode grossit d'année en année tant en Amérique qu'en Angleterre.'

genealogy of readers. Blanche's translation set a precedent, and in the 1920s and 1930s Woolf's texts were translated into French more quickly than into any other language. As French was, at this time, the *lingua franca* of Europe, these translations in turn made Woolf's writing available to readers who did not yet dispose of translations of Woolf into their mother tongue. In the case of Portugal, for example, French would continue to be the language of cultural mediation until 'well into this century' (see Abranches, 312–14; see also Lázaro, 247–8).

There is no record of any discussion between Blanche and Woolf about his translation. In a letter of thanks, Woolf simply remarks, 'I can't help feeling a little guilty that you should have spent your time translating words of mine. They read much better to me in French than in English, and again I feel deeply grateful to you for trying to convey my words to French readers' (20 August 1927; *L* 6, 516). Ten years later Woolf does record in her diary meeting the translator of *TW*, Marguerite Yourcenar. Woolf's infamous misremembering of Yourcenar's name ('Madame or Mlle Youniac (?) Not her name' (23 February 1937; *D* 5, 60), is not auspicious. And while her characterization, or caricature, of Yourcenar as 'red lipped, strenuous; a working Fchwoman' (*D* 5, 61) is picturesque, Woolf's record of the process of translation itself is frustratingly unilluminating – 'we went through *The Waves*. What does "See here he comes?" mean & so on.' Françoise Pellan's essay on translating Woolf into French begins by evoking this meeting, and proceeds to give an account both of past translations of Woolf into French, and of her own recent work – translating *TL*. Given the importance of the French language in the history of translations of Woolf, and given too the, for us, missed opportunity of the meeting with 'Mlle Youniac', it seems fitting that this paper should be partnered by a discussion of French translations from 'the other side', that is, from an English perspective. Françoise Pellan's and Mary Ann Caws's essays alone are devoted solely to the act and art of translation.

The volume opens with Virginia Woolf's reception in France.

Spain: the 1930s and beyond

If Woolf's meeting with Blanche marks 'the beginnings of her great fame in France' (Lee 1996, 566), the encounter with Victoria Ocampo had a far more direct and material influence on the translation and dissemination of Woolf's writing, as Laura Lojo Rodríguez's chapter describes. Common to both Blanche and Ocampo, however, is their autobiographical recording of the encounter with Woolf, in all its physical detail – a characteristic which seems subdued in the *Nouvelles littéraires* article when placed alongside Ocampo's description in *Testimonios*: 'Suddenly I heard her name and mine being pronounced by a friend, and when I turned my head towards that voice, her marvellous face was already facing mine' (1946, 92). Woolf can hardly have imagined that her attempts to persuade Ocampo to 'try a more personal style of writing' would result in 'Carta a Virginia Woolf' (1934), an evocation of their subsequent meeting at Tavistock Square.

These early and privileged encounters with French and Spanish culture have the advantage of making visible the writer's reception, thus initiating the double dissemination of Woolf as image and text.[7] Ocampo, appropriately enough, first met Woolf at a private view of an exhibition of Man Ray's photographs, and in their final meeting, Ocampo brings with her Gisèle Freund, the German photographer famous for her portraits of writers.[8]

Known to Ocampo as a photographer of writers, Freund was, in effect, the official portraitist of Adrienne Monnier's Parisian bookshop, one of the institutions of modern and modernist literature, La Maison des Amis des Livres; it was Monnier too who had first suggested to Ocampo that she start her own publishing house, Editorial Sur (see Lojo Rodríguez, 238). Freund's project was to assemble a photographic pantheon – in colour – for the writers of the early twentieth century, as Nadar had done for the nineteenth. These were the images projected for Woolf on 23 June 1939 in an attempt to persuade her to join Freund's collection.[9]

Woolf accepted, then regretted her acceptance, describing the shoot as a 'petty vulgar photography-advertising stunt'. But her regret is also a fear of what will happen to her image. Would it remain in what Freund described as her private collection? The photographer's use of the new colour film is read by Woolf as vulgarly commercial, but she also seems to express a superstitious sense of the photographs as too lifelike: 'life sized life coloured animated' (24 June 1939: *D* 5, 220). Woolf's fear of 'settling into a figure' (*D* 4, 85), is replaced here by the anxiety that her image is unstable, both in terms of the medium itself and as regards subsequent dissemination.[10] In an ironic reversal, the writer herself is 'afraid of Virginia Woolf' – and it is a fear that has proved well-founded, since Woolf has increasingly been received not only as text, not only as the figure behind the text, but as a cultural icon who can signify, visually, independently of her writing (Silver 1999). But this is to anticipate the

---

7 In the case of Blanche's interview, Woolf seems to have been less concerned about the text than the photograph which would accompany it. See letters of 7 and 22 August 1927 (*L* 3, 409 and 412) to Vita Sackville-West, in which Woolf claims that Blanche 'wants to substantiate his statements by a large untouched portrait' and asks Vita to take some snapshots of her as a possible replacement. The snapshots were in fact not used, the article being illustrated by Beresford's portrait of Woolf ('an old photograph of me at 19 – which is just as well').

8 Gisèle Freund (1908–2000), a German Jew and a political activist, scholar and practitioner of photography, fled to France from Germany in 1935.

9 Unable to afford to develop her images as prints, Freund's first exhibition was a slide-show, held at Monnier's bookshop on 5 March 1939. The portraits shown included, among others, Paul Valéry, André Gide, Colette, Louis Aragon, Elsa Triolet, André Breton, Jean Cocteau, Jean-Paul Sartre, Walter Benjamin.

10 Woolf never saw Freund's photographs of her. In 1941, with the help of Victoria Ocampo, Freund fled France for Argentina. In 1941 Woolf committed suicide. But the photographs were, of course, disseminated as Woolf had feared and beyond even the photographer's control. They appeared (often unacknowledged) at an early stage in French publications on Woolf and are now internationally known. For details see Luckhurst and Ravache (2000).

later reception. Freund's portraits of Woolf are initially an act of consecration, making visible the writer's last-minute entry into this photographic pantheon of the great European writers of the 1930s.[11]

The only colour photographs we have of Woolf resulted from the 'privileged encounter' with Victoria Ocampo. Yet, as Ocampo's friendship with Woolf developed, she also engaged with the writer in a dialogue which questioned the very meaning and possibility of privilege.

Hunger was a trope of the correspondence between the two women – established by Ocampo to describe the cultural deprivation of her people, taken up by Woolf who, when writing of her pleasure at the translation of her writing into Spanish, describes the language as having 'a gaping mouth but no words'. The spiritual hunger of Argentina was, as Lojo Rodríguez describes, to be sated by the reception and translation of European writers: Borges was commissioned by *Sur* to translate *ROO* – the first translation of a complete text by Woolf into Spanish. That the success of this project of translation and cultural renewal goes far beyond the initial encounter between Woolf and Ocampo is demonstrated by the richness of the final section of this volume, where Woolf is read and translated in the context of Galician and Catalan, both languages and cultures which had been suppressed by Franco's regime.

But the question most directly posed by Ocampo, and taken up by Spanish, Catalan and Galician women writers, was how to write as a woman in an underprivileged and repressive society. If Ocampo had in mind oppression under the conservative and patriarchal Argentine society, later generations of women writing in Spanish suffered similarly under Franco: 'For almost forty years the dictatorship tried to silence women's voices socially, politically and artistically, leaving future female generations apparently lacking in a tradition of their own' (Gámez Fuentes, 275). This was experienced all the more acutely when those women were Catalan or Galician, and therefore suffering also from Franco's policy of linguistic repression. As Manuela Palacios describes, there had been no literary production in Galician until 1950, and the material conditions for women writers, that is, 'the[ir] social and economic context . . . is not very different from that of Britain in the 1920s' (Palacios, 282). Paradoxically, many of Woolf's novels were translated and published in Spain under the regime, as the result of what Alberto Lázaro's fascinating archival research reveals to be a somewhat quixotic process of censorship. María José

---

11 As Simone de Beauvoir describes:

> On a spring day in 1939, Gisèle Freund invited us to Adrienne's bookshop to see her portraits . . . projected in colour upon a screen. The place was crowded with famous writers . . . . All the consecrated authors as well as the new talents with a still-uncertain future drifted across the screen before our eyes. The camera had captured them with a precision which was often cruel . . . . Ours was no Golden Age, as I am the first to admit, not being a believer in lost paradises . . . . But I keep an ardent memory of those days . . . . With their contradictions and their turbulence, the thirties had an extraordinary character, for they were, at one and the same time, a flowering and a decline. The past still lingered on in them, and even took on vivid and fecund forms; seeds of future harvests were already sprouting' (de Beauvoir 1965, ix).

Gámez Fuentes's chapter describes how women writers – Carmen Martín Gaite (one of the main translators of Woolf into Spanish), Esther Tusquets and Ana María Navales – reached to these and other of Woolf's texts, finding in her a symbolic mother for the literature they sought to establish.

The volume closes with this most vigorously and politically feminist reception of Woolf in Spain, Catalonia and Galicia.

Translation is always a privileged encounter

The meetings with France and Spain – with Jacques-Émile Blanche and Victoria Ocampo – are, of course, privileged encounters. They resonate at the beginning and end of the European reception of Woolf in her lifetime. They have the seductive advantage of being at once vivid, direct, singular and also distant, exotic. They seem to be at the origin of the reception histories of Woolf in France and the Spanish-speaking world. But we know too that, if this is not entirely a myth, nor is it anything like the whole story. The notions of the 'encounter', of 'privilege' and of Woolf's visual dissemination are insufficient to the wider story of Woolf's reception. Or at least they need rethinking. One might argue that translation itself is the most significant encounter, the underlying constant in all these accounts of reception, and it is an encounter that is perpetually renewed across Europe.

The wider and posthumous reception of Woolf in Europe involves different kinds of stories about reception, less clear in terms of narrative direction, less certain, with the passage of time, about national specificity: some of the essays in this volume make incursions into how Woolf is read now, some analyse how Woolf is read in the writing of new literary texts, others give sociological accounts of Woolf's readership. But all indicate an increase in 'traffic', as the passage into Europe becomes a multitude of crossings.

Translation: modernism, censorship, marketing

Woolf's arrival is often as part of that of modernism itself. Sometimes, this modernist reception is part of a project of translation and cultural renewal, as in the above-mentioned case of Victoria Ocampo's publishing house and journal *Sur*, or in that of the 'School of Thessalonika' (Kitsi-Mitakou 187), whose journal *Makedonikes Imeres* published in 1932 the first translation of Woolf into Greek, the short story 'Moments of Being: Slater's Pins Have No Points'. But it may also be expressive of and received into a nation's already established, native modernist literature, hence the early translations of *MD* and *TL* in France and Germany. We have already seen how readily the comparisons with Joyce and Proust are made.

Yet the seeming clarity of these examples is misleading. Ocampo's choice of *ROO* as Sur's first translation into Spanish is, for example, more expressive of her feminism than of her wider project of bringing modern European texts into Argentinian and Spanish culture. Similarly the presence of the first French and German translations is less straightforward than it might appear. The central section of Woolf's *TL* was in fact published in French before the completed novel appeared in English, an indication perhaps of the readiness, the sophistication of an already 'modernized' French reading public to receive the English Proust. Yet, as Laura Marcus's research reveals, French publishers (rather than the editors of highbrow literary reviews and little magazines) who were happy to back Woolf's modernist novels were more reluctant to experiment when it came to her feminism. Having published *TL* and *MD*, Stock proceeded to reject *O*, *ROO* and *TG*. 'Woolf's most overtly feminist texts were received by Stock as untranslatable in cultural terms' (Marcus, 334).

The German story is different again, since the post-war reception diverges into that of East and West. While in the former West Germany, Woolf's post-war reception 'continued apace' (to quote the Nünnings' account in this volume), the reception in East Germany was for decades interrupted by a censorship hostile to modernism. Woolf first appeared in the pre-war Insel Verlag translations, but her highly politicized re-entry into what had become East Germany did not occur until the 1980s, and then under the protection of her sole editor and official critic, Wolfgang Wicht. Now, Woolf's reception had become part of what Wicht terms the 'installation of modernism' in the former GDR, a process which was itself indicative of and contributed to the political changes which led to German reunification.

Although less clearly defined as such, Woolf's emergence from the censorship of communist Poland suggests a similar pattern, with a first period of 'relative silence' giving way in later years (the 1960s to the 1980s) and in the build-up to democratization, to the translation of several of Woolf's most important novels, although not of her feminist essays. Looking beyond what is the end-point of Wicht's account, democratization (and the reunification of the two Germanies), Urszula Terentowicz-Fotyga examines the proliferation of translations in Poland's new market economy of the 1990s. Woolf's novels and particularly her essay, *ROO*, became bestsellers, selling out as soon as they hit the bookstalls and shops, yet Terentowicz-Fotyga suggests Woolf's novels are still 'waiting for a faithful translator so that they will cease to pulse according to different rhythms and styles' (Terentowicz-Fotyga, 127). A similar pattern of reception occurs following the cessation of censorship under fascist rule, namely in Spain and Portugal. As Labanyi (1995) points out, it is not surprising to find in the first years of democracy following the collapse of Franco's regime, 'a substitution of social realism by modernism and an upsurge of new translations and editions of modernist authors' (Gámez Fuentes' paraphrase, 274). In post-revolutionary Portugal a similar proliferation of translations occurred, further facilitated by the end of Woolf's copyright protection in 1991. But, as Graça Abranches indicates, despite the advantages of their being more widely and cheaply available, the quality of these new translations has suffered greatly, in some cases to the extent that Woolf becomes almost 'unreadable'.

Woolf does not simply emerge and flourish in the newly democratized nations: her reception is inflected, both positively and negatively, by the pressures of censorship, whether communist or fascist, and subsequently by the demands of the marketplace.

Translations may also arrive indirectly: Ocampo's influence meant that 'in the publication history of Virginia Woolf's writings Argentina has always been recognized as the centre of pioneering translations of her texts in Spanish' (Lázaro, 249); and similarly the culture of translation in Brazil which had flourished from the early 1940s supplied Portugal with 'some exemplary Portuguese versions of modern classics of world literature', including two of its three pre-revolution translations of Woolf, *MD* and *O* (Abranches, 317).

If the political and aesthetic climate of a nation is illuminated by such histories of reception, so are the vagaries of translation itself, as the following list of first translations of Woolf (that is, of complete texts published in book form) suggests:

Swedish – *JR* – 1927
German – *MD* – 1928
French – *MD* and *TL* – 1929
Czech – *O* – 1929
Catalan – *MD* – 1930
Italian – *O* – 1933
Spanish – *ROO* – 1936
Hungarian – *TY* – 1940
Danish – *TY* – 1941
Croatian – *TY* – 1946
Portuguese – *MD* and *TW* – 1946
Dutch – *MD* – 1948
Norwegian – *TL* – 1948
Serbian – *MD* and *TL* – 1955
Finnish – *MD* – 1956
Polish – *TY* – 1958
Macedonian – *TL* – 1965
Slovenian – *MD* – 1965
Greek – *MD* – 1967
Romanian – *MD* and *O* – 1968
Icelandic – *ROO* – 1973
Slovak – *MD* – 1976
Bulgarian – *DM* – 1983
Estonian –*TL* – 1983
Basque – *TL* – 1993
Galician – *TL* – 1993
Lithuanian – *MD* – 1994

This list does, of course, somewhat blunt the contours of reception, since it neglects the many translations of short stories, essays and extracts which were published in literary periodicals at an earlier stage. Nevertheless, the first translation of Woolf – not into French, but Swedish – is unexpected. The translation of *JR* was published in a series entitled 'Den Nya Romanen' (The New Novel) devoted to new experimental writing around the world. As Catherine Sandbach-Dahlström's chapter describes, Woolf's appearance in this series 'marks her as belonging to what he [the publisher] saw as the elite of the younger authors in Europe' (Sandbach-Dahlström, 151). Yet this auspicious beginning seems to have been an anomaly in the early Swedish reception, as

Sandbach-Dahlström indicates: on the one hand, Swedish experimental modernist prose's obvious debt is 'to the male modernists', while Swedish fiction from the 1930s to the 1950s was 'of epic proportion, frequently proletarian in its roots and concerns, and thus somehow foreign to the Woolfian ethos' (Sandbach-Dahlström, 149). No further novels by Woolf were translated into Swedish until 1942, when *TY*, one of Woolf's least experimental texts, was published.

TY was, as the above list indicates, also the first of Woolf's texts to be translated into Danish (in 1941) and Polish (in 1958). This somewhat conservative and surprising choice is in both cases indicative of the political situation. As Ida Klitgård argues,'the period during and immediately after the Second World War was one of great cultural crisis for Denmark, which was occupied by Germany from 1940 to 1945' (Klitgård, 167) the sophisticated aesthetics of international modernism were thought to be of little consequence 'when the dominant concerns were national pride, unity and resistance'. Urszula Terentowicz-Fotyga describes the political climate and cultural needs of post-war Poland in similar terms, arguing that 'in a country which had to rebuild its identity national, social and economic issues became very closely linked. Consequently, the literature of the time was to a great extent "committed", and this also affected translation from other literatures. Even if formal experimentation *was* taken into account, authors who fused experimental techniques with a "social message" were preferred and Virginia Woolf was seen as too ethereal and uncommitted to fit into the "burdened" Polish context' (Terentowicz-Fotyga, 128). By the late 1950s, under the communist regime, these political and social demands had been formalized as 'socialist realism', and as such provided a climate favourable to *TY* as 'the most "social", the least experimental and so the most in accordance with the official school of literary criticism' (Terentowicz-Fotyga, 132). But we should also bear in mind that the more straightforward use of language in *TY* made it a popular choice with translators and readers alike: it suited the communist and nationalist concerns of certain European countries, but it had also already projected Woolf 'onto the best-seller lists in the United States in 1937' (Silver 1999, 74–75), and as a consequence was the book that made the most money for the author during her lifetime.

The sketch given above of Woolf's translation in Europe has drawn out the material conditions – the political climate and the demands of the market – which are likely to have determined the choice and publication of texts. Similarly, the prevailing aesthetic of a national literature can exercise a regularizing effect which might be likened to censorship. In Italy 'Virginia Woolf was appreciated as, and turned into, an example of normalized *bello scrivere* (fine writing) – a pervasive preoccupation of the 1930s and early 1940s' which obscured 'the revolutionary nature of her writing', while in the 1950s the 'prevailing neo-realist and *engagé* tendency of the time' meant that there were relatively few translations of Woolf's work at all (Perosa, 201). But if a translation itself is strong enough – a classic translation, we might say – then it can break through such constraints and demands to create its own readership and reception. Woolf may arrive in Danish in the more conservative mode of *TY*, then become established as a feminist thinker in the translation of *ROO*

(1973), but Anne Marie Bjerg's translation of *TW* in 1994 constituted 'a breakthrough in the Danish reception', placing Woolf 'definitively as a great writer on a par with other European classics [of modernism]', such as Musil, Proust and Márquez (Klitgård, 183). For the first time, Klitgård argues, Woolf's art was 'accepted in its own right instead of being an exemplar for the women's movement only. Her reputation has at last cast off the feminist burden of the 1970s whereby she was solely linked with *ROO*' (Klitgård, 183).

The feminist reception

This evaluation of Woolf's true arrival in modernist guise is, of course, as revealing of a nation's cultural priorities as it is of the quality of the translation itself. But the phrase 'feminist burden of the 1970s' is telling for Woolf's European reception as a whole. And it is echoed by Sergio Perosa's sense of Woolf's recent release from her previous colonization by feminist critics in Italy – he notes that Nadia Fusini's translations reveal 'a new Virginia Woolf, comic, laughing . . . , lovingly and perceptively recreated for the new century', adding parenthetically '(No wonder that in this view, *ROO* was less crucial than in previous feminist appraisals)' (Perosa, 216–17). Regardless of whether this is viewed in a positive or negative light, the political climate which has done most throughout Europe to establish Woolf is feminism. I have already indicated the importance of Woolf as feminist to the Spanish reception. In France, Woolf's writing was of great influence on another key feminist theorist, Simone de Beauvoir, and more generally on later French feminist theory, as the essays of both Carole Rodier and Pierre-Éric Villeneuve describe. But it should also be noted that Woolf's reception as a feminist writer was above all a popular one. *ROO* was published by small radical feminist publishers and major publishing houses alike; in the 1970s it became a best-seller in numerous European countries.

In Scandinavia, as Klitgård's above remark suggests, Woolf was claimed for the feminist movement – and Catherine Sandbach-Dahlström describes *ROO* as a 'touchstone' for Swedish feminism. But if the Danish perspective celebrates the move from Woolf as feminist to her arrival and consecration as a modernist, the Polish reception plays out and also values this development in reverse – 'the political, economic and cultural revolution of the 1990s . . . brought a complete transformation of the writer's image as the modernist edifice was replaced by a more popular picture' (Terentowicz-Fotyga, 140). This more popular picture was above all feminist, and took shape some decades after the more general European reception of Woolf as feminist in the 1970s. Prior to this revolution, the struggle for democracy had taken precedence over the question of the place of women in Polish society, but as what Terentowicz-Fotyga describes as 'the patriarchal character of the new democracy' became increasingly evident, so the feminist movement in Poland was activated, and Woolf claimed for it – *ROO* was first published in translation in 1997, and *TG* is still in the process of being translated.

This pattern of reception is not, however, common to all former Eastern European countries. In the former GDR, for example, *ROO* and *TG* were published in 1987 in the cheap and widely available Reclam edition (no such double edition was available in West Germany where Woolf's feminist essays had on the contrary been published by a small publishing house and a radical feminist press). Wolfgang Wicht, the editor of this publication, describes his presentation of the text in terms of his 'own reading of Woolf and a historically orientated, Marxist sensibility to the criticism of texts' but which 'was strengthened and enriched by international feminist theory and criticism'. (Wicht, 116). In other words, and contrary to the Polish reception, the East German 'feminist Woolf' was already published and assimilated prior to democratization, presented as part of the international feminist scene.

Graça Abranches's account of censorship under Salazar's fascist dictatorship exposes most clearly the interdependency of Woolf's poetics and politics for the Portuguese reception. Manuela Porto's translation of a selection of Woolf's short stories, and indeed the first translation of Woolf in Portugal, was published in 1951. In January 1947 Porto had spoken on Woolf at the 'Exposição de Livros escritos por Mulheres' (Exhibition of Books Written by Women), organized by the Conselho Nacional das Mulheres Portuguesas (National Council of Portuguese Women); the impact of the exhibition was such that by June 1947 'the organization was declared extinguished by the government .... No other independent women's organization would be allowed to exist for the nearly three decades that the regime was still to last' (Abranches, 316). Porto's lecture 'Virginia Woolf: o problema da mulher nas letras' (VW: the problem of women in literature) 'a passionate paraphrase, translation and appropriation of *ROO*', allowed her to 'dis-locate her analysis of the material conditions of the production of art and to denounce the situation of [women] in the political and cultural claustrophobia of Salazar's time' (Abranches, 316). Reading Woolf could be coded to carry a contemporary political message. Moreover, the very act of commentary and translation allowed women to speak when their access to an independent voice had been forbidden: 'the conscious use of translation and preface writing' allowed women 'to say by proxy that which was forbidden in their social context, that which they were not allowed to say in an autonomous text'. Translation in fascist Portugal 'allowed people to voice their muteness; and women writers, doubly silenced, would often seize this chance of "speaking culturally from the margins"' (Abranches, 317).

Yet the distance between the sense of Woolf's feminist appropriation as a burden and its revolutionary importance to nations such as Portugal and Poland is not as great as one might expect. The demand in post-revolution Portugal for translations of *ROO* and *TG* was urgent, the texts were eagerly received, but they were also poorly translated – or, as Abranches writes of *ROO* (1978), 'the most incompetent, gross and arrogantly dishonest version of Woolf's work that has been published in Portugal' (Abranches, 323). The violence, as opposed to the privilege, of this translation as encounter is done to the text in response to an extreme political situation: 'It is no doubt a measure of the strength of Woolf's ideas and prose that some of their power managed to survive the treatment to which her language was subjected' (Abranches, 323).

Different narratives of reception

The drama of Woolf's reception in these accounts of censorship and revolution makes for clear narrative lines: elsewhere, her significance as a modernist, feminist and political thinker is clearly established, but cannot be represented by an unfolding narrative as such. In addition, it could be argued that, 'At one level . . . there is no such thing as a "national" reception or at least not one that is not intersected by class, gender and generation.'[12]

This problematic – 'how do we differentiate and narrate national reception' – is directly addressed in Catherine Sandbach-Dahlström's essay on Woolf's Swedish reception. Her solution is to look at the reception history on the one hand, but also to make an insertion into how Woolf is read today, by the press and the academy, as well as, by analysing the records of provincial libraries, by the 'common reader'.

The economics of publishing in the former East Germany suggest that Woolf's 'common readers' were somewhat differently determined. Publishing was not made in response to a market economy, but according to the dictates of the state. Approval by the Ministry of Culture was required before production could begin. The print run was then limited and 'most of the copies a bookshop could get from the central distributor were sold in advance and, as a consequence, often did not turn up on the counters and shelves of the booksellers at all' (Wicht, 109). Reprints were rare, as 'the paper quota meant that issuing reprints would have delayed the publication of a next novel'. Publishers, then, 'preferred to print a new title. Thus, published books immediately became rare books' (Wicht, 109). Wicht's skilful playing of the censorship system together with the softening of that system itself meant that many of Woolf's texts were published in translation, but they were not widely available.

The lack of a market economy rather than censorship itself, as a Western reader might expect, was responsible for a limited 'common readership' of Woolf in the GDR. Alberto Lázaro's account of Woolf's reception in Franco's Spain similarly draws attention to the fact that censorship can be far from monolithic: the censors found no fault with *FB* (1944), *TY* (1946), *JR* (1946), *VO* (1946), *ND* (1947) or with the Argentinian editions of *TL* (imported in 1944) and *MD* (imported in 1945), in fact some of the reports were highly favourable; but *TW* (1953) was at first censored for what were considered morally harmful or politically incorrect 'references to the body, God, crucifixes or the Spanish language' (Lázaro, 251), then in 1957 banned altogether as 'a monstrosity that cannot be authorized'. This erratic process of censorship is far from the highly regulated, formalized but ultimately manipulable structures of GDR censorship some forty years later.

Academic production and popular consumption

There is an ironic disparity between the limited availability of Woolf's texts in the former GDR and their promotion by her one official critic, and, in the

---

[12] Correspondence with the author, 3 January 2000.

former West Germany, the proliferation of Woolf criticism, or what might be described as 'the Woolf industry'. Woolf was, of course, banned during the years of Nazi Germany. But in the 1950s she 'was virtually newly discovered', and there followed a second wave of translations and of criticism, 'testifying to a generally felt need to catch up with foreign literary currents and to distance oneself from the immediate past' (Nünning, 74). As Joyce Crick (1999, 4) poignantly observes, Woolf was

> a very apt writer for 'catching up', for it was literary modernism that had been lost under the Nazis. And by engaging with an English modernist at that, and one, moreover, whom Auerbach placed in a long view of world literature, it was possible to dissociate oneself trebly from the burden of being German.

If the Nünnings' skilful account of the various trends and stages of the scholarly reception of Woolf draws attention to the sheer wealth of response, it reminds us also of the difficulty of reading reception in specifically 'national' terms. The early narratological and formalist criticism which owes much to the work of Auerbach (an important later influence in the GDR) shades off over the years into various international critical approaches, predominant among which are Anglo-American and French feminism. Certainly, national trends persist, in the sense that one critical approach may be dominant at a certain time, but that approach is, in the later stages of Woolf's reception in Germany, unlikely to be nation-specific in itself. Indeed, it could be argued that Auerbach's analysis of Woolf is influential – and variously so – in many European countries (see Perosa on Auerbach's influence on the Italian reception, 209; Kitsi-Mitakou on his influence in Greece, 192–3, and Terentowicz-Fotyga's note on the Polish reception, 136). By contrast, French approaches to Woolf are far less porous than the German: as Carole Rodier's *état présent* of French Woolf studies illustrates, they have retained a more national flavour – with Lacanian psychoanalysis, 'theories of *écriture féminine*' and phenomenology among the most popular critical tools. The French theory of *écriture féminine*, has, in its Italian version, *scrittura al femminile*, informed the recent and highly acclaimed translations of Woolf by Nadia Fusini (Perosa, 215–17), indicating again the mobility and mutability of contemporary critical discourse.

The degree to which current readings of Woolf can be considered nation- or indeed Euro-inflected is questioned not only by her reception within the academy but also by its counterpart, the popular reception. Recent film versions of *O*, by Sally Potter (1992) and *MD*, by Marleen Gorris (1997), together with documentaries and films relating to the life and times of the Bloomsbury Group and writers and artists contemporary with them – Christopher Hampton's *Carrington* (1995) and Brian Gilbert's *Tom and Viv* (1994) – have contributed to her international profile. Urszula Terentowicz-Fotyga, for example, hesitates between attributing *O*'s recent popularity in Poland to the novel's feminist message or to the film version by Sally Potter.

But the popularization of Woolf herself has a long history of which these cinematic versions are among the most recent manifestations. There has always been, from the very earliest reviews (as the interview with Blanche indicates), a fascination with her person, but this fascination was fuelled by the publication in

1953 of *WD* (which was widely and swiftly translated), the subsequent appearance in the 1960s of Leonard Woolf's own autobiography, and finally in 1972 by Quentin Bell's *Virginia Woolf: A Biography*. Bell's biography, which has been widely translated, also fed the interest of readers eager to hear the account of an 'insider', to know more about Woolf as part of 'Bloomsbury'. The desire for an intimate account of Woolf's life has also been met by the publication of translated extracts from Leonard Woolf's autobiography (1960–69) to create *Mein Leben mit Virginia* (My life with Virginia: 1988, ed. and trans. Friederike Groth). No such text exists in English, and Groth's text, created for the German readership, has proved surprisingly popular elsewhere in Europe. It was published a year later in Italian translation as *La mia vita con Virginia* (trans. by Ilide Carmignani), with a foreword by Marisa Bulgheroni, and when, in 1991, publisher Merete Ries decided there was a market in Denmark for a biography of Woolf, she too chose to publish both Groth's selection of extracts and her original preface, changing the title to read simply, *Virginia* (trans. by Nina Lautrup-Larsen). Another specifically European take on Woolf's life, although undoubtedly influenced by Louise DeSalvo's work, is found in the German publication *Wahnsinnsfrauen* (Mad women: Amrain 1999), 'a collection of biographies of great mad or supposedly mad women. The chapter devoted to Virginia Woolf describes the writer as a female genius suppressed by male-dominated culture as represented by her father, stepbrothers and husband' (Terentowicz-Fotyga, 146). Translated into Polish as *Wielkie Szalone* (Great mad women), the book's focus on Woolf's sexuality and her attitude to her body had been largely unknown from the biographical material previously published in Poland. In Sweden, by contrast, the myth of Woolf as 'an over-refined member of the British upper classes who commonly panicked when confronted by the realities of everyday or physical life', is prevalent, reinforced, Sandbach-Dahlström argues, by the fact that her main translator is also a 'devotee of Bloomsbury' (Sandbach-Dahlström, 157).

If these biographies, some created specifically for a European readership, satisfy the reader's desire for an intimate account of Woolf's life – Bloomsbury, her marriage, her sexuality and so on – they are, in a sense, counterbalanced by Hermione Lee's *Virginia Woolf* (1996), which, a quarter of a century after Quentin Bell's account, offers the most substantial and serious version of the writer's life to date. This 'portrait of a genius and her times' (as the jacket tells us) moves skilfully between the personal and the political, it addresses the reader's interest in Woolf 'the woman', but is 'equally interested in the historical and intellectual context in which Virginia Woolf worked' (ibid.). In other words, this new 'life' of Woolf, which has already been translated into French and German and enthusiastically reviewed throughout Europe, is expressive of the richness of her reception: Woolf as political thinker, as a feminist, a woman of Bloomsbury, a modernist, as sexually abused, as a professional writer and a fragile and possibly 'insane' genius and so on. This new 'Virginia Woolf' might be multiple, but she is also iconic:

> Occurring across the cultural terrain, whether in academic discourses, the intellectual media, or mass/popular culture, the proliferation of Virginia Woolfs [both visual and verbal] has transformed the writer into a powerful and powerfully

> contested cultural icon, whose name, face, and authority are persistently claimed or disclaimed in debates about art, politics, sexuality, gender, class, the canon, fashion, feminism, race, and anger. (Silver 1999, 3)[13]

Conclusion

Is this multiple and iconic Virginia Woolf at the beginning of the twenty-first century the conclusion of the writer's reception in Europe? If so, our celebration of Woolf's arrival might also be a little uneasy, signalling as it does the internationalization of reception. Yet alongside the undoubtedly powerful international presence of Woolf as text and image, her particular and local significance is, as the contributions to this volume reveal, movingly and tangibly asserted by different languages and cultures. With every translation of Woolf a new and particular cultural encounter is made.

Certainly, Woolf's canonical status in Europe is indisputable. It is moreover also possible to distinguish the broad outlines of what tends to be a three-phase reception of Woolf throughout Europe: she is known first as a novelist, a phase which coincides with her modernist reception; subsequently as an essayist, the author of *ROO* and *TG* – this is the period of feminist reception; and, finally, as a diarist and letter writer, and, the subject of numerous biographies, as exemplary woman. But to trace this development is also to neglect that the story of Woolf's European reception in fact exposes the 'different social and cultural tempos in the various countries of the newly born European Union' (Palacios, 282). For several of the European countries represented here – Poland, the former East Germany, Portugal, Spain, Catalonia, Galicia – the emancipation of women and the assertion of democratic rights are relatively recent developments, and the reception of Woolf is both expressive of and influential in this process of political change. Here the internationalized Woolf is powerfully and locally reclaimed.

Woolf is similarly and locally influential in both the theorization and production of art. The readings, rewritings and appropriations of Woolf by other writers renew, as does translation, the specificity of encounter with the text, connecting it with contemporary literary culture in such a way as to allow her to – discuss art, gender, politics and history with the contemporary Italian left-wing politician and writer, Rossana Rossanda (Klitgård, 182); visit Santiago de Compostela (in the guise of 'Lady Woolf') and write a short story in Galician (Palacios, 289); become, together with Shakespeare and Irene Lisboa, 'a passenger in transit in postcolonial Lisbon' (Abranches, 327); meet Greek novelist Argiro Mantoglou in London's Virginia Woolf Café (Kitsi-Mitakou, 198); and revisit her own past in 'Regreso a Monks House' (Return to Monk's House), accompanied, contextually, by two Spanish women, the

---

[13] The iconic Woolf finds a biographical medium of her own in Penguin Classics' series of 'illustrated lives'. Other writers include Proust, Kafka, Beckett and Fitzgerald. Mary Ann Caws is the author of the 'lives' of Woolf and Proust in this series.

nineteenth-century Aragonese writer Maria del Pilar Sinués and the twentieth-century Aragonese painter, Julieta Aguilar (Gámez Fuentes, 264). As Woolf and her writing are read and rewritten, so they move not only intertextually, but also into other media – Galician painter Dolores Padín's polyptych *Vida, muerte y resurrección de Virginia Woolf* (Life, death and resurrection of Virginia Woolf) (1978–79) reclaims and literally revivifies the iconic Virginia Woolf.

Here, we might speak less of Woolf's arrival, her reception in Europe, than of her instigation of others' journeys, of women's journeys: as Cixous writes, 'Woman must put herself into the text – as into the world and into history – by her own movement' (Cixous 1981, 245); or, to quote Woolf's own words: 'As a woman, I have no country. As a woman I want no country. As a woman my country is the whole world' (1938, 197).

Nicola Luckhurst
Goldsmiths College, London

1 Virginia Woolf among Writers and Critics: The French Intellectual Scene

Pierre-Éric Villeneuve

From the famous 'Entretien avec Virginia Woolf' (Interview with Virginia Woolf) conducted by Jacques-Émile Blanche for the literary journal *Les Nouvelles Littéraires* in August 1927 to the intertextual character of Edward Dalloway in Julia Kristeva's contemporary de Beauvoirian saga *Les Samouraïs* (The Samurai) (1990), the work of Virginia Woolf remains a milestone on the French literary scene. The connection between Woolf and France opens up a complex epistemological space that shows, in the context of the modern intellectual revolution, one of the subtlest paradoxes of twentieth-century literature. On one hand, there is a subjective tension, almost umbilical, that crystallizes a desire to find a lost archaic memory and an ancient origin: a space of fantasy and literary stimulation. On the other hand, there emerges a collective appropriation of another literary tradition with which – in juxtaposition – Bloomsbury so often compared itself. Over the years few critics have expressed interest in the relationship between Woolf and French culture and there have been no serious studies of the critical reception of her work in France despite Woolf's influence as a novelist via translation, her importance to French feminism and the imprint she made on other aspects of cultural life there.[1]

An examination of Woolf's relationship with French criticism must acknowledge that English studies in France during her lifetime focused on the Joycean revolution. To this day French critics continue to refer (or defer) to Joyce, firm in their opinion that he is the guiding light of literary life across the Channel. This unwavering loyalty to Joyce certainly shaped Woolf's critical reception throughout the 1920s and 1930s. It would be naive to ignore the fact that Woolf's reception is concomitant with Joyce's since the latter remains, along with Marcel Proust, a standpoint for comparison in most

My thanks to Wayne Chapman and *The South Carolina Review* for permission to publish a small part of an article first published in that journal.

[1] Certainly nothing comparable to the reception of James Joyce, documented especially in Aubert and Senn 1985.

French reviews, notably albeit not nobly Louis Gillet's chronicles of foreign literature in *La Revue des deux mondes*.[2] Gillet, a Joycean, has been the most hostile critic of Woolf's work and employed his bias liberally when he offered a definitive counterbalance to the criticism of Jacques-Émile Blanche, whose reviews were more receptive to Woolf,[3] as would be those of Mayoux, Maurois and Delattre in the 1930s.[4]

It is interesting to note that these French critics foreshadowed their English counterparts. Before England, the Parisian intellectual scene was an important

---

2 Francine Lenne's analysis of Joyce's reception, 'James Joyce et Louis Gillet' (James Joyce and Louis Gillet) (1985), is most convincing. It shows how Woolf's originality was sacrificed to the Joycean revolution in the 1920s and 1930s in France. One might cite here Gillet's criticism of *O* in *La Revue des deux mondes* published 1 September 1929 (the same year *Ulysses* was published in French). Lenne notes how costly this criticism will be to Woolf's reputation in France:

> This is what Mrs Woolf has succeeded in doing: taming in a way the great bear Mr Joyce, educating, cleaning, combing, perfuming, grooming him, in fact, refining him so much that the formidable animal came out of her hands, as curly-haired as a poodle and as gentle as a lamb.... It is easy to see that Mrs Virginia Woolf's books, *Jacob's Room*, *Mrs Dalloway*, *To the Lighthouse* bear the imprint of Mr James Joyce's genius. Whatever one thinks of *Ulysses*, this strange book remains a literary landmark.... Mrs Virginia Woolf would never have written this small masterpiece of the *Lighthouse* had *Ulysses* not been constantly in her thoughts. The novelist in her preface is right in citing many authors, the great family of English humorists, Defoe, Swift, Sterne, De Quincey: her book descends from them in a straight line. Why then omit Mr Joyce, the last and greatest of this powerful race? This oversight is unfair .... Perhaps all the fantasy of *Orlando* derives, in the final analysis, from the ramblings of Mr Joyce's hero and the nocturnal visions where, half-drunk, he takes his dreams for life' ('C'est pourtant ce qu'a réussi à faire Mme Virginia Woolf: elle apprivoise en quelque sorte l'ours M. Joyce, elle l'a éduqué, nettoyé, peigné, parfumé, bichonné, bref, elle l'a si bien léché que le formidable animal est sorti de ses mains frisé comme un caniche et doux comme un agneau .... Il est aisé de voir que les livres de Mme Virginia Woolf, *Jacob's Room*, *Mrs Dalloway*, *le Phare* portent l'empreinte du génie de M. James Joyce. Quoi qu'on pense d'*Ulysses*, ce livre étrange demeure une date littéraire .... Jamais Mme Virginia Woolf n'aurait écrit ce petit chef-d'œuvre du *Phare* si elle n'avait songé tout le temps à *Ulysses* .... Le romancier, dans sa préface, a bien raison de citer ses auteurs, la grande famille des humoristes anglais, Defoe, Swift, Sterne, de Quincey: son livre descend d'eux en droite ligne. Pourquoi omettre M. Joyce, le dernier et le plus grand de cette race puissante? Cet oubli est injuste .... Peut-être toute la fantaisie d'*Orlando* procède-t-elle, au bout du compte, des divagations du héros de M. Joyce et des visions nocturnes où, dans une demi-ivresse, il prend ses songes pour la vie.' (quoted in Lenne, 159))

3 In 1965 Georges-Paul Collet already notes that 'the French intelligentsia have been reading Woolf's novels for nearly forty years .... Among them, the painter and writer Jacques-Émile Blanche (1861–1942) played an important role, since he had the privilege to introduce her to France' (1965, 73).

4 See Bibliography. Although Woolf didn't have a patron such as Valéry Larbaud and Louis Gillet in Joyce's case, critics like Maurois, Delattre and Blanche were from the very first supportive in acknowledging her singular innovation.

centre for the diffusion of Bloomsbury aesthetics and values, discerning in them similarities to *La Nouvelle Revue Française*, the intellectual élite surrounding André Gide and Jacques Rivière between the wars and consequently the French intellectuals most involved in London's intellectual scene.[5] Woolf's reception in France was also mediated by the relationship Bloomsbury maintained with Paris, starting with the Post-Impressionist Exhibition in 1910. Various contacts of Clive Bell, Lytton Strachey and Roger Fry kept the association alive, as did the group's participation in the 'Entretiens de Pontigny' in 1923 and 1925. The French connection culminated with the Woolfs' involvement in the Congrès des Écrivains in London in 1935 on the invitation of E. M. Forster, where Woolf encountered Clara Malraux, who would later translate *ROO*. Out of these contacts would emerge a relationship with Charles Mauron, a close friend of Fry and Woolf's very first translator, publishing in 1926 a translation of the second section of 'Time Passes' (Le Temps passe) before *TL*'s British publication in 1927. A growing interest in Woolf's work anticipated the acknowledgement she would receive in 1928 in the form of one of France's highest literary distinctions, the Prix Fémina-Vie-Heureuse-Anglais, for her 'elegy' *TL*.[6]

Naturally, this nascent stage of critical response to Woolf was the result of the much wider access to the works afforded by these first French translations. It should be briefly noted that today most of Woolf's texts are available in translation, with the exception of some of the essays and letters.[7] A few of the novels have recently been retranslated, including *TW* by Cécile Wajsbrot (1993) and *MD* by Marie-Claire Pasquier (1994), the first novel listed in Gallimard's luxurious 'Pléiade' edition, recently followed by *TL* by Françoise Pellan (1996).

To understand the implications of the early reaction to Woolf, it is necessary to examine the importance of the first monograph, which appeared in France in 1932. This point of departure clarifies the development of ideas within Woolfian criticism since, and by closely inspecting this criticism from the margins inward, concludes why many French intellectuals have shown an uncommon interest in her work, having appreciated its innovations, limitations, political dimensions and, most certainly, craft.

Although a certain amount of criticism came out of France during Woolf's lifetime, only one book – and an important one, too – prophesied the literary monument Woolf would become, Floris Delattre's *Le Roman psychologique de Virginia Woolf* (The Psychological Novel of Virginia Woolf) (1932). And to Virginia Woolf, it seems, this was an unprecedented occasion for a dialogue

---

5 To this effect, we can mention David Steel's excellent synthesis entitled: 'Les Strachey, Bloomsbury, Gide et le groupe de *La Nouvelle Revue Française*' (1989). Steel insists on the similarities and dissonances between the two intellectual communities.

6 It is important to understand the nature of this prize – elected by women exclusively – founded in 1904. Woolf won the prize for the English novel.

7 For a list of French translations of Woolf see the Bibliography to Françoise Pellan's contribution to this volume.

with the private self under the pressure of public image, as evinced in the writer's diary of 1932: 'Two Books on Virginia Woolf have just appeared in France and in Germany. This is a danger signal. I must not settle into a figure' (*D* 4, 85).

We should be grateful for Delattre's appreciation of the originality of Woolf's romanesque innovation in its myriad figurations. Thematic, centred on what he calls 'a typically feminine character', his criticism would be the first to uncover the possibilities of Woolf's sensibility. He also produced one of the first historical genealogies of women novelists from the beginning of the nineteenth century onwards and started a tradition by constructing a locus for Woolf's 'literary personality'. Although courageous, Delattre's reading remains circumstantial, on a theoretical level by virtue of its reflection on time in the novel, and more particularly by its Bergsonian methodology[8]. It is faithful to general opinion, perceiving Woolf's individualistic experience as a mode of 'psychic ontology' which he believes to approximate to the Joycean 'metaphysic' and Proustian 'involuntary memory'. Ultimately, he illustrated how Woolf integrates both aesthetic modes.[9] The connection with Proust could have been generated by the interview by Jacques-Émile Blanche where Woolf clearly reveals that she has persistently put the question to herself.[10] Despite recognizing Woolf's virtues, Delattre concludes: 'The work of Virginia Woolf has neither the grandeur nor the architectural solidity of certain works by male authors, nor that balance of the creative faculties which assures endurance' (1994, 125).[11] As for Delattre's own staying powers, his interpretation dominated the bulk of novel reviews after *TW*. Delattre's perspective attained closure in a chapter he wrote on Woolf and the interior monologue (1950), part of an unfinished book about the writer. Today, his view might seem quaint.

Almost twenty years separated Delattre's first book and the next major work on Woolf. In between, a series of small articles reviewed each successive novel

---

8 Delattre also published books on Henri Bergson, the main focus of his analysis of Woolf's work.

9 Delattre offers an understanding of Woolf's work which could still be useful today. I am thinking particularly of its connection with Proust which is still neglected by general criticism. Being largely influenced by English writers – namely Pater and Ruskin – Proust experienced a literary polarization similar to Woolf's.

10 In 'L'Entretien avec Jacques-Émile Blanche' (1927), Blanche insists: 'She questions me about Marcel Proust, talks about French literature; she enjoys nothing more than reading our writers, gives a very flattering image of us. "How was Proust in his youth? Tell me, tell me? How did he begin in the world? Did people understand what he was writing?"' (my translation). Delattre perceptively examined the artistic and novelistic techniques framing the psychological aspects of Woolf's prose and highlighted the principles she so radically rejected in the novels of Bennett and Galsworthy. In doing so, he assimilated Woolf's style to French novelistic aesthetics, and to the Proustian sentence with its visionary aspects.

11 'L'œuvre de Virginia Woolf ne possède ni la grandeur ni la solidité architecturale de certaines œuvres d'hommes, ni non plus cet équilibre des facultés créatrices qui en assure la durée' (Delattre 1932, 255).

until *BTA*. Imperatively philosophical, in response to the rise of French existentialism and phenomenology, Maxime Chastaing's 1951 study *La Philosophie de Virginia Woolf* ascribes Woolf's work to an uncommon tradition by drawing a peculiar connection between Hume and Woolf around which the critic elaborates what he calls a 'principle of perspective'. It is more Woolf the philosopher than Woolf the writer that emerges from his attempt to capture her metaphysics of individual experience and its relation to objects, questions at the very core of philosophical debate in France in the 1950s. In a way, Chastaing remained closer than most French critics after him to Woolf's examination of the subject–object relation within formalism, in spite of the disagreements with Woolf inherent in the overpowering Catholic tone of his argument.[12]

At the same time as Chastaing's response to Woolf, another came from within a new intellectual vanguard in France, a perspective perhaps more interesting due to its frame of analysis, especially so considering its emergence in conflict with many ideas. Outside the margins of the 'specialists', grounded not in academia but evolving from a different political agenda, this alternative reception focused on the practice of writing and was more concerned about what an intellectual standpoint means. Three of these readers of Woolf's work in particular are sources deserving of continuing reference, to remind us of her potency for them as a symbol of individualist tradition and to assimilate their respect for the actuality of Woolf's voice, which they obviously recognized as groundbreaking. They are Simone de Beauvoir, Nathalie Sarraute and Maurice Blanchot.

The cultural impact that Virginia Woolf had on the French intellectual scene, particularly on the thinking and works of writers of the generation that emerged following her death, crosses many different fields of thought, philosophy, creative writing, critical thinking and feminism, among others. Nevertheless, critics have rarely emphasized Virginia Woolf's direct contribution to the new epistemologies of post-Second World War intellectuals. That, in spite of the ever-growing field of studies dedicated to the last novels *TL* or, even more so, *BTA*, known for its examination of forms of extinction (see Beer 1996). To this day, in Woolf studies across the world, the necessary questions and answers raised by comparative readings have focused mostly on other writers' influence on Woolf. These studies have on rare occasions looked at Woolf as a central influence on the creative process of other writers; in most cases, however, this central influence has taken a more natural path with English-speaking writers: Margaret Drabble, Toni Morrison and Jeanette Winterson have in recent years been notably popular subjects of study. It is also difficult to forget the number of recollections by writers who, in their later life, admitted to their far-reaching debts to Woolf's unique craft and vision. To name but a few, one might evoke Angus Wilson (1994, 159) claiming that 'She is, I believe, the master of twentieth-century narrative technique',

12 Some have discerned 'a Catholic tone' in certain translations as well.

Stephen Spender (1951) or Auden, reflecting on *TL* as one of the ultimate masterpieces.[13]

Influence is a difficult process to evaluate in quantitative or qualitative terms: it is part of the reading process. When an author engages with what defines for him or her a *foreign* literature, numerous factors are to be considered: in most cases, the act of translation mediates the writer's voice and often becomes the only way to access the unknown. Translation imposes its range of limitations, contradictions and often after publication of a text, it creates polemics: the example of Marguerite Yourcenar's evocative yet 'polished' and utterly 'classical' version of *TW* has proved notorious. Yet, there are more tangible ways by which a paradigm of influence or reception can be read, depending on the texts. Evident and direct commentaries made by one author on another certainly form some of the best evidence that critics have in their research into reception. Commentaries made by one author on another often indicate a community of spirit, hence my interest in the literary œuvres of intellectuals such as Simone de Beauvoir, Nathalie Sarraute and Maurice Blanchot, authors who have maintained a particular connection with Woolf's literary imagination. Another factor motivating my interest in these writers is related to the prejudice by which it is often claimed that Virginia Woolf's reputation was at its lowest in the late 1940s and 1950s – a debatable assertion when one carefully examines the French intellectual scene of that period, particularly its creative writers and thinkers.

To speak of a time of liberation for French intellectuals after the Second World War is to state the obvious. The end of the war means in every respect a moment of rupture, of change and new possibilities, as expressed so often by de Beauvoir, most notably in the opening of *La Force des choses* (*Force of Circumstance*):

> We were liberated. In the streets, the children were singing:
> *Nous ne les reverrons plus*
> *C'est fini, ils sont foutus.*
> And I kept saying to myself: it's all over, it's all over. It's all over: everything's beginning. (de Beauvoir 1964, 3)[14]

Coming from three different traditions, the three authors I have chosen are very iconoclastic in their response to Woolf's voice. All are interested in the problems of the writing/speaking subject, debated extensively in French intellectual circles. Simone de Beauvoir played a crucial role as an advocate for the importance of Woolf's materialist vision. Nathalie Sarraute brought her perspective to the juxtaposition of the tropes of *psychologisme*, as explored by Woolf, in her experimentation with the inner voice as a vehicle for the

---

13 In a letter to Elizabeth dated 13 July 1942, Auden writes: 'Have just re-read *To the Lighthouse* after many years. It's a masterpiece, I think' (Auden 1995, 82).

14 'Nous étions libérés. Dans les rues, les enfants chantaient: *Nous ne les reverrons plus. / C'est fini, ils sont foutus.* Et je me répétais: c'est fini, c'est fini. C'est fini: tout commence' (de Beauvoir 1963, 1: 13).

dramatic modes of speech and their effects on fiction. Finally, Blanchot's more metaphysical reading of Woolf as a 'poet of everyday life' is an important chapter in the examination of the experience of limits; his focus finds its resonance in post-Artaud modernism and in the radical ideas of Bataille, very much taboo at the time. We shall now examine these three perspectives in greater detail.

Simone de Beauvoir: New challenges for the woman writer

> I've borrowed Monique Nathan's *Virginia Woolf* from V. Leduc; now that I've read her *Diary of a Writer,* I wanted to have another look at the extraordinary faces of this woman – what a lonely face. (de Beauvoir 1964, 413)[15]

In investigating de Beauvoir's epistemic stance as regards her intellectual debts to Woolf, I would like to begin by evoking the irony one can read in the fact that the year 1929 saw her being awarded her *agrégation de philosophie*, with a dissertation on the topic 'Liberté et contingence' (Freedom and contingency) at the Sorbonne,[16] at almost exactly the same time that Virginia Woolf was presenting to the world *ROO*. Woolf's essay was to be very well assimilated over the following years by de Beauvoir, in her own plea for women's autonomy, *Le Deuxième Sexe (The Second Sex)* published in 1949, a manifesto in which de Beauvoir challenges the ultimate questions of masculine hegemony and its cultural effects in the regulation of knowledge, power and social identities.[17] It is also in *Le Deuxième Sexe* that de Beauvoir re-examines the assumptions of the *cogito*, defining her famous paradigm of the Subject, where she opposes immanence to the transcendence inherent in the will to know. She insists that:

> The drama of women lies in this conflict between the fundamental aspirations of every subject (ego) – who always regards the self as the essential – and the compulsions of a situation in which she is the inessential. (de Beauvoir 1953, 27)[18]

---

15 'J'ai emprunté à Violette Leduc le *Virginia Woolf* de Monique Nathan; je voulais regarder de nouveau, après avoir lu son journal, les extraordinaires visages de cette femme – quel visage solitaire' (de Beauvoir 1963, 2: 183).

16 See de Beauvoir 1979, 34. This text offers a very detailed overview of de Beauvoir's intellectual itinerary.

17 As synthesized in her most famous quotation: 'One is not born, but rather becomes, a woman. No biological, psychological, or economic fate determines the figure that the human female presents in society; it is civilization as a whole that produces this creature, intermediate between male and eunuch, which is described as feminine' (de Beauvoir 1953, 273). 'On ne naît pas femme, on le devient. Aucun destin biologique, psychique, économique ne définit la figure que revêt au sein de la société la femelle humaine; c'est l'ensemble de la civilisation qui élabore ce produit intermédiaire entre le mâle et le castrat qu'on qualifie de féminin' (de Beauvoir 1976, 2: 13).

18 'Le drame de la femme, c'est ce conflit entre la revendication fondamentale de tout sujet qui se pose toujours comme l'essentiel et les exigences d'une situation qui la constitue comme inessentielle' (de Beauvoir 1976, 1: 31).

Virginia Woolf's texts are used for different reasons by de Beauvoir. One might examine the intimate interpretation of *O* in *Tous les hommes sont mortels* (*All Men Are Mortal*), where one character, Fosca, becomes the agency for a serious discussion on the fatality of existence. One could also look closely at the various techniques of *L'Invitée* (*She Came to Stay*) and its dialogue with novels like *JR* and *MD*.[19] However, let us focus more closely on *Le Deuxième Sexe*, where one finds several references to Woolf, and three lectures given by de Beauvoir in Japan in autumn 1966. In spite of her different rhetorical modes, it is essential to mention that de Beauvoir opened Woolf's textuality to a political significance that went beyond anything imagined at a time when Woolf scholarship per se (in France and elsewhere) was still predominantly interested in her narrative achievements. De Beauvoir's interpretations, in the chapter 'Formation' (The Formative Years), take an interesting turn when she engages with Woolf's modernist fiction, especially her most poetic text *TW*. In this text, she analyses the materialist contingencies inflicted on women, using one of Susan's soliloquies as an example. For instance, by describing how the 'young girl' desires to transcend her own ontological limitations, she invites us to look at how Woolf is aware of the different stages of women's maturity, in their relation to their experience of various realities, within the confines of domesticity.

Within the context of Woolf scholarship of that time, de Beauvoir was certainly among the first to suggest a materialist agenda in Woolf's exploration of a social feminine subject, in a novel like *TW*. Her approach is groundbreaking especially when one considers the enormous difficulty some readers have had to this day understanding the novel's immediate social and political potential. What is crucial is that de Beauvoir radically locates Woolf's feminist epistemology according to the writer's point of view, offering a different view of the construction of women as social entities in the public sphere. It is a position that both writers never stopped fighting for, in spite of their different historical locations as women intellectuals. Of course, while they had in common the experience of hostile and trivial responses to their feminist works, and felt the same strong sense of isolation, their status as women writers was nevertheless defined very differently, according to their particular historical contexts and the cultural stigmas surrounding their public personas.[20] This is why de Beauvoir sees Woolf's voice as a moment of

---

19 The novel *L'Invitée* (*She Came to Stay*) (1943) presents a cryptic narrative around Françoise and Xavière, the main characters. The final words 'elle était l'absolue séparation' (de Beauvoir 1943, 440) ('she was absolute separateness' (de Beauvoir 1949, 431)) may serve as a reminder of the most intricate modes of subjection found in *MD* with its famous last words 'For there she was'. The final scene of de Beauvoir's novel also resembles *JR* in the sense that death breaks in, but is never mentioned, just implied at the edge of the reading process.

20 The best analysis of the contingencies imposed on de Beauvoir in terms of her critical reception is Toril Moi's *Simone de Beauvoir: The Making of an Intellectual Woman*. In her introduction, Moi is explicit: 'To live and work in France . . . is to expose oneself to an intellectual milieu where most people take Simone de Beauvoir's lack of intellectual and literary distinction as a basic article of faith. The very same

departure. In her very wide and international public life, de Beauvoir explicitly recognized Woolf's major contribution, and on several occasions. For instance, in autumn 1966, two of her three public lectures examined Woolf's critical thinking on the experiences of women as writing subjects, formulating a new dialogue with the ideas of *Le Deuxième Sexe*.

De Beauvoir's argument is an important step in the process of social legitimization of women as public intellectuals. It is her hope that all women will find a complete autonomy. Her first lecture, entitled 'Situation de la femme aujourd'hui' (Woman's situation today), demonstrates the political relevance of the thesis of *Le Deuxième Sexe*. It argues for more rights for women in the public sphere, following Woolf in emphasizing the symbolic status of writing as a public profession. Moreover, de Beauvoir's understanding of women's experience in a bourgeois world also reflects Woolf's concerns of the late 1930s, in the way that she juxtaposes women's realities to men's according to class definitions. She notes:

> Bourgeois democracy is bourgeois by definition, meaning that it implies that a certain class is entitled to run the country; this class naturally wants to preserve its privileges, its role as leader, that is to say the established order. We are touching on an extremely important point here. What matters is giving the impression that we are living in a democracy, while maintaining the established order which is founded upon inequality. In particular, women are kept in a state of inferiority. (de Beauvoir 1979, 434) (my translation)[21]

Like the later Woolf in *TG*, de Beauvoir saturates her concept of class as being different, within the same class paradigm, as an experience and as a form of oppression for men and women. Woolf is seen here commenting on the status of 'daughters of educated men', in probably one of the most important footnotes of *TG*, easily read as pre-de Beauvoirian: 'Obviously, if the term bourgeois fits her brother, it is grossly incorrect to use it of one who differs so profoundly in the two prime characteristics of the bourgeoisie – capital and environment' (*TG* 1986, 166).

Furthermore, by telling the truth about the contingencies forced upon the woman writer, de Beauvoir brilliantly historicizes her own situation. In her other lecture, entitled 'Mon expérience d'écrivain' (My Experience as a Writer), she once again alludes to the ambiguity of defining one's own writing practices. There is, inevitably, for herself as a writer as for Virginia Woolf, the same sense of responsibility that permeates her will to tell. This form of empowerment, or responsibility, has constituted one of the bases of the modern feminist agenda, certainly since Woolf. Indeed it is easy to recall here

---

cont.
intellectuals who passionately defend every citizen's abstract right to speak are often only too eager to prevent anybody from speaking about [de] Beauvoir' (1994, 11).

21 '[L]a démocratie bourgeoise est bourgeoise, c'est-à-dire qu'elle implique que la direction du pays appartient à une certaine classe . . . . Il s'agit de donner l'impression qu'on est en démocratie, tout en conservant l'ordre établi qui est fondé sur l'inégalité. En particulier, on maintiendra les femmes dans un état d'infériorité.'

the construction of the female 'I' in *ROO* theorized as a social artefact ('I' is a convenient term for somebody who has no real being), and translated into de Beauvoir's fights for honesty, articulated via her commitment to find a 'voice' that is personal, yet, like Woolf before her, relevant to others: 'The "I" which I am using is in fact very often a "we" or a "one" which alludes to the community of my century rather than to myself' (1979, 450). Or more so: 'The "I" that I am using is an I with a general significance' (450). De Beauvoir, like Woolf, knows the risks taken by women when they are speaking subjects. She insists: 'I mean that I am I for myself alone' (456).[22]

Following de Beauvoir's logical frame of thought, her argument goes further (as an exercise in transcendence) in her last lecture, which engages with the articulation of the complex relation between 'women' and the 'artistic creation'. In her lecture entitled 'La femme et la création', de Beauvoir explores the subject of Woolf's celebrated 'Women and Fiction'. Here again, the experience of the 'I', the writing subject, is objectified as a focal point, a potential for new representations and possibilities. That said, in the light of her main agenda, one can argue that de Beauvoir is less disruptive than Woolf in her critique of the contingencies and the stigmas imposed upon the woman writer in a male-dominated literary tradition. For instance, when she alludes to the fact that Woolf

> was treated by her father like a boy; he transferred all the ambitions to her that he could have had for a boy. She was always encouraged to write; she became the writer that she became in accordance with her father's will (1979, 468),[23]

de Beauvoir is in fact neglecting the real opposition Woolf faced in her will from 1904 on, to tell her own stories as a way of transcending the contingencies of controlling family scenarios. It underlines another paradox of de Beauvoir's reading of *ROO*, which indicates a pattern of sublimation through the reading process, communicated through de Beauvoir's own ambivalence and situation in the act of writing. *ROO* radically disrupts the paternal heritage to seek new ways of reading literary history both, in a private manner, by placing Woolf and her enactments within a family genealogy, and at the same time, by publicly destabilizing the regimes of power around which knowledge was traditionally produced and from which women were alienated. Ultimately, it is what de Beauvoir, like Woolf at Girton College, invites her Japanese audience to do: she urges them to commit to their own stories.

This last of the three lectures given by de Beauvoir in Japan contains the same hopes as were envisioned by Woolf for the future of women intellectuals. Returning to the daunting photographs mentioned in the epigraph of this

---

22 'Le "je" dont je me sers est très souvent en vérité un "nous", ou un "on", qui fait allusion à l'ensemble de mon siècle plutôt qu'à moi-même', 'le "je" que j'utilise est un je qui a une portée générale', 'je veux dire que je suis je pour moi seule.'

23 'Woolf a été traité par son père comme un garçon; il a reporté sur elle toutes les ambitions qu'il aurait pu avoir pour un garçon. Elle a toujours été encouragé à écrire; elle est devenue l'écrivain qu'elle est devenue en accord avec la volonté paternelle.'

commentary on de Beauvoir, in her own construction of Woolf as 'solitaire' one can hear the echo of one of de Beauvoir's most celebrated passages: the opening of the last volume of her autobiography entitled *Tout compte fait* (All Said and Done), which is very Woolfian in tone: 'My life: it is both intimately known and remote; it defines me and yet I stand outside it. Just what, precisely, is this curious object?' (1974, 1-2).[24]

In this passage, it is clear that de Beauvoir learned from the moderns, not least Woolf, when she sees the spectrum of her life through the distance of the writing/speaking subject. Stephen Spender in his recollections of Woolf mentions that

> She seemed as detached from herself as from everyone else. Thus she would talk about herself with an objectivity which was unambiguous in her but which in others would have seemed uneasy. (Spender 1951, 156)

de Beauvoir's axiomatic sentence contains a dialectic. It encloses an object, around which the writing subject defines it/herself as 'curious'. It is probably where de Beauvoir comes closest to Woolf's powerful modes of subjectivation found in *TW*, strangely like Rhoda's disarticulation, in which the voice and the body are seen as phenomena outside 'the loop of time'. At this moment, de Beauvoir reaches what has been narrated by Woolf and what will be exemplified by Sarraute's fiction, that is, the radical possibilities of the uneventful.

Nathalie Sarraute: The tensions of the dramatic mode

> Ann Villelaur: You are often compared to Virginia Woolf. How do you feel about this?
> Nathalie Sarraute: Our resemblance and the influence Virginia Woolf has had on my writing have been extensively spoken about. I believe that our sensibilities are very much opposed. For Virginia Woolf, her entire universe, stirred up by time, rolls along through the consciousness of her characters, who are passive by nature, carried from side to side by the uninterrupted currents of moments.
>
> With me, characters are always in a state of hyperactivity: a dramatic action plays itself out at the level of their 'tropisms', these movements being very quick at the edges of consciousness. This is where our very different styles come from. (Sarraute 1961b)

If Virginia Woolf was for de Beauvoir a standard of comparison in respect to her writing practices as a form of socio-political commitment, she is, for Nathalie Sarraute, a deep source of fascination and influence hidden and dealt with in the most complex registers of ambivalence. Once again, for Sarraute, it is writing itself that becomes the paradigm of anxieties, because she is coming to terms with a very similar community of spirit and tradition. The inner

---

24 'Ma vie: familière et lointaine, elle me définit et je lui suis extérieure. Qu'est-ce au juste que ce bizarre objet?' (de Beauvoir 1972, 12).

conversation with Woolf can be viewed as productive but with more generative tensions than for de Beauvoir. Some of these tensions were clearly expressed, not without their contradictions, in Sarraute's interview with Ann Villelaur 'Virginia Woolf ou la visionnaire du maintenant' (Virginia Woolf or the visionary of the now) given in 1961 to mark the occasion of the twentieth anniversary of Woolf's death, and in Sarraute's famous collections of short essays *L'Ère du soupçon* (The Age of Suspicion) (1956).

Firstly it is important to note that Sarraute relies, in her reconstruction of Woolf's arguments, on the collection of essays in *CR 1*, written at the same time as *MD* and published in the same year (1925). It is also important to indicate that most of Sarraute's criticism of Woolf seems to engage with the ideas of the essay 'Modern Fiction', first published (as 'Modern Novels') in the *Times Literary Supplement* in 1919, thus *before* the complete publication of Joyce's *Ulysses* and six years before the publication of *MD*. The consequences are twofold and need some contextualization. Evidence shows that *MD* occupies a predominant place in Sarraute's reading of Woolf, as mentioned in her series of interviews with Simone Benmussa in *Nathalie Sarraute: Qui êtes-vous?* (Nathalie Sarraute: Who Are You?):

> S.B. You have always told me that you found *Mrs Dalloway* admirable.
> N.S. Always. From the beginning I have always loved it, just as I have never renounced for one second Proust, who overwhelmed me. I have always hated psychoanalysis and I never thought that what Proust had revealed to us could be reduced to nothing by Freudian analysis, not for a second. How tremendously I loved Virginia Woolf's works, especially *Mrs Dalloway*, her best book. I've never changed my opinion. (Sarraute 1987, 44) (my translation)[25]

These comments allow me to question a very important tension between Sarraute and her modernist predecessor, which is the definition of 'psychology' theorized by Sarraute as what controls Woolf's narrative modalities. In most articles and studies dealing with the possibility of the inner voice, the connection between Woolf and Sarraute is established around this first phase of Woolf's modernist programme in the 1920s. This emphasis on the 'psychological' becomes rather problematic if one examines the very different definitions Woolf finds to define the poetic process from the 1920s to the early 1930s, considering both *TW* and the aftermath of that novel's revolution in the narrative voice. Ethel F. Cornwell's article (1977) on the relation between Woolf's, Sarraute's and Mary McCarthy's approaches to character in fiction, or the articles by Roger Noël (1970) and Ruby Cohn (1964) focusing on the precise connection between Sarraute and Woolf, are extremely debatable in

---

25 'S. B. Tu m'as toujours dit que tu trouvais *Mrs Dalloway* admirable.
N. S. Toujours. Depuis le début j'ai toujours aimé, comme je n'ai jamais renié une seconde Proust qui a été un bouleversement pour moi. J'ai toujours détesté la psychanalyse et je n'ai jamais pensé que ce que nous avait révélé Proust puisse être réduit à rien par les analyses freudiennes, pas une seconde. Comme j'aimais énormément les œuvres de Virginia Woolf, notamment *Mrs Dalloway*, son meilleur livre. Je n'ai jamais changé d'avis.'

their assumptions, as they are interested solely in the lyrical side of Woolf's prose, viewed as antagonistic to Sarraute's project.[26] In the case of Cohn, the emphasis on the analysis of the protagonist of *Martereau* indicates, among other things, a lack of reflection on the direct influence of *JR*, and the creation of Woolf's character as petrified in the outline of objects, or the articulation in space and time of the elusive Perceval in *TW*. It would indeed be naive (to use Sarraute's expression) to imagine, following Cohn, that 'unlike Virginia Woolf who leads us with omniscience from one mind to another, Nathalie Sarraute never intervenes in the narration (1964, 176)'.[27] The use of words like 'omniscience' seems at odds with Woolf's narrative, and she doesn't quite intervene in the flow of her narrative either, even in the most private of literary genres.

Sarraute, it is fair to say, takes perverse pleasure in quoting Woolf's statements in 'Modern Fiction' to make her point: 'For the moderns "that", the point of interest, lies very likely in the dark places of psychology' ('Modern fiction', *CDML*, 5-12). It gives her a chance to create what will remain an uneasy distance. She insists that today Woolf's ideas with 'their naive confidence, their innocence of another age, would only elicit a smile' (Sarraute 1963a, 77).[28] For their differing interpretations of 'the dark places of psychology' are precisely what generates conflict in the way Sarraute and Woolf understand the inner voice. Resistant to Woolf's use of 'psychology' as she is, Sarraute fails, in her comments, to situate the real implications of Woolf's investments in 'the dark places', so close in reality to Sarraute's own modes of self-effacement: *les tropismes*. Is it possible to see, in Sarraute's respect for *MD*, yet another strategy to eradicate the obvious, or mislead the reader seeking any pattern of influence? Is *TW* not closer to Sarraute's kind of aesthetics? Woolf's investments in trying to find the right pace of inner conversation in *TW* strangely resemble Sarraute's elliptic modes of speech acts. Let us take, for example, the construction of primitive rhythms in 'Ich Sterbe', the short story that opens the collection of narratives included in *L'Usage de la parole* (*The Use of Speech*) (1980, reinventing the methods of Sarraute's first texts, *Tropismes* (*Tropisms*), published in 1939). It is primitive in the organization of the words repeated, the rhythms which reverberate in the mind of the protagonists, as an echo of Chekhov's last words which are themselves primitive in their fatality: *Ich sterbe* (I am dying). Here again, like Woolf in *TW*, Sarraute's emphasis will be on the dramatic quality and the dramatic effect found in the presentness of the dying speaking voice. Remember Bernard, trying to find 'a little language' to express the presentness of his death?

---

26 One could also cite the paradoxical example given by Cohn, when she contrasts the registers of Woolf's flexible characters with Sarraute's, through the voice of the narrator of *Martereau*, where, once again, I strongly believe an analysis of the limits of the voices of *TW* would have shown more similarities. See Cohn 1964, 173.

27 'A la différence de Virginia Woolf qui nous conduit avec omniscience d'un esprit dans l'autre, jamais Nathalie Sarraute n'intervient dans le cours du récit.'

28 '[L]eur confiance naïve, leur innocence d'un autre âge feraient sourire' (Sarraute 1956, 84).

Moreover, in *L'Ère du soupçon*, Sarraute, very much like Woolf in 'Modern Fiction', tries to justify the legitimacy of a new attitude in the novel. She seeks new roles for the reader and invites full autonomy of the speaking voice as it remains in the theatrical mode, giving the reader full responsibility for interacting with the text:

> Because theatrical dialogue, which needs no props, and during which the author does not constantly make us feel that he is present, ready to lend a hand, this dialogue, which must be self-sufficient and on which everything rests, is denser, tauter, more compact and at a higher tension than fictional dialogue: it makes greater demands on the combined powers of the spectator. (Sarraute 1963a, 106)[29]

The theatrical elements of the narrative, from dialogues to the construction of characters, are ironically the emphasis of Sarraute's criticism of the modernist movement, from Woolf, to Joyce, to Proust. If she finds a form of reconciliation in the prose of Ivy Compton-Burnett, for that matter, she sees that the voice, via the sentences, articulates the necessary tensions between what is said and what is thought. Sarraute remarks that Compton-Burnett's dialogues:

> are located not in an imaginary place, but in a place that actually exists: somewhere on the fluctuating frontier that separates conversation from subconversation. Here the inner movements, of which dialogue is merely the outcome and, as it were, the furthest point – usually prudently tipped to allow it to come up to the surface – try to extend their action into dialogue itself. (1963a, 114)[30]

One might wish that Sarraute had given more time and credit, in her reflections, to the architecture of Woolf's *TY*, constantly shifting from the modulation of the speaking voice in the actual dialogue to the reflective moment, precisely, of what was said, or more importantly, impossible to tell. On the whole, it is nonetheless a similar dislocation of the moment of speech, in the instant, that saturates Sarraute's plays with voices in her novels, or in her texts written for the theatre, like *Le Silence* (1967), where the pleasures given by the materiality of the speaking voice are found in the deepest origins of the dramatic mode: dialogue. It also gives new meaning to what is probably Woolf's and Sarraute's closest intellectual connection, that is, their fascination with the literature and traditions of the Russians. Interestingly enough,

---

29 'Car le dialogue de théâtre, qui se passe de tuteurs où l'auteur ne fait pas à tout moment sentir qu'il est là, prêt à donner un coup de main, ce dialogue qui doit suffire à lui-même et sur lequel tout repose, est plus ramassé, plus dense, plus tendu et survolté que le dialogue romanesque: il mobilise davantage toutes les forces du spectateur' (Sarraute 1956, 112).

30 'se situent non dans un lieu imaginaire, mais dans un lieu qui existe dans la réalité: quelque part sur cette limite fluctuante qui sépare la conversation de la sous-conversation. Les mouvements intérieurs, dont le dialogue ne sont que l'aboutissement et pour ainsi dire l'extrême pointe, d'ordinaire prudemment mouchetée pour affleurer au dehors, cherchent ici à se déployer dans le dialogue même' (Sarraute 1956, 120).

Woolf's generous approach to the realities of what constitutes what is foreign, in the texts of Tolstoy, Turgenev or Dostoevsky might echo Sarraute's interest in the moderns, and Woolf in particular. It is radically, for both novelist and critic, the loss of an archaic origin and soul that mediates the voice in the moment, as recalled in Sarraute's essay *De Dostoïevski à Kafka* (From Dostoevsky to Kafka), more Woolfian in its deepest elements than Sarraute would like to think:

> These subjacent movements, this incessant swirl, similar to the movement of atoms, that all of these grimaces bring to light, are themselves nothing else but action, and they only differ by their delicacy, their complexity and their 'underground' nature – to use one of Dostoevsky's favourite words. (Sarraute 1963a, 30)[31]

Maurice Blanchot: Vocation

Blanchot, in his reading of Woolf's texts over the same period, was more interested in the Woolfian question of poetics and the future of the novel. In the opening argument of the famous dialogue between Foucault and Blanchot, Foucault asserts in his essay on Blanchot 'La Pensée du dehors' (The Thought from Outside) (1966) that 'the speaking subject is also the subject about which it speaks'[32] (Foucault and Blanchot 1987, 10). This gives a tone to the dialogue between Woolf and Blanchot which follows a path both similar to and different from those explored by de Beauvoir and Sarraute in the philosophical context of the 1950s. Blanchot's response is similar in that he too is fascinated by Woolf's radical attitudes towards writing but different in that it is Woolf's experience of limits and her excess that punctuate what he calls 'the perfidious vocation'[33] (1982, 91) connecting him, as a reader, to 'the subject about which it speaks'.

This question of the speaking subject is completely empty of its elements of pathos. Blanchot's view of Woolf, then, was diametrically opposed to Sarraute's from the moment he published his first critical analysis of Woolf's works, his review of *Les Vagues* (*TW*), in 1937, for the leftist journal *L'Insurgé* (The Insurgent), later to be republished as 'Le Temps et le roman' (Time and the Novel) in *Faux Pas* (1943). Blanchot insists: 'This extraordinary adventure has only been possible because Virginia Woolf imagined a fiction from which

---

[31] 'Ces mouvements sous-jacents, ce tourbillonnement incessant, semblable au mouvement des atomes, que toutes ces grimaces mettent au jour, ne sont-eux mêmes rien d'autres que de l'action et ne diffère que par leur délicatesse, leur complexité, leur nature – pour employer un mot de Dostoïevski – "souterraine"' (Sarraute 1956, 34).

[32] '[L]e sujet parlant est le même que celui dont il est parlé' (Foucault 1994, 1: 519).

[33] 'la perfide vocation' (Blanchot 1959, 124).

all psychology is excluded' (1943, 283).[34] It is a step that anticipates his notorious interpretation of *WD* (1959), which, for a variety of reasons, is a milestone in the entire history of Woolf's reception. First, it portrays Woolf as a poet of the everyday life by examining the diary narrative. Secondly, it aims to dislocate, for almost the first time, the hierarchical relations that bound fiction and autobiography. Finally, and perhaps most importantly, Woolf, far from being second to Joyce, is in the first rank in Blanchot's philosophical investigation alongside Homer, Goethe, Rousseau and Artaud, in what Blanchot sees as 'the fascination of extremes' ('la fascination des extrêmes') (1959, 61).

In the chapter dedicated to Woolf entitled 'L'Échec du démon: la vocation' ('Outwitting the Demon: A Vocation') in *Le Livre à venir* (The Book Yet to Come) (1959), the term 'vocation' is the most crucial and resonates on a metaphysical, almost mystical level, the potential of the imagination. It is also used in a materialist fashion, with respect to the demands that writing imposes on the body. Blanchot reads Woolf in a way that gives the experience of the moment its most radical meaning:

> This is to experience the present; and what, we may ask, could be easier? Easy, maybe, yet requiring such self-effacement, such deep humility, so complete a faith in the unlimited powers of dispersion (the essence of infidelity) that the risks it involves are obvious. (Blanchot 1982, 89)[35]

Close to de Beauvoir's existentialist concept of a responsible self, the focal point is the risk taken at every step of the writing practice. Blanchot comments: 'Art reveals itself in Virginia Woolf for what it is, something terribly serious. Cheating is out of the question' (1982, 138).[36] The idea of a vocation thus incorporates the limits of artistic creation. Vocation has, for Blanchot, the same registers of dedication that he sees in the 'perverse' side of 'fidelity' (1959, 126), that is, its exclusionary aspects. Here he follows the tradition of the Stoics, which is very important for situating the philosophical implications of vocation in Blanchot's reading of Woolf. In being honest about some aspects of Woolf's life with which he sympathizes, he never falls into simple stereotypes. Implied as it is from the moment the idea of vocation is compared to a demon, Blanchot evokes by the end of his interpretation the inevitable suicide. And here, Blanchot transcends and breaks away from the logical patterns of reading suicide and allows himself to theorize about it as a point of origin, of departure.

Blanchot had much to say about what constitutes one's weakness; in respect

---

34 'Cette extraordinaire aventure n'a été possible que parce que Virginia Woolf a imaginé une fiction d'où toute psychologie est exclue' (Blanchot 1943, 283).

35 'C'est l'expérience de l'instant, et quoi de plus facile, pensera-t-on; facile, je ne sais pas, mais exigeant une telle séparation de soi, une si grave humilité, une fidélité si complète à un pouvoir illimité de dispersion (l'essence de l'infidélité) que l'on voit bien quel risque finalement il faut courir' (Blanchot 1959, 123).

36 'L'art en Virginia Woolf se montre ce qu'il est, d'un terrible sérieux. Il n'est pas permis de tricher' (Blanchot 1959, 123).

of the creative imagination, he argues, while speaking about Woolf's working habits, that:

> Hers was the indomitable strength of weaknesses – it seems that when she had reached the end of her tether she discovered untapped resources. (1982, 90)[37]

Such a comment merits a small parenthesis and explanation, because an important intertextual connection can be made with Marguerite Yourcenar's introduction to her translation of *TW* (1937).[38] The connection with Yourcenar opens yet another door into the French reception that deserves more attention. What is relevant here is not only the inevitable choice of *TW*, so rich in its dialogue with the Greeks, very appealing even then for the young Yourcenar, but the need to find a common voice for the spiritual and the intellectual: two important sides of Bernard, the born writer. Finally, it is the combination of extreme paradoxes in Woolf's writing methods that Blanchot finds the most appealing to his own sense of working constantly with contradictions. He insists:

> Yet it is the artist's prerogative to maintain, in each new work, a certain indecision in his decision, limitless within limits, and to say nothing which might impair the space of speech or his freedom to say everything. (1982, 92)[39]

Blanchot is no exception here; like de Beauvoir and Sarraute, readers of Woolf, he strongly believes in the importance of telling one's own stories.

Before concluding, I would like to explore the delicate matter of suicide, as an epistemological question, so essential to all kinds of interpretation of

---

37 'C'est là que se laisse pressentir l'indomptable force propre à la faiblesse, comme si, lorsque nous ne pouvons plus rien, se dégageait parfois la ressource d'un tout autre pouvoir' (Blanchot 1959, 125).

38 I am referring to the end of Yourcenar's introduction which anticipates Blanchot's comment:

> In the drawing room, vaguely lit by a glimmering fire, where Mrs Woolf kindly received me, I watched the pale face of a young Fate, barely ageing but delicately marked by signs of thought and lassitude, emerge against the half-light, and I said to myself that the charge of intellectualism is often brought against the keenest, most ardently living natures, who are forced by their fragility or their superabundance of strength to have constant recourse to the severe disciplines of the mind ('Dans le salon vaguement éclairé par les lueurs du feu où Mrs Woolf avait bien voulu m'accueillir, je regardais se profiler sur la pénombre ce pâle visage de jeune Parque à peine vieillie, mais délicatement marquée des signes de la pensée et de la lassitude, et je me disais que le reproche d'intellectualisme est souvent adressé aux natures les plus fines, les plus ardemment vivantes, obligées par leur fragilité ou par leur excès de forces à recourir sans cesse aux dures disciplines de l'esprit' (1937, 12–13).

39 'Le propre de l'écrivain est, en chaque œuvre, de réserver l'indécis dans la décision, de préserver l'illimité auprès de la limite et de ne rien dire qui ne laisse intact tout l'espace de la parole ou la possibilité de tout dire' (Blanchot 1959, 126).

Woolf's works (for better or worse) across the world, including her considerable reception in France. Blanchot conceptualizes suicide as inherent to the modes of Woolf's vocation as a writer, to be understood here as a moment of acute and positive consciousness: an outside. Foucault considers Blanchot's use of the outside as a kind of attraction. Outside is also a word of profound significance for Woolf. Through the notion of outside, one criticizes the usual paradigms opposing good and bad in the morality of suicide. Blanchot, like the young Virginia Stephen having a conversation with her sister Vanessa in 1905, understands the necessary elements surrounding 'the ethics of suicide'. The tone of Blanchot's last oxymoronic comments describing Woolf's particular vocation as 'that glorious degradation which Virginia Woolf chose to avoid by sinking' (1982, 93) highlights her stoic attitudes vis-à-vis the rituals of life and death.[40] If Blanchot paradoxically thinks that there is a moment of 'failure' – in itself a Woolfian concept – this point of failure can be seen as a moment where the beauty of the text certainly speaks out to the reader.

In conclusion, the critical elements elaborated by these three major figures of the intellectual scene in France following the Second World War, illustrate the complexities of an age obsessed by the will to tell and to do things differently. In the spectrum of the dark places of the living moment brought to the surface by Virginia Woolf, each of these writers has moments of uneasiness, resistance, which form a critique for no conclusive reasons except their historical positions in the act of reading. In fact, as different as these writers are, their seminal effect in their own time nonetheless indicates certain patterns of repetition. For instance, one might examine more closely the pressure forcing Simone de Beauvoir to refuse, for so many years, the implications of seeing herself as a responsible feminist subject. Furthermore, de Beauvoir's materialist views on Woolf's texts can be understood as paradoxical, if one recalls her later comments on her predecessor's works. It seems hard to imagine that, in an interview given to her most important biographer, Deirdre Bair, just before her death, de Beauvoir reiterated her passion for

> Woolf's feminist essays, because I don't agree with her novels. They don't have any centre. There isn't any thesis. (Bair 1990, 655n)

In searching, in her later life, for a semblance of 'thesis' in Woolf's works – as de Beauvoir inevitably understands it – she failed to grasp the impact of Woolf's later fictional experiments, notably *TY*. How very revealing are her comments in the interviews given in the film made by Josée Dayan in 1978, in the context of her attitude as a celebrated and rigorous woman writer: 'I have always worked extensively on what I have written, but I have not, however, tried to be a literary virtuoso – let us say like a Virginia Woolf. It is not really

---

40 '[L]a glorieuse déchéance à laquelle Virginia Woolf a préféré échapper en sombrant' (Blanchot 1959, 126).

what interested me' (Dayan and Ribowska 1979, 77) (my translation).[41] Following de Beauvoir's resistance, how more challenging it is to think that Nathalie Sarraute's repudiation of the moderns might be just another rhetorical strategy hiding the illusion that she, in fact, does accomplish something totally different, by using dialogue and sequences of speech just as they occur. When asked by Simone Benmussa if she ever met Virginia Woolf, how dramatic indeed is her aggressive or indifferent response:

> Before killing herself, Woolf herself wrote or said: 'How all these young people hate me.' And that was absolutely right. What she wrote was considered as addressing only the upper class, as stories for ladies. (Benmussa 1987, 43)[42]

Or when asked by Benmussa if she ever met Woolf, Sarraute invokes an intimidation that invites scepticism:

> What could one do? As Ivy Compton-Burnett told me later, she was a real snob. There was no way she would have met me at that time. Why? For what reason? It was not possible. (44)[43]

Finally, Blanchot is no better, dealing with his uneasiness by emphasizing 'le piège du journal' ('the diary trap'), deploring the fact that Woolf is a 'bavardeuse' ('chatterbox'), and vain,[44] contrasting the diary with the pure sense of anonymity that animates *TW*. Certainly, Woolf had experienced

---

41 'J'ai toujours beaucoup travaillé ce que j'écrivais mais je n'ai quand même pas essayé d'être une virtuose de l'écriture – mettons comme une Virginia Woolf. Ce n'est pas tellement ce qui m'a interessé.'

42 'Virginia Woolf avait elle-même, avant de se tuer, écrit ou dit: "Comme tous ces jeunes gens me détestent!" Et c'était tout à fait exact. Ce qu'elle écrivait était considéré comme ne s'adressant qu'à la "upper class", des histoires de grandes dame.'

43 'Comment veux-tu? Elle était comme m'a dit plus tard Ivy Compton-Burnett, extrèmement snob. Il n'était pas question à l'époque qu'elle me rencontre. Pourquoi? A quel titre? Ce n'était pas possible.'

44 Blanchot notes:

> But that a writer as pure as Virginia Woolf, that an artist as intent on creating a work that retained only the transparency, the luminous halo and bright contours of things, felt obliged to come back to herself in a gossipy diary, where the 'I' vents and consoles itself, that is significant and troubling. The diary seems here to be a safeguard against the dangers of writing. Down there in *The Waves* there roars the risk of a work where one must disappear. The diary is the anchor scraping the bed of the everyday, grappling onto the protuberances of vanity ('Mais qu'un écrivain aussi pur que Virginia Woolf, qu'une artiste aussi acharnée à créer une œuvre qui retienne seulement la transparence, l'auréole lumineuse et les contours légers des choses, se soit sentie comme obligée de revenir auprès d'elle-même dans un journal de bavardage où le Je s'épanche et se console, cela est significatif et troublant. Le journal apparaît bien ici comme un garde-fou contre le danger de l'écriture. Là-bas dans *Les Vagues*, gronde le risque d'une œuvre où il faut disparaître. Le journal est l'ancre qui racle contre le fond du quotidien et s'accroche aux aspérités de la vanité') (1959, 226–27).

tribulations with many of her predecessors and contemporaries. It is often part of the tactics of Woolf's most severe critics to emphasize her so-called jealous impulses. We too often forget that she was also the most generous of readers, in her comments on authors living in her lifetime, without being able to sum up what they were about.

Of these three French intellectuals, also contemporaries of Woolf, respectively thirty-three (de Beauvoir), forty-one (Sarraute) and thirty-four (Blanchot) in 1941, Blanchot as a critic gets the nearest to Woolf, when he expresses the tangible relationship that exists between texts and readers. His own answer to Michel Foucault (twenty years after Foucault's text about him) is very enlightening in the dislocations of the 'speaking subject', as it relates to the axiom raised by Foucault mentioned earlier: 'the speaking subject is also the subject about which it speaks'. Blanchot's examination of Roger Caillois's difficulty in identifying with 'Foucault's style, in its splendour and precision' (Foucault and Blanchot 1987, 64) is very revealing.[45] In fact, Maurice Blanchot's scepticism about Caillois as a reader of Foucault might also be applied to himself, Nathalie Sarraute and Simone de Beauvoir as objective writers, critics and readers of Virginia Woolf, when he argues: 'No one likes to recognize himself as a stranger in a mirror where what he sees is not his double but someone whom he would have liked to have been' (Foucault and Blanchot 1987, 64).[46]

45 'le style de Foucault, par sa splendeur et sa précision' (Blanchot 1986, 11).

46 'Personne n'aime se reconnaître, étranger, dans un miroir où il ne discerne pas son double, mais celui qu'il aurait aimé être' (Blanchot 1986, 11).

2 The French Reception of Woolf: An *État Présent* of *Études Woolfiennes*

Carole Rodier

The name of Virginia Woolf is not only closely linked with modernism;[1] it also carries connotations of difficulty. Virginia Woolf created a body of work problematic both in what it offers and what it demands, so that coming to read her works it is not unusual to feel an initial sense of alienation. This partly explains the ideological and emotional debates Woolf continually provokes. In France, this manifests itself in the overuse of critical tools in a desperate attempt to grasp the meaning(s) of her works. Indeed, as a modernist writer, Woolf was bound to tempt critics eager to apply their grids to her work. Whereas Anglo-American criticism emphasizes the historical and social contexts, the French reception of Woolf has historically taken the form of a quest for textual autonomy, whereby her works fly free of any deterministic notion of literature.

The intellectual reception of Woolf testifies to the true affective impact and reaction that she aroused in the French, and has established her as a uniquely stimulating creator. Her contribution to French feminism is undoubted. Simone de Beauvoir was instrumental in establishing her as a great writer,[2] and Woolf's influence permeates Julia Kristeva's works. Even Nathalie Sarraute,[3] although in a more ambiguous way, played a part in the canonization of

---

1 See Zéraffa 1969 and 1978. See also Lipovetsky 1983 and Gallix 1995.

2 See Pierre-Éric Villeneuve's contribution to this volume.

3 Nathalie Sarraute has always denied any comparison or even any affinity between her work and that of Woolf. She goes as far as saying that their sensitivities are diametrically opposed ('je crois que nos sensibilités sont vraiment à l'opposé l'une de l'autre') (Sarraute 1961, 3). It is true that the theme of time, omnipresent in Woolf, is absent from Sarraute's works which are characterized by the importance of the present in which her 'characters' are actively involved. Therefore, the hyperactivity of the 'tropisms' or 'sub-conversation' is very different from the stream of consciousness (see Cohn 1964 and Sarraute 1956). In fact, Sarraute can be seen to have taken Woolf's narrative ambitions a step further. See Stephen Heath (1972) for a comparison of the two writers.

Woolf. Maurice Blanchot (1959) incorporated the study of Woolf in his reflection on writing.[4] Paul Ricoeur (1984) applied to *MD* his semiotic approach. Gilles Deleuze and Félix Guattari (1980) proposed a philosophical interpretation of Woolf to explore their concepts of 'deterritorialization', 'rhizome' and 'becoming'.[5] Deleuze (1997) also analyses Woolf as part of the broader category of English writers whose works exemplify his notion of 'ligne de fuite' ('line of flight') or 'ligne brisée' ('broken line').[6]

Woolf has not only been appropriated by theoreticians. These last three decades have seen more emotional responses to Woolf. In the wake of Hélène Cixous but without her theoretical standpoint, Anne Bragance (1994) and Françoise Defromont (1995) wrote on Woolf in a very personal manner. Interestingly enough, after writing to testify to Woolf's influence on her (1982) Cécile Wajsbrot tackled the translation of *TW* in 1995. More recently, such books as *Elles ne savent pas ce qu'elles disent* (They Don't Know What They're Saying) by Maud Mannoni and *La Canne de Virginia Woolf* (Virginia Woolf's Cane) by Laurent Sagalovitsch (both 1998) reveal the pervasiveness of Woolf's influence in France. Bloomsbury has also generated many studies.[7] In 1974, Jean Guiguet directed the first international symposium, the Colloque de Cerisy-la-Salle, entitled 'Virginia Woolf et le groupe de Bloomsbury' (Virginia Woolf and the Bloombury Group).[8]

---

4 Blanchot devotes a chapter to Woolf, 'L'Échec du démon: la vocation' (Outwitting the demon: a vocation) (1959), where he analyses the process of writing and its difficulties and dangers for Woolf, and the exclusivity of vocation. Blanchot's concept of writing as a navigation, which will be taken up by Jacques Derrida (Derrida 1967), is illuminating for the Woolfian commentator.

5 Their readings illustrate the circular, not to say interactive, nature of the process at work in the study of Woolf, whose works serve as a springboard for theoreticians who then refine their notions and conceptualize a system which they apply to the work from which they have taken inspiration. Deleuze is the first philosopher to have thematized the idea of a nomadic thought; his project 'rhizome' poses a 'plane of immanence' which is not structured by any one encompassing concept, but created by the play of difference and multiplicity, or 'rhizomes'.

6 He develops the idea whereby to escape is to draw a line and this long broken line is the condition of the exploration of new worlds. In Woolf, as in many English and North American writers, writing presents a progress, a departure, a process of becoming, a passage from one state to the other which is associated with a relationship with others (Deleuze 1997).

7 See Jean Blot (Blot 1992) and G.-G. Lemaire (Lemaire 1990). See Danièle Roth-Souton's (Université Stendhal-Grenoble III) biography of Woolf in relation to Bloomsbury, *Bloomsbury côté cuisine*, 2001.

8 The Proceedings were published as *Virginia Woolf and Bloomsbury* (Guiguet 1977). One of Jean Guiguet's arguments throughout the conference was that Bloomsbury was not a cultural group in the sense that *La Nouvelle Revue Française* (NRF) or the *Temps modernes* were as they had a doctrine, a programme and a magazine to propagate their ideological positions. See also Mary Ann Caws's contribution to this volume.

I

The academic reception of Woolf parallels the intellectual reception. It is certainly inspired by it although the multiplicity of research centres in universities makes it possible for academics to explore new areas. How we set about answering the challenge posed by Woolf's works depends in part on our own personal responses. There are several ways of rationalizing Woolf's texts by resorting to the logic of a method or by circumscribing them within the framework of a clear problematic. But whatever the theoretical trend, French criticism always takes into account the epistemological break that occurred in the early twentieth century.

The publication of Jean Guiguet's exhaustive and landmark study *Virginia Woolf et son œuvre* (1962) is rightly considered as a major turning-point in Woolfian criticism, inaugurating a series of outstanding and original studies. Being scholarly, eclectic and profound, his analysis paved the way for different critical trends. It was, primarily, the first intelligent synthesis to consider the main elements of Woolf's works both from a structural and thematic point of view (problems of form, characterization, feminism, time and space, consciousness) without losing sight of the biography and the aesthetics. As the first attempt to bring to the fore the interconnection of fiction and essay, Guiguet's book provides a productive frame for other readings of Woolf and is held to be a major reference point.

Between Jean Guiguet's Cerisy symposium and the creation of the Société d'Études Woolfiennes (Society of Woolf Studies) (SEW) in 1996 by Christine Reynier and myself,[9] joined by Catherine Bernard and Catherine Lanone, Woolfian studies lacked a focal point.[10] The first symposium of the SEW was held at the University of Nîmes-Montpellier III and, by 1999, the meeting at the University of Bordeaux III (organized by Christine Reynier) had become international, welcoming participants such as Rachel Bowlby (UK), Mary Ann Caws (USA), Patricia Laurence (USA) and Pierre-Éric Villeneuve (Canada).[11]

The interest that academics who are not basically or specifically Woolf scholars take in the SEW testifies to the challenging dimension of her works as well as to their heuristic value, while the choice of topics ('Metamorphosis in

---

9 The SEW is an exclusively academic society unlike the Virginia Woolf Society of Great Britain.

10 The founding of the society was supported by several professors, such as Alain Blayac (Montpellier III), Adolphe Haberer (Lyon II), Hubert Teyssandier (Paris III), and Bernard Gilbert (Bordeaux III). The symposia of the SEW are held every two years and serve as a forum for different critical approaches. Thanks to the support of the Société d'Études Anglaises Contemporaines, (presided over by Frédéric Regard) the SEW publishes a selection of articles presented at these symposia.

11 A symposium organized by Christine Reynier and Catherine Bernard took place at Cerisy-la-Salle in July 2001. Its theme was 'À la découverte de Virginia Woolf: le pur et l'impur' (Discovering Virginia Woolf: the pure and the impure).

Woolf's Works' and 'Things in Woolf's Works') shows a willingness to break new ground. The theme of metamorphosis provided a point of articulation between theory and fiction but equally, at a micro-structural level, it allowed an exploration of both the web of metaphors underlying Woolf's writing as well as myths pervading it. The study of 'things' provided a hermeneutic key to Woolf's works; it placed Woolf at the core of the modernist debate on the dichotomy between signs and their referents, as well as nourishing a phenomenological appraisal of Woolf based on the dialectical relationship between subject and object. Thus Josiane Paccaud-Huguet's Lacanian reading of Woolf (1999) analysed the progress of the artist in terms of the movement away from objects.[12] This second theme stimulated a reflection on language, but also an exploration of sexual difference. This is the thesis developed by Frédéric Regard who argues that for Woolf sexual difference is a matter of reading: things are perceived differently by men and women.[13]

The symposia organized by the SEW give to Woolfian scholars the opportunity to test the tools provided by their research centres as well as serving as a forum for opening up new perspectives and for more general discussions on modernism.

It is illuminating to confront the SEW meetings where there is a coherence between papers with the conference on 'Virginia Woolf and the Body' held at the Maison Française d'Oxford in March 1999 and attended by French and English academics. It was an attempt to confront different approaches and bring together two different cultural traditions. Although it revealed the extent to which readers can become rooted in the cultural tradition of their own country, unable to escape its intellectual mechanisms, it proved to be a fruitful meeting for the debates it opened. The English give priority to contextual elements (whether political, the context of the World Wars, or cultural, the work of Woolf's contemporaries) whereas the French tend to focus more on textual elements (the representations of the body in Woolf's texts) and to depoliticize Woolf.

II

One could argue that the absence of any subject such as 'Women's studies' or 'Gender studies' in France (apart from the Centre d'Études Féminines at the University of Paris, Vincennes, where Héléne Cixous teaches) may explain why the works of Woolf are exploited by schools of criticism other than feminism. A panorama of the different methods and of the range of techniques used by academics to study Woolf will reveal the prominence of phenomenology. The

---

12 The movement is towards things, and subsequently from things to the Thing, which she defines as 'that which is expelled by the very interference of form' (Paccaud-Huguet 1999, 47).

13 Regard's analysis of the narrator's use of photographs in *TG* as a 'tabula rasa of reading' (Regard 1999, 117) leads to a definition of Woolf's 'arts of intercourse' (117) as an art of 'new combinations' (118) or metaphors, that is a feminine mode of writing that allows the inscription of otherness.

publication of Jean Guiguet's comprehensive book in 1962 initiated and inspired more specific studies (Marie-Paule Vigne's thesis on water imagery (1980) is one such example). It served as a matrix and thus opened the path to different critical approaches which led to new assessments of Woolf's fiction.

Jean Guiguet's interest in biography[14] and the very processes of creation, in the dynamic movement from fiction to non-fiction, was taken over by genetic criticism, which Daniel Ferrer (Item-Centre National de la Recherche Scientifique) defines as a two-fold process consisting in 'découpage' (cutting) and putting in relation (1997).[15] He studied fragments associated with the genesis of *O*.[16] The genesis of a text is to be analysed in terms of narrative transformation but this does not mean linear transformation. Daniel Ferrer stresses the fact that authorial genetics is not always reliable. It is even misleading as in the case of the preface to the American edition of *MD* in 1928, where Woolf states that Septimus did not appear in the first version and that it was Clarissa who committed suicide. But, Ferrer argues, this text is false, the claim not literally true. Then the scholar-geneticist has to propose another narrative (although he/she will not neglect the author's own version, remembering that this version expresses a retrospective point of view). Modern theory is trying to reinvigorate the old biographical approach.

If Woolf criticism cannot always be neatly categorized, Woolf appears mostly to be read through the prism of narratology, psychoanalysis and phenomenology. They are today the principal contexts in which Woolf's works are being most innovatively explored. Feminist or gender-orientated readings take place within and are subsumed into the psychoanalytical approach. All these readings reflect the widespread preoccupation with the nature of the human subject.

Still in the line of Jean Guiguet's eclectic approach, Marie-Paule Vigne (University of Bordeaux III) combined several methods, such as thematic studies, psychoanalysis, linguistics and poetics to explore Woolf's plastic representations of water. The two main aspects on which she focused were psychism and sensitivity, more specifically the notions of identity, the ambiguities of personality, the masculine/feminine dichotomy, interior time, perception, the expression of emotion, questions of existence and 'reality', the absence of clear boundaries between interiority and exteriority, and the margins of madness. To this she added the study of narratology, that is narrative techniques, poetic prose, rhythm, metaphors, as theorized by Doris Cohn, Gérard Genette and Bahktin, whom she found illuminating for the emphasis he puts on the polysemy and polyphony of enunciative voices.[17]

---

14 See Guiguet 1973.

15 For a more substantial definition, see Ferrer 1998.

16 Although these fragments (one being a passage from the *Diary* on 14 March 1927 and the other an extract from 'Suggestions for Short Pieces') seem to have nothing in common, the link was established retrospectively and explicitly by Woolf herself.

17 Bahktin coined the term 'dialogism' based on the idea that all discourse is in dialogue with prior discourses on the same, given subject, as well as with discourses still to come. Each culture consists in a 'polyphony' of discourses retained in the collective memory (stereotypical discourse and the sophisticated literary text alike), and in

Christine Reynier's (University of Bordeaux III) narratological approach (1988) deals with the 'bolts of iron beneath the surface' (*TL*). In her doctoral thesis on Woolf's narrative technique as implemented in *MD*, *TL* and *TW*, she shows that Woolf's so-called impressionistic technique was something of a myth. In her later work she considers Woolf's relatively less known works such as her short stories and biographies, giving less a structural or thematic reading than an analysis of the metafictional dimension of those texts and of the way in which they shed light on Woolf's better-known fiction and essays. Her postgraduate teaching also explores the way in which Woolf's fiction and theoretical works are interconnected.

What is striking is that the significance of the First World War for Woolf's writing (both fictional and non-fictional), which is one of the topoi of English criticism, is more or less neglected in France. In fact, after Jean Guiguet, the only real attempt to concentrate on the historical aspect of Woolf's works was made by Hubert Teyssandier (University of Paris III) (1988).[18] Hubert Teyssandier directs a group of researchers concerned with the relations between literature and the arts, that is, literary and artistic intertextuality.[19] The second axis of Hubert Teyssandier's research deals with the study of recurrent forms in literature, that is undulatory movements, phenomena of intermittence (in general all the motifs of alternance, oscillation and vibration). He applied this approach to *TW* (Teyssandier 1997) focusing on Woolf's obsession with undulation, and more particularly with ripples, with the movement of the waves providing the structuring pattern of the novel and its network of images. This oscillatory phenomenon also functions at a metaphoric level, and is combined with pendular movements to constitute a unifying imaginary structure, a poetics of unity; it includes the pulsations of the body, the pulsations and withdrawals of consciousness, the rhythms of life and the alternating movements in the cosmos. Woolf's texts are, according to this reading, based on an association of the vibrations of sunlight ('flicker'), the undulation of the waves and sound waves. Teyssandier shows how all these undulatory phenomena are inscribed in the web of the narrative and how they generate interferences between the luminous, sonorous and liquid elements, thus creating a unified vision of reality. In Woolf's poetics, undulation affects space-time in its totality, so that the 'literary space' (*espace littéraire*), as in the case of the image of the wave, implies both cycle and alternance. Ultimately, undulation refers to the fluctuating consciousness, taking us back to the question of identity and the problematics of the self. Teyssandier shows how the pattern of the waves running through Woolf's texts composes a writing of unity, of universal interconnection.

Whatever the approach, all reveal an attempt to map Woolf's mental world. Pointillist studies of phenomenological topoi have ontological implications

---

cont.

relation to which each speaking (or writing) subject has to situate him/herself in a 'dialogical' process.

18 See also Catherine Bernard's stimulating analysis of Woolf's essays (1999).

19 The Équipe d'accueil EA 179.

and verge on psychoanalysis; they give an insight into the workings of the fantasizing process and the alienation of the subject. In the wake of Teyssandier's thematic approach but more phenomenologically orientated, André Topia (University of Paris III) (1977) has studied the visual processes in Woolf, and in particular optical phenomena, showing that Woolf's colours fluctuate in their symbolical values, and also that they conspire in the dissolution of shapes. His phenomenological approach, undeniably influenced by Merleau-Ponty, focuses on the relationship between the perceiving eye and its object, on light as a central metaphor of perception and the eye, and on the ambiguous status of colour that lies in the tension between opacity and transparency, between matter and light. Topia shows the Woolfian preoccupation with relating the vibration of coloured surfaces to a geometrical framework and analyses transparency as an intermediary between a sheer enjoyment of surfaces generated by burning colours and an idealistic standpoint that affords a glimpse of the essences behind these surfaces. Topia's studies of Woolf deal with the usual phenomenological notions of outline, boundary, separation, substance, etc., concluding that the multiplicity of colours is not dissolved but transformed into one substance. He analyses this spectrum of colours as a chromatic equivalent of Woolfian immanence which makes the same unique substance circulate through the fragments of the visible world. Thus, there is a constant 'tropism' of perception towards the invisible world, or, rather, towards a 'mysterious' mode (a 'non-visual' one). Believing that the modifications taking place in the characters themselves can be measured against the fluctuations of luminous intensity, Topia shows the close association in Woolf between colour and texture, between colour and a transparent and impalpable film, as well as the links between the constitution of identity and luminous fluctuations. Opposite processes take place in Woolf's apprehension of the material world: the solidification of outlines is denied by the liquefaction of substances; yet this is only an apparent contradiction. Woolf's vision of matter is based on a paradox according to which the sharp outlines are counterbalanced by fusion and fluency, culminating in the link between the intensity of light and fantasy. Like fantasy, light brings objects to the fore in sharp outlines only to cheat the perceiving subject of a true revelation. Light is also paradoxical: the 'edges' it brings about are also 'wedges'. The recurrent metaphor of the 'unsealing' reveals an obsession with liquefaction, with an amorphous reality. From the study of physical phenomena ontological conclusions can be derived: it is in the discrepancy between contents without an envelope and an envelope without contents that the fluctuations of the Woolfian being are encapsulated.

Phenomenology or the philosophy of perception, as practised by Merleau-Ponty, proves appealing to scholars of Woolf in that it articulates the drama of consciousness in her work. It is based on the Heideggerian notion of 'being-in-the-world' and its correlative notions of body, world, process of perception, chiasm, essence, form, intentionality, invisible, nothingness, logos, ontology and dialectic. The topos of vision-representation pervades the work of Liliane Louvel (University of Poitiers). Alongside problems of narration in the strictest sense she concentrates on parallels between writing and the visual arts, taking as references the works of Derrida, Rosolato and Lyotard. She analyses instances of what she calls 'pictorial description' (phenomenological and pictorial transfiguration) and its underlying 'process of sublimation as one which metonymically shifts desire from one object onto another' (Louvel 1999, 42), as a kind of aesthetic redemption. This method is also the line adopted by Catherine Lanone (University of Toulouse II) and Chantal Delourme (University of Lille III) who study Woolf in the light of Heidegger, Derrida, Blanchot, Deleuze and Merleau-Ponty.[20] Catherine Lanone considers *JR*'s 'rhizomatic' mapping based on a metonymic logic as initiating 'a deconstruction which many a postmodern writer might envy' (Lanone 1999, 89).

Catherine Bernard (University of Paris VII), who has written extensively on contemporary English fiction and on the theory of representation in the modern and postmodern eras, shares a similar interest in poetics and aesthetics. Her analyses deal with notions of un/defamiliarization, the tension between a disordered reality and the narrative order within the broad framework of the modernist dismantling of the episteme, of the breaking down of the strategies of representations. What interests her more specifically is the paradigmatic structure of Woolf's texts based on the building up of recurring schemata, the elaboration of thematics by means of structural metaphors and the play between points of view. She uses the critical tools of feminist criticism, 'new historicism' and 'cultural studies'. Her analysis of Woolf's essays (Bernard 1999) throws light on the farthest limits of the modernist paradigm shift and the failure of the representational apparatus, in particular of the metaphorical process. What she calls 'urban nomadism' (Bernard 1999, 124) deterritorializes writing as it dislocates the self. It illustrates the dismantling of representation at work in Woolf's writing, the defamiliarization of perception which is characteristic of modernity.

Frédéric Regard's (École Normale Supérieure, Lyon) interest in Woolf's aesthetic and philosophical issues is best exemplified in his article 'Clapham Junction 1910' (1997) where he deals with the nature of her writing and with her priorities as a writer who wants to represent life and who confronts the fundamental problems inherent in the philosophy of writing.[21] He shows that 'Mr Bennett and Mrs Brown' does not announce a system of writing but discovers it and experiences it, integrating it to the point where it is transformed into an anchorage point so that the slippages of Edwardian realism become just as open to condemnation as the daring modernist innovations of the Georgians. This text serves as an illustration of Woolf's position born out of a double movement, which is both ideological and ethical. Referring to Lyotard (1971), Frédéric Regard shows the originality of Woolf's processes based on the deconstruction of narrative identity and on the prominence of vision as both the horizon and the core of discourse. Conceiving her own topology of knowledge and truth, Woolf transforms her characters into an

---

20 Chantal Delourme is about to publish a book on *TL* through Éditions Ellipses.

21 He is one of the three major contributors to the *History of British Literature* for the Presses Universitaires de France. He is currently writing a book on the theory and practice of contemporary feminine writing for the Presses Universitaires de France.

anamorphic presence, a force of heterogeneity which acts upon the order of the discourse. Frédéric Regard then proceeds to analyse the Woolfian metaphor as part of the 'tunnelling process' (*TG*) on which Woolf's writing is based in connection with Derrida's study of dreams (1967) and Ricoeur's conception of metaphoric language (1975). Regard's reflection on 'things' (conceived as material objects by Heidegger) in his re-appraisal of *TG* takes the form of an exploration of gender and aesthetic issues. Psychoanalytic theory allows Regard to read Woolf's essay polemically as 'an anti-"feminist" text where the metaphysical question addressed to the object is paradoxically exposed as ... a gender-productive strategy' (Regard 1999, 108). Lacanian echoes pervade his article which shows that the writing 'I' does not conform with the Law of the letter and that the feminine enunciator positions herself in the realm of difference, the difference of a subject who refuses a Truth imposed on her. Regard shows that Woolf's political and philosophical intentions in *TG* inform a strategy of undermining the male law of metonymic associations and of providing an aesthetic solution to the war. *TG* is revolutionary in that it reveals Woolf's intuitions concerning the gender-determined perception of objects and presents the necessity of a change in the representational system and of a new reading of objects that would not be gender-determined. The ethos of Woolf's engagement being based on the art of combinations (see n. 13), Regard analyses Woolf's 'arts of human intercourse' (*TG*, 34) as a new erotic link superseding the masculine law of desire. These new combinations are based on the art of metaphorical combinations which makes possible the inscription of otherness, of a difference or *différance* (Derrida 1972),[22] that is to say a deferral of her own presence, which is the very essence of feminine writing. Woolf's project of an ethos inflected by gender relies on aesthetics, and her feminine inscription is 'a mode of production whose address is a poetic *espacement*' (Regard 1999, 120). As we have seen in the case of Catherine Lanone, Regard's approach illustrates a typical aspect of criticism: the fact that Woolf is displaced to analyse postmodernism.

Feminist literary critics 'reshape' modernism, through explorations of the place of women writers in the modernist period, of female and feminist relationships.[23] Claire Joubert (University of Paris VIII) is interested in issues of feminist criticism, in particular in the poetics of sexual difference, and of the feminine, and concentrates on the workings of *sexion* as a signifying activity. Through her examination of the concept of *écriture féminine* ('feminine writing'), Joubert is led to explore its critical potency, that is the poetics to which it is linked. She studies Woolf's strategies in fiction, which consist in the exposing of *sexion*, that is, in displaying the play of the paternal metaphor and

---

22 The feminine subject is 'différante' in that it is both a presence and an absence, a difference that is first and foremost a deferral or a displacement of the self (Derrida 1972). The writing 'I' in *TG* asserts herself against the masculine order.

23 See also Lecercle's study of the 'feminine sentence' in the light of Lyotard's, Derrida's and Deleuze's works (Lecercle 1997). His conclusion is that Woolf's writing displays a stylistic polarity (masculine/feminine) endowed with a political value of subversion.

in using language in order to stage its inherent faults (Joubert 1999b). Feminine textuality, beyond the definition of literary sub-categories such as 'feminine', calls for a notion of poetics as a critique of discursive techniques centred on the very concept of *signifiance*. Her study takes as its epistemic object the text itself, the textual problematics of 'gender' or sexual difference, femininity in its relation to language. The female subject in the text is not to be considered as Woman but through representation, thus emphasizing the critical nature of literature shared by both author and (theorist) reader. She explores narrative and poetic constructions where the grammar of desire and the sexual order of discourse take part in a symmetrical pattern. She analyses Woolf's fiction as a description of the symbolic order, as the presentation of a world colonized by signs and polarized around the paternal metaphor. The Lacanian overtones of this analysis play with semiotics to explain the workings of sexuation: sexual identity is first and foremost a position in language, being acquired through a sequence of exploratory positionings within the discursive order. Joubert's aim is to present the feminine as related to the enunciative standpoint, in considering sexual difference as an issue that undermines the symbolic order, which implies the prevalence of 'parole' over 'langue'. Joubert analyses the various strategies underlying the elaboration of a 'poétique de la parole' at work in Woolf's writings, the dramatization of the dispossession and exile of the speaking subject through the motifs of polyphony, of irony or pastiche, that is to say all those enunciative devices which disperse the authorial position. The further implications of this reflection deal with the connection between the feminine state of alienation in language and the enunciative position of the reader. Therefore, this shift in perspective calls for reading as an enunciative operation unfolding the workings of signifying processes.

Psychoanalysis is widely represented in Woolfian criticism. At the University of Lyon II, where English studies go under the heading of the so-called 'École Lacanienne' led by Adolphe Haberer and Josiane Paccaud-Huguet, Woolf is often at the centre of debates. Attached to this school of criticism are Woolf critics such as Denise Ginfray and Michelle Rivoire (both University of Saint-Étienne). Lacanian poetics is not to be dissociated from a structuralist focus on literature as being first and foremost a linguistic phenomenon. This implies a study of the functions of language, of the status of the narrator in fictional works, of intertextuality and dialogism.[24] Their research has a solid foundation in psychoanalytic theories though it never departs from a strict observance of the linguistic functioning of the text and of the linguistic performance it displays in relation to a problematics of the subject. This global approach is twofold: it tries to take into consideration structuralist and post-structuralist theories so as to open up the text's potential for broader interpretations ranging from aesthetics and creativity to ethics, identity and art.[25] As a further stimulus for discussion and logical step in the

---

24 For a survey of Bakhtin's theory see Bakhtin 1987.

25 The major references are: R. Jakobson's *Essais de linguistique générale* (Essays in general linguistics), R. Barthes's *Le Plaisir du texte* (The Pleasure of the Text) and *S/Z*, C. Greimas's *Sémantique structurale* (Structural Semantics), G. Genette's

psychoanalytic apprehension of any work of art as production of a human subject motivated by loss and desire, Lacanian critics rely on Freudian concepts, such as the Oedipal triangle, the work of mourning, imaginary identifications and sublimation. Lacan's revisitation of Freud's theories, in particular the famous 'mirror-stage', constitutes interesting material for the critic. The concept of 'otherness' is key in that it points to the various ways the unconscious writes itself into the gaps and accidents of the text, mainly through the devices of metaphor and metonymy. Notions such as the paternal metaphor, the three registers of the unconscious, foreclosure, *jouissance*, *la langue* prove to be appropriate when it comes to articulating the drama of subjectivity in its relation to the issue of artistic creation.

This articulation turns out to be one of the main concerns of Woolfian scholars. When combined with narratology, psychoanalysis can reveal what is at stake in Woolf's literary creation, as exemplified by *L'Ancrage et le voyage* (The Anchorage and the Voyage) by Françoise Pellan (University of Bourgogne-Dijon), which is eclectic in its sources of inspiration (Lacan, Serge Leclaire, André Green, Blanchot, Derrida, Rosolato, Lyotard), but rigorous in its methodology. Pellan's concern is the relationship between the novels and the essays, and the linguistic idiosyncrasies of Woolfian prose. More precisely, she considers the duality of Woolf's works, the different modes of writing or genres which were sometimes born of conflicting motivations. Pellan examines the literary theory contained in the essays, as well as the fantasies, obsessions and conflicts linked to Woolf's personal history and which are inseparable from her literary activity. The first part of the book deals with Woolf as a reader, in particular with reading as a stimulus and as a basis of her literary theory, showing that Woolf's work as an essayist is in line with the logic of her literary activity. The very duality of Woolf's production testifies to the perpetual to-ing and fro-ing motion between reading and writing; the former enabled her to circumscribe a space of her own in which she could identify herself as a writer. Pellan shows the therapeutic value of literary filiation as a means of exorcising the anguish of discontinuity, of re-establishing a continuity through her anchorage in the literary background of her native country. In the second part, she proceeds to analyse Woolf's fiction as exemplifying modernism and the anxieties it conveys. Defining modernist prose as a break from ideology and the subsequent liberation of a signifier ('signifiant') from a preconceived signified ('signifié'), Pellan shows that writing cut Woolf off from her predecessors and meant more than simply

---

cont.

Figures I-III (Figures of literary discourse) and *Palimpsestes* (Palimpsests), T. Todorov's *Littérature et signification* (Literature and meaning), L. Dallënbach's *Le Récit spéculaire: essai sur la mise en abyme* (The mirror in the text) and J. L. Austin's *How to Do Things with Words*. See also Henri Quéré's illuminating readings (1994). Linguists too find in Woolf rich material for analysis. Pierre Cotte (Université de Paris-Sorbonne) (1996) wrote a detailed analysis of the opening pages of *ROO* in which he exposes a semantic and enunciative theory of syntax. Pierre Cotte supervised Linda Pillière's thesis 'Quelques aspects du style de Virginia Woolf' (Some aspects of Virginia Woolf's style) (1997).

following in their footsteps; in finding a balance between 'preserving' and creating, Woolf was embarking on a quest for self-discovery. The movement from fiction to criticism is one between two different ways of using language, one that undermined the writer's self and one that strengthened it by giving her the illusion of mastering language. Yet Woolf needed the linear progress of literature and the ability to position herself in line with her predecessors. Pellan speaks about the urgency in Woolf of a compensatory imaginary anchorage and of her need to reinforce it through her critical discourse. The novels, usually considered in isolation from the rest of her works or considered in a global thematic perspective, are analysed, in Pellan's book, as the landmarks of a subjective progress and as the marks of the desire which generated them. Pellan examines the meaning(s) of poetic writing ('intransitive' writing to adopt Barthes's terminology (Barthes 1973, 89)), as a source both of frustration in that it stirred up a desire she could not assuage and of delight ('Jouissance') in that it gave her the sense of her existence and of communicating with others ('l'Autre'). The recurrent words to be found in the *Diary* ('pleasure', 'suffering', 'necessity', 'desire' and 'quest') refer to the meaning of writing, to writing as a perpetual initiation process and as a perpetual struggle with words. Woolf's dilemma lies in the urgency of her desire to write and her reluctance to renounce the illusory mastery of meaning. Its resolution will be the invasion of writing by the uncontrollable power of the imaginary, the manifestation of which was a deep-seated fantasy of death.

III

All these experiments and explorations have revealed the wide-ranging character of Woolfian studies in France and, as Freud writes in *Beyond the Pleasure Principle*, to desire an ending would be to desire the end of desire, to desire death or the death of the readability of Woolf's works.

The pluri-disciplinarity of the so-called 'Critique de l'imaginaire' (Criticism of the Imaginary) as conceptualized by Bachelard, Jean-Pierre Richard and Gilbert Durand and as practised by the 'École de Grenoble' offers a comprehensive understanding of Woolf, as well as opening up Woolfian studies.[26] Before I undertook my thesis 'L'Imaginaire Woolfien' (The

---

[26] The 'École de Grenoble' is the school of criticism practised at the Centre de Recherches sur l'imaginaire (University Stendhal-Grenoble III), which is a pluri-disciplinary research centre founded in 1966 by Professors Gilbert Durand, Léon Cellier and Paul Deschamps. It provides a forum for the exploration of the 'imaginaire' from cross-cultural, theoretical perspectives. It holds regular seminars and an annual conference, and issues a yearly publication. It is at the centre of a national (Angres, Bordeaux, Dijon, Lille, Montpellier, Nice, Paris-Sorbonne, Paris V, Paris VIII, Perpignan, Poitiers, Tours) and international (Barcelona, Bucharest, Cracov, Minho, Moncton, Québec, Récife, St Petersburg, São Paulo, Thessalonica, Naples, Verona) network composed of more than sixty 'laboratories'. The scientific project of this centre finds its unity and coherence in the reflection on both the 'imaginaire' and the symbolical imagination as they were first explored by

Woolfian Imaginary) (1997), only Marie-Paule Vigne had applied this methodology to her work on water imagery and Frédéric Monneyron in his comparative study of the myth of the androgyne (Monneyron 1995).

Durand developed Bachelard's polyphonic approach to create a method based on a systematized typology of images through myths and symbols. The notion of the 'imaginaire' is associated with a praxis which consists in concentrating on the way in which symbols and archetypes work as part of a network and in tracking down their metamorphoses. The corpus of images in Woolf's works (the web of perceptions, sensations, leitmotifs and persistent obsessions) is organized according to wider and underlying structures or patterns (that of the Fall for example). Jean-Pierre Richard sees the act of reading as provoking echoes, discovering new connections, linking 'sprays of convergence' ('faisceaux de convergence'), and exploring the 'undergrowth of the text' ('les sous-bois du texte') (Richard 1996, 9-10). This methodology concentrates on the evolving reality of the text as it gradually discloses its layers of meaning and as it shapes the heterogeneous nature of the Woolfian sensibility; it brings to the fore the dialectical process induced by the conflicting values of images. Durand's classification in *Les Structures anthropologiques de l'imaginaire* (The Anthropological Structures of the Imaginary) (1969) offers a methodical framework to Blanchot's view according to which a work of art is made up of the intimacy and violence of contradictory movements which are never reconciled (Blanchot 1955). The 'imaginaire' as a dynamic system made up of irreducible invariants and polarities is based on two regimes of images: *diurnal* (dealing with the entropy of time) and *nocturnal* (structured around the process of euphemization or reversion of values), which help to analyse the drama of self-development and the aporetic movement underlying Woolf's fiction. Yet, despite the useful categories provided by these schemata, or 'regimes', texual phenomena assert themselves in an irreducible alterity, contributing to the design of a fixed enigma which resists conclusive interpretation.

One can read Woolf in the light of Bachelard's 'isomorphism principle' according to which an image remains the same, or at least retains its value and connotations through the successive stages of its manifestation in the text (the network created, for example, by the association of the house, the womb and the grotto, as echoed in micro-symbols such as the shell). The plasticity of the

---

cont.

Bachelard and Mircea Eliade, and subsequently by Gilbert Durand, whose epistemology bears a conjunction of influences; anthropological, philosophical, psychological or literary theories and methods have been created and developed with reference to, and sometimes confrontation and/or collaboration with the works of Georges Dumezil, Ernest Cassirer, Roger Caillois, Henri Corbin, Claude Lévi-Strauss, Bachelard and Paul Ricoeur. From this background (the elements taken from psychology, anthropology, philosophy and literary criticism), this reflection has developed in relation to the philosophy of language, to the structural methods or 'ontology' that we find in Durand's works, and, in a more strictly literary domain, to the works of Charles Mauron, Georges Poulet, P. Albouy, J. Starobinski, N. Frye, M. H. Abrams, R. Girard, H. R. Jauss and J. P. Richard.

functioning of perception also implies a principle of reversibility applied to images and metaphors which can take on different values, as embodied in the correspondences between images and in the exchange of their qualities: water and hair, wine and blood, man and the universe. The 'reversibility principle' which is at work in Woolf's fiction fulfils a function in the psychic structure. Negative images such as the abyss, darkness or the archetype of the Fall reappear in other forms: the schema of descent derives its meaning from the two archetypes of night and of the cavity and the schema of bodily intimacy is contained in the archetype of the womb. The 'euphemization' process operates at several levels, in particular as a strategy to negate the omnipresent schema of antithesis and restructure the imaginary world in creating a metaphorical web. The magnification of small objects is an example of that. The magnifying eye tries to capture reality and to pierce its opacity of meaning, to abolish the chiasm, the phenomenological distance (the 'béance' in Lacanian terms) between the Self and the world.

The 'imaginaire' is at the junction of the subject and the object; it is a nexus between the microcosm and the macrocosm, that is to say, consciousness in a time-space structure. The psychological conquest of space is manifold: through the exploration of the 'flesh' ('la chair' according to Merleau-Ponty (1964)) of the world which resists perception, through the interplay of different substances and symbols, and also through a metaphorical strategy such as the web or the labyrinth which becomes the positive metaphor of a process of awareness. Beyond the imaginary processes which actualize a reversal of values and a transfiguration of images, the stages of a spiritual progress emerge, which consists of an exploration of the hermeneutic objects of phenomenology; it corresponds to a sharpening and refining of perception, an intuition of the 'invisible reserve' (Merleau-Ponty 1964, 199) expanding beyond perception. This process culminates in a regeneration of language, in the advent of 'les choses mêmes du fond de leur silence' ('things in themselves from the depth of their silence') (Merleau-Ponty 1964, 18).

The aims of the 'Critique de l'imaginaire' are those of literature itself, or at least literature as Woolf conceived it, that is to say as an opening-up of the novel genre, as a hermeneutic act based on a creative and critical consciousness in novelist and reader. The act of reading then becomes an act of self-understanding.

IV

From these samples of responses to Woolf's works emerges a vision of Woolf's 'espace littéraire' as a kind of laboratory for critical theory. The French reception of Woolf over the last decades has followed critical fashions and bears their influence. Woolf has been an object of academic study as well as an inspiration for the great theoreticians and writers who shaped the intellectual landscape in modern and postmodern France. Feminist issues are always subsumed by aesthetic issues. The guideline of this reception is a preoccupation with language as an enunciation process and as the web of metaphors it displays.

Academics have drawn substantially on their critical a priori in an attempt to find a key capable of unlocking aspects of Woolf's works. However, the protean nature of her writing demands an openness to suggestion. There is a common awareness that Woolf's art is open-ended and that, consequently, any attempt to draw ready-made conclusions about it runs the risk of debasing it and stifling Woolf's voice in theoretical logorrhoea. The reader is challenged to respond to Woolf in an imaginative and creative way and is certainly not frustrated at having to leave her mystery intact.

Although the list of these seminal readings of Woolf is testimony to the vigour with which commentators tackle her works, it would be wrong to see the reception of Woolf as a movement towards any final word, and it should not mask Woolf's attack on system-builders. In the interzone between loose eclecticism and staunch theory lies the Woolfian wish for 'a system that did not shut out' (*WD*, 2 October 1932).

3 Translating Virginia Woolf into French

Françoise Pellan

Virginia Woolf appears to have been remarkably indifferent to what her translators did with her texts, and did to her texts, in any language, including French. Although she could read the classics of French literature, as well as contemporary writers, in the original, there is no evidence that she ever closely examined, or even dipped into, any of the French translations of her works that were published in her lifetime. Nor did she welcome her translators' occasional queries very warmly: 'I'd like to see you', she once wrote to Ethel Smyth, 'But what's the use of seeing you against some intolerable necessary bore – this refers to a French translator who's wasted one of my rare solitary evenings' (*L* 6: 109; 24 February 1937). The visitor in question was none other than Marguerite Yourcenar, who was translating *TW* and had come to London with a list of questions to submit to the author. She was to be disappointed, since after a few brief, non-committal replies, Virginia Woolf quickly turned the conversation to the current political situation in Europe. This was 1937, and Virginia Woolf could understandably feel more concerned about the impending danger of a new world war than about the potential damage caused to her text by 'Mlle Youniac', as she called her in her Diary (*D* 5, 60; 23 February 1937). Moreover, since she was working on *TG* at the time, and nervously waiting for the publication of *TY*, she would have been particularly reluctant to cast her mind back to such a different type of book as *TW*. The fact remains, however, that, whatever the circumstances, Virginia Woolf chose to ignore what became of her novels in translation. This may seem surprising on the part of such a meticulous writer, one who spent so much time rewriting, revising and polishing her texts, even at proof stage, on the part, too, of an author obviously concerned with her image and whose reputation abroad largely depended on the work of her translators. Her detachment in the matter, however, is entirely consistent with the grim view she took of the translating process. To quote from one of the essays in *CR*: 'When you have changed every word in a sentence . . ., have thereby altered the sense a little, the sound, weight and accent of the words in relation to each other completely, nothing remains except a crude and coarsened version of the sense' ('The Russian Point of View', *CE 1*, 238-39). She goes on to speak of 'mutilations' and to compare the effect of a translation to 'some terrible catastrophe'. No wonder, then, that concerning the translation of her own texts, Virginia Woolf should have washed her hands of the whole business.

All translations are damaging, but they are nonetheless a necessary evil, and the catastrophe they amount to may be 'terrible' to a greater or lesser extent. For example, Charles Mauron did a fine job translating *O* (1931) and *FB* (1935), whereas Maurice Lanoire made a mess of *TL* (1929): the translation is at best clumsy, often grossly inaccurate and generally careless; for example, omissions abound, including a whole paragraph, while the text of one section runs on into the next without any break.

Marguerite Yourcenar's translation of *TW* is an entirely different case and far more difficult to assess. As a text, it is undoubtedly very beautiful, and a pleasure to read. As a translation, it is deeply, almost insidiously, unfaithful to the original. Let me take a few examples to illustrate my point. They are all drawn from the beginning of the text, the first series of speeches directly following the descriptive prelude. It is early morning, six children, three boys, three girls, are lying in bed in a house by the sea and their voices rise in turn to express their immediate sensations on waking up. The same narrative tag is used to identify all six speakers: 'said Bernard', 'said Susan', 'said Rhoda' etc. Not so in the French translation: although 'said' is always literally translated as 'dit' in the case of the first five speakers, 'said Louis' is systematically rendered as 'murmura Louis', up until his seventh intervention. I suppose that Yourcenar objected to the sound of 'dit Louis', because the diphthong partly echoes the vowel sound of the verb. Personally I do not find 'dit Louis' particularly shocking to the ear, and anyway Yourcenar reconciled herself to this phrase in the second part of the section. But the point is that the change of verb alters the effect and significance of the text. Why should Louis murmur when Bernard and the rest all plainly 'say'? This sets him apart from the other five, whereas the original text suggests that all six of them are equally close to and different from one another. Yourcenar did not scruple either to tamper with the syntax of these first speeches. Here are two examples:

> 'I hear something stamping,' said Louis. 'A great beast's foot is chained. It stamps, and stamps, and stamps.' (*TW* 1972, 6)
> J'entends le piétinement d'une gigantesque bête enchaînée, murmura Louis. Elle frappe la terre... Du pied elle frappe continuellement la terre... (*Les Vagues* (*TW*), 17)

> 'A shadow falls on the path,' said Louis, 'like an elbow bent.' (*TW* 1972, 6)
> Une ombre pareille à celle d'un bras replié s'étale sur le sentier, murmura Louis. (*Les Vagues* (*TW*), 17)

In English, each brief speech follows a strict logical pattern: the visual or auditory perception of the outside world comes first, followed by the image it triggers in the speaker's consciousness. By altering the syntax and fusing together perception and image, Yourcenar distorts the original effect of immediacy: the perception is not given raw but as if already filtered through an interpreting mind. This appears even more obvious in the following example:

> 'The birds sang in chorus first,' said Rhoda. 'Now the scullery door is unbarred. Off

they fly. Off they fly like a fling of seed. But one sings by the bedroom window alone.' (*TW* 1972, 7)
Le bruit de la porte de l'office interrompt le chœur matinal des moineaux, dit Rhoda. Les oiseaux se sont envolés, dispersés comme une poignée de grains. Mais un pinson solitaire continue son chant à la fenêtre d'une chambre à coucher. (*Les Vagues* (*TW*), 18–19)

The translation here is at once syntactically, grammatically and lexically distorting, since, not content with altering the order of the clauses, verbalizing a cause and effect relationship which is only implicit in the original, and substituting a perfect tense for the simple present, 'fly', Yourcenar turns the scullery into a pantry, and, worse, arbitrarily identifies the unspecified birds as sparrows before introducing a solitary chaffinch as a last picturesque touch, thereby spoiling the stylized, almost abstract quality of the original setting.

As a writer herself, Marguerite Yourcenar could draw on the resources of her own language more skilfully, more subtly than an ordinary translator, hence, I repeat, the undeniable beauty of *Les Vagues*. But perhaps she was also more tempted to superimpose her own vision onto Virginia Woolf's, hence to slip into her own style. She took just as many liberties with all the texts she was to translate in later years, and, judging from what she wrote in the preface to her translation of early Greek poems, she felt entirely justified: translations must be faithful, but, she adds, what is true of women is also true of translations: fidelity alone is not enough to make them tolerable.[1]

This is amusingly put, but highly questionable. Personally, I believe that fidelity is actually all that might be required of a translation, and that is precisely where the difficulty lies .... Turning to my own experience as a translator of *TL*, I must confess that perfect fidelity to the original was my own private lighthouse, my own inaccessible goal. The problem is naturally that, like practically everything Virginia Woolf wrote, *TL* is a poetic text in the full sense of the term, one meant for the ear as well as for the eye, to be apprehended at once intellectually, imaginatively and sensually. As it was rarely possible to safeguard each and every element of significance in a given verbal segment, literal meaning, connotations, sound, rhythm, I constantly found myself in the frustrating position of having to choose the lesser evil and sacrifice whichever element seemed to me *relatively* dispensable. Let me give a few examples of the countless problems I came across, some of which were perfectly insoluble, while others involved at least a regrettable loss.

Let me begin with the image of the alphabet which is repeatedly used to convey Mr Ramsay's difficulties as a philosopher. He can reach the letter Q, but can go no further. R is beyond his reach. The image is of course easily translatable. But how unfortunate that the letter Q should sound in French exactly like the three-letter equivalent of 'arse': 'cul' .... Now, since R, the letter that eludes Mr Ramsay happens to be the initial of his name, and hence

---

1 'Il n'y a, certes, de bonne traduction que fidèle, mais il en est des traductions comme des femmes: la fidélité, sans autres vertus, ne suffit pas à les rendre supportables' (Yourcenar 1979, 36).

the symbol of his identity, I had no choice but to let him stick at Q. But as a result, the whole passage which, in English, merely raises a faint smile at the expense of the character, comes perilously close to sounding ludicrous – and indelicate – in French.

In the case of nouns denoting specific objects, animals, flowers, etc., the translator's freedom is equally restricted, whatever the impoverishment suffered in the transfer. For instance, the text contains several references to the red-hot pokers that grow in the Ramsays' garden. The name is splendidly evocative. Not so its French equivalent, 'tritoma'; hence, too, the problem raised at one point by a fine metonymic association of words made possible by the polysemy of 'poker':

> the thick hedge, guarded by red-hot pokers like brasiers of clear burning coal (*TL* 1974, 35)
> la haie, flanquée de tritomas aussi flamboyants que des charbons ardents (*Vers le Phare* (*TL*), 59)

In order to maintain some amount of verbal play and textual logic, I chose to modify the syntax, turning the simile into a clause of comparison and the noun 'brasier' into an adjective, and to play on the polysemy of the word 'flamboyant' which, as an adjective, means 'flaming red' or 'flamboyant', as a present participle, 'blazing', and which can also be a noun denoting an exotic tree, in English a flame tree. Thus 'flamboyant' can serve as a logical link in the verbal chain connecting a plant and burning coal. This is certainly not as satisfying as the original wording, but I could think of no better solution.

In many cases, however, the text allowed, and even encouraged me to take some liberty with the signified and give priority to the signifier. See, for instance, this extract from the last section but one of 'Time Passes', after the cleaners, workers and gardeners have made the house ready for the Ramsays and their guests:

> And now as if the cleaning and the scrubbing and the scything and the mowing had drowned it there rose that half-heard melody ... (*TL* 1974, 218)
> Alors, comme si le nettoyage et le récurage, le fauchage et le jardinage l'avaient étouffée, s'éleva cette mélodie à peine audible ... (*Vers le Phare* (*TL*), 221)

Sound and cadence mattering more than the particular meaning of each of the verbal nouns, it seemed to me essential to keep four words with the same ending. Cleaning and scything were no problem. Scrubbing literally means 'brossage', but in connection with 'nettoyage' I preferred the four syllables of 'récurage' (scouring) and the French for 'mowing'; 'tonte' sounds so ugly that I had no hesitation in substituting the general activity of gardening.

I felt equally free in the case of the image used to convey James's emotional response to his father's interruptions and relentless demands for Mrs Ramsay's sympathy:

> like a beak of brass, barren and bare (*TL* 1974, 62)
> comme un bec de bronze, sec et stérile (*Vers le Phare* (*TL*), 82)

The alliterative game here is all important. So I turned the metal to bronze and the bareness to dryness: 'bec de bronze' has the same hard effect as 'beak of brass', while 'sec et stérile' has a different, though no less aggressive, spiteful hissing sound.

I must confess that, while Virginia Woolf's constant play on assonance and alliteration always struck me as an exciting challenge, her no less skilful use of onomatopoeia inevitably made my heart sink. For there, English has an undeniable advantage over French. Faced with such delightfully mimetic wording as 'She leapt splashing through the shallow waves' (*TL* 1974, 119) or 'He would whizz his plate through the window' (305), I could only acknowledge defeat and resign myself to the dullness of 'Elle sauta dans les vaguelettes' (*Vers le Phare* (*TL*), 133) or 'Il lançait son assiette à toute volée par la fenêtre' (297).

The wealth of onomatopoeic terms in English and their relative scarcity in French is only one aspect of an essential difference between our two languages and the way we use them. French is more abstract than English. In ordinary speech, whatever the context, an educated English speaker will express himself more vividly, will use images more spontaneously than a French speaker. It follows, not only that writers in English will resort to similes and metaphors more often than their French counterparts but also, and more to the point, that an English reader is less likely than a French reader to object to a concrete image in a literary text on the grounds that it clashes with the tone of the passage. I daresay nobody would raise an eyebrow on reading that Jasper swung Lily's hand 'like a pump-handle' (*TL* 1974, 39). Yet the literal translation 'comme un bras de pompe' would definitely strike a false note. And since the simile is vivid but not particularly significant I did what seemed the natural thing to do in French and replaced it by an adverb, 'vigoureusement' (*Vers le Phare* (*TL*), 62).

A strikingly original and even more untranslatable image is to be found in the dinner scene, when Lily Briscoe becomes aware of Charles Tansley's discomfort and frustration:

> Sitting opposite him could she not see, as in an X-ray photograph, the ribs and thigh bones of the young man's desire to impress himself lying dark in the mist of his flesh. (*TL* 1974, 141)
> Assise en face de lui, ne voyait-elle pas, comme sur une radiographie, le désir qu'avait ce jeune homme de faire impression se dessiner en noir sur le flou de sa chair. (*Vers le Phare* (*TL*), 152)

Unlike the pump-handle, the ribs and thigh bones of the young man's desire arrest the attention of an English reader, although the searing vision the image conveys is no more likely to raise a smile than the equally bizarre analogies to be found in metaphysical poetry. A literal translation, on the other hand, would send French readers into fits of laughter, especially as we have only one word for thigh-bone, the medical sounding 'fémur'. Naturally, the image of the X-ray photograph had to be kept, but it seemed to me sufficient: any further reference to ribs and thigh bones would have seemed grotesquely over-explicit. So I left them out. But then, the metaphor recurs in the next paragraph:

> to go to the help of the young man opposite so that he may expose and relieve the thigh bones, the ribs, of his vanity (*TL* 1974, 141–42)
> aller au secours du jeune homme en face d'elle afin qu'il puisse exposer l'ossature de sa vanité (*Vers le Phare* (*TL*), 152–53)

Since, here, the analogy with an X-ray photograph is only implied by ribs and thigh bones, I had no other solution than to find an acceptable equivalent for them, hence my choice of the general term 'ossature' (skeleton).

No doubt the worst problem of all was the title of the novel, *To the Lighthouse*. I knew, of course, that since 1929, Virginia Woolf had mainly been known in France as the author of *La Promenade au phare*. But the title had always struck me as inaccurate and misleading. 'Promenade' suggests leisure and pleasure, but certainly not the tension, desire, aspiration, effort and struggle associated with the characters' metaphoric attempts to reach the Lighthouse and connoted by the preposition 'to'. The second translation into French, which came out three years before mine, was entitled *Voyage au phare* (1993), which is definitely better, but still rather odd, considering that the lighthouse in the novel can be seen just across the bay. Above all, it seems to me that, whatever the noun chosen, a nominal phrase as such betrays the dynamic quality of the original title. Hence my decision to keep the same structure, preposition, article and noun. Yet, though 'Vers le phare' does convey the idea of movement towards a potentially inaccessible goal, it is not as significant as 'To the Lighthouse', which can also be read as a dedication, read, in other words, as the title of the poem by Shelley quoted in the novel: 'To Jane…'. 'Au Phare' would have kept the dedicatory effect, but the dynamic sense would have been all but lost and the title as a whole would have seemed much too short. So 'Au Phare' had to be rejected. But of course it is the very word 'lighthouse' that most suffers from being translated into French. 'Phare' sounds unfortunately short and dull compared to 'lighthouse' with its two sonorous diphthongs. Moreover, unlike 'phare', 'lighthouse' is a descriptive noun, one which relates the object of James's desire to the lighted house which so dazzles Paul Rayley when he returns from the beach late in the evening that he can only murmur to himself, 'Lights, lights, lights' (*TL* 1974, 123–24).

So, yes, the very title proves Virginia Woolf right: translating is indeed an impoverishing, coarsening and mutilating process. Yet, for all the loss and consequent sense of frustration, it is also a highly rewarding experience, one which made me throughout tremendously happy, as a reader that is. Before I translated it, I thought I knew this text inside out. I had read it attentively so many times over the years. But then, page after page, from first to last, I came across little gems, stylistic beauties, subtleties which had escaped my attention and further increased my admiration for the work and its writer. In short, this experience confirmed my belief that, though translators are certainly very useful, language teachers fulfil a far more important task in that they give their students access to the thing itself, the original text as an irreplaceable source of pleasure.

4 A Virginia Woolf, with a French Twist

Mary Ann Caws

It was, in the beginning, Roger Fry who put his friend, the Provençal writer and translator Charles Mauron, in touch with Virginia Woolf – it was not for nothing that Mauron was called 'Bloomsbury's man in France' (King 1978, 76). In 1927, he translated the central part of *TL* for the French journal *Commerce* even before its publication. This translation is fully the equal of the amazing rendering of *O* made subsequently by Mauron, the translator of E. M. Forster, T. E. Lawrence, D. H. Lawrence and Henry James, whose sensitivity to the English language has not been, in my view, equalled by any other translator of Woolf.

Mauron went on to found the school of psychocriticism, based on his work with Stéphane Mallarmé, of which the origin was the commentaries he had done for Roger Fry's translations, and which he published, in augmented form, with Julian Bell in 1936 for *New Directions*. It was to Mauron that Vanessa Bell had turned when she had wanted to dissuade Julian from going to Spain during the Spanish Civil War, and to him that Virginia Woolf wrote one of her most moving letters, saying that he, more than anyone else, could speak of Roger Fry, and that he was in fact the French critic whom she most trusted.[1] His integrity endeared him to her, and seemed unusual: for in general, Woolf had a rather jaundiced idea of French critics.

She herself, making many trips to France, with Vanessa to Paris in her youth, with Vita Sackville-West through Burgundy, and several times with Leonard, had been tempted for a moment to settle down in France. This would have been in a tiny house called La Boudarde, near Cassis, where Vanessa and Duncan Grant were spending much time from 1928 on, in a *mas* called La Bergère, on the property of Fontcreuse, where Colonel Teed and his partner Jean Campbell lived and produced a superb wine still available now in Cassis.

That she did not in the long run settle in France had to do with Leonard's dislike of it, and with her own dissatisfaction with her ability to speak the

[1] Unpublished letter; my thanks to Alice Mauron for sharing its contents with me.

language. Janie Bussy, the daughter of Lytton Strachey's sister Dorothy Bussy – who had married an always impoverished French painter, Simon Bussy, a close friend and erstwhile classmate of Henri Matisse – tried to teach her a sufficient amount for her to feel at home in France. But Virginia, too sensitive to words to adapt to a foreign atmosphere as had her sister the painter, remained English to her very roots, and never settled there.

However, she became progressively more celebrated, as we know, by French critics and in France, even as certain problems remained as to her relationship to the group of friends loosely termed the 'Bloomsbury Group'. In 1974, Anne Heurgon-Desjardins, the *grande patronne* of the château at Cerisy-la-Salle, decided to dedicate one of Cerisy's famous ten-day meetings, or *décades* (which carried on the tradition her father, Paul Desjardins, had started at Pontigny) to Virginia Woolf and that group: 'Virginia Woolf et le groupe de Bloomsbury'.[2]

She had asked Jean Guiguet, author of a celebrated study of Virginia Woolf (1962), to organize the meeting. The timing of the theme was particularly apt, since Quentin Bell's biography had just been translated into French, Viviane Forrester had just spoken of Woolf on the radio, and had published a small volume on the subject, and Guiguet himself had just written in *Études anglaises* a piece on 'Virginia Woolf devant la critique' (1973). More and more Woolfian theses were appearing every year, and she had become clearly à la mode in France as in England.

There was, at Cerisy, a fine gathering of scholars French and English, including David Daiches, Peter Fawcett, Viviane Forrester, David Garnett, Anthony Inglis, Hermione Lee, Jean Pace, Marie-Paule Vigne and, of course, the stalwart regulars such as Maurice de Gandillac and Clara Malraux.

Guiguet began by avowing his perplexity, with a typically French question, having to do with classification, terminology and specificity. Guiguet's object had to do, it seems, with a separation he would prefer to have made between sociology and literature: the ascription of importance to the grouping was not, he thought, essential to the consideration of Woolf as a writer. Why, he asked Anne Heurgon-Desjardins, *were* we talking about the Bloomsbury group? Was it a group? Why? Was it not simply a label conferred by the journalists who needed one? To back up his scepticism on the subject, he quoted Clive Bell's *Old Friends* of 1956: 'Bloomsbury never existed' (Guiguet 1977b, 14). And the ensuing conversations often turned about the problem – how would Woolf's writing have been different had she been part of a different 'group'?

As one might expect, a French parallel was found in the group around the *Nouvelle Revue Française*, which had included Jacques Copeau, Jean Schlumberger, Roger Martin du Gard and André Gide at the centre of it all.[3] Alas, lamented one participant after the other, if only the Bloomsbury group had a

---

2 As was also traditional, the proceedings of the deliberations were published; see Guiguet 1977 in Bibliography.

3 In fact, the memory of Gide was held in such high esteem that the first time I was privileged to be invited to Cerisy, I was shown the bed of André Gide, kept royally in the centre of the main room, rather like the body of Lenin. I was duly impressed.

journal! What a needed cohesion it would have given them! How typical of the English temperament that its youth did not get around to this, Guiguet remarked (1977a, 28). Oh, the English lethargy. So un-French. The very notion of an English group seemed to teeter in the balance. Now, retrospectively, it may seem of great interest to us that all this was of such concern: but I think it has to do with the very French desire to pin things down now. That desire, so un-English, is also very un-Virginia Woolf, and thereby hangs much of the tale.

In answer to Guiguet's query about the group's very existence, Clara Malraux pointed out that in 1936, in London for the Congress of Revolutionary Writers in London, where she had met Woolf for the first time, she had been shown a part of London and told it was there that the Bloomsbury group had its origin and continuance (Guiguet 1977a, 21). And Anne Heurgon-Desjardins stressed the fact that it had existed for at least ten years previously, for when Lytton Strachey and his sister Dorothy Strachey Bussy, the translator of André Gide, came to Pontigny in 1923, there was no question at all whether Bloomsbury as such existed. It did, then, it had and it would from then on, for all intents and purposes (Guiguet 1977a, 30).[4]

Guiguet continued, however, by comparing the reaction of 'journalists' as opposed to 'les gens sérieux' ('serious people') toward such an idea of grouping (Guiguet 1977b, 17). He thought the idea of Bloomsbury as incoherent, vague and unuseful as that of existentialism. Journalists, he said, spoke of 'existentialists and existentialism', whereas 'les gens sérieux' (presumably, like those gathered at Cerisy and those who would read the proceedings later) would speak of individual figures within it: Strachey, Fry, Woolf, the way they had spoken not of 'existentialists' but rather of Sartre, Camus, and Gabriel Marcel. That this point should have been discussed at such length is characteristic of the French reception of Woolf and others, and reminiscent of what happens with many French editors and translators of Woolf, wanting to pin down her poetic writing to a more graspable style.[5] The former were referring to a vague ambience, the latter to precise thoughts. The general label Bloomsbury, like existentialism, is a vague, inconsistent term, that should be scratched from any serious critical vocabulary (Guiguet 1977, 17).

Guiguet continued by comparing the non-existence of this group to the gathering of friends in Woolf's *TW*, where the empty centre, Percival, continues to be awaited. Perhaps, he said, the centre would eventually arrive.

As Hermione Lee pointed out, the unity of the group had been said, by J.K. Johnstone (among others), to derive from the philosophy of G. E. Moore.[6]

---

[4] The remarks by Malraux and Heurgon-Desjardins are printed in the group discussion following Guiguet's 'Introduction'.

[5] Oh, laments Pierre Nordon, in the notes to his translation of *Kew Gardens and Other Short Stories,* when will she ever get down to naming her subject (1993, 64)? Even the writers Clara Malraux and Marguerite Yourcenar will overspecify terms in their translations.

[6] I was told by Nigel Nicolson that his mother, Vita Sackville-West, was teased by Virginia Woolf for not knowing the difference between George Moore and G. E. Moore!

Peter Fawcett, certainly the expert in that epoch, in this sort of Anglo-French relation, discussed the extent to which Lytton Strachey, Virginia Woolf, and Roger Fry were so intimately connected to France, and entered into some detail with the comparison between the *NRF* group and the Bloomsbury group, reminding the company how Gide had been called, by one of the group, 'France's Bloomsbury'. Discussing the relation of the Strachey family to France (how intelligent it would have been, Lytton was fond of exclaiming, just to have been born French), he spoke of Les Ruches, Marie Souvestre's school outside Fontainebleau where the two eldest Strachey girls had been sent, Lady Strachey being a friend of Marie Souvestre, and how, when the school was transferred to Allenswood, she sent two more of her daughters there. Roger Fry was, of course, the most French of them all, and felt more appreciated as an artist in France.[7] But, as everyone in France and England seemed to agree, Virginia Woolf was always and remained deeply English.

Among the speakers, Marie-Paule Vigne was perhaps the one who treated the work of Woolf the way most scholars of Woolf have tended to. Her reflections around the theme of water deal quite specifically with the use of the image in Woolf's writings: fluidity, reflection, the flow of time, the relation to death and the unfathomable and unconscious depths. She pointed out the order of frequency: water, sea, wave, river and, far down the list, the pool and the lake, and ended by the proposition that for Virginia Woolf, 'real life was perhaps at the bottom of the water' (Vigne 1977, 206).

For Raissa Tarr, Woolf's writing, so 'typically feminine', was further proof of the fact that 'a woman cannot write a novel like Joyce or Proust' (!) – this attitude is even now prevalent in some academic circles in France (Guiguet 1977a, 246).[8] Then Jean Guiguet admitted that he found it unlikely that any man could truly appreciate the problem in *ROO*, since it had not been his experience 'as an adolescent almost contemporary with the publication of this book in 1929 that women had been at all held back intellectually' (Guiguet 1977a, 259).[9] At any rate, however, he did venture to agree with Françoise Pellan about the significance of *TG* particularly since he found it more general than *ROO*, addressed as it was to the actuality of Fascism (259).

The entire discussion was at once typical of the Pontigny–Cerisy tradition, combining general speculation, thematic analysis, sociological and psychoanalytic considerations, and unusual in that the problem of and the importance of the idea of group and individual genius was constantly in play.

Anthony Inglis, who had been called upon to represent 'anti-Bloomsbury', instead called, with great sobriety, for a more sustained discussion of Woolf's

---

7 For further details on the relations between the group and France, see Caws and Wright 1999.

8 'Au risque de mécontenter une partie de cet auditoire, permettez-moi de dire que l'œuvre de Virginia Woolf me semble typiquement féminine. Je ne crois pas qu'une femme puisse faire un roman comme Joyce ou Proust.' (Tarr's remarks and Guiguet's subsequent observations are made during a group discussion.)

9 'D'après mon expérience d'adolescent presque contemporaine de la publication de ce livre (1929), je n'ai pas eu l'impression que les femmes en ce temps-là aient été brimées intellectuellement.'

writings in the light of recent criticism. And that is, of course, what is taking place now in France. Monique Nathan's most useful collection of critical writings for the collection 'Écrivains de toujours' (1989) gives an idea of the various kinds of approach, and the continuing enthusiasm for Woolf is testified to by the French association devoted to the analysis and criticism of her work, organized originally by Christine Reynier at the University of Bordeaux.[10]

Interest in Virginia Woolf is unlikely to subside: it will, no doubt, increase, even with a French (and generalizing) twist to it. Virginia herself would, no doubt, have been amused by it all, then and now. I think she would have been particularly amused in the long run, even if she was, as Françoise Pellan points out, pained in the short run, to see what different kinds of translations she received.

Although it was not discussed at Cerisy, where the subject of translation seems not to have arisen (not even in relation to a once-mentioned appearance of Dorothy Bussy, who did attend a Pontigny meeting, and appears in a celebrated photograph with André Gide, whose translator she was, at a breakfast), it ties into the central discussion there of contacts between England and France in relation to Bloomsbury. Perhaps it is more recently that we take the topic of translation so seriously. In any case, in order to connect with Françoise Pellan's discussion of her own translation, I shall take just one case, that of the translations of *O*, for that permits me to join the discussion of Bloomsbury and the Bloomsbury contacts in France which did take place at Cerisy. Charles Mauron's splendid translation of *O* permits us to see what difference there is between a truly great rendering and an ordinary one.[11]

As Francoise Pellan remarks in Chapter 3 in this volume, the reputation of Charles Mauron's translation of *O* is a very good one. For excellent reasons, I would say, and shall bear out my comment with a few salient passages in Mauron's superb translation, comparing them with another, competent but undistinguished. Clearly, one of the best ways to see the quality of any translation is to place it alongside another, and Virginia Woolf's faith in Mauron as a translator is fully justified. Mauron, Roger Fry's good friend, also translated Woolf's *FB* and the middle section of *TL*, but I wish to limit myself to the case of *O* and to a very few passages within it.

What Pellan says about the particular qualities of the English language and its particular difficulties of translation into French should be kept in mind in the consideration of the following passages, crucially interesting in their rendering for those and additional aspects of the problem. It is in general the colourfulness of English that the formalities of French so often fail to grasp, sometimes through the fault of the language, but sometimes through a certain lack of imagination which makes its irremediable mark upon the translated text. It falls flat. Not that it is 'horrid', in the language of a familiar nursery

---

10 The proceedings of the meeting on the topic of 'Virginia Woolf's Objects' have been published in a special issue of *Études britanniques contemporaines* (1999), with contributions by scholars from England, France and America.

11 I have previously discussed Mauron's translations in Caws and Wright 1999, 351–67.

rhyme, but it is not touched with genius. In such readings, a French reader might well be saying to herself: well, of course, what important topics and how wonderfully Woolf handles them, but I really don't quite grasp the greatness of her style. . . . Whereas, in the case of Mauron's translation, the French reader sits up and takes notice. There it is, Woolf's quirkiness, right on the French page. Perhaps not the very same identical quirks, but the unflatness, the bends and stretches, the shiny spots: the whole garment appears, and not behind some scrim. This brief piece is written in honour of Charles Mauron's translation.

> For once the disease of reading has laid hold upon the system it weakens it so that it falls an easy prey to that other scourge which dwells in the ink pot and festers in the quill. The wretch takes to writing . . . a poor man, whose only property is a chair and table set beneath a leaky roof (*O* (1956), 74)
>
> 1. Quand cette peste de lecture s'est emparée de l'homme, elle l'affaiblit tant qu'il devient une proie facile pour l'autre fléau – celui qui se tapit au fond de l'encrier et purule au bout de la plume. Le malheureux est pris de la rage d'écrire . . . sa chaise et sa table branlantes sous un toit crevassé. (*O*, trans. Mauron, p. 56)
> 2. Une fois que la maladie de la lecture exerce son emprise sur l'organisme, elle l'affaiblit tant que l'individu devient une proie facile pour cet autre fléau qui gîte dans l'encrier et couve sous la plume. Le malheureux se met à écrire . . . une chaise et une table sous un toit qui prend de l'eau. (*O*, trans. Pappo-Musard, p. 605)

The roof is indeed leaking, it takes in water, but the cause is, of course, that the roof is 'crevassé', a word that you can roll around in your mouth. You can feel the Provençal joy in words in Mauron's translations. For he knew how to profit from the actual richness of French humour to capture the real funniness of Woolf. Wherever the high colour of French words could prevail, he had it prevail. All the way through his *O*, Woolf's own kind of humour is kept, even enhanced. French was never funnier than in Mauron's handling of it, when it should be handled that way. He picks up the tone and plays with it lovingly, in what seems to me again part of the Provençal genius, a conscious and consciously understood exaggeration. So the writing wretch is not just taken with a 'maladie' but with 'la peste', and this plague does not just hatch in the quill – 'couve' – but actually festers there: 'purule'. This 'wretch' does not just start to write, as in the other translation ('se met à écrire') but is actually seized by madness: 'pris de la rage', and so on.

What else he captures, here and elsewhere, and quite astonishingly, is the rhythm of the English. When Woolf breaks off, over and over, in a tease, he does precisely the same thing, never missing a beat. Instead of Pappo-Musard's quite correct 'Une chaise et une table sous un toit qui prend l'eau', he brings the scene into close-up, with rapidity: the poor man's chair, his table, his broken roof . . . of course, a roof in need of repair lets water in, no need to say it!

And yet at times, when the humour is quieter in the original, he can be quieter:

> Here she took up her lodging and began instantly to look about her for what she had come in search of – that is to say, life and a lover. (*O*, 190)

The wit here, of course, resides in the irony of the 'instantly' and in the confidence of our hero/ine in the notion of the instant availability of those things, and others. Mauron speeds on even more quickly: putting a simple colon after 'what she had come in search of' ... 'that is to say' which does the trick neatly:

> C'est donc là qu'elle s'établit et qu'elle se mit immédiatement en quête de ce qu'elle était venue chercher: c'est-à-dire, la vie et un amant. (Mauron, 674)

The other translation is quite correct, but does not wear its irony so crucially upon its sleeve:

> Aussitôt installée, Orlando se mit en quête. Elle était venue chercher à la ville: la vie et un amant. (Pappo-Musard, 123)

Another passage in *O* seems to be modelled on the formal model of the celebrated 'Comices' scene in Flaubert's *Madame Bovary*, in which the interruption outside and the seduction inside are set in an implicit/explicit dialogue for the amusement of the reader. Woolf too plays here on the in and out of it all:

> Is nothing, then, going to happen this pale March morning to mitigate, to veil, to cover, to conceal, to shroud this undeniable event whatever it may be? For after giving that sudden, violent start, Orlando – but Heaven be praised, at this very moment there struck up outside one of these frail, reedy, fluty, jerky, old-fashioned barrel-organs which are sometimes played by Italian organ-grinders in back streets. Let us accept the intervention, humble though it is, as if it were the music of the spheres, and allow it, with all its gasps and groans, to fill this page with sound. (*O*, 292)

> Ne va-t-il donc rien arriver, en cette pâle matinée de mars, pour atténuer, voiler, recouvrir, envelopper cet événement (quelqu'il soit), indéniable? Car, après avoir sursauté de façon si soudaine et si violente, Orlando .... Mais Dieu soit loué, juste à cet instant monta du dehors, frêle, sillotant, fluté, sautillant, démodé, le chant d'un orgue de Barbarie .... Acceptons cette intervention, si humble que nous la jugions, comme si elle était la musique des sphères, et permettons-lui, avec ses hoquets et ses grognements, de remplir du moins cette page. (Mauron, 182)

Here the wit about the event (whatever it is) is undeniable. And it is the wit that counts, as well as the deliberate delay of the sound of the organ, and the rough and tumble nature of the 'hoquets et grognements'. The subtle irony of its being allowed, if not to fill the universe, to fill at least this page, is undeniably rendered.

> Rien ne va-t-il donc arriver, en cette pâle matinée de mars, pour atténuer, voiler, couvrir, dissimuler, déguiser cet événement indéniable, quelle que soit la nature! Car après avoir soudain et violemment sursauté, Orlando .... Mais, le ciel soit loué, au même instant résonna dehors l'un de ces vieux orgues de Barbarie, fragiles, nasillard, flutés, saccadés, dont jouent encore .... Acceptons cette intervention, aussi humble soit-elle, comme si c'était la musique des sphères, et permettons à l'instrument, qui halète et ahane, de remplir de bruit cette page. (Pappo-Musard, 735)

For me the final clincher is a combination of two brief and impossible-to-render plays on words, the second repeating and teasing about the first, both of which have their play in rhyme so that the translation too has to play on rhyme or all is lost. Here, Mauron makes the very best of a difficult situation, and that is surely one of the best ways to judge any translation:

> and to be taking from its case a cigarette or cigar, and to be flinging a cloak under (as the rhyme requires) an oak . . . and we rise, and our eyes (for how handy a rhyme is to pass us safe over the awkward transition from death to life) fall on – (here the barrel-organ stops playing abruptly). (*O*, 293-94)

1. et qu'on prend dans son étui une cigarette, ou même un cigare, et qu'on étale son manteau sous (la rime l'exige) un ormeau . . . alors nous nous redressons et nos yeux abaissons (car une rime s'avère bien utile pour franchir sain et sauf le col malaisé qui sépare la mort de la vie) sur . . . . (Mais l'orgue de Barbarie s'interrompt soudain.) (Pappo-Musard, 736–37)
2. et encore prendre dans son étui une cigarette ou même un cigare, jeter son manteau (comme la rime le demande) sous un ormeau . . . et nous nous levons, et nos regards vont (comme une chanson est commode pour nous aider à franchir sans encombre la pénible transition de la mort à la vie!) tomber – (l'orgue de Barbarie s'arrête net.) (Mauron, 182–83)

This is not a simple repetition of the rhyme: repetition of sound, but a deliberately awkward rendering in order to make fun of it all. That, after all, is often the point. Mauron knows how to have fun and how to share it. This is, I submit, one of the goals of such a translation.

5 The German Reception and Criticism of Virginia Woolf: A Survey of Phases and Trends in the Twentieth Century

Ansgar and Vera Nünning

Virginia Woolf and the Germans, or, on German ineffectiveness and effusiveness about Woolf

Even though Virginia Woolf's scattered observations on Germany and the Germans are in general rather unfavourable and unflattering, she was not at all displeased with the interest they displayed in her work, as her letter to Harold Nicolson of 19 February 1928 shows: 'The Germans are apt to be very effusive and very ineffective about translating and writing, but I think MD will soon appear in German, and any notice is likely to be to my good' (*L* 3: 460). The degree of German ineffectiveness may be debatable, but they have certainly been very effusive both in translating Woolf's works into German and in writing books and articles about them. Woolf could not have foreseen just how effusive the Germans would actually be, but she was certainly correct in predicting that any notice was likely to be to her good.

The unprecedented degree of German effusiveness about Woolf has meanwhile not only turned Woolf into a canonized modern classic, it has also resulted in a very profitable and prolific Woolf industry, with both sales figures and the annual number of journalistic and academic publications on her life and works soaring to impressive heights. Just how extensive the interest in her works actually is, is reflected in the fact that a Collected Works in German from S. Fischer Verlag is being published to wide acclaim. This major enterprise, under the able editorship of Klaus Reichert, has made many of her writings available in German for the first time and has introduced the common reader to hitherto unknown facets of her œuvre. It includes new translations of her novels, four volumes of essays, five of diaries and three of letters, making more than half of her letters available to the German reading public. The translations of Virginia Woolf's autobiographical writings which were published in the collection *MB* (1976, ed. Jeanne Schulkind), *Augenblicke: skizzierte Erinnerungen* (1981), and of selections of Leonard Woolf's five-volume autobiography, which appeared in German under the telling title *Mein Leben mit Virginia* (1988, ed. and trans. Friederike Groth), also served to shed new light on a previously 'unknown' Virginia Woolf. A number of American and English studies of Woolf's life have also been translated into German, including the biographies by Quentin Bell (1977, first pub. in English in 1968) and Lyndall Gordon (1987, first pub. 1984), Spater and Parsons's *A Marriage of True Minds* (1980, first pub. 1977) and Louise DeSalvo's controversial book *Virginia Woolf: The Impact of Childhood Sexual Abuse on Her Life and Work* (1990, first pub. 1989). The fact that most of these publications have been widely reviewed not only in scholarly journals, but also in most of the daily and weekly papers testifies to the great and widespread interest Woolf enjoys in Germany today.

Moreover, since the end of the Second World War literary scholars and critics in Germany have published about sixty books and almost one hundred scholarly articles dealing with Woolf's life and works. When Annegret Maack concluded her review essay in 1978 by suggesting that the publication of archival materials was more likely to give a fresh impetus to Woolf scholarship than the deluge of secondary literature lavished on Woolf's novels, she was prescient indeed. The accessibility of her letters, diaries, memoirs and essays, in combination with recent developments in feminism and in other aspects of literary theory, has completely altered Virginia Woolf's image and reputation in Germany. Anyone familiar with her German reception in the decades just before and just after the Second World War could be forgiven for failing to recognize any likeness between the old cliché of Woolf as an apolitical aesthete, impressionist novelist and fragile invalid, who spent her sheltered life in the ivory tower of Bloomsbury writing experimental novels, and the present view of her as the figurehead of feminism and as a politically engaged critic, essayist and novelist, a highly versatile writer very much aware of and coping successfully with challenging personal, social and political issues. The great and growing number of new books and articles appearing every year in Germany shows that she has never before enjoyed such great popularity in this country and that the fundamental rethinking of Woolf's place in the development of English literature, literary criticism and feminism is not confined to Britain and the USA but is proceeding apace abroad as well.

Despite the effusiveness of the German common reader and critic alike, the German reception and criticism of Virginia Woolf like her European reception as a whole is a field which has yet to be fully mapped. Up to now, no comprehensive attempt has been made to survey the subject, let alone to introduce English-speaking readers to it.[1] We shall begin by setting out the different phases of German Woolf criticism that are by now discernible,[2]

---

1 As Füger (1980, 17) has pointed out, the history of the post-war German reception of Virginia Woolf has yet to be written. For short surveys of German Woolf criticism and the reception of Woolf in Germany, see Füger (1980), Nünning and Nünning (1996) and Crick (1999).

2 The term 'German Woolf criticism' is meant to refer to critical contributions from the German-speaking countries. The focus will be mainly on studies published by

focusing on the last five decades. But instead of proceeding author by author, the survey will focus on the different phases and trends of twentieth-century German Woolf criticism, with the goal of introducing readers to German contributions to Woolf scholarship by providing an overview of the main developments in both the reception and criticism of her work, and by identifying critical trends, commonalities and new directions of research that have opened up.[3]

The early reception of Woolf's works in Germany: the beginnings of stylistic, thematic and feminist criticism

The history of German Woolf criticism goes back to the 1920s and 1930s. In her lifetime, Woolf's works were well received in Germany and gained ever greater critical acclaim, though Woolf herself does not seem to have been fully aware of this. In his pioneering work on the early reception of Woolf's works in Germany, somewhat misleadingly entitled *Eine 'Extravagante Engländerin': Untersuchungen zur deutschen Frührezeption von Virginia Woolf* (A 'Flamboyant Englishwoman': Studies in the Early German Reception of V.W.), Wilhelm Füger (1980) has shown that the first phase of German Woolf criticism begins in the mid-1920s and extends to about 1937.[4] Füger's tremendously useful reference guide, which is descriptive rather than analytic, provides an invaluable source of information on both journalistic criticism and academic studies of Woolf's works in Germany during the 1920s and 1930s. He carefully reconstructs both the early reception of Woolf in German-speaking countries and the history of German Woolf criticism up to 1941, when she already enjoyed an international reputation as an experimental author of the first rank.

The concise summary of his findings deserves to be quoted in full, because it not only succinctly delineates the first phase of Woolf's appearance on the German cultural scene, it also conveys something of the flavour of the first

---

cont.

German critics, but pertinent contributions from Austrian and Swiss Woolf scholars will also be taken into consideration.

3 Since a short survey cannot discuss every contribution to German Woolf criticism, the focus will be on a selection of the most important full-length studies and articles, particularly academic studies that deserve to be better known in English-speaking countries. German Woolf criticism in this chapter refers primarily to that written in the Federal Republic of Germany to 1989 and in the reunited Germany since 1989. What happened in the former German Democratic Republic is a different story. For a detailed account of Woolf's reception in the GDR up to 1989, see Wolfgang Wicht's contribution to this volume (and Crick 1999).

4 For details of the early reception of Woolf's works in the German-speaking countries, see Füger (1980), to whose carefully documented study the following paragraphs are indebted. Füger also provides a comprehensive bibliography of the secondary literature published in or translated into German up to Woolf's death (107–11). For full bibliographical data of all the publications discussed below, see the bibliography of German Woolf scholarship accompanying the present article.

journalistic reviews, many of which celebrated her as a pioneer of new literary forms and as a new kind of psychological novelist:

> The earliest German reactions to her writings can be found, since 1923, in studies and surveys of the contemporary English novel. As a rule, these publications mention her briefly among a host of minor authors, often in connection with typical catchwords such as 'impressionism', 'mysticism', or 'psychological novel'. By the end of the twenties, however, critics gradually became aware – partly in the wake of the French – that Virginia Woolf's success as an artist was more than an ephemeral blossom of literary fashion. Between 1928 and 1934, four of her novels [*MD, O, TL* and *TW*] and three of her essays were translated, and throughout the same period numerous reviews and essays were published that endeavoured to make a wider public familiar with her writings. This wave of journalistic criticism ebbed away rather abruptly in 1935, not least under the influence of a political climate that favoured a growing hostility to experimental literature in general. (Füger 1980, 103)

In the wake of the first translations and journalistic criticism a number of German monographs and dissertations were published during the 1930s, some of which established two main lines of investigation that would extend through the 1960s and 1970s: namely the exploration of the stylistic peculiarities of Woolf's fiction and of the themes of her works, especially with respect to their feminist potential and to their delineation of female characters.[5] Ingeborg Badenhausen's monograph *Die Sprache Virginia Woolfs: Ein Beitrag zur Stilistik des modernen englischen Romans* (1932) (V.W.'s Language: A Contribution to the Stylistics of the Modern English Novel), which provides a thorough treatment of Woolf's language, stands in the tradition of stylistic analysis developed by such Romance scholars as Curtius, Spitzer and Voßler. It devotes chapters to Woolf's syntax, her use of adjectives and adverbs, and her use of free indirect discourse. This book laid the foundations for more detailed investigations of Woolf's prose style. Two pioneering dissertations, Ruth Gruber's *Virginia Woolf: A Study* (1935) and Gertrud Lohmüller's *Die Frau im Werk von Virginia Woolf: Ein Beitrag zur psychologischen und stilistischen Untersuchung des neuesten englischen Frauenromans* (1937) (Woman in V.W.'s Works: A Contribution to the Psychological and Stylistic Investigation of the Most Recent English Women's Novels) explore thematic and stylistic aspects of Woolf's novels in order to shed light on what they regard as the feminine and feminist qualities of her works. Gruber's and Lohmüller's dissertations anticipate many of the issues raised by contemporary feminist criticism.

By focusing on the style and theme of Woolf's fiction, by looking in detail at the woman writer's need to search for her own language, and by emphasizing the close analysis of her works, these three critics established both the main subjects and the prevailing methodological approaches that continued to preoccupy German Woolf critics until well into the 1970s.

---

5 See Badenhausen (1932), Gruber (1935) and Lohmüller (1937). We should like to thank Professor Willi Erzgräber for drawing our attention to these doctoral dissertations and their impact on German Woolf studies. For a concise summary and their reception in Germany, see Füger (1980, 63–84).

Moreover, in contrast to the journalistic criticism of the previous decade they provided German readers 'with more substantial insights, especially as regards Virginia Woolf's narrative technique, her concept of reality, and the feminist aspects of her œuvre. Yet these efforts did not result in a real breakthrough, either, since the imminent war brought them to a practical standstill', as Füger (1980, 104) observes. He also provides a balanced and shrewd summary of the impact that the first phase of Woolf's reception in Germany had, comparing it to English and French criticism of the same period:

> Seen as a whole, the early reception of Virginia Woolf in the German-speaking countries can be understood as part of a general process that, between the wars, gradually established the author's fame outside her mother country. Although the results attained in this field of criticism cannot, in their majority, seriously compete with the oft-times more subtle insights gained by English and French critics of that period, they deserve adequate attention on account of their quantity as well as of their occasional quality. By their joint impact, they eventually convinced a small circle of connoisseurs at least that Virginia Woolf had to be appreciated as a first-rank author, whose literary art demanded and justified the comparison with modern classics like Proust and Joyce. Despite all critical praise, however, she did not become a favourite of the wider reading public. (Füger 1980, 104)

At the end of the 1930s, however, the very promising first phase of the German reception and criticism of Virginia Woolf came to an abrupt and untimely end through the Nazis' deep-seated hostility to all experimental art. As soon as they had seized power in 1933, the critical climate had begun to change, and the change affected British citizens and experimental authors. While both the experimental novelists and critics in Weimar Germany had been intensely open to foreign literary currents (see Crick 1999), such currents were ruthlessly suppressed during the second half of the 1930s and even more so after the beginning of the Second World War. It was not long before Woolf's name appeared on the third list issued in 1942 by the *Reichspropagandaministerium* of the Nazis, who officially outlawed and banned Woolf and many other British writers as 'enemy authors' (*Feindautoren*).

The heyday of formalism: German Woolf criticism from the 1950s until the mid-1970s

It was only after the end of the Second World War that a second phase of German reception and criticism of Woolf began. It was ushered in, as Füger points out (1980, 17; 100-01), by the publication of Erich Auerbach's seminal study *Mimesis: Dargestellte Wirklichkeit in der abendländischen Literatur* (1946) (*Mimesis: The Representation of Reality in Western Literature* (1953)), but it was not until the 1950s that a real breakthrough became apparent (see Füger 1980, 17). Wolfgang Wicht, arguably the most sophisticated and undogmatic Woolf critic to publish in the former German Democratic Republic, succinctly summarizes the impact Auerbach's famous chapter on *TL* had on Woolf studies: Auerbach's influential reading of the novel shifted attention to the formal features of Woolf's fiction, since it pointed to the disappearance of the omniscient narrator, to the blurring of the narrator's and characters' voices, and to the multi-perspectival and subjectivized representation of the fictional world (see Wicht 1985b, 137).

Auerbach's book not only ushered in a renaissance of Woolf studies in Germany but it also brought critical attention to the formal properties of her novels. The well-known final chapter of *Mimesis*, entitled 'Der braune Strumpf' (The Brown Stocking), which is devoted to a close reading of a famous passage from *TL*, raised many of the issues that later Woolf criticism has tried to come to terms with, developing ever more refined analytical tools: e.g. the intricate problem of narrative perspective, the epistemological implications of multi-perspectivism and Woolf's subtle treatment of time. Moreover, post-war German Woolf criticism profited from the fact that pertinent English works on Woolf published during the 1940s gradually became available on the Continent. The influence of Auerbach and others can be seen in Erik Wiget's book *Virginia Woolf und die Konzeption der Zeit in ihren Werken* (1949) (V.W. and the Concept of Time in Her Works) (1949) and in the first two German dissertations on Woolf to appear after the war (in 1952), Aloysia Isenberg's 'Studien zur Erzählkunst Virginia Woolfs' (Studies in V.W.'s narrative art) and Margot Walter's 'Strukturanalysen von Romanen Virginia Woolfs' (Structural Analyses of V.W.'s Novels), both of which provided close structural readings of Woolf's novels. Wilhelm Borgers's 1953 dissertation on *TW* broke new ground at the time in that it compared Woolf's experimental novel with impressionist and post-impressionist art. With hindsight, Borgers's work looks like an early forerunner of what has come to be known as 'inter-art studies', which explore the formative influence of post-impressionist painting on Woolf's writing or other aspects of intermediality.[6]

German critics' concentration on Woolf's narrative technique was further encouraged by two other epoch-making events of post-war German criticism, the publication of Franz Stanzel's ground-breaking article on the narrative situation in *JR, MD* and *TL* (1954), and of his seminal monograph *Die typischen Erzählsituationen im Roman: Dargestellt an 'Tom Jones', 'Moby Dick', 'The Ambassadors', 'Ulysses'* (1955), a very influential book providing a thorough treatment of the typical narrative situations in the novel, which appeared in an English translation in 1971 (Narrative Situations in the Novel: 'Tom Jones', 'Moby Dick', 'The Ambassadors', 'Ulysses'). The Austrian scholar Franz Stanzel has arguably done more than anyone else in his generation to develop a new conceptual framework for the study of narrative techniques in Germany, an approach which fostered a much better understanding and appreciation of Woolf's formal experiments and her specific contributions to modernism. The terms that Stanzel coined for the study of point of view in fiction, e.g. *auktoriale Erzählsituation* (authorial narrative situation) and *personale Erzählsituation* (figural narrative situation) or

---

[6] For later and more sophisticated contributions to this field, see Erzgräber (1974), Kross (1998) and Mosthaf (2000); see also Wolf's (1996; 1999) pioneering work on the crossing of boundaries between literature and other media.

the distinction between *erzählendes Ich* (narrating self) and *erlebendes Ich* (experiencing self), soon became familiar and usable words in schools but also in many reviews, indicating that his influence was not confined to the academy. Moreover, together with scholars such as Käte Hamburger and Eberhard Lämmert, Stanzel's publications served to inaugurate a new approach to the study of fiction which has come to be known as *Erzähltheorie* (narrative theory) or *Narrativik* (narratology).

This narratological line of inquiry has proved to be continuously and particularly fruitful in Woolf criticism since the 1950s. It can be traced back to Stanzel, or even further back to stylistic critics like Leo Spitzer and theorists who carried out pioneering work on the problems of *erlebte Rede* (free indirect discourse). In the most recent phase of German Woolf criticism, a number of relevant books have underscored just how illuminating the tools of narratology can be for enhancing the understanding of Woolf's subtle experiments with narrative perspective (see pp. 94–5 below).

But to return to the 1950s, the decade in which the previously banned and largely forgotten Woolf was virtually newly discovered in Germany. In addition to a second wave of translations, which S. Fischer Verlag began to publish in 1954, there was also a second wave of academic criticism, testifying to a generally felt need to catch up with foreign literary currents and to distance ourselves from the immediate past. As Joyce Crick (1999, 4) astutely observes, Woolf was 'a very apt writer for "catching up", for it was literary modernism that had been lost under the Nazis. And by engaging with an English modernist at that, and one, moreover, whom Auerbach placed in a long view of world literature, it was possible to dissociate oneself trebly from the burden of being German'.

It may largely be attributed to Auerbach's and Stanzel's wide-ranging influence that the second phase of German Woolf criticism, which extends from the 1950s till about the middle of the 1970s, was dominated by formalism. A generation of German Woolf critics emerged whose overriding concern for the next twenty years was the exploration of the formal, stylistic and structural innovations of Woolf's experimental novels.[7] Albrecht Neubert's (1957) book about the development of free indirect discourse in the English novel, Ludwig Borinski's (1963) investigation of Woolf's radical stylistic experiments and Robert W. Weber's (1965) subtle analysis of the structural function of the chimes of Big Ben in *MD* (see also Hasler 1982) stand out among the stimulating contributions during this second phase of German Woolf criticism.

Although academic critics were already beginning to explore many facets of Woolf's novels during the second phase of her German reception, interest in her works was by no means confined to university English departments. Hilde Spiel's essay of 1953, 'Virginia Woolf: Bildnis einer genialen Frau'

---

[7] There are very few exceptions to this predominant trend of formalism, e.g. Kröger's (1955) dissertation on Woolf's essays, Stürzl's (1956) appreciation of her novelistic art in the light of her diary and Pasternak's (1962) shrewd analysis of Woolf's comic sensitivity.

(V.W.: A Portrait of a Woman of Genius), an introductory piece very much in the vein of Woolf's own essayistic, non-methodological method, may serve as a reminder that reception is as much the affair of the common reader as of the professional critic (see Crick 1999). In contrast to the much more specialized academic studies mentioned above, the Austrian refugee Hilde Spiel did a splendid job in introducing the common reader in Germany to Woolf's life, to Bloomsbury and to the stylistic and formal characteristics of Woolf's novels. Spiel's highly readable essay, which was reprinted as the introduction to the German translation of *MB, Augenblicke: Skizzierte Erinnerungen* (1981), has projected a very influential image of Woolf as 'a woman of genius' and done much to make her better known to the German reading public at large. As Theodor Adorno's (1958) essay on the standpoint of the narrator in the modern novel illustrates, Woolf had at that time also begun to find a place in much wider discussions of modernism.

During the 1970s most German critics were still primarily concerned with illuminating Woolf's textual practice. This is the subject of a number of studies exploring the relationship between form and content in her novels by offering chronological work-by-work analyses or close readings of Woolf's modernist fiction. In his cogently argued monograph *Bildstruktur und Romanstruktur bei Virginia Woolf: Untersuchungen zum Problem der Symbolkonstitution in 'Jacob's Room', 'Mrs Dalloway' und 'To the Lighthouse'* (The Structure of the Image and the Structure of the Novel in V.W.'s Works: Studies in the Problem of the Constitution of Symbols in *JR, MD* and *TL*), Klaus Schwank's (1975) formalist approach to the structural functions of images, leitmotifs and symbols in Woolf's prose fiction, for example, shows how traditional methodologies can be made to yield productive readings. In addition, a number of fairly sophisticated close readings of individual novels and short stories explored the ways in which meaning is conveyed through the imagery, rhythm and structure of Woolf's writing. Some of this criticism tends toward summary but often the critical comments are still of interest today. Erzgräber's illuminating interpretations of *MD* and 'The Shooting Party' (1971; 1973), Stadtfeld's reassessment of *BTA* (1973) and Maack's careful analysis of the structure of *Jacob's Room* (1977) stand out in that they show the virtues of solid close reading at its best.

As a result of this predominant interest in Woolf's formal experimentation with narrative technique, German Woolf criticism from the early 1950s through to the middle of the 1970s was mainly concerned with her literary modernism as it is reflected in *MD, TL* and *TW*. In line with the dismissive attitude of many earlier critics, the majority of critics tended to ignore Woolf's early novels and her critical writings, reserving all their praise for the modernist novels.[8] *TW* and, to a lesser extent, *MD* and *TL* have always been the

[8] This is also true of a number of dissertations (e.g. Brandt 1968; Dölle 1971; G. Winter 1977) and articles which try to give a general overview of Woolf's development as a writer, e.g. Hilde Spiel's (1953) well-known essay, Fricker (1966), Hamburger (1976), Fischer (1971) and Otten (1986).

undisputed favourites with German critics.[9] Like many critics in the 1950s and 1960s (see Maack 1978, 235), most adopted a teleological perspective, whereby *TW* constitutes the quintessential Woolf achievement. The majority of German critics were censorious of the works that preceded it (unless they could be shown to be evolving toward this perfect model) as well as those that followed it. Erika Dölle's book *Experiment und Tradition in der Prosa Virginia Woolfs* (1971) (Experiment and Tradition in V.W.'s Prose) was then the first German study that called into question the widely accepted modernism of Woolf's works, drawing attention to the traditional means of representation which Woolf relied on, but emphasizing that Woolf's novels demonstrated the limits and failure of conventional techniques. Moreover, alongside some other critics of the 1970s (e.g. Erzgräber 1974, Weber-Brandies 1974), Dölle did not limit herself to interpreting the novels, but also made substantial use of Woolf's essays to illuminate her aesthetic concerns.

A book that deserves to be singled out as one of the rare German contributions to Woolf criticism in the 1970s, underpinned by theory and reflecting a sense of history, is Ingeborg Weber-Brandies's highly sophisticated study *Virginia Woolf – 'The Waves': Emanzipation als Möglichkeit des Bewußtseinsromans* (1974) (V.W.'s *TW*: The Emancipatory Potential of the Stream of Consciousness Novel), which remains the most outstanding discussion of *TW* published in German.[10] The major contribution of this well-researched and persuasively argued book, something which sets it apart from many of the somewhat reductive formalist readings of Woolf's works in the 1960s and 1970s, is Weber-Brandies's fresh attempt to produce an appreciative assessment of Woolf's artistic achievement in the light of its historical and social context. Influenced by the Frankfurt School, Weber-Brandies proceeds from the hypotheses that events in art and society are closely interrelated and that artistic form can be seen as crystallized content. She is alert to particularities, recognizes the partiality of her method, and refuses to force a coherence that would belie the intricate texture of Woolf's novel. As the first German critic to bring in sociological and psychoanalytical approaches to Woolf criticism, Weber-Brandies managed not only to break new interpretative ground but also to provide a very fruitful framework for investigating Woolf's textual practice.

The ongoing upsurge of academic Woolf criticism was, however, just one of a number of clear signs that Woolf's novels were in the process of acquiring the status of canonized modern classics in Germany during the 1960s and

---

9 This preference of German critics for the canonical modernist classics is clearly reflected in the number of publications devoted to each of Woolf's works. No less than six book-length studies along with several articles on *TW* have been published in Germany since 1950, while *MD* and *TL* are the subject of more than a dozen articles each.

10 For other important works on *TW*, see the monographs by Brandt (1968), Grünewald-Huber (1979) and Müller (1993), and the very perceptive readings more recently offered by Bettinger (1993, 179–205), Wenner (1998, 76–146), Rogge-Wiest (1999, 161–236) and Neukirchen (1999, 99–154).

1970s. She had by then managed to secure a firm place in general introductions to the modern English novel (e.g. Fricker 1966), in reference works portraying major modern writers (e.g. Fischer 1971) and in collections of articles providing model interpretations of works that were regarded as exemplary modern classics (e.g. Hüllen 1966; Erzgräber 1971; 1973), *MD* being the great favourite with both the editors of such collections and many academic critics and teachers at the time. Such publications, which were mainly aimed at a student readership in German-speaking countries and whose main goal was to acquaint students with the works of major authors, both assured and enhanced Woolf's popularity in Germany, making her better known to a wider range of readers than ever before.[11]

Another sure sign of Woolf's canonization in Germany is the fact that her works have received more and more coverage in prestigious and widely distributed reference works since the 1960s. The seminal twelve-volume *Kindlers Literatur Lexikon*, arguably one of the most comprehensive reference works on world literature, is a case in point. The fact that the original version of this encyclopaedia, the first volume of which was published in 1965, already contained eight entries on Woolf's novels (on *JR, MD, TL, O, TW, FB, TY* and *BTA*), while the completely revised and enlarged 20-volume *Kindlers Neues Literatur Lexikon*, which was published between 1988 and 1992 and which has since sold a great number of copies in both hardback and especially paperback and student editions, features no less than eleven comparatively long articles on an ample selection of her works,[12] is interesting for a number of reasons. First, it testifies to a marked increase in Woolf's popularity since the 1960s. Second, the new articles that were added to *Kindlers Neues Literatur Lexikon* reflect changes in the literary and intellectual climate that occurred between the 1960s and the late 1980s: in addition to completely revised and updated versions of the entries on *JR, MD, TL, O* and *TW* and to new articles on *TY* and *BTA* there were new entries on *VO, CR1, RO* and *TG*, which nicely redressed the balance between her experimental modernist novels, once the only focus of attention in Germany, and her allegedly more conventional 'other' novels and essays, which had for a long time suffered from either neglect or critical condescension. Third, these shifts of balance towards both her early and late novels and towards her essays clearly demonstrate that a new wave of interest was underway from about the mid-1970s, one which has had far-reaching implications for the German reception and criticism of Virginia Woolf, implications which fully came to the fore during the third and fourth phases.

---

[11] For other general introductions to her work that appeared later, see Kohlhagen (1983), Otten (1986), Lavizzari (1991a) and Schneider (1993).

[12] See Dittmar (1992), Kluge (1992a; 1992b; 1992c), A. Nünning (1992a; 1992b; 1992c), V. Nünning (1992a; 1992b; 1992c) and Schoeller (1992).

Beyond formalism: German Woolf criticism from the mid-1970s to the mid-1980s

A third phase of German Woolf criticism, which roughly extends from the 1970s up to the mid-1980s, is characterized by a shift from formalism to other analytical modes. One of the new concerns was Woolf's biography. A second was Woolf's conceptions of the nature and functions of art and of the artist. A third was Woolf's early reception, both in England and in Germany, and the history of Woolf criticism.

The number of general introductions to Woolf's life and works, primarily addressed to the common reader, testifies both to the increased interest in her biography and to the popularity that Woolf had by then acquired in Germany. The short introductory critical biographies by Riley (1983) and Wiggershaus (1987), the richly illustrated biography by Waldmann, which appeared in the popular paperback series *rowohlts monographien* in 1983, and Klein's (1984) long and more substantial, but budget-priced biography are more or less résumés of the state of knowledge about Woolf's life. All four are published in series, but none is overburdened with the kind of plot summary of an author's work which the format usually demands. They offer fairly traditional biographical narratives, interspersed with information about cultural contexts and commentary on Woolf's works. Moreover, they all tend to jump easily from Woolf's life to her fiction, and vice versa, without problematizing the complex relationship between life and art. Compared to English and American biographical Woolf criticism, to which all of these books are heavily indebted, they seem largely derivative, and none really breaks new ground.

The opposite is true of those studies which explore Woolf's conceptions of art and the artist. A number of critics in the late 1970s and early 1980s focused on Woolf's essays in order to reconstruct her views of the nature and functions of art.[13] Closely connected to this interest in Woolf's conceptions of art and the artist was a new concern for the function rather than just the formal features of her fiction.[14] The East German critic Wolfgang Wicht's pioneering work on Woolf's aesthetics marks an important breakthrough in German Woolf studies in that it takes into account Woolf's aesthetic and ethical norms as well as her social experience. Moreover, Wicht was the first German critic to stress the interrelation between the fictional worlds of the novels and historical reality, emphasizing that Woolf's aesthetics and her formal innovations 'implement a radically recast ideological consciousness of art and its functions' (Wicht 1985b, 140).

A third area explored in Germany for the first time was Woolf's early reception, both in England and in Germany. Füger (1980) carefully documents

---

13 See Wicht (1978; 1980; 1981) and Drescher (1979); on aesthetic and poetological issues, see also Bisanz's (1981) article on Woolf's fictitious critic Nicholas Greene, Erzgräber's (1981; 1984b) subtle observations on what he argues is a specific Woolfian aesthetics of the moment and Hillgärtner (1988).

14 For the relationship between function and form in Woolf's novels, see Drescher (1979), Erzgräber (1984a; 1991b; 1999) and Wicht (1978; 1980).

both contemporary reactions to Woolf's works in Germany and the beginnings of German Woolf criticism. Gerd Egloff (1978) reconstructs the contemporary reception of Woolf's novels in England in the 1920s from a sociological point of view. Whereas Füger's approach is primarily descriptive, Egloff explores the interplay between social conditions, cultural norms and aesthetic forms, taking into account the horizon of expectations of the middle classes.

Quite a number of other critical works published in the 1970s and even in the late 1980s, however, continued to explore a perennial concern in Woolf studies, namely the ways in which her aesthetic values and her personal background are related to the themes and formal properties of her novels. A case in point is Peter te Boekhorst's (1987) close analysis of the use of the literary leitmotif and its functions in the novels of Woolf and other modernist writers. Also relying on close analysis, Andrea Beck's *Konstitution von ästhetischen Sinnsystemen in sieben Hauptwerken Virginia Woolfs* (1988) (The Constitution of Aesthetic Systems of Meaning in Seven of V.W.'s Major Works) investigates the relationship between 'the aesthetic structure and ideological message' ('der ästhetischen Struktur und ideologischen Aussage') in seven of Woolf's major novels (Beck 1988, 14). She offers long, interpretative summaries of individual novels but does not really relate them to their 'philosophical and aesthetic background' ('philosophischen und ästhetischen Hintergrund') (see 295ff.).

Familiar in approach, though much more complex in analysis than other German studies on Woolf, Willi Erzgräber's work is unsurpassed in German Woolf criticism, both in quantity and in quality, and compares well with the very best international work recently done on Woolf. With a dozen full-length articles and a highly acclaimed monograph on Woolf, Erzgräber has done more, perhaps, than anyone else in Germany to encourage adequate critical views of Virginia Woolf.[15] Although it is a critical commonplace by now that aesthetic movements in the arts, especially post-impressionist painting, are vital to a full understanding of Woolf's own aesthetic concerns, Erzgräber's pioneering article of 1974, 'Nachimpressionistische Anschauungen über Kompositionstechnik und Farbsymbolik in Virginia Woolfs Roman *To the Lighthouse*' (Post-impressionist Conceptions of Compositional Technique and Colour Symbolism in V.W.'s *TL*), was the first study to give the subject the attention it deserves. Erzgräber persuasively shows both Woolf's affinity to the theoretical views of the leading post-impressionists with respect to techniques of composition and colour symbolism and the impact of these views on the structure and texture of *TL*.

Erzgräber's (1982a) monograph on Woolf's works, which has recently

---

15 Some of Erzgräber's relevant articles are now readily available in a splendid recent collection of his essays (1995). It is no exaggeration to speak of an Erzgräber-school of German Woolf criticism, since not only have his publications had an important impact on Woolf's reception in Germany, but Erzgräber has also supervised a number of excellent dissertations on Woolf, e.g. Weber-Brandies's (1974) groundbreaking monograph on *TW* (see above), and the books by Wenner (1998), Rogge-Wiest (1999) and Neukirchen (1999) discussed below.

appeared in revised form (1993), is arguably the most comprehensive and perceptive examination of her art of fiction published in German to date. Erzgräber casts his net extremely widely, providing an appreciation of the form and the themes of Woolf's novels, by highlighting the individual traits that set them apart and make them unique. He is also one of the few German critics to try to relate Woolf's writings to their cultural background in order to demonstrate how both contemporary thought and her intellectual heritage influenced her artistic and political attitudes. Erzgräber traces the influence Woolf's father and members of the Bloomsbury Group had on her philosophy of life and art. Moreover, he carefully delineates the development of Woolf's new concepts of novel-writing by providing a series of sophisticated and penetrating readings of both her novels and her feminist pamphlets. His interpretations of the novels demonstrate how Woolf experimented with narrative voice, with the treatment of character and with narrative structure in order to express her particular vision of reality.[16] His specific analyses of the ways in which Woolf's presentation of private life and public life in *ND* expresses her veiled social criticism, of the relevance of moments of vision in *MD*, and of Woolf's views on history, which are reflected in *BA*, could each be the point of departure for much broader investigations.

Moreover, Erzgräber has managed to dispel the idea that Woolf was either just an ethereal aesthete or just a radical feminist, since he takes into account both the complex formal texture of the novels and the political implications of Woolf's modernist project. Erzgräber (1982a; 1984) was also the first German critic to draw attention to the historical awareness and the social criticism directed against contemporary England that appear in Woolf's novels. In his analyses, the literary and the historical are inseparable. His readings have been strongly endorsed by German Woolf critics of the 1980s and 1990s, and the resourcefulness and insight of Erzgräber's work have substantially enhanced German understanding of Woolf's achievement as a novelist, critic and feminist.

Given the deluge of books published on Woolf every year since the 1970s, together with hundreds of articles and doctoral dissertations, it is hardly surprising that some German critics turned their attention to surveying the history of Woolf criticism. Annegret Maack (1978) was the first to produce such a survey. The non-specialist and the professional scholar alike will find Christoph Schöneich's (1989) concise, informative and balanced overview of the results of Woolf criticism a useful starting point. Covering both the history of international Woolf criticism and the state of the art, his text-orientated guideline is a good synthesis of recent studies of Woolf's life and works. The bibliographical essay appended to Erzgräber's (1982a, 196-223) monograph provides another useful overview of the history of Woolf criticism. And most recently, the authors of the present paper have tried to provide surveys of

---

[16] On Woolf's concept of reality and on the ways in which specifically modern forms of experiencing reality are depicted in her novels, see Hackenberg (1957), Villgradter (1966), Brandt (1968), Jackson (1973), Maack (1977) and especially V. Nünning (1990, 31–58) and Erzgräber (1999).

major developments, new methodologies and important results in Virginia Woolf criticism of the 1980s (see Nünning and Nünning 1991b) and in post-war German Woolf criticism (see Nünning and Nünning 1996).

Recent trends in the German reception and criticism of Woolf

The most recent phase in the German reception and criticism of Virginia Woolf begins in the mid-1980s. Since the Woolf centenary in 1982, an *annus mirabilis* in English Woolf criticism, which produced a significant number of excellent critical works, her writings have been the subject of ever more intense study in Germany. Moreover, in addition to the increase in academic and journalistic criticism, there has been a tidal wave of interest in her life and work since the end of the 1970s. It has been fed by two main sources (see Crick 1999, 7-10), the great fascination that her biography and the lives of her Bloomsbury contemporaries have exerted on a host of readers, and the rise of the women's movement and feminism.

The unprecedented degree of interest that the German reading public has displayed in Woolf may partly be attributed to the fact that, over the last two decades, the amount of information on the author that is readily available in Germany has increased substantially as a result of the accessibility of her letters, diaries, memoirs, essays and holograph notes. Whereas the majority of critical works published in Germany up to the mid-1980s were primarily concerned with exploring the formal and thematic aspects of Woolf's novels, her literary criticism and her feminist essays have only recently begun to receive the scholarly attention they deserve.

In the most recent phase of the German reception and criticism of Woolf, four new trends have emerged. At the risk of some oversimplification, these may be designated 'the feminist discovery and appropriation of Woolf as a feminist figurehead', 'the turn towards history', 'the discovery of Woolf as a literary critic and thinker' and 'the rise of theory', with a recent narratological turn of German Woolf criticism resuming and further developing the formalist tradition initiated by Stanzel. The first and arguably most influential trend has led to a discovery of Woolf as the initiator and originator of feminist criticism, who first addressed many of the issues that have preoccupied the women's movement and feminism ever since, a trend which has led to her canonization as a feminist icon and figurehead. The second of these trends is represented by works that focus on the significance of history in Woolf's novels, on her views on history and on her ambivalent relationship with her literary heritage. The third and equally innovative trend in German Woolf criticism of the late 1980s and 1990s is characterized by an interest in Woolf's non-fictional writings, thus reversing the tendency to concentrate almost exclusively on her novels. This has at last resulted in the discovery of Woolf as a literary and cultural critic. Such studies have begun to look more closely at the author's methods of composition and her philosophical, aesthetic and feminist concerns. The final trend can be attributed to the general rise of literary theory. Whereas most German Woolf critics in the 1970s and 1980s still adhered to traditional critical approaches and to well-established value judgements, others began to absorb literary theory and the analytic techniques of feminist theory and psychoanalytic criticism. Some of the most sophisticated recent contributions to Woolf criticism have managed to refine and modify the formalist approach developed by eminent scholars such as Stanzel so as to be able to combine new forms of cognitive narratology with broader historical and cultural concerns.

Though these four trends are closely intertwined, what we have called the feminist discovery and appropriation of Woolf stands out in a number of ways. First, in contrast to the other recent trends, it is not confined to academic criticism: it has had a far-reaching influence on the general German reception of Woolf, involving academia, the women's movement and the common reader so dear to Woolf. Second, it has profoundly changed Woolf's public image, alerting the German public (not just the reading public) to a hitherto unknown Woolf. Third, it has led to a revision of the Woolf canon, in fact resulting in a complete inversion of the previously existing hierarchization between her modernist novels and her feminist essays, which had for a long time been almost completely ignored in Germany. Therefore we have decided to devote a separate section to the feminist strand of the German reception and criticism of Woolf, though, chronologically speaking, it runs more or less parallel to the other recent trends. Since the feminist discovery of Woolf, in fact, precedes the other trends by a couple of years, dating back to 1978, it also provides a convenient bridge between the third and the most recent phase in the German reception of Woolf.

The feminist discovery and appropriation of Woolf as a 'feminist figurehead'

While the discovery of Woolf as a literary critic and the other recent trends outlined above have largely been confined to the academic reception of her works in Germany, the widespread attention devoted to her feminist essays arguably represents an upsurge of interest, bringing a noticeable critical reassessment of her works in its wake. The recuperation of her feminist essay *ROO* and her anti-fascist pamphlet *TG* dates back to the end of the 1970s when these texts were first translated into German and brought out by fringe publishers:[17] *Ein Zimmer für sich allein* (*ROO*, trans. Renate Gebhardt) in the Gebhardt Verlag in 1978, and *Drei Guineen* (*TG*, trans. Anita Eichholz) in the same year by the feminist publisher Verlag Frauenoffensive. The influence that these two essays have had on the reception of Woolf and on her public image in Germany can hardly be overestimated. *ROO* has not only turned into a real long-term bestseller, it has also entailed a wholesale revision of Woolf's public image.

As in Britain and the USA, the German women's movement and feminist criticism have turned Woolf into an idealized figurehead, a cultural icon to be

---

17 *ROO* was rediscovered rather than discovered by German feminists in the late 1970s, having already been the subject of a short article by Else Arnheim (1930–31).

adored and a role model to be emulated. Gisela von Wysocki's short book *Weiblichkeit und Modernität: Über Virginia Woolf* (1982) (Femininity and Modernity: On V.W.), for instance, goes a long way to stylize Woolf into an icon of the twentieth-century woman writer as victim and rebel. Susanne Amrain's more down-to-earth biographical study *So geheim und vertraut: Virginia Woolf und Vita Sackville-West* (1994) (So Confidential and Intimate: V.W. and V.S.-W.) capitalizes on the interest in Germany in readable narratives about Woolf's life. Although this engaging and chatty book offers a wealth of anecdotes and details about Woolf's lifestyle and her relationship with Sackville-West, these are hardly new. Moreover, it provides only one side of the story, offering nothing fresh for those who have kept up with English and American Woolf scholarship.[18]

With regard to her German reception, it is only since the end of the 1970s that the feminist Woolf has begun to emerge from the shadow of her other self, the modernist author of experimental novels. The women's movement and feminist criticism contributed significantly to that emergence, perceiving (and conceiving) her primarily as a political and cultural icon. In the wake of the translations of *ROO* and *TG*, Woolf soon enjoyed unprecedented popularity with a continuously growing number of feminist critics and readers. Her growing fame rested as much on her life as on her works, both representing paradigmatic ideals that supporters of the women's movement could readily identify with, as Bettinger observes:

> Every emancipation movement must reconstruct its own history in order to recognize the mechanisms of oppression and to liberate itself from the role of victim. For this phase of feminism, the phase of the reconstruction of its own history, Virginia Woolf was almost predestined to become a figure with whom to identify, her biography paradigmatic in providing many instances of the oppression of women. (Bettinger 1993, 12)[19]

In feminist literary theory and criticism, and in its more recent incarnation of gender studies, references to Woolf abound, with *ROO* being German feminists' all-time favourite. Examples here are legion since an introductory bow to Woolf has become so much of an established topos (see Crick 1999, 7) that in some cases it is now hardly distinguishable from a cliché. There is a long list of feminist publications that make more than just a passing reference to

---

18 For other recent biographical studies, see Amrain (1992), Bettinger's article 'Woolf in Spain' (1995) and her overview of recent Anglo-American research on friendship between women (1998a), and H. Winter's *Virginia und Leonard Woolf* (1999), which is intended for the common reader. See also Hartung's (1982) essay on the occasion of the Woolf centenary and the piece by Klein and van Behr (1986).

19 'Jede Emanzipationsbewegung muß die eigene Geschichte aufarbeiten, um die Unterdrückungsmechanismen erkennen und sich aus der Opferrolle befreien zu können. Für diese Phase des Feminismus, die Phase der Rekonstruktion der eigenen Geschichte, war Virginia Woolf als Identifikationsfigur geradezu prädestiniert, liefert ihre Biographie doch paradigmatisch viele Momente der Unterdrückung von Frauen.'

Woolf's most popular feminist essay, however, ranging from Silvia Bovenschen's influential book *Die imaginierte Weiblichkeit: exemplarische Untersuchungen zu kulturgeschichtlichen und literarischen Präsentationsformen des Weiblichen* (1979) (Imagined Femininity: Exemplary Studies in Cultural and Literary Presentations of the Feminine) to the groundbreaking anthology *Genus: zur Geschlechterdifferenz in den Kulturwissenschaften* (1995) (Gender: On Gender Difference in Cultural Studies), edited by Hadumod Bußmann and Renate Hof.[20]

Important though such references to her feminist essays have no doubt been for Woolf's rapidly growing popularity with German readers, at least as important for spreading the word, or the image of the feminist icon, is G.C. Beresford's famous 1902 photograph of Woolf, reproductions of which have sold in countless numbers in Germany. (It may be mentioned as an aside that this paper was also written under the famous picture of the young Virginia.) Beresford's stylized photograph arguably did more than anyone or anything else not only to popularize Woolf in Germany, but also to establish a highly clichéd view of her as a fragile female genius.[21] Alexandra Lavizzari is right when she astutely observes that

> In parallel with biographic documentation, photographic documentation has perhaps been even more conducive to turning her person and life instead of her work into the centre of public interest. Ever since Woolf stopped having control and jurisdiction over the construction of her 'image' for the public, posterity has increasingly turned away from the mature author and typified the entranced twenty-one year old Miss Stephen, as she is immortalized in a photograph of 1903, as the genius Virginia Woolf. (1991b, 8)[22]

---

20 In lieu of countless other examples, see Kohlhagen (1983, 117), who calls ***ROO*** 'the first plea for the independence of the woman writer' (das erste Plädoyer für die Unabhängigkeit der schreibenden Frau'), and the chapter by Winnett and Witte (1985) on 'Ästhetische Innovationen' (Aesthetic innovations) in the first edition of a very successful German history of women's literature, *Frauen – Literatur – Geschichte: Schreibende Frauen vom Mittelalter bis zur Gegenwart*, which, like Bovenschen's book, uses *ROO* as the point of departure, calling Woolf's essay a 'text which is as canonical for feminist studies as it is problematical' ('In diesem für die feministische Wissenschaft ebenso kanonischen wie problematischen Text', 318).

21 For the importance of Beresford's and Man Ray's photographs for Woolf's (in some ways curiously reductive) German reception, see Lavizzari (1991b, 8–9) and Bettinger (1993, 9–19).

22 'Parallel zur biographischen Dokumentation hat die photographische vielleicht noch stärker dazu beigetragen, Person und Leben statt Werk in den Mittelpunkt des öffentlichen Interesses zu rücken. Seit Woolf selbst keine Entscheidungsbefugnis mehr hat über die Konstruktion ihres "Image" für die Öffentlichkeit, hat sich die Nachwelt zunehmend von der reifen Schriftstellerin abgewandt und das entrückte einundzwanzigjährige Fräulein Stephen, wie es auf einer Photographie von 1903 verewigt ist, zum Genie Virginia Woolfs typisiert.'

Thus, whether the enormous increase in popularity and fame that Woolf has enjoyed through her being turned into a feminist figurehead and model woman of genius has actually resulted in a greater German familiarity with her works or in a more refined critical appreciation is debatable. There are, in fact, quite a number of indications that the opposite is true: while more people than ever before may now be familiar with the name ('Virginia Woolf? Isn't she the feminist who . . .?'), the level of familiarity with her novels and her literary innovations does not seem to be much higher in Germany now than it was twenty or thirty years ago. Moreover, in feminist theory, references to Woolf's works are mostly confined to a very small number of texts, with *ROO* invariably receiving the lion's share, followed by *TG* and *TL*, and the same issues tend to be emphasized time and again. In sum, the interest of the wider German reading public has become so focused on Woolf's biography and her feminist views that it has tended almost to eclipse her novels, a development which the editor of a recent collection of essays attempts to redress (see Lavizzari 1991b, 14). Whether this is actually necessary may be debatable but the important, and salutary, impact that the rediscovery of her feminist essays has had on her German reception should certainly not be underestimated, let alone denigrated. With regard to the German reception of her work, the feminist appropriation of Woolf has in fact resulted in a wholesale revision of her public image, turning her into a feminist icon that has assumed a symbolic place in popular culture and consciousness.

Recent interest in Woolf's non-fictional writings, particularly that resulting in the reassessment of *ROO* and *TG*, has also led to academic deconstructions of the old cliché of Woolf as an apolitical aesthete and to a greater appreciation of her political and feminist commitments. Exploring Woolf's awareness of the material impediments and ideological constraints that women writers have to overcome in a patriarchal society, Wicht (1985a) made the first sustained effort to locate *ROO* and *TG* in terms of Woolf's intellectual development and succeeded in encouraging serious interest in these important feminist texts. In his well-argued book *Emanzipation bei Virginia Woolf: Eine Studie zu ihrer nichtfiktionalen Prosa* (1986) (Emancipation in V.W.: A Study of Her Non-fictional Prose), Thomas Riedl asserts the importance of Woolf's nonfictional prose, which had previously been largely ignored by German Woolf criticism, and provides a close analysis of her feminist pamphlets. Like Klein (1984), Riedl focuses on the concept of 'emancipation', which he defines broadly as the mental and moral liberation of men and women from prejudices and inhibiting constraints. In contrast to those critics who reproach Woolf with what they regard as a 'flight into androgyny' and who claim her to be a wholehearted advocate of some particular feminist stance, Erzgräber (1991a) argues that in *O*, which he discusses alongside *ROO*, androgyny functions as a metaphor for the emancipation of both sexes.[23] Drawing on feminist theory in

---

[23] On the conceptualization of androgyny, see Klinner (1995) and also chapter 6, 'Androgynität, Feminismus und die Emanzipation beider Geschlechter' (Androgyny, feminism and the emancipation of both sexes) in Nünning and Nünning (1991a), who interpret Woolf's ideal of androgyny in the light of her unremitting

order to elucidate Woolf's political stances and writing practices, Helga Quadflieg (1991) provides an overview of Woolf's attitudes toward feminism and the women's movement and discusses her proposal for rewriting literary history.

In addition to these and other substantial explorations of feminist aspects of Woolf's works,[24] German feminist theorists have recently begun to reconstruct Woolf's role as a pioneer feminist critic and to take stock of the many issues that can be traced back to her essays. To give but one or two examples: Woolf's ideas of 'thinking through our mothers', establishing a tradition of female writing, and of a 'woman's sentence' figure prominently not only in the chapter 'Feministische Zugänge – "Gender Studies"' (Feminist Approaches – "Gender Studies") of the bestselling textbook *Grundzüge der Literaturwissenschaft* (An Outline of Literary Criticism) (see Erhart and Herrmann 1996), they also recur again and again in other German publications on feminist theory and criticism.[25] Lena Lindhoff, for instance, devotes an informative chapter of her widely circulated and useful textbook *Einführung in die feministische Literaturtheorie* (Introduction to Feminist Literary Theory) to 'Virginia Woolf und die Frage nach einer weiblichen Tradition' (V.W. and the Question of a Female Tradition), which does not ignore what the author considers to be 'the many unresolved contradictions in her essay [*ROO*]'[26] (1995, 34). Calling Woolf 'the "mother" of the history of women's literature'[27] (XI), Lindhoff also refers to *ROO* throughout and uses Woolf's works (especially *TL*) as a touchstone to test, illustrate and criticize the feminist theories she discusses. Lindhoff's brief overview of Woolf's most noteworthy achievements as a feminist critic deserves to be quoted at some length, because it aptly summarizes those aspects of her work that have played a crucial role in her German reception since the end of the 1970s:

---

cont.

struggle for unity and relate it to her conviction that cultural progress demands the emancipation of both sexes and cooperation between free individuals rather than confrontation.

24 See also Riedl (1986), Maassen (1990), Nestvold-Mack (1990), Erzgräber (1991a), Hof (1991), Quadflieg (1991), Bettinger (1993; 1998a) and Würzbach (1998), most of which are briefly discussed below, pp. 95–6. See also Hesse, Knight and Pfister (1984) on the New Woman.

25 See Bovenschen (1979, 10–12), Burmann and Hof (1995, 5, 33, 187–88, 190, 192) and Schabert (1997, 10–11). Though the range of material here is vast, it is doubtful whether it would repay detailed investigation because this strand of the German reception of Woolf is as repetitive and reductive as it has no doubt been influential. Anyone who uses the well-known phrase 'Who's Afraid of Virginia Woolf?', as Loster-Schneider (1999), like Toril Moi (1985) and Erzgräber (1982b) before her, does in her introduction to an interesting German collection of feminist essays, is capitalizing on Woolf's popularity rather than on that of Edward Albee's play.

26 'der vielen ungelösten Widersprüche in ihrem Essay'.

27 '"Mutter" der Frauenliteraturgeschichte'.

> Virginia Woolf is the first woman to write the history and social history of (English) literature written by women. She is the real initiator of feminist literary studies, not just with regard to chronology, but also in respect of the audacity and radicality of her questioning of patriarchal values in culture. Long before Simone de Beauvoir, she began to historicize the patriarchal definition of femininity and to attribute it to the social allocation of roles. In contrast to Beauvoir, she tried at the same time to situate herself as a woman within a female tradition, and made significant contributions to its reconstruction. With her search for specifically female cultural values beyond ontological stipulation she can be considered to be the 'mother' of the theories of difference. (Lindhoff 1995, 31)[28]

Woolf has indeed by now become generally recognized as an important forerunner of present day feminist theory and criticism in Germany. In the most systematic and comprehensive research report on the subject to date, Natascha Würzbach (1998) shows that Woolf's critical writings on the subject of women and literature anticipated a broad range of the issues that later came to be important theoretical considerations in present-day feminist literary criticism. By carefully delineating the ideological changes within the women's movement and the development of feminist literary criticism, Würzbach examines and explains both the reasons why Woolf's ideas failed to be adequately appreciated during her lifetime and the subsequent rediscovery and revaluation of her views on the subject of women and literature. Like Toril Moi (whose 1985 book *Sexual/Textual Politics: Feminist Literary Theory* has also been translated into German (see Moi 1989), further strengthening the feminist strand of Woolf's German reception), Würzbach does a good job of 'rescuing' Woolf for feminist politics and literary theory. Her article also shows how closely intertwined Woolf's appropriations by the women's movement and by feminist criticism in academia have been in Germany since the late 1970s.

The turn towards history: the discovery of Woolf as a literary critic and the rise of theory

The second recent trend in German Woolf criticism, the turn towards history, which has nothing to do with the new-historicist school of literary theory, has led to a reassessment of the functions of traditional narrative modes in Woolf's

---

[28] 'die Virginia Woolf ist die erste Frau, 'die Geschichte und Sozialgeschichte der (englischen) Literatur von Frauen schreibt. Sie ist die eigentliche Initiatorin der feministischen Literaturwissenschaft, nicht nur in chronologischer Hinsicht, sondern auch im Hinblick auf die Kühnheit und Radikalität ihrer Infragestellung patriarchalischer Werte in der Kultur. Lange bevor Simone de Beauvoir begann sie, die patriarchalische Bestimmung von Weiblichkeit zu historisieren und auf eine soziale Rollenzuweisung zurückzuführen. Anders als de Beauvoir versuchte sie aber zugleich, sich als Frau innerhalb einer weiblichen Tradition zu situieren, zu deren Rekonstruktion sie Wesentliches beigetragen hat. Mit ihrer Suche nach spezifisch weiblichen kulturellen Werten jenseits ontologischer Festlegungen kann sie als "Mutter" der Differenztheorien gelten.'

fiction, of the concepts of history underlying her works,[29] and of her complex attitude towards her own literary heritage. Having thoroughly explored the experimental quality of Woolf's fiction, critics in Germany have recently become increasingly aware of the fact that the evaluation of her place in modernism is far more complex than literary histories have tended to suggest. The turn towards history and concern with the issues raised are clearly evidenced in Sabine Hotho-Jackson's fine monograph *Zwischen Tradition und Moderne: Geschichte bei Virginia Woolf* (1990) (Between Tradition and Modernity: History in V.W.), which stands out among the publications that focus on Woolf's views of history. Hotho-Jackson explores the ways in which history played a formative role and had a continuing influence on Woolf's criticism and fiction. Her book is a persuasive blend of formalist criticism, literary-historical analysis and biographical commentary. In addition to contributing to our understanding of Woolf's views of history, Hotho-Jackson illuminates the thematic and narrative structures of *O* and *BTA*. Three other important features of her book are the systematic use she makes of Woolf's essays, letters and diaries in order to reconstruct Woolf's concept of history, her convincing reassessment of the mixture of traditional and specifically modern narrative modes in Woolf's fiction, and her insightful analytical commentary on Woolf's use of recurrent metaphors of history like the tree and the house. Hotho-Jackson demonstrates Woolf's essentially conservative view of history, shedding light on how Woolf presented her notions of history in her fiction as well as raising questions about her ambivalent attitudes towards her cultural heritage.

In addition to Hotho-Jackson's seminal monograph, several other publications exemplifying the turn towards history deserve brief mention.[30] One of them is Fritz-Wilhelm Neumann's book *Der englische historische Roman im 20. Jahrhundert* (1993, 108–33) (The English Historical Novel in the Twentieth Century), which includes a very interesting chapter on Woolf's 'physiognomic world-picture' ('Virginia Woolfs physiognomisches Weltbild') presenting a number of fine observations on Woolf's historical novels (i.e. *O* and *BTA*; see also Schabert 1981). Another one is Hotho-Jackson's (1998) original and penetrating comparison of the ways in which Woolf and Ingeborg Bachmann appropriate history for their own revisionary purposes. Instead of locating Woolf in either the male modernist tradition or the conventional 'masculine' kind of historical novel, A. Nünning (1999) argues that it might be more rewarding to see her novels that engage with history as part of a female tradition of revisionist historical novels and attempts to situate *TY* and *BTA* in the yet to be written history of this tradition.

---

29 On the concepts of history underlying Woolf's works, see also Schwank's (1984) balanced assessment of *O* as a work situated squarely between historiography and fiction, and Maassen's (1987) analysis of the narrative and thematic structure of *BTA*.

30 See also Mengel (1986), Glaser (1998b) and Richter (1996), which includes a chapter on 'Bloomsbury and History' (77–98), discussing, among other writers, Leonard Woolf (78–80) and Virginia Woolf (87–94).

The turn towards history has also led to reassessments of some of Woolf's previously neglected works. During the last two decades, German critics have, for instance, begun to analyse *O* and *BTA* as achievements in their own right. Though there are a number of important reassessments of *O*,[31] Ina Schabert's painstaking and cogently argued book *In Quest of the Other Person: Fiction as Biography* (1990) deserves to be singled out for providing a very perceptive and illuminating analysis of Woolf's unconventional biographical novel within the conceptual framework of the new literary genre known as fictional biography. Moreover, Schabert (1990, 4) draws attention to Woolf's role as 'a pioneer of fictional biography as concerns both its theory and practice', while also delineating the significance of this genre for the development of twentieth-century fiction. *BTA*, which had previously been the subject of only one German article (Stadtfeld 1973), has also greatly profited from the turn towards history; it has finally and deservedly been canonized, and is even included in the seminal *Kindlers Neues Literatur Lexikon* (see A. Nünning 1992a). In their convincing rereadings, Maassen (1987) and Hotho-Jackson (1990, 265-370), for instance, have shown that conventional forms of historical narration are rejected as inadequate in *BTA* and that innovative aesthetic modes impose order and meaning.[32] By comparison with Woolf's innovative 'historical' novels (i.e. *O* and *BTA*), *VO, ND* and *TY* have as yet received relatively little critical attention in Germany, but there are clear indications that their fortunes will improve: like *CR, ROO* and *TG*, two, *VO* and *TY*, have made it into *Kindlers Neues Literatur Lexikon* (see V. Nünning 1992c; A. Nünning 1992c), and after a surprisingly long period of neglect all have been the subject of a fair number of appreciative rereadings during the 1990s.[33]

It may also be attributed to the turn towards history and culture that Woolf's experimental uses of time – one of the favourite issues of German Woolf criticism since the end of the 1940s[34] – have recently been reexamined within the wider frameworks of cultural history. In a wide-ranging article on the concept of time in modernist literature, Stephan Kohl (1998) carefully delineates how new notions of time (e.g. Einstein's and Bergson's concepts)

---

31 See Schwank (1984), V. Nünning (1988), Hotho-Jackson (1990, 147–264), Schabert (1990, 66–84) and Webel (1999, 388–91), who examines the literary strategies Woolf uses in *O* for the deconstruction of biological gender. In comparison to Hotho-Jackson's (1990, 147–264) and Schabert's (1990, 66–84) highly illuminating rereadings of *O*, Antor's (1998, 416–19) rather perfunctory discussion of the novel fails to offer anything essentially new.

32 For other incisive recent rereadings of *BTA*, see I. Weber (1986), Bartschi (1991), Olejniczak (1994, 236–40), Hotho-Jackson (1998) and especially Neukirchen (1999, 155–97); see also Blöcker (1966) and A. Nünning (1992a).

33 See, however, the chapters on these novels in Erzgräber (1982a), A. Nünning's (1991) article on Woolf's Victorian heritage, Bettinger's (1993, 72–107) observations on Woolf's use of metaphors in Woolf's first two novels, Rogge-Wiest's (1999, 57–86) perceptive and lucid analysis of forms of subjectivity in *VO* and Thume's (1997) exploration of the role of quantum logic in *TY*.

34 See Wiget (1949), R.W. Weber (1965), Erzgräber (1980; 1981; 1984b), Smuda (1981), Hasler (1982) and Wenner (1998).

were taken up and transformed by Woolf and other modernist writers and how literature became one of the major fields of the discursive negotiation of time as a central aspect of the process of modernization. Examining what he calls the 'dialogue between literature and scientific writings' ('des "Dialogs" zwischen literarischen und naturwissenschaftlichen Schriften') (173), Kohl analyses in great detail such issues as the subjectivization of the experience of time, the phenomenon of simultaneity, discontinuity and the evocation of 'idyllic timelessness' ('idyllische Zeitlosigkeit') (171), which served as a means of compensation for the ubiquitous experience of acceleration as a central aspect of the process of modernization. Arguing along somewhat similar lines, Annette and Linda Simonis (2000) also provide a broad and thorough exploration of the concept and representation of time in the modernist novel, giving particular attention to Woolf.

Some German Woolf critics have recently turned their attention to Woolf's ambivalent relationship to her own literary heritage. Among the studies which investigate the relationship between Woolf's modernistic aesthetics and her cultural inheritance there are Martin Brunkhorst's (1993) article on Woolf's views of the Restoration Comedies and Irmgard Maassen's (1992) striking observations on the impact of romantic concepts of the artist on Woolf's works. Examining Woolf's attitudes to the 'great tradition' of English fiction, other critics have argued that it oversimplifies Woolf's art to interpret her novels as a rejection of traditional narrative modes in favour of an exploration of consciousness. In his narratological analysis of Woolf's ambivalence toward her Victorian heritage, Ansgar Nünning (1991) explores the complex process of assimilation and revision of traditional narrative modes in *VO, ND* and *TY*. These articles correct both the one-sided view of Woolf's revolt against the Victorian patriarchal society and the equally one-sided emphasis on the 'experimental' aspects of her novels. Moreover, by establishing a context for approaching Woolf's complex attitude to her literary heritage, these studies demonstrate how much the appreciation of Woolf's works is enhanced by placing them in broader diachronic and synchronic cultural frameworks. Taken together, these studies have succeeded in illuminating the importance of history and literary heritage in Woolf's works.

Moreover, though Woolf's short fiction has yet to be investigated in detail,[35] both the turn towards history and an increased concern with her aesthetics have led to original new readings of some of her short stories, opening up new horizons. Two recent articles by Bernd Engler suggest that an investigation of Woolf's short fiction can shed much light on her aesthetics and her view of history. One (Engler 1987) analyses the ambivalent mixture of realist narrative conventions and the underlying innovative aesthetics in 'An Unwritten Novel'.

---

35 For some noteworthy German contributions on Woolf's short fiction, see, however, Villgradter's (1966) instructive article, Erzgräber (1973), Häußler (1982), Engler (1987, 1993), Lavizzari (1991c) and I. Weber (1994), whereas Geraths's (1999) observations on 'The New Dress' are rather superficial. Bernd Engler (Tübingen) is currently writing a book-length study on Woolf's short fiction, focusing on her role as a precursor of postmodernist poetics.

In another highly original article, Engler (1993) provides a wealth of information on and insights into one of Woolf's most neglected works, 'The Journal Of Mistress Joan Martyn'. Sharing Hotho-Jackson's interest in Woolf's views on the functions and problems of historiography, Engler persuasively argues that this text can be seen as an early forerunner of what has come to be known as 'historiographic metafiction'. In addition, a number of recent monographs primarily concerned with exploring Woolf's novels from different theoretical angles also demonstrate that her short fiction is at last beginning to receive a fair share of attention in Germany. Elfi Bettinger (1993, 63–71) devotes an interesting chapter to Woolf's use of metaphors in 'Phyllis and Rosamond', while Claudia Wenner (1998, 47–75) provides detailed and sophisticated interpretations of 'The Moment: Summer's Night' and 'Moments of Being: "Slater's Pins Have No Points" ', focusing on Woolf's depiction of moments of being. Gunilla Neukirchen's (1999, 34–66) subtle observations on 'The Mark on the Wall', 'The Lady in the Looking-Glass' and other short stories also contribute to a better understanding of Woolf's short fiction.

The new interest in Virginia Woolf's essays and reviews

A third trend of recent German Woolf criticism is the new interest in Woolf's literary essays and reviews, which have rarely been given the scholarly attention they deserve. Like the discovery of Woolf's ambivalent relation to her literary heritage, the exploration of her aesthetic and feminist concerns has also opened up new perspectives for German Woolf studies. Among the major features explored in the 1990s are Woolf's aesthetics, her political and feminist commitments, and her views on such diverse issues as patriarchy, the social system and pacifism. These new lines of development can be seen as the result both of the publication of Woolf's personal writings – of her essays, diaries, letters and manuscripts – and of the vitality of feminist literary scholarship.

Recent studies of Woolf's non-fictional writings have also highlighted an important new field of inquiry: the philosophical implications of her art and her underlying aesthetic concerns. Heinz Antor (1986) provides a general introductory overview of Bloomsbury's philosophical, aesthetic and literary theories, and Jürgen Klein (1985) explores Woolf's idea of the new novel. By revealing Woolf's preoccupations while composing her novels, Vera Nünning (1988) elucidates Woolf's processes of composition and points to the conscious artist at work. In her monograph *Die Ästhetik Virginia Woolfs* (V.W.'s Aesthetics), V. Nünning (1990) tries to correct the prevailing view that Woolf's aesthetic theory lacks unity, is naive and, at best, partially formulated. The subtitle of her book – *Eine Rekonstruktion ihrer philosophischen und ästhetischen Grundanschauungen auf der Basis ihrer nichtfiktionalen Schriften* (A Reconstruction of Her Philosophical and Aesthetic Assumptions on the Basis of Her Non-fiction Writings) – indicates its scope. Nünning examines Woolf's notions of 'reality', 'personality' and 'history', reconstructing Woolf's theories of literary creation and reading, her concepts of form and the autonomy of art, her views on the differences between art and propaganda, and her assumptions about the aims of literary criticism. The study demonstrates that Woolf, far from being the impressionistic or subjective critic she is usually taken to be, was in possession of a coherent and sophisticated aesthetics, even if this is not explicitly formulated in any one of her essays. Woolf's aesthetics is shown to rest upon such principles as wholeness, order and formal perfection and to display comprehensiveness, sophistication, coherence and unity.

A number of other recent studies have provided reassessments of Woolf as one of the last of the great English essayists and critics. Working from a feminist perspective, Renate Hof (1991) gives an overview of the themes and forms of Woolf's essays and reviews. And in a collection of essays called *Classics in Cultural Criticism*, Irmgard Maassen (1990) provides an introduction to Woolf's work as cultural critic. Pursuing some of the significant unifying strands in her literary criticism, Vera Nünning (1991) examines Woolf's view of the common reader as the natural companion of the essayist and analyses the critical precepts, aims and methods of Woolf's literary criticism.

Despite the vast number of books and articles published on Woolf in Germany during the last two decades, her reputation as a thinker continues to suffer from a kind of critical condescension. In their revisionist introduction to Woolf's nonfictional writings, Vera and Ansgar Nünning (1991a) try to redress the balance by looking at Woolf's role as literary critic, essayist and political thinker and by setting the explicitly feminist issues within the context of the wider humanistic concerns of her works. They argue that the essay genre has a strong affinity with Woolf's epistemological perspectivism and that the form of the essay is particularly well suited for conveying Woolf's subjective point of view. Moreover, they relate her literary criticism to her humanistic belief that reading literature can liberate people from social and moral constraints. Taking into consideration Woolf's concern with and awareness of the relationship between hierarchy, patriarchy, Fascism and war, they also elucidate the challenging assertion developed in *TG* that war and the oppression of women in the home spring from the same source, a source which she referred to as 'subconscious Hitlerism'.[36]

The increasing influence of contemporary literary theory on Virginia Woolf studies

A fourth trend in the most recent phase of German Woolf criticism is marked by the increasing influence of contemporary literary theory. While most of the formalist and thematic studies published in Germany in the first three decades after the Second World War were fairly traditional in methodology, some German Woolf critics since the early 1980s have become aware of recent developments in literary theory and have begun to reassess Woolf's works in the light of such approaches as reader-response criticism and psychoanalytic theory. Their work differs considerably, however, in terms of the ideology and methods adopted by the authors.

---

[36] Virginia Woolf, 'Thoughts on Peace in an Air Raid' (in *DM*, London: The Hogarth Press, 1981, pp. 154–57, here: 155.)

Quite a number of books on Woolf's fiction published during the 1980s and 1990s are direct theoretical projects. Three of them are based on the frameworks provided by psychoanalytic theories. Like Elisabeth Grünewald-Huber's (1979) cogent textual analysis of *TW*, Gabriele Schwab's *Entgrenzungen und Entgrenzungsmythen: Zur Subjektivität im modernen Roman* (1987) (Delimitations and Myths of Delimitation: On Subjectivity in the Modern Novel) provides a thorough analysis of the same novel, reading Woolf's works against the background of psychoanalysis (see also Schwab 1981). The rise of theory is also reflected, albeit in a very specialized way, in Marlene Müller's (1993) detailed Lacanian reading of *TW*, which draws on the methods of poststructuralism and psychoanalysis (see also Müller 1985). She takes care to distinguish between the psychoanalytical content and the specific literary treatment of the themes she explores, but her approach runs the risk of treating characters as if they were actual people, and even feminist theorists have found fault with it, pointing out that such readings within a Lacanian framework might tell us more about Lacan than about Woolf's novels (see Lindhoff 1995, 92–93). Providing a subtle and revisionist phenomenological approach to Woolf's notion of moments of being, Claudia Wenner's *Moments of Being: Zur Psychologie des Augenblicks bei Virginia Woolf* (1998) (Moments of Being: On the Psychology of the Moment in V.W.) also draws on psychological and psychoanalytical models to uncover the textual patterns and significance of mystic moments in two of Woolf's short fictions and *TW*.

Three other sophisticated theoretical studies demonstrate that Woolf criticism in Germany, just like the development of literary theory at large, has recently followed a course away from the structuralist project of identifying and systematizing the 'properties' of texts in the directions of a poststructuralist awareness of the dynamic potential of language (see Bettinger 1993, 33) and a growing interest in the complex interplay that exists between texts and the interpretative choices and strategies involved in the dynamics of the reading process.[37] Making use of the theoretical framework of reader-response criticism, Verena Olejniczak's ambitious monograph *Wirkungsstrukturen in ausgewählten Texten T.S. Eliots und Virginia Woolfs: Eine Untersuchung zur Lesewirkung moderner englischer Literatur* (1987) (Patterns of Response in Selected Works of T.S.E. and V.W.: An Analysis of Reading Effects of Modern English Literature) examines the ways in which notions of self and identity are transmitted, or constructed, in the reading process of *JR* and *BTA*. Focusing on the textual conditions of aesthetic response, she attempts to define the 'basis of appeal' ('Wirkungsprinzip') in Woolf's novels and to identify those textual strategies which guide the reader's responses and prevent the achievement of interpretative wholeness he or she may strive to achieve. Following upon

[37] For this general reorientation of much of German Woolf criticism, see Olejniczak (1983; 1985), Schwab (1981; 1987) and Bettinger (1993). Though such a project is well beyond the scope of the present paper, it would indeed be interesting and rewarding, as Bettinger (1993, 29) suggests, to trace the correlations that exist between the phases and preferences of German Woolf criticism outlined above and changing trends in literary theory at large.

Harald Weinrich's theory of metaphorical fields, which emphasizes the productivity of the metaphorical process, Elfi Bettinger's thorough study *Das umkämpfte Bild: Zur Metapher bei Virginia Woolf* (1993) (The Contested Image: On Metaphor in V.W.'s Texts) explores Woolf's use of metaphors in her early and modernist novels from a feminist point of view, providing in-depth readings of all Woolf's novels from *JR* to *TW* except for *O*. A Woolf book of a completely different colour, Gunilla Neukirchen's *Aktive Spiegelungen: die Konstituierung des Subjekts im Werk Virginia Woolfs* (1999) (Active Reflections: The Constitution of the Subject in V.W.'s Work) offers a very subtle account of Woolf's conception of 'a dialogic subject' (199). Starting out from Lacan's concept of the mirror stage and profitably drawing on Mikhail Bakhtin's suggestive notions of dialogism and polyphony, Neukirchen persuasively demonstrates 'that both the motif of the mirror and the paradigm of mirrorings' are 'constitutive structural elements' ('daß sowohl das Motiv des Spiegels als auch das Paradigma der Spiegelung ... ein konstitutives Strukturelement [sind]', 199) of Woolf's novels and that Woolf conceives of the 'I' as a 'polyphonic I in a polyphonic society' ('ein vielstimmiges Ich in einer vielstimmigen Gesellschaft') (200). Different, but thoroughly self-conscious theoretical agendas govern Olejniczak's, Bettinger's and Neukirchen's readings, which contribute much to a better understanding of both Woolf's novels and the methodological and cultural implications involved in interpretations.

Closely related to the general rise of literary theory is the narratological trend in German Woolf criticism. While many studies continue to draw on the toolkit provided by narratology, they tend to combine analysis of the formal features of Woolf's novels with broader questions concerning literary criticism and cultural history. Among the works that might be subsumed under this heading,[38] Monika Fludernik's (1993; 1996) and Gudrun Rogge-Wiest's (1999) books deserve to be singled out for special praise. Following in the footsteps of her former teacher Franz Stanzel, the internationally renowned Austrian narratologist Monika Fludernik has published two seminal monographs, which, while not being solely or even primarily concerned with Woolf, frequently refer to her novels, contributing substantially to a more subtle and analytically more refined appreciation of Woolf's narrative techniques: *The Fictions of Language and the Languages of Fiction: The Linguistic Representation of Speech and Consciousness* (1993) provides a comprehensive 'guidebook on free indirect discourse in its fullest spectrum' (82), which throws much new light on the narrative and stylistic modes Woolf uses for the representation of consciousness. Counteracting many of the shortcomings of structuralist narratology, Fludernik's *Towards a 'Natural' Narratology* (1996) provides a resolutely diachronic and cognitive approach, which allows her to follow developments in written narrative in English from the late Middle Ages

---

[38] On the distinctive German tradition of narratological Woolf criticism see e.g. Stanzel (1954), Neubert (1957), Adorno (1958), Erzgräber (1965; 1982a; 1984a), Hamburger (1976), Smuda (1981), R.W. Weber (1981), Schabouk (1990), A. Nünning (1991) and especially Jahn (1996).

up to the twentieth century and to reassess the 'novel of consciousness' (168–72).

While interest in problems of narrative technique and perspective may seem to have waned since the halcyon days of formalism, Gudrun Rogge-Wiest's *Wahrnehmung und Perspektivik in ausgewahlten Romanen Virginia Woolfs* (1999) (Perception and the Use of Perspective in Selected Novels by V.W.) demonstrates that the analytic tools of narratology can yield interesting results when they serve interpretative concerns that are vital for a better understanding of particular novels and their place in literary and cultural history. Drawing on Fludernik's new cognitive approach to narratology, V. Nünning's (1990) insights into Woolf's aesthetics and various theories of perception, Rogge-Wiest argues persuasively that Woolf used literary conventions 'both as a means of communication with the reader and as frames or schemata which correspond to a specific interpretation of reality' and that ' "perception" is the frame of reference by which important themes of the texts[,] like subjectivity and the problem of cognition, can be connected with each other' (267). Her theses are forcefully brought home in long analytic chapters on *VO, JR, MD* and *TW*, in which she demonstrates that 'the representation of the everyday experience of perception' provides 'a basis for the communication with the reader by means of which she [V.W.] draws him into the text so that he can experience the limits of perception and cognition himself' (268).[39]

In addition to these central developments in recent German Woolf criticism, a number of other studies which cannot readily be related to any of these trends indicate further new directions in research. One of these is Werner Wolf's brilliant article (1996) on intermediality as a new paradigm for literary studies, delineating a very promising approach for what he calls 'literature-centred investigations of the border crossings between literature and other media' ('eine literaturzentrierte Erforschung der Grenzüberschreitungen zwischen Wortkunst und anderen Medien'). Both his penetrating reading of Woolf's 'The String Quartet', which serves as a case study in the 1996 article, and his more recent and wide-ranging monograph *The Musicalization of Fiction: A Study in the Theory and History of Intermediality* (1999) demonstrate just how productive this approach to the relationship between literature and music actually is. The same holds true for two less ambitious studies focusing on the relationship between Woolf's works and visual art: Meike Kross (1998) reappraises and situates Woolf's post-impressionist aesthetics of the novel within the cultural contexts of Bloomsbury and Charleston, Pont-Aven and Provence, while Franziska Mosthaf (2000) draws on the analytic tools of narratology and intermediality in order to provide a new view of the forms and functions of the treatment of painting in *TL* and other novels from the nineteenth and twentieth century.

Moreover, a number of excellent readings of individual novels have recently

---

39 Fludernik's and Rogge-Wiest's volumes are primarily for those who already have a very good command of narratology, but anyone interested in Woolf will also find them very illuminating and useful.

been published by German critics.[40] Four of the most noteworthy are highly sophisticated interpretations of the interrelationship between the structure and themes of *TW* by Erzgräber (1991b), Roughley (1994), Wenner (1998, 76–146) and Rogge-Wiest (1999, 161–236). Similarly, a number of recent readings of *TL* have also taken German Woolf criticism measurably beyond earlier commentaries: these include Irmgard Maassen's (1991) exploration of the significance of art, tradition and modernity, Sabine Volk-Birke's (1993) analysis of the relevance of epistemological issues and the problem of perception in that novel, Jürgen Klein's (1995) observations on the role of social criticism and the search for meaning, and especially Christian Moser's (1990) perspicacious and original article on the revision of aesthetic modes of perception.

Two books with greater scope, reaching across a broad spectrum of writers, but which deserve notice because each has an interesting chapter on Woolf, are Ruth Nestvold-Mack's (1990) monograph on the use of the fictional female perspective in literature and Lothar Fietz's (1994) wide-ranging book on the transformations of the myth of man's loss of totality and completeness.[41] Nestvold-Mack shows how Woolf deploys the central female consciousness in *O* in order to voice social criticism and to deconstruct fixed gender roles and stereotypes. And Fietz explores how Woolf depicts the experience of isolation and fragmentariness and how she, in spite of her scepticism, still clung to the myth of personal wholeness and completeness as a potential mode of existence.

Of broader interest than most of these fairly specialized academic studies is a collection of essays on Woolf edited by Alexandra Lavizzari (1991a) and published by the prestigious Suhrkamp Verlag. It has an amazingly wide focus for an anthology, including articles on all of Woolf's novels plus three contributions that deal with her roles as critic, essayist and feminist (V. Nünning 1991; Hof 1991; Quadflieg 1991), and cover a broad selection of her essays. The collection not only reflects the increased popularity that works previously regarded as 'minor' now enjoy in Germany, but also makes a modest attempt to intervene in the dynamics of the German reception of Woolf, trying to redirect the attention of the wider reading public from the feminist icon Woolf became in the 1970s and 1980s to the novels and essays themselves. Unlike some of the studies mentioned above, the essays collected

---

40 It would be remiss on our part not to make at least brief mention of some other interesting recent interpretations, even though they do not fit in well with any of the general trends we have tried to outline. These include Heidi Marek's (1990) essay on the reception of *MD* in Elio Vittorini's *Piccola Borghesia*, Verena Olejniczak's (1994) general, but perceptive introduction to Woolf's prose fiction and Brigitte Glaser's (1998a) analysis of the role that the motif of 'death-in-life' plays in Woolf's novels.

41 See also Dietrich Jäger's (1998) case studies in the phenomenology of narrated spaces, which include an interesting chapter on the multi-perspectivist presentation of the setting and of other aspects in *TL* (244–53), and Detlev Gohrbandt's (1998) monograph on the reading process, which contains a chapter inquiring into the constraints which text and context impose on the reader's productive responses, referring particularly to Woolf.

in the Lavizzari anthology, while taking up a number of issues in current literary theory, are theoretically less ambitious, preferring instead to tread more traditional methodological ground.

Over and above these trends in academic, journalistic and feminist German Woolf criticism, there are many other unmistakable signs that Virginia Woolf's canonical status in Germany is no longer in any doubt at the end of the second and the beginning of the third millennium. She figures prominently, for instance, in introductions to the history of the twentieth-century English novel mainly aimed at a student readership in German-speaking countries,[42] e.g. in A. Nünning's *Der englische Roman des 20. Jahrhunderts* (1998) (The English Novel in the Twentieth Century), which includes chapters on Woolf's programme for a new kind of novel, on Bloomsbury and the cultural contexts of modernism and on Woolf's experiments with new forms of novels. In his brilliant survey *Der englische Roman von Joseph Conrad bis Graham Greene*, Willi Erzgräber (1999, 125–72) devotes a long chapter to her works, entitled 'Virginia Woolf: Der Roman als Instrument der Wirklichkeitsentdeckung' (V.W.: The Novel as an Instrument of Discovering Reality).

Woolf has also acquired a firmly established place in all of the standard literary histories, two fairly recent German histories of English literature, which have already gone through several editions, being cases in point (Fabian 1991; Seeber 1999). The second and completely revised edition of the equally widely read history of women's literature, *Frauen – Literatur – Geschichte: Schreibende Frauen vom Mittelalter bis zur Gegenwart* (Women – Literature – History: Writing Women from the Middle Ages to the Present), edited by Hiltrud Gnüg and Renate Möhrmann and published by Metzler Verlag, also includes a chapter on Woolf, which, significantly, discusses her novels as a 'highpoint' of 'aesthetic innovation' (see Wende 1999, 533 and 536). Moreover, courses on Virginia Woolf are regularly offered at almost every German university, her novels and feminist essays being very popular with students.[43]

In addition, Woolf is now very well represented in almost all the standard German reference works and encyclopaedias of world literature and of literary theory. The budget-priced one-volume *Lexikon der Weltliteratur: Hauptwerke in Charakteristiken und Kurzinterpretationen* (Encyclopaedia of World Literature: Major Works in the Form of Characterizations and Short Interpretations) (1968), edited by Gero von Wilpert, contains five (albeit very short) entries on *VO, O, TW, TY* and *BTA*, while the five-volume *Harenbergs Lexikon der Weltliteratur: Autoren – Werke – Begriffe* (1989) (Harenberg Encyclopaedia of World Literature: Authors – Works – Terms), which is richly illustrated and obviously directed at a very wide readership, includes five comparatively long

---

42 See Otten (1986), Haefner (1990), Jahn (1996) and Würzbach (1996).

43 Despite some critics' efforts (e.g. Erzgräber 1982a; 1982b), it is only rarely that Woolf's novels are taught in secondary schools in Germany, but some of her short fiction (e.g. 'The Mark on the Wall', 'The New Dress') occasionally appears in anthologies and collections of essays designed as study aids (see, most recently, Geraths 1999).

entries, one on Woolf and one each on *MD, TL, O* and *BTA*, plus an article on the 'Bloomsbury Group'. There are also entries on Woolf in such widely used recent encyclopaedias as the *Metzler Lexikon Literatur- und Kulturtheorie: Ansätze – Personen – Grundbegriffe* (Metzler Encyclopaedia of Literary and Cultural Theory: Approaches – Theorists – Technical Terms) (see Antor 1998b) and the *Metzler Autorinnen Lexikon* (Metzler Encyclopaedia of Female Writers) (see Bettinger 1998b), and even the *Lexikon literaturtheoretischer Werke* (Encyclopedia of Works of Literary Theory) features an excellent entry on her essay 'Modern Fiction' (see Engler 1995), a remarkable feat for a writer who used to be belittled as an impressionist critic at best. In short, in addition to the soaring sales figures of the German translations of Woolf's novels and feminist essays, there are numerous sure signs of 'arrival'.

Germany is a foreign country – they do things differently there: on the specificity of the German reception and criticism of Virginia Woolf

In contrast to authors whose popularity has waxed and waned over the years, Virginia Woolf's German stock has continuously risen since the end of the Second World War. It is partly due to excellent work on her writings by such eminent scholars as Willi Erzgräber, Ingeborg Weber and Wolfgang Wicht, and partly, no doubt, due to the many parallels that the women's movement and feminist criticism have discovered between their own agendas and Woolf's feminist essays. Moreover, Hollywood's interest in her novels – manifested in films such as *Mrs Dalloway* (1997) (directed by Marleen Gorris) – has also been to her good, making her works familiar to people who would have been unlikely to have read her novels, even in German translations.

Whether Virginia Woolf would have liked it or not, her life no longer belongs to those of the obscure, and her works have definitely acquired the status of canonized classics in Germany. Woolf the pioneer critic, who did not tire of arguing for the opening up of the canon and who did more than anyone else in her generation to bring to light a tradition of forgotten or neglected female writers once considered 'minor', has not only been discovered by feminist critics in Germany, she has herself been canonized as one of the greatest English authors. Moreover, she has not only kept almost as many professors busy as James Joyce, she has also become a household name for a wide range of German readers. The flourishing German Woolf industry, second, perhaps, only to the Shakespeare industry, has been very busy catering for all tastes, producing not only a host of specialized single-author studies for those who have spent many years avidly reading Woolf's fiction, but also fine companions for the recently initiated.[44] This holds true for the English and American Woolf industries as well, of course, but in other respects Germany is

---

[44] See Riley (1983), Waldmann (1983), Klein (1984), Wiggershaus (1987), Schöneich (1989), Nünning and Nünning (1991a), Lavizzari (1991a), Amrain (1994), H. Winter (1999) and especially Erzgräber (1982a; 1999).

arguably a foreign country: they do things differently there, even as far as the reception of Woolf is concerned.

The most obvious particularities and even peculiarities of the German reception of Virginia Woolf, especially with regard to the earliest phases, can of course be explained only if one takes the changing political contexts into account: the auspicious, but short-lived, contemporary response to her work in Weimar Germany benefited from an openness to foreign literary currents, while her German reception was prematurely cut off when the Nazis seized power in 1933, suppressed experimental fiction and banned 'enemy authors' (*Feindautoren*) (see Crick 1999, 2–3). Both Woolf's continuously growing fame in post-war West Germany and the near-suppression of her works in the German Democratic Republic are also inexplicable without reference to the wider political, cultural and aesthetic contexts, with the doctrines of socialist realism being anything but conducive to fostering interest in the former Eastern Germany in kinds of writing which did not fit the pattern of the nineteenth-century model of realism (see Crick 1999). The history of the reception and criticism of Woolf in the German Democratic Republic is given in Wolfgang Wicht's chapter 'Installing modernism'.

Despite the fact that nowadays the different countries in Europe and their English departments no longer live in splendid isolation or blessed insularity, there is still an obvious divergence in both national traditions of Woolf studies and in her reception. If one compares German Woolf criticism to the development of Woolf studies in English-speaking countries, for instance, a number of obvious differences emerge. First, Woolf's early and late 'novels of fact' have seemed far less relevant to German critical concerns than her experimental modernist novels. Second, compared to the wholesale revision of traditional views on Woolf in the USA, the old cliché of Woolf as a modernist writer or even as an apolitical aesthete has proved to be much more lasting in Germany than anywhere else. Third, the great majority of German critics, in contradistinction to many of the studies published in the USA or in France, have until very recently refrained from the application of theory to Woolf's writing. Contemporary French feminist theory, deconstruction or other poststructural textual theories, for instance, have exerted less influence on German Woolf studies to date than in the USA. Fourth, in contrast to the new-historicist trend in Anglo-American literary theory, only very few German Woolf critics have turned to biography and cultural history as an effective basis for illuminating the relationship between Woolf's ideas and her writings.

Most important of all, perhaps, the political themes of Woolf's novels and the ethical and moral power of her writing were largely ignored by German critics until the 1980s. In contrast to much recent American work, German Woolf criticism has not sought to trace the appearance of Woolf's political concerns in her fiction or to consider her narrative practice mainly in terms of her personal life, her feminist politics or the politics of gender. German critics have also had very little to say about the ways in which Woolf's views of the relationship between literature and politics influenced her prose style, narrative technique or choice of themes. It is probably no coincidence that it was a Marxist critic from the former German Democratic Republic,

Wolfgang Wicht, rather than a critic from the Federal Republic, who first sought to trace the appearance of Woolf's political concerns in her essays and fiction by looking at her works mainly in light of her aesthetics and her feminist politics.

On the other hand, recent German Woolf criticism has opened up territory for further exploration. This is the case, for instance, with many of Erzgräber's publications, with Hotho-Jackson's book on the significance of history in Woolf's works and with Engler's articles on her short fiction. Moreover, a number of German publications have emphasized the need for closer attention to Woolf's aesthetic theories and to her conceptions of the nature and function of art, questions which have arguably not received the attention they deserve in Anglo-American Woolf criticism.[45] Some recent German publications have also shown that Woolf's importance as a literary critic and her theory of art, her processes of composition and her ambivalent relationship to her literary heritage surely all deserve thorough study.[46] In addition, recent German publications on her non-fictional writings may serve as a reminder that Woolf has yet to be properly situated, not only in the history of the English essay, but also in the development of feminist theory and of cultural criticism.[47] Another distinctive German tradition that deserves to be singled out is that of studies in narrative technique, which has had some noteworthy impact on German Woolf criticism, with seminal studies like Stanzel's (1954), Fludernik's (1993, 1996) and Rogge-Wiest's (1999) standing out from a broad range of publications in this field. In sum, the most recent phase of German Woolf criticism has managed to indicate future directions of investigation and to remind the reader that there are still stimulating new areas of research which are likely to generate further interest in Woolf's work and thought, in Germany as well as in other countries.

The great and growing number of books, articles and dissertations that appear every year indicates the continuing 'effusiveness' of the Germans about Woolf, and the plethora of academic publications and journalistic notices has certainly been to her good. The deluge of secondary literature lavished on her works testifies, moreover, to the fact that the rethinking of Woolf's place in the development of English literature, literary criticism and feminism is proceeding apace in Germany. Being no longer regarded as the impressionist novelist or 'flamboyant Englishwoman' she was once thought to be in Germany, someone whose novels were known only by the select few, Virginia Woolf has come to acquire the status of a veritable 'cult figure' by the end of the millennium, the '"original mother" of feminism'[48] for some and a

---

45 See Wicht (1978; 1980; 1981) and V. Nünning (1988; 1990).

46 See Hotho-Jackson (1990), Maassen (1990) and V. Nünning (1988; 1990; 1991).

47 See Erzgräber (1991a), Hof (1991), Maassen (1990), Quadflieg (1991) and especially Würzbach (1998).

48 See Erhart and Herrmann (1996, 510), who refer to her as 'die feministische "Ur-Mutter" Virginia Woolf'. See also Bettinger (1993), who provides a sketch of how Woolf was turned into a cult figure ('Kultfigur' (10)) and an ideal figure that feminists could readily identify with ('Identifikationsfigur' (12–13)).

canonized modern classic with which every student and even the common reader is familiar. The Woolf industry has become so productive, prolific and polyphonic that even with regard to the German reception and criticism of Virginia Woolf, 'fifty pairs of eyes' are no longer 'enough to get round that one woman with' (*TL*, 303).[49]

---

[49] The quote refers to one of Lily Briscoe's reflections about Mrs Ramsay; we have previously used it as a title for our review article on developments of Woolf criticism in the 1980s (see Nünning and Nünning 1991b).

6 Installing Modernism: The Reception of Virginia Woolf in the German Democratic Republic

Wolfgang Wicht

I

In East Germany, the public reception of Virginia Woolf began in 1977. Insel-Verlag Leipzig published *Mrs Dalloway*, in the admirable early translation by Thesi Mutzenbecher, for which Insel-Verlag had held the copyright since 1928. Insel continued to be the main publishing house of the writings of Virginia Woolf until the demise of the German Democratic Republic in November 1989 and the political incorporation of its territory into the Federal Republic of Germany on 3 October 1990. Other works followed *Mrs Dalloway* at more or less regular intervals, *Die Fahrt zum Leuchtturm* (*TL*) (in the old 1931 Insel-Verlag translation by Karl Lerbs) in 1979, *Orlando* (translated by Lerbs, revised by Heide Steiner) in 1983, *Die schmale Brücke der Kunst: Ausgewählte Essays* (The Narrow Bridge of Art: Selected Essays) in 1986,[1] and *Die Wellen* (*TW*) in 1988. An edition of 'Gesammelte Kurzprosa' (based on *CSF*) was prepared for Insel-Verlag by the editor (Wolfgang Wicht) and was being translated; its publication was planned for 1990. But the end of the GDR

[1] It is not to be confused with another book of the same title (see *Die schmale Brücke der Kunst* 1994). This later edition is an eloquent example of Western ignorance of East German culture and, possibly, the arrogant assumption that Insel-Verlag Leipzig no longer existed in its Leipzig structure and would not be in a position to defend its copyright. A reviewer of the Wagenbach edition in *Frankfurter Allgemeine Zeitung* (the leading German daily) told his readers that 'four essays by Virginia Woolf are translated here for the first time' ('mit vier erstmals übersetzten Essays von Virginia Woolf') (Maar 1994). Naturally, the reviewer was wrong. I sent a letter to the cultural editor of the *FAZ*, who answered that he had passed it to the reviewer. The reviewer never replied to it. This incident would not be worth mentioning, if it were not a metonym of the post-1990 state of German–German relations.

was the end of all Insel-Verlag projects. *BTA* was on the agenda to be published in the early 1990s; a scholarly recommendation for submission to the Ministry of Culture was sent (by the present author) to the publishing house on 26 June 1989. Verlag Philipp Reclam jun. Leipzig published *Ein eigenes Zimmer-Drei Guineen* (*ROO-TG*) in 1989 (repr. 1992). *Die Fahrt zum Leuchtturm* (*TL*) was reprinted in a low-priced (*c.* £1.10) paperback edition by Aufbau Verlag Berlin in 1987.

As one can see from the publication dates, for Insel-Verlag and myself the edition of Woolf's works was inspired by the idea of a 'publication in progress'. Practically simultaneously with the Leipzig edition, S. Fischer Verlag (Frankfurt) scheduled a Complete Edition, edited by Klaus Reichert. There was, however, no contact between the two editors at that time. The East and West German editions appeared quite separately from each other. In the East, the intervals between the books were dictated by the economic capacity of Insel-Verlag. After all, it was not one of the big publishing houses; it was allocated a limited quota of printing paper and hard currency, required to pay royalties to the estates or agents of Western writers or their West German publishers who held the copyright for German translations. Under these circumstances, it was extremely helpful that the early agreements between Hogarth Press and Insel-Verlag predated the latter becoming an East German publisher. Insel-Verlag Leipzig gave the Woolf project a kind of celebrity status, which had the personal approval of its director Roland Links. In particular, the Woolf series was a major concern of Günter Gentsch, one of the editors.

The beginning of the reception of Virginia Woolf in East Germany in 1977 coincided with the beginning of the worldwide change in the writer's reputation, marked by 'a wholesale revision of traditional views about Woolf' from 'the old cliché of Woolf as a fragile invalid and apolitical aesthete, who spent her sheltered life in the ivory tower of Bloomsbury writing experimental novels', to 'the present view of her as "one of the first socialist feminist critics"' (Marcus) (Nünning and Nünning 1991, 41). It also coincided with the transition from (according to Nünning and Nünning 1996) the second to the third phase of German Woolf criticism.[2] From the mid-1970s, the study of Woolf's biography, aesthetics and awareness of social problems superseded the previous close attention to formal properties and narrative technique. Concurrently, it was the time when at least a minority of intellectuals and artists in East Germany began to cast severe doubt on the validity of the Stalinist ultra-dogmatic repudiation of modernism. Anti-modernism had been an affirmed focal aspect of offical cultural politics since Walter Ulbricht's (the then Party leader) philippic at the infamous 14th Plenary meeting of the Central Committe of the Socialist Unity Party in 1961, which explained to the

[2] As Füger (1980) has aptly documented in detail, the first phase extends from the mid-1920s to Woolf's outlawing by the Nazis in 1942. The second phase begins with Auerbach's *Mimesis* in 1946. For an assessment of the critical reception of Woolf in post-war Germany, see also Vera and Ansgar Nünning's essay in this volume.

rank and file of the Party and the general public that 'the confrontation [with imperialism] teaches us that it is impossible to create works of art which stimulate the socialist thinking and feeling of the working masses by using formalist, decadent or even modernist formal means, borrowed from late bourgeois art' (Ulbricht 1961, 131).[3] From then on, doctrinal opinion suspected even Romanticism to be decadent. Modernism was made taboo or to serve a bogeyman function.

This is the point where the autobiographical factor enters into the public recognition of Woolf. It is a point defined by the intersection of my personal interest, as reader and scholar, in her novels and the objectively emerging differentiation of post-Stalinist culture in East Germany. In retrospect, the 1970s inaugurated a curious juxtaposition of official tendencies to stabilize the sanctioned political-ideological system and cautious but determined deviations from dogmatism. Those critics, however, whose approach was not dogmatic always faced the challenge of assessing and then questioning the thresholds of political legitimacy in order to judge how far it was advisable to overstep them. Alternative literary (cultural, scholarly) 'philosophies' and practices were only effective when they operated within the wider boundaries of the ideologically inscribed social order. They in fact belonged to this order and were caught in the prison-house of its linguistic codes, which they in turn used in order to broadcast coded messages. With this proviso, the cultural situation in East Germany was marked by growing and deepening discontinuity and friction between official cultural politics (along with its theoretical and philosophical discourses of legitimization) and attempts at their modification, reformation, anti-dogmatic liberalization or even subversion.

The writings of Woolf played a minor but nonetheless paradigmatic part in this plot. Woolf emerged as one of the champions of Western modernism, next to Proust, Joyce, Kafka and Faulkner, who more or less simultaneously attracted the attention of publishers and critics. She was seen to deserve relative importance because of her female, not particularly feminist, sensitivity and her portrayal of women as fictional protagonists. Potentially, the experience of reading coincided with the social emancipation of women, which was a remarkable phenomenon of East German society. On the whole, the publishing and discussion of Virginia Woolf was a result and a part of the fundamental re-orientation which gained ground among a cultural elite. For this reason, the examination of Woolf's reception inevitably broadens to a panoramic enquiry into ideology. This in turn establishes a vital need for the critic to apply methods of discourse analysis, which annul the logocentric conception of speech and meaning, acknowledge the materiality of language, attend 'to the performative utterance' (Derrida 1977, 192) and emphasize that communication is a special effect of language.

Since I was involved both in the theoretical discussions (modestly) and in

---

[3] 'Die Auseinandersetzung lehrt: Mit formalistischen, dekadenten oder sogar modernistischen Gestaltungsmitteln, die aus der spätbürgerlichen Kunst entnommen werden, kann man keine Werke schaffen, die das sozialistische Denken und Fühlen der Werktätigen bereichern.'

the editing of Virginia Woolf (exclusively), this essay is necessarily written from an autobiographical perspective. Paradoxically, as a matter of priority, personal experience lends itself, I hope, more effectively to an impartial assessment of cultural and ideological processes in the GDR than the (often biased) gaze from outside, because the archive of printed documents is to a considerable extent determined by dominant ideological patterns and its stylistic adaptation to Party lingo, or embedded in a veil of allusions. Thus, the de- and reconstruction of cultural discourses is primarily a task for insiders. Any later reading of the discourses of that time obviously needs to be versed in these practices. On the other hand, I feel that the position of the 'involved critic' is significantly uncertain. Criticizing my own convictions and texts, I cannot exactly decide to what degree I am completely free from the restrictions of the philosophical and political contexts which 'wrote' the texts of the past. Assessing my anti-dogmatic activities, I cannot deny my complicity in the existing social system. Well-read in, for example, Derrida and Catherine Belsey, De Man and Christopher Norris, I am inclined, albeit hesitatingly, to admit that my own reading is supported by the reasonings of critical theory, which in turn teaches us to suspect the objectivity of subjective authorship. Using modernist key terms, I can only promise to do my best to analyse my subject in a 'disinterested, depersonalized' way. My chapter will deal first with editing Virginia Woolf, an exemplary case of the general practice of publishing Western literature, and then with the wider field of cultural and theoretical discussion.

II

My own attraction to Woolf has its roots in reading *TL* and *O* as a student in the late 1950s. Then, in the middle of the 1970s, Woolf became a main focus of my interest, beside Joyce and Eliot, as the perception grew that the orthodox castigation of modernism needed urgent and fundamental renegotiation. An awareness was growing that realism, which had been favoured as the *ne plus ultra* method of artistic production since the Soviet Writers Congress in 1934, was a historically legitimate but ideologically charged form of representation. In this context, reading Auerbach's *Mimesis* (1946), with its famous chapter on *TL* ('The Brown Stocking'), turned out to be not only of methodological consequence – as it was for the formal leanings of post-war German Woolf criticism – but, now, of incisive epistemological and axiological importance.[4] It was extremely important to learn that in his essay on *TL*, Auerbach testified to the disappearance of the omniscient security of

---

[4] Further publications stimulating my interest were Quentin Bell's biography *Virginia Woolf* (1972), Bernard Blackstone's monograph *Virginia Woolf* (1949), a special issue on Woolf of *Modern Fiction Studies* (1972) and, last but not least, Ingeborg Weber-Brandies's *Virginia Woolf, 'The Waves': Emanzipation als Möglichkeit des Bewußtseinsromans* (1974) (which I got as a review copy), which has remained a seminal German Woolf study ever since.

the narrator, to the ambiguity as to whether certain speech acts belong to a character's or the narrator's voice, to the reflection of objective reality through the consciousness of the characters, to the movement away from the predominance of outer events and to the presentation of several individual stages of consciousness which correspond to shifts of point of view and fictional time (see Wicht 1985a, 137). On a more abstract level, Auerbach's reading foregrounded the notion that form was itself a means of conveying meaning. This surprising insight (at least for someone of my scholarly education) counterpoised and finally reversed the rationale underlying realism, socialist realism, vulgar materialism and Lukácsian literary criticism, which taught us that the content determines the form. Urged by the challenge to counterbalance the pivotal position of realism, which was acute for someone working as a university teacher in the field of English studies, I decided to write a book-length study on metafictional problems represented in the works of Woolf, Joyce and Eliot. It was accepted as a second doctoral thesis (*Habilitationsschrift*) by the Pädagogische Hochschule Potsdam in 1978 and was published as a book in 1981. To my surprise, the book was out of print in less than no time. I suggested a reprint to the Akademie-Verlag, but the publishers shelved the idea, whether for economic or political reasons is still unclear.[5]

By the mid-1970s, courageous editors in publishing houses, not to speak of the reading public, felt that the essentialist conception of realism had to be subverted and decentred. In the case of Woolf, it happened that contingency met necessity. I chanced to meet Günter Gentsch at a conference in 1975, I think. We talked about English literature, modernism, Woolf and Joyce, and publishers' politics. In the end, Gentsch came up with the idea of giving the publication of *MD* a try and asked me to support it by writing a scholarly reader's recommendation and doing some editorial work, such as providing notes and writing an editor's essay as an Afterword ('Nachwort'). Gentsch then persuaded the director of Insel-Verlag to include the novel in their publishing plan for 1977.

There were two major prerequisites for getting a novel published in East Germany. The first was partly internal; the directorial board of a publishing house had to agree to add the book to the yearly plan of publications, which was clearly delimited by the quota of paper and money. The external aspect of the matter was that the plan of a publishing house had to be approved by an advisory board of the Ministry of Culture. The second prerequisite was that the Ministry of Culture had to be asked to give its official blessing to the publication of a particular book. Though I learned by experience (obtained from editing works by Woolf, Joyce, Eliot, Yeats, Jean Rhys and Heaney) that

---

[5] A curious anecdote may be added. A good friend of mine told me that a man in Thuringia, a very common reader, had bought the book at the local village grocer's, not really knowing what it was about. After all he thought that it was 'a pretty good bargain'. Be that as it may, the episode tells us a lot about the imponderables of the dissemination of cultural products in the GDR. At the same time, it was impossible to get the book through a university bookshop in East Berlin, since it was already out of print.

the Ministry was liberal in confirming the projects, the potential for (self-) censorship was ingrained in the system and certainly operated in other cases. But on the whole there was ample, and in the 1980s widening, room to move, if a publisher really wanted to enter it.

It was compulsory for every publishing house to submit to the Ministry of Culture a scholarly reader's recommendation of a particular book, called *Verlagsgutachten*. The publishers usually asked an expert working in the relevant field in a university to write it. In most cases, writing merged with ritual and 'righting', since the publisher's editor and the scholarly editor (paradoxically often identical with the author of the recommendation) by now acted in silent or open complicity. On its ritualistic surface, the commentary located the literary object within the right frame of official cultural politics.

In the case of a novel by Virginia Woolf, for instance, the recommendation would foreground that its general tendency was 'humanistic' (a much preferred catchword), that the writer had sympathies with the working class though belonging to an elite coterie, that the narrative contained a critique of capitalist alienation, that the œuvre belonged to the heritage of world literature, that publication of the particular book would enrich socialist society and testify to the cosmopolitan liberal-mindedness of socialist culture (*Weltoffenheit*, or openness to the world) was a favourite term of the Party oligarchy). The recommendation would also give a short outline of the plot, the characters and the implied (humanistic) meaning of the novel, and finally emphasize its universally acclaimed advances in narrative technique and the beauty of its language. It would avoid introducing the word modernism or foregrounding the experimental character of the fictional discourse. Correspondingly, I carefully avoided the emotive word 'modernism' and its hypostatized antidote 'realism' in the *Nachwort* to the Leipzig edition of *Mrs Dalloway*. It was arranged in the following order: a reference to 'Mr Bennett and Mrs Brown' and its main argument, selected biographical details, the change of paradigm in the arts about 1910, a short reading of *MD* which stressed the narrative method of free indirect discourse and a final statement about Woolf's poetic representation of an alienated world. Referring to 'Mr Bennett and Mrs Brown', I emphasized Woolf's refutation of Bennett, Galsworthy and Wells on the one hand and her narrative innovations on the other. The issue raised by the afterword was, of course, the realism-modernism controversy and the conflict between the partisan defenders of the one and the other. Though eschewing a theoretical debate proper it signalled a tacit challenge to the ruling realist paradigm.

Once the publication of *MD* (or the other books) was approved by the Ministry of Culture, Insel-Verlag signed a contract with the scholarly editor, which fixed the framework of his/her contribution, such as size and deadline, and the notes, royalties, copyright, etc. At a later stage, the publisher's editor, who had a nose for style and the logic of an argument, would discuss the *Nachwort* with the book editor, drawing attention to possible discursive improvements, but – in my experience – never interfering in its outline and ideas. Translation was completely in the hands of the publishing house. The fact that Insel-Verlag held the copyright on the old translations by Mutzenbecher and Lerbs certainly helped to start the Woolf project; no royalties had to be paid to West German publishers. Since Lerbs's German version of *O* fell far short of Woolf's text, Gentsch asked Heide Steiner, an excellent East German translator, to revise it. In the case of *TW*, Insel-Verlag approached S. Fischer Verlag and bought the translation by Herberth and Marlys Herlitschka, who monopolized the early West German Woolf market after the war. Insel-Verlag commissioned completely new translations for the edition of selected essays. Reclam Verlag acted analogously when it published *Ein eigenes Zimmer-Drei Guineen* (*ROO-TG*) (1989). A greater number of the essays were the first German editions, with the exception of those published in the earlier Western editions of *Der schiefe Turm: 5 Essays* ('The Leaning Tower': Five Essays) (1957) and *GR* (*Granit und Regenbogen*) (1960). *Drei Guineen* (*TG*) came out in the low-priced Reclam paperback aiming at mass circulation, some time after its publication by a marginal feminist publishing house in Munich (1978).[6] The first West German publication of *ROO* (*Ein Zimmer für sich allein*) was also prepared by a small printing press (1978). It was then taken over by the prestigious Frankfurt publishing house Fischer-Taschenbuch-Verlag, which regularly re-issued it during the 1980s and 1990s. By 1995 it had a circulation of 120,000 copies, indicating that the pamphlet had won a kind of (feminist) cult status in West Germany.

The success of getting *Mrs Dalloway* into print fostered the idea of regarding it as the beginning of a serial publication of Woolf's works, which in the end would tend towards a Complete Edition. During the following years I acted as sole editor. The reason for this exclusivity was the simple fact that I was and remained the only scholarly critic of Virginia Woolf in East Germany during the whole period. This fact, however, was nothing special given the conditions of a small academic subject such as English Studies at the six universities of the GDR, the Pädagogische Hochschule Potsdam and the Institute of Literary History at the Academy of Sciences, where only a handful of professors taught English Literature. Some of them specialized in Shakespeare, the others more or less became experts in a particular field. Since the early 1970s, I opted for British and Irish modernism and contemporary literature. At undergraduate level, I gave considerable space to Woolf in my lectures on twentieth-century English literature. The students were expected to have read at least one novel by Woolf for their final examinations. It is my guess, however, that she was neglected in other universities.

It was one of the advantages of this situation that in editing Woolf's works a consistent policy could be pursued, based on close cooperation with the publishing house. The disadvantage, perhaps, was that this precluded possibilities of discussion and a louder pro-modernist voice. More broadly, however, my concern with Woolf became part of the ongoing debate about literary and methodological openness. Elsewhere, in the primary field of literature itself, Woolf's fictional and non-fictional writings reverberated (as Joyce Crick has pointed out in a paper she gave at the launch of the present

---

6 The first edition of 1978 does not figure in *Deutsches Bücherverzeichnis 1978-80*, the bibliography of all printed books in Germany. The essay I contributed to the Leipzig book was pre-published in *Sinn und Form* (see Wicht 1985b).

Reception project) in the works of a number of East German woman writers, such as Christa Wolf, Brigitte Struzyk, Irmtraud Morgner and Sigrid Damm (Crick 1998, 9-10).[7] As usual, literature was more flexible than criticism.

The sociological reception of Woolf's novels, essays and pamphlets by the East German common reader is beyond the scope of this paper. But I would like to give the following brief indication. The first edition of the books (the print run was up to 10,000, *Drei Guineen-Ein eigenes Zimmer* 20,000) was out of print immediately. Most of the copies a bookshop could get from the central distributor were sold in advance and, as a consequence, often did not turn up on the counters and shelves of the booksellers at all. With the exception of the paperback edition of *Die Fahrt zum Leuchtturm*, the paper quota meant that issuing reprints would have delayed the publication of a subsequent work. Insel-Verlag always preferred to print a new title. Thus, published books immediately became rare books, only available in public libraries, or by chance in a second-hand bookshop or through circulation among friends. The number of books on sale in proportion to the number of prospective readers was distorted. The literary market place, i.e. the relationship between those who buy and those who sell books, was not organized along the principles of the exchange value of the 'commodity', but rather regulated by its use value. Since this was high, availability was low.

The widespread interest in modernist literature was rooted in a number of reasons. First, East German readers felt an urgent need to bridge the period between the 1920s and the 1970s, during which time fascist and communist rulers alike had ostracized innovative and experimental Western literature and art, labelling modernist works 'degenerate'. With the publication of Woolf, Joyce, Proust, Faulkner, Yeats, Eliot, Kafka and a representative selection of current American writers in the 1970s and to a larger extent in the 1980s, a new, semi-official, canon of modernist writing took shape alongside the established canon of realism and socialist realism. Second, within the boundaries of a political system which, in contrast to its traditions, was orientated to the East, Western art held exotic attraction for the reader. It symbolized an alterior space which could not be entered and at which people directed their gaze, curiously blending admiration with critical distance. Third, on a different level, modernist literature offered an alterior space compared to official politics and the wooden rhetoric authorizing it. Woolf's elegance of style was an antidote to the humourless dullness of officialese and the journalistic, critical and philosophical discourses infected by it. As for literary reception, one may say that the art-versus-politics antinomies of linguistic utterances sensitized readers to the political implications of the seemingly apolitical modernist experiments. Fourth, parallel to this, modernism was seen as an alternative to the adulatory literary representations of working-class and revolutionary heroism as well as to the defining ideological principle of *Volkstümlichkeit*, a translation of the Russian *narodnost*, that is, literature with

[7] This is the place to say that deep appreciation is due to Joyce Crick for her careful reading of the first version of the present essay and her suggestions which considerably improved what I tried to express.

popular appeal, ideology, source and subject matter. Since many readers mistrusted the ideal socialist world promised to them (according to the ruling discourse threatened only by the military, economic and moral aggressiveness of imperialism) and recognized that 'contemporary history' was an 'immense panorama of futility and anarchy' across the political systems, they began to appreciate forms of narrative which presented – as Eliot said in his review of *Ulysses* – 'a way of controlling, of ordering, of giving shape and a significance to' this panorama (Eliot 1975, 177). Fifth, the readers discovered, if unconsciously, the importance and appeal of artistic form. They realized that vision and meaning were inseparable from language, structure and formal patterns. Thus, last but not least, and quite innocently, new and unexpected pleasures of reading were engendered.

III

Desires of this kind paradoxically originated in the pressures of political power and the enclosure of the country by material and ideological frontiers, which the rulers erected to isolate the socialist system geopolitically. Once the repression of Western art could no longer be practically maintained, its impact was gradually changing 'pure' socialist culture, and finally uprooted the system from within. In pragmatic terms, the system had never been monolithic. Individual opinions and conceptions prevailed even within the Party nomenklatura; Party politics always steered a zig-zag course between orthodoxy and liberalization. When the novels of Virginia Woolf were published, *Neues Deutschland* (New Germany), the daily newspaper of the ruling Socialist Unity Party, printed laudatory reviews. It may be that they were shaped by the subjective open-mindedness of the reviewers, who had their own ideas of cultural values. But the decisive factor was that they were printed in the Party's daily, which thus gave authorized blessing to the activities of the Insel-Verlag and promoted the dissemination of Woolf's writings. Woolf's novels were also reviewed in *Junge Welt* (Young World), the daily of the Socialist Youth Organization (*FDJ*), which was widely read by younger people, and *Sonntag* (Sunday), a cultural weekly, which was much favoured by intellectuals.

To give a sense of the flavour of these reviews, a presentation of selected quotations may be instructive. The item on *Mrs Dalloway* in *Junge Welt* begins with a general statement, suggesting that 'the English novelist Virginia Woolf ranks as one of the precursors of modern narrative. Her method of uncovering streams of consciousness ... had a seminal influence on literary style. In many cases, she went to the extreme. One example of the new departure is *Mrs Dalloway*'.[8] The (somewhat pedestrian) reviewer continues with a short outline

---

[8] 'Die englische Erzählerin Virginia Woolf zählt zu den Wegbereitern modernen Erzählens. Stilbildend wirkte ihre Methode, Bewußtseinsströme freizulegen ... Oft hat sie diese Methode ins Extrem getrieben. Ein Beispiel für die damals neuartige Form ist der Roman *Mrs Dalloway*.'

of the story, stressing Woolf's criticism of English class bigotry (Teissler 1977, 8).[9] *Mrs Dalloway* was not (yet) reviewed in *Neues Deutschland.* But it was at least listed in the newspaper's regular column of selected 'Book News' on 13/14 August 1977 (p. 14). Two years later, *TL* was presented through a remarkably sophisticated and appreciative review by Hans-Jürgen Geisthardt, who was a member of the editorial staff of *Neues Deutschland.* Geisthardt wrote:

> This novel by Virginia Woolf was published at the time of sweeping politicization of literature on the Continent, and in Germany in particular (1927). It is a kind of reversal or turning away from public affairs. For the writer, the sensations of the soul or the mind ... are reality proper. Reality is not even comprehensible through individual impressions; for Virginia Woolf, it only exists as the interior life of women or men. As a consequence, a narrative structure is produced which is opposed to the traditional novel. The novel becomes a 'non-novel' ... Historical movements evaporate and we enter a world of vague and strenuous movements of consciousness. Social backgrounds become indistinct. Nonetheless, this book is a document of the social self-determination of the middle classes. It is a product of Virginia Woolf's poetic programme. (1979, 14)[10]

Geisthardt foregrounds Woolf's description of female figures and Mrs Ramsay's 'challenging existence' ('herausforderndes Dasein'), and is careful to stress the poetic beauty of her language, which casts the stream of consciousness in 'a vast number of precious lyrical expressions' ('eine unübersehbare Summe von kostbaren Lyrismen') (1979, 14). It is worth noting that Geisthardt, the *Neues Deutschland* editor and critic, does not criticize Woolf's modernism from the traditional dogmatic position which *Neues Deutschland* by and large was still defending, but rather describes it in order to intimate its innovatory potential.

The *Junge Welt* review of *Orlando* (1983) begins with a reference to the previous two novels which appeared in East Germany, informing the reader that 'following *Mrs Dalloway* and *Die Fahrt zum Leuchtturm*, Virginia Woolf's best-seller *Orlando* has just been published in the exquisitely devised series of separate editions of her œuvre'. Following a synopsis of the plot and structure of the book, the reviewer arrives at the conclusion that 'Virginia Woolf has

---

9 All quotations of sources written in German are translated into English by the author of this essay.

10 'Zur selben Zeit, da auf dem europäischen Festland und zumal in Deutschland die Literatur eine durchgreifende Politisierung erfährt (1927), erscheint in England dieser Roman von Virginia Woolf. Es ist eine Ab- und Umkehr gegenüber dem Öffentlichen; die Autorin erhebt die Empfindungen der Seele, des Gemüts ... zur eigentlichen Realität. Wirklichkeit ist nicht einmal über den individuellen Eindruck erfaßbar, ihr Vorhandensein beschränkt sich für Virginia Woolf auf inneres Erleben. Daraus entsteht eine dem herkömmlichen Roman entgegengesetzte Erzählstruktur. Der Roman wird "kein Roman" ... Statt historischer Bewegung also deren Verflüchtigung in schwindende und bemühte Bewußtseinsinhalte. Soziale Horizonte verschwimmen dabei. Das Buch ist dennoch ein künstlerisches Dokument sozialer Selbstbestimmung späten Bürgertums. Es ist das Ergebnis von Virginia Woolfs poetischem Programm.'

written a novel about the distress and anxiety prevalent in her times. But there is also much hope in this book, a declaration of love for creative, free, many-faceted and inconsistent human beings' (Neissner 1983, 8).[11]

In *Neues Deutschland*, Irene Skotnicki wrote of *Die schmale Brücke der Kunst*:

> According to Virginia Woolf, the capacity of literature to enrich the life of the reader is almost boundless. One is happy to accept her invitation to read when turning to her own essays, since this woman's wealth of ideas, wit and sagacity instantaneously cast their spell over us ... All in all, the texts help us to understand more precisely the aesthetic conceptions of Virginia Woolf, who is one of the pre-eminent figures on the English literary stage in the first half of the present century. The struggle of the writer, who was of middle-class origin, for the innovation of literature with regard to contents and form – especially of the novel – was based on a deep insight into the fundamental interrelationship between art and social structures and classes. The demand for changes in literature resulted from a remarkable cognition of social processes. This is illuminated by the present – excellently selected and edited – volume. What the book reveals is an artist of fascinating subtlety. For me, Woolf's 'Memories of a Working Women's Guild', her introduction to an anthology containing autobiographical reports of proletarian women, is a genuine discovery. (1987, 14)[12]

Reviewing *Die Wellen* (*TW*) (1988), Skotnicki describes the experimental quality of the novel and the desires of its characters. Her summary reads:

> Like other novels by Virginia Woolf, the writing of *TW*, published in 1931, is marked by her endeavour to innovate epic narrative. This aim is derived from a

---

[11] 'In der Insel-Reihe schön gestalteter Einzelausgaben der Werke Virginia Woolfs erschien nun nach *Mrs Dalloway* und *Die Fahrt zum Leuchtturm* ihr Verkaufsschlager *Orlando* ... Virginia Woolf hat einen Roman geschrieben über ihre Zeit mit allen Bedrängnissen und Ängsten. Und es ist viel Hoffnung in diesem Buch, eine Liebeserklärung an den schöpferischen, freien, vielseitigen, widersprüchlichen Menschen.'

[12] 'Für nahezu unerschöpflich hielt Virginia Woolf die Möglichkeiten der Literatur, das Leben des Lesers zu bereichern. Ihrer Aufforderung zum Lesen folgt man in bezug auf ihre eigenen Essays nur zu gern, ziehen uns Gedankenreichtum, Witz und Scharfsinn dieser Frau doch schnell in Bann ... In der Zusammenschau aber tragen die Texte dann dazu bei, daß wir das Kunstverständnis Virginia Woolfs genauer erfassen, die zu den herausragenden Persönlichkeiten der englischen Literaturszenerie der ersten Hälfte unseres Jahrhunderts gehört. Das Ringen der aus dem Bürgertum stammenden Schriftstellerin um eine Erneuerung der Literatur – namentlich des Romans – in Inhalt und Form lag die Erkenntnis von der grundsätzlichen Gesellschafts- und Klassengebundenheit der Kunst zugrunde. Die Forderung nach Veränderungen in der Literatur resultierte aus bemerkenswerten Einsichten in gesellschaftliche Prozesse. Dies vor allem macht der vorliegende – in Auswahl und Edition vorzügliche – Band deutlich. Er zeigt eine Künstlerin von faszinierender Vielschichtigkeit. Eine Entdeckung für mich in diesem Zusammenhang: Virginia Woolfs "Erinnerungen an eine Vereinigung arbeitender Frauen" – ihre Einleitung zu einem Band mit Lebensberichten von Frauen aus dem Proletariat.'

> sensitively and astutely realized awareness of her, the capitalist, world in a condition of crisis. New narrative techniques, incisive changes of form and structure, an interiorizing organization of poetic language and a wealth of metaphoric and symbolic images became the new hallmarks of the novel. Virginia Woolf is one of the eminent representatives of modern literature. The significance of *TW* is often reduced to its experimental character. But the novel is much more than an interesting experiment for the contemporary reader. It is a novel which assigns Virginia Woolf a place among the greatest writers. (1989, 14)[13]

In *Sonntag*, Karl-Heinz Magister (1989) glosses *The Waves* 'as the most experimental novel by Virginia Woolf after *MD*, *TL*, and *O*' ('Der Roman *Die Wellen* gilt nach *Mrs Dalloway* und der Biografie *Orlando* als das experimentell am weitesten vorangetriebene Werk Virginia Woolfs'). Like Joyce and Lawrence,

> she annulled the dominant fictional conventions of the nineteenth century, giving priority to narrative form over narrated contents. A 'realistic' picture of reality is no longer imagined, but rather – beyond any ruling ideological apologetics – the rendering of subjective psychical processes and conflicts, which condenses social life in a distinctive manner and tries to set out ways of alternative thinking. She finished with the omniscient narrator, who was replaced by the frequently alternating narrative voice within the 'stream of consciousness'. (1989, 12)[14]

Magister then goes on to give a short reading of the novel.

In the face of the prevailing dogmatism of official East German cultural politics these reviews of the novels by a prototypical modernist writer were remarkable for strongly commending Woolf to the readers' attention.

---

13 'Wie andere Werke der Virginia Woolf stand auch die Entstehung des Romans *Die Wellen*, erschienen 1931, ganz im Zeichen der Bemühungen um Erneuerung des epischen Schreibens. Dieses Streben leitet sich her aus dem sensibel gespürten und scharfsinnig erfaßten krisenhaften Zustand ihrer, der bürgerlichen Welt. Neue Erzähltechniken, tiefgreifende Form- und Strukturveränderungen, ein ganz von der Innerlichkeit der Aussage getragene poetische Sprache, ein Fülle von assoziationsreichen und symbolträchtigen Bildern wurden zu neuen Kennzeichen des Romans. Virginia Woolf ist eine der Großen der modernen Literatur. Die Bedeutung des Romans *Die Wellen* wird nun aber häufig vornehmlich an seinem experimentellen Charakter festgemacht. Doch das Werk ist weit davon entfernt, nur als interessantes Experiment für den heutigen Leser von Belang zu sein. Es ist ein Roman, mit dem Virginia Woolf ihren Platz unter den "großen Künstlern" einnimmt.'

14 'Wie diese brach sie mit allen wesentlichen Erzählkonventionen des 19. Jahrhunderts, indem sie die erzählerische Form gegenüber der Komponente des Inhalts zum wesentlichen Faktor der Kunst aufwertete. Nicht ein "realistisches" Abbild der Wirklichkeit wurde mehr anvisiert, sondern – außerhalb der herrschenden ideologischen Apologetik – eine Verdeutlichung der inneren psychischen Vorgänge und Konflikte im Menschen, die auf ihre besondere Weise gesellschaftliches Leben verdichteten und eigene geistige Alternativen zu setzen suchten. Schluß wurde gemacht mit dem allwissenden Erzähler, der sich jetzt weitgehend als personell oft wechselnde, berichtende Instanz im "Bewußtseinsstrom" manifestierte.'

Invariably, they gave prominence to the innovative aspect of Woolf's narrative. In other words, they emphasized, with positive implications, the importance and validity of non-realist literary forms. Distancing narrative innovation from the customary privileging of realism in Party cultural politics and theory, the reviews appropriately reflected the blurred contours between official doctrines and the various, and varying, shapes of critical, theoretical, cultural and artistic discourses. Obscurity was a permanent characteristic of the cultural system as a whole, which was steadily becoming even more uncertain. The discontinuities within this contingent 'socialist' cultural practice are difficult to define, even from a considerable distance. But they warn us not to believe in metaphysical generalizations, such as 'Stalinism', 'system of injustice' ('Unrechtssystem'), 'oppression', 'state socialism', 'cultural dictatorship', 'censorship' etc., which are rather reductive terms, ruling out complexity and merely providing a distorted picture of the East German situation.

Aside from this polemical side-swipe at excessive and incongruous political wrangling, critical assessment must attend to the uncertainties of the situation. Returning to Virginia Woolf, one cannot but point out the peculiarity of a setting where the reviews of her novels in Party or Party-aligned newspapers helped to establish modernist literature within the consciousness of the common reader and the realm of literary theory. Collaterally, the appraisals in the 'leading' newspapers supported the plan of editing further works by Woolf. Making use of the information in the *Nachworte*, they corroborated the critical policy forwarded by the editor. Thus, the inclusion of essays in editions of Woolf had the dual function of supplying the reader with additional knowledge, and, once the essays were taken up by the reviewer, of publicizing hitherto suppressed narrative performances.

Here is a further example illustrating the line of argument in the afterwords, which also throws some light on the language of criticism available and possible at the time. In *Die Wellen* (*TW*), my reading of the novel centres upon the suggestion that

> 'the extreme difficulty of the form', which Virginia Woolf herself (according to an entry in her diary of 9 April 1930) considered to be 'the furthest development so far', eventually engenders a profound analysis of social and spiritual hopelessness. At the same time, the difficulty of the form is a radical challenge to the conventional narrative of the middle-class realist novel, which, ideologically, tended to degenerate into apologetics. The production of a new form signified the development of far-reaching ideational alternatives expressed through works of art. The mendacity inherent in pseudo-optimistic wishful thinking could be exposed. The other side of the coin was the loss of the reader's easy empathy, of which Virginia Woolf was thoroughly aware. Abandoning an action-packed plot, she abstained from the usual means of emotionally triggering off the empathetic immersion of the reader in the epic story. The text calls for intense mental activity. (Wicht 1988, 293)[15]

---

[15] 'Die "extreme Schwierigkeit der Form", die Virginia Woolf selbst in einer Eintragung vom 9. April 1930 für "die bis jetzt weitestgehende Entwicklung" hielt, realisiert letztlich eine extreme Tiefenanalyse der gesellschaftlichen und geistigen Ausweglosigkeit. Sie ist ebenso die äußerste Herausforderung der konventionellen

The author of a *Nachwort* certainly counted on the East German reader's sensitivity to the employment of catchwords and particular formulations. In the quoted passage, 'hopelessness' is not used in a pejorative sense, as in dogmatic anti-modernist jargon; it is a metaphoric signifier describing common features of the human situation in the twentieth century (not alien to the German reader's own experience), which Woolf analysed 'profoundly'. The paradigmatic significance of anti-realist aesthetics and narrative innovation is openly proclaimed and positively assessed. Amounting to a heretical reversal of the normal pro-realist denunciation of modernism, realism in turn is dismissed as 'pseudo-optimistic wishful thinking' and a 'degenerate' literary method. It is only in retrospect that I am becoming aware that I shunned the term 'modernism' even at that late date when, in accord with postmodernism, it had become common currency, though disinterested scholarly terminology was still in conflict with older biased shades of meaning. Since I had tried to formulate a revision of the officially abusive word 'modernism' much earlier (see Wicht 1981, 234), its omission from the *Nachwort* to *Die Wellen* cannot be reasonably explained *post festum*. I tend to assume that it was after all an essay written for the 'common reader', which forbade theoretical debates about the use and misuse of conceptual signifiers.

In my earlier editorial essays, a partly calculated and partly politically unconscious adherence to linguistic codes of officialese fused with illustration of Woolf's poetological thinking. A typical example is a passage from the afterword to *Die Fahrt zum Leuchtturm* (*TL*) (1979), where I adopted the old shibboleths of verbal abuse in order to explain and sanction the assumptions of the writer. On the linguistic surface, the discourse aligned with the ruling norms; but in effect it overturned the dominant notion that bad capitalism necessarily produces the bad art of modernism.[16] All editorial essays included

cont.

Erzählweise des bürgerlich-realistischen Romans, der ideologisch zur Apologetik zu verkommen drohte. Die Schöpfung dieser neuen Form erschloß weitreichende geistige Alternativen im Bereich der Kunst. Mit ihr wurde es möglich, die Verlogenheit scheinoptimistischer Wunschbilder zu entlarven. Die Kehrseite der Sache, die Virginia Woolf durchaus fühlte, war allerdings eine Einbuße an Leserwirksamkeit; denn mit der Preisgabe der handlungsreichen Erzählung verzichtete sie auf ein probates emotionales Auslösemoment für die intensive und oft unbewußte Anteilnahme am epischen Geschehen. Der Text fordert die engagierte geistige Auseinandersetzung.'

16 The passage in question argues: 'Under the social conditions of monopoly capitalism, Virginia Woolf sceptically reviewed a literary method where literary figures acted within a panorama of outer circumstances and, struggling with these conditions, arrived at a certain state of self-identity. The assertive belief in the bourgeois order and its humanist potential had passed. It was replaced by the knowledge of being powerless and paralysed by social structures regulated by money and anonymous powers. Unable to believe in the scientific philosophy of the proletariat, a turning away from the social field and a turning towards the individual was a consistent thing to do. The limitation of the literary subject, however, also caused its intensification. Based on highly refined feminine sensibility, Virginia Woolf discovered the most intimate stirrings, feelings and

in the East German publications of Woolf's works centre on the shifting relationships between art and life, the writer's anti-realist aesthetics, the correlation of vision and truth, the historicity and changeability of reality. Conspicuously and ambiguously, the afterword to *O* (1983) quotes a reflection Woolf raises in 'Notes on an Elizabethan Play' (*O* 1983, 314). Her argument there serves to characterize the narrative structure of the novel, but implies a much wider potential of meaning. Imagining the reality of a man called Smith, living in Liverpool, Woolf suggests (and these words are quoted) that 'we know indeed that this reality is a chameleon quality, the fantastic becoming as we grow used to it often the closest to the truth, the sober the farthest from it' (*CR 1* 1975, 74). For the implied reader in the GDR, this (carefully selected) quotation explained the novelist's poetological intentions in the authorial sense, but equally it evoked a general insight into the 'chameleon quality' of social reality, which was deeply political, pointedly negating the Party philosophy of a logical, natural progression towards 'developed' socialism and communism.

Apart from these individual politics of discourse, embedded in the increasingly indeterminate paradigm of cultural politics in general, my essays of the 1980s signal a gradual shift of attention from the poetological to the political in the writings of Virginia Woolf. This focus, which had been immanent in the essays from the beginning, gained prominence in the essay 'Die Ermordung des Hausengelchens' (The Murder of the Angel of the House), which was first published in *Sinn und Form* (Meaning and Form) (the most important bimonthly cultural periodical in the GDR) in 1985 and subsequently reprinted as the Afterword to *Ein eigenes Zimmer-Drei Guineen*. The political aspect of consideration, which was originally nourished by my own reading of Woolf and a historically orientated Marxist sensibility to the criticism of texts, was strengthened and enriched by international feminist theory and criticism. The latter became a (still marginal) topic of discussions and debates within the English and French departments of the universities and

---

cont.

thoughts of differently structured individuals, striving to find out how they can safeguard their personal values through their actions and mutual relationships.' ('Unter den gesellschaftlichen Bedingungen des Monopolkapitalismus begegnete Virginia Woolf einer literarischen Methode mit Skepsis, welche die Gestalten in einem Panorama äußerer Umstände agieren und in der Auseinandersetzung mit der Umwelt ein gewisses Maß an Selbstverwirklichung erreichen ließ. Der Glaube an eine bürgerliche Ordnung mit humanistischen Potenzen war dahin; das Wissen vom Ausgeliefertsein, der Ohnmacht gegenüber einer von Geld und anonymen Mächten regulierten Gesellschaft hatte ihn ersetzt. Ohne die wissenschaftliche Weltanschauung des Proletariats konnte die Abwendung vom sozialen Bereich und die Hinwendung zum Individuum nur folgerichtig sein. Die Einengung des literarischen Gegenstandes führte allerdings auch zugleich zu seiner Vertiefung. Mit einer außerordentlich feinen femininen Sensibilität förderte Virginia Woolf innere Regungen, Gefühle, Gedanken von individuell unterschiedlichen Gestalten zutage, um zu erwägen, wie sie sich in ihren Handlungen und in ihren Beziehungen zueinander ihren eigenen Wert erhalten ... können.') (Wicht 1979, 259-60)

among female writers (see the names mentioned above).[17] The American feminist approach had recently discovered Woolf, and it too influenced my thinking, in particular through the collections *New Feminist Essays on Virginia Woolf* (1981) and *A Feminist Slant* (1983), edited by Jane Marcus. International feminism was certainly also influential in persuading Gabriele Bock of Reclam-Verlag to plan the publication of *ROO* and *TG* together in one edition. The political argument in 'Ermordung' was supported by Naomi Black's assertion that Woolf's frame of mind is hallmarked by 'what today seems clearly political behaviour' (Black 1983, 297). The essay quotes Black and then goes on to state:

> Academic criticism has largely repressed this thought up to the present. Analysing the condition of women as a typical special case within the social space, the writer's [Woolf's] interweaving of the aesthetic with the political was highly intense in her novels and essays. To demand the liberation of women from their economic, social, psychic and physical dependence on family and society meant, as a consequence, to insist on fundamental socio-political changes. (Wicht 1989, 284)[18]

In this essay, I tried to make the political inscription of Woolf's feminism easier to understand by giving an account of her sympathy for the National Society for Womens' Service and by enlarging on her considerations of war and peace as well as her poetological principles.

Ambiguity is perhaps the common denominator which defines the politics of the essays on Virginia Woolf. Ambiguity was a stylistic means of appropriating an experimental writer and modernist aesthetics in a society which was dominated by centralistic ideology and a dictatorial state apparatus, but which was also subverted by disintegrative forces. The ambiguity of writing was comparable to a fundamental ambiguity pervading the socio-political order at large. Though this order was structurally embedded in the Eastern Soviet system, it always balanced between East and West in varied ways, economically, politically and culturally. The only stable factor, about which no doubt was allowed, was the leadership of the ruling political oligarchy. In the long run, however, the frictions between a dictatorial regime and the ambiguities of contingent social practice were destabilizing the thrones of absolute power. Such a process of destabilization was a distinctive hallmark of the East German conditions in the 1980s.

---

17 On a broader social and theoretical scale, where the practical professional, personal and cultural emancipation of women was at the centre of attention, Western feminist conceptions hardly managed to gain a foothold.

18 'Diesem Gedanken hat sich die akademische Kritik bislang weitgehend verschlossen. Gerade dadurch, daß die Schriftstellerin die Lage der Frau als typischen Spezialfall sozialer Verhältnisse analysierte, erreichte – in ihren Romanen wie in den Aufsätzen – die Durchdringung des Ästhetischen und des Politischen höchste Intensität. Die Befreiung der Frau aus der ökonomischen, sozialen, psychischen und physischen Abhängigkeit der bürgerlichen Familie und Gesellschaft zu fordern, zieht letztlich die Konsequenz grundsätzlicher gesellschaftlicher Wandlungen nach sich.'

IV

In the fields of criticism and culture, a theoretical and deeply ideological debate about the principal questions of literary (artistic) representation amply contributed to the advance of liberation. Functionally, this debate had two distinct aspects. On the one hand it contained and maintained a utopian projection of socialism and the idea of establishing a neo-Marxist methodology, but beyond that it was also subversive, attacking dogmatism, ideological clichés and the interference of Party authority. As I indicated above, the fundamental reversal of the assessment of the realism–modernism controversy and the reconsideration of the relationship between form and content (which in the end rightly tended to shun the term 'content') were of major theoretical significance. Virginia Woolf was one of the key writers figuring in the East German change of paradigm.

The wider field of debate which made for this change of paradigm requires some discussion. As early as 1973, the study *Gesellschaft Literatur Lesen* (Society Literature Reading) (Naumann 1973), influenced by the West German reader-orientated theory of Wolfgang Iser and Hans Robert Jauss, was seminal in giving a critical assessment of the ruling gnoseological conception of the deterministic dependence of literature on 'reality' and the writer's consciousness. By contrast, the autonomy of the literary text was emphasized as being functionally relevant and open to its active reception by the reader. Though Naumann and his fellow authors (who worked at the Institute of Literary History of the Academy of Sciences) explicitly confessed to historical and dialectical materialism as the conceptual basis of their argument (it guaranteed that this volume could become a kind of officially accepted handbook), their book paved the way for the rapid re-orientation of literary theory and cultural practice. Further development was not so much determined by specialists in German literature but rather by scholars specialized in French and English/American literatures. A detailed exploration of these activities is still a blank area on the map of East German literary theory. First approaches in English studies are a short outline of the critical/ideological situation since the 1950s by Riese (1983, 759-61), the inquiries into Shakespeare reception in the GDR, presented by Weimann (1999a) and Guntner and McLean (1998), and a number of contributions to the anthology *Amerikanistik in der DDR: Geschichte-Analysen-Zeitzeugenberichte* (American Studies in the GDR: History, Analysis, Contemporary Testimonies) (Schnoor, 1999), among them new papers by Weimann (1999b) and Riese (1999).[19] The intricate explorations of Shakespeare on the East German stage and in East German criticism give, metonymically, a picture of the typical features of the whole.[20]

---

[19] A first short description of the reception of Joyce was pioneered by the late Ulrich Schneider (1991, 145-50). For Woolf, the outline by Nünning and Nünning (1996) also deserves mention.

[20] On the other hand, an essay dealing with literary criticism and theory from the 1970s up to the mid-1980s (Thierse and Kliche 1985), which gives an account of developments post-*Gesellschaft Literatur Lesen*, is largely descriptive. Moreover, it is

During the 1980s, the cause of modernism, new theoretical approaches and innovations in all art forms and on the stage were promoted by an increasing number of individuals who distanced themselves from the discourses of socialist metaphysics. The essence of what was happening is well described by Robert Weimann, who was a proponent, if not the prophet, of unorthodox new thinking. His account focuses on the proceedings of the German Shakespeare Society, but in fact it has far wider significance. He argues:

> It was difficult to think of a more forcefully challenging body of discourses than the emerging alliance, as yet scarcely differentiated, between poststructuralism, neo-Marxism, and feminism. For those who were prepared to look (and refused to follow Professor Erich Hahn [one of the most prominent philosophical dogmatists], chairman of the council of GDR philosophers, in his call for putting the whole postmodernism issue on the index of the Central Committee) the challenge was formidable: it comprised basic issues of epistemology, historiography, and semiology and was unsettling especially to those positions that had gone into the orthodox uses of Shakespeare as 'heritage'. (1998, 132)

Since the late 1970s, an increasing and ever more effective trend in the arts and in criticism was 'to turn the hitherto unchallenged notion of realism into a state of crisis' ('daß der ... bislang unangefochtene Realismusbegriff selbst in die Krise gebracht wurde' (Weimann 1999a, 961); and to show the ruptures

---

cont.

intentionally distorting because it studiously avoids any mention of the theoretical revolution which was going on in French, English and American studies (in spite of Riese's abstract of 1983, which the authors must have known). The principal thesis of the authors was 'that a new phase of seeing the functional interrelationship between social development, literature and aesthetics, which orients itself towards the development of mature socialism, has gained foothold since the beginning of the 1970s' ('daß der entscheidende Einschnitt für den neuen, an der Entwicklung des reifen Sozialismus orientierten Funktionszusammenhang von Gesellschaftsentwicklung, Literatur und Wissenschaftsgeschichte am Beginn der siebziger Jahre liegt'). The reasons for 'the divergences informing the concept of literature' were 'ultimately and decisively informed by social, educational, cultural and political motives which established the dominant role of various fundamental social functions of literature and various fundamental social needs in socialist society' ('Gründe für die ... deutlichen Divergenzen im Literaturbegriff' lagen 'letztlich und entscheidend in der die Literaturauffassung tragenden gesellschafts-, bildungs-, kultur- oder kunstgeschichtlich motivierten *Dominantsetzung* verschiedener sozialer Grundfunktionen der Literatur und verschiedener sozialer Grundbedürfnisse im Sozialismus') (Thierse and Kliche 1985, 280, 291). Even the style of the discourse betrays that it presented a refined affirmation of the Party line. It is quoted here because it aptly illuminates the Shangri-la of Party-aligned theoretical illusions, which actively or indirectly checked an open debate. Parallel to the partial description by Thierse and Kliche, Weimann published a long essay which insisted on the formal and autonomous existence of a work of art and made a plea for poststructuralist methodological insights (1985). It 'met with a widespread lack of understanding in East German literary criticism' ('traf ... auf ein weit verbreitetes Unverständnis in der Literaturwissenschaft der DDR') (Riese 1999, 203).

('Bruchstellen') (959-60) existing within the dominating cultural terms of realism, humanism and *Volkstümlichkeit*. The difficulties of even defining their metaphysical universality were historically documented by the ongoing official attempts at clarification, which always ended in Jesuitical casuistry. A vital need had grown for theoreticians and artists to free the methodology of literary interpretation from vulgar materialism and ideological bias, with their focus on the three principles of *reflection*, *determinism* and *teleology* (see Wicht 1991, 93-94). They were no longer willing to accept the perceived guiding principle that the value of a work of art is decreed by the extent to which its contents 'reflected' contingent reality, the degree to which economic conditions and ruling or alternative (working-class) ideology 'determined' its superstructural existence, and the potential it contained in projecting a *teleological* social progress to the final state of socialism.

The necessity of re-orientation was clearly formulated in an essay by Weimann published in 1980. It was a date when, as in 1910, all relations were shifting and conduct, politics and literature changed (see *CDB*, 96-97). Aptly giving voice to the inevitable intersection of socialist possibilities and innovative claims, Weimann declared that the 'self-definition' of literary theory was not autonomous but had as its 'presupposition its consciously realized functions in the general context of a socialist conception of society and culture' (1980, 13).[21] For a while, up to 1984, Weimann tried to formulate his radical revision by redefining the term 'realism' itself. Then, 'representation', 'authority' and 'mimesis' (which he had used earlier) became the keynote words. Typically, they figure in the title of his *Shakespeare* book of 1988 (see Weimann 1988a).

To a considerable extent, culture and cultural politics in the GDR were marked by antagonistic positions and conceptual differences, which, however, very often applied identical norms and practices of language. Since the early 1980s, the most advanced critics recognized that the thorough investigation of cultural processes, including the positions of both the critical object and subject, must be based on a discriminating analysis of the given discourses. This insight was becoming the guiding principle of a new functional self-determination of literary theory and criticism, which tried to catch up with international theoretical developments (see Weimann 1980, 15). Consequently, a (widening, though still minority) number of critics appropriated neo-Marxism (Williams, Althusser, Eagleton, Jameson, Said, Lentricchia, Graff), poststructuralism and deconstruction (Foucault, Barthes, De Man,

---

21 'die Problematik eines disziplinären Selbstverständnisses, das aus seinem ureigensten Begründungszusammenhang heraus keine Autonomie oder auch nur Isolation duldet, vielmehr eine bewußte Funktionssetzung im Gesamtzusammenhang einer sozialistischen Gesellschaftkonzeption und Kultur zur Voraussetzung hat'. In contrast to Thierse and Kliche, who (five years later!) *passively* adapted their discourse to the ruling dogma, Weimann, using similar discursive formulas, *actively* asked for conceptual revisions within the given space of social practice, which was nothing less than to invoke the constructive power and effective social role of criticism, intruding on petrified ideological structures through purposive action.

Derrida, Hartman), reader-orientated theory (Iser, Jauss) and Bakhtinian heteroglossia. The publishing practice of editing Virginia Woolf and a whole spectrum of modernist literature was a parallel venture. In fact, the one cannot be separated from the other, since both were complementary aspects of the larger process of internal liberalization and diversification, providing a valuable antidote to the sanctioned rituals. A complex critical history of these processes cannot be the subject of the present article; it has still to be written.

Returning to Woolf and an autobiographical perspective, I may add that my critical and editorial activities happened to converge. To accompany the publication of *Mrs Dalloway* and *Die Fahrt zum Leuchtturm* (*TL*), I wrote an article on Woolf's poetological thinking for the *Zeitschrift für Anglistik und Amerikanistik*, the East German Quarterly of English Studies. Rereading this paper, the extent to which it established a symbiosis of a typical East German Marxist discourse with an urgent drive to consolidate the reception of Virginia Woolf strikes me as odd. I shall cite it at some length because it provides, to my mind, an exemplary insight into both the earliest academic attempt to approach Virginia Woolf and the transitional phase of the theoretical destabilization of the dominant concept of realism. The anonymous opposition, which the text obviously tried to take in, was not only the Party establishment but equally the dogmatic faction among the scholars and teachers who represented English Studies in the East German universities. I also detect now how much I was influenced by my Greifswald University teacher Joachim Krehayn, whose versatile diplomacy in writing speaks through the first passage I shall quote. The core of diplomacy was care, which had to be taken to mediate one's message through the accepted forms of language. The intention was to bring into the country the contraband of a Western modernist writer, pretending at the same time that the import would be completely legal. The subjective position was messianic and to this extent nonsensical. The academic author believed that the cultural merchandise in fact *was* legal and could be integrated into socialist society, which, as a consequence, would become better, richer, more human, open-minded, liberal etc.

Legitimizing myself with Lenin's dictum (always good!) 'that socialists "must take hold of the legacy of culture which capitalism left to us and build socialism from it" [Lenin 1970, 55]', I called for a positive consideration of Woolf's essays

> in Marxist-Leninist literary theory and aesthetics which, though under different social and ideological circumstances, is urgently concerned with the appropriation of the literary heritage, the function of art and the interaction between the writer, the literary text and the reader ... Furthermore, an examination of her writings is necessary with regard to the desires and needs relevant to the reception of Woolf in the socialist order of the GDR. (Wicht 1978a, 6)[22]

---

[22] 'Gemäß dem bekannten Satz Lenins, daß die Sozialisten "von der gesamten Kultur Besitz ergreifen, die der Kapitalismus hinterlassen hat, und aus ihr den Sozialismus aufbauen" müssen, sind Virginia Woolfs Essays in wesentlichen Aspekten bedenkenswert und aufhebungswürdig in der marxistisch-leninistischen Literaturtheorie und Ästhetik, wo Probleme der Erbeaneignung, der adäquaten

An analysis of 'Mr Bennett and Mrs Brown', *ROO*, 'The Leaning Tower' and a number of other essays leads to the central significance of Woolf's conception of 'truth'. The foregrounding of this topic acted as a foil to the enforced reputation of (socialist) realism, which was defined as the true reflection of the truth of life. Extolling the utter divergence of Woolf's conception from the brisk materialism of Stalinist dogma, the essay attempted to cut methodological and theoretical bonds which were hierarchical, oppressive and canonical.

I argued that truth, for Woolf, was the polar star around which the constellations moved.[23] Referring to the beginning of *ROO*, the essay emphasized that, according to Woolf's polemic, truth in fiction is deeper than truth mediated through a mere mirroring of reality. The creative imagination of the writer creates truth, even if it lies:

> The essence of truth cannot be found in outer appearances. To mediate truth, the task of the writer is to look beneath the surface and to give life to the essential features of a situation through the structure and language of a fictional work, which thus communicates them to the reader. (Wicht 1978a, 18)[24]

Needless to say, this understanding of truth, which was derived from imagination, subjectivity and the deconstruction of dominating discourses,

---

cont.

Abbildung komplizierter Sachverhalte in der Literatur, der Wirkung der Kunst, des Zusammenhangs von Schriftsteller, Werk und Rezipienten ... aktuell anstehen ... Die Untersuchung ihres Werkes ist weiterhin notwendig in Hinblick darauf, was den Bedürfnissen und Notwendigkeiten der Rezeption in der sozialistischen Gesellschaft der DDR entspricht.'

23 'No other problem and no other term compares with this concept in her writings. She did not conceive of truth statically as "truth of imagination", as some Western critics think, maintaining instead that it is a criterion assessing the complex interconnections between art and reality, authorial intention and the work of art, meaning and reader reception .... Her concept of truth is not identical with the idealistic notion of absolute truth, put forward by Wordsworth ("general and operative") or Shelley ("eternal", "unchangeable"), nor with Henry James's classification of it as a quintessential dimension, besides beauty, which an outstanding writer brings to fruition.' ('Kein anderes Problem und kaum ein anderer Begriff wurden in ihren Schriften so häufig bemüht wie künstlerische Wahrheit. Diese war in ihren Überlegungen aber nicht, wie manche bürgerliche Kritiker meinen, statisch "truth of imagination", sondern sie war für das komplizierte Verhältnis von Kunst und Wirklichkeit, Autorenabsicht und Werk, Werkaussage und Leserverhalten das Wertkriterium .... Ihr Wahrheitsbegriff ist weder mit den idealistischen Konzeptionen einer absoluten Wahrheit verwandt, wie sie vor ihr Wordsworth ["general and operative"] oder Shelley ["eternal"; "unchangeable"] gekennzeichnet hatten, noch mit der Definition als – neben Schönheit – schlechthin von einem hervorragenden Schriftsteller erreichte feststehende Größe, wie sie etwa Henry James vornahm.') (Wicht 1978a, 18)

24 'Ihr [der Wahrheit] Wesen liegt nicht in der äußeren Erscheinung. Die Aufgabe des Schriftstellers bei der Wiedergabe der Wahrheit definierte sie folglich darin, hinter die Oberfläche zu blicken, in den Strukturen und Einzelheiten des Kunstwerks das Wesentliche zu beleben und zu kommunizieren.'

undermined the acknowledged system of Marxist-Leninist 'dialectical and historical materialism'.

The final passages of the paper tend to mitigate the radical implications of this theoretical consideration. A quotation of Woolf's vision of 'classless society' in 'The Leaning Tower' tempers her dream with an allusion to her 'highbrow' middle-class background and the naivety of her political beliefs. I stated categorically:

> First, she trusted in the noble rhetoric of the politicians who outlined a new post-war order; second, influenced by Labour Party economic theories, she placed her trust in the reformist effects of a new income tax scheme, which would even out the differences between the social classes; third, she was convinced that democratic school reforms and better education would redeem the working class from cultural and social subordination. Clearly, Virginia Woolf's position was a long way from a working-class scientific philosophy of life. Indisputably, however, her ideals were humanistic and democratic, and followed the great tradition of humanist thinkers in English culture. (Wicht 1978a, 20)[25]

This conclusion fluctuates between insight, absurdity and ideological idiom. But despite the deficiencies in personal courage or individual methodological precision, the argument as a whole is nevertheless highly illuminating. It represents the typical tactical means of disconnecting art from the traditional linear conventions of realist fiction and, above all, from the Soviet precepts of realism.

The context of the general debate is illuminated by the proceedings of a conference 'Literature and Revolutionary Progress', staged by the Institute of Literary History of the Academy of Sciences in 1977. The topic of Section 2 of the conference was 'Western European and North American Literatures: New Aspects of the Development of Realism'. The title convincingly testifies to the still dominant institutional position of realism. In his preface to an anthology of the papers given at Section 2, Günther Klotz stuck with the ruling conventions, asserting the commanding role of realism in the arts. But he distinctly dissociated himself from a dogmatic view, pointing out the need to re-enter a debate of the theory of realism and to revise the Stalinist confrontation of realism with modernism. Looking back (in some anger), he argued:

---

[25] 'Sie vertraute erstens den gefälligen Reden der Politiker von einer neuen Ordnung nach dem Kriege; zum zweiten glaubte sie ausgesprochen reformistisch und sichtlich unter dem Einfluß ökonomischer Theorien in der Labour Party an die klassenbeseitigende Wirkung der Einkommensbesteuerung; und zum dritten äußerte sie die Überzeugung, daß durch demokratische Schulreformen und eine erhöhte Bildung die Arbeiterklasse aus ihrer kulturell und gesellschaftlich unmündigen Rolle erlöst werden könne. Deutlicher wird kaum an anderer Stelle, wie weit Virginia Woolf von der wissenschaftlichen Weltanschauung des Proletariats entfernt war. Unübersehbar ist jedoch auch, daß ihre Ideale humanistisch und demokratisch waren und sich an die Tradition der großen Leistungen humanistischer Denker in der englischen Nationalkultur anfügen.'

> Writers such as Proust, Kafka, Musil, Joyce, Woolf and Dos Passos were not published, decadence was not the issue and a general suspicion of literary innovation and experiments prevailed. This situation is changing; but analytical studies of modernism in its historical development are not yet in existence and adequate theoretical generalizations not introduced into the current theory of realism. The present volume offers different positions and methodological suggestions. Meanwhile, there is a growing body of opinion which suggests that modernism created aesthetic value (Satonski), that its aesthetic experiences and techniques made a substantial contribution to world literature (Weimann) and that its attempt to convey the moral and social chaos of late capitalism drew nearer to reality than the stories narrated in the style of the nineteenth century, which dissolve social contradictions in the order of narrative and thus pacify conscious political activity (Wicht). (Klotz 1980, 14–15).[26]

Klotz's argument deserves attention because it gives a unique historical eyewitness account of the shifts in cultural and intellectual life at that time. My own contribution to the conference was a modified version of the *Zeitschrift für Anglistik und Amerikanistik* essay. Its rationale, however, was expressed in a less inhibited way. Referring to the London post-Impressionist exhibition of 1910 and its controversial reception, I drew the conclusion that

> even the brief mention of this controversy between the traditionalists and modernists obliges us to presume that the unhistorical and abstract placing of realism and modernism in juxtaposition with each other cannot satisfy the requirements of the present stage of socialist cultural revolution and the Marxist-Leninist examination of the bourgeois cultural heritage. (Wicht 1980, 36)[27]

Moreover, this thesis was central to my book on Woolf, Joyce and Eliot

---

26 'Autoren wie Proust, Kafka, Musil, Joyce, Woolf, Dos Passos wurden bei uns nicht veröffentlicht, eine Beschäftigung mit den Dekadenten stand nicht zur Debatte, und zeitweilig herrschte ein nahezu generelles Mißtrauen gegen literarische Neuerer und Experimente. Das hat sich geändert, ohne daß allerdings eine historische Aufarbeitung des Modernismus im Rahmen der Literaturentwicklung bereits geleistet wurde und ohne daß deren Verallgemeinerungen bereits in die gegenwärtige Realismustheorie eingebracht worden wären. Der vorliegende Band bietet auch dazu unterschiedliche Stellungnahmen und methodologische Vorschläge an. Inzwischen mehren sich Stimmen, die davon sprechen, daß der Modernismus ästhetische Werte schuf (Satonski), daß einige seiner ästhetischen Erfahrungen und Techniken in die Weltliteratur eingingen (Weimann) und daß er in dem Versuch, das sittliche und gesellschaftliche Chaos der spätkapitalistischen Gesellschaft als solches zu vermitteln, der Realität näherkam als im Stile des 19. Jahrhunderts erzählte Geschichten, weil jene die gesellschaftlichen Widersprüche in der Ordnung des Erzählens aufheben und damit dem aktiven Zugriff einer politischen Bewußtheit entziehen (Wicht).'

27 'Schon die Andeutung dieser Kontroverse zwischen Traditionalisten und Modernisten drängt den Denkansatz auf, daß die unhistorische Gegenüberstellung von Realismus und Modernismus als abstrakte Größen für die gegenwärtige Etappe der sozialistischen Kulturrevolution und der marxistisch-leninistischen Auseinandersetzung mit dem bürgerlichen Kulturerbe nicht mehr genügen kann.'

(Wicht 1981). The writers' names figuring on the title page were meant to be provocative. On the whole, this study strongly favoured literary modernism and Virginia Woolf, while also being studded with what Mary Reynolds correctly called 'polemical phrasing' (1982, 635). The underlying idea of appropriating Woolf within the socialist East German order was taken up by Hans-Jochen Sander, who reviewed the book in *Zeitschrift für Anglistik und Amerikanistik*, emphasizing that this 'first complex Marxist study of Woolf's, Joyce's and Eliot's poetology and literary innovation' has 'practical cultural relevance, thoroughly explaining the importance of Woolf's and Joyce's writerly liberal humanism for their reception in socialist society' (1983, 72).[28] With a distant view from America, Reynolds recognized my book's insistence that many rebellious forms of literature mirrored a spiritual crisis in the bourgeoisie; from this perspective Woolf is described as a self-conscious innovator stimulated by increasing awareness of a widening chasm between the English writer and his society (Reynolds 1982, 634). In 1991, from a West German perspective, Ulrich Schneider called the study the most substantial contribution to the process of Joyce's, Woolf's and Eliot's re-valuation in the GDR, but correctly criticized some conclusions which did not revise Lukács's biased attacks on modernist art (Schneider 1997, 323). As early as 1983, Utz Riese, one of the outstanding critical avantgardists in the GDR, put forward a fundamental critique of some of my theoretical assumptions, censuring, for instance, the continuous belief in the individual subject which is in a position to develop her or his creative potential, even if she or he is powerless in face of adverse social structures. What Riese had in mind was 'another kind of critical inquiry' ('eine andere Art der Befragung') which aimed at the deconstruction of logocentrism and social idealization (1983, 762). In uncoded text, he held that it was by now appropriate to discontinue critical diplomacy, to deconstruct one's own critical discourse and to quash the universalist approval of humanism and subjective possibilities.

Riese's review anticipates the tendencies of thinking in the later 1980s. For Riese, *Woolf, Joyce, Eliot: Kunstkonzeptionen und Künstlergestalten* (Woolf, Joyce, Eliot: Concepts of Art and the Figure of the Artist) was a 'breakthrough' ('Durchbruch'; 1983, 761); but in 1983 he fittingly upheld that the transitional period from ideological literary criticism to deconstructing modes, and from essentialist realism to a broad acceptance of (post)modernism must be brought to an end. It was a time when modernism became a legitimate literary, cultural and political issue. It was a time when the Woolf project was firmly installed and gradually taken for granted as one facet of East Germany's many-faceted culture.

---

[28] 'erste[n] marxistische[n] Komplexstudie zu Poetologie und Kunstinnovation bei V. Woolf, J. Joyce und T. S. Eliot' 'liegt ihre kulturpraktische Relevanz im vertieften Erschließen des bürgerlich-humanistischen Kunstbeitrags von V. Woolf und J. Joyce für die Rezeption in der sozialistischen Gesellschaft'.

V

The appropriation of modernism, of which Virginia Woolf was a part, and the theoretical re-orientations in criticism were activities emanating from a somewhat schizophrenic mindset, which hesitated to recognize the perversities of the ruling political system, because it entertained, defended and wanted to preserve utopian Marxist ideology and philosophy, on which the political system based its authority in contrast to its own political practice. Through individual refashioning, the system of Party texts, co-texts and con-texts was changed dramatically. This process was marked by a deep rupture. The introduction, translation and production of con-texts of Otherness opposed the self-enclosed dogma of Party politics, and simultaneously affirmed and redefined it. In the concrete case, the reception of Virginia Woolf and the wider endeavours to make modernism acceptable were (subjectively) considered to be inevitable in order to reform socialist society from within, not as means of introducing the alterity of the other (old, dying, corrupt, exploitative or whatever) social system. Objectively, however, the reception of Western culture, literature and cognitive systems contributed to the spiritual undermining of the Eastern order, which in the end proved incapable of surviving economically and politically. In retrospect, one is inclined to presume that culturally East Germany was in no small measure re-united with the West before the socio-political changes of 1989 became historical reality.

Scrutinizing the reception of Virginia Woolf in East Germany, one becomes immediately aware that the establishment of a 'Western' canon created a two-way functional force. In one direction, the internal one, Woolf's novels played a prominent role in widening the readers' horizon of literature and subverting the ruling ideological patterns of dogmatism. In the other direction, reflecting back on the writer herself, the critical (and possibly also the readerly) appropriation of Woolf was marked by a distinct turn toward politics. Woolf became a model for the political reading of novels which was primarily concerned with locating modes of resistance in a literary text, which in turn presupposed the existence of repressive forces in socio-economic reality. As a consequence, the methodological heritage of Marxist historicism proved to be still productive, if it was modified and qualified by post-structuralist approaches. But the political aspect of the reception of Woolf also issued a strong warning about the unquestioned reproduction of the traditional ways of historical analysis.

The most advanced scholarly conceptions in East Germany at the end of the 1980s, notably in Shakespeare criticism and a mere handful of studies in modernism and postmodernism, were characterized by a tendency to merge linguistic and deconstructive with historical analysis, to embed the historicity of a literary discourse within a system of signs and discourses which constitute the actual historical place, to unearth the politics of the form. In a way, the end of the reception and criticism of Virginia Woolf in East Germany introduces the subject of ongoing theoretical and methodological discussions. The end is a denouement and potentially a new departure.

7 From Silence to a Polyphony of Voices: Virginia Woolf's Reception in Poland

Urszula Terentowicz-Fotyga

Although in the second half of the 1990s the delicate profile of Virginia Woolf became a common sight in Polish bookshops and her name began appearing on the pages of women's magazines, the beginnings of the writer's reception in Poland were far less promising. Her work was for a long time overlooked by the reading public for a number of reasons. On the one hand, the facts of the political, social and literary situation put Virginia Woolf among those writers for whom the climate was not favourable, for what distinguished the Polish literary scene from those of most countries discussed in this volume was the scope and persistence of historical and political pressures. In fact, in the recent history of Poland there were only relatively short periods of time when the cultural and literary scene could develop quite freely and independently. On the other hand, when the disadvantages resulting from the political, economic and social pressures were not so strong, other factors worked against the popularization of Virginia Woolf's œuvre in Poland. At different times elements such as the state of research into English modernism, the number and quality of translators and the choice of works to be translated all contributed to her remaining relatively unknown to the general public for a long time. Even though the last decade of the twentieth century witnessed an increasing fascination with the writer – and she seems to write herself much better into the contemporary Polish context than other modernists – many of her works are still waiting to be discovered. What seems equally important is that her novels are waiting for a faithful translator so that each of them will cease to pulse according to different rhythms and styles.

Virginia Woolf's reception in Poland may be divided into three phases. The first, which lasted until the late 1950s, when political and social pressures were strongest, was the time of relative silence. The second, encompassing the next three decades, brought the translation of her most important works: *MD*, *TL*, *TW*, *TY* and a collection of essays. At this time, Virginia Woolf was read mainly as a canonical writer, interesting from a historical perspective yet not truly significant for the contemporary literary scene. Finally, the last decade of the twentieth century witnessed the reversal of this perspective. A growing interest in her life made Virginia Woolf a 'personality' as well as a literary figure. She is no longer treated as an obsolete author of difficult novels addressed to a limited number of more sophisticated and demanding readers. Due to the translation of her more popular works such as *FB* and *O* she appears far more committed to contemporary issues and much more approachable and affable.

Naturally, in the first decades of the twentieth century the silence in response to Virginia Woolf was not complete and the factors causing the silence were far from homogeneous. These were very turbulent years in Polish history. The new country, which in 1918 regained independence after over a hundred years of partitions, had to cope not only with the aftermath of these partitions and the First World War, but also face the difficulties brought by the world crisis of 1929 and the approaching Second World War. Obviously the economic situation had direct implications on the book market and it meant, in broad terms, limited contact with other cultures as few magazines could afford foreign correspondents, and resources for translation, publishing and academic research were scarce. In a country which had to rebuild its identity national, social and economic issues became very closely linked. Consequently, the literature of the time was to a great extent 'committed', and this also affected translation from other literatures. Even if formal experimentation *was* taken into account, authors who fused experimental techniques with a 'social message' were preferred, and Virginia Woolf was seen as too ethereal and uncommitted to fit into the 'burdened' Polish context.

The second part of the thirties witnessed a gradual turning away from realism in Polish prose and as a result greater interest in formal experimentation in foreign literature. This tendency is reflected in the growing number of articles devoted to English modernism, in which Virginia Woolf features as one of its most prominent representatives. Interestingly, Woolf receives far higher acclaim than does James Joyce from many critics of this period, a situation which will change in the years to come. In a study entitled 'Stare i nowe w powieści współczesnej' (The Old and the New in the Contemporary Novel) (1933) Aniela Gruszecka highlights the contrast between old and new tendencies in the English novel, citing the example of *TL*. She sees the text's main novelty in the replacement of the traditional notions of 'plot' and 'character' with the non-hierarchical order of motifs ruled by the progress of an individual psyche. In a mode which sounds pleasantly outdated to the contemporary ear, Gruszecka praises Woolf for her courage in creating a new form and a unique vision of reality, independent of the ready-made patterns of traditional fiction and everyday life. In 1936 another article discussing modern writing techniques and using the example of Virginia Woolf's fiction was published by *Kurier Literacko Naukowy* (Journal of Literary Studies) – an important chronicle of pre-war art, literature and science (Świątek 1936). Woolf is described as the most talented, original and independent of the contemporary women writers. Though the choice of the novels discussed – *ND*, *TL*, *O*, *TW* and *FB* – seems rather arbitrary, Świątek grasps the unique character of each. He sees the novelty of Virginia Woolf's fiction as lying primarily in the new conception of time and self understood as constant and unremitting 'becoming'. Pointing to the growing inwardness of Virginia

Woolf's characters, he links the disintegration of a coherent self to what he calls 'impressionist psychology' (psychologia impresjonistyczna) (8), which he finds characteristic of all her novels. Although Świątek claims that women's fiction is less 'burdened' (obciążona) (8) with social and political questions, he sees Virginia Woolf's respect for the uniqueness of individual visions of reality as the product of a truly democratic culture. The emphasis laid by both Gruszecka and Świątek on the individual character of Virginia Woolf's creation does not seem accidental. Their opinions reflect the two myths of English culture which permeated the Polish mind at this time: the myth of Imperial England and the myth of a Western parliamentary democracy (see Kurowska 1987). Both, in contrast to the geopolitical reality of Poland, made for a picture of an England whose political and social stability created favourable conditions for the development of its citizens and independent artistic creation. Although in the reality of the post-war years official opinion will make the 'threat of imperialism' and 'anarchy of individualism' key terms in communist propaganda, this nostalgic vision of English culture will survive in the 'private world' of Poles.

In 1937 *Wiadomości Literackie* (Literary News) published two reviews of *TY* and in 1938 a short article devoted to Bloomsbury. The author of all of them, Quidam (Wiktor Weintraub) quotes amply from foreign sources and blames Polish publishers for their random publishing policy. His first review of *TY* is rather short and, only several months later, Quidam analyses it in more detail speaking very favourably about its author. The article devoted to Bloomsbury reveals that Weintraub's knowledge of the topic must have been rather limited as he calls Bloomsbury a school and regards Edith Sitwell and her brothers as the most distinguished members of the group.

Just before the war Roman Dyboski, one of the most distinguished literary scholars of the time, published a long essay entitled 'O powojennej literaturze angielskiej' (On Post-war English Literature) (1939) in which he traces the process of gradual departure from realism in the works of Lawrence, Joyce and Woolf, among others. Similarly to Świątek, he sees the new conception of time as central to all modernist literature and thought. Although Dyboski questions whether any further development in radically anti-realist literature is possible, he praises the psychological quality of Woolf's prose, in which, he writes, the stream of consciousness technique reaches 'the summit of subtle psychic artistry' (wyżyny subtelnego artyzmu psychicznego) (20). Apart from Dyboski's study, 1939 brings yet another important event in the history of the writer's reception in Poland. Wanda Melcer gives a lecture on Woolf's writing to the Polish Academy of Literature. It seems a peculiar whim of fortune that the lecture was to be published in the first September issue of a popular literary weekly – *Wiadomości Literackie*, which due to the outbreak of the war never appeared. What remains is a very favourable report written by Stanisław Brucz, which gives an idea of the lecture's scope (1939). Apart from the writer's biography – her philosophical, intellectual and literary background – Melcer discussed Woolf's conception of time and her peculiar kind of impressionism, which is contrasted with the methods of Joyce and Proust.

Although the articles published in the 1930s prepared the ground in a natural way for the direct reception of Virginia Woolf's fiction, readers had to wait until the late 1950s for the first translation into Polish of a novel by Woolf. The reason why none of her works was translated for another two decades, apart from the originally unfavourable climate for experimental literature, was the difficulty of Woolf's prose. Since for centuries Poland had had much closer links with French culture, the English language was known by only a limited group of people at the beginning of the twentieth century. The first English Department was opened in 1908, and even in the 1930s the number of English language students was relatively low. As a consequence, there were comparatively few translators and hardly any who were sufficiently qualified to tackle a more challenging literary text (Kurowska 1987, 37–38). When the situation began to improve and translators and the reading public were ready to face the challenge of Woolf's fiction, the war broke out, followed by a harsh post-war reality, which dashed hopes for a quick development in research and publishing.

The censorship imposed by the communist regime proved most severe in the decade that followed the war.[1] According to socialist realism the quality of a literary text was determined by its devotion to social and political issues, and characters were to serve as models personifying progressive socialist ideas. All texts which did not give a simple and unequivocal picture of reality were deemed suspicious and formal experimentation was thought to contain a coded political message. Woolf's interest in the human psyche and the complexity of individual experience was considered dangerous and harmful escapism and, although most modernist writers were treated as potentially subversive, the 'bourgeois' character of her fiction only made matters worse.

Very characteristic of the new critical method is Marian Promiński's article 'W stronę Virginii Woolf' (Towards Virginia Woolf) published in *Życie Literackie* (Literary Life) – a literary weekly edited by the Cracow branch of the Association of Polish Writers (1957). It is worth a closer look not only because it exemplifies the peculiarity of contemporary terminology and argumentation but also because it offers a new interpretation of English culture. Promiński analyses factors responsible for the failure of modernist fiction using the example of *MD* and *TL*. For him, modernist authors are sick individuals who do not distinguish between the world of childhood fears and repressions and that of the adult, which tends to be ruled by moral and social principles. Therefore, endless modernist analysis 'leads from nowhere to nowhere' (wiodą znikąd do nikąd) (4) and ultimately proves infantile or pseudo-artistic (it is difficult to decide which of the two is thought by Promiński a greater offence). The meaninglessness of its investigations, however, is only one of the novel's faults. Another is the complexity of form, which looks like 'a deliberate nonchalance and negligence of the struggle for simplicity and lucidity' (zakrawa to na programową nonszalancję i zaniedbanie trudu prostoty i jednoznaczności) (5) on the part of the author. For Promiński even if the complexity of the analytical process *is* occasionally justified, ultimately, it should lead to 'an unequivocal and intentionally unambiguous end'

---

1 An interesting analysis of the problem is offered in an unpublished study by Alicja Kędzielska devoted to the reception of English literature 1945–65.

(jednoznaczny i intencjonalnie jednokierunkowy wynik) (5). Having discussed the symptoms of the modernist disease Promiński offers an analysis of its origin. It results, he claims, from the boredom and stagnation of narcissistic writers, who live in a reality deprived of significant social upheavals and, finding nothing interesting in what surrounds them, turn to their inner worlds for inspiration. Seen from this perspective, Promiński's article seems to put the outbreak of the Second World War in a positive light as such historical tremors clearly break the glass of artists' artificial isolation and bring literature back onto the safe territory of realism.

Similar faults are ascribed to modernist fiction in Bronisław Wiśniewski's article 'O powieści subiektywistycznej' (About the Subjectivist Novel) (1956), which, though more subtle and less ideological, derives from the same school of criticism as Promiński's. In a polemic aimed at Leon Edel's *The Psychological Novel* (1955), Wiśniewski questions the applicability of Edel's usage of the term 'psychological novel' for the discussion of such writers as Henry James, Virginia Woolf and James Joyce and suggests an alternative: 'subjectivist novel'. Psychological fiction, he claims, aims primarily at understanding human behaviour, and the exploration of an individual mind simply fulfils the function of explaining man's 'subjective reactions' to 'objective stimuli' (obiektywnych bodzców i subiektywnych reakcji) (203). Thus, the difference between Wiśniewski's and Edel's definition of the term comes down to a different definition of a human being. For Wiśniewski a man is essentially a social and rational being:

> Human behaviour is the most genuine and only reliable picture of inner life ... The psychological novel recognizes the complexity of the inner structure of man yet at the same time believes that a certain hierarchy of stimuli and motifs controlled by general tendencies is indispensable; it attributes importance to ethical principles and to the controlling function of the mind. (Wiśniewski 1956, 203)[2]

The paradox of Wiśniewski's argument lies not in his theoretical stance but in the analysis which follows. Having pointed out the novelty of modernist fiction and suggested an alternative term, in his analysis of individual authors he applies the standards of the traditional psychological novel that he himself recognized as inapplicable. Thus, he measures the 'weight of social thought' (ładunek myśli społecznej) (206) in *Ulysses*, concluding that 'Joyce is creative only as an artist' (Joyce jest odkrywczy wyłącznie jako artysta), and sees Virginia Woolf's 'persistent silence' (uporczywe milczenie) and 'indifference' (indyferencja) about social matters as the main factor responsible for the incomprehensibility of her fiction (206). Thus, it is only natural that Wiśniewski finds Woolf's vision of man as autonomous and individual absurd

---

[2] 'Postępowanie człowieka jest najwierniejszym i jedynym sprawdzalnym obrazem jego życia wewnętrznego ... Powieść psychologiczna uznaje skomplikowaną strukturę wewnętrzną człowieka, ale jednocześnie zakłada konieczność istnienia pewnej ustalonej tendencjami ogólnymi hierarchii bodźców i motywów, docenia znaczenie nakazów etycznych i kontrolującej funkcji umysłu.'

and unconvincing. Like Promiński, Wiśniewski criticizes the complexity of the novels' form and admits that he finds the poetic metaphors and symbolism in *TW* impossible to understand. His conclusion that Virginia Woolf 'despite great talent will always remain an elitist, difficult and incomprehensible writer' (207) does not come as a surprise.[3]

Clearly, given the critical climate of the decade that followed the war there was no possibility of Virginia Woolf's fiction being published. The situation improved slightly in the second half of the 1950s. 1956 was the year of change in the Polish political scene and, although hopes raised by the change at the top of the Communist Party proved largely futile, there was a noticeable improvement in publishing. The beginning of the 1960s marks a surge in the translation of modernist literature and soon three novels by Woolf are published: in 1958 *Lata (TY)*, in 1961 *Pani Dalloway* (*MD*) and a year later *Do latarni morskiej (TL)*. While official opinion remains critical of the novels, considering them nihilistic, her works, like those of many writers from behind the Iron Curtain, live a different life among readers. For the intellectual elite of the time, reading literature uncommitted to political questions was an act of personal resistance, a retreat from the uniformity imposed by the communist system. In this sense the individualistic character of modernist fiction offered a particularly liberating experience.

Today, it is difficult to understand why the first novel by Woolf translated into Polish was *TY*. The reason might be that it seemed the most 'social', the least experimental and so the most in accordance with the official school of literary criticism. It was also the first novel to be reviewed soon after publication in Britain. Finally, it might have been dependent on the language – certainly more transparent and easier than in her other works. It is clear, however, that in terms of the presentation of Virginia Woolf to the Polish reading public it was not the best choice. As one of the early reviewers put it:

> Introducing Virginia Woolf to the Polish reader through *TY* the publisher played the unfortunate part of a maid who presented her elderly though still beautiful lady in inappropriate clothes. Her slightly risqué dress was meant for close friends, from whom nothing has to be hidden, who are acquainted with the lady's idiosyncrasies and extravagances but also know and value her numerous virtues. The meeting was not really successful. (Krzeczkowski 1958, 2)[4]

It must be added that the uneven and occasionally awkward translation by Małgorzata Szercha was in part responsible for the failure of the meeting. As Krzeczkowski rightly comments, the appearance of *Lata* as the first of Woolf's

---

3 'mimo wybitnego talentu pozostanie zawsze pisarzem elitarnym, trudnym i niezrozumiałym'.

4 'Przedstawiając polskiemu czytelnikowi Virginię Woolf od strony *Lat* odegrał wydawca niefortunną rolę pokojówki, która swą niemłodą ale jeszcze piękną panią sprezentowała nowym znajomym w nieodpowiedniej sukni. Nieco ryzykowna toaleta przeznaczona była dla przyjaciół, przed którymi nia ma potrzeby zbyt wiele ukrywać, obytych z ekstrawagancjami damy i jej dziwactwami, ale znających równocześnie i ceniących jej liczne zalety. Spotkanie nie bardzo się udało.'

works in Polish creates an unfavourable situation both for this novel and for others. The experiment attempted in *Lata*, he writes, looks different when seen as the culmination of a certain vision developing gradually in Woolf's writing. When deprived of this context, it looks estranged and abandoned.

The reviewers' opinions reflect the tension between their excitement about the first translation of a novel by Woolf and their dissatisfaction with the publisher's choice. Most admit to a sense of disappointment, but point to different reasons for their dissatisfaction. The writer's purpose, the portrait of 'an ordinary mind on an ordinary day', writes Krzeczkowski, succeeds in a compact time structure yet fails when extended over a longer stretch of time. Therefore, the novel although 'exquisitely written' (świetnie napisana), ultimately proves 'perfectly indifferent' (doskonale obojętna) (2). Łapiński, expressing his otherwise very appreciative opinions of the novelist, concludes that in *Lata* 'vision' damaged 'facts'. What the reader is left with is a phantom world, a complete disintegration of forms and the novel's final effect is that of tedium and numbness (1958). Such opinions prevail although there are reviewers who find the represented world much more 'tangible' and 'real'. Julian Stawiński, for example, praises the wide social panorama, which makes the family history part of 'the forces shaping the fate of individuals and society' (sił kształtujących losy jednostek i społeczeństwa) (1958, 982).

Most at odds with critical opinions is Zbigniew Dolecki's review entitled 'Kronika wielkiego przemijania' (The Chronicle of Time Passing) (1958). In his enthusiastic reading of *Lata* he analyses the elements found in Virginia Woolf's other novels – the importance of the 'moment' in the novel's time structure, the sensuous and poetic quality of the language, and the depth of the philosophical message. Unlike most critics, who see Virginia Woolf primarily as a stream of consciousness writer and repeatedly evoke the names of Joyce and Proust, Dolecki does not look for similarities in terms of writing technique but concentrates on the novel's mood, atmosphere and 'message'. Thus, he sees in *Lata* the beauty and tragedy of Wilder's plays, the absurdity later found in Beckett's works and a vision of reality echoing Hemingway's *nada*.

Critical reaction to the next two novels published in Poland, *Pani Dalloway (MD)* and *Do latarni morskiej (TL)*, is in fact quite uniform. The reviewers are unanimous in their evaluation of these texts as Virginia Woolf's masterpieces and their excellence remains indisputable. However, since the two novels enter the Polish literary scene together with the works of the new wave of experimental fiction, most critics find it necessary to redefine Virginia Woolf's position in the literary tradition. The writers most frequently cited in the context of Woolf's method are Joyce and Proust, but in contrast to the reviews published before the war, primacy is almost unanimously given to the two male writers and the originality of Woolf's method is often undermined.[5] A closer look, however, proves that although repeated in most reviews, this opinion is never discussed in detail. In fact, Joyce's superiority seems more of

5 Different opinions are expressed by, among others, Kasiński (1962) and Czerwiński (1962).

an exemplar than a critically proven thesis. At that time his only works translated in full were *Dubliners* and *A Portrait of the Artist as a Young Man*; *Ulysses* was known only from several short extracts. Leszek Elektorowicz in his article devoted to the contemporary state of Joyce research in Poland writes that Joyce is instead known theoretically, through other writers using the same or similar techniques:

> If his name occasionally appears in various reviews, it usually serves as a vague symbol of some rather undefined writing school or even a kind of *bête noire* of contemporary literature, a beast rapacious though unknown. (Elektorowicz 1963, 7).[6]

The tendency to take Joyce's superiority for granted leads to some openly mistaken and unsubstantiated claims in the evaluation of Woolf's work, such as that of Tomasz Burek who described her as Joyce's great admirer and a conscious follower of the author (1961).

More substantial and analytically interesting are those reviews which see Virginia Woolf's fiction in the context of American literature of the time, in particular the works of John Dos Passos. Henryk Bereza explores the similarity in the two writers' usage of simultaneity and notes that the same technique was used for totally different effect by each (1961). While in Dos Passos, simultaneity results in the representation of the world as unified and deprived of individuality, in Virginia Woolf's fiction the unity is of a transcendental character and the essence of reality lies in the unlimited diversity and uniqueness of human experience. Tomasz Burek likens their artistic visions of external reality, though he finds the tone and character of their works completely different (1961). If Dos Passos is desperate and violent, Woolf is intimate and subdued.

For many critics the most significant factor defining Woolf's position in twentieth-century literature is the context of the contemporary wave of experimentation, especially the *nouveau roman*. Seen from the perspective of the most recent writing techniques, they argue, Virginia Woolf's works have lost much of their power and revolutionary novelty. As a result, although her role in the literary tradition is unquestionable she is not 'alive' from the point of view of a contemporary reader:

> Virginia Woolf's prose does not pass the test of time well, today she is studied like a specimen. (Lam 1962, 60)[7]

> These days she is read a bit as a historical figure. The world she describes has no equivalent in contemporary reality. (Klimowicz 1962, 2)[8]

---

6 'Jeśli nazwisko tego pisarza pada niekiedy w recenzjach, to służyć ma ono zazwyczaj jako mglisty symbol jakiejś bliżej nieokreślonej szkoły pisarskiej lub zgoła jako *bete-noire* literatury współczesnej, zwierzę drapieżne choć nieznane.'

7 'Proza Virginii Woolf nie wytrzymuje dobrze próby czasu, studiuje się ją dzisiaj jak preparat.'

8 'Dziś czytamy ją z nastawieniem trochę historycznym. Swiat, o którym pisze, nie ma juł ładnego odpowiednika w rzeczywistości.'

The portrayal of Virginia Woolf as a writer of mainly historical importance is in tune with the image of her as an elitist and hermetic novelist, the author of difficult novels for a small group of more demanding readers – the image that was to pervade the Polish mind for the next three decades.

It takes fifteen years for the next significant publication of Virginia Woolf's work to appear – a collection of critical essays entitled *Pochyła Wieża* (The Leaning Tower). In the meantime several sketches and essays were published by various periodicals.[9] Most of these reappeared in *Pochyła Wieża*.[10] The collection contains thirty-six essays from *CR*, *DM*, *M*, *CDB*, *GR* and *CE*. The essays were translated by Aleksandra Ambros (the editor) and Ewa Zycieńska and completed with notes on the publishing, historical, cultural and literary background. The collection reflects three areas of Virginia Woolf's critical interest: prose writing, the history of English literature and the issue of women's fiction. To the first group belong, among others, 'Nad Książką' (Reading), 'Nowoczesna Powieść' (Modern Fiction), 'Esej O Krytyce' (An Essay in Criticism), 'Sztuka biografii' (The Art of Biography) and the title essay 'Pochyła Wieża' (The Leaning Tower). Among the essays devoted to famous writers are those on Joseph Conrad, Jane Austen, George Eliot and Charlotte Brontë. The advantage of the collection, as indicated by its reviewers, is its representativeness both in terms of Virginia Woolf's critical ideas and the topics of the essays, which, given their chronological order, offer a coherent and complete view of English literature from the time of the Elizabethans to that of Woolf's contemporaries.

The reception of the volume is almost unanimously enthusiastic. Even those who criticize Woolf's novels speak very favourably of the essays. The main focus is on Woolf's critical method, which, although referred to differently by different reviewers, is generally contrasted with structuralism. Most speak very favourably of the personal tone of Virginia Woolf's criticism even if they admit that it is rather archaic and obsolete. Since Woolf does not adopt the position of a distant observer but crosses the borderline between the subject and the object, writes Teresa Walas, 'the reality of the subject and the reality of the theme merge making for this unique polyphony of an essay ... [and] reveal[ing] most unexpected aspects of the observed object' (1978, 36).[11] For Mirosław Ratajczak, Woolf's intimate reading of literature and her free and

---

9 'Joseph Conrad' (1958); 'Pani w zwierciadle' ('The Lady in the Looking Glass: A Reflection') (1959); 'Modern Fiction' and 'The Russian Point of View' published together under the title 'Dwa szkice o powieści' (1963); 'Zgon Ćmy' ('The Death of the Moth') (1963); 'Madame de Sévigné' (1963); 'Sztuka biografii' ('The Art of Biography') (1963); 'Literatura współczesna' ('Modern Fiction') (1969); 'Prezentacja' ('The Introduction') (1973); 'Kobiety i powieść' ('Women and Fiction') (1974).

10 Not found in *Pochyła Wieża* are: 'Zgon Ćmy' (The Death of the Moth) and 'Kobiety i powieść' (Women and Fiction).

11 'Rzeczywistość piszącego i rzeczywistość tematu nakładają się na siebie, tworząc tę właśnie jedyną w swoim rodzaju polifonicznosć eseju ... [i] ukaz[ując] niespodziewane cechy oglądanego przedmiotu.'

easy approach to cultural tradition are strikingly different from the approach characterizing Polish readers:

> Our attitude to our literary tradition is more tense, more self-conscious, more official . . . From our point of view literature must still fulfil a mission. (1978, 131)[12]

Many critics see Woolf's focus on concrete and tangible detail as the greatest asset of her approach and speak very favourably of the sociological aspect of her criticism. When analysing nineteenth-century fiction, writes Jacek Popiel, Woolf uses the method of 'structural homology', that is she 'tries to detect the homology between the structure of the world represented in a literary work and the structure of the world of a given social group' (1979, 149).[13]

After the period when Virginia Woolf's reception in Poland was shaped almost entirely by reviews there is a noticeable increase in academic research into Woolf's fiction in the mid-1970s. The scale and pace of its development is reflected in the growing number of master's theses written at Polish universities: from one thesis written in the 1950s and two in the 1960s there is an increase to sixteen in the 1970s and seventeen in the 1980s (Carter 2001). The growing interest in Virginia Woolf's work is also reflected by the rise in the number of articles published in academic periodicals.

Three studies published during this period of increasing academic interest cover those aspects of Virginia Woolf's writing which had previously remained relatively unknown.[14] Marianna Abrahamowicz in her essay 'Virginia Woolf as a Short Story Writer' (1960) analyses five short stories from *HH* ('The Mark on the Wall', 'The Lady in the Looking Glass', 'An Unwritten Novel', 'The Searchlight' and 'The Legacy'). For Abrahamowicz a short story proves particularly interesting material for discussion of Woolf's method because it might be expected to reveal a strong tension between generic devices and her artistic temperament. One might expect, writes Abrahamowicz, that Woolf's 'intangible' reality is not capable of creating a successful short story which needs a compact plot and a well-defined climax. Surprisingly her works turn out to be so powerful that 'classical, well-built short-stories prove "unreal" in their very realism'. Accordingly, when the novelist tries to follow the rules of the genre, as in 'The Legacy' she fails and it turns out that:

> A definite plot, tangible, concrete situations hinder her, check her in communicating her inner meaning to the reader. She seems . . . at her best not when her starting point is a well-ordered, crisply cut story, but just a Manx cat, an unidentified spot on the wall, or the dreamy void of an empty mirror. (1960, 45)

---

12 'Nasz stosunek do własnej tradycji literackiej jest bardziej napięty, skrępowany, oficjalny . . . W naszych oczach literatura wciął musi 'pełnić jakieś posłannictwo.'

13 'Woolf zmierza do wykrycia homologii między strukturą świata ukazanego w dziele literackim a strukturą świadomości określonej grupy społecznej.'

14 Polish studies were preceded by the translations of Auerbach's *Mimesis* (1968) and David Daiches's study of Virginia Woolf's fiction from *The Novel and the Modern World* (1976).

Jadwiga Ćwiąkała-Piątkowska in her essay 'The Feminist Pamphlets of Virginia Woolf' (1972) explores the political and literary questions of *ROO* and *TG*. While Woolf's literary theory, writes Piątkowska, was quite uniform and in harmony with her art, her 'political diagnosis was erroneous and confused' (276). Piątkowska is particularly critical of *TG*, which she calls an 'odd and irritating book' (279), 'more a testimony of the writer's anguish than a sample of coherent writing' (276). At the core of the pamphlet's incoherence, she claims, lies a mistaken idea of the addressee: 'Virginia Woolf seems to be speaking of the female sex as opposed to the male sex while in fact she is speaking about a tiny group within the upper-middle class' (274), 'a tiny educated elite of women, whose importance in politics she exaggerated out of proportion' (279). As a result, in her political and social appeals she absurdly assigns 'the gigantic task of preserving peace' (274) to a tiny social group. Piątkowska contrasts the novelist with the older generation of feminists and contends that Woolf's political ideas were not only incoherent and naive but also outdated. In fact, she totally disregards the impact of her work on the feminism of the 1960s and thus fails to give a proper, more contemporary perspective to the two pamphlets.

Three years later *Kwartalnik Neofilologiczny* (Modern Language Quarterly) published Krystyna Stamirowska's study 'Virginia Woolf's Concept of Reality and Some Theories of Her Time' (1975). The critic analyses *MD* and *TL* seeking points of convergence between her fiction and the theories of William James and Henri Bergson. Exploring the representation of the duality of time and the corresponding duality of reality Stamirowska slightly ambiguously contends that:

> In the two novels different aspects of this discrepancy are emphasised. In *MD* the contrast and opposition between two types of reality are constantly related to the problem of understanding and interpretation of other people's inner life and reality in general. In *TL* V. Woolf's chief concern is the analysis of human experience with regard to the basic split: man participates in the two types of reality and in the two kinds of time. Human life considered in the aspect of time and duration, and permanent effects of the two are in the focus of attention. (1975, 209–10).

In 1975 echoes of the growing interest in Virginia Woolf's life which developed in Britain are heard in Poland. Before that time, knowledge of Woolf's life was limited to basic facts. Often the family and intellectual background were emphasized and her suicide was interpreted differently by different critics. Only a short extract from her Diary was published in *Kierunki* (Directions) in 1958 and the choice of the fragment (August–September 1940) describing the novelist's war experiences seems to reflect the editor's attempt to bring the facts of her life closer to the Polish perspective. In 1975 *Literatura na Świecie* (World Literature) publishes an article entitled, slightly inappropriately, 'Renesans Virginii Woolf we Francji' (Virginia Woolf's Renaissance in France) (Korotyńska 1975). Katarzyna Korotyńska discusses the shift in studies of Virginia Woolf away from her writing towards a fascination with her life. Her essay is accompanied by a translation of Lehmann's memoirs of his friendship with the Woolfs, the first such detailed and personal account of the writer's life (Lehmann 1975).

The first Polish study which reflects the tendency to read Virginia Woolf's life and work together was published in 1985 in *Twórczość* (Creation) – an influential and versatile monthly journal of literature and criticism. Maria Niemojewska's long sketch entitled 'Nie bój się więcej ...' (Fear No More ...), written in a very warm and intimate tone, not only gives new information about the writer's life but also adds new elements which reshape her profile.[15] Probably for the first time the image of Virginia Woolf as a daring experimenter, an upper-class lady and an icon of the London intellectual and literary elite is completed with a picture of a sensitive and vulnerable woman, whose childhood traumas generated many of her works. Niemojewska discusses the importance of the writer's formative years for her adult life as well as for her fiction: the death of her mother, the tyranny of her father, the lifelong complex due to a lack of formal education. More attention is given to the importance of an unspecified mental illness, her suicidal character, and her lesbian inclinations, though her childhood sexual abuse is overlooked, and, for some unspecified reason, Gerald Duckworth is called 'the most gentle man in the world' ('najłagodniejszego człowieka pod słońcem') (87). At the same time Niemojewska remains very critical of Leonard Woolf and his impact on the writer's life; she calls him 'possibly the flattest and most down-to-earth man in the world' ('chyba najbardziej płaskim i rzeczowym człowiekiem na świecie') (85–86) and considers him a complete bore, who was a totally unsuitable match for the imaginative and oversensitive novelist.

For Niemojewska the dominant feature of Virginia Woolf's personality, hidden behind snobbery, toughness and a craving for fame, is her feeling of insecurity; the feature which is also partly responsible for the faults in her writing. While her best novels are those in which she delves deepest into her own complex and fascinating self, her extreme self-consciousness, writes Niemojewska, prevents her from expressing it openly.

> Instead, she keeps hiding behind a meaningless idea of poetry. Her girlish prattle and the shallow exaltation which fill her novels seem to me a desperate escape from the truth which might prove too dangerous to herself and incomprehensible to others. As long as this psychic experience lives in the experiences of her characters and the reader is aware of it, the truth in her work is alive. She was truly a disabled genius, who, until the end of her life, remained a small, terrified girl who sings and dances only to disarm and ingratiate herself with adults. (1985, 95)[16]

---

15 She writes, for example, about the *Dreadnought* Hoax and about the relative poverty of the early years of the Woolfs' marriage; she also discusses in detail the role of Bloomsbury both in the writer's life and on the contemporary literary scene.

16 'W miejsce tego kryje się ciągle za tu nic nie znaczącym pojęciem poezji. Cały ten panieński szczebiot, płytka egzaltacja, które wypełniają jej powieści, sprawiają na mnie wrażenie rozpaczliwej ucieczki przed prawdą, która mogłaby okazać się zbyt groźna dla niej samej i – niezrozumiała dla innych. Jak długo to psychiczne doświadczenie żyje w doświadczeniu jej bohaterek i jak długo czytelnik jest tego świadomy, tak długo prawda jest czymś żywym w jej dziele. Był to w sumie zaiste geniusz kaleki, wiecznie przestraszona mała dziewczynka, która tańczy i śpiewa, tylko po to, by rozbroić i przypodobać się dorosłym.'

Thus, Niemojewska values *MD* and *TL* most and remains repelled by *FB*, which she calls 'a truly horrible book, pervaded by a pretentious, pseudo-playful tone adopted by supercilious ladies when talking to servants or children' (96).[17] Niemojewska is both fascinated and disappointed by the writer. Although Woolf's input into the European literary tradition is unquestionable, her field of interest remains rather limited. Niemojewska believes that Woolf did not take full advantage of her talent and for this she blames her conformism, cowardice, and ... Leonard. Refusing to delve into the deepest layers of her extraordinary mind, claims Niemojewska, Woolf betrayed both herself and her readers.

Three years later another article devoted to Virginia Woolf's life was published by *Kultura* (Culture). Agnieszka Baranowska's 'Sekretna wiadomość' (A Secret Message) (1988), which hinges on three key concepts – death, madness and suicide – could be read as a compact version of Quentin Bell's biography and although Poole's *Unknown Virginia Woolf* is also mentioned it does not contribute significantly to Baranowska's vision of the writer's life. 'Sekretna wiadomość' is a chronological and factual presentation of the novelist's life, which has no pretensions to moulding opinions about either Woolf herself or her fiction. Although Baranowska clearly lacks the lightness of Niemojewska's style, her dry and verbatim report nicely complements Niemojewska's emotional and impressionistic tone. Occasionally, however, her attempt to give maximum factual information results in a rather peculiar conglomeration of unrelated statements which, although significant and obvious for those familiar with the writer's life, may sound slightly absurd for those who are reading her biography for the first time. An interesting aspect of Baranowska's essay is the attempt to convey the duality of Virginia Woolf's character. The clash of her candour and sociability with the tragedy and gloom of some aspects of her life is reflected in the choice of the two strikingly different portraits of the novelist: the first, by Beresford, portrays Virginia Woolf as a young, beautiful, almost ethereal girl, the second, by Gisèle Freund, shows the sharp and tragically experienced face of a sad, ageing woman.

The first, and so far the only, full-length study of Virginia Woolf's novels was written not by a literary critic but by an art historian, and this may be partly responsible for the originality of his approach to *MD*. Zbigniew Juszczak (1981) argues against those critics who compare Woolf's works with those of Conrad, James or Proust and point to their impressionistic qualities. Virginia Woolf, he argues, belongs to a totally new epoch in the history of art – that of abstract painting. For Juszczak *MD* first and foremost explores the nature of a creative act. Juszczak focuses on the motif of a yellow curtain, which, he claims, is the key to the understanding of the text. The moment when Ralph Lyon beats the curtain back and Clarissa realizes the success of her party is her 'moment of vision', the ultimate experience of form, when chaos is transformed into coherent shape and the external world into a higher reality of art. Although the novel is deprived of an artist at the level of the plot it

---

[17] 'naprawdę książką okropną, utrzymaną w pretensjonalnym, pseudołartobliwym tonie w jaki wpadają czasem wyniosłe damy w rozmowie ze słułbą lub dziećmi'

should be read as 'a portrait of the artist'. The analysis leads Juszczak to a theoretical discussion of the nature of form, which he defines in neo-Platonic terms. Though offering a fresh look on the novel, Juszczak's highly abstract theoretical considerations are written in an obscure way, which overshadows the analysis and makes the reading of his work an arduous task.

After the silent years of martial law in Poland, translation of the Woolf canon is completed and crowned with the publication of *Fale* (*TW*) in 1983. The most difficult of Virginia Woolf's novels is also that which is most beautifully translated. Lech Czyżewski managed to meet the challenge posed by the poetic prose of the text and to render its specific rhythm and imagery. Despite its success in terms of translation, *Fale* did not arouse much response from critics. The voices that made themselves heard reflect the dichotomy of responses which the novel had evoked in Britain fifty years before. While Anna Kołyszko (1983) in her enthusiastic review cherishes the notion of Virginia Woolf's 'uneventful reality' ('bezwydarzeniową rzeczywistość') (35) and clearly finds the novelist's venture into the inner worlds of the six characters fascinating, for Danuta Ulicka (1984) the represented world is extremely artificial and the characters unconvincing. The elevated language and excessive focus on formal experimentation, she writes, strip the characters of psychological authenticity. Although many critics share this opinion, the argument that follows proves to be spurious. Ulicka repeats the objections traditionally put forward against stream of consciousness novels without noticing that, if *Fale* can be seen as artificial and unconvincing, it is so rather for its departure from the typical stream of consciousness novel. In this sense her claim that in the novel the psyche is in 'the domain of chaos and muddle of dark forces' ('domena chaosu i bezładu ciemnych mocy') (148) is groundless. The formal soliloquies of the six speakers are far from the disorderly, broken language of Molly Bloom and can in fact be read as too orderly and formal rather than the reverse. Although differing in their overall evaluation of the novel, both reviewers see the text as being primarily about the experience of an individual in the world of others and consequently neglect the differences between the six speakers' visions of reality.

Kołyszko's description of *TW* as one of 'the classics long consumed and absorbed by Europe' ('klasykę dawno przetrawioną i wchłoniętą przez Europę') (35) reflects the approach which dominated Woolf's reception from the 1960s to 1980s – that Woolf was a difficult but no longer revolutionary writer. The 1990s, however, brought a complete transformation of the writer's image as the modernist edifice was replaced by a more popular picture. The political, economic, and cultural revolution of the 1990s, which brought freedom of speech and a free market economy, opened totally new perspectives for the development of publishing. Previously, all Virginia Woolf's works were published by large, state-owned publishers: PIW, Czytelnik, and Wydawnictwo Literackie. In the 1990s all texts apart from a second edition of *Pani Dalloway* (*MD*) were published by new, private publishers. Under the old system the publishing process was not only long and largely ineffective, but also, in varying degrees, controlled by censorship. At the same time, due to the lack of any competition the publishers did not have to hurry, and this had a positive effect on the quality of translation and editing.

The advantage of the new system is its flexibility and a quick publishing process. Within four years six texts appeared in bookshops: in 1994 *FB* and two different translations of *O*, in 1997 *Własny Pokój* (*ROO*) and the second edition of *Pani Dalloway*, and in 1998 the second edition of *Fale* (*TW*). *TG* is in preparation. The main disadvantage is that the quality of publication is no longer assured, as is clearly apparent when the first and second editions of *Fale* are compared. Although published in the same brilliant translation by Lech Czyżewski, the second has a number of editorial errors.

Since the fortunes of Woolf's works began to be determined by the rules of the market economy there has been a complete change in the profile of the published works. Although *Pani Dalloway* and *Fale* had second editions, they are not the triggers of the writer's popularity but, rather, sell in the wake of interest kindled by her more popular works. In this sense the translation of *O* might be seen as a turning point in the writer's reception. It was the first 'popular' novel by Virginia Woolf published in Poland. Its popularity was further enhanced by its appearance in two 'competitive' translations and the production of Sally Potter's film. However, the factor that seems most vital is that in *O* we can find most issues that will prove crucial to Virginia Woolf's reception in the 1990s: autobiographical elements, feminist and lesbian themes and a widely defined question of transgression. Thus, although the novel did not receive a large number of reviews on publication, it has since become the main point of reference in the discussion of Virginia Woolf's life and work.

The two translations of *O* differ not only in overall mood and tone but also in their solutions to some major translation problems, which are crucial to the novel's meaning. Tomasz Bieroń's free and playful version (*Orlando* (O) 1994a) takes full advantage of rich stylization, relying heavily on archaisms and neologisms. The style is light, even frivolous. He plays with his role as the (re)creator of the text and completes *O* with his own notes concerning the process of translation. He claims, for example, that Orlando's poem was translated by a renowned, Polish, modernist poet, his/her great devotee. Such acts of transgression on the part of the translator, the novel's reviewer rightly contends, are in accordance with the conventions of the text, whose main character transgresses time, space and sex boundaries (Jarniewicz 1996). Next to Bieroń's 'creative' approach to *Orlando*, Wójcik's word-by-word translation sounds rather flat and plodding (*Orlando* (O) 1994b). Although literally closer to the original it fails to reflect the playful nature of Virginia Woolf's text and occasionally sounds artificial and rough in Polish.

However, the main problem faced by the translators was connected with the linguistic implications of the change of Orlando's sex. Polish is an inflected language, and female names have different endings than male, which poses the problem of how to translate the name of Woolf's character. Each translator offered a different solution yet neither is wholly satisfactory. Wójcik left the original male ending thus violating the rules of Polish grammar. Bieroń changed it into Orland*a*, which made the change of sex seem much more radical and complete than in the original version thus distorting the harmony implied in the idea of androgyny. Jarniewicz sees this peculiar situation as, yet again, reflecting the shifting nature of the text:

> It seemed inevitable that the novel, which flickers with a variety of forms and identities, will also appear in a variety of shapes in Polish ... The Polish Orlando has maintained his/her androgynous nature and appeared simultaneously in two forms: male and female. Hence, we have both Orlando and Orland*a*. (1996, 328).[18]

A similar problem will be faced by the translator of *Własny Pokój* (*ROO*), who, when forced to provide the lecture's addressee with a sex, chooses to speak to a female reader, which, naturally, strengthens the feminist tone of the text.

Orlando proves trailblazing in other respects too. In Jarniewicz's review of the novel the term 'modernist' shifts for the first time to 'postmodernist' as he speaks of the 'aesthetics of fragmentation' (1996, 326), 'the great book of change' (324) and 'the play that mocks the human (male?) tendency to classify and define' (325).[19] Apart from the idea of transgression exhibited on all levels of the text, Jarniewicz focuses on the figure of Vita Sackville-West and, briefly, on a wider context of sapphic literature. The same tone dominates the reception of the next novel – *FB*. Rafał Księżyk in his review points to the text's 'contemporary postmodern aura' ('współczesną postmodernistyczną aurę') (1994, 21) discernible in its neglect of all hierarchies. He notes that the element that lies at the root of all of Woolf's works is her deep mistrust of language. The power of *FB*, Księżyk believes, lies in the choice of narrative point of view, which limits the role of language in rendering experience and thus gives the reader a more direct contact with reality. His comment that few works have the advantage of being, like *FB*, interesting to both a literary critic and a nine-year-old child, indicates that the image of Woolf as abstract and difficult is gradually becoming somewhat outdated.

Critical responses to *O* and *FB*, placing these works in the perspective of contemporary literature, reflect one of the trends in Virginia Woolf's reception in the 1990s. Another centres on the publication of *Własny Pokój* (*ROO*) and is connected with the changing climate of feminist thought in Poland. The reason why feminist issues have become urgent in Poland only in the last decade are too complex to be discussed in detail. The core of the problem, however, was formulated by Maria Janion, a renowned literary scholar and feminist critic who, in her book *Kobiety i duch inności* (Women and the Spirit of Otherness) confesses:

> At the end of the 1980s I believed that Solidarity must win independence and democracy for the whole society first and only then focus on the female question and the improvement of the situation of women. (1996, 326).[20]

---

18 'Wydawało się rzeczą nieuniknioną, że powieść, która nieustannie mieni się wielością form i tożsamości, pojawi się w Polsce również pod wieloma postaciami ... Polski Orlando zachował swą androgyniczmą naturę i pojawił się naraz pod dwiema postaciami: męską i kobiecą. Mamy bowiem zarówno Orlanda jak i Orlandę.'

19 'estetyka fragmentu', 'wielką księgą przemian', 'granie na nosie ludzkiej [męskiej?] tendencji do klasyfikowania i definiowania'.

20 The problem was also the subject of hot debate in the popular daily *Gazeta Wyborcza* in the summer of 1999. The debate is worth mentioning also because two articles refer briefly to Virginia Woolf's works.

This opinion, shared by many contemporary women, soon proved mistaken as hopes for equality were gradually thwarted by the increasingly patriarchal character of the new democracy, which brought a gradual activation of the feminist movement.

ROO was quoted in feminist literature before its actual translation. In the first Polish history of women's literature *Cudzoziemki* (Strangers), Grażyna Borkowska refers to Woolf's idea of women's solidarity and her diagnosis of the social and cultural conditions of women writers (1996, 69). Maria Janion in *Kobiety i duch inności* also cites the essay when discussing Virginia Woolf's life and work. Janion draws attention to the striking similarities between the lives and ideas of Virginia Woolf and her Polish contemporary – Maria Komornicka. Both were daughters of noble families, members of liberal, anti-philistine artistic groups and suffered from an unspecified mental illness, which Janion sees as the manifestation of a spiritual conflict. For both, a stay in Cambridge brought an acute sense of exclusion and resulted in a sharp criticism of male-dominated society. Although both believed that a woman artist must transgress the limits of her sex, each understood this transgression differently. While Woolf came up with the idea of androgyny, Komornicka underwent a process of sexual transfiguration, demanding to be referred to and treated as a man. Komornicka clearly lacked Woolf's belief in women's solidarity and therefore, despite a number of striking similarities, her fate was different from that of Virginia Woolf. She was rejected by both men and women and became 'a great illegal figure in the history of Polish literature' (Janion 1996, 253–62).

The factor that contributed to the essay's becoming an important voice in feminist discussion was partly connected with the publication process. *Własny Pokój* (*ROO*) was translated by a feminist critic – Agnieszka Graff – brought out by a publishing house devoted to gender-related literature – Sic! – and completed with an introduction written by a feminist critic and one of the most talented contemporary writers – Izabela Filipiak.

Critical discussion of *Własny Pokój* (*ROO*) focused on two main questions: Virginia Woolf's definition of women's writing and her impact on contemporary feminism with a special focus on the Polish context. The reception was dominated by enthusiastic, pro-feminist voices, the only negative one being that of Wacław Sadkowski (1997), whose more critical stance is reflected in the comparison that he uses to describe Virginia Woolf's role in the feminist movement. For Sadkowski the role of the essay is analogous to that of the Communist Manifesto, whereas other reviewers place Virginia Woolf in a very distinguished context. Aneta Górnicka-Boratyńska writes that:

> Virginia Woolf is for contemporary feminist thought what John Stuart Mill is for today's liberals, Freud for psychoanalysts and neo-psychoanalysts, or Nietzsche for the postmodern critics of culture. (1997, 71)[21]

[21] 'Virginia Woolf jest dla współczesnej myśli feministycznej tym, kim John Stuart Mill dla dzisiejszych liberałów, Freud dla psychoanalityków i neopsychoanalityków albo Nietzschec dla postmodernistycznych krytyków kultury.'

Graff evokes a theological context, calling *ROO* 'a kind of Bible for feminist literary criticism' ('swoistą biblią feministycznej krytyki literackiej') (1997, 299).

Although Sadkowski, at some point of his review, calls his tone jocular, it is, in fact, more patronizing and mocking than jocular and this is reflected in the ironic title, 'Lęki i wdzięki Virginii Woolf' (Virginia Woolf's Charms and Qualms). Sadkowski in a benevolent and patronizing way shows the pitfalls of Woolf's reasoning. Her 'excessive radicalisation of non-conformist ideas and their literary overrefinement' ('nadmiernej radykalizacji nonkonformistycznych poglądów i ich literackiego przerafinowania') (10), he argues, not only negatively affected her writing of the 1930s but ultimately also endangered her own well-being and led to her suicide. For Sadkowski the core fault of the essay lies in the narrow treatment of the problem of discrimination. In a world where discrimination is so universal, that which concerns women is only of minor importance. Sadkowski's claims are characteristic of the contemporary anti-feminist position and are a perfect reflection of the argument formulated by Janion – the once dominant and now challenged belief in the necessity of establishing a hierarchy of discriminations. What Sadkowski does not seem to notice is that he transfers the situation of a communist regime, where discrimination and lack of freedom were so universal that sex was not a political category, onto the totally different reality of Britain in the 1920s. If Sadkowski worries about Virginia Woolf's 'qualms' he truly enjoys her 'charms', which he apparently considers more suitable for a woman. Thus, in *Własny Pokój* (*ROO*) he praises the descriptions of autumn, Woolf's typically feminine 'intimidation by the piles of professional books', 'courting the reader with her lack of academic discipline', as well as her 'authorial insecurity, fear of being rejected or even slighted by literary critics' (10).[22] These opinions, in which Sadkowski is quite isolated, prove that the irony of the essay escaped his attention. Other critics differ not only in the evaluation of Woolf's writing temperament but see her 'charms' as a conscious and deliberate game with the reader.

> [Woolf] formulates thoughts like a naive girl, yet with the sharp intelligence of a child (or an artist) who calls out 'The Emperor has no clothes'; she asks seemingly stupid questions yet expects (particularly of men) honest answers; she wonders, she is astonished, yet all these rhetorical figures are designed to demonstrate and prove her thesis. (Beszczyńska 1997, 43)[23]

---

22 'onieśmielenia stertami książek z zakresu tzw. literatury przedmiotu', 'kokietując czytelnika tym, łe nie nabrała nigdy akademickiej dyscypliny', 'niepewność autorska, obawa przed odrzuceniem czy nawet niedocenieniem przez opinię literacką'

23 'Formułuje myśli niby jak pierwsza naiwna, lecz z przenikliwą inteligencją dziecka (lub artysty) wołającego "król jest nagi"; zadaje pozornie głupie pytania, lecz oczekuje (głównie od mężczyzn) uczciwych na nie odpowiedzi; dziwi się i zdumiewa, lecz te figury stylistyczne służyć mają wyłącznie zademonstrowaniu i udowodnieniu bronionej przez nią tezy.'

In the chorus of appreciative opinions different elements are seen as the essay's greatest asset. For Grzegorz Grochowski (1997), who finds Virginia Woolf's feminism rather obsolete (his review is entitled 'Feminizm w stylu retro' (Retro Feminism)), the essay's value lies primarily in its ingenious form, which reverses the essay-novel of the 1920s. Borrowing such novelistic techniques as fictionalization of the represented world, focus on concrete detail and extended metaphorization, Woolf greatly enriches the possibilities of the genre. Grochowski also praises Woolf's method of getting at the true sense of experience through detailed analysis of its individual components. This method, analogous to that of Proust, is seen as the embodiment of the modernist concept of epiphany. Many critics point to the unity of the essay's 'form' and 'content' seeing it as an important aspect of Woolf's definition of women's literature. The model formulated by Woolf, they claim, is one of the most valuable and up-to-date problems tackled in *Własny Pokój*. Unlike most reviewers, the essay's translator, Agnieszka Graff, believes that in the essay the writer does not give a uniform definition of women's literature. The two opposing concepts found in *Własny Pokój*, writes Graff, that of 'difference' and that of 'androgyny' ('różnicy i androgynii') (1997, 298) are, in fact, equally legitimate and 'the whole text is not conceived as a uniform theory of women's writing, but is a story of how difficult it is to formulate such a theory' (311).[24]

Another element discussed by many critics is the essay's significance for the contemporary Polish reader. Izabela Filipiak (1997), in the introduction to *Własny Pokój*, writes that Woolf's analysis of the factors limiting the intellectual activity of women should be considered in the light of the present-day situation of women in Poland. Zofia Beszczyńska finds the essay very valuable for contemporary (Polish) women though at the same time remains bitter about the potential female readership. Few women, she argues, read such literature and those who do probably do not give it enough attention. The reflection necessary for the reception of Woolf's text is not a popular activity in a country where the term 'feminist' is often considered offensive.

The fact that *Własny Pokój* is considered by many critics, particularly feminist ones, significant for contemporary Polish women is reflected in the essay's appearance in the popular media. Its publication was the theme of a programme 'Ogród Sztuk' (The Garden of Arts) shown in 1998 on the second channel of national TV, which in addition offered a retelling of the writer's life. *Własny Pokój* also found its way into the popular women's magazine, *Wysokie obcasy* (High Heels). Kinga Dunin (1999) quotes from the essay when mocking the chauvinistic ideas of the magazine's male reviewer and cites Virginia Woolf as *the* woman writer missing from the survey concerning the most popular books of the twentieth century.

Virginia Woolf's popularity in Poland continues to be enhanced by the growing interest in her life. The articles published in the 1990s, unlike the previous ones, tend to focus on a specific aspect of the writer's biography. Izabela Filipiak's 'Virginia Woolf, *Orlando*, i stare Bloomsbury' (Virginia

---

[24] 'Całość tekstu jest pomyślana nie jako jednorodna teoria kobiecego pisarstwa, lecz jako opowieść o tym, jak trundle taką teorię zbudować.'

Woolf, *Orlando* and the Bloomsbury Group) tells the story of the writer's life at the time of Old Bloomsbury (1998). Filipiak portrays the whole Group as continually and consciously transgressing social boundaries and sees androgyny as its major manifestation. When highlighting the model of an androgynous society she contrasts the group's members with 'celebrities of Polish culture of the 1990s' ('znanych ludzi kultury lat dziewięćdziesiątych w Polsce') (115), who, unlike the adventurous Bloomsburians, would never dare to transgress their gender-bound natures. A different aspect of Woolf's life is discussed in my article 'Virginia Woolf: biograficzna fikcja czy fikcyjna biografia' (Virginia Woolf: Biographical Fiction or Fictional Biography) (Terentowicz 1998a). Analysing the contemporary state of Woolf research, I point to the advantages and pitfalls resulting from the inseparability of life and writing and trace how different phases of Woolf's reception in England shaped her image and affected the fortunes of individual works. Yet another view of the writer's life can be found in *Wielkie Szalone*, a translation from the German book *Wahnsinns-Frauen*, a collection of biographies of great mad or supposedly mad women (Amrain 1999). The chapter devoted to Virginia Woolf describes the writer as a female genius suppressed by male-dominated culture as represented by her father, stepbrothers and husband. Attention is focused on Woolf's sexuality and her attitude to her own body, both of which were largely neglected in the biographical sketches previously published in Poland.

Apart from the growing interest in the writer's life, the 1990s have also witnessed a significant increase in research into Woolf's individual works. Within the first eight years of the decade thirty-three MA theses were written on Virginia Woolf, which doubled the number from the whole period up to the 1990s. Among English department students, Virginia Woolf is now the third most popular female British novelist, after Iris Murdoch and Jane Austen, and is soon likely to move into second position (Carter 2001). If statistics can reflect the growing interest in Woolf's work it may be worth looking at the amount of space devoted to the writer in the histories of English literature. In Przemysław Mroczkowski's 1981 book there is only one page on Virginia Woolf. In Bałutowa's history of the English novel of the twentieth century (1987) approximately nine pages are devoted to her work. In the history of English literature of the twentieth century that is in preparation for PIW, to which I am contributing a chapter on Virginia Woolf, about fifty pages will be allocated to the writer's life and work.

It is characteristic that academic discussion focuses on the works which were previously little known and are presently less popular. Justyna Kostkowska, in her study of Virginia Woolf's representation of character (1992), analyses *JR* and *TW*. She argues against Bennett's opinion which blames the writer for her inability to portray convincing, life-like characters, though she admits that Woolf's aims were, in fact, impossible to fulfil. Kostkowska explores the writer's own theoretical stand as expressed in 'Mr Bennett and Mrs Brown', and in the light of these considerations analyses the two novels, focusing on issues such as the abandonment of the omniscient narrator, the multiplication and internalization of points of view, the idea of composite identity and the importance of imagery and symbolism.

A detailed analysis of *TW* is also the subject of my two complementary articles: 'Triptych of Non-Verbal Search for Reality: The Female Mind in *The Waves* by Virginia Woolf' (Terentowicz 1996) and 'The World and the Word in *The Waves* by Virginia Woolf' (1995). The first article argues against the categorizations of male and female elements formulated by Hermione Lee in *The Novels of Virginia Woolf*; the second addresses the problem of the modernist struggle with language, and sees the six characters as representing different approaches to verbal communication. In another article, entitled 'Centre and Periphery in *To the Lighthouse*', I analyse the space-time dichotomy at different textual levels (Terentowicz 1998b). The split into spatial ('The Window' and 'The Lighthouse') and temporal ('Time Passes') parts at the level of composition is harmonized with the clash of the human (spatial) and the phenomenal (temporal) perspectives at the level of the represented world. The symbolic unity of Mrs Ramsay and the lighthouse means that the journey to the periphery of the world undertaken by the characters in the last part of the novel can be seen as the return to its emotional centre, represented by Mrs Ramsay.

In terms of Woolf's general reception, the main disadvantage of analytical studies devoted to particular novels is that most are written in English and so cannot reach the general public. As a result, the popular reception of Virginia Woolf's life and work in the 1990s is to a large extent shaped by feminist critics, who focus primarily on the writer's feminism, the question of transgression and androgyny. Consequently, for the general reader in the 1990s, Virginia Woolf is associated primarily with two works, *O* and *ROO*. Although neither her diaries nor any full-length biography of Virginia Woolf have been published so far, the story of her life, with the scandalous madness and suicide, is a recognized feature.[25] It is not accidental that in the 1990s three out of the six published books appeared with her portrait by Beresford on the front cover. The fact that Virginia Woolf's face has become a publishers' marketing tool suggests that for readers it is not only a recognizable image, but also a kind of lure. Although saying that Virginia Woolf has become a popular cultural icon might be an exaggeration, she has certainly been adopted by the reading public. Whether as a mother figure or as an advocate of androgyny, a mad woman or a sharp-minded intellectual, a victim of male-dominated culture or a clever and uncompromising trespasser of social boundaries, she is no longer the distant and slightly obsolete author of a few once revolutionary works.

---

25 Apart from the Diary and a full-length biography, the list of exceptions includes the first three novels, *BTA*, *RF*, the letters and most of the short stories.

8 'Literature is no one's private ground': The Critical and Political Reception of Virginia Woolf in Sweden

Catherine Sandbach-Dahlström

> Literature is no one's private ground; literature is common ground. It is not cut up into nations; there are no wars there. Let us trespass freely and fearlessly and find our way for ourselves. It is thus that English literature will survive this war and cross the gulf – if commoners and outsiders like ourselves make that country our own country, if we teach ourselves how to read and to write, how to preserve, and how to create.
>
> ('The Leaning Tower', *WE*, 178)

To start this essay on the reception of Woolf in another country with a quote from a text devoted to the fate of literature in England might seem perverse. However, as the epigraph suggests, Woolf's dislike of the erection of national borders extended to literature as well. 'The Leaning Tower' ends with a denial of boundaries and a Utopian gesture towards a future where the constraints of class and nation would cease to determine literary value. The reader from a different country will, of course, always already be an Outsider displaced from the type of understanding that characterizes a national interpretive community. In other words, lacking the kind of cultural coding engendered by class and national affiliation, certain aspects of Woolf's life and writing may be opaque to them. The reception of Woolf in Sweden has thus sometimes been formed by the ideological preconceptions of the culture and some responses appear as reading against the grain or even as misunderstanding. Be that as it may, much Swedish response is sensitive and perceptive; presumably because Sweden's engagement in the wider project of modernity has enabled a number of Swedish critics to explore the literary territory that lies beyond the more superficial differences of place and national culture. Woolf's status as a modernist experimenter has been recognized from the start and her politics have often received a good press. Moreover, Woolf's standing in Sweden endorses the doctrine of *CR,* and other essays, namely that the true critic is the general reader who approaches the text without the disadvantages of a classical education or the blinkers of received notions of value.

My prime focus then is upon the response of the 'common reader', the critical and political reception in the press and in the universities, rather than upon Woolf's influence on Swedish fiction. My own sense is that any such influence upon the major writers has been of lesser importance. There are a number of explanations for this. Firstly, Swedish experimental modernist prose's obvious debt is to the male modernists. Joyce's internal stream of consciousness has been an important and acknowledged influence, as has 'D.H. Lawrence-inspired [*sic*] primitivism and sexual mysticism', which according to Ingemar Algulin, 'swept through Swedish literature around 1930' (1989, 192). In the succeeding years other important sources of inspiration have been Hemingway, Faulkner, Kafka and Sartre (Algulin 1989, 204). Secondly, much of the important Swedish fiction of the 1930s to 1950s is of epic proportion, frequently proletarian in its roots and concerns, and thus somehow foreign to the Woolfian ethos. This applies very definitely to one of the most important woman novelists of this period, Moa Martinsson (1890–1964). Moreover, prominent present-day women writers such as Sara Lidman and Kerstin Ekman continue a tradition of representing the fast-vanishing peasant way of life in the more remote parts of the country, and the latter in particular has departed ever more from her original realistic mode, moving towards a magic realism with roots in a Christian mysticism that is philosophically divorced from Woolf's epiphany. Agnes von Krusenstjerna (1894–1940) is the only contemporary with whom Woolf, primarily for reasons of class, is supposed to have an affinity. However, von Krusenstjerna's openly Freudian eroticism is a far cry from Woolf's studies in repression. Krusenstjerna's critique of gender characteristics is similar to Woolf's, but since there is no evidence that she had read *O* this may be evidence of a post-Freudian acceptance of bisexuality rather than anything else (Svanberg 1989, 381).

If Woolf's influence on the actual form of fiction has been marginal, her presence on the cultural scene is assured. In the course of investigating her reception in Sweden I have discovered that her work is known and appreciated by several categories of reader, and that prominent members of the Swedish cultural elite have often acknowledged her importance. I have also discovered that the 'Woolf' known to the Swedes is as composite and varied a creature as indeed is the 'Woolf' of Anglo-America.

*

As in Britain and America, interest in Woolf has exploded in the last twenty years. In the 1960s and 1970s, even if several works had been translated, the Swedish common readers and university students of English would often have known of her through grudging comments in literary historical reference works. One such notes somewhat patronizingly that 'Virginia Woolf's novels were highly valued earlier; but today her aestheticizing art must only attract a smaller number of readers' (Levander and Annergren 1971, 197, quoted by Ritamäki 1991, 246).[1] Similar views were to be found in widely used

---

[1] 'Virginia Woolfs romaner värderas tidigare mycket högt; i dag torde hennes estetiserande författarskap locka endast ett mindre antal läsare.' Levander and

textbooks like Anthony Burgess's *English Literature* (1958) or Walter Allen's *The English Novel* (1954). Burgess dismisses Woolf as hard to classify and of lesser importance than Jane Austen, while Allen – though trying to be fair – finds it hard to conceal his distaste for Woolf's aesthetic. 'At present,' he writes in 1954 of Woolf's declining reputation:

> The reaction against her work is probably at its greatest, and I must admit to sharing it. Much of her fiction seems to me marred by portentousness, and I cannot escape the feeling that from time to time the exercise of sensibility has become an end in itself. Nor do the moments of revelation and illumination always seem illuminative in any very real sense; they are rather a succession of short, sharp, female gasps of ecstasy, an impression intensified by Mrs Woolf's use of the semi-colon where the comma is ordinarily used. All the same, it is difficult not to believe that the future will see her as an indubitable minor master of the novel, who expressed with lyrical intensity her apprehension of the beauty and terror of life. (1954, 351)

Although the cultural climate has changed, this conception of Woolf as important primarily as a modernist experimenter took time to change and continues to inform some of the literary handbooks encountered by students at the equivalent of sixth-form colleges. Sverker Göransson remarks in 1972 on how 'Woolf's prose is softer and more impressionistic and sensitive than Joyce's, whereas her register and ambitions are significantly more restricted than those of the Irishman. Where he wishes to give a complete picture of life, she provides us with a psychologically penetrating depiction of the educated English upper class whose taste and cultural refinement do not differ noticeably from her own' (Göransson 1972, 363).[2] Similarly Joyce's pre-eminence is reasserted in a number of ways in an adapted dictionary of famous twentieth-century writers (*Vem är vem i världslitteraturen* (Who's Who in World Literature) (1998)). Apart from praising Joyce's superior skill (her career is defined in relation to his, but not the reverse) the volume also offers a visual image of a youngish middle-aged man looking assertively out at the reader. In contrast, the photograph of Woolf is of an adolescent, crouched in her father's shadow; her body language expressing the inhibitions and uncertainties typical of this phase of life. Joyce's life and career is figured as a heroic struggle – against glaucoma and the intolerance of critics and authorities – whereas Woolf is represented as publishing her own work for (a coterie of) her friends and as failing finally in the struggle with life (Goring 1998, 170, 343).

Responses like this are familiar to the historian of taste or literary reputation, and in several ways the Swedish 'reception' reproduces features

---

cont.

Annergren also observe that Joyce and Lawrence are the truly central figures of the time. Woolf, however, is regarded as even more subtle than Forster (197).

2 '[Hennes prosa] är av mjukare mera impressionistisk och sensibel [karaktär]', '[hennes] register och ambitioner är betydligt mera begränsade än irländarens: där han vill ge en total bild av livet ger hon en psykologiskt inträngande skildring av bildad engelska överklass, vars smak och kulturella förfining inte skiljer sig uppseendeväckande från hennes egen.'

well known to us from the Anglo-American scene. In 1927 when *JR* first appeared in an authorized Swedish translation it was in a series entitled 'Den Nya Romanen' (The New Novel) devoted to new experimental writing around the world. The choice of novels – the Czech writer, Karel Čapek's *Krakatit* (1925; trans. 1926); the Americans, Christopher Morley's *Thunder on the Left* (1924; trans. 1926), and Willa Cather's *The Professor's House* (1925; trans. 1927); as well as Austrian, Leo Perutz's *Zwischen neun und neun* (Between Nine and Nine) (1918; trans. 1927) – now seems idiosyncratic and very much reflected the interests of the publisher, Hugh Geber. In including Woolf, however, Geber marks her as belonging to what he saw as the elite of the younger authors in Europe. Nonetheless, the reception of *JR* suggests that the critical climate in Sweden at this point closely resembled that in Britain. Novels were expected to provide the satisfactions of realism, to offer plot and conventional studies of 'character'. Much of the critical comment simply repeated the incomprehension of British critics schooled in 'materialism'. One of the leading daily papers remarked that whereas 'Miss Virginia [sic] might please the Seventh Day Adventists of the literary world', the novel 'gave an impression of confusion where artifice was more powerful than art' (Lutherson 1988).[3]

A fascinating example of the critical climate at the time comes from Arthur Lundquist in 1933. A modernist poet, an important critic and later one of the most dominant figures of the Swedish Academy, Lundquist is evidently torn between dissatisfaction and admiration. Repeating the usual accusation that, being an upper-class lady, Woolf lacked contact both with conditions of the ordinary world and her own body, he remarks, on the one hand, that despite her 'fertile imagination and inexhaustible creative power', Woolf's writing is the result of a cool need for sublimation and consequently lacks 'sexuality, sensuality, contact with skin and body and with the secret deep self' (Lundquist, 1933, 44).[4] He is seduced on the other hand by the poetry of *TW*. Here Woolf fully captures the stream of consciousness: 'a river of strong, shifting impressions, an-ever changing flood of landscapes, cities and situations'. Indeed, 'she is on her way towards an independent subjective poetics which to the modern mind that follows her on this path is an experience quite without banality' (1933, 47).[5]

Although there is evidence of an endemic interest in Woolf's writing, particularly among intellectuals such as Lundquist, its full importance was not recognized until the 1980s in response, no doubt, to the explosion of critical

---

[3] 'Romanen gör ett trasigt och förvirrat intryck, förkonstling är starkare än konsten ... kanske kan "Miss Virginia" behaga "de yttersta dagarnas heliga litteratur sekt"' (Lutherson quotes Carl-August Bolander in *Dagens Nyheter*, 1927).

[4] '[Hon besitter] en alstrande fantasi, en artistisk skaparkraft av till synes outtömliga resurser ... [de saknar] sexualitet, sinnlighet, kontakten med hud och kroppar, med det hemliga, mörka jaget.'

[5] 'en flod av starka, brokiga intryck, en ständigt förbirinnande flod med landskap, städer, situationer ... hon är på väg mot en oavhängig, subjektiv dikt och för moderna hjärnor är det en upplevelse utan all banalitet att följa henne på denna väg.'

studies and the re-visioning work of feminist criticism.[6] An early dissertation, Kerstin Elert's *Portraits of Women in Selected Novels by Virginia Woolf and E. M. Forster* (1979), while very lightweight in itself, can be thought of as initiating this trend. Since then Woolf's aesthetic has increasingly been the subject for serious review in academia in general, and in departments of English in particular. Adrian Velicu's thesis, *Unifying Strategies in Virginia Woolf's Experimental Fiction* (1985), in acknowledging the scope and seriousness of contemporary Woolf criticism is representative of the re-evaluation that has characterized the last two decades of Anglo-American scholarship. Ironically, it may also be that Norwegian Toril Moi's much-publicized re-evaluation of Woolf in *Sexual/Textual Politics* (1985) has contributed significantly to Woolf's reputation. In addition, scholars such as myself with their roots in the English-speaking world have carried out some of the task of dissemination. Mark Troy, a distinguished American student of modernism, in an essay entitled 'A Wedge-Shaped Core of Darkness' (1988), contributed to the ongoing reassessment by tracing the influence of Conrad on Woolf's writing, while my own early contribution is an essay, 'The Moth and the Fish', which draws attention to some recurring images for the creative process in Woolf's œuvre (Sandbach-Dahlström 1986).[7] These contributions are, however, rather disparate: it would not be possible to speak of the emergence from English departments of a Swedish 'school of Woolf'.

While academic criticism has slowly but surely freed itself from the influence of the literary histories, it seems that the textbook views have had little impact on common readers. It may be that they gain their information from book reviews or direct contact with British culture. Whatever the source of inspiration, there is every indication from the evidence of book sales, the number of translations, as well as library holdings and borrowing statistics, of Woolf's early and abiding popularity.

Who reads Woolf? If library holdings are anything to go by a great many people do. Woolf's texts have been made widely available and the fact that no other English modernist enjoys a similar coverage suggests her pre-eminence. E. M. Forster comes a poor second, and D. H. Lawrence lags far behind. The public libraries' database fascinatingly reveals that translations of *ROO* and *TL* are held from north to south, in towns and villages even in very remote areas.[8] Where immigrant groups are fairly large there are also translations into Polish and Finnish, Spanish and Serbo-Croatian. But admittedly more demanding texts, *TW* or *MB,* are only held in the larger cities and richer suburbs.

These holdings reflect an official policy, of course. Swedish public libraries have traditionally disseminated high culture throughout the country in

---

6 Early critical studies of Woolf's writing were bought by Swedish libraries – see for instance the Nobel Library's holding of Winifred Holtby's *Virginia Woolf* (1932) and Ruth Gruber's *Virginia Woolf: A Study* (1935) in the Royal Library.

7 I mention these two essays particularly since they are directed to a Scandinavian readership in the first place. Mark Troy has also published an essay on patriarchal myth in *BTA* outside Sweden (1998).

8 BURK at www.btj.se

accordance with democratic ideals of mass education that would have delighted the Woolf of 'The Leaning Tower'. Parliamentary bills regulating the libraries have even insisted on it being their duty to promote quality works.[9] Typically then, the official policy of the central public library for the county of Jämtland (in the sparsely populated north) is the purchase of works of literary and stylistic merit which 'stimulate the imagination and extend the readers' understanding of their own reality as well as that of others'.[10]

Needless to say holdings are one thing, readers another. However, several Woolf novels are regularly borrowed. A random check indicates that the figures after 1993 for Alingsås – a small Swedish town in the west where the translations of *TL* and *MD* are often taken out – are typical. The original texts are also borrowed, though to a lesser extent. The same goes for the translations of *O* and *BTA*. If we compare these statistics with those for Lawrence the differences are suggestive. The translation of *Women in Love* has been borrowed regularly, though only once in 1999, and by no means as often as the Woolf texts. No one has ever borrowed the translation of *Aaron's Rod* or Lawrence's poetry. On the other hand, *Lady Chatterley's Lover,* both in the original, in translation and as an audiocassette, is more popular even than Woolf's novels. The explanation for this latter statistic lies presumably beyond issues of purely literary value. Be that as it may, the figures as a whole mark Woolf's privileged position as a 'classic' author.[11]

As I have indicated, up until the 1980s only a smaller selection of works was available in translation. Despite the enthusiasm of some literary figures for Woolf's work, few of her books were translated in the early years. Following *JR* the next text to be published in Swedish was *TY* (Åren) in 1942 to be followed in the 1950s by *TL* (Mot fyren) (1953) and Jane Lundblad's excellent translation of *ROO* (Ett eget rum) (1958). This volume also contained 'On Not Knowing Greek' and 'How One Should Read a Book' from *CR*. Otherwise, until a magazine translation of 'Professions for Women' (Kvinnor och yrkesliv) appeared along with an introductory essay by Brita Enoksson (1988), the only other essays to be published were 'Montaigne' and 'Jane Austen' from *CR* along with 'The Leaning Tower' in a volume with that name (Det lutande tornet) (1952). Following the translation of *MD* and *MB* the 1980s saw the publication in Swedish of several of the lesser known works, *O, FB, TG* and Susan Dick's *CSF*. This process owes much to the enthusiasm and empathetic involvement of the translator, Margareta Ekström, and the illness

---

9 See 'Proposition 1984/85:141: Om litteratur och folkbibliotek' (Bill entitled 'on literature and public libraries').

10 '[Stor vikt läggs vid litteratur] som har god språklig och litterär form, som stimulerar fantasi och inlevelse och som vidgar läsarens förståelse för sin egen och andras verklighet.' *Medieurvalsprinciper för Jämtlands Läns Bibliotek* (Principles of Selection for the County of Jämtland's Public Library, 1998), Ostersund: Jämtlands Läns Bibliotek, 1998.

11 The figures from the County of Jämtland's Public Library show that *TL* in translation is the most frequently borrowed of all. *ROO* comes a poor second.

that interrupted her work was an unfortunate break in the chain.[12] *BTA* was not translated until 1993. *The Voyage Out* as well as most of the essays remains untranslated to this day, while *Night and Day*, on the initiative of the translator Maria Ekman, appeared at last in April of 2000.

Translations vary in quality needless to say. Jane Lundblad's scholarly translations of *ROO* and *TW* (1980) hold their own today,[13] but Ingegerd Wiking's translation of *BTA* contains a number of inaccuracies that actually affect meaning. The translation of *TL* now seems outdated and pedestrian; unfortunately, the major publishing house has recently reissued it in a cheap pocket edition. Considering the unwillingness of Swedish publishers to market their own classics, the interest they have nonetheless shown in Woolf is actually remarkable. Over the years the translations have been printed and reprinted, both by leading firms and smaller publishers whose policy it is to promote avant-garde writing or satisfy minority interests. Several of these editions have introductions by critics and these are often excellent. For instance, *TL* has a very perceptive introduction by a prominent literary figure, Anders Österling, who appreciates how Woolf 'captured the play of memory and momentary insights, the flashing rhythm of the senses, the mysterious and incomprehensible nature of time passing that is recorded in the life of the human soul' (1953, 5).[14]

Translators are important disseminators of knowledge about Woolf too, but in this respect they may be less than successful. In a postscript to *BTA*, for instance, Wiking emphasizes Woolf's anguish upon completing her books while making little attempt to address the content or implications of the novel (139–41). A similar emphasis on the personal is to be found in Jane Lundblad's postscript to *TW* where the parallels are drawn between Orlando and Vita Sackville-West and Percival and Thoby Stephen, and where the rhythm of the waves beating on the shore is placed against Woolf's own death 'in the waves' (1980, 279).

Other introductions accept the often repeated view that Woolf's ambitious project is somehow a failure. Per Erik Wahlund's introduction to *Det lutande tornet* repeats the not uncommon view that Woolf is more successful as an

12 I had very much wished to interview Margareta Ekström in connection with writing this piece. Sadly she has been afflicted by a stroke and is unable to speak. Ekström was born in 1930 and is a prominent writer of short stories. She has also published a number of novels dealing primarily with the theme of love which have been praised for their psychological sensitivity. She was the leading translator of Woolf in the 1980s, complementing the existing distinguished translations of the major texts with *O, FB*, *TG* and Susan Dick's *CSF*.

13 A university lecturer with a PhD on Hawthorne, Lundblad was a much respected expert on literature in English in Stockholm in the 1950s and 1960s.

14 '[fångade] spelet av minnesbilder och ögonblicksbelysningar, sinnesintryckens ilande rytm, det mysteriöst ogripbara i själva tidsförloppet, sådant det avspeglar sig i mänskligt själsliv'. Unfortunately, however, the emphasis on Woolf's refinement now in contrast to Joyce's animal force appears once again here: '[hennes romaner saknar] spontanitet, energi, egentlig livskraft'. (Her novels lack spontaneity, energy or any real life force.)

essayist than a novelist. Wahlund clearly does not feel at home with Woolf's aesthetic aims. The novels, we learn, are without 'spontaneity, energy, and true life force'. Moreover:

> Glittering poetically like the sun on the sea, what are Virginia Woolf's novels but an inadequately objectified testimony to her own problems of adjustment? There is nothing final or rounded about them. They present irredeemably anonymous human destinies, seen through the eyes of others or living in their memory .... In Virginia Woolf we encounter refined psychological details and nuances on the verge of the precious, and it is hard to feel at home with her sensitive souls. (Wahlund 1952, 7)[15]

Ekström's critical introductions, as I shall have cause to consider below, are lightweight and subjective. It may too have been her somewhat uncritical admiration for Bloomsbury that promoted the translation of Quentin Bell's biography in 1991. (It was followed by Frances Spalding's illustrated, coffee-table selection of letters, *Paper Darts,* the following year.) The decision to publish was an expression of the enthusiasm of the publisher's editors, partly for Woolf, but also for Bell's book, which they saw as being in the best tradition of English literary biography.[16] I am told by the publisher, Forum, that despite enthusiastic reviews both books sold badly and were quickly remaindered. Ironically though, at just this moment reviewers on national television and in the press recommended Bell's book. As a consequence all the remaining copies were sold overnight: the book has, however, not been reprinted. Personally I cannot regret this since translations of both Bell's life and *Paper Darts* reproduce the Woolf/Bloomsbury cult for foreign consumption, and emphasize the details of the life at the expense of Woolf's significance for literature.

As no other life has been translated – and in the light of the commercial failure of the Bell biography it is unlikely that any will be – the Swedish common reader who cannot, or does not, read English will only have access to other perspectives through the mediation of critics and reviewers. Luckily, the Swedish papers have provided both information and much useful and well-informed criticism. New material published in Britain (Andrew McNeillie's edition of the essays for instance) and new Swedish translations are reviewed as they appear, and reissues of the older translations have provided occasions for retrospective reviews.[17]

---

15 'Och vad är Virginia Woolfs' romaner annat än bristfälligt objektiverade och poetiskt havskimrande vittnesbörd om hennes egna anpassningssvårigheter? Det har inget avrundat eller slutgiltigt över sig .... Det är en till preciositetens gräns förfinad detalj och valörpsykologi som möter oss hos Virginia Woolf, och vi har svårt att känna oss hemma bland hennes sensitivor och mimoser.'

16 The publisher had produced reprints of both *MD* and *TL*. Unfortunately my informant, Viveca Petersson, who worked for the company at the time, does not remember who actually suggested Bell's biography. Nor does she really know why so much time elapsed between the original publication and the decision to translate.

17 For McNeillie see Malmberg 1994.

As in the English-speaking world, the Swedish reading public's interest in Woolf's writing is accompanied by a fascination with the life and with Bloomsbury. Not surprisingly then, the Swedish edition of Bell's biography was reviewed in many places. Due no doubt to the wonderful translation many critics were seduced by the rhetoric and aesthetics of this work. With notable exceptions, such as Olof Lagercrantz's account of August Strindberg (1979), Sweden lacks the tradition of literary biography so typical for Britain and America. Critics were impressed by the skill with which Bell described his aunt's life and accepted – more or less at face value – the authority of his privileged account. As one of them wrote, 'This life of Virginia Woolf is a wonderful piece of writing. The book is like a good friend to whom one returns with joy and from whom one would never be separated' (Söderberg 1991, 4).[18] This same critic, moreover, was particularly delighted by Bell's version of Woolf's mental illness and the treatments to which she was subjected, seeing it as a welcome counter-balance to the excesses of feminism. (Söderberg is known for her anti-feminist views and is presumably referring to American feminist criticism, perhaps even to Jane Marcus, though this is purely speculative.) Despite all the praise, there are a couple of qualifying voices, however. Interestingly, it is in the socialist paper, *Arbetet* (Work), that Carl-Eric Nordberg recognizes that Bell's detailed account of the social scene, the drawing-room existence from which Virginia Woolf rises like a phoenix, actually inadequately veils the demons that tormented her soul (1992, 4).[19] Sara Danius (a critic with a PhD in comparative literature) writing in the major national newspaper – and from a wider knowledge of Woolf scholarship – places Bell against DeSalvo and, while recognizing that DeSalvo is writing a book on incest rather than a biography of Woolf, suggests acutely that Bell's urbane manner conceals a number of family skeletons (1992, 4).

Like Bell's life, *Paper Darts* has been extensively reviewed – more than the translation of *BTA* and *TG* – and the commentators, naturally enough, repeat the information it contains about Bloomsbury and Woolf's private life, highlighted as these aspects are by the principles of selection upon which the book is based. As an introduction to a reality other than that of Sweden's common readers it also presents a somewhat skewed perspective on British middle-class life. (Not so surprisingly, some of the reviewers have difficulty in distinguishing between the intelligentsia to which the Stephen family belonged and the aristocracy to whom they were only rather distantly related.[20]) It is obvious, in fact, that Spalding's collection, while providing a useful

---

18 'Biografin over Virginia Woolf är skön författarkonst. Boken blir en vän man återvänder till med glädje och helst skulle aldrig skulle vilja skiljas ifrån.'

19 Nordberg came to Bell direct from Anthony Burgess's autobiography where Woolf was viciously attacked for her ladylike qualities and hypocrisy, and dares to make the radical suggestion that both writers were actually tormented by the same need to grasp the fleeting moments that lead us steadily towards our deaths.

20 One example of the kind of misunderstanding that can arise is to be found in a review of the reprint of *JR* which records that Woolf was born into the English aristocracy and that her first books were modelled on the Elizabethan novel (Källestål 1989).

introduction to the visual aesthetics of Woolf's circle, has reinforced the common perception of her as an over-refined member of the British upper classes who commonly panicked when confronted by the realities of everyday life or physicality. As one reviewer puts it somewhat acidly, 'The reader of *Paper Darts* is strengthened in the belief that this woman must have lived an outwardly good life with few financial worries, surrounded by authors and artists drenched in intellectual stimulus, and with time to spend on creative work without being disturbed by housekeeping problems or the need to earn a living' (Söderberg 1993, 4).[21] There is one dissenting voice, however: in *Arbetarbladet* (The Workers' Sheet) Anne Brugge proposes that the drama suggested by this collection of letters resembles a performance of *Hamlet* where everybody dies at the end. Brugge remarks shrewdly that a small selection of letters (there are after all more than 4000 preserved) cannot tell us the truth about a person's life, and refreshingly she questions the face value of Virginia Woolf's often-reprinted suicide letter to Leonard. 'What indeed would one write,' she asks with some sarcasm, 'if one were reasonably well brought up and perhaps ashamed at having reached the limits of one's endurance?' (1995, 4).[22]

★

Woolf's reputation among reviewers has its equivalent among Swedish scholars. She is now widely read and taught in departments of Comparative Literature and articles have appeared in prominent journals. In 1991, for instance, *Tidskrift för litteraturvetenskap* (Journal of Comparative Literature) published two interesting pieces by Mona Sandquist and Margareta Petersson. Independently of Patricia Laurence's *Reading of Silence* (1991), Sandquist argues that the repression of homosexual desire, Lily's for Mrs Ramsay and Carmichael's for Andrew, as well as the unspoken tensions in the Ramsay (Stephen) marriage, produces a series of textual displacements or gaps. Although she does not relate this to the famous ellipses, Sandquist's account is convincing when she remains close to the text: she provides a compelling reading of the troubled emotions of the Ramsays' relationship suggested by the tale of the fisherman and his wife as well as by the apocalyptic tone of some passages ('Never did anybody look so sad. Bitter and black, halfway down in the darkness in the shaft which ran from sunlight to the depths' (*TL* (1977), 31). The return to the autobiographical element at the end of this essay is less original or interesting in itself, and represents the – to my mind – unfortunate need for the kind of biographical explanation that bedevils Woolf studies generally.

---

21 'De som tar del av 'Din tillgivna Virginia' stärks i sin övertygelse att det måste har varit ett ytligt sett gott liv hon levde denna kvinna med få ekonomiska bekymmer, omgiven av författare och konstnärer i ett flöde av intellektuell stimulans med tid att ägna sig åt konstnärligt skapande utan att störas av varken hushållsbekymmer eller knegamödor'. Not surprisingly another reviewer, in a socialist newspaper, repeats the often-voiced accusations of snobbery by picking out Woolf's reaction to Maynard Keynes's choice of a wife and remarks too upon the ingratiating tone of the letters to Ottoline Morrell (Nordberg 1993).

22 'Vad skriver man om man är någorlunda väluppfostrad och kanske skäms för att inte härda ut.'

Margareta Petersson's study of the rhythmic patterns in the novel engages more with other criticism and is more cogent. The novel's movement, she argues, is 'characterized as an oscillation between dispersal and gathering where dispersal is thematically marked by destruction, darkness and mortality whereas re-gathering denotes unity and light' (1991, 23).[23] In a third essay, Christina Sjöblad discusses the allusions to Renaissance art, the more specific correspondences between Mrs Ramsay and the Madonna, and particularly the form of the triptych which, she believes, determines the tripartite structure of the book (1992). A significant aspect of her article is its dependence on Anglo-American criticism, indicating the powerful influence of American criticism in particular on the study of women writers.[24] An equally significant feature of all three articles is their focus on the aesthetic and philosophical aspects of Woolf's fiction rather than on issues of androgyny or gender politics. Sjöblad's essay with its emphasis on Mrs Ramsay's mythical status is even conceived as a response to those feminists (unfortunately she does not name them) who have criticized Woolf's reactionary endorsement of Victorian womanhood. For Sandquist and Petersson, however, these issues remain a part of the unspoken in their texts.

Petersson speaks of double exposure in *TL* and much the same could be said of the configuration of 'Woolf' in the Swedish context. There is the Bloomsbury, aesthetic Woolf, and there is the political Woolf. The contrast is suggested by the translators' introductions to *ROO* and *O* respectively. Jane Lundblad writes in the former of the extent of Woolf's political contacts, remarking that the reader who pays attention 'soon notes that he [sic] is in the company of someone who was not only historically and literarily trained but was also politically schooled' (1958, 6).[25] Ekström, in contrast, finds that the diaries reveal 'not the fine lady with the long pearl necklace and the cutting irony' but a perpetually girlish figure 'with a clear view of the shifting nuances in the seasons of nature and of man' (1982, 221).[26] Of course Ekström cannot avoid mentioning the gender role-playing in *O*, yet this phenomenon is explained only in terms of the private life, while the novel's bitter critique of male writers and critics, as well as the wider ideological implications of its deconstruction of identity, are passed over. In this Ekström is true to her refusal to acknowledge the feminist Woolf outright. Criticizing Lundblad for writing in the introduction to *TW* that Woolf stood 'on the feminist battlefront', Ekström writes elsewhere: 'I have difficulty in associating her with

---

23 '[Rytmen i boken som helhet] kan karaktäriseras som en växling mellan upplösning och hopsamling, där upplösningen tematiskt sett kännetecknas av destruktion, mörker och förgänglighet, hopsamlingen av helhet och ljus.'

24 Sjöblad cites Stevie Davies's *Virginia Woolf: 'To the Lighthouse'* (1989), Blotner's 'Mythic Patterns in *To the Lighthouse*' (1956) and Moi (1985).

25 'märker snart att han befinner sig i sällskap med en inte bara historiskt och litterärt utan också politiskt bevandrad person.'

26 'I stället för den fina damen med de långa pärlhalsbanden och den rakknivsvassa ironin, lär man känna en läs och livshungrig evig flicka med vaken blick för de skiftande nyanserna i naturens och människonaturens årstider.'

any kind of front or barricade. She struggled bravely with death within her, death in life, until she took her life in the waves' (1981, 3).[27]

Biographical criticism, presumably because of a formalist bias in the universities, is uncommon. The biographical point of view appears mostly in reviews and translators' notes where, as we have seen, the familiar tale of incest and madness is rearticulated for foreign consumption. Students, in contrast, commonly adopt an either/or approach to Woolf, either aesthetics or gender politics. Following upon the success of Sally Potter's film, *O* is often the chosen text for the latter, although students also choose to write feminist analyses of Clarissa Dalloway or Mrs Ramsay as Victorian women.[28] *O* is, however, especially popular because it accommodates the ongoing critique of gender dichotomy, and because it is amenable to 'queer' studies and to current theories of gender as performance. One particularly successful student essay from the University of Lund, by Nina Björk, has even resurfaced as part of a recent popular feminist polemic entitled: *Under det rosa täcket : om kvinnlighetens vara och feministiska strategier* (Under the Pink Coverlet: Femininity and Feminist Strategies) (1996).

Some students note that *O,* far from being a representation of androgyny, or a questioning of gender roles, actually deconstructs the whole relation between gender and identity or the self. One title sums this trend up rather neatly 'Orlando through the Centuries: She Was a Man, He Was a Woman' (Kane 1997).[29] In a related vein, a graduate student extends the argument beyond gender to discuss the connection between ageing bodies and the fear of death and sexuality in *MD*. She suggests that:

> Woolf dissolves the differences between the sexes by dissolving personality and the body itself: 'But often now this body she wore ... this body, with all its capacities, seemed nothing – nothing at all' (*MD*, 11). The characters become no-body at all. Thus the difference between man and woman in this constellation of characters [Clarissa, Peter, Septimus] is not distinct (Posti 1997, 3).

In March of 1999 a prominent literary journalist and popularizer of English works, Ruth Halldén, noted that although '[Woolf] was more of a poet than an epic writer and her novels were thought by many to be far too free floating and mysterious ... the modern reader is so inured to this mode that they hardly experience the difficulties' (1999, B3).[30] This is true of university students who have not grown up with nineteenth-century realism as the norm

---

27 'Jag har svårt att förknippa henne med några som helst fronter eller barrikader. Med döden inom sig, döden i livet, kämpade hon tappert tills hon tog sitt liv i vågorna.'

28 See for instance Gabriella Westerlund's 'Killing the Angel in the House: Women's Roles in Virginia Woolf's *To the Lighthouse*' (1998).

29 A similar idea is explored in another student paper, Linda Svenneros' 'Identity in Virginia Woolf's Orlando: Gender – Intrinsically Connected with Sex or Not?' (University of Gothenburg, 1999).

30 'Hon var mycket mer av poet än epiker, och hennes romaner ansågs av många alltför utsvävande och gåtfulla. Dock är läsare av i dag så härdade att de knappt ser svårigheterna.'

– and in the case of Swedish students scarcely met with it during their education – but rather with the narrative provided by moving pictures, or indeed with the anti-narrative provided by MTV. In the light of the cinematic effects of much of Woolf's prose, then, it is hardly surprising that these younger readers can approach her without being troubled by fragmentation, lack of obvious plot or conventional character description. Student writing that does not deal with the gender issue commonly looks appreciatively to aesthetic and structural qualities in her work. Much of this writing is sophisticated and even original. Maura Tavares's 'Virginia Woolf Paints with Words: Pictorial Qualities in *Jacob's Room* and *Orlando*' (1996) presents a series of fascinating correspondences between textual features and Impressionist and post-Impressionist painting. Tavares's Scandinavian background allows her to note the connection between Munch's elliptic modes of painting (in *Evening in Saint-Cloud*) and Woolf's 'eyeless' picture of Jacob (1996, 20). From the University of Gothenburg, Helena Svanberg's 'Multiple Voices: The Relationship between Discourse and Consciousness in Virginia Woolf's *Mrs Dalloway*' uses Kristeva, Foucault and a number of prominent critics of Woolf (Geoffrey Hartman and Harvena Richter, for example) to map the multiple discourses present in the novel, and thereby to demonstrate how 'language proves to be both liberating and repressive' for both Septimus and Clarissa (1998, 30). A similar constructive use of literary theory is seen in Annelie Arvström's 'Performance as Narrative and Narrative as Performance in Virginia Woolf's *Between the Acts*' where she argues for a reading which sees the whole narrative and not only the pageant as performance (1998).

In its awareness of aesthetic issues university students' figuration of 'Woolf' is rather different to that of Swedish common readers. It is also different from the political 'Woolf' who has always been recognized and admired. *ROO* is, as noted, available all over the country and has been regularly reprinted. In addition it has – as elsewhere – functioned as something of a bible for feminists. A major project for the reclamation of Swedish women writers and for feminine criteria of value characteristically took Woolf's notion of the common sitting-room as its pivotal idea (Holm 1981). Similarly Birgitta Svanberg's (1989) re-evaluation of von Krunsenstjerna's series returns repeatedly to the essential death of the domestic angel as a trope for female resistance, while the concept of the woman's sentence from *ROO* is the starting point for an important dissertation on 'women's language' in the works of three American poets, Adrienne Rich, Susan Griffin and Beverly Dahlen (Shima 1993). *ROO* is not only a significant text for literary scholars, of course. As in so many other countries, middle-class women in general, and feminists in particular, continue to use it as a touchstone for their own thought. Fairly recently, a leading political scientist, Maud Eduards, arguing that liberation from the established power structures can come from women acting together, concluded her essay with the final visionary passage from *ROO* (1992, 269). It is here, we may remember, that Woolf evokes the significance of the collective experience, 'the common life which is the real life'. For even if the privacy of a room of one's own enables writing, the intellectual freedom granted women by the change in their material conditions, the 'five hundred a year' and the individual space, are equally the necessary conditions that will enable women to escape the constraints of the private sphere.

Annelie Brännström Öhman (1995) makes similar use of Woolf's text for political purposes in an essay in an issue of *Kvinnovetenskaplig Tidskrift* (The Swedish Journal for Women's Studies).[31] *ROO* functions here as a controlling trope for the intellectual space occupied by the woman writer or academic, and Öhman suggests that this intellectual space is potentially boundless and analogous to the tracts visited by the explorer, the archaeologist or the anthropologist – or indeed any kind of research scientist. Although Woolf often views the outer world from a window, Öhman also argues that the intellectual space posited by *ROO* and elsewhere is without the walls that separate the outer from the inner world, the public from the private, the soul from society (1995, 9-11). The use of Woolf's feminist polemic for didactic purposes is characteristic of international feminism and in this respect Sweden is no different. The year before, for instance, the same journal had printed a longer essay by an American philosopher, Jane Roland Martin, that she had presented at the University of Umeå. Starting from John Stuart Mill's postulate in *The Subjection of Women* that learned women are a contradiction in terms, Martin reads *TG* as an extended warning to women of the danger of losing the civilized virtues they possessed before they began the struggle for entry into the professions. Indeed, Martin's essay is a challenge to professional women to cherish their ability to function as troublesome intruders – 'Outsiders' in Woolf's sense – who will maintain 'the humane values of consideration and care for others' (1994, 3–17).

Interestingly the salience of this thought was apparent to some Swedish readers right from the start. In stark contrast then to its very mixed reception by Woolf's immediate circle, the original publication of *TG* was the occasion for more than one perceptive article. Writing in *Hertha*, the liberal feminist journal of the day, Örjan Lindberger, a prominent literary scholar, critic and Anglophile, sympathetically recounts the main arguments of *TG*: that the socialization of men in Britain is ontologically the same as that which gives rise to the fascist leadership in Europe; that the only way for women to prevent war is to enter the professions, noting also that, paradoxically, this will only be an effective strategy if women maintain the virtues of their Outsider status (1939). In the same year, considering *TG* and *TY*, Margit Abenius celebrates Woolf as 'a free, fearless spirit, a witty and subtle intelligence with an undercurrent of dynamic feeling' while picking up on Woolf's warning to women not to enter the professions on the terms created by men (1939, 41).[32] In thus acknowledging one of the central arguments of the text, Abenius also notes sourly that the readers of a literary journal would be well advised to recognize the dangers of the 'intellectual prostitution' which produces 'the rotting pile of indifferent words that poison us all, that destroy our courage, that soil our culture and restrict intellectual liberty and thereby inexorably lead to war' (1939, 43).[33] Personally, I take consolation

---

31 This issue, 2–3 (1995), also contains a longer extract from Jane Lundblad's translation of *A Room of One's Own*.

32 'en fri, alldeles orädd ande, en kvick och subtil intelligens med en underström av dynamisk känsla.' Abenius was a respected literary scholar and cultural critic, with a special interest in the Finnish-Swedish poet Karin Boye.

in the company of women, living and dead, who have heard the voice that urges us to embrace 'mental chastity' (*TG* (1982), 95) and to resist the seductions of money, fame and honour; those, in other words, who have recognized the uncomfortable honesty of *TG*.

It is to this text that I have often returned in my own work, even if I have come to the conclusion that in its form it too is an example of the collusion that it mocks.[34]

*

It is not so surprising that intellectuals in Sweden have been able to embrace both the political 'Woolf' and the aesthetic 'Woolf' – or more properly that they have been able to discern the cooperative co-existence of both elements. Secular idealism is congenial to the Swedish spirit: modernism and radical politics have been associated with one another. Thus an important aspect of Lindberger's article is the connection he makes between Woolf's feminist politics and her fictional methods. The qualities that women have been forced to embrace over the centuries explain

> the purpose behind the choice of motif and singular form of her novels. The novels are meant to move in space and not to be constructed systematically. Men construct philosophies of life; men try to envision a life as the consequence of dramatic events, men use novels to demonstrate their ideas or to make propaganda for political or social ends. Virginia Woolf achieves artistic effects in her books by placing apparently unconnected details of everyday life beside one another. Large sections of these works are to be read in the same way as we study a still life by Cézanne or Braque. It is possible that it is for this reason that she may appear to a later age simply as an experimenter. She is more; there is existential seriousness and depth in her books just as there is wit and intelligence. But in order to provide a counterbalance, and to reduce the pressure of the weight of tradition upon those women writers who will come after her, she has chosen to write in a manner that as far as possible differs from the literary tradition as men have created it. (Lindberger 1939)[35]

---

33 'den ruttna högen av likgiltiga ord som förgiftar oss alla, slår ner vårt mod, smetar ner kulturen och binder den intellektuella friheten och därigenom obevekligt leder till krig.'

34 See 'Conversing about Collusion' (Sandbach-Dahlström 1996) and the monograph with the same title (forthcoming) where I perform a detailed analysis of the semantic consequences of the form of *Three Guineas* and consider the ambivalences of Woolf's feminism.

35 'det avsiktliga motivvalet och den säregna formgivning i hennes romaner. Romaner skall röra sig i rum och vara systematiskt byggda. Män konstruerar livsåskådningar; män försöker se ett liv som en följd av dramatiska händelser; män använder romaner för att exponera sina idéer eller för att göra propaganda för politiska och sociala syften. Virginia Woolf når den konstnärliga effekten i sina böcker genom att ställa bredvid varandra skenbart sammanhangslösa vardagliga detaljer. Stora delar av dem ska läsas ungefär på samma sätt som man ser på ett stilleben av Cézanne eller Bracque. Det är möjligt, att hon just därför kommer att för en senare tid framstå som blott och bart experimentator. Hon är mera; det finns livsallvar och djup in hennes böcker liksom det finns kvickhet och intelligens. Men hon har valt att skriva

As I have implied, for many readers at present there is either a political or an aesthetic Woolf; a neurotic, refined upper-class lady or a radical feminist polemicist. A trend that has made no great impact on student writing, for instance, is Woolf's conflation of gender politics with textual strategies. Some professional critics note the connection however. One of them writing of *TW* remarked on how 'Woolf's original prose gracefully wound itself around her untiring struggle for women's liberation' (Frostin 1980, 2).[36] Significantly, some of Sweden's most important (and male) critics have combined an appreciation of both factors. Torsten Ekbom in the postscript to the 1988 reprint of *JR* emphasizes Woolf's radical importance in literary history. Presenting her 'method' of describing a person indirectly, and thus of course questioning the usual notion of personality, Ekbom writing of how Jacob is reached through absence notes that:

> She had certainly been influenced by the contemporary modernist art that art-historian Roger Fry had shown in London some years earlier – the post-Impressionists and the futurists, Picasso, Matisse. There is something of Seurat's heraldic stylization over the scenes in *Jacob's Room*; it is a pointillist or cubist portrait of fragments put together as in a kaleidoscope. (1988, 235)[37]

Similarly, the reception of *ROO* emphasizes its rhetoric as well as its politics. Carl Axel Westholm, writing in 1986 for the Uppsala paper read by many academics, notes that 'the argumentation in this polemic is not only witty and imaginative, but also characterized by a desire to change the state of affairs' (1986).[38]

As has been noted, Swedish intellectuals' ready recognition of Woolf's radicalism dates from the earliest publication of her work. Writing in 1933, Arthur Lundquist already knew that Virginia Woolf was attempting to modernize literature. If he was still uncertain as to her success at that time, when he returned to Woolf on the occasion of the 1980 translation of *TW* – a novel he had first read fifty years previously and always admired – it was with a full recognition of Woolf's achievement. Although his comments are to be found in a newspaper review, they represent a small gem of criticism, which

---

cont.
på ettsätt, som så mycket som möjligt avviker från den litterära tradition, som skapats av män för att åstadkomma en motvikt och lätta trycket av dess tyngd åt de kvinnor som kan komma att skriva efter henne.'

36 'Tydligt framträder Virginia Woolfs originella skrivarsätt som graciöst slingrar sig kring denna outtröttliga kamp för kvinnans frigörelse, i romanen *Vågorna*.'

37 'Säkert hade hon fått impulser från det samtida modernistiska måleriet som konstkritikern Roger Fry några år tidigare hade visat i London – postimpressionisterna och futuristerna, Picasso, Matisse. Det finns något av Seurats heraldiska stilisering över scenerna i *Jacob's Room*, ett pointillistiskt eller kubistiskt porträtt av kalejdoskopiskt sammanfogade facetter.'

38 'Samtidigt kännetecknas argumenteringen i denna tendensskrift inte bara av spiritualitet och infallsrikedom utan också av målmedveten vilja att få en ändring till stånd.' Understanding of the interrelation of form and theme is also implicit in the same critic's remark that *O* and *TG* are amongst Woolf's most readable books.

comes close to Woolf's own understanding of the role of 'personality' – of the essence of the writer's mind present in the text. Lundquist's summing-up points to the variation in Woolf that makes so many interpretations possible. In his 1980 critique he brings together the formal with the biographical, the personal with the political, the singular with the multiple:

> More than anywhere else Virginia Woolf reveals herself in this book as the manifold human being, complex to the verge of disaster and disintegration; composed of a multitude of possibilities deprived of the space that would enable their release. She is composed of too many elements: she is too talented, too sensitive and highly intelligent. Male and female qualities exist side by side in tragic opposition to one another instead of working together harmoniously. Insofar as she complains about women's fate in a male-dominated world it is because the male elements in her own personality are being suffocated. Her vision is of an integration of male and female rather than a strict division of the sexes. In this she is percipient, a model and a precursor not only as the moulder of the prose poem but also in her insight into the quality of life itself. (1980, 3)[39]

'I am', says Bernard, 'not one and simple but complex and many' (*TW*, 56). So too the 'Woolf' read, admired and in all her many shapes present in Sweden today is as much a focus of interest as ever. Judging from the variety of response to her writing and the fascination she clearly exerts upon many different kinds of reader, it seems in effect that as Enobarbus says of Cleopatra, 'Age cannot wither her, nor custom stale her infinite variety'.

---

[39] 'Virginia Woolf avslöjar sig i denna bok mer än någon annanstans som den mångfaldiga människan, den intill upplösning och olycka sammansatta, med alla möjligheter som inte får rum att förlösas. Hon rymmer för mycket, hon är alltför begåvad, överkänslig och högt intelligent, med kvinnliga och manliga egenskaper sida vid sida, genom omständigheterna i tragisk motsättning till varandra i stället för samverkande i harmoni, i balans. I den mån hon klagar över kvinnans öde i en mansdominerad värld är det främst för att de manliga egenskaperna inom henne förkvävs. Vad som föresvävar henne är en integrering av kvinnligt och manligt i stället för en hårt ensidig könsåtskillnad. Däri är hon förutseende och förebildlig, en föregångare inte bara i prosapoetisk form utan i insiktsfull livsmedvetenhet.'

9 Waves of Influence: The Danish Reception of Virginia Woolf

Ida Klitgård

I shall pass like a cloud on the waves. Perhaps it may be that though we change, one flying after another, so quick, so quick, yet we are somehow successive and continuous we human beings, and show the light through. But what is the light?
Virginia Woolf, *WD*, 4 January 1929

Introduction

The appearance of Virginia Woolf in Denmark rides on waves of enthusiasm. Although the epigraph expresses Woolf's concern with life as either very solid or very shifting, it might also be said to characterize how the Danish reception of Woolf has experienced surges of interest according to national and international cultural paradigm shifts. Cultural responses to Woolf have indeed been highly variable in Denmark, and Woolf studies – if there is such a thing – have suffered many hardships over the years. But, if Woolf has not always enjoyed widespread popularity, she has persistently been held in high regard by critics, creative writers and, not least, one particular publisher who has played a determining role in her reception. At present, Woolf is no longer just a passing cloud reflected in the flood of literary currents, and it is the aim of this chapter to explain how this transition has come about.

Until the 1990s, the popular and academic reception of Virginia Woolf in Denmark were more or less inseparable, as Danish writers and academics often make themselves heard in the media – most literary critics in the papers have academic backgrounds. Yet, contrary to male modernist writers, such as T. S. Eliot and James Joyce, Woolf was considered neither interesting nor important enough to be included in serious scholarship. There has been no extensive academic tradition for reading Woolf other than in student classrooms and as a topic of student essays and the occasional master's thesis. Her general preoccupation with gender and politics has given Woolf public appeal, as has her presence as myth and icon, whereas her literary accomplishment has generally been neglected in favour of internationally recognized male modernists. This circumstance must be viewed in the light of the late reception and adoption of modernism in Denmark in the 1950s and 1960s. It was only later, with the new international attention to women's aesthetics, that Woolf was received as a modernist writer of note, as will be discussed in detail in the following sections.

Woolf's breakthrough in Denmark took place with a controversial feminist writer's translation of *ROO* in 1973. Woolf was suddenly 'discovered' and appropriated by the feminist movement as a heroic foremother of women's rights. While her image as icon or myth persisted in the accounts of male critics throughout the 1980s, the new international scholarly interest in the nature of women's aesthetics, which brought about a renaissance in Woolf studies, encouraged Danish women writers and critics to read Woolf as a great writer in her own right, on a par with other male high modernists, and as a source of creative inspiration. A number of polemical feminist writers, who did not always agree with the established feminist movement, expressed their debt to Woolf's vision, themes and style. And one female Danish scholar in comparative literature and women's studies broke new ground for an interest in Woolf within academia as well as in the media.

The aim of this chapter is not to provide an outline of the sociological, political or theoretical reception of Virginia Woolf. Instead, I want to study the chronological development of responses in the cultural elite as international and national modernism gradually comes to the fore, and as the publication of Danish translations increases. Thus, my study focuses mainly on the impression and impact Woolf's works and reputation make on the contemporary popular audience, and how this view changes over time in line with cultural development in Denmark. The source material, then, is text-orientated and includes a number of exemplary and illuminating works in the form of translations, reviews, creative responses and criticism since the publication of the first Danish translation of a novel by Woolf in 1941 to the latest remark on her role in 1999 alongside other historical giants in a special millennium supplement of a national Sunday paper. Owing to paucity of texts before the 1970s, the main focus will be on the 1980s and 1990s where responses to Woolf are plentiful.

Due to the porous divide between popular and academic reception in Denmark, the two will accompany and support each other in my chronological investigation. So, this study does not claim to be exhaustive, but rather a representative survey of multiform texts dealing with Virginia Woolf's literary and critical standing in the small Scandinavian country that is Denmark.

1920–70: Woolf's entry into the slow-moving current of modernism

During the First World War and subsequently in the 1920s, some of the international 'isms' left but few traces in Danish literature which until then had been immersed in a strong realist tradition. The only major international influences were German expressionism and Italian futurism which inspired Johannes V. Jensen (1873–1950)[1] and two other major poets and novelists,

[1] Johannes V. Jensen was awarded the Nobel Prize for Literature in 1944.

Emil Bønnelycke (1893–1953) and Tom Kristensen (1893–1974) who was also a personal friend of James Joyce. Joyce asked him to translate *Ulysses*, but the project fell through. (In 1949 *Ulysses* was translated into Danish for the first time by Mogens Boisen.) Kristensen translated part of T. S. Eliot's *The Waste Land*, and in 1930 he wrote *Hærværk* (Havoc), a novel much inspired by Joyce's stream of consciousness technique. Danish expressionism was marked by nihilism and chaos, fear of the mindlessness of technological civilization and a growing fascination with the dangerous depths of the mind.

Expressionism was succeeded to a degree by surrealism, but even though these movements were forerunners of the much later Danish modernist movement, they remained marginal phenomena in Danish literature of the time. The Danish literary scene did not keep abreast with international literary events, remaining predominantly influenced by working-class social realism which dealt with the class struggle and social portrayals of people's lives and fates.

The 1930s were dominated by a split between cultural leftism and a rather heterogeneous group of mainstream, conventionalist writers with a broad conservative appeal among readers. Karen Blixen (Isak Dinesen) occupied a place apart as her fiction, dominated by mythological wisdom, merged aristocratic conservatism with rebellious femininity. She won an international reputation with her *Seven Gothic Tales*, published originally in English in 1934 and in Danish (*Syv fantastiske fortællinger*) in 1935.

The period during and immediately after the Second World War was one of great cultural crisis for Denmark, which was occupied by Germany from 1940 to 1945. There was no time for the sophisticated aesthetics of international modernism when the dominant concerns were national pride, unity and resistance.

In this respect it is interesting to note that the first Danish translation of a novel by Virginia Woolf was one of her less experimental novels, *TY* (Aarene gaar). It was translated in 1941, the year of her death, and published by Hagerup in Copenhagen. Until 1953, while Hagerup was still an independent company, it specialized in popular-nationalist publications, school and children's books. It seems obvious that Woolf's death prompted a sudden interest in her work, but it is not clear why *TY* was chosen as the first publication. My guess is that it was regarded as more accessible to a wide audience than were Woolf's more experimental novels. And as Hagerup were at this time concerned above all with the entertainment value of fiction, the translator Paula Biehe, who was principally a translator of French novels, strove for explanatory equivalence in terms of content, often missing Woolf's lyrical tone and cadence. Biehe's translation is in accordance with the description of *TY* on the back of the book: 'In terms of its subject and setting this novel is in many ways reminiscent of Galsworthy's *Forsyte Saga*, as it is the respectable London upper classes which are being portrayed.'[2] The translation

---

[2] 'Ved emne og Milieu kan den i flere Måder minde om Galsworthys *Forsyte Saga*, idet det er den borgerlige Overklasse med London som baggrund, der er skildret i bogen.'

aims to entertain the reader rather than bewitch or astonish with a poetically sophisticated style. Besides, for Biehe the translation of Woolf was an anomaly, and she translated nothing further by her.

In his review 'Virginia Woolf paa Dansk' (Virginia Woolf in Danish), printed in the social democratic paper *Socialdemokraten*, 16 December 1941, Svend Erichsen opens with the statement that this novel is a literary milestone. It is about time Woolf were translated, he argues, claiming that in France every educated person has read her at some point. At a time of limited media, Denmark was predominantly influenced by German-French rather than Anglo-American currents. After the Second World War, however, Anglo-American thought gradually gained a footing.

Erichsen describes her thus: 'She is elegant and composed, bordering on indolence, cool and perspicacious, but not deep, as her characters have no depth' (1941).[3] Perfectly in agreement with the paper's social democratic ideology, Erichsen thinks Woolf's characters are superficial because they belong to the British upper classes marked by tradition and civilization, but also, surprisingly, by beauty and wisdom. The British upper classes, says Erichsen, are like a caste system, rotating in a closed circuit at the centre of the British Empire.

It is obvious that Erichsen senses how Woolf's novel breaks with the unquestioned social realism of Danish literature. Woolf's portrayal of life is fragmentary, he says, as it dissolves into separate moments – a kind of anti-Pantheism. But such moments, and Woolf's philosophy in general, nevertheless comprise a homogenous whole. Erichsen then goes on to compare her method with Jules Romains's collectivism and *unanimisme* – this comparison is the very same topic of Allen McLaurin's much later essay on 'Consciousness and Group Consciousness in Virginia Woolf' (1984). Erichsen says that Romains's idea is to connect a number of singular events and singular lives into a mosaic. This is, however, not Woolf's purpose. Her purpose is to break life down into fragments without piecing them together into a whole, claims Erichsen. But the final, general impression of her novel is nevertheless one of homogeneity as 'life is stronger than any theory' (1941).[4] Erichsen concludes that Woolf may not be the kind of writer the times crave, given the German occupation and the need for a belief in national unity, but she is an important figure in European literature, and thus it is a blessing that she has been translated into Danish.

In sum, Svend Erichsen's review demonstrates great confusion between views of Woolf as a person, as a member of the British bourgeoisie and as a writer. He is torn between praise and a sharp critique of Virginia Woolf. His review does not concentrate on Woolf's writing but is heavily tainted by the political situation and Erichsen's socialist bent.

Just prior to Denmark's release from the German occupation on 5 May 1945, *MD* was published in a Danish translation by Aage Brusendorff, by the

---

3 'Hun er fornem og rolig indtil det indolente, kølig og klartskuende, men ikke dybtskuende, fordi de Personer, hun skriver om, ikke er dybe.'

4 'livet er stærkere end alle teorier.'

country's biggest publishing house, Gyldendal. It appeared in a series called 'Verdensromaner' (World Novels). Brusendorff (1906–86) was a film historian who had written a major encyclopedia on films (1939–41), and was the first curator of Denmark's Museum of Film from 1942 to 1960. He also translated F. Scott Fitzgerald's *The Great Gatsby*, Edgar Lee Masters's *Spoon River Anthology*, James Joyce's *A Portrait of the Artist as a Young Man* and *Dubliners*, John Cleland's *Fanny Hill*, Henry James's *The Turn of the Screw*, and D. H. Lawrence's *The Rainbow*.

The war made *MD* an obvious choice for translation in 1945. Brusendorff's translation may, however, seem old-fashioned and grandiose to modern readers, and, probably as a consequence, a new translation by Jørgen Christian Hansen was published in 1984.

In his review, 'London set gennem bølgende vand' (London Perceived through Waters of Fluctuation), for the national paper *Politiken* (Politics), 6 March 1945, the above-mentioned Expressionist poet and novelist Tom Kristensen gives an impressionist and lyrical celebration of Virginia Woolf's *MD*. He speculates about what the object for literary depiction might be if one were standing on a pier: the solid truth at the bottom of the sea, with its beetles and blobs of seaweed? Or the green, crested waves with their reflections of light and soothing regularity which give us a sense of rhythm and time? Is it superficial to portray the surface, asks Kristensen?

Woolf chooses to stay on the surface of things, he says, instead of reaching for the concrete as in realist fiction, and it is this very surface of occasional impressions, interruptions, digressions, which blows on the waves of our minds. He ends this astonishingly beautiful review with the conclusion that, when we are in our fifties, like Mrs Dalloway, we become extremely vulnerable because every experience carries layer upon layer of earlier experiences with it. In Woolf's novel, and in reality, 'life becomes a geology of sadness' (Kristensen 1945).[5] This personal view may be related to the fact that Kristensen's own literary production reached its climax in the 1920s, and after his publication of *Hærværk* in 1930, his creativity waned. He went on to assume an important position as critic and translator of international literature, introducing and translating writers such as Joyce, Remarque, Hemingway, D. H. Lawrence and T. S. Eliot.

Another review, which is really a feature article, by the notoriously outspoken literary historian of the time, Jens Kruuse, 'En poetisk roman' (A lyrical novel), *Jyllandsposten* (Jutland Post), 16 March 1945, elaborates on Woolf's style and the new reading practice demanded for lyrical prose. His long review begins with a discussion of the physiologically different responses to the reading of poetry and prose in the reader. The reader of prose is split, feels compelled to go on and on towards the end, is absorbed – as if controlled by a demon. The reader of poetry is tranquil and undergoes an intense feeling of wholeness. Kruuse's point is that *MD* miraculously merges poetry and prose allowing a happy conjunction of excitement and peacefulness in the reader,

---

[5] 'Livet bliver en vemodets Geologi.'

who at once strives for the conclusion and indulges in pauses of profound contemplation.

At the end of this review Kruuse deplores the translator's painfully deficient knowledge of English language and customs. But Brusendorff is, to Kruuse's mind, one of Denmark's best literary translators as he has a magnificent feel for poetry and the novel as a whole. Kruuse jokingly asks whether the Danish League of Translators would consider sending Brusendorff to England for three years, and then make him *translator laureatus*. As translators in Denmark in general at the time did not have professional training or academic educations in English (most were writers, artists, essayists or otherwise men of letters), translations usually document major problems between literariness and localness. Danish translators at the time might have been very gifted as writers themselves, but their knowledge of foreign customs and idioms was limited. Today, many translators have academic backgrounds in the language of the books they translate and also better means of research.

From an overall point of view, in spite of the ongoing Second World War and the lengthy German occupation of Denmark, the reviews of *MD* reveal greater interest in the particularities of Virginia Woolf's style than in her personality, as was the case in the review of *Aarene gaar* (*TY*) in 1941. Perhaps the expectation that the war was coming to an end allowed for new energy, a new faith in experiment and trust in the freedom of art and aesthetics unencumbered by the often bleak outlook of social realism. This change in the literary climate was, for example, taken up by a newly founded publishing house, Borgen, which from the outset specialized in new works in Danish, primarily poetry, visual art and non-fiction. Borgen's first publication in 1949 was a small pamphlet, printed in 300 copies, containing a translation of Woolf's essay *LYP* (Brev til en ung digter) by a fairly unknown writer, Martin Melsted. The choice of this particular essay functioned, I believe, as an appeal to young Danish writers to reconsider literary history and then to begin to write.

In the post-war period this growing fascination with aesthetic experiment and loss of restraint developed in the literary and intellectual milieu of the cultural magazine *Heretica* (1948-53). Greatly inspired by T. S. Eliot (a number of essays and part of *The Waste Land* were translated into Danish in 1948), *Heretica* wanted a new poetry drawing on the experience of the tensions between fear and courage, falsehood and truth, and, as a result, international modernism at last had a voice on the Danish literary scene. In 1949 Joyce's *Ulysses* was first translated into Danish.

In the 1950s an authentic Danish 'modernism' saw the light of day. It took modernity for granted and found an adequate means of expression to render this fact. The speculative essayist and novelist Villy Sørensen (1929–2001) established a new and apparently 'absurd' narrative technique which took as its starting-point a keen awareness of language and the loss of identity through psychological splitting. Villy Sørensen is often said to have been our second-greatest philosopher after Søren Kierkegaard. Another literary innovator was the prolific 'angry young man' at the time, Klaus Rifbjerg (1931–), whose poetry, stories and novels describe life as it is painfully felt by sensitive individuals through a saturation of linguistic energy, much in the same vein as Joyce in *Dubliners* and in Hemingway's fiction.

This renewed interest in artistic form, language, psychology and absurdity was perhaps the reason why a selection of Virginia Woolf's essays was translated into Danish in 1953. The collection, *Et London-Eventyr og andre Essays* ('Street Haunting: A London-Adventure' and Other Essays), was translated by Niels Lyhne Jensen and published by Steen Hasselbalchs Forlag in Copenhagen. The following essays were chosen for translation: '*Robinson Crusoe*', 'Modern Fiction', 'On Being Ill', 'Street Haunting: A London-Adventure' and an extract from *ROO* called 'Shakespeare's Sister'. As the translator's preface explains, these essays give a panorama of Woolf's ideas on literary history, her reaction to realism, the constituents of modern literature, human consciousness, the creative imagination and feminist issues.

Niels Lyhne Jensen explains that the aim of this publication is the representation and evaluation of a literary period which was first received in Denmark in the 1950s. We must bear in mind that in spite of the new faith in experiments, this decade was increasingly characterized by pessimism and an intense use of keywords such as confrontation, alienation and concretism. The Danish writers of the 1950s involved themselves in a rather hectic search for experiments. The state of the arts perhaps led Lyhne Jensen to admit that contemporary literature could not live up to the international experimental literature of the 1920s, even though it was regarded as the model. And it is only now, writes Jensen, after a requisite interval, that we can distinguish what is really original from the merely sensational. As Woolf is a renewer of the art of fiction on a par with Henry James, Joyce and Proust, these essays are invaluable in an evaluation of modernist literature of the 1920s and onwards, Lyhne Jensen concludes (1953, 7). In his review of this collection, 'Bloomsburys første lady' (The First Lady of Bloomsbury), for the intellectual paper *Information*, 15 April 1953, Niels Kaas Johansen agrees by concluding that writers who have become stuck in the social realist ditch ought to be forced to read this selection of essays. No further essays by Virginia Woolf have been translated into Danish since this publication.

In the Aschehoug series 'Levende Litteratur' (Living Literature), a Danish translation of *FB* by Mogens Boisen was published in 1953, as were translations of novels by Tolstoy and Aksel Sandemose. It is uncertain why *FB* was chosen for publication rather than any of Woolf's more important novels. One of the editors of this series, and the translator of this particular edition, was Denmark's greatest, most productive and unique translator, the late Mogens Boisen (1910–87) who actually had the rank of lieutenant colonel in the Danish army. In addition to more than 800 translations of world literature, which include Herman Melville's *Moby Dick*, Thomas Mann's *Doktor Faustus* and Andre Malraux's *Antimemoirer* (Antimémoires), the crowning glory of Boisens's lifework is as many as *three* published translations of Joyce's *Ulysses* (1949, 1970 and 1980 – based on a number of different manuscripts). Boisen became internationally renowned for being the best translator worldwide of this nearly untranslatable novel. Why he wanted to translate *FB* rather than, say, *TW*, considering his talents for 'difficult' fiction, remains a mystery. But he always worked on several translations at the same time, alternating between difficult texts and easier pieces, for entertainment and relaxation. Perhaps *FB* fell into Boisen's second category.

Boisen's translation of *FB* is overall an accurate, smooth and natural version of the original which is written in a more 'realistic' style than most of Woolf's experimental novels. However, Boisen was also notorious for being careless when the mood took him, and so there are some under-translations of lyrical descriptions. In the last chapter with Flush in a marketplace in Florence we learn that 'The sun burnt deliciously through the lily leaves, and through the green and white umbrella' (*FB* 1968, 147). Boisen translates: 'Solen brændte mellem liljebladene og på den grønne og hvide parasol' (*Flush: historien om en Cocker Spaniel* (*Flush*) 1953, 132). He leaves out a translation of 'deliciously', omits the comma before the afterthought about the colours of the umbrella and lets the sun burn 'på', that is 'on' the umbrella rather than 'through' it.

The next sentence 'The marble statue tempered its heat to a champagne freshness' (*FB* 1968, 147) becomes 'Marmorstatuen mildnede dens hede til perlende kølighed' (*Flush: historien om en Cocker Spaniel* (*Flush*) 1953, 132). Here Boisen has omitted the freshness of champagne and substituted it with a metonym 'perlende', that is 'sparkling'. He naturalizes the unusual metaphor, and thus some of Woolf's originality is lost.

In short, it is odd that the collection of essays by Woolf, which called for conventional realism to be abandoned and was thus in line with the 1950s craving for literary experiments, was not followed up by translations of her major novels to prove the point. Instead, the jocular *FB* was translated by our greatest translator, who could, and perhaps should, have devoted his talents to one of her more stylistically challenging texts. Not until 1962 was one of her major novels translated, *O*.

In the 1960s and in the beginning of the 1970s the Danish literary scene developed from an engagement with the styles and themes of 'absurdity' (Benny Andersen, Peter Seeberg, Ivan Malinovski, Jess Ørnsbo) towards a constructivist or formalist modernism (Hans-Jørgen Nielsen, Inger Christensen, Svend Åge Madsen, Per Højholt). As modernism took off, so other trends emerged, such as an existentialist–historical documentarism in Thorkild Hansen's fiction; existentialist realism in Tage Skou-Hansen and Erik Aalbæk Jensen; contemporary realism in Christian Kampmann and Henrik Stangerup's novels; and autobiographical, social and psychological portrayals of women's lives in Tove Ditlevsen's poetry and prose.

Yet even in this period, as before, it was not one of Woolf's most technically experimental novels, such as *TL* or *TW*, that was translated, but *O*, by Jørgen Årup Hansen in 1962. *O* was published in the series 'Bekkasinbøger' (Snipe Books) by Gyldendal in Copenhagen, and reprinted in 1983 and 1992. Together with *TY* and *FB*, it presents Woolf as either a realist, decadent or playful novelist, rather than a serious modernist writer. Ironically, *MD* alone represented Woolf's genius in the slow, incoherent introduction of her œuvre in Denmark. This may be due to the fact that the Danish literary milieu, that is a host of male writers, looked predominantly for inspiration in imagism, in the lyric poetry of T. S. Eliot and in Joyce, that is to say 'hard-core' male high modernists, rather than in a woman novelist such as Virginia Woolf. In spite of the highly commendatory reviews by two major literary figures in Denmark,

Tom Kristensen and Jens Kruuse, Woolf was not yet generally judged and acknowledged on her merits as an important innovator of prose writing on a par with James Joyce. Consequently, Danish readers of the 1960s might very well have formed the impression that she was nothing but an exponent of the British upper classes who while away their time writing books about pets and aristocrats.

1970–99: The feminist surge and its repercussions

The international student revolt in 1968 certainly put an end to any further ideas of translating Woolf's major novels. The rebellion resulted in a heated ideological debate, and thus all interest in 'extravagant' literary experiments was lost. Throughout the 1970s a new kind of working-class literature came to the fore, and especially a so-called women's literature (Jette Drewsen, Vita Andersen, Dea Trier Mørch and Suzanne Brøgger) which created quite a stir in popular culture. A harsh ideological critique of the function and expressions of literature, undertaken in Marxist scholarly circles, contributed to forcing novelists to empty the everyday, the private and the intimate of any ideology, resulting in what is termed 'confessional writing'. Moreover, chopped-up prose became a favourite style in poetry as it resembled everyday speech.

Against this background, and in this rather non-aesthetic current, it comes as no surprise that Virginia Woolf was more or less 'discovered' for her merits as a spokeswoman of the women's movement in Britain rather than as a writer of experimental fiction. All of a sudden, she became an 'icon' for the women's movement and received no substantial reception in the academic world. In 1973 the Danish writer Elsa Gress (1919-88) together with her son David Gress-Wright, undertook a translation of *ROO* (Eget værelse), published by Samleren in Copenhagen (reprinted in 1978 and 1994).

Elsa Gress is said to be our first major debater of women's issues after the Second World War. She wrote novels, short stories, radio and television plays, essays on cultural criticism and memoirs. Gress's feminist convictions were based on a general humanism which focused on the rights of the individual and their opportunities for self-realization. She disagreed strongly with the main body of feminists in the 1970s who were influenced by American and French thought. They saw Gress's humanism as dominated by male values. Gress also disagreed with the feminist idea that motherhood is a cultural artifact. In her view, motherhood creates and changes culture as the creation and development of language is inextricably bound up with the linguistic contact between mother and child. Gress's disagreement with the established women's movement resulted in an extremely polemical body of works which expressed her anger at regimentation, Danish self-sufficiency and nationalism.

In the preface to the edition, Elsa Gress states that *ROO* is as topical on today's heated feminist agenda as it was in 1928:

> For it embodies the kind of understanding between *both* sexes that we must reach in order to avoid stagnation within sexual 'racism' and mutual abuse. But it embodies

> this understanding without yielding an inch in the question about justice and reasonableness and human compassion. (Woolf 1973, 7)[6]

Thus, Gress used Woolf's writing as a springboard for expressing her own vision about equality between the sexes *without* falling into the pitfall of creating a war between them, which was, to Gress's mind, the great mistake made by contemporary feminists. This preoccupation with mutuality is emphasized by the fact that she and her son co-translated the text.

In the 1980s and 1990s writers began to tire of formless forms and confessions about intimate daily life. A new generation of modernist writers emerged, such as the poets Michael Strunge, Bo Green Jensen, Pia Tafdrup and Søren Ulrik Thomsen, who were inspired by rock music and a new consciousness of the body, as well as by romanticism and symbolism. Writers also developed a greater awareness of religious and mythological themes. Danish prose writers of the 1980s became deeply involved in mixed genres, such as prose and memoirs in the work of Suzanne Brøgger, and realism and formalism in Peter Seeberg and Jens Smærup Sørensen. The world-wide fascination with 'magic realism' is also present among certain contemporary Danish writers, such as Ib Michael and Peter Høeg, whose novels have gained great international acclaim. Even though recent years have witnessed several postmodern attempts at minimalism and an increasing focus on the body in the text, Danish literature is now characterized by great diversity after a long literary tradition which, roughly speaking, alternated between realism and the absurd.

With the 1980s departure from the trivialization of the aesthetic, the novels of Virginia Woolf received fresh interest. Feminism had paved the way for a flourishing interest in women's literature. In the early 1980s, the full body of Woolf's prose works, which had long been ignored and neglected by a male-dominated modernist scene, was at last properly and coherently introduced to a Danish audience.

Before looking in detail at responses of the 1980s and 1990s, I want to take a synthesizing backward glance at the work of translators, critics and writers so far and compare it with subsequent developments. In this early period, the choice of translations appears scattered, random and rather ill-conceived. It is easy to see how Woolf was not taken seriously. None of her translators can be considered real 'experts' on her œuvre with full knowledge of the peculiarities of her style. In most cases it looks as if the publishers wanted to give Woolf a try, then abandoned the idea. Perhaps her books, or upper-class reputation, did not sell very well in a country whose literary roots are firmly planted in (social) realism. And interestingly, all the critics, writers and reviewers I have found pre-1980 have been men. But with Elsa Gress's translation of *ROO*, nearly all subsequent writers, critics and reviewers expressing their debt to Woolf are

---

[6] 'For den rummer den forståelse af *begge* køns dilemma, som vi må og skal frem til, om vi ikke bare skal stå i stampe i gensidig køns-"racisme" og skældsordsudveksling. Men den rummer forståelsen uden at give sig en tomme i spørgsmålet om ret og rimelighed og menneskelig medfølelse.'

women. With the 1980s there is a major shift from male negligence to female exhilaration. This new 'discovery' of Woolf is engendered by the translations of her major works, as well as by an almost invisible incorporation of academic thought and international feminist theories in the press, thanks to Tania Ørum, a Danish female scholar in modernist and women's studies.[7] I will return to her achievements further on.

This new appreciation of Woolf as a great writer began with the translation of *TL* by the publisher Merete Ries (1938) in 1982.[8] Like the Hogarth Press, her small independent publishing house, Rosinante (also founded in 1982), was located in the basement of her villa in the suburbs of Copenhagen. This was where she was first visited by, and discovered the talents of, Danish publishing's 'golden egg', Peter Høeg. Ries had earlier been editor for the publishers Gyldendal (1966-80) and Tiderne Skifter (1981-82). She became chief editor of Rosinante when it was bought by the major publishing house Munksgaard in 1989. Since 1997 she has been director of literature for Ejnar Munksgaard's Booksellers and Publishers. In the early 1980s, when Ries was head of Rosinante, a series, or programme, of Danish translations of Virginia Woolf was initiated: *Til fyret* (*TL*) in 1982 (reprinted 1991 and 1999), *Tre Guineas* (*TG*) in 1983 (translated by Inger Christensen) and a new improved translation of *MD* by Jørgen Christian Hansen in 1984 (reprinted 1990 and 1998). Thus, Rosinante has been a key factor in the reception of Virginia Woolf, republishing old translations and commissioning new ones.

In the critic May Schack's review of *Til fyret* (*TL*), 'Den sandhed som øjeblikket skaber' (The truth of the moment), in *Politiken*, 13 October 1982, she commends Merete Ries for the daring venture of translating *TL*. Schack explains that in Denmark Woolf is known above all for *ROO*. Besides giving a description of the structure of the novel and its characters, Schack interprets the novel not as a feminist manifesto in the style of *ROO*, but as primarily a portrayal of two different women's, Mrs Ramsay and Lily's, opposed ways of life. However, *TL* also reflects sexual politics as the two women's ways of life are reconciled through a mutual desire for perfection, a vision of truth beyond triviality. Mrs Ramsay strives for this by bringing the moment to perfection, whereas Lily seeks the truth through painting.

The same year, in response to the translation and first Danish performance of Edna O'Brien's play *Virginia* (1980), which dramatizes Woolf's split between her husband Leonard and Vita Sackville-West, two major introductions to the background, life and art of Virginia Woolf were published in two

---

[7] Tania Ørum holds a degree from the Department of English, University of Copenhagen (UC), has worked at the Centre for Women's Studies (UC) and is now Associate Professor in Comparative Literature at the same university. She is one of Denmark's most prominent names in gender studies and modernist literature. She is also the only Danish scholar who has written extensively on Virginia Woolf.

[8] Merete Ries has also translated the work of other authors, in particular many of the novels of Doris Lessing, suggesting that Woolf and Lessing are her favourite novelists.

distinguished Danish newspapers: the newspaper critic Ebbe Mørk's presentation in anticipation of the theatre première, 'Myten Virginia Woolf' (The Myth of Virginia Woolf) (Mørk 1982) and Tania Ørum's essay introducing the novel *TL*, 'Men bemærkede han blomsterne?' (But Did He See the Flowers?) (Ørum 1982).

Both essays consider Woolf's life and art, but whereas Ørum's slightly academic article describes the status of Virginia Woolf in Denmark, tells us the story of the great artist and analyses *TL*, Mørk's essay dwells on her life and friendships with other writers, including Vita Sackville-West. Ebbe Mørk views Woolf more or less as a myth or an icon. He is fascinated by the marked changes of Woolf's face throughout her many portraits and photos:

> No portrait of Woolf is insignificant but radiant with the changing moods of her mind – quite often a kind of awkward elegance as in piano compositions by Debussy. (Mørk 1982)[9]

This rather odd observation about Woolf's image would seem to connect with her growing status as icon in the women's movement, but also for women writers and, later, the Danish intellectual milieu in general. This proposition is supported by a scholarly article, 'Ikke kun det skønne billede: et kalejdoskopisk blik på et portrætfotografi af Virginia Woolf' (Not Just a Pretty Picture: A Kaleidoscopic View of Virginia Woolf's Portrait) by Dorte Buhl, Birgitte Fogh and Regitze Petri, published in the first issue of the cultural magazine *Luftskibet* (Airship) (1984). The photo of Woolf taken by George Beresford in 1903 is not just a picture of female vulnerability, it is argued. The three critics trace several dualisms in Woolf's facial expression, such as weakness and strength (physically and mentally), intimacy and distance, as well as both male exteriority and female interiority.

Tania Ørum, on the other hand, gives us a more detailed introduction to the status of Woolf in Denmark. She explains how Woolf's writing differs tremendously from Danish women's literature of the 1970s and early 1980s, as her development of personal material is extremely controlled, and she concentrates on intense moments in women's daily lives, in contrast with Danish women writers' either 'confessional writings' which represent formless talk, or realist novels which attempt to incorporate entire life stories or historical periods. Ørum indicates that, internationally, a cultural paradigm shift has occurred, moving from a general orientation towards the political and realist content of art to a new interest in aesthetic expression, and accordingly her article functions as a plea for a wider consideration of a possible female aesthetic. Ørum's analysis of *TL* seeks to define what constitutes such a female aesthetics in Woolf's universe.

Since her first comments on Woolf in the media, Tania Ørum has in fact come to play a major role in the discovery of Virginia Woolf in academic circles. Her contributions to the study of Woolf in Denmark have always been

---

[9] 'Intet portræt af hende er ligegyldigt, men lyser af sindets vekslende stemninger som i klaverstykker af Debussy.'

up to date with international critical and theoretical research. In latter years, she has published a number of articles on the relations between Woolf, gender, genre and modernism, but here I want to focus on her major critical work on women's literature in England since the eighteenth century: *Pamelas døtre* (Pamela's Daughters) (1985). The purpose of the book is to retrieve women's writing from the merely social, political and historical frame offered by the women's movement of the 1970s. As Ørum detects a growing international preoccupation in the 1980s with women's aesthetics, so she senses an opening for women's writing to be judged according to its aesthetic values irrespective of any feminist content. In her work, then, Ørum poses the highly topical question of whether women novelists write like men, or whether there is a specifically female way of writing. The book is structured around two major sections: one on historical considerations of culture, history, sociology and the genre of prose, starting with Samuel Richardson's portrayal of Pamela, and including readings of Katherine Philips, Aphra Behn, Mary Delarivier Manley and women's Gothic fiction; and one section comprising close readings of Charlotte Brontë's *Jane Eyre* and Virginia Woolf's *TL*. Throughout the book, Ørum does not refer to the Danish reception of Woolf, but predominantly to international theory, such as French and Anglo-American feminist thought. Thus, it might be described as an international study, written in Danish. The book claims to be intended not only for specialists in the field of English literature, but also for a wider audience interested in the relations between fiction, gender and history.

One of Ørum's arguments is that the typically female conflict of identity that she traces throughout the tradition of the novel from 1700 to the present parallels the conflict of identity in the study of women's literature. In *ROO*, for instance, Woolf directs our attention to her struggle for individual identity as both woman and writer by looking back at women's mothers. This outlook unites considerations of both womanhood (expressed in family relations) and writing (expressed in her attempt to delineate her own 'room' in literary history.)

I will not pursue the detail of Ørum's reading of *TL*, but just want to note how Ørum's readings of Brontë and Woolf demonstrate her point that English women's literature displays a great variation in style, so that no fixed demarcations between men's and women's writing can be made at a technical level. Although the content differs between the two sexes, their varied aesthetic expressions prove that gender is more ambiguous and flexible than is conventionally assumed by cultural historians. There is no one-to-one relationship between a particular literary technique and a particular gender. This means that Woolf can at last be judged according to her merits as a writer, and not according to her gender.

Back in 1982, another attempt to redefine Woolf was made by the academic Lotte Thrane. The cultural magazine, *Hug!* (Cut!), edited by, among others, Merete Ries, brought out an issue on women's art incorporating an extended extract from Ries's new translation of *TL*, as well as a popular introduction to Virginia Woolf by Thrane, 'Den knivskarpe ligevægt: introduktion til Virginia Woolf' (The Razor-edge Balance: An Introduction to Virginia Woolf). Thrane opens her essay with an *état présent* of the Danish reception of Woolf.

Either Woolf is categorized as a feminist spokeswoman of women's rights for equality and freedom, that is to say as an 'analytical–critical egghead with a cool–humorous outlook' or as a 'passive victim of the Victorian education of girls and of Victorian patriarchal society' (Thrane 1982, 25).[10] These views represent two versions of Danish feminist studies: one focusing solely on *ROO*, the other taking sociological circumstances into consideration.

Instead, Woolf must be viewed as a *whole* person, a whole woman, says Thrane. In support of Ørum's plea, Thrane draws our attention to the new focus on women's aesthetics in international women's studies. Virginia Woolf's writings will now be seen in a different light.

Thrane then goes on to discuss Woolf's life and in particular her concept of 'the angel in the house'. There follows an analysis of *TL*. Thrane's thesis is that Woolf's understanding of her own female and male sides proves to be limited in her personal administration of them, but when she gives them aesthetic form in her novels, she transgresses all such boundaries. This relationship is symbolized in the character of Lily whose sexual needs are sublimated in artistic creation. This female character's art then represents *both* liberation (she forgets about her difficult femininity when she paints) *and* compensation for relationships with other people. Thus, by more or less identifying Lily with the author, Woolf is seen to tell the story of her own divided self in a novel which attains mythical qualities.

Taken together, Ørum and Thrane are correct in forecasting a renewed interest in Woolf's art as an expression of the complicated relationship between men and women. Another artistic response to the translation of *TL* is the Danish writer Vibeke Grønfeldt's interpretative paraphrase of the novel, 'Kinesiske æsker: en parafrase' (Chinese Boxes: A Paraphrase) in the literary journal *Luftskibet*. The journal was edited by a host of leading Danish writers of the time, and the contributions included short pieces of prose, poetry and literary criticism. Vibeke Grønfeldt (1947–) is one of our most important woman writers of the 1970s and still going strong. Together with other writers of this period, she was active in making language and narration the themes of texts, and this makes her a 'difficult' writer. Apart from her surprising narrative structures and constructions, she is noted for her preoccupation with psychological and social limits between people who are either marginalized, lonely, fearful or falling apart. And like Elsa Gress, Grønfeldt disagrees with the perhaps rather too neat categorizations of men and women in many feminist studies.

Grønfeldt's six-page creative and impressionist interpretation of *TL* is chronologically structured and embroiders on the significant images that connect the characters. Grønfeldt for instance rephrases certain characters' thoughts and desires:

> – I'm in love with you, says the painter Lily Briscoe to Mrs Ramsay. – No, I mean in this place, in everything.

---

[10] 'analytisk-kritisk egghead med køligt-humoristisk overblik'; 'passivt offer for victoriansk pigeopdragelse og mandssamfund.'

> – The weather is no good for a trip to the lighthouse, announces a snake in the garden.
> Something might happen. Something must happen. They must go on and on trying to get something out of every little detail. They must, in thousands of ways, try to get the same out of the others as the others get out of their own thoughts, body, life. (Grønfeldt 1982, 76)[11]

This piece is an unconventional review of the novel prompted, I think, by the Danish translation, as well as by a writer's personal appreciation of Woolf's aesthetics and interest in the relationship between lonely souls, be they men or women. The text expresses Grønfeldt's own thematic concerns by merging her personal style with that of Virginia Woolf.

The following year *TG* (*Tre Guineas*) was translated by our greatest living woman poet Inger Christensen (1935–) who emerged during the constructivist, formal modernism of the 1960s. She has also translated numerous other important books by internationally acclaimed writers. As the book-jacket blurb reveals, Woolf's essay was marketed as of great immediate interest to issues of rearmament, capitalism and sexual politics. And the result is an adequate, naturally smooth translation which attempts to capture and preserve the pictorial effect of Woolf's precise and concrete illustrations of her points.

Newspaper critic May Schack's review, 'Forsørgelse er afhængighed' (Maintenance Equals Dependence), in *Politiken*, 23 November 1983, finds this essay interesting from a feminist analytical point of view, but deplores Woolf's insistence that women should stay out of all wartime issues altogether. To ignore patriotism and the glorification of war is all very well, but hardly a sufficient strategy of action, she argues. The text strikes us, claims Schack, as a resigned acceptance of women's powerlessness and freedom from responsibility. Schack doubts whether such a point of view is what we need at present. Instead the book can be enjoyed as a splendid and insightful picture of women's powerless situation at the beginning of this century.

In 1984 *MD* was translated for the second time, by the late Danish novelist Jørgen Christian Hansen (1956–89). Hansen updated Aage Brusendorff's translation of 1945. Hansen's translation captures the more natural flow of everyday language (more so than Brusendorff's), without neglecting the text's lyrical intensity. However, Hansen is at times a little too relaxed. At the end of the novel Peter Walsh asks what it is that fills him with 'extraordinary excitement' (*MD*, 213). Hansen translates 'excitement' into 'ophidselse' which can relate only to agitation or to sexual excitement in Danish. Brusendorff's 'bevægelse', which is the equivalent of 'movement' *and* affection, something that touches the heart, is thus more adequate and attentive to Peter Walsh's emotions. This new translation of *MD* was reprinted in 1990 and 1998.

Jørgen Christian Hansen was a lecturer at the Department of English,

---

[11] 'Jeg er forelsket i Dem, siger malerinden Lily Briscoe til Mrs Ramsay. – Nej, jeg mener i stedet, i alt. – Det bliver ikke vejr til at tage til fyret, meddeler en slange i haven. Noget kan ske. Noget må ske. De må blive ved og ved med at få noget ud af hver detalje. De må på tusinde måder sikre sig at få det samme af de andre, som de andre tager sig af deres tanker, krop, liv.'

University of Copenhagen, and the writer of a successful trilogy in the classic modernist tradition. In 1989 a collection of his autobiographical essays *Den skrigende Buddha* (The Screaming Buddha) was published posthumously. Included in this collection is an essay dedicated to the strange life of Virginia Woolf titled 'Virginias værelser: Virginia Woolf' (Virginia's Rooms: Virginia Woolf). Of all writers, Hansen says, Virginia Woolf is the one with whom he feels the greatest kinship; she is his 'literary sister'. He has read all her works, letters and diaries to such an extent that he claims he is beginning to think like her. Hansen also refers to R. D. Laing's studies in madness and to Woolf's mental illness as valuable in the creation of certain characters in his own novels (Hansen 1989, 45). Madness fascinates Hansen too, but he is touched above all by Woolf's depictions of childhood, especially in *TL* (1989, 45). The rest of the essay is a long biographical introduction to Woolf.[12]

Hansen's piece, however limited, is the first autobiographical response to Woolf that I have traced, and it is perhaps surprising that it should be written by a man. His text can be compared with a much later personal response from one of Denmark's leading women writers, Suzanne Brøgger (1944–).

Suzanne Brøgger is the author of essays on cultural criticism and women's issues, translator of Doris Lessing, and her many novels from the early 1970s to the present express her contempt for the institution of marriage. Influenced by the sexual liberation of the 1970s, Brøgger is convinced that love must be freed from suffocating gender roles. The illusion of monogamy leads only to self-denial and disintegration. Brøgger has been interpreted as promiscuous, but her own view is that Western society is at fault for having severed sexuality from our being, our very existence. Brøgger's vision and aim are to reintroduce the importance of eroticism as seduction, play, game and experiment – a way to make life whole. Eros is the basic force of life, and we should not try to suppress it. Like Virginia Woolf, and Karen Blixen, Brøgger has become an icon, a myth-like figure or an enigmatic sphinx, playing various roles in the media and managing either to enrage or to fascinate the public.

Inspired by Hermione Lee's new biography, *Virginia Woolf* (1996) (which has not been translated into Danish), Suzanne Brøgger wrote a feature article for the paper *Weekendavisen*, '"Jeg ville skrive om døden, men livet brød ind som sædvanlig"' ('I Wanted to Write about Death, but Life Interfered as Always'). She writes of her 'fear' or 'anxiety' about Woolf's importance and influence: Woolf's writing may be tantalizing but her personal life was complex in the extreme. Brøgger begins:

> By instinct, a woman writer will always try to avoid Virginia Woolf carefully. Or rather frantically. For she is the kind of archetype of the sexed art of writing which always draws your attention to the problem that if you base your (sexual) life on the production of words, you will have to commit suicide when the words no longer

---

12 Hansen also dedicates chapters to Joyce, whose *Ulysses* was a bible to him, Baudelaire and Lautréamont, who worshipped the beauty of madness, D. H. Lawrence, Dorothy Richardson, Rachel Ingalls, Doris Lessing and Edwin Muir, who, like Hansen, underwent a transition from realism to myth.

sustain you. And how long will they sustain you? Silence is to be the aim. (Brøgger 1997, 2)[13]

Brøgger nevertheless describes, celebrates and reflects on Woolf's life-long need to turn chaos into order, 'to create a language where language normally breaks down' (Brøgger 1997, 2).[14] She comes to define Woolf's soul as porous as a sieve. 'She let reality pass through every hole in herself, and she survived by translating this penetration into words' (Brøgger 1997, 2).[15] By turning memories into fiction she created some kind of order in what had been total chaos in her soul. But in 1941 the mental overload was beginning to weigh her down: Brøgger describes the sieve breaking, and Virginia Woolf drowning in 'voices'.

In comparison with Jørgen Christian Hansen's autobiographical response, both texts develop into extensive accounts of Woolf's life and the historical background to it. But whereas Hansen's creativity is indebted to the myth of Woolf's personal life and mental instability, her reputation as icon, Brøgger's response focuses more elaborately on her personal anxiety about adopting Woolf's difficulties in coming to terms with her own identity in relation to language. These two responses from creative writers, a man and a woman, parallel Mørk and Ørum's introductions to Woolf in the press in 1982. We recall that Mørk also dwelled on the mythic image of Woolf, whereas Ørum directed our attention to Woolf's texts and female aesthetics. The tendency to divide Woolf into either icon or writer in her own right might be gender-related.

Unlike Brøgger, Jette Lundbo Levy, a scholar in Danish literature, did not present Woolf as porous in 'Den store vægring ved historien og politikken' (The Great Resistance to History and Politics), a chapter in her work of cultural criticism, *Modstandens figurer: fiktion, historie og køn* (Figures of Resistance: Fiction, History and Gender), published by Rosinante in 1987. On the contrary, here Woolf is presented as a woman with very strong opinions, and her perspectives on women's role in history are rendered as essential and incontestable. The chapter is shaped as a fictive dialogue between Woolf and the modern Italian left-wing politician, author and editor of *Il Manifesto*, Rossana Rossanda.

The general scope of this book is to shed light on modern culture's obsession with gender. Gender differences do not just express an absence characteristic of women in history, they have also become a starting point from which we can hope for new cultural patterns and paradigms. All the writers dealt with in Lundbo Levy's study have these ideas as their starting point, and

---

13 'Som kvindelig forfatter går man instinktivt i en stor bue uden om Virginia Woolf. Eller rettere, man springer. For hun er en slags arketype for den kønnede skrivekunst, der altid minder én om, at hvis man baserer sit (køns)-liv på at producere ord, så er man nødt til at tage sit eget liv den dag ordene ikke længere kan bære. Og hvor langt bærer ord? Det er stilheden man stiler imod.'

14 'at skabe sprog på det sted, hvor sproget ellers bryder sammen.'

15 'Gennem alle hullerne lod hun virkeligheden gennemtrænge sig og hun overlevede ved at omsætte penetrationen til ord.'

their attempts to change things become, for them, a kind of mental archaeology.

By making a book on this subject into a series of fictive dialogues, Lundbo Levy provides a reconstructed, *symbolic* solution to these issues of gender. All writers, Virginia Woolf, Rossana Rossanda, Peter Weiss, Christa Wolf, and the Danish Kirsten Thorup and Hans Christian Andersen, scrutinize and criticize Western society as well as reflect on the relationship between history, subjectivity, gender and form in what can be called an *aesthetics of resistance* (Lundbo Levy 1987, 9). This concept includes a vision of and trust in how the course of history might change if women were to take part in the creation of what has been a male-dominated society. This aspect is for example characteristic of Woolf, says Lundbo Levy. With her, as with the other writers, there is a major tension between analysis and vision.

According to Lundbo Levy, modern writers concerned with gender and society require new experiences and new ways of understanding in order to break familiar habits of women's marginality. The long dialogue between Woolf and Rossanda about art, gender, politics and history seeks to open new pathways, illustrate new solutions to such problems, in a symbolic way rather than in a conventional critical analysis of Western civilization.

The basic purpose of the dialogue between such different women as a politically active feminist like Rossanda and an 'ethereal novelist', as Woolf is presented here, is to analyse how their different points of view on womanhood and history can be combined in a fruitful new perspective on women's role in history. The chapter opens with Rossana Rossanda's strong visions about changing Italian society, but she does not quite know how to turn theory into reality. She's working on an article on the current situation in Poland, but her prospects of finding any *real* solutions to various problems have become bleaker over the years. Then Woolf enters the room, but Rossanda is sceptical about how she might contribute to the problem, as Woolf is, in her view, the 'high priestess of narcissism' (Lundbo Levy 1987, 15).

Their discussion begins with Rossanda blaming Woolf for writing 'unreal' novels. She does not, for instance, understand *TL*, but Woolf answers that Rossanda's historical and political 'realities' are false as they are in principle male-dominated and full of abstract rules that kill life as it is really lived. Mrs Ramsay's dinner party is more real than anything, claims Woolf, as it is a work of art about human relations.

After a second discussion about anti-fascism in *TG* and Antigone's role as first evidence of the conflict between the state and the freedom of the individual, Woolf expresses her concern with modern women's denial of womanhood. Fear of being a woman, she says, will lead only to a renunciation of one's own wants in favour of a higher idea, which will ultimately result in ignorance of *other* people's wants. The ascetic ideals of political institutions, such as the ones Rossanda is part of, force people to lose the use of their senses. By insisting on one idea only, others will be lost or shut out. In defence of her aesthetic, Woolf says that her stories portray how acceptance of womanhood in general can make characters turn away from the narrowness of focusing on personal wants and lives (Lundbo Levy 1987, 23–24).

Rossanda then confesses to Woolf that her slogan, 'Liberty, equality and fraternity' does not seem to have caught on among Italian women. What is she to do? During the last part of the conversation, Woolf helps Rossanda to understand that she needs to keep her eyes open, to resist becoming enclosed in the single dimension of radical politics: Rossanda should see the beauty in dignity and hope, not only focus on problems and injustice, and should consider events in the mix so as to fathom how history changes, all of which means abstaining from isolating and categorizing issues and events in the name of left-wing politics (Lundbo Levy 1987, 24–25). The essence of Woolf's argument is that Rossanda needs to be in close contact with real people out there in the real world, in order to encourage and inspire a feeling of *real* solidarity among women. Rossanda must look for patterns instead of differences.

After Woolf has left, Rossanda can eventually finish her article by emphasizing the need to fight for freedom, openness and dialogue (Lundbo Levy 1987, 27). In short, in spite of their differences of opinion, Woolf and Rossanda agree that history and people's bearings on history will change only if women also have a say, become visible and take an active share in traditionally male-dominated Western societies. Interestingly, when comparing Elsa Gress's, Tania Ørum's, Vibeke Grønfeldt's, Lotte Thrane's and now Jette Lundbo Levy's conception of Virginia Woolf, all embrace her as spokeswoman of the insistence on *not* creating a war between the sexes and *not* focusing on and maintaining rigid differences between men and women, as was the case in the more militant feminist movements of the 1970s. Woolf's aesthetics and political stance have been embraced by Danish women writers and critics who do not belong to the schools of dogmatic feminism. They have found in Woolf the perfect means of emphasizing the need for mutuality, flexibility, dialogue and understanding between the sexes.

In 1991, after the new 'discovery' and creative use of Virginia Woolf in the media and in the rise of women's studies during the 1980s, Merete Ries felt the time was ripe to publish a translated biography of Woolf in 1991. Nina Lautrup-Larsen translated selected extracts from Leonard Woolf's *Autobiography* (1960-69) and called the Danish publication *Virginia*. It also contains a translation of Friederike Groth's preface to the German edition, *Mein Leben mit Virginia* from 1988.

Three years later *TW* was translated as *Bølgerne* by Anne Marie Bjerg and published by Rosinante (reprinted 1997). Anne Marie Bjerg is a highly acclaimed, prize-winning translator of texts from English and Swedish, including a new translation of James Joyce's *Dubliners*. Her translation of *TW* is perhaps a breakthrough in the Danish reception of Virginia Woolf. It establishes her definitively as a great writer on a par with other European classics. Her art is accepted in its own right instead of being an exemplar for the women's movement only. Her reputation has at last cast off the feminist burden of the 1970s whereby she was solely linked with *ROO*.

The translation received a series of exhilarated reviews which reflect the reception of the original text. In her diary Woolf wonders: 'Really, this unintelligible book is being better received than any of them . . . And it sells – how unexpected, how odd that people can read that difficult grinding stuff!' (*WD* 175). The following is a representative selection:

May Schack finds the novel astonishingly modern in its treatment of the opposition between a stable identity and the dissolution of the 'I'. Schack also praises Woolf's attempt to catch and depict emotions, especially the way in which they are re-experienced in the moment of recollection (Schack 1994).

Lars Ole Sauerberg calls the novel 'hypnotic reading' ('hypnotisk læsning'), referring to the new reading experience demanding that readers sustain their concentration at all times. The reader will experience an almost hypnotic sensation in which Woolf's ethical message and aesthetic style will melt into something incredibly beautiful and touching. As with Proust's *À la Recherche du temps perdu* this novel is about the nature of memory, existential continuity and the possible ways in which people can involve themselves with each other emotionally (Sauerberg 1994).

The Danish translation of *TW* is a major event, according to the late poet and famous reviewer Poul Borum. He describes it as a novel of great pain, tenderness and human understanding, so rich and multitudinous that it can be read over and over again. This, together with Proust, Musil and Márquez, is one of the novels of the year, infers Borum (Borum 1994).

Jette Lundbo Levy regrets that it is impossible to write a review which does this novel justice. She claims that it is a great reading experience and intellectual challenge in its profound description of the relationship between language and the world. *TW* has not won all hearts, and Levy suggests that it is because it is simply too big, too sublime, as it is both immensely fascinating in terms of style and, in terms of themes, prone to inspire the reader with fear; the novel simply challenges our inherent conceptions of what it means to exist (Lundbo Levy 1994).

These reviews all stake out Woolf's status by describing the sublimity of her vision and style and by comparing her with established classics of modernism.

In her review, however, Tania Ørum recounts that she did not finish her reading the first time she tried to tackle *TW*. She found it too abstract and monotonous. It was not until she had become acquainted with the writings of Freud that she became fascinated by the psychological drama in Woolf's treatment of human development. The second time Ørum tried reading the novel, she became absorbed and learned how to read it slowly so as to digest every single memorable observation and wording. The novel invites the reader to sink into a sea of interpretations which, Ørum claims, will always remain impressed on his or her mind (Ørum 1995). The same might be said of the general reception of Virginia Woolf in Denmark – all the above sources demonstrate the extent of the popular interpretations of her life and works (and the responses are in their own right both impressed and impressing) from which, however, an academic reception is largely absent.

Summary

The lack of a substantially theoretical approach to Woolf in Danish scholarship is counterbalanced by the fact that the fusion of popular and academic reception in the media and cultural/literary magazines expresses a desire to read Woolf according to her own spirit. In her essay 'The Leaning Tower' (1940)

Woolf says that 'the germ of a theory is almost always the wish to prove what the theorist wishes to believe. Theories then are dangerous things' (Woolf 1972, 163). On a par with Woolf's own beautifully lyrical and impressionistic essays, some of the noteworthy responses to Woolf by creative writers in Denmark for the past twenty years have been written in the same impressionistic manner, and a few even as either lyrical, interpretative paraphrases of her novels or as heated dialogue between feminists. One translator in particular, Anne Marie Bjerg, has excelled in striking and sustaining the right Woolfian note.

As Woolf says at the end of 'The Leaning Tower':

> Literature is no one's private ground; literature is common ground. It is not cut up into nations; there are no wars there. Let us trespass freely and fearlessly and find our own way for ourselves. It is thus that English literature will survive this war and cross the gulf – if commoners and outsiders like ourselves make that country our own country, if we teach ourselves to read and write, how to preserve, and how to create. (CE 2: 181)

Thanks to the pioneering work of Merete Ries, who had Woolf properly and widely introduced in Denmark, and the new academic trail blazed by Tania Ørum, Virginia Woolf's writings have, over the past twenty years, inspired Danish responses which are filled with enthusiasm, admiration and respect for her visions and achievements as woman and writer. The women writers, critics and translators who have expressed gratitude to Woolf in public have made her vision their own. Woolf suffuses the media and popular intellectual culture, such that knowledge of her life and writing will gradually become common ground in Danish literary and academic circles. In fact, she is well on her way as a special supplement on the history of the past millenium in the Sunday edition of *Politiken*, 26 December 1999, ranks her contribution to world history as worthy of a place on a list of national and international historical giants, including Mahatma Gandhi (1922) and Adolf Hitler (1925), listed immediately before her, and succeeded by Joseph Stalin (1931) and the Danish architect and writer Poul Henningsen (1934). The brief text accompanying a photo of Woolf epitomizes her historical status: 'with her sophisticated impressionistic style, her novels and essays such as *A Room of One's Own*, Virginia Woolf came to play a crucial role in women's politics' (*Politiken* 1999, 15).[16]

---

16 'kommer med sin raffinerede impressionistiske stil, sine romaner og essays som *ROO* (*Eget værelse*) til at spille en vigtig kvindepolitisk rolle.' It is interesting to note that, despite this celebration of Woolf's significance, the year of publication of *ROO* given is incorrect.

10 'The Country of the Moon' and the Woman of 'Interior Monologue': Virginia Woolf in Greece[1]

Katerina K. Kitsi-Mitakou

The year 1932 initiated a reciprocal relation between a country and a person, for there can be 'sympathies between people & places, as between human beings', as Virginia Woolf observes in a diary entry during her second visit to Greece (*D* 4: 8 May 1932). Late in April 1932 Leonard and Virginia Woolf travel by train through Paris and then at Venice embark on a ship, which takes them down the Adriatic and round the southern coast of Greece to Athens. 'One night at Venice then on down the Adriatic with Venizelos on board, passing the islands all day yesterday' (*L* 5: 20 April 1932) – Woolf had got as close as possible to the heart of Greek history. The inter-war period, which in most European countries had started in 1918, started in Greece in 1922, after the Asia Minor disaster – only ten years after the recovery from Turkey of Macedonia, Crete, and the Aegean Islands in 1912. The state of Greece was in ruin as it had lost almost all its lands in Asia Minor, and the refugees swarmed into Greece. Eleftherios Venizelos, who had managed to overthrow the monarchy and institute a republic in 1924, was unable to stop another military *coup d'état* that restored the monarchy, and effective power passed into the hands of Ioannis Metaxas who instituted a dictatorial regime. Poverty, pain, exhaustion: Woolf is subtle enough to observe and record in her diary:

---

[1] Research for the present study has been conducted in the libraries of Thessaloniki (Library of Modern Greek and Medieval Studies, Libraries of the Greek and English Departments of the Aristotle University, City Library, and Vafopoulio Library) and Athens (National Library of Greece, Library of the Parliament (Benakios) and Gennadios Library). I would like to thank Argiro Mantoglou and Miltos Pechlivanos who helped me enrich my bibliographical references and Mary Mike, my colleague from the Department of Medieval and Modern Greek studies, for her ardent support and enlightening comments. Final thanks, as always, to Professor Jina Politi.

> Greece then, so to return to Greece, is a land so ancient that it is like wandering in the fields of the moon. Life is receding (in spite of that donkey). The living, these worn down, for ever travelling the roads Greeks, cannot master Greece any longer. It is too bare too stony, precipitous for them. We met them always on the high mountain passes paddling along beside their donkeys, so small, existing so painfully, always marching in search of some herb, some root, mastered by the vast distances, unable to do more than dig their heels in the rock. Such solitude as they must know, under the sun, under the snow, such dependence on themselves to clothe & feed themselves through the splendid summer days is unthinkable in England. The centuries have left no traces. There is no 18th 16th, 15th all in layers as in England – nothing between them & 300 B.C. somehow <dominated> conquered Greece & still holds it. So it is the country of the moon; I mean, lit by a dead sun. (*D* 4: 2 May 1932)

The trips to Sunium, Aegina, Marathon, Corinth, Mycenae, Nauplia, Sparta, Delphi are like (if one could use Conrad's words here) 'travelling back to the earliest beginnings of the world' (1993, 1783); *her* world, as in her visit to the Parthenon she meets her own 'ghost', 'the girl of 23, with all her life to come' (*D* 4: 21 April 1932);[2] the world of the Ancient Greek poets and philosophers whom she had been studying and admiring ever since she was a girl; the world of Byzantium powerful enough to restore her religious feelings: 'all that is in me of stunted and deformed religion flowered under this hot sensuality, so thick, so yellow, so waxen; . . . Why, we almost wept, we pagans' (*L* 5: 4 May 1932). The present of Greece is the past of England, it is 'England in the time of Chaucer', it is Greece in the year 300 BC, it is her own past. This is perhaps what makes Greece 'far and away the loveliest country now left – quite unspoilt – in fact, uncivilized' (*L* 5: 2 May 1932).

Tuesday 10 May 1932. Thessaloniki is on Virginia Woolf's way to Yugoslavia from where she will take the Orient Express back to England. There is just one short, passing remark in her diary: 'At Salonika (1.30) *they* came in to ask about money [my italics]' (*D* 4: 10 May 1932). 'They', refugees, poor, famished, worn out, homeless people: Salonika/Thessaloniki was saturated with such a population. Still, the city was trying hard to forget the wounds of the past and move forward. On the one hand, pain and misery. On the other hand, the University of Thessaloniki, newly founded in 1926, the second university established in Greece after the University of Athens, with only one school in the beginning, the School of Philosophy. At the same time a group of literary people, prose-writers mostly, start publishing a new periodical with the title *Makedonikes Imeres* (Macedonian Days); its first issue comes out in March 1932. The name of Virginia Woolf, as well as the first translation of her work, appears for the first time in Greece in *Makedonikes Imeres*: a translation of her short story 'Moments of Being: Slater's Pins Have No Points' (Stigmes zois: I karfitses tis Slater then tripoun). In their effort to break away from the long-standing tradition of the *roman de mœurs*, regional novels that dominated the literary scene of Greece from 1880 to 1900, this

---

2 Woolf refers here to her 1906 visit to Greece with her sister, her brothers and her friend Violet Dickinson.

group who were given the name the 'School of Thessaloniki' (S. Xefloudas, Y. Delios, A. Yiannopoulos, N. G. Pentzikis) despite the fact that each of them had his own unique style, turn towards the West for an alternative future.

Some have spoken of a lack of cultural tradition and of a literary establishment in Thessaloniki (Christianopoulos 1958, 13); others have ascribed their being influenced by the West to the geographic position of the city: the dull and cold wintry climate of a northern city which seeped into the misty, dreary representation of the world found in these writers (Vitti 1987, 388), or to the seclusion of the city and its inhabitants, 'people', as Kitsopoulos records, 'inaccessible, inexpressive, reserved' (1962, 1782). This turn inwards, he continues, is 'a kind of escape from reality', a way to be free from 'former conventions, and to express themselves better in relation to the city they lived in' (1782).[3]

And this is where a country and a person converge: Woolf had discovered the past in what for Greece was the present; the 'School of Thessaloniki' was discovering in Woolf their future. And so, past, present and future were interwoven in modernist fluidity.

In the first issue of *Makedonikes Imeres* P. S. Spandonidis in his article 'Kathreftismata' (Reflections) observes the new tendency in art to move away from realism and its extreme manifestation, which he calls naturalism. After Bergson, James, Schiller, Dilthey and Brunetière, Spandonidis points out, Truth will never be static or fixed again. Art seeks for a Truth that is fluid, it becomes subjective, 'expressionistic', as he calls it, and objects are subjugated to subjects. Art is 'an inward look, into inner life that is flowing, art is expression' (Spandonidis 1932, 30).[4] The term 'interior monologue' makes its entrance into Greek scholarship, along with the names of Gide, Werfel, Whitman, Claudel and Joyce. It is defined by Spandonidis as a 'reflection of the unconscious', an effort to 'express thought at the stage of its construction, before thought falls into a plan, before it turns to reason', 'the quintessence of poetry, as poetry too is an expression of the unconscious' (1932, 31).[5] English fiction of the modern period is, according to Piniatoglou in a later issue of *Makedonikes Imeres*, the only truly important work of our century; D. H. Lawrence, Mansfield, Woolf, Joyce are acclaimed (1932, 393). Speaking of the 'Literature of the young', Spandonidis makes the connection between Woolf and two young writers, Karavias and Kastanakis: they have escaped from the web-like literature of the 'spider', as he calls it, where everything is 'complete,

---

3 'anthropi disprositi, dihos ameses ekdilosis, singratimeni', 'ena idos figis apo tin pragmatikotita', 'etsi eleftheronontan apo progenesteres simvatikotites kai borousan na dosoun kalitera ton eafto tous kai ti shesi si tous me ta pragmata tis polis opou zousan'.

4 'expressionistiki', 'I tehni etsi ginete mia enorasi tis esoterikis zois, pou kila kai mia ekfrasi'.

5 'ena kathreftisma tou iposiniditou', 'Prospathi na ekfrasi ti skepsi sto stadio tis ikodomiseos, protou bi se shedio, protou gini *logiki*', 'o esoterikos monologos egizi tin pemptousia tis piiseos, giati kai I iisi ine ekdilosi tou iposiniditou'.

interconnected, and consistent' (1934, 25).[6] As in Woolf, 'no explanations are given, life is purposeless', Spandonidis says using A. Maurois's words (1934, 25).[7]

It is the treatment of such issues as the elements of poetry in fiction, the technique of interior monologue and the fluidity of time that most of these writers admire in Woolf.

'What is missing from most literary production of Greece is poetry in its wider sense', S. Xefloudas writes in his article 'Sholia' (Comments) in 1935 (159).[8] The generation after the war had been trying hard to create a new literature; 'there are some novels', he writes, 'coloured with those wonderful colours that only poetry can depict, novels in which reality is surrounded by a halo whose light extends to an interminable depth. Everything in these novels is covered by an imaginary aura, they have their own temperature, they live in an endless dream, they are flooded by an imperceptible music' (Xefloudas 1935, 161–62).[9] Mrs Dalloway, he continues, 'transfer[s] us incessantly to the magic world of the truest poetry, of the purest beauty'. 'In order for us to feel this beauty, we must let our soul unite with that of the writer, and worship all those figures that speak so softly .... These silent confessions ... this inexplicable sorrow that overcomes the soul of the characters' must become part of us (Xefloudas 1935, 162–63).[10] In 1955 Stelios Xefloudas writes an essay *To sinhrono mithistorima* (The Modern Novel). Virginia Woolf is here also mentioned among the leading figures of the modern novel, along with Proust, Kafka, Joyce and Faulkner. Xefloudas points out the musicality, poetry and melancholy in the writings of Woolf (1955, 25), her intermittent oscillation between past and present (70) – influenced as she has been by Bergson – and her use of interior monologue (86–87), all of which have been dynamically adopted by Greek novelists who wished to break away from the *roman de mœurs*.

More influenced than any other writer of the 1930s by Virginia Woolf, Yiorgos Delios starts writing about Woolf in 1938 in *Makedonikes Imeres*. In his article 'Apopsis gia to angliko mithistorima' (Views on the English Novel), Delios observes the shift of emphasis from the outside to the inside, the

---

6 'i logotehnia tis arahnis', 'teliomena, allilendeta kai sinepi'.

7 'Then exigi tipote, de dini sti zoi kanenan skopo'.

8 'ekino pou lipi sti megaliteri logotehniki mas paragogi, ine i piisi stin pio platia tis simasia'.

9 'Iparhoun kapia mithistorimata hromatismena me ta exesia ekina hromata pou monaha i piisi bori na mas ta zografisi kai opou i pragmatikotita ehi giro tis ena fotostefano pou to fos tou makreni s' ena vathos atelioto. Ola s' afta ine skpasmena me mian atmosfera fantastiki, ehoun mia diki tous thermokrasia, zoun mesa s' ena atelioto oniro, ola ta plimmirizi mia mousiki pou molis akougete'.

10 'I kiria Dalloway tis Woolf ... mas metafer[i] adiakopa sto magiko kosmo tis pio alithinis piisis, tis pio agnis omorfias', 'Gia na niosoume tin omorfia afton ton vivlion hriazete ... na enosoume tin psihi mas me ekini tou dimiourgou, na latrepsoume oles aftes tis morfes pou mas milan toso siga .... Aftes i siopiles exomologisis ... afti i thlipsi i anexigiti kapote pou plimmirizi tin psihi ton prosopon'.

constant preoccupation with the unconscious in modern writers such as Proust and Joyce, a tendency influenced by the study of psychoanalysis. Woolf, Delios continues, quoting her famous passage from 'Modern Fiction' ('Examine for a moment an ordinary mind') (Woolf 1993, 1923), frees herself completely from the conventions of fiction. Her mind, her time is adapted to the rhythms of modern life, moving in and out of the present and the past in its effort to capture everything that surrounds us. No explanation is given, no conclusions are drawn. We are to love life as it is offered to us, as comedy, as tragedy, as 'true poetry' (Delios 1938a, 214).[11] The same thoughts are continued in the next issue of *Makedonikes Imeres*. Woolf's characters, Delios observes, are not even vague, remote reflections of reality, as they have no materiality, no substance. They throw light on one another with their thoughts, their memories, their feelings, their moods, and a great part of them has to be illuminated by the imagination of the reader. But they will never be autonomous, independent creatures, as it is impossible really to know anyone completely. Delios draws examples here from *VO*, *TL* and *O*, and ends by comparing *MD* with *Ulysses*. Unlike Joyce, Delios says, Woolf does not attempt to include everything in her works, she limits her search to the inner world, where 'everything is soft, aerial ... everything acquires a magic touch' (1938b, 247).[12]

Delios's interest in Woolf is manifested also in the two books that he published: *To sinhrono mithistorima* (The Modern Novel) in 1939, and *Dio Anglides pezografi: Virgina Woolf & Katherine Mansfield*: *Dokimia kai metafrasis* (Two English Prose Writers: Virginia Woolf and Katherine Mansfield: Essays and Translations) in 1963. In the first of these books, Delios starts by making passing references to English women novelists of the nineteenth century (Jane Austen, Charlotte Brontë, George Eliot) in order to point out that the creative abilities of modern women writers have caused a 'peaceful' ('iriniki') revolution in the literary life of England. He mentions the names of Rose Macaulay, Margaret Kennedy, Katherine Mansfield and, of course, Virginia Woolf. Delios focuses on Woolf in the rest of his book, whom he considers one of the most, if not the most important modern English writer. He is aware that his book is the first sizeable attempt in Greece to approach Woolf's work in all its extent and depth (47), and he appears to be familiar with it, summarizing and commenting on almost all her fictional and critical writings, such as *CR*, *ROO*, *VO*, *ND*, *JR*, *TL*, *MD*, *O* and *TW*. Despite the fact that Delios's writing appears to be more descriptive at certain points in his book – something unavoidable since he writes at a time when Woolf's texts have not yet been translated into Greek – he is perceptive enough to detect Woolf's total liberation from the tyranny of plot, her impressionism, her silences that at times can reveal more than speech, the mist surrounding her characters, the dreamy atmosphere, her attempt to present the multiplicity of time and point of view, the influence of Henri Bergson's theories on time, her emphasis on memory, her use of interior monologue, most of all, a pervasive tendency to melancholy.

---

11 'alithini piisi'.

12 'ta panta ine lepta kai etheria, ... ta panta apoktoun mian opsi magiki'.

A large part of Delios's book, *To sinhrono mithistorima*, appeared again in 1963 in *Dio Anglides pezografi: Virgina Woolf and Katherine Mansfield*: *Dokimia kai metafrasis*. Delios adds here a new section which deals with Woolf as an essay writer and critic. By referring to and quoting from *CDB* and *GR*, he characterizes her as a systematic and sensitive critic. When writing about a certain period Woolf tries to recreate the mood and the atmosphere, to help the reader become acclimatized to a certain time in history. Woolf's criticism is 'impressionistic' ('empressionistiki [*sic*]') (1963, 61), Delios continues, as she manages to make her readers participants in the specific historical moment of the writer she studies. He also speaks of Woolf as a woman writer abstaining from any active struggle for the equality of the two sexes. She is interested in the education and cultivation of women. The famous passage on Shakespeare's sister is quoted at this point; the end, however, is missing. The section about Judith's pregnancy and death is perhaps too cruel to be translated by Delios, and in contradiction with his mental image of a kind and refined lady. The section on Woolf contains also translations of 'Three Pictures' (Ikones Tris), 'Moments of Being: Slater's Pins Have No Points' (Stigmes zois: I karfitses tis Slater then tripoun), and two excerpts from her *Diary* (26 January 1940 and 8 March 1941).

In the 1940s and 1950s a number of translations of Woolf appeared for the first time in the Athens journal *Nea Estia* (New Vestal): in 1945 'Apospasmata apo *Ta kimata*' (Selections from *TW*), in 1946 'To stihiomeno spiti' ('The Haunted House'), in 1949 'Ikones tris' ('Three Pictures'), in 1950 'I kiria kai o kathreftis' ('The Lady in the Looking Glass'), in 1955 'Virginia Woolf: Apo to Imerologio [1940–41]' (Virginia Woolf: from her diary [1940–41]). In 1948 there was also a translation in the journal *Alexandrini Logotehnia* (Alexandrine Literature): 'To mithistorima pou then graftike' ('An Unwritten Novel'). During that period a number of articles, or excerpts from books written by English critics on Woolf and English literature appeared in translation in the journal *Angloelliniki Epitheorisi* (English-Greek Review): in 1946 John Lehmann's 'Virginia Woolf', followed by a translation of her short story 'The Legacy' (I klironomia), and Elizabeth Bowen's 'English Fiction at Mid-Century' (To angliko mithistorima sto diastima tou mesopolemou), in 1947 Rosamond Lehmann's 'The Future of the Novel' (To mellon tou mithistorimatos), and in 1950 Henry Reed's 'The Novel since 1939' (To angliko mithistorima apo to 1939). I will not attempt to comment on these articles here, as they are by non-Greek critics; I only wish to point out that here Woolf's use of interior monologue, her preoccupation with rhythm, her obsession with her characters are once again stressed.

Despite the fact that there was such a warm reception of Woolf in the 1930s by the 'School of Thessaloniki' and, as we have seen, numerous translations of her short stories in literary journals, the first translation of a novel appeared quite late, in 1967 *I kiria Dalloway* (*MD*), and six years later a much improved translation (closer to Woolf's style and making a more creative use of the Modern Greek language) of the same novel by a different translator and with a slightly different title *Mia imera tis kirias Dalloway* (A Day of Mrs Dalloway). By the end of the 1970s interest in Woolf as a woman writer began to rise. Translations of selections from four different texts by Woolf appeared in the feminist journal *Skoupa* (Broom) in 1979: 'A Sketch of the Past', 'Women and Fiction' from *ROO*, selections from *D* and from *TG*.

It is in the 1980s really that a new surge of interest in Woolf took place, and carried on into the 1990s too, as is manifested by the numerous translations of her books, in many cases of the same book by different translators: in 1980 *Ena diko sou domatio* (*ROO*), in 1981 *Mehri to Faro*, in 1982 *Sto faro* (two different translations of *TL*), in 1982 *Tris ginees* (*TG*), in 1984 and 1986 *Ta kimata* (*TW*) by three different translators, in 1984 *Orlando*, in 1987 and 1996 *Ena stihiomeno spiti kai alla diigimata* (*HH*), in 1987 *To domatio tou Jacob* and in 1988 *To domatio tou Iakovou* (*JR*), in 1987 again *Ellada kai Mais mazi* (Greece and May Together: A Selection of Letters and Diary Entries During Woolf's Visit to Greece in 1932), in 1988 *Ginekia portreta: dokimia kai kritiki* (a selection of essays from *BP*),[13] in 1990 a third translation of *MD, I kiria Dalloway*, in 1991 *Ta hronia* (*TY*), in 1992 *FB*, in 1996 *Leshi ginekon kai alla diigimata* ('A Society' and Other Short Stories),[14] in 1997 *Gramma s'ena neo piiti* (*LYP*, with a commentary by Aris Berlis), in 1998 *Gia tin agnia ton arheon ellinikon* ('On Not Knowing Greek'), and *Skotonontas ton angelo tou spitiou* ('Killing the Angel in the House'), in 1999 *Dokimia* (Essays).[15] Many of these editions came out more than once, an indication that the public's interest in Woolf has increased significantly from the 1980s onwards. Translations of short stories and excerpts from diaries and letters appeared from time to time in journals, as, for example, in 1980 'Pos diavazoume ena vivlio' ('How Does One Read a Book?'), in 1983 'To simadi ston tiho' ('The Mark on the Wall'), in 1994 'Mia isagogi sto *Sinesthimatiko taxidi*' (AN Introduction to *A Sentimental Journey* [i.e. excerpts from 'The Sentimental Journey]), in 1996 'Gramma apo tous Delfous' ('Letter from Delphi' to Vanessa Bell, 2 May 1932) and in 1998 'Epangelmata ginekon' ('Professions for Women').

It is in the 1980s also that a serious attempt was made towards a critical reading of Woolf, and this was located mainly in the scholarly journal *Diavazo* (I read) in two special issues, one on English Literature which came out in 1982,[16] and the second on Virginia Woolf in 1986. In 1982 Aris Berlis wrote about 'Virginia Woolf and the Novel'. His effort to see Woolf, a leading figure, he says, in modern fiction along with Proust and Joyce, from a critical point of

---

13 'A Woman's College from Outside', 'Men and Women', 'Praeterita', 'Dostoevsky the Father', 'Maria Edgeworth and Her Circle', 'Jane Austen and the Geese', 'Mrs Gaskell', 'Wilcoxiana', 'Shelley and Elizabeth Hitchener', 'The Girlhood of Queen Elizabeth', 'The Diary of a Lady in Waiting', 'Queen Adelaide', 'Elizabeth Lady Holland', 'Lady Hester Stanhope', 'The Memoirs of Sarah Bernhardt', 'Lady Strachey'.

14 'The Mark on the Wall', 'The Duchess and the Jeweller', 'Kew Gardens'.

15 Translations of 'How Should One Read a Book?', 'Pictures', 'Professions for Women', 'Personalities', 'The Artist and Politics', 'Three Pictures', 'Old Mrs Grey', 'The Decay of Essay Writing', 'The Modern Novel'. Reviewed by Roumboula 1999 and Spinou 1999.

16 In the same year a Greek translation of Peter Faulkner's book *Modernism* was published which contains a chapter on Woolf 'Kritika dokimia tis Virginia Woolf' (Virginia Woolf's critical essays).

view is to a great extent influenced by Erich Auerbach's article 'The Brown Stocking' in his book *Mimesis*, from which he quotes extensively in his article. (Berlis was using the English translation of *Mimesis*, as the book had not been translated into Greek.) He summarizes four basic points from Auerbach's article: the lack of objective narration, the multiplicity of consciousness, the conflict between external and internal time, the emphasis on unimportant, everyday facts. The importance of this article lies in the fact that it initiates Greek readers, through Auerbach, into a close reading of the literary text and into basic narratological concepts. This is something which Olympia Karagiorga's book, *Virginia Woolf: Mia megali agnosti* (Virginia Woolf: A Great Unknown), does not aspire to do. The book, which also came out in 1982, is a collage of passages from various works by Woolf gathered together in thematic units ('I am in love with life', 'The two worlds', 'Unborn selves', 'Human nature is implacable', 'Private room', 'Let's live together freely' are some of the titles of the chapters). The writer's voice is in a sense an echo of the fragmentary, stream of consciousness voices one comes across in Woolf's writings, and the reader has the impression that such confusion is, after all, desirable.

The special issue of *Diavazo* on Woolf in 1986 is a collection of nine articles by Greek scholars and poets, all women. Maria Koutsoudaki's article 'Pia ine i kiria Dalloway' (Who Is Mrs Dalloway?) focuses on Mrs Dalloway's character, her empty life despite her social success, her adolescent love for Sally Seton, her virginity which, as she says, is very close to Septimus Smith's aversion to fleshly love, while at the same time she draws parallels between Mrs Dalloway's and Virginia Woolf's lives. Both Clarissa and Woolf (and Septimus, of course) listen to the birds singing in Greek and manage to transform those moments of madness into moments of mysticism and creativity (30). Her article 'O "Ellinas" Iakovos: I Ellada sto *Domatio tou Iakovou*' (The 'Greek' Jacob: Greece in *Jacob's Room*) centres on Jacob's love for and debt to Ancient Greek civilization, as they are manifested throughout the novel, and remarks also on Woolf's own debt to Ancient Greek tragedy with which she was very familiar. The theme of the novel, she says, does not concern only Jacob's personal drama; it is the tragedy of mankind, of every human being, who, like Jacob, wishes to achieve the state of the perfect fighter and citizen while still retaining his personal characteristics (48).

In this same issue, Afroditi Panagi's article 'To thema tou kallitehni sto *Pros to faro* tis Virginia Woolf' (The Theme of the Artist in Virginia Woolf's *To the Lighthouse*) has been influenced to a great extent by her readings of Joan Bennett's *Virginia Woolf: Her Art as a Novelist* (1945), Arnold Kettle's *Introduction to the English Novel* (1951), and Leon Edel's *The Modern Psychological Novel* (1964). She is more interested in Lily Briscoe's struggle to portray Mrs Ramsay, in the relationship between the two women, and the symbolism of the trip to the Lighthouse that is finally accomplished at the end of the novel. Maria Anastasopoulou's article 'To lirko mithistorima kai i Virginia Woolf' (The Lyrical Novel and Virginia Woolf) is to a great extent a brief summary of Ralph Freedman's book *The Lyrical Novel* (1963), and presents Woolf as one of the most important representatives of the lyrical novel. Liana Sakelliou-Schultz's '*Ta kimata* kai i "ipogia" metaphora tous' (*The Waves* Bearing Us

'Under Ground') explores waves as the basic structural and thematic pattern in Woolf's novel. The relationships between the characters/speakers are 'underground' relationships, organic, not obvious; life, like the waves, does not change, it is a succession of repetitive acts. Efi Lambadaridou's 'Diania kai fantasia ston *Orlando* tis Virginia Woolf' (Intellect and imagination in Virginia Woolf's *Orlando*) characterizes O as a record of English society and literature, a psychological novel in which both the intellect and the Imagination of its creator are harmoniously combined in order to trace the process that man/woman has followed in his/her desire for poetry. Sofia I. Kazakou's 'I feministiki apopsi tis Woolf mesa apo dio dokimia tis' (Woolf's Feminism in Two of Her Essays) depicts Woolf as a socially active writer who recorded and denounced all discrimination against women. For the first time in Greece Woolf is presented as the forerunner of the modern feminist movement, for, Woolf, as Kazakou says, had touched upon most of the issues that modern feminists have to face, such as women's exclusion from higher education and certain professions, women's unpaid housework, their poverty, their pacifist nature, their imprisonment in the house, etc. Finally, this special issue of *Diavazo* also contains two short articles: 'O erotas sto ergo tis Virginia Woolf' (Love in Virginia Woolf's Work), translations from various passages from Woolf that deal with the theme of love, and 'Ena gramma tis Virginia Woolf gia tin Ellada' (A Letter by Virginia Woolf about Greece), a translation of Woolf's letter to Ethel Smyth, 4 May 1932.

In 1991–92, 1993 and 1994, I published a series of articles on Virginia Woolf in Greek magazines, which form part of my book *Feminist Readings of the Body in Virginia Woolf's Novels* (1997), originally a PhD thesis submitted at the University of Thessaloniki in 1994.[17] The book examines the extent to which the image of the female body in Woolf's novels is moulded by the current ideology as well as the degree to which it deviates from it. As becomes evident after a close analysis of five of her novels, Woolf's attempt to speak of the body as a woman follows the two-fold process that the French feminist Hélène Cixous spoke of in the 1970s: it breaks up, it destroys and then it 'foresee[s] the unforeseeable', it 'project[s]' (1981, 245). In her early novels Woolf is mainly preoccupied with destroying patriarchal notions of the body, which she inherited and had been forced to accept. As Woolf questions Victorian and Christian definitions of the body, the body appears absent, dismembered or fragmented. In the later stages of her writing, however, woman seems to be able to overcome the 'lack', she discovers her body and its lost organs and pleasures and inscribes the first signs of a female writing.

Chapter 1 focuses on the mouth and the stomach as organs of submission and resistance in *VO*. Rachel, the young heroine, is enmeshed in an ideology that entraps woman within her own body, her reproductive system and excludes her from any creative or intellectual activity. The book begins as a typical *Bildungsroman* but turns out to be an important denial, a reversal of the patriarchal model. Rachel refuses to be part of a world in which the female body is debased to an animal-like existence, and becomes incompatible with

---

17 So far this is the only PhD thesis on Virginia Woolf written in Greece.

any kind of creative activity, a world in which male desire devours its prey, and woman is trichotomized into mother, virgin, or whore. In her effort to escape from her strange, inimical body, Rachel strives to emaciate it by refusing food. Her anorexic body as a rejection of femininity and maternity fails, however, to offer any alternatives to the problem of the female body, as it turns into a corpse, an 'abject'.

Chapter 2 explores the ways in which Christian ideology is challenged in *MD*. Clarissa Dalloway's virginity, her ascetic figure, her woodenness clearly allude to Byzantine hagiographies, or fifteenth-century Flemish paintings of the Virgin Mary. Virginity and asceticism, however, move towards new directions in Mrs Dalloway's case: her virginity, rendered as a conscious denial of a male-centred sexuality, is a sign of power and autonomy; her asceticism is accompanied by her ability to arouse sexual desire in others; her breastlessness is a sign of her failure to nourish the milk of patriarchy. Finally, her experiencing a religious apocalypse, a mystical/erotic feeling when women come to confess to her gives a new perspective to her sexuality, leaving, though, the question of the female body still unresolved, as Clarissa's desire is spoken in male terms.

Chapter 3 is a reading of *TL* as a novel that bridges Woolf's earlier attempts at deconstructing with her later attempts at re-constructing the body. Mrs Ramsay is the archetypal mother figure, the faithful mirror of male desire, the pubic deltos upon which male desire is inscribed. She perceives herself as 'a wedge-shaped core of darkness' (*TL* 1998, 85), 'a centre of complete emptiness' (241), the lack, which Lacan defines as 'The Woman' (1982, 152). In her attempt to portray this eternal mother-figure, Lily, the female artist, refuses deliberately to benefit from the masterpieces of the great artists of the past. With the help of her 'Chinese' (*TL* 1998, 24), meditative eyes, Lily manages to create a new vision of Mrs Ramsay, a vision that consists primarily in revisioning. The process of painting becomes a 'tunnelling' into the past, a re-experiencing of the maternal body and its transformation into a space of recollection. Moreover, Lily's final move of drawing an eliminating line at the centre of her painting announces a shift in female perception; it is both a representation and a denial of the emptiness. This double negation, the denial of an absence, announces a presence, and bares the potential of a female gaze.

The fourth chapter examines the issue of female desire in *O*. Assuming that the generic 'he' which characterizes Orlando in the sixteenth century is a mere disguise for the female pronoun 'she', then Orlando's unquenched desire for her poem would be a quest for a female text/language that could express female desire. In the novel body and text are interdependent and interchangeable. Being written by an androgynous biographer, Orlando's body and text undergo a process of censoring and editing, which, nevertheless, renders them voiced, utterable. The male presence/voice is there to foster the female in its first steps of expression. Puzzled and shocked by the outcome, the biographer can do no more but accept this strange, veiled presence, Orlando's 'muffled' (Cixous 1981, 256) clitoris. Rejoicing at the rediscovery of her clitoral nature, Orlando celebrates her hysteria (for the 'clitoral' woman is a hysteric, as Freud assures us), and the text overflows with blanks, gaps, inconsistencies, sudden eruptions and, ultimately – ecstasy. This 'greater ecstasy' (*O* 1998, 149) comes when Orlando is finally capable of locating it in the poem, which had for centuries been incubating in her breast. Written in 'white ink' (Cixous 1981, 251), the female text is engendered by and engenders a female body.

Chapter 5 is a reading of *TW* as a novel undulating throughout to the rhythms of the female body. The novel accommodates a series of binary oppositions: the past is juxtaposed to the present, the part to the whole, the male writer to the female writer, life to death. The bodies of the three female characters, however, eventually erase these oppositions. Jinny, Rhoda and Susan, representing respectively the erotic, the virginal and the maternal female nature, borrow the male discourse of flowers in order to speak of their bodies. They are not, though, dead flowers killed by a male metaphor; the three women assume an active part as they violate, deflower their bodies themselves. Jinny invites men to plunder her body, which unfurls like a fern. Rhoda becomes one with her petals and, finding no one to share her garland with, throws herself into the waves to be consumed by the water and the flowers forever. And Susan, having exploited the reproductive potential of her body, like a field bearing crops in rotation, 'crack[s] with the winter cold' (*TW* 1998, 108). The three male and the three female characters unite finally in the image of the six-sided carnation which expunges gender and identity differences, and flow into the same element, the troubled, regenerating, alleviating sea of the womb. Bernard, the voice of the male author, gives up his efforts to measure the sea, to dry her up, and allows himself the pleasure of being hushed by the waves.

A fresh interest in Woolf in the 1990s coincided with the impressive increase in the number of translations of foreign literature into Greek; from 1990 up to 1996 there is a rise of 81.8 per cent, according to a study published in the Greek periodical *Ihneftis* (quoted in M. Hartoulari's 1998 article 'Apo ton Lord Byron eos ton Koundera: Dio erevnes gia ti metaphrasi sta ellinika xenon vivlion kai ellinikon se xenes glosses' (From Lord Byron to Kundera: Two Studies of Foreign Books Translated into Greek and Greek Books Translated into Foreign Languages)).[18] In the second half of the 1990s translations of Virginia Woolf's essays, followed by a number of reviews in newspapers, orientated the Greek public towards Woolf the essay writer. *LYP* is described by V. Rouvalis as 'timeless' in his article 'Ena gramma panda epikero' (A Timeless Letter) (1998). If Woolf were to write a letter to young poet today, Rouvalis says, she would make an exact copy of her original letter, for the danger of forgetting oneself, of striving after fame remains the same irrespective of the age one lives in. Her 'On Not Knowing Greek' should teach us Greeks how to approach Ancient Greek with modesty, P. Boukalas states in his article 'Boroume arage na gnorisoume tous arheous?' (Could We

---

18 Translations of English literary texts have been at the top of the scale since 1944, when English was taught as a second language for the first time in Greek public schools. The National Centre of Books (Ethniko Kentro Vivliou) under the supervision of Konstantinos Kasinis has been working towards compiling a complete list of all translations into Greek since 1500 and the results are to be published soon.

Ever Know the Ancient Greeks?) (1999) and Y. Faraklas in 'Then xeroume ellinika' (We Don't speak Greek) (1999) agrees that Woolf's essay reminds us that we don't really speak Greek; our familiarity with certain ancient Greek words that are still in use in Modern Greek makes us believe that we speak the language, but this is just an illusion.

In 1999 Argiro Mantoglou's translation of nine essays by Woolf is an important attempt to throw light on Woolf's critical writings. Prose and fiction are closely interrelated in Woolf's case, A. Mantoglou contends in her introductory note, as in both the same themes recur, a conflict between the internal and the external world, a tendency to focus on the inner world of her characters. Her essays are preparations/experiments for her novels, her contact with worldly reality, according to L. Tsirimokou in her article 'Amethodi methodos' (Method-less Method) (1999). At the same time, she continues, her writing is 'musical, fluid, beyond rules, with internal and subterranean nuclei', following 'a method-less method she leads her reader to the kernel of her thought through a series of multiple whirling circles'.[19] D. Kapsalis in his article 'I anagnostria' (The Female Reader) (1997) discovers in Woolf's critical writings the 'professional reader of literature'.[20] Quoting Harold Bloom, Kapsalis characterizes Woolf's feminism as a lifelong love for literature; being a woman forgetting that she is a woman she aims at experiencing human nature in all its depth.

Woolf's contribution to the question of female writing is emphasised in A. Mantoglou's article 'Ginekia apotypomata sta tihi tis hartinis polis' (Female Footprints on the Walls of the Paper City). This article appears in a special issue of *Vivliothiki* (Library) (the book supplement of the newspaper *Eleftherotypia*) on 'Female Writing'. Having spoken of the fluidity of female texts (texts not necessarily being written by women) and of their tendency to incorporate the most indefinite forms, Woolf is recognized by A. Mantoglou as a forerunner of the French feminists, Irigaray, Kristeva and Cixous, who also tried to define *écriture féminine*. Associating parrots with female voices in her article 'I papagali tis grafis' (The Parrots of Writing) (1999), Mantoglou examines the role of parrots in texts written by women. There are cases in which the parrot, she says, like 'The Angel in the House', has to be violently killed by the woman writer. When the voice of the parrot becomes a reproduction of male-centred speech, he must die (1999, 115–16).

In 1999 Edna O'Brien's plays *Virginia* and *Orlando* (a translation of Robert Wilson and Darryl Pinckney's adaptation of the novel for the theatre) were put on in Athens, making Virginia Woolf known to the wider public. Both performances were quite successful, provoking a great number of reviews

---

19 'mousiki, refsti, dihos oratous kanones, me esoterika kai ipogia kentra', 'mia amethodi methodo na odigi anepesthita ton anagnosti mesa apo pollaplous peridinomenous kiklous ston pirina tis skepsis tis'.

20 'o epangelmatias anagnostis tis logotehnias'.

in newspapers.[21] Michael Cunningham's book *The Hours*, a book that borrows themes, characters and extracts from Woolf's diaries and letters, as well as its title from an early draft of *Mrs Dalloway*, was translated into Greek (*I ores)* in 2000. This 'postmodern pastiche', the need to imitate the style of a writer from the past, to recall and repeat the past, A. Mantoglou claims in her review of the book ('*I kiria Dalloway* tis Woolf "stihioni" s' ena sinhrono mithistorima' (Virginia Woolf's *Mrs Dalloway* 'Haunts' a Modern Novel)) (2000b) can be interpreted in various ways. It may be an indication that fiction, like life, has a limited set of plots, it may express the author's love and respect for Woolf's genius or it may simply be a proof that inventing new forms and styles today is almost impossible after the revolution of modern fiction. Can a writer in the twenty-first century entrapped in a glorious past, she asks, ever write of the present? Cunningham, she believes, has managed to create an original piece of work through imitation and repetition.[22]

Mantoglou herself is haunted by the glorious ghosts of the past. Her novel *Virginia Woolf Café*, published in 1999, is a symphony of different times and voices, a desire to deconstruct and rewrite the past and heal its wounds. Ella, Thomas Hardy's heroine in his short story 'An Imaginative Woman' from the *Wessex Tales*, visits Anna, the writer/narrator in Mantoglou's story who lives in London in 1996. Hardy himself admitted the fact that Ella's character had been hastily portrayed and was left almost incomplete; the female poet commits suicide out of grief for the male poet whom she has secretly admired but never had the chance to meet. As Ella returns from the past, she wishes to be the heroine of a different story, one that does not promote conventionally male-centred beliefs about female creativity. And Anna is called to write this new story. The idea of female creativity is redefined in Anna's version, as Ella refuses to be determined exclusively in relation to her sexuality or to be the victim of it. Ella's desire is for poetry – clearly an echo of Orlando's love for his poem above all, a love which replaces his early craving for 'Life and a lover' (*O* 1998, 177) and later in the novel, 'Life! A Husband!' (233) – and the death of the male poet becomes in the modern version a source of power and inspiration for her. At the same time, Anna is in the process of writing the story of Emma (Aima is the Greek word for blood), her modern heroine who is born miraculously out of the flames of her burning manuscripts and demands that her story be written too. Virginia Woolf's voice urging female writers to kill the 'Angel in the House' comes to haunt Emma, and at the end of her story, her body becomes a fire consuming the male lover who has betrayed her. The desire to burn part of the past even at the cost of burning part of herself is, as I have argued in my own book, a dominant motif in

---

21 For reviews of *Virginia*, see Mantoglou 2000c, Mikelidis 2000, Toulatou 2000 and Vatopoulos 2000. For reviews of *Orlando*, see Georgakopolou 1996 and 1999a, Georgousopoulos 1999, Hatziandoniou 2000, Hatziioannou 1999, Hatzivasiliou 1999, Loizou 1999 and Loverdou 1999.

22 For other reviews of *I ores*, see Katsoularis 2000 and Papaspyrou 2000.

Woolf's writings. Anna, Ella and Emma, like Woolf, can write only by turning blood into ink.[23]

This is not the end of the relationship which started sometime in 300 BC: '[I] felt as if a knife had scraped some incrusted organ in me, for I could not find anything lacking in that agile, athletic beauty, steeped in colour, so that it was not cold, perfectly free from vulgarity, yet old in human life' (*D* 4: 8 May 1932). In the year AD 2000 Virginia Woolf's texts are being read and re-read, written and re-written by Modern Greek authors, as if this same knife scrapes some incrusted organs in them. Some feel the need to declare their debt to Woolf openly, like Yiorgos Himonas who has borrowed her name for the title of his book, *Pion fovate i Virginia Woolf?* (Who Is Virginia Woolf Afraid Of?), a collection of various essays and talks on diverse subjects that begins with Virginia Woolf's vision of a poetic novel, a poet/novelist, and agrees with her that the greatest novels have been structured upon 'unripe, green poetic ideas' (1999, 17). Others prefer to remain silent, letting readers and critics draw their conclusions. The influence of Virginia Woolf on Modern Greek writers is an area that has not been researched yet, but the land of Greece is fecund despite its bareness, as Woolf herself observes in a letter to Vanessa Bell (*L* 5: 2 May 1932) and may prove to be fruitful.[24] There are still a number of books, essays and short stories that have not been translated into Greek; there are still many critical articles to be written about her in Greek. And the soil is prosperous: Virginia Woolf is taught in the courses on 'modernism' at the University of Athens and at the University of Thessaloniki; at the University of Thessaloniki a course on 'Virginia Woolf and the Bloomsbury Group' is offered. We can only hope that it will bear more fruit.

---

23 For reviews of *Virginia Woolf Café*, see Athanasopoulos 1999 and Papageorgiou 1999.

24 Two modern women writers, Mando Aravandinou and Nana Isaia, have expressed their love of Virginia Woolf and there have been attempts to compare their writing with Woolf's (such brief remarks are made, for example, in the newspaper articles by Y. Aragis 'Katastrophikes shesis' (Destructive Relationships) (1999) and L. Sakelliou-Schultz 'Lernees Idres' (Lernaean Hydras)). An attempt to draw parallels between Woolf and the Modern Greek writers of the inter-war period is made by D. Behlikoudi in her unpublished doctoral thesis 'To neoelliniko mithistorima tou mesopolemou kai i Virginia Woolf: mia singritiki prosengisi' (The Modern Greek Novel between the Wars and Virginia Woolf: A Comparative Study) (1999). The section on Woolf's influence upon Greek writers, however, is only a very small part of her thesis, and Behlikoudi limits herself to simply juxtaposing on the page excerpts from Woolf, Delios and Xefloudas and drawing vague and general conclusions rather than making a comparative analysis.

11 The Reception of Virginia Woolf in Italy

Sergio Perosa

Translations

Early Italian translations of Virginia Woolf were mostly by women (as Emilio Cecchi, a leading critic of the period, perceptively observed in 1946). She was first translated in the 1930s, as a 'curiosity', and an example of poetic writing. *O* was her first book to be translated, in 1933; *Flush: vita di un cane* (*FB*: the subtitle, 'Life of a Dog', gave the surprise away) was issued in 1946. (Such casual encounters were also mirrored in E. Cecchi's own experimental translation of 'Dr Burney's Evening Party' in 1945, and in the critical response of those years.)[1] In between, *TL* was translated (with the title *Gita al faro*) in 1934 by Giulia Celenza, an inspired and distinguished translator, who had turned Swinburne's *Atalanta in Calydon* and Shakespeare's *A Midsummer Night's Dream* into beautiful Italian: Celenza indulged in poeticisms, fading hues and dreamy atmospheres, even in excess of Virginia Woolf's own style. After twelve years of silence,[2] Alessandra Scalero, who had translated *O*, brought out her translation of *MD* (1946); 1950 saw translations of *JR* (*La camera di Giacobbe*) by a well-known Italian writer, Anna Banti, and of *HH* by Desideria Pasolini (*La casa degli spiriti*). As will be shown in the next section, critical response to these books was appreciative, but rather lukewarm – though they were issued by Mondadori, one of the leading publishers of the period, in their prestigious series, 'Il Ponte' (The Bridge) and 'La Medusa'. As for the translations, editorial conventions, or fears, and imperfect knowledge, were responsible for a high degree of 'regularization': Virginia Woolf's free indirect speech (and 'interior monologue') was made explicit with the insertion of arbitrary inverted commas, or turned into straight third-person narrative; names of characters had to be given in Italian. In a way, Virginia Woolf was

---

1 For full bibliographical references, see the Bibliography, which is an integral part of this chapter.

2 An article in *Meridiano di Roma*, 22 August 1937, announced, and gave a specimen of, a translation of *TY* by A. Scalero, copyright by Mondadori. The book, however, was never published.

appreciated as, and turned into, an example of normalized *bello scrivere* (fine writing) – a pervasive preoccupation of the 1930s and early 1940s in Italy; the revolutionary nature of her writing remained hidden.

The 1950s saw relatively few translations – possibly owing to the prevailing neo-realistic and *engagé* tendency of the time, when Virginia Woolf was likely to be considered an elitist, escapist, snobbish, high-society and non-committed author. Choices seem to have been random: *VO* was translated twice (as *Il lungo viaggio* (The Long Voyage) in 1951, as *La crociera* (The Cruise) in 1956), *TY* in 1955 (*Gli anni*), *TW* in 1956 (*Le onde*), both translated by Giulio De Angelis, who would become the author of the first Italian translation of Joyce's *Ulysses* in 1960. They were followed by *Notte e giorno* (*ND*) in 1957 (this time by a less known, small publisher), so that most of her fiction was now available in Italian. A great deal of interest – critical and otherwise – was raised by the translation of *WD* (*Diario di una scrittrice*) in 1959: this caused, as it were, a typical deviation, in so far as a concern with the technical or human side of the writer seemed to have gained the upper hand, while her fiction was temporarily pushed into the background. In fact, another period of silence is perceivable, reaching to the mid-1970s: during this interval, only a relatively small selection of her essays was issued, *Per le strade di Londra* (Through the Streets of London) (1963), from *CR 1-2*, *DM* and *TM*; *Una stanza tutta per sé* (*ROO*) was added at the end in a 1974 reissue; they were all translated by Livio Bacchi Wilcock and J. Rodolfo Wilcock – the latter a writer and a fine translator. The translations of Monique Nathan's monograph on Virginia Woolf in 1962, and of Bernard Blackstone's in 1965, show that interest in her was present but mild, and that there was a tendency to rely on foreign books to sustain her reputation (the 'Group 63' (63 Group) avant-garde movement, so influential in breaking the rule of neo-realism and social engagement, seldom used Virginia Woolf as a 'text').

The late 1970s, however, marked the breakthrough of Virginia Woolf into the Italian editorial market and cultural consciousness, on two accounts: a renewed interest in the nature of her personality, her fictional methods and contribution to literature; and the upsurge of feminism (this breakthrough was heralded by the translation of Quentin Bell's biography in 1974, and clinched by that of Phyllis Rose's biography in 1980).

The translation of *TG* by Adriana Bottini in 1975 seems in retrospect less important than that of *MB* by the same writer in 1977 (with the influential introduction by Jeanne Schulkind), while it is significant that *BTA*, translated by Francesca Duranti and Franco Cordelli, with a 'writerly' introduction by the latter, had to wait for a small publisher to issue it in 1978. The first, *Le tre ghinee*, was for feminist critics, but was not widely known; the third, *Tra un atto e l'altro*, was presented as the work of an experimental writer; the second, *Momenti di essere*, worked very well from both of these perspectives, and had a great impact due to the novelty and intensity of Virginia Woolf's self-revelation.

Two typical examples (one of which verges on the personal) will be highlighted here. In the mid-1970s Mondadori, still a leading publisher and the holder of the copyright for most Virginia Woolf titles, asked me to edit a Virginia Woolf volume in their 'Meridiani' series – roughly equivalent to the French 'Pléiade', and thus establishing the canonical status of a writer. Yet the persistent uncertainty about her real value was betrayed by the fact that I was asked to make the volume as slim as possible (not exceeding 1000 pages); existing translations (most of them already in-house) had to be used when available. My decision was then to privilege early Virginia Woolf by including *MD*, *TL*, *O* and *ROO*, three of her essays relating to fiction-writing, plus selected passages from the then available *Letters* and from *WD*, that directly referred to, and clarified, the works included in the volume (hence the title *Romanzi e altro* (Novels and other pieces). Notes and chronology were kept to a minimum, though the introduction (see next section) could expand on a definition of her importance as a fiction writer. Translations had to be silently emended, when mistakes were obvious, and brought to some kind of consistency; yet it proved impossible to free them from the blemishes and the limitations noted above (Virginia Woolf's free indirect speech still in inverted commas, etc.). In any case, the Meridiani volume appeared at the right moment, had good press reports, and went through an unanticipated number of editions, contributing to the revival of Virginia Woolf in a significant manner. On my part, it had been planned with a view to a possible second volume, if conditions improved, which would accommodate late Virginia Woolf, from *TW* to *BTA*, with a similar correlation of essays, letters and diary entries. When some years later the possibility was considered, it turned out that the publisher, who had so wisely invested in Virginia Woolf at an early stage, had let some of the crucial translation copyrights expire (they usually last twenty years); the one-volume edition was still selling, and nothing was done about the second. (This is mentioned not in personal regret, but as an indication of the vagaries to which translations, even of successful authors, are often subjected.)

Meanwhile, the impact of a feminist interest in Virginia Woolf began to be felt in publishing, as well as culturally and academically. A 'Virginia Woolf University' was established in Rome in 1977, and the militant magazine *donna WFD* (woman WFD) often used her as a champion: both sponsored meetings, conferences and the publication of pamphlets, translations and tributes (e.g. *Virginia Woolf: Lettere* (Selections from *L*), ed. Pia Candinas, 1981; *Progetto Virginia Woolf: Parole, Immagini* (Project Virginia Woolf: Words, Images), ed. C. Bertea and others). A typical phenomenon was the upsurge of small presses specializing in women's writing that took up Virginia Woolf as a banner, and indeed as a backbone, for their publishing ventures (some were short-lived). This had two results: a series of translations of out-of-the-way, less known or less canonical, experimental, early or discarded works, and a series of reissues or retranslations of canonical works – for the most part with appropriate and lengthy, often enthusiastic or strongly committed, introductions.

One such press was La Rosa: they brought out, for instance, *La famiglia Pargiter* (*TP*), translated by Alide Cagidemetrio, in 1981, a new translation of *ND* by Maria Vittoria Malvano in 1982, and a translation of *FC* by L. P. Ruotolo and M. V. Malvano in 1983, with a long introduction by Barbara Lanati.[3] Another, more long-lived and successful one, was La Tartaruga,

[3] Rather surprisingly, *FC* was re-translated by S. Bartoli and A. Tesauro for a small publishing house, Sellerio, in 1992.

which had brought out *MB* in 1977; in 1980 they issued a translation of *MT* (*Lunedì o martedì: tutti i racconti*), in 1981 *Le donne e la scrittura* (*W&W*) translated by A. Bottini, and in 1988 a new and really comprehensive collection of *Tutti i racconti*, with translations by A. Bottini, Masolino D'Amico, Francesca Duranti, based on Susan Dick's edition of *CSF*. Il Saggiatore (which for a while was a subsidiary of Mondadori) reissued *Per le strade di Londra* in 1974, adding the first translation of *ROO*, which was then published separately in 1980 with an introduction by Marisa Bulgheroni: in 1979 they had brought out *La signora dell'angolo di fronte* (essays), and in 1982 they had Grazia Livi, a distinguished writer in her own right, translate *LS* (*Scene di Londra*). Savelli – then a radical left-wing publisher – published Virginia Woolf's introduction to Margaret Llewelyn Davies's *Life as We Have Known It* (*Lettera a Margaret Llewelyn Davies*) (1980); this was the first time a declared left-wing publisher 'took on' Virginia Woolf.

Reissues of particular note were *Le onde* (*TW*) (in an economic and very popular series by Rizzoli, BUR, 1979) and *WD* (Mondadori, 1979). Einaudi, *the* leading left-wing publisher, which had previously been impervious to Virginia Woolf (as they had been to Henry James, and for similar reasons: both for being considered upper-class and 'decadent'), decided to ride the wave. Much against the advice of many (myself included) that they bring out only a sizeable selection of *L*, they decided on a full translation of the six volumes. Only the first four volumes, however, were published (in good, accurate translations) between 1980 and 1985, while, as a partial gesture of reconciliation and further commitment, they reissued M. V. Malvano's translation of *ND* in 1987.

However, a stream of new, in a sense 'revolutionary' translations was clearly visible elsewhere. These were prepared by, and went hand in hand with, the critical reappraisal of the 1980s and 1990s (see next section); in particular, they were fostered by the new feminist awareness and set in full motion by the fact that in the early 1990s Woolf's copyright expired, and big and small publishers alike had prepared for new ventures (this was an interval that lasted only for a few years, in that soon the copyright period was extended to seventy years after the author's death).

The 1990s saw an incredible number of new translations and an impressive revival of Virginia Woolf titles on all fronts. New translations of novels were brought out in very inexpensive single volumes by a Rome publisher, Newton Compton: *MD* (translated by P. F. Paolini, 1992), *TL* (translated by A. L. Malagò, 1992), *TW* and *O* (both translated by M. Del Serra, 1992 and 1994), *ND* (translated by P. Meneghelli, 1996), all with a standard introduction by Armanda Guiducci. The main aim was to reach for a new market, especially of younger people; although no new principles seemed to be at work in the translations, the inexpensiveness of the volumes assured a wide circulation of these texts. The same purpose was served by A. L. Zago's edition of *Romanzi e racconti* (Novels and Short Stories) in Mondadori's popular series 'Gli Oscar', where she included *JR* in A. Banti's version, *MD* in A. Scalero's, *TW* in G. De Angelis's, and supplied her own version of *TL* and of a selection of short stories.

Most of Virginia Woolf's works of criticism were duly and repeatedly translated: *Leggere, recensire* (Reading, Reviewing), selected essays, translated by A. Bottini for a small publisher, Marcos y Marcos (1990), *Ore in biblioteca e altri saggi* ('Hours in a Library' and Other Essays), translated by Daniela Daniele for La Tartaruga (1991), a publisher still active in the diffusion of Virginia Woolf texts, *Volare su Londra* (Flying over London), translated by E. Pea, Marcos y Marcos (1992), with a preface by Grazia Livi, and a complete, two-volume translation of *Il lettore comune* (*CR 1–2*) by Daniela Guglielmino, issued by 'il melangolo', a subsidiary of Einaudi (1995–96). In 1995 Mirella Billi edited and translated a sizable selection of Virginia Woolf's *Ritratti di scrittori* (Portraits of Writers) for another small publisher, Pratiche.

A new development was the publication of bilingual texts: simultaneously in 1995, *ROO* was issued in a new translation by M. A. Saracino with facing English text, introduction and a very comprehensive bibliography, in a specialized series by Einaudi, while M. Billi prepared a similar edition of *JR* for Marsilio Editore in Venice (this time with the title *La stanza di Jacob*). Both editions were meant to make Virginia Woolf available for school and university curricula. Most of these titles also indicate that the task of translating Virginia Woolf into Italian had been almost completely re-appropriated by women, as in the early stages. This had good, but also bad sides to it: a partial danger was of making her a writer for women only.

The most remarkable development in this vogue was represented by Nadia Fusini's new series of translations, which began with *TL* (with the new title *Al faro*) in 1992, went on to *MD* in 1993 (both for Feltrinelli, a new, important publisher to take on Virginia Woolf) and *TW* for Einaudi (now a full convert) in 1995, and continued till 1998, as we shall soon see. With a strain of feminist awareness (but not bias), a scholarly knowledge of English and a particular sensibility for writing (she is a university professor of English and the author of several novels), Fusini was intent on introducing and applying new principles of translation to Virginia Woolf texts. These can be summarized as: a less poetic, more direct approach; the search for the right, expressive word, not for the blurred murmur; a more immediate, fluent rapport with language, privileging a crystal-clear, rather than poetically suffused, style, the cutting edge, the quick move, the forceful turn of phrase.

Typical of this aim was the new title for *TL*, *Al faro*, which does away with the equivocal and pleonastic previous title, *Gita al faro*: 'gita' is an excursion, a pleasure party; *Al faro* has the poignancy and the urge of a command, a yearning, a driving purpose.[4] After all that had been written on language, after the newly acquired awareness of linguistic and stylistic devices, Virginia

---

[4] I give three examples of this tendency in three random places of the novel: Mr Ramsay's 'But ... it won't be fine' *TL*, 1:1, was 'Però non farà bel tempo' in G. Celenza; it becomes 'Ma non farà bello'. 'Ah, but she was relieved', about Lily Briscoe (in 3:13) was 'Però ella s'era anche alleviata d'un peso', very elegant and *recherché*; it becomes, more appropriately, 'Ah, ma ora si sentì sollevata'. Her final realization, 'yes ... I have had my vision' (in 3:13) was 'Ho avuto anch'io una visione' – which was not strictly correct; 'Sì ... ho avuto la mia visione' in the new version.

Woolf's free indirect speech could now be accommodated into Italian easily; the characters' thoughts and impressions could be given within the narrative flow and not in inverted commas. For Fusini, poetry lay not in dream-like sequences, but in an adherence to facts: her new versions kept this very much in the foreground. She seemed to be translating from the point of view of Lily Briscoe – from the artist's, rather than the woman's, point of view. As she put it in her later 'Translator's Note' to *TW*: 'Translation is a reading, but an active reading; it is therefore fatiguing, nerve-racking.' Reading is passive, not all words are grasped, and a protecting veil operates between the radiance of the word and the reader: 'Translation, instead, is violence, a tremendous exertion ... the text in front of us, as if it were the Tables of the Law, imposes on us with the overbearing force of something not ours ... It calls on us, anyway, it appeals to us, it defies us' (Fusini 1995, 284–86).[5]

These new translations were brought together in 1998 in a two-volume 'Meridiani' edition, edited by her, which did justice, exactly twenty years later, to the original intention of presenting Italian readers with the full range and scope of Virginia Woolf's fiction and other writings. Times and the cultural climate had radically changed: Mondadori could now trust 3000 pages of Virginia Woolf to reach a wide audience, superseding its own previous 1978 edition; the existence of new translations made competition viable and prosperous; a feminist, lucid and concrete writer (rather than a poetically minded dilettante), Virginia Woolf could have a monument erected to her memory, and to her stature.

Volume 1, *Romanzi* (Novels), comprised *JR* in Anna Banti's translation, *MD*, *TL* and *TW* in Fusini's translations, *O* in A. Scalero's and *BTA* in F. Wagner's and F. Cordelli's, Volume 2, *Saggi, prose, racconti* (Essays, Prose, Tales), with a separate introduction, offered a selection of nine short stories (translated by F. Duranti and Fusini), eighteen essays (mostly in existing translations by L. B. and J. R. Wilcock, and M. D'Amico), *ROO* in M. A. Saracino's version, *TG* in A. Bottini's, *FB* in A. Scalero's, *RF* (first translated by Fusini), two pieces from *MB* and over 100 pages of letters (eighteen translated by Fusini for this edition, the rest selected from existing editions of letters by Einaudi and other publishers). Introductions and chronologies were spacious; notes and commentaries abundant and even too meticulous (the danger of such bulk being that the books become unmanageable and the writer is canonized beyond readability). As in the 1930s and early 1940s, translations were predominantly by women, but the feminist bias was avoided in an effort to make Virginia Woolf into a cornerstone and at the same time a central figure of twentieth-century literature (see next section).

A further – final? – step in the acceptance and canonization of Virginia Woolf is represented by a translation of *D* in the process of being completed in two volumes for the same Mondadori series (translated by Bianca Tarozzi,

---

[5] 'La traduzione è una lettura, ma attiva; è perciò faticosa, snervante'; 'È violenza, invece, la traduzione. È fatica, tremenda. ... Quel testo che abbiamo di fronte, come fosse le tavole della legge, si è imposto a noi con la prepotenza di qualcosa che non è nostro ... E comunque ci chiama in causa, ci appella, ci sfida.'

edited, introduced and annotated by S. Perosa). This was originally to have been a relatively small selection; now almost the full text will be given, with the excision of only repetitive or very minor and obscure entries. For copyright reasons, *PA* could not be considered for this edition. Once *PA* is translated – possibly by some small publisher – and when a comprehensive edition of her essays, now scattered in various and overlapping volumes, is brought together, one can rest assured of Virginia Woolf's full acceptance in Italy, after the slow beginning.

Critical response

Italy was one of Virginia Woolf's 'late conquests'. She was first encountered in the late 1920s and 1930s, but reviewed and considered by leading critics and writers – both male and female – who were active before the Second World War. First she was seen as an example of symbolic, psychological and experimental writing; as a representative of *bello scrivere*, partially in unison with the non-committed, 'escapist' form of literature prevailing in the Fascist period, and as a 'curiosity' to be sympathetically accepted. A common attitude was to praise her elegance and her measure, her 'spiritualism', as against James Joyce's coarseness and profusion.

This is shown by the pioneering Anglicist Carlo Linati, in an article in *Corriere della sera* (Evening Post) (24 January 1927), and by Umberto Morra's lengthier essay in *Il Baretti* (27 May 1928), where her 'composition' is praised and extolled, and Marcel Proust begins to be paired with her as a more verbose counterpart. Both pieces gave a brief account of her career to date. Morra would return to Virginia Woolf as a representative of the 'new English novel' in the magazine *La cultura* (Culture) (January 1931), showing some unease about *O* ('a queer and total novelty', 'outside the strict province of art')[6], and would write about *TW* in *Pegaso* (Pegasus) (March 1932); Linati was to insist on her grace and coquetry, her pleasantness and humanity, as against Joyce's heaviness, in *Emporium* (January 1935).

Mario Praz, by then an established Anglicist and a very active reviewer and essayist, as early as 1930 in an article in *La Stampa* (The Press) surprisingly wrote about *ROO*, which he considered an eccentric work, noting that if equality had prevailed, Virginia Woolf would not have been born (!), but highlighting her special kind of androgynous fiction. The following year (and again in 1945) he would concentrate on *TW* as a 'lyrical soliloquy', stressing its 'tone of musical illumination', its harsh but calm light, its symbolism and its irony: 'a rich *féerie* of poor things', in which everyday events are imbued with

---

6 'Bislacca e totale novità', 'fuori della stretta provincia dell'arte'. On Virginia Woolf's early reception, see Elio Di Piazza's very uneven *Virginia Woolf nella critica italiana* (1975).

magic and spiritual resonance (Praz 1931).[7] In 1933 he devoted an article to *FB*, tracing its pedigree back to the Italian scholar Lorenzo Malgarotti, but proclaiming it the masterpiece of its kind. (A sign of the seriousness with which he wanted to treat Virginia Woolf is provided by the fact that Praz wrote an article on her for the Italian *Enciclopedia Treccani* (1937).)

Emilio Cecchi, too, was active in bringing Virginia Woolf to the fore. He was all for *TL*, to which he devoted a preface and an article in 1934, on the occasion of its Italian translation, praising its 'tightrope walker' quality, its taut form (and its translation), and also a longer article in 1946. He delineated Virginia Woolf's web of relations and affinities – with Joseph Conrad, William and Henry James, Proust and Joyce, Bergson (for her 'interior monologues'), stressing her interest in the eighteenth century, her humanism and her adherence to life, her almost too precious *sensiblerie* counterbalanced by common sense, the purity and fullness of her narrative time and tone, and the 'sonata form' achieved in *TL*: 'a masterpiece of psychological counterpoint'.[8] In 1945 he concentrated on her posthumous collection of essays, *DM*, specifically for the meticulous stylistic care given to essay composition, and himself translated 'Dr Burney's Evening Party'.

In his book on Virginia Woolf's critical reputation in Italy, *Virginia Woolf in Italia*, Elio Di Piazza maintains that the insistence on the musical metaphor was a way of belittling her literary achievement: she was praised for doing something that was *not* strictly literature. A sense of her potential limitations lurked within the official welcome: writing in the *Nuova Antologia* in 1933, Salvatore Rosati denied her real break with Victorianism, for instance, and saw her as a 'mere parenthesis' in the development of English fiction. Pietro Rebora in 1938 insisted on her 'psychological materialism': here, too, it must be noted that an insistence on her 'analytical' powers (i.e. her psychological probings) had a double edge in the Fascist period – it was something outlandish, not part of our classical tradition.

Mixed feelings about her acceptance and her value characterize the period after the Second World War. It is true that in 1947 she had pride of place in the title of M. Praz's anthology *Prospettive della letteratura inglese da Chaucer a Virginia Woolf* (A Prospect of English Literature from Chaucer to Virginia Woolf), and that three profiles of her appeared in the short-lived proto-feminist magazine *Pensiero femminile* (The Feminine Mind), as a striking anticipation of what was to follow years later. But the prevailing and 'correct' attitude was then all in favour of neo-realism, socially committed fiction, political engagement, and in that cultural climate Virginia Woolf's reputation and 'relevance' were doomed

---

7 'Tono di illuminazione musicale', 'ricca *féerie* di cose povere'. Linati's and Praz's articles were also influential in that they were reprinted in the former's book *Scrittori angloamericani* (British and Amerian authors) (1942) and the latter's *Cronache letterarie anglosassoni* (Anglo-Saxon literary chronicles), 1–2 (1950–51.) Enthusiasm for Virginia Woolf was shown in Pavolini 1933.

8 'Un capolavoro di contrappunto psicologico'. Cecchi's contributions were also influential in that they were collected in his volume *Scrittori inglesi e americani* (British and American authors), 1935 and 1946 (enlarged edition).

to suffer. She – and Bloomsbury: the views of F. R. Leavis and others had spread to the continent – attracted the suspicion or the stigma of snobbishness, aristocratic elitism, aloofness from the problems of real life, disengagement and a devotion to art for art's sake. This attitude may be summarized in Sandro De Feo's article of 1954 in *L'Europeo* (The European), where she was charged with snobbishness, sentimentality and detachment from reality; similar views were expressed in 1960 by Maria Grazia Biovi in an essay in *Paragone* (Comparison), one of the best literary magazines of the period, where she expressed annoyance at Virginia Woolf's digging a trench between the self and the world, and as late as 1974 in a TV programme by Lalla Romano, by then an established and influential writer. This goes to show that women, too, were reluctant to acknowledge her literary achievement.[9]

Critics like Cecchi and Praz were now less in the forefront of 'militant' criticism. Those writing on her inclined to a kind of lukewarm, qualified admiration, almost damning with faint praise; others were ready to ignore her (as they did Henry James). Typical examples are provided by S. Rosati, again, who in a 1950 essay in *English Miscellany* (the leading magazine for English studies, edited by Praz), was rather severe in his overall appraisal. Even Desideria Pasolini, in the introduction to her translation of short stories, *La casa degli spiriti* (*HH*) (1950), while writing of Virginia Woolf's daring rebellion against literary conventions, and of her stream of consciousness technique, insisted on her kind of 'scientific experimentalism' and her intellectualism, which was only partially redeemed by her poetical flights, and emphasized her 'lack of spiritual synthesis', of real characters, and her rather limited vision of life.[10]

Cecchi confronted the accusation so often raised against her, of a lack of real characters, in his 1950 article 'La Woolf e il "personaggio"' (Woolf and 'Character'), but his insistence that Virginia Woolf's characters live in our imagination as 'musical themes' was rather unlikely to pacify critics on this issue. Giorgio Melchiori's well-documented essay 'L'attimo come unità di tempo nella narrativa' ('The moment as a time-unit in fiction'),[11] rescued

---

9 It is noteworthy that in 1954 the fashionable magazine *Prospetti* (Prospects) chose to publish a long essay by William Troy, 'Virginia Woolf e il romanzo della sensibilità' (Virginia Woolf and the Novel of Sensibility), which brought together three previous contributions of his (from 1932, 1937 and 1952!), and was basically the expression of his difficulty in coming to terms with her: her style was artificial, metaphorical, a cultivation of language for its own sake; her charm was false, her authority, weak, her beauty, sterile; she suffered from a disease of the will, and indulged in purely formal variations; only after her death could she be given an adequate, but not a very important place.

10 Here is a typical sentence: 'in her lack of a spiritual synthesis, closed as she was in a psychological (i.e. scientific) view of life, she ended by stiffening her characters, depriving them of humanity, and of life itself' ('mancandole proprio la facoltà di una sintesi spirituale, chiusa come era in una visione psicologica (e cioè scientifica) della vita, finiva per irrigidire i suoi caratteri togliendo loro l'umanità e la vita stessa').

11 Originally in *Lo spettatore italiano* (The Italian spectator) (Melchiori 1951), in English in his volume *The Tightrope Walkers* (whose subtitle was *Studies of Mannerism*

Virginia Woolf from marginalization by showing her capacity – together with T.S. Eliot, Ezra Pound, and Joyce – to do full justice to the 'moment of being' (be it impression or epiphany) and to the fullness of the moment of vision; but it also conceded that Virginia Woolf had found no narrative form to replace the traditional ones, and that her endless experimentation compromised real development.

Women writers came to the rescue: Gianna Manzini in 1947, Anna Banti in 1952, with a perceptive article on 'Virginia Woolf's Humanity' ('Umanità della Woolf') – the title is revealing in itself – where she was seen as 'compromised by family, friends, and home traditions'; her books were 'still and brilliant in the constellation of the most valuable works of the first half of the century', and yet (Banti wrote, significantly), it is 'precisely in this astronomical harmony of subtleties, uncanny correspondences and demonstrations, that the failure ... of an intellect too eager for life and expression takes shape'.[12] Another aspect soon emerged, which was to last for decades afterwards: Virginia Woolf's greatest contribution to literature was identified in her early phase, to 1930. For a long time we would have a halved, or cloven, Virginia Woolf for critical consideration.

Two events in the 1950s and 1960s allowed Italian culture to keep Virginia Woolf, if not to the fore, at least as a half-hidden, not to be subdued, presence, in spite of all the cultural and political odds against her in the Cold War years. The first was the appearance in Italian translation in 1956 of Erich Auerbach's monumental and influential study *Mimesis*, which became a sort of bible for supporters of realism and neo-realism (its subtitle was curtly and incorrectly given in Italian as *Il realismo nella letteratura occidentale* (Realism in Western Literature)). There Virginia Woolf was luckily included at the conclusion – if not at the culmination – of an impressive 'realistic' tradition, from Homer to Dante, from Rabelais to Zola, and Auerbach's masterly appraisal of her particular achievement not only kept her in the very best company, but invited a form of acceptance even by socially committed critics. He rightly insisted that in her novels almost everything is reflected in the characters' consciousness, but it was not a form of uni-personal subjectivism: Virginia Woolf had managed to achieve the representation of a pluri-personal consciousness, a convincing combination of inner and outer time, shifts in point of view and a stylization of narrative material; to capture, in fact, the symbolical omni-temporality of the event. The first and the last point, in particular, rescued Virginia Woolf from neglect and allowed for her consideration in times of 'realistic' awareness.

---

cont.

in Modern English Literature) (Melchiori 1956), then in its (expanded) Italian translation, *I funamboli: il manierismo nella letteratura inglese contemporanea,* 1963.

12 'Compromessa da famiglia, amici, tradizioni di casa'; 'fermi e brillanti nella costellazione dei primi valori del cinquantennio'; 'proprio in questa astronomica armonia di sottigliezze, di arcane rispondenze e dimostrazioni, si configura la sconfitta ... di un intelletto troppo avido di vita e di espressione' (reprinted in Banti 1961, 1966, 1969).

The second event which counteracted and dispelled doubts about Virginia Woolf's standing as a writer, was the appearance, first in English, then in Italian translation in 1959, of *WD*. Most critics – militant and academic, literary as well as social – were irresistibly drawn to it: from S. Rosati to G. Melchiori, from Agostino Lombardo to Grazia Caliumi, from S. De Feo to M. L. Astaldi, from G. B. Angioletti to Aldo Camerino, from Maria Bellonci, another well-known writer, to A. Banti (to name only a few). In retrospect, it may seem almost an obsession or an infatuation. Such keen interest in *WD* allowed for two emphases: one was Virginia Woolf's painstaking, absorbing seriousness as a writer, her commitment to technique, composition, experimentation and her acceptance of the painful burden of the writer (an appealing aspect for Italian culture); the other was that the book appeared and could be debated as a testing ground for technical, 'writerly' matters. The writer as technician, grappling with questions of invention, point of view, narrative stance, structuring, etc., fighting daily and directly not only with the angel of art, but with the frightening blank page to be written, exercised a strong appeal for writers and critics of diverse allegiances.[13]

Attempts to rescue Virginia Woolf for the Left were made in the early 1960s in articles by the young Umberto Eco (1962), Enzo Siciliano (1963), Giansiro Ferrata (1963) in *Rinascita* (Rebirth), the official Communist magazine, and others, partially, at least, on the strength and inspiration of *WD*. They culminated in Vito Amoruso's first serious attempt to deal with her on an academic, as well as socially committed, Marxist, level. His 1968 monograph, *Virginia Woolf*, emphasized her 'existential and restless form of spiritualism' as against 'contemporary materialism', her reliance on an aristocratic, art-for-art's-sake, decadent tradition; yet she was at the head of an ideal genealogy of contemporary fiction, with Joyce and Proust, and did represent (as Auerbach had shown) the last and most innovative form of Western realism. Her central theme was the crucial art/life, literature/reality relationship, but with a cognitive strain. Amoruso saw in her the tragic end of a Victorian-Decadent tradition, and insisted upon her encountering a final impasse, a dead end, a form of impotence. This led him to emphasize her early fiction (180 pages to reach *TL*, 33 for the rest), which was to become almost standard procedure in the following years. Realism and symbolism, the combination of inner and outer reality, of aesthetic perfection and a keen sense of life, of traditional and experimental ways, were the keys used by Amoruso to make Virginia Woolf's dealings with alienation, her increasing escape into subjectivity, her human isolation, and the like, acceptable. Yet an art which took itself on as a subject

13 A third factor can be taken into account: M. Praz's insertion of a final chapter in the 1960 edition of his widely read and consulted *Storia della letteratura inglese* (A History of English Literature), 'L'età dell'ansia' (The Age of Anxiety), where Virginia Woolf was quite extensively presented in the network of her cultural relations (G.E. Moore and his 'moods', Bergson and *pointillisme*, Mallarmé for the role of the 'inexpressible', Tolstoy, Joyce and stream of consciousness, etc.), and in the long series of her novels; her solipsism was conceded, the 'musical metaphor' was insisted upon, but Virginia Woolf's tragic awareness, her sense of anxiety and of imminent disaster were also emphasized.

was doomed to a tragic consummation: *TW* became a clear symptom of the failure of bourgeois attempts at controlling and expressing life. Virginia Woolf had shown and embodied the crisis inherent in *aesthetic* art.

This attitude prevailed in the 1960s and early 1970s. A form of sober interest was re-directed to, and re-awakened in, her life by the translation of Quentin Bell's biography in 1974, and was reflected in Mirella Billi's 1975 monograph, *Virginia Woolf*, which managed to present and illustrate the whole range of her achievements – from family conditions to Bloomsbury, from *VO* and *ND* as dynamic moments to *JR* as a novel of transition, from *MD* as a series of epiphanies to *TL* as combining the case for life (Mrs Ramsay) and art (Lily Briscoe), from the androgynous vision of *O* to the peak of *TW* (based on sensations produced by events and transformed by individual sensibilities, and on a total elimination of whatever is outside psychic reality), from *TY* to *BTA* as a pageant, to her masterly essays, social as well as literary. Billi gave us Virginia Woolf 'in the round', not halved. This kind of appraisal was confirmed by the publication of *MB* (translated 1977); it almost coincided with Sergio Perosa's edition of *Romanzi e altro* (1978), and with the rise of feminist criticism and awareness in precisely those years, for which Virginia Woolf soon became a presiding spirit and a full-fledged example.[14]

MB, which came partly as a surprise, was widely reviewed and discussed in papers and magazines: according to Jeanne Schulkind's introduction, it showed a coming together of personal involvement with artistic perception, the unity of memory and fiction, the connection of then and now, past and present, a sense of society as well as of invisible presences. Rather than starting with Virginia Woolf, my introduction to the 'Meridiani' volume stressed the way in which the novel had been transformed by her sensibility and her fiction, and presented her as one of the masters of the twentieth-century tradition in her exploration of consciousness, her psychological subtlety and her experimentation with new forms. While always 'vibrating on the edge of dissolution, and

---

14 An article by Giuseppe Tomasi di Lampedusa, the well-known author of *Il gattopardo* (*The Leopard*), in *Corriere della sera* (1978), also contributed to this particular trend: she was equated with Joyce and Proust (though she was a master of 'fluid', not past, time), and was considered the author of five masterpieces, a writer of European importance. *BTA* was seen as a fantastic *Midsummer Night's Dream;* her novels were like 'diagrammi che al capezzale dei ricoverati all'ospedale segnano ora per ora la febbre' ('charts by the beds of hospital patients that hourly mark their temperature'; reprinted in Lampedusa 1991, 2: 402). The poet Attilio Bertolucci, in his 1978 foreword to *O*, reconsidered it no longer as a *curiosità*, but as 'a metaphor for England in her social and cultural transformation over three centuries'. In a review of 1978, M. Praz saw *O* as a series of metempsychoses of characters in the Bloomsbury group. The 1978 introduction to *BTA* by Franco Cordelli (then a budding novelist) was in a sense a missed chance: he tried a non-analytical critical method, and in a long series of short notations wrote of her 'superior Bohème' (almost an apartheid), of her alienation and loss of self, of her prose merging with poetry, of her peculiar voice and black humour, of her use of a theatrical stance, but was sceptical about her literary criticism, and showed misgivings about a feminist reconsideration: Virginia Woolf was essentially and above all a writer.

seeming to deny itself', the Virginia Woolf novel 'opened up undreamt-of possibilities'.[15] Fluid and formless, she was also lucid and cutting, drawing arabesques on the wall but leaving a clear-cut sign. Questions of highbrow and lowbrow, snobbishness and disengagement, Bloomsbury and aestheticism were best left aside, or in the background: the crucial element was Virginia Woolf's adventure with the novel.

Hence a clarification of her cultural background and literary pedigree was proposed: William James for the stream of consciousness (though in the mind, rather than the subconscious), Bergson for *durée*, Roger Fry for the concept of vision, G. E. Moore for that of moods, Freud, Joyce and Proust, but only in a limited way. Her poetics, as expressed in a number of essays ('Mr Bennett and Mrs Brown', 'The Narrow Bridge of Art', 'Modern Fiction'), was highlighted, as well as her reliance on subjectivity *and* objectivity (her love for London, Defoe, Jane Austen and Henry James): she consciously – and defensively – alternated between poetic experiments and factual books, critical and otherwise (*TL*, *MD*, *TW* were set against *O*, *TY*, *FB*); contrary to previous strictures, *BTA* was seen as the greatest effort at reconciliation between the two modes. Letters and diary entries provided a running commentary and a counterpoint to her fiction; as with Henry James, one had to rely on, as well as be wary of, their over-determining presence, the risk of their controlling our response. Uneasiness about her aristocratic ways and her poetic flights had to be dispelled by an appreciation of the openness and fluidity of her novels. (Similar ideas were expressed in my introduction to *MD* in 1979: stream of consciousness was applied to the level of consciousness; one was confronted not by subjectivity, but by a multi-personal representation of the mind in action.)

The coincidence of these presentations of Virginia Woolf's achievements with the forceful rise of feminist criticism brought her reputation to its highest peak. Feminist criticism was at first enthusiastic, militant and somewhat confused. It then turned into problematic, scholarly assessments; finally – in the late 1980s and 1990s – it merged fruitfully with a concern with, and an appreciation of, the ways and means of *la scrittura al femminile* (gender writing). Generalizations – and some representative examples only – are needed to deal with this unprecedented spread of Virginia Woolf studies.

An example of the first type was provided by Paola Zaccaria's short monograph of 1980, *Virginia Woolf: trama e ordito di una scrittura* (Virginia Woolf: The Warp and Woof of Writing), which started from Virginia Woolf's feminist essays, *ROO* and *TG*, as 'elements of a feminist education', and ended with a consideration of the inescapable position of women, for whom writing is a way of distinguishing their true from their 'tamed' nature. In opposition to previous studies, an interesting reversal took place: starting from the later, feminist essays, Zaccaria proceeded backwards to earlier concerns – androgyny in *O*, wordy silence in *TW*, the warp and woof of *TL* (another of her passionate and militant contributions along these lines was in the magazine

---

15 'Vibra costantemente sull'orlo della dissoluzione, sembra negarsi ad ogni passo, eppure si apre ad impensate possibilità'.

Confronto letterario (Literary Comparison (Zaccaria 1988)). On the borderline between the first and the second type, one might consider Erina Siciliani's contribution in her volume *Tele con strani disegni* (Canvases with Strange Designs) (1984), Grazia Livi's in her *Da una stanza all'altra* (From One Room to Another) (1984), Nadia Fusini's early essay in her volume *Nomi* (Names) (1992a), Anna Brawer's monograph on *TL*, *Ritratto come autoritratto* (Portrait as Self-portrait) (1987).

Of particular interest in the second area – that of problematic, scholarly assessments – were Marisa Bulgheroni's 1980 introduction to *ROO*, and Barbara Lanati's introduction to *Freshwater* (*FC*) (1983). In the first, Virginia Woolf's metamorphosis as a woman and as a writer was charted and extolled: her essays turns into a story, this story into an invective, and her analysis into aphorisms; poetic reverie coexists with visionary thrusts, and, eventually, games with paradoxes; Virginia Woolf erases herself from the scene, like Shakespeare's sister. In the second, Lanati expanded on the question of the woman trapped, of woman becoming a word, a sign, a symbol, i.e. writing and art. Virginia Woolf's feminism was eventually an invitation to plunge into language, to use writing as a demonstration of existential unease. Hence a tendency – in this, as well as in other contributions of similar type – to lay emphasis on young Virginia Stephen (usually Virginia, for short), on the woman *before*, or *after*, she became a writer, *pre-existing* or *renouncing* writing, going back to her origins or forward to her death. The translation of Phyllis Rose's *Woman of Letters* in 1980 supported this tendency, which was also strengthened by the impact of, and the controversy aroused by, the Italian publication of *La mia vita con Virginia* (My Life with Virginia) in 1989; this selection from Leonard Woolf's autobiography of passages related to their married life, based on the German edition *Mein Leben mit Virginia*, with an apt and balanced foreword by M. Bulgheroni, 'Leonard & Virgina', revived a great deal of interest in her life as a woman as well as a writer.[16]

The balance – or the dialectics – between the writer and the woman was hard to attain: a temptation to be content and to identify with the woman only, as if her writing were something superfluous, not to be reckoned with, was lurking in the early feminist criticism of Virginia Woolf. That of a more scholarly, academic type came to fruition in Lilla Crisafulli Jones's and Vita Fortunati's essays in the volume *Ritratto dell'artista come donna* (Portrait of the Artist as a Woman) (1988). For the former, Virginia Woolf was marked by nihilism, obsessed with death: art was the only, fragile barrier against it; her only character (going back to a perennial controversy) was the mind; as crises and raptures enter her fiction, turning it into meta-fiction and meta-writing, hers becomes a typically feminine 'aesthetics of crisis' (incidentally, Crisafulli

[16] Bulgheroni wrote of a 'marriage novel' (or romance?: 'romanzo coniugale'), of a truce between two solitudes, and that 'Virginia Woolf does not ask Leonard Woolf to accompany her in her in-depth paths ... but to receive her on the surface when she comes back' ('Virginia Woolf non chiede a Leonard Woolf di accompagnarla nei suoi percorsi di profondità ... ma di accoglierla in superficie quando vi fa ritorno').

was the first to suggest a tentative comparison of Virginia Woolf with the Italian writer Pirandello). For Fortunati, *O* operated in a parodic, comic dimension: its irony, too, showed the way in which women writers appropriate meta-fiction as a means of expression. Both essays I take to represent a mature way of re-reading and re-assessing Virginia Woolf in terms of feminine identity as well as artistic achievement.

Other ways of assessing Virginia Woolf's achievement were of course pursued: by Alide Cagidemetrio, for instance, in her 1982 introduction to *La famiglia Pargiter* (*TP*), which started from the feminist debate, but stressed Woolf's new way of attempting a twentieth-century kind of historical novel; or by Carla Apollonio in a 1989 structural-linguistic study of *MD* and *TL*, *L'enigma del tempo* (The Enigma of Time); or by Roberto Bertinetti, in his 1985 academic volume, *Virginia Woolf: l'avventura della conoscenza* (Virginia Woolf: The Adventure of Knowledge), where an analysis of *VO*, *MD*, and *BTA* was meant to show her not as an 'instinctive' writer, but rather as a thinker committed to a search for the fullness of the individual. And the novelist Grazia Livi, in her afterword to *Scene di Londra* (*LS*) (1982), admitted that, if as a woman Virginia Woolf was saved by writing, her femininity was almost always neutralized by and assimilated into the person of genius.

Yet the prevailing – if not the only – interest, well into the 1990s, remained feminist criticism. This is again exemplified by a long series of contributions. Armanda Guiducci's *Virginia e l'Angelo* (Virginia and the Angel, 1991) was a 'writerly', empathetic biography, in which 'Jenny' was seen killing the 'Angel in the House': the emphasis was on her youthful experience (indeed, nightmare) of sexual harassment by Gerald, on her 'Victorian' repression by father and family, her complex relations with Nessa and her friends, her shunning of sex, her lack of formal education, her striving for personal, psychological and intellectual independence, her social awkwardness and snobbishness and her 'liberation' through art. Her art was seen as a 'lyrical sinewing of sensations'; most of the attention, however, was given to her feminism in the 1920s, her nervous breakdowns, her de-sexualized marriage ('a personal vengeance on Bloomsbury'), her refusal of 'masculinity', and her half-hearted espousal of socialism. Pride of place was given to *ROO* and *TG*, and to her exploration of feminine creativity: bisexuality and androgyny rule and provoke the creative mind. Working on the 'cracks of female consciousness', Virginia Woolf is masterly in the delineation of female characters.[17] A sense and a premonition of death hover over all her writing career; suicide is the beginning and end of her life.

Here was a full, painstaking portrait of the woman as pained writer; yet we also had – as previously in Amoruso and others, though from a different perspective – a Virginia Woolf cut into two halves: Guiducci's narrative practically stops in 1929 (260 pages to this date, fewer than 50 to the end, with

---

17 'Nervatura lirica della sua scrittura'; 'una personale rivalsa contro Bloomsbury'; 'fessure della coscienza femminile' (in Dorothy Richardson's phrase). Virginia Woolf's was a 'journey on the lucid thread of madness' ('percorso sul filo lucido della follia').

no mention of *TY*). The same attitude was betrayed in her standard introduction to a series of new translations in the 1990s (see Guiducci 1992), where a distinction was made between Virginia Woolf's feminism and that of the 1970s and 1980s, though *ROO* was a 'little bible' for both, and she was presented as the greatest avant-garde woman writer of the century.

A special number of the magazine *Merope* was devoted to Virginia Woolf in 1992, and leaned heavily on this aspect. Of particular interest there was Mirella Billi's contribution, which emphasized her Victorian heritage, the cultural as well as human influence of Leslie Stephen, and her particular recovery of female writing through the form of biography, portraits, impressions and visions.[18] So, understandably, did M. A. Saracino's introduction to her bilingual edition of *ROO* in 1995, which drew a great deal on Virginia Woolf's youthful experiences and her feminist commitment: the book was 'the founding text of contemporary reflection on women and writing', an invective against patriarchal culture, the palimpsest of the 'great exclusion' of women from History, and of their recovery through writing. (A third example of mature feminist criticism was provided by Oriana Palusci's contribution in her *Le dimore del tempo* (The Dwellings of Time) (1996), where Virginia Woolf's 'discourse on the language of gender' was taken as a starting point for an analysis of her use of family dwellings in *MD* and *O*.)

The final, prolonged exploration and definition of Virginia Woolf's feminism turning into a perfect example of *scrittura al femminile* was by Nadia Fusini in a series of contributions by a writer–critic who is free from academic shackles, can write with inspiration and is personally involved in that specific problem. In an early essay in 1977, 'Sulle donne e il loro poetare' (On Women and Their *Poiesis*) in the magazine *nuova DWF* (new DWF), Fusini had already defined some of the quandaries and the potentialities of gender writing. In a note to a 1982 edition of *ND* she had stressed Virginia Woolf's 'realistic' writing as a way of overcoming 'an envy of reality' (represented by Nessa and her family), her vying with Austen and George Eliot, while recognizing a distance between writing and being, her early shift towards a 'night word' in *JR*, and the attainment of a 'transparent', absolute word in *TW*, as an attempt to unravel the I/you tangle. In *TW* a third voice beyond 'I' and you was reached, so that the writer herself was dispossessed, shirking mimesis and encountering a denial of narration, eventually finding herself 'without words'.

Fusini's views on these matters developed in the 1990s, thanks to her close work as a translator. In her 1992 introduction to *Al faro* (*TL*), she stressed its

---

18 In her many contributions on Virginia Woolf, however, M. Billi kept away from feminist considerations as such. In her volume *Il testo riflesso: la parodia nel romanzo inglese* (The Reflexive Text: Parody in the English Novel (1993)), she saw O as a form of 'critical and alien vision', a parody and an ironic deconstruction of the novel, precisely because Virginia Woolf stood outside it in a critical way; yet it was a crucial moment, leading to *TW*. In the same way, Billi's introduction to her bilingual edition of *JR* (1994) was a balanced study of its experimental nature: *JR* was a kind of *Bildungsroman* in reverse. In Billi 1999, she correlates *JR*, in part, with T. S. Eliot's *The Waste Land,* in tone and in the application of the crucial principle of juxtaposition.

elegiac tone, its dialectics of memory and nostalgia, its impersonal 'I think', and Virginia Woolf's identification with Lily Briscoe over the problems of expression and of the unbreakable link between the sensory and the intelligible. There lay the crux: 'to get at the vision . . . one would have to sacrifice presence';[19] there – in the discovery of the symbolic dimension of language – representation gave way to poetry, language to rhythm, to rapture and miracle. In her subsequent introduction to *MD* (1993), Fusini still insisted on the role of nostalgia, time and organic growth, as means of expressing the variety and importance of life, where the 'I' is cancelled out, but where death lays siege to human possibilities. In her 'Translator's Note' appended to *TW* (1995), she dwelt on the middle-aged quality of the book, born of Eos, the Dawn, and yet following the movement of the wave in a crucial counterpoint of what flows and what is still; soliloquies are turned inwards in a pure present, while the impersonality of poetry is reached through a kind of multiple language. We are 'stunned', in the end, by the alternation of movement and stasis, caught in a timeless energy without entropy.

All these threads came to fruition in Fusini's two introductions to the two 'Meridiani' volumes she edited in 1998 (*Romanzi* and *Saggi, prose, racconti*). In the first, 'Virgo, la stella' (Virgo, The Star) (Fusini 1998a), she wrote of Virginia Woolf's 'irrefutable greatness' as an experimental writer, a peer of Conrad, James, T.S. Eliot, though she had learned how to tune her language differently. Writing about elusive life, Virginia Woolf behaved like a scientist connecting inner and outer reality, the self and the world; although dramatically sought-after, form is sudden configuration; language transmutes life into word. While *TY* was, understandably, almost ignored (for being too realistic, too regressive, late-Chekhov), *TW* pursued the extreme link with language, the extreme point of escape or collapse for consciousness; while *BTA*, an 'empty vessel', aimed at silence at the centre. As a woman writer, Virginia Woolf sought to embody life in words, revealing, however, that life itself is elusive, that there is no salvation in literature; in her final experiments, she turned a kind of post-modern somersault.

The quality of her feminine writing was even better pursued in Fusini's second introduction, 'La foresta della prosa' (The Forest of Prose), dealing with Virginia Woolf's essays and 'biographical' writings. Her essays, too, are considered 'writerly', written in a creative, metaphorical prose: there she could stand perfectly *al femminile* (in the feminine), obsessed with form, in order 'to recreate the process of thought' in an empathic, rather than logical, mode, by blurring the boundaries between the 'I' and the subject of her discourse. Writing for the common reader, Virginia Woolf followed an open 'chain of thought'; while reading, we have the impression that creation is at work: her essays are art, with a soul, not science. From this perspective, *RF* and *FB* are just as realized as her fiction: there, too, a woman can show how 'to write life', how to be hungry for life in the presence of death, to smile in the throes of anguish. This was a new Virginia Woolf, comic, laughing (as in many of her

---

19 'Per poter giungere alla visione . . . si dovrà sacrificare la presenza'; writing moves in a void.

letters), lovingly and perceptively recreated for the new century. (No wonder that in this view, *ROO* was less crucial than in previous feminist appraisals.)

This insistence on the high quality of Virginia Woolf's essays, letters, and diaries tied in very well with a widespread trend of the 1990s. At no other time were her 'non-fictional' works given so much critical attention. In 1994 Giovanni Luciani devoted a full-length academic book to a study of her literary criticism, *La polvere della lettura* (The Dust of Reading); yet it was left to essays and introductions to expand on the impact and revolutionary nature of her essays. In her introduction to *Ore in biblioteca e altri saggi* (1991), Paola Splendore insisted on the central role that reading and reviewing had in Virginia Woolf's experience: her essays in *DM*, for instance, were perfect equivalents of her later novels. Mirella Billi (in her introduction to *Ritratti di scrittori* (1995)) perceived in her 'portraits of writers' the creation of non-conclusive formal models, which were well in keeping with *scrittura al femminile*: there, too – and in her generational conflict with her father – Virginia Woolf founded a tradition. Writing a short note for the translation of *CR 1-2* (1995-96), D. Guglielmino confirmed this new awareness (as my forthcoming introduction to *D* will do also).

We no longer have a Virginia Woolf divided into two halves: the critical response has accommodated an 'all-round' Virginia Woolf, who is seen in her web of relations with parents, relatives, friends, contemporary fellow-writers and forerunners, and with writing as such – feminine as well as traditional and experimental writing.

12 'A gaping mouth, but no words': Virginia Woolf Enters the Land of Butterflies

Laura Maria Lojo Rodríguez

For Maruja
in loving memory

I

In November 1934, Virginia Woolf and Victoria Ocampo met at an exhibition of Man Ray's photography in London. For Woolf, Ocampo was at this time just one of 'these opulent millionaires from Buenos Aires' – or, as Roger Fry had termed her, a 'South American rasta' (*D* 4: 263). For Ocampo, Woolf was the admired writer whom she began reading at Sylvia Beach's suggestion in 1929, when *ROO* was published.[1] The meeting between Woolf and Ocampo was not a chance occurrence: Aldous Huxley – whom Ocampo had met in 1930 and who subsequently became one of her great friends – knew that the Woolfs had been invited to attend the exhibition, and thus introduced the two women.

In spite of the pejorative words which Woolf had used to describe Ocampo in her diary, she did not remain indifferent to the physical and spiritual charm of the South American intellectual. Ocampo was full of interesting stories and Woolf was eager to listen: [2] 'Anyhow she was very ripe & rich; with pearls at her ears, as if a large moth had laid clusters of eggs; the colour of an apricot

[1] Sylvia Beach's greatest glory was to publish James Joyce's *Ulysses* in Paris. Along with the Spanish philosopher José Ortega y Gasset, Beach advised Ocampo to set up a publishing business (Hermes Villordo 1993, 241).

[2] Ocampo had just returned from a trip to Italy, where she was received by Mussolini. In their first meeting, Woolf and Ocampo talked alternately in French and in English about South America, the Duce, Ocampo's unhappy marriage and feminism (*D* 4: 263).

under glass' (*D* 4: 263).[3] For Virginia Woolf, Victoria Ocampo was an example of remote and exotic exuberance, in much the same style as the box of orchids which Victoria had sent to her after their meeting: 'You are too generous. And I must compare you to a butterfly if you send me those gorgeous purple butterflies [orchids]. I opened the box and thought "This is what a garden in South America looks like!"' (*L* 5: 348–49). Indeed, South America seemed to Woolf a remote and distant country, a 'land of great butterflies and vast fields', of 'wild cattle and pampas grass' (*L* 5: 365).

Some years later, in 1946, Ocampo published an essay – included in the collection *Testimonios* (Testimonies) (third series) – entitled 'To the Argentine Students', in which she commented upon Woolf's butterfly imagery:[4]

> Virginia imagined that I came from a city (Buenos Aires) where clouds of the most splendid butterflies follow us in the gardens and superbly tanned young men wear tropical garments and have cool drinks under brightly coloured umbrellas. The butterflies she may have taken from Darwin, I said to myself, who does indeed tell of how the *Beagle* was one day assaulted – ten miles off San Blas Bay – by a real flock of butterflies, to the point that the sailors said that it 'snowed butterflies'. But where do the young men under the umbrellas come from? From nowhere. From Virginia Woolf, purely and simply. (1946, 95) [5]

From this moment onwards, the relationship between the two women ripened quickly: Woolf invited Ocampo to dinner, and they exchanged experiences drawn alike from their rich personal and professional lives. Woolf was to become a lifelong influence on Ocampo; their first encounter was to have great resonance, and Ocampo preserved its excitement and intimacy in everything she wrote on Virginia Woolf.

In the same essay, Ocampo recorded how interested Woolf seemed to be in

---

3 The terms in which Virginia Woolf spoke of her first meeting with Ocampo are strikingly similar to those used to describe the encounter with Vita Sackville-West at Long Barn in 1927. Vita was at the time well known as a writer, and had just been awarded the Hawthornden Prize for her poem *The Land*. Woolf was impressed by Vita's aristocratic provenance, which she translated into images of opulence and exoticism: 'Such opulence & freedom, flowers all out, butler, silver, dogs, biscuits, wine, hot water, log fires, Italian cabinets, Persian rugs, books – this was the impression it made . . . Vita very opulent, in her black velvet coat with the baggy pockets, pearl necklace, & slightly furred cheeks' (*D* 3: 144).

4 'Virginia se imaginaba que yo llegaba de una ciudad (Buenos Aires) en que nubes de las más espléndidas mariposas nos persiguen en los jardines, mientras jóvenes soberbiamente bronceados y de indumentaria tropical toman bebidas frescas bajo los quitasoles de vivos colores. Las mariposas pueden haberle venido de Darwin, me decía yo, quien cuenta, en efecto, que el *Beagle* fue asaltado un día, a 10 millas de la bahía de San Blas, por una verdadera manga de mariposas, a tal punto que los marineros decían que 'nevaban' mariposas. Pero, ¿de dónde vienen los jóvenes con los quitasoles? De ninguna parte. De Virginia Woolf pura y simplemente.' Unless otherwise indicated, all translations of Spanish quotations are my own.

5 Virginia Woolf did indeed have a copy of Charles Darwin's *The Journey of 'The Beagle'* in her library. For a development of this point, see Beer 1996.

the particulars of her life: 'What is curious about her way of asking questions is that she talks to one about the most personal things in the most impersonal manner, the most scientifically objective' (1946, 94).[6] Woolf gradually developed an interest not only in those exotic aspects which surrounded the glamorous Ocampo, but also in her cultural background – including her language, which 'has a gaping mouth, but no words' (*L* 5: 349).

In spite of their quite different personalities – Woolf considered Ocampo too impetuous; Ocampo was in turn hurt by the little or no significance which she felt she had in Woolf's life[7] – there were many similarities which inevitably brought them together. As Bernice Hausman has argued (1990, 204), Victoria Ocampo had a particular set of writers with whom she corresponded frequently and on whom she modelled herself as a writer and literary critic: Rabindranath Tagore, T. E. Lawrence, Aldous Huxley and Virginia Woolf. But Ocampo's relationship with Woolf differed from her relationships with other writers because she identified herself with Woolf both as a writer and as a woman.

Victoria Ocampo's critical writings and autobiography are equally revealing of a woman who moved away from traditional and patriarchal notions of literary criticism in order to express her experience as a woman reader. In Ocampo's critical writings about Woolf and her work, she emphasized Woolf's treatment of the feminine and of women's relationship to literature. Ocampo was undoubtedly one of Virginia Woolf's first feminist readers and, as a result, she was eager to promote her discovery by publishing most of Woolf's work in the literary journal she ran – *Sur* (South) – while encouraging other women writers to express themselves, as she herself had been encouraged by Woolf.

---

6 'Sin embargo lo que hay de curioso en su manera de interrogar es que le habla a uno de las cosas más personales en la forma más impersonal, más científicamente objetiva.' Woolf's curiosity reminded Ocampo of Anna de Noailles whom she had met in 1928: 'Anna de Noailles would also ask abundantly; but would leave no time to answer. Virginia Woolf, on the contrary, waits and wants an answer' (1946, 94).

7 Ocampo was aware that she might have no real existence for her heroine. Woolf, in contrast, used Ocampo's friendship to arouse jealousy in Vita Sackville-West: 'I am in love with Victoria Okampo [*sic*]', Woolf told her (*L* 5: 335). Significantly, in her autobiography – published posthumously – Ocampo talks about Woolf's great beauty as comparable only to that of her lover, Julián Martínez: 'The architecture of his face (the bones) was of an astonishing beauty that I did not find again until I met Virginia Woolf' ('La arquitectura de su rostro (los huesos) tenía una singular belleza que no he vuelto a encontrar hasta que conocí a Virginia Woolf') (1991, 140). In the 1950s Vita Sackville-West and Victoria Ocampo became friends; Vita would reassure Ocampo about her friendship with Woolf: 'I don't think it is in the least true to say that you had no real existence for her, because she often talked to me about you even before I had met you. It is true that there was an uncertain reality about her unless you knew her very intimately. One always felt that she might take flight any moment and disappear', Sackville-West to Ocampo, 7 July 1954, quoted in Meyer (1979, 128).

II

Victoria Ocampo was born in 1890 in Buenos Aires, to an aristocratic family. The privileges and enslavement of such a background presented a contradiction that she was never able to resolve. Ocampo's social and economic background was to condition both her professional life and the controversial impact she exerted on the Argentine society of her time (Abella 1996, 17). As was typical for any woman of her class, she was taught at home in French and in English; Ocampo, like Virginia Woolf herself, did not, however, have access to regular education.

She married according to her class, an event which would result in a dramatic change in both her personal and professional life: her marriage was a failure. In trying to dissolve her marital vows, Ocampo started her rebellion against the constrictions which oppressed her as a member of a privileged class and as a woman, against her family, official education, the church, the government's political and economic regime and, in short, against the 'conventional lies of civilisation' (Anderson Imbert 1962, 22).

Yet Ocampo never renounced the privileges of her social position and, as a result, was unable to break with her family, her class or her past. The same society which prevented her from having access to a college education, from becoming an actress or from divorcing her husband did, however, allow her little 'treats', even if these were scandalous for a woman of her time: Ocampo was, for example, able to live and travel alone, to cultivate male friendships, to develop a literary vocation and to run a magazine and a publishing house (Sebreli 1993, 31).

Victoria Ocampo was a woman who was profoundly committed to the history, culture and traditions of her own country, despite the fact that she was often criticized – especially during the years in which she ran the literary journal *Sur* – for paying too much attention to foreign culture. Once Argentina had won political independence in 1810,[8] the extremely arduous task remained of gaining *spiritual* independence: they were a people with no past, because their history was either too remote or too painful for them to remember. Those who had been born in the Old World were inextricably linked to the particular cultural expressions of their country, but Argentina had none. Eduardo Avilés, a South American writer, raised the question:

> What should the American artist's attitude be as regards the European? To assimilate efforts, to adopt energy, to exploit discoveries, but this is all for the sake of American art. The impulse of this art will be realized by a process of assimilation, which may even become a transfusion ... It is vital that two personalities should arise, face to face, both with their feet firmly planted on the ground: the personality of Europe

[8] For a brief insight into Argentine politics during the first half of the twentieth century, see Botana and Gallo 1984.

and the personality of America. Political dependence is broken, why should intellectual dependence subsist? (Jarnés 1984, 25)[9]

Such was also the view of the young Victoria Ocampo, who was determined to make her passion for art and literature her profession: Ocampo was a major representative of those Argentine intellectuals who looked towards Europe as a means of ridding themselves of the cultural inferiority of their country. Ocampo intended to build a cultural bridge between Europe and America: her spiritual 'hunger' led her to travel incessantly through Europe and the United States in order to meet those whom she held to be the most relevant intellectual figures of her time: José Ortega y Gasset, Rabindranath Tagore, Hermann von Keyserling, Paul Valéry, Aldous and Julian Huxley, Benjamin Fondane, Waldo Frank, Drieu La Rochelle, André Malraux, Karl Gustav Jung, Anna de Noailles and Virginia Woolf herself, most of whom would become regular contributors to her journal *Sur.*

One of the most influential figures in the development of Ocampo's professional life was without any doubt the Spanish philosopher and humanist José Ortega y Gasset, and through him Ocampo gained international relevance. Ortega and Ocampo had met in Buenos Aires in 1916, where he had been invited to give a lecture. At thirty-three, Ortega was already a well-known figure within Spanish academic circles: he was a professor of Metaphysics at the University of Madrid and had specialized in German philosophy. Seven years later, in 1923, Ortega founded the journal *Revista de Occidente* (Journal of the Western World), which was widely available in Europe and America, and a publishing house of the same name. From 1924 onwards, Ortega began his regular contributions to the Buenos Aires periodical *La Nación* (The Nation) with a study on Marcel Proust which was significant for its original conception of literary criticism.[10]

During those years, Ocampo had initiated her own literary career by submitting an article entitled 'De Francesca a Beátrice' (From Francesca to Beatrice) to Paul Groussac, director of the Buenos Aires National Library: it was rejected. Ocampo's first published work – 'Babel' – was published in *La Nación* in 1924, but it was not well received by the conservative society of Buenos Aires: 'In those years, the attitude of Argentine society towards a woman writer was not indulgent. What Jane Austen had said in the nineteenth century was still true: "A woman, if unfortunate enough to know something,

---

[9] '¿Cuál debe ser la actitud americana ante lo europeo? Asimilar fuerzas, adoptar energías, explotar descubrimientos, todo en beneficio del arte americano. La vigorización de este arte se hará mediante un proceso asimilativo, llegándose, si es posible, a la transfusión misma .... Es preciso que se alcancen dos personalidades, una frente a otra, ambas bien plantadas sobre sus piernas: la personalidad de Europa, la personalidad de América. Roto el vasallaje político, ¿por qué ha de subsistir el intelectual?'

[10] For an analysis of Ortega's influence on the South American intellectual world, see García Pinto 1984 and Ortega 1984. Soledad Ortega also includes some unpublished correspondence between herself and Victoria Ocampo.

should hide it as carefully as she can" ... For this I received a shower of insults' (Ocampo 1981, 105).[11]

Ortega, however, was aware of Victoria Ocampo's potential as a writer: in 1924, he published in *Revista de Occidente* the work which Ocampo had dedicated to Dante, 'De Francesca a Beátrice' and, in 1926, her short story 'La Laguna de los Nenúfares' (The Pool of the Water Lilies). Yet, as Blas Matamoro has pointed out (1975, 228), Ortega himself suggested to Ocampo that she move away from the essay in order to concentrate her efforts on more personal forms of writing, such as memoirs or letters, the genesis of Ocampo's forthcoming *Testimonios*, fluctuating between reveries, memoirs, traditions, social chronicles, critique of manners, biography of forefathers, letters and diaries (Sebreli 1993, 30).

Towards the end of the 1920s, Victoria Ocampo felt ready to begin a new adventure, which was considered as ill-suited for a woman as was that of becoming a writer: she founded a literary journal and a publishing house, which were conceived as a cultural bridge between America and the rest of the world. Thus, on 1 January 1931, the first number of *Sur* appeared: it was sold primarily in Madrid and Paris. Its editorial board included, among others, Jorge Luis Borges, María Rosa Oliver, Pierre Drieu de La Rochelle, Alfonso Reyes, Pedro Henríquez Ureña, Waldo Frank and José Ortega y Gasset; Ocampo was the board's director. In June 1931, Benjamín Jarnés summarized the spirit of *Sur* in *Revista de Occidente*:

> An anxiety to excel themselves ... drives the vehement youth of South America, who are moving towards a personal literature, full of native themes and stimuli ... This is, we believe, the aim of *Sur*, which is published in Buenos Aires by Victoria Ocampo. This is a magazine whose dynamic and vital line does not reject any foreign vigour, a magazine which belongs, according to its own editor, 'to those who had gone to America, to those who think in America, and to those who are of America'. That is why the magazine, thought in American and for the Americans, is so full of European thought, because it is also written for all good Europeans. (Jarnés 1984, 28)[12]

The 1930s and 1940s represented the period of Ocampo's greatest glory and popularity; her success would be diminished after the establishment of Perón's

---

11 'En aquellos días, la actitud de la sociedad argentina hacia una mujer escritora no era indulgente. Lo que decía Jane Austen en el siglo XIX continuaba siendo cierto: "Si una mujer es lo suficientemente desafortunada de saber algo, debe esconderlo lo mejor que pueda" .... Por ello recibí una lluvia de insultos.'

12 'Un afán de superarse a sí mismo encauza las vehemencias jóvenes de Sudamérica hacia una literatura personal, rebosante de temas y estímulos indígenas .... Este es, creemos, el propósito de la revista *Sur*, que publica en Buenos Aires Victoria Ocampo. Revista en cuya línea dinámica, vital, no se desdeña ningún vigor ajeno; revista que es – en palabras de la propia editora – 'de los que han ido a América, de los que piensan en América y de los que son de América' ... Por eso, la revista, pensada en americano y para los americanos, está tan llena de pensamiento europeo, está también escrita para los buenos europeos.'

regime. According to Doris Meyer, 'during those years Victoria presided as a queen over a cultural court in Buenos Aires, most of whose members were self-willed or forced *émigrés* from France, Spain and other Latin American countries. The plenitude of life there, in the years previous to Perón, offered a great contrast with France at war' (1979, 102).

III

Throughout her professional life, the struggle to liberate women from the oppression of conservative Argentine society was a major preoccupation for Victoria Ocampo. Her entire life and work was a 'testimony' to her rebellion against the Victorian inheritance which prevented women from having any active role in public life by limiting their legal rights as individuals. In her writing Ocampo often rejected sexist theoretical positions such as those of Montherlant, Keyserling and Ernesto Sábato (Sebreli 1993, 33). In practice, Ocampo protested in 1935 against a bill which was designed to suppress the few legal rights which years earlier had been granted to women. In 1954 she supported a law for the legal recognition of natural children;[13] she even advocated a policy of birth control in 1975.

The right of women to have a place in the public realm was something which Ocampo championed with her own example. From the outset of her career Ocampo was concerned with how women might express themselves in writing; she wanted to find a tradition of women writers with whom she could identify. Towards the end of the 1920s Ocampo met in Paris one of the literary figures that she most admired from her adolescence, Anna de Noailles, but was disappointed by the French poet's obvious anti-feminism.[14]

Soon after this encounter, Sylvia Beach was to suggest to Ocampo that she read Virginia Woolf's latest book, *ROO*. This reading was a revelation: Ocampo considered Woolf one of the greatest women writers and defined her, years later, as 'the most precious gift that England has given me' ('el más precioso regalo que me ha hecho Inglaterra') (1946, 92). According to Ocampo, Woolf was one of the few women writers – along with Emily

---

13 See Ocampo 1954b.

14 In an encounter which would mirror that of Ocampo and Woolf a few years later, the Argentinian was intimidated by this writer who was at the time extremely popular, and who received her languidly on a sofa in an artificial and self-conscious pose. Yet Ocampo was disappointed by Noailles's vision of women: according to Noailles, women were naturally inferior to men, there existing only a few notable exceptions of whom she was one (Ayerza and Felgine 1991, 105–06). One of the topics in the conversation which Woolf and Ocampo held at their first encounter was precisely this meeting between Ocampo and Noailles, as Woolf records in her diary: 'And so to Mme de Noailles, dying of extinguished vanity in a small flat. She lay in bed, bedizened, covered with dozens & dozen of veils &c: began plucking them off; was never still a moment; lighting lamps & putting them out; demanded worship; was not old, but had outlived her fame. Nothing wrong with her but the death of her great fame' (*D* 4: 263–64).

Dickinson and Emily Brontë – who 'felt the world', who offered a 'poetic vision of things and beings'. For, 'who can adequately describe a woman's world but a woman herself?' (1963, 76–77).[15] Ocampo consistently used Woolf's texts – as well as her own constructed image of the writer she so admired – to identify and clarify her image of herself.[16] In 1946, at a conference for Argentine students of the 'Association for English Culture', Ocampo once more evoked their first encounter, romanticizing the figure of Woolf, which did not prevent her, however, from developing a criticism of Woolf's writing which was acutely perceptive:

> Suddenly I heard her name and mine being pronounced by a friend, and when I turned my head towards that voice, her marvellous face was already facing mine. Imagine a mask which, though deprived of life and intelligence, were beautiful. Imagine that mask filled with life and intelligence to the point that it seems to have been modelled by them. Imagine all that and still you will not have imagined the charm of Virginia Woolf's face; a charm of the most happy union of the material and the spiritual in a woman's face ... Her forehead and grey hair were hidden under the broad rim of a hat which made her face even more delicate and pale. What age? Clarissa Dalloway's; hardly over fifty, but I do not think she had ever been more seductive, though she may have been differently so. Everything that this woman has understood, felt, thought, adds to her beauty and underlines it. One wonders how she has managed not to think anything vulgar, not to feel anything low, since no vulgarity, no ugliness has left a mark on her face. (1946, 92–3)[17]

Their first meeting was followed by a series of letters and visits which, Ocampo felt, partly satiated her intellectual 'hunger' ('hambre'), the particular

---

15 'sentido del mundo' 'una visión poética de las cosas y de los seres' '¿Y quién puede describirnos adecuadamente el mundo de la mujer sino una mujer?'

16 In her contribution to this volume Manuela Palacios argues that the Virginia Woolf text that has had the most durable impact in Galicia is *ROO*. Like Victoria Ocampo, Galician women writers may have felt that that particular work of Woolf's provided a landmark on their long road towards social and intellectual emancipation.

17 'De pronto, oí su nombre y el mío pronunciados por un amigo, y al volver la cabeza hacia esa voz, el rostro maravilloso ya estaba vuelto hacia el mío. Imaginen ustedes una máscara que, aún sin vida, sin inteligencia, fuera hermosa. Imaginen esa máscara impregnada de vida y de inteligencia a tal punto que parece haber sido modelada por ellas. Imaginen todo eso y todavía se habrán imaginado mal el encanto del rostro de Virginia Woolf; encanto del más feliz encuentro de lo material y de lo espiritual en una cara de mujer .... Su frente y su pelo gris quedaban ocultos bajo el ancho borde de un sombrero que le hacía más delicada la cara y más pálida. ¿Qué edad? La de Clarissa Dalloway; apenas pasados los cincuenta; pero no creo que haya sido nunca más seductora, aunque lo haya podido ser de otro modo. Todo lo que esta mujer ha comprendido, sentido, pensado, se agrega en este momento a su belleza y la subraya. Se pregunta uno cómo se las ha arreglado para no pensar nada vulgar, para no sentir nada bajo, pues ninguna vulgaridad, ninguna fealdad han dejado marca en su rostro.' I am grateful here to Nicola Luckhurst, who indicated that this description was used to caption Virginia Woolf's photograph in a celebratory survey of British *Vogue* magazine (Howell 1975, 61).

expression that she used to refer to her eagerness for knowledge, as a result of her being an officially 'uneducated woman' – as she saw herself – from a country deprived of a strong literary tradition. A few days later, Victoria Ocampo was invited to dinner at Tavistock Square (*D* 4: 265); throughout December 1934 Woolf and Ocampo exchanged letters and presents (the exotic orchids which Woolf was to identify with Ocampo herself and her distant native country). When Ocampo left England towards the end of that month, they continued to correspond and talk about women and literature. It was then that Ocampo first explained to Woolf her project of translating some of Woolf's works into Spanish (*L* 5: 358). Throughout the following year the two women informed each other of their intellectual projects: Woolf received a copy of 'Carta a Virgina Woolf', and promised to write an article for Ocampo's *Sur*. Yet their correspondence also shows a growing sense of intimacy, as both writers spoke too of their private lives. Every time Ocampo travelled to England, she visited Woolf, even inviting her and Leonard on one occasion to give a lecture at the PEN International meeting in Buenos Aires (*L* 6: 13). Through Woolf, Ocampo also met Vita Sackville-West (*L* 4: 309). At all times Woolf was informed of Ocampo's intellectual projects, but above all of those which concerned Ocampo's criticism of her work and the translation of her texts which Ocampo was supervising. Their relationship was to be continued even after Virginia Woolf's death: Ocampo never stopped revisiting her by recomposing her reveries on her dear friend and acknowledging the debt she felt she owed to the British writer.

Ocampo specially credited Woolf with having encouraged her to go on writing; as a result, Ocampo sent Woolf a piece of criticism on Aldous Huxley – presumably 'Huxley en Centroamérica' (Huxley in Central America) – which would be published the following year (1935) in Madrid by Ortega y Gasset's Revista de Occidente imprint as part of Ocampo's first anthology of criticism entitled *Testimonios*. Woolf wrote: 'I'm so glad you write criticisms not fiction. And I'm sure it is good criticism – clear and sharp, cut with a knife, not pitchforked with a rusty old hedge machine.' But at the same time Woolf suggested – as had Ortega himself some years earlier – that Ocampo try a more personal form of writing: 'I hope you will go on to Dante, and then to Victoria Okampo [*sic*]. Very few women yet have written truthful autobiographies. It is my favourite form of reading' (*L* 5: 356).

Woolf's suggestions had a prompt effect on Ocampo: in 1935 she would begin her autobiography, which remained unpublished until after her death. Yet in December 1934, only a few days after their first exchange, Ocampo published an article in the *Revista de Occidente* journal entitled 'Carta a Virginia Woolf' (Letter to Virginia Woolf), which Ocampo would choose as the preface for her *Testimonios*, published the following year. On the one hand, this first critical essay on Woolf charts the relationship between a woman writer and her feminist reader; yet in its form, it also evokes Woolf's and Ocampo's private correspondence in which the themes of mirroring and reflection appear as 'testimonies' of Ocampo's modelling of her own literary figure. 'Carta a Virginia Woolf' is a reflection of the two women's relationship, a metaphorical room where they speak to each other about women, literature and the ways in which Woolf changed literary discourse.

Ocampo begins by recalling her first interview with Virginia Woolf at Tavistock Square, as if she were peering through a window watching the English writer and her Argentine admirer converse (Hausman 1990, 207). The warm atmosphere which surrounds the two women in Woolf's living-room as opposed to the chilly fog which permeates the London streets outside emphasizes the significance which Ocampo chose to give their first meeting: 'Outside, all the fog of London. Inside, up there, in the light and warmth of a *livin-room* [*sic*] with panels painted by a woman, two other women talk about women. They examine each other, they question each other'.[18]

Yet Ocampo is very conscious of the different things which they expect from each other, of the cultural gap which keeps them apart. They speak about what it is like to be a woman writer and for Ocampo this means that she must differentiate her own experience from Woolf's:

> These two women look at each other. They have different gazes. One seems to say: 'Here is a book of exotic images to leaf through.' The other: 'In which page of this magic history will I find the description of the place where the key to the treasure lies hidden?' But of the two women, born to different backgrounds and climates, one Anglo-Saxon, the other Latin and American, one backed by a formidable tradition, the other with a void at her back ..., it is the richer who will emerge enriched by the encounter. The richer will immediately have reaped her harvest of images. The poorer will not have found the key to the treasure. All is poverty in the poor and riches in the rich. (1935, 9–10)[19]

Yet, Ocampo feels that some similarities exist between them which bring them together in spite of all that has been said. Woolf confesses: 'Like most uneducated Englishwomen, I like reading.'[20] Ocampo is one of Woolf's most fervent women readers, though she goes further in saying: 'I would like to state publicly, Virginia: "Like most uneducated South American women, I like writing"' (1935, 10–12 [in English in the original]). Woolf's original statement and Ocampo's revision of it are ironic: both women had been widely – though privately – educated, both were well-read writers, both established their distance from a masculine literary tradition. The point of difference lies in the fact that Ocampo asserts her South American identity against the English-

---

18 'Afuera, toda la niebla de Londres. Dentro, allá arriba, en la luz y la tibieza de un *livin – room* [*sic*], de paneles pintados por una mujer, otras dos mujeres hablan de mujeres. Se examinan, se interrogan.'

19 'Estas dos mujeres se miran. Las dos miradas son diferentes. La una parece decir: "He aquí un libro de imágenes exóticas que hojear". La otra: "¿En qué página de esta mágica historia encontraré la descripción del lugar en que está oculta la llave del tesoro?" Pero de estas dos mujeres, nacidas en medios y climas distintos, anglosajona la una, la otra latina y de América, la una adosada a una formidable tradición, y la otra adosada al vacío ... es la más rica la que saldrá enriquecida por el encuentro. La más rica habrá inmediatamente recogido su cosecha de imágenes. La más pobre no habrá encontrado la llave del tesoro. Todo es pobreza en los pobres y riqueza en los ricos.'

20 The phrase is inserted in English in the Spanish original.

woman, as a means of finding a place of her own as a woman writer in a non-existing Argentine literary tradition.

As noted above, Ocampo's 'Carta a Virginia Woolf' occupied a prominent position in her first collection of essays: the preface. Ocampo, who saw herself as a wandering figure deprived of a literary tradition, felt that her hunger could be satiated in part by that woman who 'was building between us a bridge of words' (Ocampo 1934, 171).[21] Thus, Ocampo acknowledges a debt to Woolf when publishing her *Testimonios*:

> Your name, Virginia, is linked to these thoughts. For it was with you that I spoke lately – and unforgettably – of this wealth, born of my poverty: hunger. All the articles collected in this volume ... testify to my hunger. My hunger, authentically American! In Europe, as I said to you a few days ago, it seems that you have everything but hunger. (1935, 10–11)[22]

As a woman writer herself and as an active feminist, Ocampo was deeply concerned with the way in which women expressed themselves as well as with the social conditioning which predetermined their writing, and in this she coincided with Woolf: 'You give a great deal of importance to the fact that women should express themselves, and that they should do it in writing' (1935, 11). Like Woolf, Ocampo felt that masculine literary production did not satiate her hunger: 'You find that men's books account only very partially for the psychology of women. You even find that men's books speak rather imperfectly about themselves' (11). Moreover, the necessity of vindicating a place for women in literature is also, Ocampo argues, a 'selfish' effort: 'My only ambition is to come to write one day, more or less well, more or less badly, but like a woman ... For I understand that a woman cannot relieve her feelings and thoughts in a masculine style, for she cannot speak with a man's voice' (12).[23]

The body of 'Carta a Virginia Woolf' discusses Woolf's *ROO*. This essay was particularly significant for Ocampo: on the one hand because it was through her reading of it that she had first become acquainted with Woolf, but also because the book claimed a place for women in literature. This was indeed a discovery for Ocampo, who felt that 'my eyes, fixed on those lines, no longer

---

21 'tendía entre nosotras un puente de palabras.'

22 'Su nombre, Virginia, va ligado a estos pensamientos. Pues con usted fue con quien hablé últimamente – e inolvidablemente – de esta riqueza, nacida de mi pobreza: el hambre. Todos los artículos reunidos en este volumen ... son una serie de testimonios de mi hambre. ¡De mi hambre, auténticamente americana! Pues en Europa, parece que se tiene todo, menos hambre.'

23 'Usted da gran importancia a que las mujeres se expresen, y a que se expresen por escrito .... Encuentra usted que los libros de los hombres no nos explican sino muy parcialmente la psicología femenina. Hasta encuentra usted que los libros de los hombres no nos informan sino bastante imperfectamente sobre ellos mismos .... Mi única ambición es llegar a escribir un día, más o menos bien, más o menos mal, pero como una mujer .... Pues entiendo que una mujer no puede aliviarse de sus sentimientos y pensamientos en un estilo masculino, del mismo modo que no puede hablar con voz de hombre'.

perceive in the manner of eyes, but like a hand pressed against a chest' (1934, 174).[24] Ocampo's discussion of Woolf's ideas moves from agreement toward revision and rearticulation: Ocampo revises Woolf's analysis of women and literature while defining her own experience – which was to some extent different from Woolf's – as a woman reader in a distant, 'exotic' and conservative Spanish-speaking country.

Ocampo argues, for instance, for a more passionate – and less critical – approach to women's writing: she identifies with Charlotte Brontë whose books, Woolf had said, are 'deformed by spasms of indignation, by rebellion against her own destiny' (1935, 13).[25] For Woolf, however, Jane Austen seemed a much better writer, for she writes, 'in spite of her sex, without bitterness, without rage' (14).[26] Woolf seems to consider that anger and indignation are out of place in a literary text, and she argues that the oppression of women has had a negative effect on their writing (Hausman 1990, 211). But for Ocampo this indignation which 'deforms' texts such as Charlotte Brontë's is especially significant when placed against her own cultural background: 'If only perfection is moving, Virginia, there's no doubt that I've lost before I start' (1935, 14). For Ocampo, the disparity between Austen and Brontë is due to 'differences of character' ('diferencias de carácter') (14), a judgement which could well apply to Woolf and Ocampo themselves when they review women's writing.

Ocampo carefully insists upon difference and articulates it: for herself, as for Brontë, 'suffering, which convulses her books, translates into a moving imperfection. By vindicating her cause, it is my own that I vindicate' (1935, 13–14). In the conservative society in which Ocampo was born and grew up, she often had to stand up for her rights in a combative and furious manner, and found that the 'purely patriarchal society' (16 [in English in original]) where Austen and Brontë had lived did not differ much from her own: 'In a similar atmosphere ... I started to write and to live; similar, but worse, Virginia. To write and to live in such conditions is to have a certain courage. And to have a certain courage, when one is not insensitive, is already an effort which absorbs, without our being conscious of it, all our faculties' (16).[27] Ocampo – like Brontë – felt herself to be emotionally involved in the text, while Woolf distances herself from it according to a more rigid critical practice. As Hausman has suggested (1990, 213), their different attitudes towards literary texts and reading practice are also repeated in the narrative form which each woman utilizes for her criticism.

---

24 'Mis ojos, fijos en estas líneas, no perciben ya a la manera de los ojos, sino a la manera de la palma de una mano apoyada en el pecho.'

25 'deformados, por las sacudidas de indignación, de rebeldía contra su propio destino.'

26 'a pesar de su sexo, sin amargura, sin odio.'

27 'este sufrimiento, que crispa sus libros, se traduce en una imperfección conmovedora. Defendiendo su causa, defiendo la mía también .... En un medio semejante ... comencé yo a escribir y a vivir; semejante, pero peor, Virginia. Escribir y vivir en esas condiciones es tener cierto valor. Y tener cierto valor, cuando no se es insensible, es ya un esfuerzo que absorbe, sin darnos cuenta, todas nuestras facultades.'

Yet Virginia Woolf's use of the essay is by no means conventional: she consciously detached herself from both the form and aim of the kind of criticism which was practised in 1920s England, and which was for the most part dominated by male figures such as Desmond MacCarthy, John Middleton Murry or T. S. Eliot. According to Woolf, the principle which should control the essay was not – as these male writers conceived it to be – the correction of readers' taste; the essay should be designed 'to amuse in 1500 or 2000 words' (*E* 3: 212); the 'principle which controls it is that it simply should give pleasure' (*E* 4: 216). By doing this, Woolf was effectively rejecting the principle of authority which functioned as a remnant of the nineteenth-century positivist approach to understanding and interpretation: 'To admit authorities, however heavily furred and gowned, into our libraries and let them tell us how to read, what to read, what value to place upon what we read, is to destroy the spirit of freedom which is the breath of those sanctuaries' (*E* 4: 397). A possible consequence of Woolf's rejection of the authority supposedly held by the critic could be her desire to 'cloak' herself under the impersonal 'one', who is the narrator of most of her essays.

While the voice may tend to impersonality, Woolf herself described her essays as 'personal', a quality inscribed in their very form. Ocampo is, however, more direct, using a private literary form made public. Her insistence upon difference and their different readings of women's writing does not separate the two women, but rather enriches – as she suggests in the very first paragraphs of the essays – their relationship. Thus, Ocampo concludes her essay by paying homage to all those women who, like Shakespeare's imaginary sister, have struggled to find a voice of their own – to articulate their difference – in the mainstream of male voices:[28]

> And if, as you hope, Virginia, all effort, however obscure, is convergent and hastens the birth of a new form of expression which has not yet found a propitious climate to bloom, may my effort be united to that of those many women, either unknown or famous, who have worked in the world. (1935, 17)[29]

As I have argued above, Victoria Ocampo had been an active feminist who rebelled against the constrictions of Argentine patriarchal society: the insertion of the personal woman into the public, male-dominant sphere was for her a political act. Although Ocampo's feminist perspective is also 'integral to her literary methodology' (Hausman 1990, 209), she wrought her arguments with renewed energy having received Virginia Woolf's encouragement. In her essay 'La Mujer y su Expresión' (Women and their Expression) – which was originally a radio broadcast, and then published in 1941 as part of the second

---

28 For a more detailed consideration of Victoria Ocampo's feminism, see Kaminsky 1980.

29 'Y si, como usted espera, Virginia, todo esfuerzo, por oscuro que sea, es convergente y apresura el nacimiento de una forma de expresión que todavía no ha encontrado una temperatura propicia a su necesidad de florecer, vaya mi esfuerzo a sumarse al de tantas mujeres, desconocidas o célebres, como en el mundo han trabajado.'

series of her critical writings, *Testimonios* – Ocampo argues for the necessity of women's 'self-realization' ('autorrealización') (1941, 281), however difficult this may be, since 'women in general, and South American women in particular, are not at all prepared to achieve that victory. They do not have the necessary education, freedom or tradition' (282).[30]

IV

When a few months later Victoria Ocampo returned to her native country, she was determined to share 'England's most precious gift' and to introduce Virginia Woolf's works to Argentine society. Woolf had been delighted by Ocampo's 'Carta a Virginia Woolf' and she wrote to the author: 'I don't usually like appearing as a private person in print, but on this occasion I can find no fault, and like what you say very much and thank you for it. When will the book be out?' (*L* 5: 365).

Virginia Woolf always seemed to be jealous of her privacy and she was careful to separate it from her professional activity. In a lecture read for the National Society for Women's Service in 1931 – later to become her essay 'Professions for Women' – Woolf confessed: 'These were the two adventures of my professional life. The first – killing the Angel in the House – I think I solved. She died. But the second, telling the truth about my own experiences as a body, I do not think I solved' (*WE* 2: 105). Woolf had an unpleasant experience with Ocampo which had to do with Woolf's reluctance to appear as a 'private person'. In June 1939 Ocampo appeared at Tavistock Square with her friend, the photographer Gisèle Freund; she intended to persuade Woolf to sit for a photographic session. Woolf was outraged by Ocampo's behaviour:

> Yes, London broke in fairly vigorously yesterday. Ocampo bringing Giselle Freund & all her apparatus, which was set up in the drawing room, & all the lit. gents & ladies shown on a sheet ... No getting out of it, with Okampo [*sic*] on the sofa, & Freund there in the flesh. So my afternoon is gone in the way to me most detestable & upsetting of all. A life sized life coloured animated photograph .... Such are one's friends – & their deformities (*D* 5: 220).

Yet Woolf had started to develop a deep interest not only in Victoria Ocampo as a friend, but also in the personal circumstances that surrounded her:

> And you are about to voyage to the land of great butterflies and vast fields: which I still make up from your flying words. What a strange broken life we live – what phantoms! But do not let me drift into the bog. Tell me what you are doing: whom you see: what the country looks like, also the town; also your room, your house, down to the food and the cats and dogs and what time you spend on this and that. (*L* 5: 365)

---

30 'lo mal preparada que está actualmente la mujer en general y la sudamericana en particular para alcanzar esa victoria. No tiene ni la instrucción, ni la libertad, ni la tradición necesarias.'

And of course, as a writer, Woolf was fascinated by language, and Spanish was no exception:[31] 'How interested I am in your language, which has a gaping mouth but no words – a very different thing from English' (*L* 5: 349). As Patricia Laurence has pointed out, Woolf was often 'drawn to the musical but sometimes intelligible sounds of other languages' (1999, 1). Woolf, who could not speak Spanish, regarded the language as a cryptic succession of 'exotic' sounds – so different to English – which very much fitted her vision of the Spanish country itself. In 1905 Woolf had reviewed for the *Times Literary Supplement* Rowland Thirlmere's *Letters from Catalonia and Other Parts of Spain* (1905) and Somerset Maugham's *Sketches and Impressions in Andalusia* (1905). For Woolf, Catalonia – the state which first received *MD* in translation within the borders of Spain, as will be shown below – 'is a place which, like many others, possesses sunsets and stars and mosquitoes and cathedrals' ('Journeys in Spain', *E* 1: 45).

Far more interesting is Woolf's account of her own experience travelling in Andalusia for the first time, which she recorded in her essay 'An Andalusian Inn' (1905). She describes Spaniards as a kind and hospitable people: 'We should be made to feel that silver is a most vulgar coin in which to pay such hospitality, and that that noble virtue – long dead among the innkeepers of our own country – still flourishes in Spain' (*E* 1: 50). Woolf's subtle irony falls on the British party who appear ridiculous in their attempts to communicate with the Spaniards, searching 'feverishly for a word of his own among the Ss and the Zs', drawing out their sentences from a conversation-book: 'A sentence in a conversation-book is something of the nature of an extinct monster in a museum: only the specially initiated can tell you that it is related to the live animal. It was at once obvious that our specimen was hopelessly extinct, and, further, a terrible doubt insinuated itself that it was the nature of what we asked as much as the language in which we asked it that was unintelligible' (*E* 1: 50–51). The party is described as desperately and unsuccessfully searching for the Spanish word for 'inn', while 'scraps of vehement Spanish penetrated . . . and somehow seemed to be concerned with us'. Woolf concludes that 'Spanish is a fierce and bloodthirsty language when heard under these conditions' (*E* 1: 52). Yet Woolf's inability to speak Spanish did not prevent her from visiting the country on numerous occasions.

As a writer, Woolf was obviously interested in other languages and their literatures. In 1917, when the Woolfs set up the Hogarth Press, they sought primarily to provide a forum for works which had formerly been unavailable in English. Her discovery of the Russian novelists aroused in her a desire to learn their language, and in this S. S. Koteliansky came to the Woolfs' assistance. Koteliansky himself had directed Virginia Woolf's interest towards the need to write for a much wider audience than that originally imagined for the Hogarth Press, pointing out the relevance of publishing translations. 'We've been seeing a Russian called Koteliansky' – Woolf wrote to David Garnett – 'who says that to write for a small public is damnation' (*L* 2: 167–68).

---

31 For a brief but illuminating insight into Woolf's translation into foreign languages, see the special issue of *Virginia Woolf Miscellany* (54, Fall 1999) devoted entirely to this subject.

Woolf was, however, also very conscious of the need to publish works in translation in order to approach a literary tradition which would otherwise have been missed: 'It is amusing sometimes to freshen one's notion of a great, and thus semi-mythical, character by transplanting him in imagination to one's own age, shore, or country village' (*E* 3: 113). Such were Ocampo's thoughts when she first envisaged the project of translating Woolf's works into Spanish. The prospect of having *ROO* translated into Spanish was, for Woolf, fascinating: 'The Lawrence has come – a magnificent looking book, though I can't read a word of it, and I shall be proud to see A Room look like that'. She also advised Ocampo as to which books would be more suitable for translation: 'I think the Room is the best to begin on: then perhaps, if you want another, Orlando or The Lighthouse'. The passage of time had the effect of making these books appear 'strange' to Woolf, 'like faces seen in my childhood – those remote books, about which I felt so passionately, as I wrote them' (*L* 5: 358). Ocampo's project of translating them into Spanish would, on the one hand, preserve this 'remoteness' since they would appear in the exotic, remote land of the 'great butterflies' but it would also make them appear 'brand new' to a somehow 'remote' readership.

Victoria Ocampo did not translate *ROO* herself, but encouraged the young Jorge Luis Borges to carry out the project. Borges had been one of Ocampo's first collaborators on *Sur*, established by Ocampo in 1931, and it was here that he published a significant part of his œuvre. Borges, who was then a promising young writer, had already published several books and also had some editorial experience, for he had been the director of the literary journal *Proa* (Prow) from 1924 to 1925. Like Ocampo herself, Borges had been concentrating his literary efforts on trying to create a literary tradition which would move away from provincial conservatism towards wider horizons. In his work *Prólogos* (Prologues) (1977), Borges summarized his literary attitude as follows:

> At the Tucumán Conference we decided not to be Spanish any longer; our task was to found, as had the United States, a tradition which should be different. To find such a tradition in the country we had detached ourselves from would have been an evident contradiction in terms; to find it in an imaginary native culture would have been absurd. We opted for Europe. (Borges 1977, 16)[32]

In his youth, Borges had taught himself to a great extent by reading the *Encyclopaedia Britannica*. English literature was – more than that of any other country – present in his work. Borges did not only study carefully those writers in whom he took a greater interest – namely Chaucer, Shakespeare, Donne, Swift, Yeats, Wilde, Conrad, Joyce, T. S. Eliot, Emerson, Whitman, Poe, Hawthorne, Melville or Faulkner – he also translated many of them into

---

32 'En el Congreso de Tucumán resolvimos dejar de ser españoles; nuestro deber era fundar, como en los Estados Unidos, una tradición que fuera distinta. Buscarla en el mismo país del que nos habíamos desligado hubiera sido un contrasentido; buscarla en una imaginaria cultura indígena hubiera sido absurdo. Optamos por Europa' (quoted in Waissbein 1984, 59).

Spanish. Tradition, along with imitation, creation and translation constitute, according to Borges, the steps towards the construction of national European literatures. And Borges had a special interest in translation: he had learnt, as had Ocampo, to read and write simultaneously in two languages; translating texts and conversations from one language into another was not unusual for him.

Yet, as Ana Gargatagli has pointed out (1993, 273–74), Borges seems to have developed throughout his career a particular poetics concerning translation. Knowledge of foreign – especially European – literature was a necessity for avant-garde writers in Argentina, and translation was often the means by which it could be made known. As Borges himself explained, 'I believe that our tradition is the whole of Western culture, and I also believe that we have a right to this tradition' (2000, 426).[33] By stating this, Borges was coming to terms with the – often criticized – cosmopolitan spirit of *Sur*, which aimed to make European writers who had been consecrated by European critics accessible to the Argentine readership.

Un cuarto propio (*ROO*) was published in *Sur* between 1935 and 1936; and in 1936 Woolf's essay appeared in book form, published by Editorial Sur, as did *Orlando* – also in Borges's translation – in 1937. The circumstances which surround Borges's translation of both works have always been controversial and equivocal (Gargatagli 1993, 10–11). In Argentina many doubted that Borges had been the sole translator, a doubt which had been spread by Borges's great friend and *Sur* contributor, José Bianco. Borges himself helped to maintain the ambiguity concerning Woolf's translation when in a broadcast interview of 1982, he ironically remarked:

> Now I am going to confide to you – since it is just the two of us – a secret: the book [*Un cuarto propio (ROO)*] was really my mother's translation. I did revise the translation a little, in the same way that she revised my translation of *Orlando*. The truth is that we worked together. Yes, *Un cuarto propio* interested me less . . . well, the subject is, of course, a mere vindication of women and feminism. But since I am a feminist myself, I do not need a vindication to convince me, for I am already convinced. (Ferrari and Borges 1982, 306)[34]

This is, indeed, an obscure point in Borges's biography. However, and as Gargatagli has indicated (1993, 13), both *Un cuarto propio* and *Orlando* had been published prior to the death of Borges's father, Jorge Guillermo Borges (1938). According to Borges himself, his mother – Leonor Acevedo – only began

---

33 'Creo que nuestra tradición es toda la cultura occidental, y creo también que tenemos derecho a esa tradición' (Borges 1989, 272).

34 'Ahora voy a confiarle, ya que estamos solos los dos, un secreto, y es que ese libro [*Un cuarto propio* (*ROO*)] lo tradujo realmente mi madre. Y yo revisé un poco la traducción, de igual modo que ella revisó mi traducción de *Orlando*. La verdad es que trabajábamos juntos; sí, *Un cuarto propio* (*ROO*), que me interesó menos . . . bueno, el tema, desde luego, es digamos un mero alegato a favor de las mujeres y el feminismo. Pero, como yo soy feminista, no requiero alegatos para convencerme, ya que estoy convencido.'

translating after her husband's death and, therefore, could not have collaborated with her son in translating Woolf into Spanish. It is possible, then, that Borges and his father translated Woolf together, or that he carried out the task on his own, and that he was willingly teasing his readers and critics, as he so often did. Borges may also have been saying something about the female tradition – or lack of it, in this case – and the vindication of women, which is the very subject of Woolf's essay by having his mother appear as the sole translator of *ROO*. The statement of mother–son collaboration – that is, a male–female translation of *O* – could be also read as suited to the subject-matter of the text.

Orlando was well received by South American intellectuals: Laura Ayerza (1991, 398) has described how Gabriel García Márquez took Woolf's novel as inspiration for his *Cien Años de Soledad* (One Hundred Years of Solitude); Borges himself chose it as one of the greatest English novels in his *Introducción a la Literatura Inglesa* (Introduction to English Literature) (1965). According to Borges, 'Orlando, the hero of [Woolf's] most famous novel, is not only an individual, he is the archetype of an ancient family. He lives three hundred years, and during his long story he changes sex' (1974, 67).[35] Victoria Ocampo herself was fascinated by it, and in 1938 she published an essay entitled *Virginia Woolf, Orlando y Cía* (Virginia Woolf, Orlando and Co.). Just as Virginia Woolf herself warns her readers that the text is a hoax, so Ocampo chooses to begin by breaking her readers' expectations about the words which follow:

> I am going to speak to you as the '*common reader*' [in English in original] of Virginia Woolf's work. I am going to speak to you of the image I keep of her. Do not expect to hear pure literary criticism; you'd be disappointed. For my encounter with the author of *Orlando* has given me once more – among other things – the certainty that nothing that I have imagined about this woman, dreamed for her, defended in her name is false, exaggerated or in vain. And in thinking of Virginia Woolf, I cannot forget it for one moment. (1938, 7).[36]

Just as Woolf's *O* is not a conventional novel, so Ocampo's criticism moves away from convention. As is the case throughout her œuvre, Ocampo becomes emotionally involved with the text she is dealing with; in order to justify herself, she speaks as the 'common reader' of Woolf's texts would, and begins by borrowing her definition. The common reader 'differs from the critic and from the scholar in reading only for pleasure, without having to

---

35 '*Orlando*, el héroe de su obra más famosa, no es sólo un individuo; es el arquetipo de una antigua familia, vive trescientos años y en el largo tiempo de su historia cambia de sexo' (Borges 1965, 98).

36 'Voy a hablarles a ustedes como 'common reader' [*sic*] de la obra de Virginia Woolf. Voy a hablarles de la imagen que conservo de ella. No esperen ustedes oír crítica literaria pura; se decepcionarían. Pues el encuentro con la autora de *Orlando* me ha traído una vez más – entre otras cosas – la certidumbre de que nada de lo que yo había imaginado de la mujer, soñado para ella, defendido en su nombre, es falso, exagerado ni vano. Y al pensar en Virginia Woolf no puedo olvidarlo ni un momento.'

worry about transmitting his/her knowledge. The common reader does not have a method, only a passion: reading' (1938, 46).[37] In following Orlando's story through the centuries, Ocampo also comes closer to the relationship between women and literature; at that time, she suggests, Argentina was not much different from Elizabethan England:

> Things seem to have changed a great deal since then, and to hear of those prehistoric customs makes us smile. We must note, however, that if they have changed for men, they have hardly begun to change for women. All those women who have written have repeated, in one way or another, Jane Austen's gesture of hiding her manuscript under blotting paper when visitors or servants entered her room. (1938, 26)[38]

Indeed, little had changed for women in 1930s Argentina. In discussing Orlando's self-awareness as a woman, Ocampo argues that women have always been subservient to men's image of them, which has nothing to do with nature, but with civilization: 'Women are not natural, nor obedient, nor chaste, nor perfumed, nor adorned, and they only come to be so by submitting to the most unpleasant discipline' (1938, 30).[39]

Five years after Virginia Woolf's death, Victoria Ocampo gave a lecture to the students of the 'Asociación de Cultura Inglesa' ('Association for English Culture'), which was subsequently included in her third series of *Testimonios*. In this lecture, Ocampo traces the history of her progressive discovery of English culture – language, tradition, and literature – Virginia Woolf, according to Ocampo, being one of its greatest achievements. She tried to wake in her students her own passion for the English literary tradition, 'one of the richest literatures that exists' (1946, 81).[40] Ocampo acknowledged her debt to Miss Ellis, the English tutor of her adolescence who not only taught her the language, but also made a gift to her of the English literary tradition:

> Shakespeare and Milton, Byron and Shelley, Hazlitt and Johnson, Spencer and Chaucer, Keats and Dickens, the Brownings and the Brontës, Eliot and the two Lawrences, and my dearest friends, one of whom has died so tragically, Virginia Woolf and Aldous Huxley. Without Miss Ellis, I would have been able to reach them only indirectly. I would not have been able to see them other than through the transparent, but hard and cold glass of translation. (1946, 82)[41]

---

37 'difiere del crítico y del erudito en que lee exclusivamente por placer y sin preocupación de tener que transmitir sus conocimientos. No tiene un método sino una pasión: la lectura.'

38 'Las cosas parecen haber cambiado mucho desde entonces y nos hace sonreír el relato de costumbres de trogloditas. Conviene advertir que si han cambiado para los hombres, apenas empiezan a cambiar para las mujeres. Todas las que han escrito han hecho, de uno o de otro modo, el gesto de Jane Austen ocultando su manuscrito bajo un secante cuando los visitantes o los criados entraban en su cuarto.'

39 'Las mujeres no son naturales ni obedientes, ni castas, ni perfumadas, ni revestidas de adornos, y que sólo llegan a serlo sometiéndose a la más molesta disciplina.'

40 'una de las literaturas más ricas que existen.'

41 'a Shakespeare y a Milton, a Byron y a Shelley, a Hazlitt y a Johnson, a Spencer y a Chaucer, a Keats y a Dickens, a los Brownings y a las Brontës, a Eliot y a los

For – and this is the message which Ocampo wished to transmit to her audience – 'knowing languages is one of the most effective ways of widening our horizons, thus placing ourselves in a position of receiving the inheritance to which we are entitled' (1946, 99).[42] Ocampo's own ability to speak several languages had made her contacts with foreign intellectuals possible; among these acquaintances, Ocampo cherished in particular her memories of Virginia Woolf, whose physical and intellectual charm she was eager to share with her students: 'As soon as Virginia was there, the rest disappeared. Virginia, tall and thin, wearing a silk blouse whose blues and greys perfectly harmonized with her silvery hair.' Woolf's physical appearance seemed merely to be a sign of a deeper psychological beauty: 'Virginia is as able to speak marvellously as to write marvellously. By saying this, I am confessing that I could not, without an effort, leave her side .... She managed to write in such a way that she had transformed the modern novel' (1946, 96).[43] Yet the romantic image which Ocampo had of Woolf did not prevent her from making an acute analysis of Virginia Woolf's novelistic method:

> I still see her, I see her always at her house in Tavistock Square with her snoring dog. This is the woman, I think, who can be cited among the most famous contemporary English writers. This is the woman whose novels seem '*herbaceous borders*' [English in the original] of the gardens in her country, a mixture of flowers, spots of colours which seem to sprout in happy disorder and where, however, everything is inspired foresight, confident selection, art and discipline. (1946, 97)[44]

The imagery of exuberance which indicates Woolf's novelistic method – those 'herbaceous borders' – seems to be particularly apt, since Woolf herself used it to refer to the private world of imagination. The flower imagery seems to stress the beauty of Woolf's prose, yet Ocampo places special emphasis on words such as 'selection' or 'discipline'. Woolf's prose has frequently been

---

cont.
Lawrence, a Shaw y, en fin, a mis queridos amigos, uno de los cuales ha muerto tan trágicamente, Virginia Woolf y Aldous Huxley. Sin Miss Ellis no hubiera podido acercarme a ellos sino indirectamente. No hubiera podido verlos sino a través de los vidrios transparentes, pero duros y fríos, de las traducciones.'

42 'conocer idiomas es uno de los modos más eficaces de ensanchar nuestro horizonte y de ponernos en condiciones de recibir la herencia que nos corresponde.'

43 'Pues en cuanto Virginia estaba allí, lo demás desaparecía. Virginia, alta y delgada, con su blusa de seda cuyos azules y grises armonizaban admirablemente con el plateado de su pelo ... Virginia Woolf es tan capaz de hablar maravillosamente como de escribir maravillosamente. Con esto estoy confesando que yo no podía, sin esfuerzo, irme de su lado ... se las arregla para escribir de tal manera que ha transformado la novela actual.'

44 'Todavía la veo, la veo siempre en su casa de Tavistock Square con su perro roncador. Esa es la mujer, pienso, que puede citarse entre los escritores más famosos de la Inglaterra contemporánea. Esa es la mujer cuyas novelas se parecen a los "herbaceous borders" [*sic*] de los jardines de su país, mezcla de flores, en manchas de color, que parecen brotar en feliz desorden y donde sin embargo todo es previsión inspirada, selección segura, arte y disciplina.'

labelled as 'impressionistic' and 'lyrical', a definition which appears to ignore the technical precision which Woolf always sought to achieve in her prose. Indeed, Ocampo's description of Woolf's style is very similar to Woolf's account of the process of writing and finding order in experience:

> Movement and change are the essence of our being .... Let us say what comes into our heads, repeat ourselves, contradict ourselves, fling out the wildest nonsense, and follow the most fantastic fancies without caring what the world does or thinks or says. For nothing matters except life; and, of course, order (*CR 1*, 63).

Ocampo would write again on Virginia Woolf in 1954, in response to the publication of *WD*. As Bernice Hausman has argued (1990, 220), Ocampo commented on the vicious effects of men's censorship on women's writing by discussing Leonard Woolf's editing of his wife's diaries and the influence which Sir Leslie Stephen exerted on her daughter. These were precisely the barriers that Ocampo herself had to overcome: despite her strong relationship with her father, he objected to her early desire to become an actress (and here Ocampo capitulated) and subsequently to her projects of running her own literary journal and press, projects which Ocampo – who was by then more mature and self confident – did not, however, renounce. Ocampo also found this ambivalence in Woolf's relationship with her father: 'Though it is true that Leslie Stephen would impose a great deal of Victorian taboos on his family, he also gave his daughters entire freedom to read any book from his library, quite an intellectual attitude' (1954, 26).[45]

Ocampo did not like the editorial intervention of Leonard Woolf in his wife's diaries. She felt that he had interfered with her access to Woolf by manipulating the text: 'Readers pause perplexed. They would like to know more. They would like to know why. The omission is flagrant. What is there behind this remark?' (1954a, 21).[46] Ocampo considers textual access crucial, not only to her personal relationship with Virginia Woolf, but also to Woolf's reception as a woman writer.

V

In spite of the relevance of *Sur* as a literary journal, the business proved ruinous in economic terms for Ocampo, and her fortune decreased dramatically. Although *Sur* was never a commercial but a cultural business – this was Ocampo's own definition – she decided to heed the advice of both Ortega y Gasset and Sylvia Beach and of Adrienne Monnier, who suggested that she should found a publishing house which would run alongside the journal.

---

45 'Si es cierto que Leslie Stephen imponía buena cantidad de tabúes victorianos a su familia, les daba a sus hijas entera libertad para leer cualquier libro de su biblioteca, actitud bastante intelectual.'

46 'Aquí el lector se queda perplejo. Querría saber más. Querría saber por qué. La omisión es flagrante. ¿Qué hay detrás de esa reflexión?'

Ocampo, who was reluctant to undertake a new business, tried to find an outlet for her publications in Spain – more specifically in Catalonia – through her friend María de Maeztu. However, Spain was at the time shaken by the Civil War, and Ocampo's name was inextricably linked to *Sur*, in which several items had condemned Franco's totalitarian regime.

These economic difficulties eventually led Ocampo and a group of collaborators to found in 1939 Editorial Sudamericana, which then published all the titles formerly published by Editorial Sur. As Victoria Ocampo herself explained, 'the name Sudamericana was a result of the impossibility of keeping the name "Sur" for the publishing business, "for this word had a revolutionary stamp"' (Hermes Villordo 1993, 242).[47] Ocampo's first partners in this new adventure were Oliverio Girondo and Alfredo González Garaño, who had, from the beginning, worked with Ocampo on *Sur*; they were later to be joined by Antonio López Llausás, a prominent intellectual who had lost his possessions under Franco's dictatorial regime and was, as a result, exiled in Buenos Aires.

The impact of Editorial Sur and Editorial Sudamericana was invaluable for the Spanish-speaking world. To mark the twentieth anniversary of the founding of *Sur*, its secretary Guillermo de Torre wrote a triple issue entitled *Evocación e Inventario* (Evocation and inventory). De Torre reminded readers that Malraux had anticipated in *Sur* the publication of D. H. Lawrence's *Lady Chatterley's Lover* and enumerated Sur's publications, many of which had appeared in translation almost simultaneously with the originals, as, for example, Martin Heidegger's *¿Qué es la Metafísica?* (What Is Metaphysics?):

> Thus it was *Sur* which published the first Aldous Huxley in Spanish *Contrapunto* (Point Counter Point) – which continues to be his masterpiece; the first D. H. Lawrence, *Canguro* (Kangaroo); the first Malraux, *La Condición Humana* (The Human Condition); the first Joyce, *Exiliados* (Exiles); the first Virginia Woolfs, *Un cuarto propio* (*ROO*), *Orlando* y *Al Faro* (*TL*); the first Chekhov, *Las Revelaciones de la Muerte* (Revelations of Death); the first Michaux, *Un Bárbaro en Asia* (A Barbarian in Asia) (Hermes Villordo 1993, 270).[48]

Indeed, the works published by the publishing houses Sur and Sudamericana were distributed throughout the whole of South America and Spain. After Borges's *Un cuarto propio* and *Orlando*, many other titles by Woolf followed: *Al faro* (*TL*) (1938), translated by Antonio Marichalar;[49] *La señora Dalloway* (*MD*) (1939), translated by Ernesto Palacio; *Tres Guineas* (*TG*) (1941), translated by Román J. Jiménez; the journal *Sur* also published 'Pasa el tiempo' ('Time Passes') (1938) in Marichalar's translation and 'Reflexiones

---

47 'pues esta palabra tenía un deje revolucionario.'

48 'De esta suerte le correspondió [a *Sur*] dar el primer Aldous Huxley en castellano, que sigue siendo su obra maestra, *Contrapunto*; el primer Malraux, *La condición humana*; el primer Joyce, *Exiliados*; los primeros Virginia Woolf, *Un cuarto propio, Orlando* y *Al faro*; el primer Chekhov, *Las revelaciones de la muerte*; el primer Michaux, *Un bárbaro en Asia*.'

49 For more on Marichalar, see Luis Alberto Lázaro, Chapter 13 in this volume.

sobre la paz durante una incursión aérea' ('Thoughts on Peace in an Air Raid') (1947), translated by B. R. Hopenhaym.

The work undertaken by the group 'Sur' was, paradoxically, more often read in Spain than in Argentina. There are several reasons for this. Firstly, some Argentine intellectuals heavily criticized the literary activity of *Sur*, for its efforts to endow Argentina with a literary tradition whose foundations were in Europe – especially France and the United Kingdom. Secondly, many of the intellectuals who collaborated on *Sur* were Spanish exiles, who still preserved strong bonds with their native country. And thirdly, Victoria Ocampo herself was a figure who was well known on the Spanish literary scene, primarily through her connections with María de Maeztu and, above all, with Ortega y Gasset and his *Revista de Occidente*, in which she had published several texts, among others 'Carta a Virginia Woolf', as early as 1934.

Curiously, Ocampo's 'Carta a Virginia Woolf' – which is, among other things, Ocampo's own rendering of her reading of *ROO* – was nearly simultaneous with the first translation of Woolf in the Spanish state. *MD* 'travelled into the Spanish state through Catalonia', as Jacqueline Hurtley has argued (1991, 121):[50] *MD* was published in Badalona in 1930, only five years after its appearance in England, and some eight years before Woolf's next work – *FB* – would be translated again in Barcelona.[51] As Hurtley has pointed out, *MD* did not arrive in Spain by accident; it was part of a publishing project undertaken by Marcelí Antich i Camprubí and Josep Queralt I Clapés – directors of Proa Editions in Badalona – whose aim was to stimulate the modern novel in Catalonia.

The decay of the novel as a genre could be applied to the whole of the Spanish state, a situation which José Ortega y Gasset had already analysed in his 1925 essay 'Ideas sobre la novela' ('Ideas on the Novel'):[52]

> Publishers complain that novels do not sell well, and it is true that the reading public buys fewer novels while the demand for books of a theoretical character is relatively increasing .... There exists a definite number of possible themes for the novel .... This, I believe, is now happening to the novel. It has become practically impossible to find new subjects .... It is not for nothing that the novel is called 'novel'. (Ortega y Gasset 1948, 57–59)[53]

In spite of the obvious differences that exist between them, it is curious to see how Ortega published his essay on the decadent state of the present novel

---

50 For an analysis of this translation into Catalan, see Hurtley 1991.

51 *Flush* appeared in *Quaderns Literaris*, 211–12 (1938), trans. Roser Cardús.

52 For a comment on Ortega's essay, as well as an overview of the development of modern English literature, see Baquero Goyanes 1955.

53 'Los editores se quejan de que mengua el mercado de la novela. Acaece, en efecto, que se vende menos novelas que antes y que relativamente aumenta la demanda de libros con contenido ideológico .... Existe en la novela un número definido de temas posibles .... A mi juicio, esto es lo que hoy acontece en la novela. Es prácticamente imposible hallar nuevos temas .... Por algo se llama al género "novela", es decir, "novedad"' (Ortega y Gasset 1964, 162–63).

the year after Woolf's 'Mr Bennett and Mrs Brown' (1924). Like Woolf, Ortega felt that the traditional novel – or rather, the conventions on which it relied – were exhausted and, as a result, it had ceased to interest the Spanish reading public. And, again like Woolf, Ortega considered that the modern novel should place emphasis on character – 'the novel is, above all, imaginary psychology' (1948, 211)[54] – rather than on conventional plot construction:

> What then pleases is not so much the fortunes of the characters as their self-presence. We enjoy seeing these people before us and being admitted to their inner life, understanding them, and living immersed in their world or atmosphere ... the important thing is not *what one sees* but that what one sees is something human, whatever it may be. (Ortega 1948, 61–63 [adapted translation])[55]

According to Ortega, the modern novel needed these innovations in the manner of, for instance, Dostoevsky, whom Ortega regarded as 'one of the greatest innovators of the form of the novel' (1948, 76), whose fiction succeeds in 'never appearing sham and conventional' (79).[56] Woolf shared this admiration for Dostoevsky, the 'great genius who is beginning to permeate our lives' (*E* 2: 83). For Woolf, Dostoevsky was also one of the great reformers of the novel. Unlike some traditional writers, who 'reproduce all the external appearances – tricks of manner, landscape, dress, and the effect of the hero upon his friends', Dostoevsky has the 'power of reconstructing those most swift and complicated states of mind, of rethinking the whole train of thought in all its speed, now as it flashes into light, now as it lapses into darkness' (*E* 2: 85) (McNeillies edition).

As I have described above, the aim of Edicions Proa was to awaken a new interest in the novel in both practitioners and readers. Thus, Proa published several Catalan authors, old and new, as well as translations of nineteenth-century foreign classics – such as Balzac, Dostoevsky and Tolstoy – alongside the contemporary: André Gide, Aldous Huxley and Virginia Woolf (Hurtley 1991, 122). Yet, after Proa's pioneering effort, there was a period of silence which, chronologically speaking, coincided with the outbreak of the Spanish Civil War and its aftermath; Woolf's works had to wait another decade to be translated in the Spanish state. This may be contrasted with the activity of the Argentine publishing houses Sur and Sudamericana; under Ocampo's supervision they were translating a great deal of Woolf's novels in this very same period.

The late 1940s saw a slow modification in the structure of Franco's regime, as Spain was forced to open up its frontiers and to ask for economic help. As

---

54 'La novela es, sobre todo, psicología imaginaria' (Ortega y Gasset 1964, 211).

55 'Lo que complace no es tanto el destino o la aventura de los personajes, sino la presencia de éstos. Nos complace verlos directamente, penetrar en su interior, entenderlos, sentirnos inmersos en su mundo y en su atmósfera ... lo importante no es *lo que* se ve, sino *que* se vea bien algo humano, sea lo que quiera' (Ortega y Gasset 1964, 165, 167).

56 'uno de los más grandes inovadores de la forma novelesca' ... 'nunca aparecen falsos, convencionales' (Ortega y Gasset 1964, 181, 184).

José-Carlos Mainer has argued, the modification of Spain's economic structure also meant the establishment of a timid basis for ideological change (1938, 395). This situation allowed innovations within the publishing market in Spain's two cultural capitals, Madrid and Barcelona. Yet – in broad terms – the publishing houses in Madrid focused primarily on the existing bond between Spain and the work of exiles, whereas Barcelona tended to publish European works which had played a seminal role in the process of cultural innovation. It is not surprising, therefore, that most of Woolf's works were – and still are nowadays – published in translation by editorial houses in Catalonia.

Prominent within this European-centred publishing effort was the figure of Josep Janés i Olivé who,[57] through his contacts with the British ambassador, Sir Samuel Hoare, and the first representative of the British Council Walter Starkie, published numerous works by twentieth-century British writers, such as Joseph Conrad, Aldous Huxley, James Joyce and Virginia Woolf. Janés's publishing house launched the following Spanish translations in 1946: *Los años* (*TY*) and *El cuarto de Jacob* (*JR*); in 1947, *Noche y día* (*ND*); and in 1956, *Obras completas* (The Complete Works) which included *TY, JR, ND* and *TL*. The text of *To the Lighthouse* in *Obras completas* was a reprint of Antonio Marichalar's translation of 1938 for Ocampo's Sur Editorial, thus revealing the continuing relationship between the Argentine and Spanish editions of Woolf's work.

In Barcelona in 1955 the collection entitled 'Biblioteca Breve' (Short Library) was published and promoted by Carlos Barral, whose aim was to 'establish a *back-list* [in English in original] of the more relevant recent authors' (Barral 1978, 139)[58] while at the same time competing with other editorial houses such as Sudamericana, which was at that point in its heyday. The first volume of the collection was Frederick J. Hoffman's *The Modern American Novel 1900–1950* (La novela moderna norteamericana 1900–1950), translated by J. M. Castellet: and Hoffman was soon followed by Robbe-Grillet, Duras, T. S. Eliot, Heinrich Böll and, in 1967, *Una habitación propia* (*ROO*) translated by Laura Pujol.

As José-Carlos Mainer has argued (1998, 403), the renewal of the Spanish publishing scene was accompanied by a proliferation of cultural magazines, and this was also the case in Buenos Aires, as described above. These journals provided a propitious framework for approaching both Europe and the cultural world of the exiles. *Ínsula* (Isle) was one of the first to be founded in 1946, directed by José Luis Cano and Enrique Canito: although its primary focus was the cultural activity of the exiles, it also provided a panorama of both European and American literature. As early as 1947 – just a year after the establishment of *Ínsula* and, significantly enough, a year after Janés's publishing house had launched the first translations of Virginia Woolf – Norman Nicholson published an article entitled 'Panorama de la literatura inglesa contemporánea' (Panorama of Contemporary English Literature). As the title suggests, Nicholson analysed the development of the contemporary British novel of the first quarter of the twentieth century. According to Nicholson, the period

57 For an analysis of Josep Janés's editorial policy, Hurtley 1984, 1985 and 1986.

58 'establecer una *back-list* con los autores recientes más relevantes.' For an analysis of the significance of Barral's editorial project, see Gracia 1995.

prior to the outbreak of the First World War had been dominated by writers such as Bernard Shaw, H. G. Wells, Arnold Bennett and John Galsworthy, whom Nicholson defined as 'realists', primarily concerned with 'the solid surface of life and interested in man as a social being' (1947, 2),[59] which sounds like a paraphrase of Woolf's 'Mr Bennett and Mrs Brown'.

Nicholson explored the work of writers such as James Joyce, D. H. Lawrence, E. M. Forster, Lytton Strachey and Aldous Huxley who, he felt, embodied a reaction against 'realism' by 'rejecting, each in their own way, the doctrine of inevitable progress while moving away from a civilisation based on such doctrines' (1947, 2).[60] Nicholson paid special attention to the work of Virginia Woolf:

> Virginia Woolf has triumphed by discovering her own form of novel. Virginia Woolf, like Joyce, utilized in her novels the 'stream of consciousness'. Yet, while Joyce took the multitudinous experience of life and tried to make order of it by means of his technical control, Mrs Woolf preferred to select and to give her work a form of delicate prose which resembles lyrical poetry more than any other fiction of our time. (1947, 2)[61]

Only two years later, the director of *Ínsula* – Enrique Canito – interviewed Vita Sackville-West for the magazine. Canito asked Sackville-West about 'The Land', her poem which had been awarded the Hawthornden Prize and which Canito described as the 'modern *Georgics*'. But the connection with Virginia Woolf is inevitable and thus Canito asked: 'I know you are Virginia Woolf's friend. What is your opinion about her influence on English literature?', to which Sackville-West answers: 'Virginia Woolf's legacy to English literature is indeed very precious .... She presents a perfect work of art, which is in itself a closed circle' (1949, 2).[62] Yet, Vita Sackville-West appeared not only inextricably linked to the figure of her friend Virginia Woolf, but also to the character recreated in *O*, a novel which was very present in the imagination of Spanish readers (*O* had probably reached the Spanish state through Borges's translation under Ocampo's supervision).[63] Significantly, Canito – whether intentionally or not – confused Vita's 'The Land' with Woolf's recreation of it

---

59 'la sólida superficie de la vida, y les interesaba el hombre como ser social.'

60 'rechazaban la doctrina del progreso inevitable, y repudiaban la civilización basada en esa doctrina'.

61 'Virginia Woolf ha triunfado al descubrir su propia forma en la novela. Virginia Woolf, como Joyce, utilizaba en sus novelas la "corriente de conocimiento". Pero mientras Joyce tomaba la total experiencia multitudinaria de la vida e intentaba poner un orden en ella por la fuerza de su control técnico, Mrs Woolf prefería seleccionar y dar a su obra una forma de prosa delicada que se asemeja más a la poesía lírica que a cualquier otra ficción de nuestro tiempo.'

62 'La aportación de Virginia Woolf a las letras inglesas es muy valiosa ... presenta una obra perfecta, que es en sí misma un círculo cerrado.'

63 There exist a great number of references to the connection between cultural life in Argentina and Spain, in which Ocampo invariably emerges as an outstanding figure through her work in *Sur*. See, for instance, Garrido 1949 and Torre 1951.

in *Orlando*, 'The Oak Tree'. Vita smiled indulgently and answered:

> I have already told you that my poem is 'The Land'. You are mistaking me for Orlando; indeed, when Virginia Woolf wrote that famous book she sought inspiration in my family traditions, in my castle Knole, and probably in myself in order to write *Orlando*, that apology for the spirit of continuity through the centuries and their changes, which is probably the most outstanding feature of the English soul.[64]

Yet Canito was reluctant to disentangle the real Victoria Sackville-West from Orlando, and concluded the interview with the line: 'I say farewell, I do not know if to Orlando or to Lady Victoria, but still I keep thinking of the magic world of *Orlando*' (6).[65]

Virginia Woolf proved to be a significant influence, not only in Britain, but for the whole of the European literary scene, and Spain was no exception. The year after Janés's publication of Woolf's *Obras completas* (Complete Works) (1956), José García Lora wrote in *Ínsula* about Woolf's possible influence on Spanish writers,[66] more specifically centring on the writer Azorín. Lora found a surprisingly large number of similarities between the two writers, and was particularly struck by their way of dealing with the relationship between self and time:

> Both writers are concerned with the fleetingness of the moment, become dismayed when it fades, and are fascinated by the paradox of its eternal return. The ambivalence of time – which flies and remains, which destroys things leaving them intact, which finishes them off in order to introduce them again, nearly identical, years later, which connects the self with other selves and the present with past times – is a key concept in both Virginia Woolf and Azorín. (1957, 9, 12)[67]

Lora offered a brief analysis of some of Virginia Woolf's novels – *MD*, *TL*, *O* and *BA* – paying special attention to the existing similarities between these novels and some of Azorín's works. He also commented on Woolf's *ROO*:

---

64 'Ya le he dicho que mi poema es "The Land". Me confunde usted con Orlando; y, en efecto, Virginia Woolf, al escribir este famoso libro, tuvo presente y se inspiró en las tradiciones de mi familia, en mi mismo castillo solariego de Knole, quizá en un trasunto mío, para esa apología que es *Orlando*, del espíritu de continuidad a través de los siglos y sus mudanzas, acaso el carácter más saliente del alma inglesa.'

65 'Me despido, y ya no sé si de Orlando o de lady Victoria; pero largo tiempo pienso en el mundo mágico de *Orlando*.'

66 For the influence of Virginia Woolf on Spanish writers, see the articles by Manuela Palacios and María José Gámez Fuentes in the present collection.

67 'Preocupa a los dos escritores la fugacidad del momento, les desconsuela su paso y les fascina la paradoja de su eterno retorno. La ambivalencia del tiempo que huye y permanece, que destruye las cosas dejándolas intactas, que acaba con unas para volverlas a presentar, casi idénticas, al cabo de los años, que enchufa en un yo otros yos y en el presente otras épocas, es directriz de Virginia Woolf y uno de los epicentros de la obra de Azorín.'

> [Woolf] considers so-called civilization as an exclusively male product, from whose construction women had been excluded. Women have to prove – when they are allowed to – their intellectual capability. In the essay *A Room of One's Own*, the writer proposes that economic independence is the foundation on which women's intellectual independence must rest. (1957, 9).[68]

Thus Virginia Woolf was a well-known writer – at least within literary circles – in Spain, from the early 1930s when Ocampo published 'Carta a Virginia Woolf' in *Revista de Occidente* and the first translation of *MD* reached the Spanish territory. Woolf was primarily regarded as an innovator of the novel as a literary genre, and was seen as an example to follow by Spanish writers in their attempt to give a new turn to the decaying Spanish novel.

In the early 1960s, Guillermo de Torre – who was well-acquainted with Woolf's work and has written criticism on her œuvre – founded the collection 'El Puente' (The Bridge), an editorial project under the auspices of the Barcelona editorial house Edhasa. In the course of an interview for *Ínsula*, De Torre explained the editorial policy of 'El Puente':

> The new collection, which Sudamericana from Buenos Aires will publish jointly with Edhasa from Barcelona, will assume a symbolic title . . .: 'The Bridge', which will tend to group under its arch Spanish writers from both shores, Spaniards inside and outside Spain unified by a common spirit of strictness and rigour, as well as likeminded Hispanic and foreign writers following this same line. (1962, 3)[69]

The editorial house Edhasa was founded in 1946 by Antonio Lopez Llausás, born in Barcelona and exiled in Buenos Aires where, from the beginning, he had been one of Ocampo's collaborators at *Sur* and Editorial Sudamericana. Llausás's task as an editor in Sudamericana allowed him to introduce into Spain banned books by, for instance, Rosa Chacel, Francisco Ayala and Max Aub, as well as by other foreign writers also banned by censorship.[70] Yet, as José-Carlos Mainer has argued (1998, 408–09), Spanish censorship – camouflaged under the name 'Servicios de Orientación Bibliográfica' ('Services of Bibliographic Orientation') – softened with the arrival in 1962 of the new Minister of Information, Manuel Fraga Iribarne, today president of the Galician state.

As a result of its bonds with Sudamericana, Edhasa published in 1978

---

68 'Woolf considera la llamada civilización como producto exclusivamente masculino, en cuya elaboración no ha participado la mujer. Esta tiene que demostrar – cuando la dejan – su pujanza intelectual. En el ensayo *Una habitación propia* (*ROO*) la escritora expone que la independencia económica es la base sobre la que ha de asentarse la independencia intelectual de la mujer.'

69 'La nueva colección que publicarán conjuntamente la Sudamericana de Buenos Aires y la Edhasa de Barcelona asumirá un título simbólico: "El Puente", y tenderá a agrupar bajo sus arcos a escritores españoles de las dos orillas, españoles de dentro y de fuera de España, unificados por un común espíritu de exigencia y rigor, además de algunos afines hispanoamericanos y extranjeros.'

70 I am grateful to Josep Menguá Catalá (from Edhasa's literary department) for the information given on this point.

Virginia Woolf's *O*, translated into Spanish by Jorge Luis Borges, as well as *Al faro* (*TL*) translated by Antonio Marichalar. In the 1980s Edhasa published in its collection 'Clàssics Moderns' ('Modern Classics') *Orlando* (1985), *Els Anys* (*TY*) (1988) and *Les ones* (*TW*) (1989), all translated into Catalan by Maria Antonia Oliver, under the direction of the poet Francesc Parcerisas, who had a great interest in Woolf.

More recently, the editorial house Lumen has translated into Spanish nearly all Virginia Woolf's work, both fiction and non-fiction. The project started with Antonio Vilanova, who recommended Woolf to Lumen editor Esther Tusquets. Tusquets in turn became fascinated by Woolf, and commissioned Andrés Bosch to translate her works into Spanish.

VI

From the 1930s to the end of the 1960s Buenos Aires was undoubtedly regarded as the capital of the Spanish-speaking cultural world. Argentina's booming economy and the strong bonds of identity which linked the country to Spain enabled cultural activity to flourish that was promoted by Argentine intellectuals and also by European – but especially Spanish – exiles, fleeing war-shaken Europe.

The figure of Victoria Ocampo emerged and 'presided like a queen' over them; her pioneering literary activity aimed to provide Argentina with a solid cultural background and a national identity which, as a former colony of Spain, the country seemed to lack. Ocampo regarded the Argentine people as the rightful heirs to the European literary tradition, and she was determined to spread this tradition through her work at *Sur* as well as through the translations she supervised in her publishing houses.

Virginia Woolf was for Victoria Ocampo the epitome of the woman writer; Woolf had encouraged her to use language to express herself. Ocampo was thus one of the first feminist readers of Woolf's work, and felt it was her task to share it. Ocampo's first critical piece on Woolf – 'Carta a Virginia Woolf' – was published in Spain in 1934, one of the earliest introductions of the figure of Virginia Woolf to the Spanish reading public. Her article would appear the following year as the preface to her first collection of literary criticism *Testimonios*, published by *Revista de Occidente*. Woolf had helped to satiate Ocampo's 'hunger for literature', of which her *Testimonios* were an expression, and the prominent position of 'Carta a Virginia Woolf' in this collection gave Ocampo a means of acknowledging her debt.

While Spain was being shaken by the Civil War, Ocampo was in Argentina undertaking the promotion of Woolf's novels, whose translation she trusted to brilliant intellectuals such as Jorge Luis Borges or Antonio Marichalar. The works edited by Sur and Sudamericana were also distributed in Spain; many of Victoria Ocampo's closest friends – such as Guillermo de Torre, Antonio López Llausás and José Ortega y Gasset – ran publishing houses in Spain which would publish Woolf's work. Victoria Ocampo had eventually succeeded in her effort to 'share the most precious gift that England has given me', not only in Argentina, but in the whole of the Spanish-speaking world.

13 The Emerging Voice: A Review of Spanish Scholarship on Virginia Woolf

Alberto Lázaro

Virginia Woolf is nowadays recognized in Spain as a leading exponent of the modernist movement and one of the most influential feminist writers whose works have merited detailed scholarly attention. A wide range of Spanish editions of her novels, diaries, letters, biographies and critical studies is within the reach of the general reader, and her art is also admired by numerous critics and literature specialists who have studied her writings from many different approaches. However, the Spanish reception of Virginia Woolf has not always been so rich and varied. Although her genius was already proclaimed during her lifetime, there was not a great deal of criticism written in Spain on Virginia Woolf until the last quarter of the twentieth century, or at least the Spanish response seemed belittled for many years by comparison with the critical attention accorded to her in other European countries. Nevertheless, an analysis of Spanish scholarship on Virginia Woolf shows how her writing has steadily risen to prominence, from the early passing references of the 1920s to the longer critical articles and book-length studies of the 1990s.

Robin Majumdar's *Virginia Woolf: An Annotated Bibliography of Criticism 1915–1974* includes a large number of articles and books which were published in various European cities, highlighting the importance of Virginia Woolf in the literary life of France, Germany, Italy or Finland. However, no reference is made to critical pieces from Spain. The only items in Spanish come from Argentina, like Lila Rillo's *Katherine Mansfield and Virginia Woolf* (1944) and Inés Verga's *Virginia Woolf's Novels and their Analogy to Music* (1945), or from Chile, like M. E. Clare's *Algo sobre Virginia Woolf* (Something on Virginia Woolf) (1965). The total absence of critical material on Virginia Woolf from Spain in Majumdar's bibliography suggests a grim picture of the reception of her writings in this country during the middle decades of the century. It is true that she received little attention among the Spanish critics of the time, partly because French rather than English culture still dominated the Spanish literary intelligentsia,[1] but this does not mean that her work was

[1] French was the main foreign language at Spanish schools and universities, and,

completely ignored. Early references to Virginia Woolf in a Spanish journal can be found in *Revista de Occidente* (Journal of the Western World), a prestigious monthly publication founded in 1923 by José Ortega y Gasset.[2] One of the major contributors to this journal who introduced the name of Virginia Woolf to Spanish readers is Antonio Marichalar. In 1928 he published in *Revista de Occidente* an article about Lytton Strachey entitled 'Las "vidas" y Lytton Strachey' (The 'Lives' and Lytton Strachey), placing his work within the context of the so-called 'Georgians', a term applied to a group of young writers including James Joyce, T. S. Eliot, D. H. Lawrence and, of course, Virginia Woolf, who despite their difficult beginnings would become, according to Antonio Marichalar, the 'classics of tomorrow' (352). The article continues with a discussion of Lytton Strachey's biographies, supported by a couple of long quotations in Spanish from Virginia Woolf's pamphlet *Mr Bennett and Mrs Brown*, which had appeared four years earlier. Citing her opinions on Lytton Strachey, Antonio Marichalar shows not only some knowledge of her critical work, but also his esteem and respect for her ideas; the phrase used to introduce the quoted material clearly confirms this statement: 'Let's listen to a subtle and authoritative voice; Virginia Woolf speaks' (354).[3]

After these early allusions to Virginia Woolf as a novelist and literary critic, Antonio Marichalar refers specifically to *MD* in another article entitled 'Nueva dimensión' (New Dimension), also published in *Revista de Occidente* in 1929. Here he looks at the narrative density of the new novels that are written in an extremely slow tempo, at a time when everything in society is moving very quickly. Consequently, he mentions Joyce's and Proust's works as key examples of this type of fiction, as well as Virginia Woolf's *MD*, whose action takes place within a single day (Marichalar 1929, 381–82). But, if this is no more than a passing reference, two years later Antonio Marichalar offers a more detailed description of her narrative in the same journal. This time he writes on the crisis of the purely fictional story, overshadowed by the more intellectualized novels of Marcel Proust, André Gide, James Joyce, D. H. Lawrence, Aldous Huxley and Virginia Woolf, which were all very well received, as the title of his piece – 'Último grito' (The Latest Craze) – suggests. He praises Virginia Woolf's innovative contribution to the fictional representation of reality, describing her peculiar technique as poetic, feminine and impressionistic, although he admits that her fiction is at times difficult and confusing: 'People and things are ground into a fine mist which tones

---

cont.

although British authors, like James Joyce or Virginia Woolf, were also translated and reviewed, French writers, like Marcel Proust, were more likely to be the subject of critical discussion. We should also bear in mind that the first modern language departments at Spanish universities were not established until the 1960s.

2 José Ortega y Gasset, the Spanish philosopher and humanist, greatly influenced the cultural and literary life of Spain in the twentieth century; the first period of his journal (1923–36) witnessed the publication of valuable articles on art and literature, showing a clear preference for new experimental trends.

3 'Escuchemos una voz sutil y autorizada; Virginia Woolf habla'.

everything down. We do not see clearly through her pages, and it is useless to try to clear the pane: the heat is on the other side, in the hearth of the work itself' (Marichalar 1931, 102).[4]

It is hardly surprising that Antonio Marichalar is the author of these early comments on Virginia Woolf's work in Spain, considering how much he contributed to popularize the work of French, British and American writers. He was particularly interested in the new tendencies of modernist fiction, introducing also the names of James Joyce and William Faulkner to the Spanish reader.[5] It is interesting to note that Antonio Marichalar's criticism of Virginia Woolf mentioned above was written before any of her texts had been translated into Spanish. He subsequently became the translator of the first edition of *TL* in Spanish, published in Buenos Aires in 1938.[6] In the publication history of Virginia Woolf's writings Argentina has always been recognized as the centre of pioneering translations of her texts into Spanish, as is attested by the first Spanish versions of *ROO*, *O*, *TL* and *MD* which were published in Buenos Aires in the 1930s. Undoubtedly, this fact becomes an important factor in assessing the reception of her work. However, there is an earlier version of the central section of *TL*, 'Time Passes', which was published in Madrid, under the title 'El tiempo pasa', in *Revista de Occidente* in 1931. Although the translator's name is not given, this early text is very different from Antonio Marichalar's, and three complete sections are missing (1, 5 and 10). It is a suggestive version which predates the Argentinian piece by seven years and also precedes Jorge Luis Borges's translation of *ROO*, traditionally considered as the first text by Virginia Woolf in Spanish.[7] Nevertheless, the fact that Antonio Marichalar may not have been the only one who presented her writings to Spanish readers in the early 1930s does not diminish the significance of his role in spreading her name in this country.

One of the leading intellectuals responsible for much of the interest in Virginia Woolf generated in Argentina was Victoria Ocampo, a distinguished literary critic who was well acquainted with the work of contemporary European authors.[8] Victoria Ocampo is primarily known for the valuable

---

4 'Seres y cosas se esmerilan en una fina niebla que todo lo esfumina. No vemos claro a través de sus páginas, y es inútil frotar con la mano: el calor está al otro lado, en el hogar de la obra misma'.

5 For details of the importance of Antonio Marichalar in the reception of James Joyce in Spain, see García Santa Cecilia 1997, 30–42.

6 The translation of the second part of the novel, 'Time Passes', first appeared in the same year under the title 'Pasa el tiempo' in the journal *Sur*, also in Argentina. The fourth edition of B. J. Kirkpatrick's *Bibliography of Virginia Woolf* states that this translation of 'Time Passes' was 'presumably' made by Antonio Marichalar (Kirkpatrick and Clarke 1997, 395); if one reads this text and the Spanish edition of *TL*, there can be no doubt that Marichalar is the translator of both.

7 Again, B. J. Kirkpatrick's bibliography presents Jorge Luis Borges's translation of *ROO* (published in a series of articles in *Sur*, Buenos Aires, 1935–36), as the first Spanish version of a text by Virginia Woolf, when in fact this anonymous translation of 'Time Passes' was published in Madrid four years earlier.

critical work done in her native Argentina, but she also contributed to the understanding of Virginia Woolf's work in Spain. In 1934 she published, in *Revista de Occidente* of course, a monographic article on Virginia Woolf entitled 'Carta a Virginia Woolf' (Letter to Virginia Woolf),[9] where she remembers a meeting with the English writer at Tavistock Square. This is, in fact, a good excuse to write about Virginia Woolf's ideas as they were expressed in *ROO*. Victoria Ocampo deals with the main feminist concerns of this extended essay, emphasizing the significance of women's writing, the historical constraints of female creativity and the importance of 'male' and 'female' qualities in all writers. She also reviews Virginia Woolf's comments on Charlotte Brontë and Jane Austen, but above all she speaks very highly of the figure of Shakespeare's sad sister: 'The delightful story of Shakespeare's sister that you narrate in such an inimitable way is the most beautiful story in the world' (Ocampo 1934, 176).[10] Victoria Ocampo's 'letter' is a key document in the assessment of Virginia Woolf's work, because it raises feminist issues which were to dominate much critical thought in later years. Moreover, one might reasonably suppose that such 'advanced' ideas contributed towards stimulating the debate on the condition of women and sexual difference in a Spanish society that had just won the battle for women's suffrage.[11]

The devastating effects of the Spanish Civil War were certainly felt in the literary scene of 1940s Spain. The economic depression as well as the political and cultural isolation the country endured did not facilitate access to the work of Virginia Woolf or other foreign writers. In addition, the state intervention in publishing policy reached a greater intensity. In 1938 new laws were passed to regulate book production with clear instructions to editors, who were to pay particular attention to three basic aspects: 'orthodoxy, morals and political rigour'.[12] Censorship kept the production and importation of books under strict control, and literature was asked to conform to ideology. Domingo Pérez Minik, in his 1973 survey of the foreign novel in Spain, stated that Spanish translations of English novels were scarce, and that consequently writers such as James Joyce, Aldous Huxley and Virginia Woolf had been largely ignored (209). Perhaps this is a rather too negative statement. Although the political, economic and literary situation was indeed difficult, Pérez Minik somewhat exaggerates the extent to which these authors were unknown in Spain at that time. Valeriano Bozal offers a much more positive view and asserts that, despite all legal restrictions and cultural constraints, translations of con-

---

8 For a full discussion of Ocampo's relationship with Virginia Woolf see Laura Lojo's chapter in this volume.

9 This article was later included at the beginning of Victoria Ocampo's book entitled *Testimonios* (Testimonies), published in Madrid in 1935.

10 'La deliciosa historia de la hermana de Shakespeare que de modo tan inimitable cuenta usted, es la más bella historia del mundo.'

11 Spanish women acquired the right to vote in national and local elections in 1931.

12 For a discussion of the censorship situation in post-war Spain, see Bozal 1969 and Abellán 1980, which minutely examines the draconian censorship laws and practices of Franco's regime, including many illustrative examples from a wide range of literary works.

temporary English novels doubled in number during the 1940s (1969, 86).

It is important to note that in the decade after the war several books by Virginia Woolf came out in Barcelona: *FB* (1944), *TY* (1946), *JR* (1946), *VO* (1946) and *ND* (1947). Censorship did not pose a serious problem for the publication of these books.[13] On the contrary, some of the censors' reports included highly favourable comments. One of them stated that *FB* was a biography which displayed 'much wit and skill'.[14] Another one described *ND* as a 'novel of considerable literary interest'.[15] And the censor's report on *VO* also comprised a laudatory description:

> Poetical novel, all written in a lyrical tone. Various types of people are described, apparently vulgar characters, which are given artistic representation through a fine psychological and imaginative vision. There is hardly any plot and it is of no significance, being a mere pretext for the poetic representation of the characters. Its literary value is considerable and genuine.[16]

Similarly, the censors did not find fault with the Argentinian edition of *TL* and *MD* and gave the go-ahead for their importation in 1944 and 1945 respectively.[17]

TW, however, did not fare so well. In 1953 the publisher Fernando Baeza wanted to print what he described as a 'selection of the most important twentieth-century English fiction': Arnold Bennett's *The Old Wives' Tale*, Aldous Huxley's *Point Counter Point* and Virginia Woolf's *TW*. But the board of censors decided to forbid the publication of *Point Counter Point* and allow the other two novels to come out with several suppressions. In the Penguin edition of *TW* read by the censor there are several marks in red ink striking through those parts considered to be morally harmful or politically incorrect – references to the body, God, crucifixes or the Spanish language.[18] In 1957 *TW* became subject to the scrutiny of the censors again and, although one of them saw nothing wrong in the novel, another one suggested cuts in twenty-nine pages and ended the report with the following comment: 'Of undoubted

---

13 *HH* and *DM* also got past the censors in 1945 and 1947 respectively; see File 5300–45, Box 7.729 and File 626–47, Box 7.946. Most files on censorship of this period are found in the 'Fondo de Cultura' at the Archivo General de la Administración (Alcalá de Henares, Madrid). I should like to express my gratitude to the archive staff for their unstinting help and friendly guidance on how to find my way through the complexities of these files.

14 'mucho ingenio y destreza'; see File 2579–43, Box 7.148.

15 'Novela de considerable interés literario'; see File 163–46, Box 7.765.

16 'Novela poemática, escrita toda ella en tono lírico. Se describen diversos tipos de gentes, caracteres vulgares en apariencia, a los que a través de una fina visión psicológica e imaginativa se les confiere virtualidad artística. El argumento casi no existe y carece de importancia, siendo un mero pretexto para la presentación poética de los personajes. Su valor literario es considerable y genuino.' See File 8416–43, Box 7.315.

17 See File 4574–44 bis, Box 7.459 and File 4442–44, Box 7.455.

18 See File 384–53, Box 10.170.

literary quality; but in my opinion a monstrosity that cannot be authorized'.[19] The ban imposed on the novel was finally lifted in 1972, when the publishing house Lumen included it in a collection entitled 'Palabra en el tiempo' (Word in Time).[20]

Over and above all these considerations, it remains true that Virginia Woolf's work won serious critical acclaim in the literary circles of the time, especially in two publications: *Escorial* (Escurial) and *Ínsula* (Isle). We should note, for example, Alberto Palancar's discussion of *TW, MD* and *TL* in his article on the contemporary novel published in *Escorial* in 1944, which regarded Virginia Woolf as the great practitioner of what he called the 'pictorial novel' (141–43). The following year this journal also included a review of contemporary English criticism by Denis Brass, who brought to the fore the topical interest of *CR* (322–25). In contrast, a less flattering reference in *Escorial* was made by the South African poet Roy Campbell, who, during a brief stay in Spain after the war, wrote a critical piece on the English literature of his time and flagrantly disregarded Virginia Woolf, together with Rudyard Kipling, Henry James, E. M. Forster and Joseph Conrad. He did so, because, in his view, 'their influence upon current thought and contemporary sensibility cannot be compared to that of the irresistible tidal surge' (Campbell 1949, 1036).[21] More enthusiasm was exhibited by the reviewers from *Ínsula*, an independent literary journal founded in 1946 that regularly transmitted literary news from Britain. In its first year, María Manent underlined the 'highly poetic value' of Virginia Woolf's pages (1946, 4) and William Plomer offered an admiring introduction to her personality and work, focusing on her feminist views, her use of the stream of consciousness and her concern with the human spirit. Just one year later, *Ínsula* also included another reference to Virginia Woolf in an article by Norman Nicholson that presented her as an important innovator who tried to capture in her novels 'the subtlest sensation of experience' (1947, 2).

Undoubtedly other allusions to Virginia Woolf could be tracked down in different journals of the time,[22] but what deserves special attention is Ricardo Gullón's study of Virginia Woolf included in his volume *Novelistas ingleses contemporáneos* (Contemporary English Novelists) (1945). His is an enlightening survey of the contemporary English novel which contains stimulating introductions to fourteen writers, providing both information and original analysis. He chose those representative novelists who had already reached the Spanish reader in translation, including sections on Hardy, Conrad, Mansfield, Joyce, Lawrence, Huxley and a chapter on 'Virginia Woolf o la novela en

---

19 'De indudable calidad literaria; pero a mi juicio un engendro que no puede autorizarse.' See File 1182–57, Box 11.638.

20 See File 10378–72, Box 675.

21 '[S]u influencia sobre las corrientes del pensamiento y la sensibilidad contemporáneas no es de las que se puedan comparar con la oleada irresistible de la marea.'

22 See, for example, Marian Baquero's two articles on the contemporary novel in *Arbor* (1948; 1949); they both refer to the impressionistic style of Virginia Woolf's *TY* to illustrate his views on novel writing.

crisis' (Virginia Woolf or The Novel in Crisis). Ricardo Gullón sees her fiction, from *JR* onwards, as a refreshing attempt to overcome the lack of depth from which many contemporary novels suffered. The originality of her art, it is argued, resides in the narrative method, which consists of placing characters within the context of their conflicting memories and observing them as they try to work out their meanings. This often leads to the major themes of isolation and lack of spiritual communication between people, a tragic and anguished message that is only partially covered up by the musical language of her prose. On the whole, this is a favourable critical evaluation of Virginia Woolf, in which *FB* comes off best of all her books (Gullón 1945, 163–65), whereas *O* only succeeds as a 'museum piece' rather than a literary work (163). After this seminal essay, Virginia Woolf often reappeared in much of Ricardo Gullón's criticism of fiction, particularly in his well-known studies of the lyrical novel, where there were comparisons with Spanish novelists, such as Azorín and Gabriel Miró, and a sense that a kind of lyrical mode was flourishing in European narrative.[23]

The following decades saw growing interest among Spanish critics and scholars in Virginia Woolf's work. Together with passing references in general articles on the state of the novel,[24] there emerged a series of more specialized critical items which added to the picture of Virginia Woolf presented by earlier reviewers. Again, it is *Ínsula*, with its characteristic policy of opening the door to foreign literature, which provided some examples of a more sophisticated response. Firstly, in 1957 José García Lora offers a stimulating comparative study of Virginia Woolf and Azorín, showing how both authors have in common their treatment of time, their poetic prose and their class-consciousness; they even share a similar talent for inventing historical characters to support their arguments – Shakespeare's sister in Virginia Woolf's *ROO* and a new Cervantes in Azorín's *Aventuras de Miguel de Cervantes* (Adventures of Miguel de Cervantes). Another *Ínsula* reviewer, Concha Castroviejo, revived the feminist line of criticism opened up by Victoria Ocampo in the 1930s and praised the style and validity of *ROO* nearly forty years later. It is interesting to observe that this review was published in the emblematic year of 1968, on the occasion of a new Spanish translation of Virginia Woolf's essay edited in Barcelona the previous year, at a time when the establishment in Franco's Spain did not welcome the rise of 'revolutionary'

---

23 In *La novela lírica* (The Lyrical Novel) (1984), for instance, Ricardo Gullón makes extensive use of Virginia Woolf's theories of the novel and illustrates his arguments with manifold references to *MD*, *TL* and *BTA*.

24 An example of this type of reference can be found in Edmundo Meouchi's article on the presence of the American novel in Spain (1953, 12), published in Madrid, where Virginia Woolf appears as one of the main creators of the modern novel; Mariano Baquero (1954, 10) and Ernesto Sábato (1964, 15) also allude to Virginia Woolf's use of the interior monologue; likewise, Domingo Pérez Minik devotes a few lines in his *Introducción a la novela inglesa actual* (Introduction to the Contemporary English Novel) to describing her views on novel writing (1968, 100–04).

ideas – whether social, political, religious or, indeed, feminist.[25] That same year Emilio Sosa brought a new approach to her work by emphasizing the importance of 'vision' in her creative method. In 'Visión y técnica novelísticas de Virginia Woolf' (Novelistic Vision and Technique of Virginia Woolf), a chapter included in a broad study of fiction, he revealed how she seeks to transcend immediate reality and apprehend the essential reality of things 'in special moments of inner expansion, when the subject comes into contact, by a kind of elective affinity, with something external, an object or a particular landscape' (Sosa López 1968, 46).[26] Such epiphanic moments in which her characters undergo a spiritual transformation were also perceived by the Spanish philosopher José Luis Aranguren who, in 1974, wrote about her fiction as an expression of anti-solipsism (with the characteristic dissolution of the 'I' in the universe and the description of life outside itself), an aesthetic stance largely inspired by the influential British philosopher G. E. Moore.[27]

All the critical acclaim that Virginia Woolf's works received from Spanish critics and reviewers of the time was surprisingly contradicted by the anonymous censor who lifted the ban on *TW* in 1972.[28] His report began with the acknowledgement of Virginia Woolf's reputation in Britain, but then it questions the significance of her work in the 1970s: 'Her writings must have seemed very modern in the 1930s and 1940s; but, today, thirty years after the novelist's death, her works have neither interest nor modernism'.[29] Unable to classify the text in terms of a specific genre, the censor describes the novel as 'boring', marred by 'unending monologues', 'digressions' and 'useless details'. Most importantly, the psychological style is a mere 'pretension' that leads to incoherence, something that 'anticipates the mental state of the writer'.[30] One wonders what triggered such an adverse judgement on *TW*: were the opinions expressed in this report genuine? Or was the censor justifying the existing ban on the novel? Whatever

---

25 For an illuminating discussion of the situation of women during the Franco regime see Gallego Méndez 1983, 198–99, which describes the female members of the Falange state party as anti-feminist women who tried to consolidate patriarchal society, while denying their own right to be free and equal.

26 'en momentos especiales de expansión interior, cuando el sujeto entra, por una especie de afinidad electiva, en comunicación con algo exterior, un objeto o un paisaje determinado'.

27 Aranguren (1974a) had already discussed Woolf's life and work in a previous review of Quentin Bell's *Virginia Woolf: A Biography* entitled 'Virginia Woolf y su época' ('Virginia Woolf and her time').

28 File 10378–72, Box 675.

29 'Su literatura debió parecer muy moderna en los decenios de los 30 y los 40; pero hoy, treinta años después de la muerte de la novelista, sus obras no tienen ni interés ni modernismo.'

30 Here is the literal transcription of the whole paragraph: 'Esta novela, relato o lo que sea, pues su estilo narrativo no permite una verdadera catalogación de género, es aburrida, con interminables monólogos, escaso diálogo y divagaciones, plenas de pormenores que resultan inútiles. La pretensión de un estilo psicológico queda en minuciosidad que no aporta nada al retrato de los personajes. A veces son cosas sin ilación, sensaciones sueltas que, quizás, anticipen el estado de ánimo mental de la autora, muerta dramáticamente el 25 de marzo de 1941.'

the reasons, this is just an isolated, special example of hostile criticism directed at Woolf's fiction in a much more favourable atmosphere.

The development of English studies at Spanish universities in the 1960s marked a watershed in the reception of Virginia Woolf's work in Spain. The first full professor of modern philology in the field of English literature was appointed in 1961 at the University Complutense of Madrid, and then modern language departments in other universities followed suit. Although it was a slow process at the beginning, there was a gradual increase in the number of literary scholars who included contemporary English fiction in their syllabus, did some research on it and published their results in academic publications such as *Filología moderna* (the first journal of this sort in the field of modern languages), founded in Madrid in 1960. Their articles obviously tended to focus on more specific issues or make a close analysis of particular literary texts. This means that the vagueness and generalization characteristic of previous Virginia Woolf criticism gave way to more detailed and elaborated critical responses. An early example of this academic approach appeared precisely in the sixth volume of *Filología moderna* (1966-67), in an article by Cándido Pérez Gállego specifically concerned with the structure of *TL*. Pérez Gállego argued that the apparent three-part division of the novel – which presents a time before, during and after the events – is eroded as the journey towards the inner self of the characters shows that everything remains the same, thus revealing 'the most trivial aspects of human life, which we have, however, so many times "mythologized"' (130).[31] Similarly, another logical outcome of this increasing literary critical activity within academia was the appearance of doctoral dissertations, which often became full-length books of particular relevance. The first doctoral thesis on Virginia Woolf in Spain was defended by Manuel Míguez at the University of Santiago de Compostela in 1974, and, most curiously, also focused on the structure of her fiction. This time the author set out to demonstrate how an analysis of the structure of *MD*, *TL* and *TW* reveals an extraordinary coherence of plot, point of view and characterization.[32]

Although the validity and weight of all these antecedents to current scholarship on Virginia Woolf cannot be denied, the full emergence and expansion of Woolf criticism in Spain is actually to be traced in the last quarter of the twentieth century. In this period a large number of general articles, reviews and non-academic critical pieces have continued to be published in a wide range of cultural and literary publications: *Ínsula* has remained a valuable source of information on foreign literature in general and Virginia Woolf in particular;[33] two Catalan literary journals, *Camp de l'arpa* (A Field Near

---

[31] 'los aspectos más triviales de la vida humana, pero que tantas veces hemos "mitificado"'.

[32] In 1977 another doctoral thesis on the narrative methods in Virginia Woolf's fiction was defended by María Lozano at the University of Saragossa.

[33] See Domingo Pérez Minik's review of *BTA* (1980) or Cándido Pérez Gállego's descriptive article 'Quién teme leer a Virginia Woolf?' (Who's Afraid of Reading Virginia Woolf?), which appeared two years later.

Barcelona) (1976; 1978) and *L'Avenç* (Progress) (1982), have included some critical pieces written by Marta Pessarrodona, a translator of Virginia Woolf's work;[34] *Cuadernos hispanoamericanos* (Spanish-American Journal) has offered an enticing biographical article on the tensions in her career written by Flora Guzmán (1982); and *Quimera* (Chimera) has incorporated, among other things, an informative feature on the Bloomsbury Exhibition staged in Barcelona in 1986.[35] However, it is in the academic arena where the presence of Virginia Woolf has been much more noticeable. Such is the quantity and diversity of Spanish academic criticism of her work over the last decades that it is difficult to organize a discussion of it into clear-cut categories or approaches. What is quite certain is that these approaches are in line with the methods and styles of contemporary literary theory, including textual studies, historical contextualizing, close reading, narratological analysis, biographical focus, stylistic concerns, feminist issues and comparative readings. Moreover, since most of these recent Spanish critical responses come from scholars who work in the area of English studies, their research makes extensive use of British and American Woolf criticism.

As could be expected, much current critical writing considers the nature of Virginia Woolf's art as a novelist. A significant full-length treatment of her narrative is Carlos Herrero's *Virginia Woolf: proceso creativo y evolución literaria* (Virginia Woolf: Creative Process and Literary Evolution) (1996b),[36] a volume which traces the evolution of Virginia Woolf's novelistic practice with detailed analysis of individual works. Drawing from her diaries and critical works, Carlos Herrero outlines the main changes that mark her method of composition, where he discovers an 'eternal renewal' (200). This type of comprehensive work on Virginia Woolf's narrative is not common among Spanish scholars, who prefer to focus on a particular novel or topic. That is what Oscar Sanz, for instance, does in his article 'The Handkerchief as Suggested Symbol in Virginia Woolf's *The Waves*' (1988) published in *Miscelánea*, the journal of the Department of English Philology at the University of Saragossa. Here he illustrates the wide range of meanings the handkerchief conveys in *TW*, a symbol used over twenty-five times in the novel to represent the characters' feelings and personalities. Likewise, María Eugenia Perojo, in her essay ' "That fluidity out there": El tiempo como factor estructural y temático en *To the Lighthouse*' ('That fluidity out there': Time as a Structural and Thematic Factor in *To the Lighthouse*) (1993), pays specific attention to the centrality of time in the narrative of *TL*, tracing Virginia

---

[34] In *Camp de l'arpa* Marta Pessarrodona published an article on the significance of *MD* and two years later, in 1978, another interesting piece on the references to Joyce in Virginia Woolf's diaries and letters; she also contributed a couple of articles to the dossier on the Bloomsbury Group published in *L'Avenç* in 1982.

[35] Carme Riera recounts his visit to this exhibition in 'Una tarde en Bloomsbury' (An Afternoon in Bloomsbury) (1986). The exhibition was open from 17 September to 31 October and had a great public response (approximately 20,000 visitors); for further details, see Pessarrodona 1987.

[36] It is based on a doctoral thesis defended at the University of Valladolid in 1992.

Woolf's notion of time back to the works of philosophers such as Heidegger and Bergson, as well as the poetic tradition, particularly Shakespeare's sonnets.

It is interesting to see how discussions of *MD* vastly outnumber those of any other novel. Even when the critical piece deals with a broad issue, like Pilar Hidalgo's 'Virginia Woolf: el contexto inglés' (Virginia Woolf: The English Context) (1980), this novel takes up much of the space. The reason for this may lie in the novelty of its narrative technique, in the attractiveness of its characters or, perhaps, in its sophisticated feminism; whatever the case, *MD* has often occupied a central position in Spanish studies of Virginia Woolf. There is a book-length study of the novel by Catalina Montes, entitled *En torno a 'Mrs Dalloway' de Virginia Woolf* (On *Mrs Dalloway* by Virginia Woolf) (1980), whose main focus of attention is on the 'heroine': what she represents, how her split personality relates to the main themes of the book and how the other characters bolster her image in the novel. Besides this, Catalina Montes skilfully draws an analogy between *MD* and Shakespeare's *Cymbeline*, claiming that both raise issues about 'the human condition, the nature of life and death, fidelity; also, both question the capacity to govern' (1980, 17).[37] Another challenging parallel in the book is the one between Clarissa Dalloway and Doris Kilman, something that will appear again two years later in Montes's essay 'Algunas consideraciones sobre Doris Kilman, en *Mrs Dalloway*, de Virginia Woolf' (Some Considerations on Doris Kilman, in *Mrs Dalloway*, by Virginia Woolf).[38] Finally, the last chapter comments on the significance of the mad scenes in the shaping of the novel, connecting Septimus Smith's plight with that of the war poets, and Wilfred Owen's in particular.[39] A more recent article by Isabel Carmen Anievas on *MD* uses a stylistic approach to analyse the various technical tools Virginia Woolf employed in her 'journey into the inner mind'. She distinguishes between external presentation (omniscient description and indirect interior monologue) and internal (free association, broken syntax, anaphora, anacoluthon, repetition, images and symbolism), and concludes that 'the aim of the journey Virginia Woolf undertakes in this novel is not the actual inner mind, but a conscious artistic attempt at re-creating the inner mind' (Anievas Gamallo 1992, 169).

Virginia Woolf's work as a critic, essayist and diarist is now again at the forefront of current Spanish criticism, as it was for Antonio Marichalar in 1928. In this respect, it is appropriate to underline the importance of Dámaso López's studies, detailed and rigorous works which provide a number of insights into Woolf's theories of fiction and feelings about her own creative

---

[37] 'la condición humana, la naturaleza de la vida y de la muerte, la fidelidad, también las dos cuestionan la capacidad de gobernar'.

[38] This essay was originally a paper read by Catalina Montes at a conference organized by the Asociación Española de Estudios Anglo-Norteamericanos (AEDEAN), held at the University of Oviedo in 1981.

[39] Catalina Montes also addressed the issue of Septimus Smith's madness in her paper 'Locura y muerte de Septimus Warren Smith en *Mrs Dalloway* de Virginia Woolf' (The Madness and Death of Septimus Warren Smith in Virginia Woolf's *Mrs Dalloway*), read at the 1980 AEDEAN conference at the University of Salamanca.

process. In a 1980 essay published in *Arbor* he traces the development of Virginia Woolf's narrative, taking into account the comments about her novels that appear in her diaries. The result is not particularly flattering to the author: her constant hesitation between traditional and experimental techniques is due to her wish to synthesize both forms, but that is something she could never accomplish (López García 1980, 86). A few years later, Dámaso López (1993) published a book, based on his doctoral thesis, on the literary criticism of the Bloomsbury Group, which he sees as following two complementary directions, as it receives the influence of classical rhetoric on the one hand and of romantic theories on the other. Nevertheless, he avoids any reductionist premise and emphasizes the many divergent and often contradictory views of the different authors. The chapter on Virginia Woolf, however, admires the coherence, uniformity, comprehensiveness and self-criticism that characterizes her critical work, while stressing the author's endeavour to maintain a fine balance between reason and feelings. In a similar vein to Dámaso López's first essay on her diaries, Carlos Herrero's article 'Virginia Woolf y la pasión de escribir' (Virginia Woolf and the Passion for Writing) (1992) seeks in her diaries the answer to the question she often posed, 'What is the use of writing?', and provides a helpful overview of a range of responses, including the purely aesthetic, the therapeutic, the nihilistic and even the socio-political.[40] Finally, there is an interesting scholarly essay by Luisa-Fernanda Rodríguez entitled 'Diarios de artista: Virginia Woolf' (Artists' Diaries: Virginia Woolf) (1998), which places her autobiographical writings in the context of the English tradition of diary writing, the narcissistic trends of modernism and the necessity to articulate the female condition.

This last insight leads to the Spanish feminist approach to Virginia Woolf, which mainly focuses, as one might expect, on her critical and autobiographical work. And it is precisely with her autobiographical essays that Aránzazu Usandizaga is most concerned in *Amor y literatura: la búsqueda literaria de la identidad femenina* (Love and Literature: The Literary Quest for the Female Identity) (1993). This book is a rigorous discussion of the role of female characters in western literature, placing special emphasis on British writers. The author argues that when the romantic novel loses ground at the end of the nineteenth century a new feminine voice emerges, and it is mainly in the autobiographical writings where women characters are fully portrayed. The volume includes a section on Virginia Woolf's *MB*, which is seen as being primarily concerned with following the matrilineal line in its stories as well as confronting some critical issues concerning the theory of the autobiographical mode. In another recent feminist essay, '*Una habitación propia*: las utopías de las mujeres en los años 20 en Gran Bretaña' (*A Room of One's Own*: Women's Utopias in the 1920s in Britain) (1998), Sally Alexander suggests an analogy between Virginia Woolf's *ROO* and Kathleen Woodward's *Jipping Street*. Both were written at the end of the 1920s and, although their setting is very different – a sitting-room in Bloomsbury and a poor suburb in South London – the two

---

[40] In another recent essay (1996a), Carlos Herrero returns to Woolf's letters, diaries and essays to look at her views on her contemporaries.

works show the feelings of the women of that time, their lack of education, economic independence and intellectual freedom; for both authors the room of their own does not represent a utopian solution, only 'a provisional place, a place where they can meditate, a retreat to uncertainty, to the unknown' (Alexander 1998, 150).[41]

But not all feminist responses deal with Virginia Woolf's essays. An example of feminist criticism of Virginia Woolf's fiction is an essay by a male critic, Rafael Galán, entitled ' "El hecho fértil": *Orlando*, de Virginia Woolf' ('The Fertile Fact': *Orlando*, by Virginia Woolf) (1996). In fact, it uses an interdisciplinary approach to emphasize the importance of this novel in Woolf's quest for new ways of writing fiction and for its representation of female identity. Rafael Galán refers to the metaphor of 'the fertile fact' used by Virginia Woolf in 'The Art of Biography' (*CE* 4: 228) in order to consider the writing of *Orlando* as a multiple creative act. Among the themes he discusses are the revision of the biographical discourse, the place of the individual in history and the sexual features of the protagonist. This novel also becomes the focus of an essay by Ana I. Zamorano, 'The Carnivalesque Body of the Hermaphrodite: A Reading of Woolf's *Orlando*', whose starting point is Bakhtin's definition of the grotesque body of the carnival and its resemblance to the traditional notion of the hermaphrodite, which serves 'to relativize and therefore to deconstruct traditional notions of masculinity and femininity' (1997: 647–48). Ana Zamorano then shows how *O*, with its parodic spirit, explores the satiric implications of Bakhtin's dialogism and its assertion of a relationship of non-exclusive opposites.

Within this context of feminist criticism, the volume of essays edited by Mercedes Bengoechea, *La huella de Virginia Woolf* (In the Footsteps of Virginia Woolf) (1992), merits special attention. It brings together fourteen papers read at an international conference of specialists in women's studies held at the University of Alcalá de Henares in 1991 to commemorate the fiftieth anniversary of Virginia Woolf's death. As the title suggests, the main focus of this book is to examine her seminal contribution to twentieth-century literature and it includes essays by two writers, Maggie Gee and Ana María Navales, who admit to being most indebted to Virginia Woolf: the former for her 'commitment to form' (1992, 35), the latter for being an inspiration in the writing of *Cuentos de Bloomsbury* (Bloomsbury Tales) (1991).[42] Other contributions include a study of Virginia Woolf's style by Mercedes Bengoechea, a reading of *ROO* in the light of 'écriture féminine' by Esther Sánchez-Pardo,[43] an analysis of the paintings of women in Woolf's narrative by

---

41 'un lugar provisional, un lugar donde pensar, una retirada hacia la incertidumbre, hacia lo desconocido'.

42 For a discussion of the influence of Virginia Woolf on Ana María Navales, see María José Gámez Fuentes's contribution to this volume.

43 In another essay on the mother figure in Virginia Woolf Sánchez-Pardo tries to show how, after her mother's death, Woolf sought 'maternal protection' (1996, 198) in other women of her circle – including Caroline Emelia Stephen, Vita Sackville-West and Ethel Smyth – and describes the mother–daughter relations that are also represented in her fiction.

Manuela Palacios, and two discussions of the mark she left on contemporary feminist criticism by Jane Moore and Teresa Gómez. The book opens with a sparkling essay by Isobel Armstrong, 'Virginia Woolf: Founding Feminist or Anxious Influence?', which studies the influence of Virginia Woolf on contemporary women's fiction. It presents two different responses to Virginia Woolf's sway: on the one hand, there is 'an anxious influence, making for a troubled sense of both sexuality and class in later writing' (Armstrong 1992, 12), and Anita Brookner's *Hotel du Lac* is discussed within this framework; on the other hand, there is a 'liberated sense of a multiple subject which . . . leads to an element of fantasy, openness and play' (12), and makes *O* the real antecedent of Angela Carter's *Nights at the Circus.*

The comparative approach has also borne some other fruits. Comparative studies have no long tradition in Spanish academic circles. The Spanish Association of General and Comparative Literature (SELGYC) was founded in 1974 and the first issue of its review, *1916*, was published three years later. However, since the 1970s several scholars, such as Claudio Guillén, Darío Villanueva or Antonio Prieto, have made valuable incursions into this field and have contributed to its development with various works on a wide range of authors.[44] An early exercise in the comparative study of Virginia Woolf with other writers from the English-speaking literary world is Catalina Montes's 1982 article 'Voces de T. S. Eliot en *Mrs Dalloway*, de Virginia Woolf' (Voices of T. S. Eliot in Virginia Woolf's *Mrs Dalloway*), where she examines specific intertextual relationships between Woolf's *MD* and Eliot's *The Waste Land* – images, symbols, topics, characters.[45] Discussing Montes's works above, we have already referred to the parallels she has drawn between *MD* and *Cymbeline* on the one hand, and Septimus Smith and Wilfred Owen on the other; but this essay on Woolf and Eliot falls more clearly within the scope of the comparative approach. The same could be said of her other essay '*To the Lighthouse*: un viaje en el espacio de la imaginación' (*To the Lighthouse*: A Journey in the Space of the Imagination), published in 1991. Here she establishes a convincing comparison between *TL* and the Romantic theory of imagination, particularly as it is expressed in Wordsworth's *The Excursion.* Sometimes comparative studies combine elements of other lines of inquiry, as in the case of Aldolfo Campoy's article (1993), an interesting piece of research which explores some similarities between Virginia Woolf and Emily Dickinson from linguistic and feminist points of view. Following Julia Kristeva's theories about the ineffability of language, he sets out to demonstrate how Virginia Woolf's fiction and Emily Dickinson's poetry take their strength from and are at the same time bound by the limitations of language.

These articles testify to the interest of recent comparative contributions in foreign rather than indigenous writers. The formal and thematic comparisons between Virginia Woolf and Azorín made by José García Lora and Ricardo

---

44 For further information regarding the situation of comparative studies in Spain, see Morales 1999, 55–60.

45 In a later article (1990) Catalina Montes wrote again about this relationship between *MD* and *The Waste Land.*

Gullón have given way to other studies that suggest analogies with a wide-ranging variety of writers, not only from an English literary tradition but also from such different countries as Israel, Belgium or Portugal. We should note, for example, M. E. Varela's article (1993), printed in a journal of Arabic and Hebrew studies published by the University of Granada, which points to some affinities between Virginia Woolf's work and the impressionistic and lyrical narrative of the Israeli novelist Binyamin Tammuz. Similarly, María Alzira Seixo (1994), in an essay included in the proceedings of the ninth Spanish Association of General and Comparative Literature conference, examines the concept of the journey motif in three different works: Virginia Woolf's *To the Lighthouse*, Henri Michaux's *L'Espace du dedans* (*The Space Within*) (1994), and José Saramago's *A jangada de pedra* (*The Stone Raft*) (1986).

Apart from these critical responses to Virginia Woolf's work from specific fields of research, we could also put together a miscellany of critical material dealing with a great variety of concerns and topics. This heterogeneous collection should include an informative survey of Virginia Woolf's three visits to Spain by J. A. Díaz (1982), a doctoral thesis on the myriad connections between Woolf's fiction and painting by Manuela Palacios (1992),[46] an article on the Spanish translations of her work by Luisa-Fernanda Rodríguez (1997) and a review-article on Hermione Lee's biography by Laura Lojo (1997). In addition, we should not overlook the importance of some introductions to the Spanish editions of her works. While it is true that most of them simply consist of a brief exposition of some biographical data and a general description of her work, there are some scholarly exceptions which are worth looking at.[47] There are three very good critical editions of *TL* (1999), *MD* (1993) and *TW* (1994) published in Madrid by Cátedra which include detailed rigorous introductions by distinguished Spanish Woolf scholars. Dámaso López is the editor and translator of *TL* and María Lozano is the author of the critical introductions to the other two novels, both comprising over 100 pages and constituting monographs in their own right. Written in an academic style, they all display an impressive knowledge of Virginia Woolf and offer thoughtful and discriminating analysis of her work, providing at the same time valuable discussions of the literary, social and personal contexts of the novels with numerous bibliographic references.

This brief review of Spanish scholarship on Virginia Woolf makes no pretence at completeness. There will surely be omissions and most of the critical items included here certainly allow for more extensive treatment, but hopefully there is enough material to trace the main directions and developments in Spanish criticism of Virginia Woolf and show how her work has gained persistent and increasing attention in this country. The passing references to her work in general articles of the 1920s gradually increased in

---

46 See her chapter in this volume. Before finishing her thesis Manuela Palacios also published an illuminating article on this topic, in which she likens Virginia Woolf's work to a cubist picture (1990, 500).

47 Another notable exception for its literary flavour is the preface to *MD*, written by the Peruvian novelist Mario Vargas Llosa for the 1989 Círculo de Lectores edition.

quantity and became more specialized in scope during the following decades, until the vast expansion of longer and rigorous scholarly works took place during the last quarter of the twentieth century. All this significant growth of research on Virginia Woolf naturally coincided with the development of English studies at universities and the proliferation of translations and critical editions of her works. It is undeniable that at the beginning many allusions to Virginia Woolf in Spanish essays and reviews were inserted in broad surveys of contemporary fiction, so that her reception was usually linked to that of other celebrated modernist writers such as James Joyce, Marcel Proust or William Faulkner. However, the essays by Victoria Ocampo in the 1930s, Ricardo Gullón in the 1940s and José García Lora in the 1950s represent early examples of Spanish Woolf criticism in which her work is discussed separately. Of course, they are somewhat leisurely pieces that lack the scholarship and critical rigour of more recent monographs and essays, but they retain their value because of their pioneering treatment of a number of issues that recur in later reception, such as the idiosyncratic brand of experimentalism in her narrative, her sophisticated feminist concerns and her insightful literary criticism.

In conclusion, Spanish critical responses to Virginia Woolf have reflected the diversity of her work and include a great variety of interests: from feminist studies to comparative readings, from stylistic approaches to history of ideas, from narratological analyses to studies of pictorial motifs. Nevertheless, not all of these areas have been explored with the same profusion. Woolf's short fiction and her biographical work have been almost ignored when compared with the attention paid to her novels, essays, letters and diaries.[48] Similarly, some theoretical approaches, such as deconstructionist, neo-Marxist and psychoanalytical theories, have seldom if ever been applied. All in all, Virginia Woolf has generally been admired by Spanish critics and reviewers, and her work has been accorded high praise for its originality, variety, complexity and authenticity. But, what is the future of Woolf study in Spain? Will she maintain this privileged position for long? Time will tell. It is impossible to foresee the new paths that future criticism and literary theory may follow. Yet, surely Virginia Woolf will be prominent on university syllabuses and a popular subject of critical studies. In Spain, as in other countries of the Western world, she will be chiefly remembered for the role she played in both the modernist fiction of the twentieth century and early feminist discourse.

---

[48] There is an interesting essay by María Antonia Álvarez on the narrative strategies of 'Kew Gardens' (1997); then, Manuela Palacios (1992), Carlos Herrero (1996b) and Laura Lojo (1999) included a discussion of Virginia Woolf's short stories in their doctoral dissertations; and, as we have seen above, Ricardo Gullón praised the originality of *FB* in his 1945 study.

14 Virginia Woolf and the Search for Symbolic Mothers in Modern Spanish Fiction: The Case of *Tres mujeres*

María José Gámez Fuentes

Within the framework of the present project on the reception of Virginia Woolf in Europe the volume of short stories *Tres mujeres* (Three Women) (1995) constitutes a challenging textual case. Navales (1942–) takes the mythical figure Virginia Woolf has become in the field of women's studies and converts her into a fictional character through whom to construct an exploration of the female artist's relation to language and representation without overlooking the influence of specific cultural and historical contexts. For Navales places the figure of Virginia Woolf alongside two Spanish artists: María del Pilar Sinués, a writer, and Julieta Aguilar, a painter. Our choice of *Tres mujeres* is based on the multiple intertextual directions that Navales's project opens up for the discussion of Woolf's reception in Spain. The aim of this chapter is to analyse the cultural significance of re-creating/re-writing/re-textualizing the figure of Virginia Woolf for Spanish women's relationship to textual representation and, consequently, to contribute towards offering new insights into the understanding of Virginia Woolf's European impact. From a Spanish theoretical perspective, this work attempts to follow the line opened by authors such as Martín Gaite (1992, 25–34) and Valls (1989) who assert the need to reflect upon the influence of Woolf's work on Spanish women writers. Needless to say Woolf's influence upon modern writers goes beyond Navales's work and through our study we will tackle, when relevant, other authors' œuvres.

To those not familiar with contemporary Spanish writing I should start by saying that Ana María Navales is a multifaceted female writer of poetry, short stories, essays and novels. Her poetry has been translated into English, Romanian, Swedish, Albanian, Italian and Bulgarian. Translations from Québec and Bulgaria of her book of short stories *Cuentos de Bloomsbury* (Bloomsbury Tales) (1991) are due to be published. Both this book and *Tres mujeres*, along with several research papers published in Spanish (Navales 1993; 1996a; 1996b; 1999), are the result of a long-standing interest in the

Bloomsbury group in general, and Virginia Woolf in particular. This permeates all of her short stories concerning the famous group, and the reader familiar with Bloomsburian lives can trace in the fictional narratives reminiscences of real events and facts, such as Virginia Woolf's problems with clothing, the nuances of her personal relationships both with her husband and other women, and her continuous struggle within her writing. One must not forget, though, that we will be dealing throughout our analysis with narrative events and not with real-life ones, despite the echoes of the latter that the former may bring. Nevertheless, as Encinar (1996, 604) notes in reference to *Cuentos de Bloomsbury*, this connection between fiction and reality is a further intertextual element that enters the readerly game when played by an audience familiar with Woolf's life and work.[1]

Tres mujeres is composed of three stories: 'Regreso a Monk's House' (Return to Monk's House), 'La dama escritora' (The Lady Writer) and 'Julieta de los espíritus' (Juliet of the Spirits). The first of these has the character of Virginia Woolf as the protagonist. The other two texts recreate respectively the lives of two Spanish women: María del Pilar Sinués (1835–93), an Aragonese writer of popular literature for women, and Julieta Aguilar (1899–1979), an almost unknown Aragonese painter. The different short stories in this publication are not new; they have previously appeared in the same or in alternative form in other writings by Navales.[2] Their discourse is not unfamiliar either in the field of women's literature, for they echo issues of great interest in the exploration of the area between language and female experience that Woolf herself dealt with. Although this is a theme that permeates all her work and has been widely researched (Hawkes 1981; Marcus 1981a; Rosenman 1995; Stimpson 1992), *ROO* is the text that doubtless best encapsulates Woolf's thought on the subject and where she advocates the resurrection of female forerunners.

Nevertheless, the originality of *Tres mujeres* consists in combining the three characters with Navales's own writerly project. Indeed, the author adopts the first-person pronoun to address the reader from her position of woman writer in the introduction to the book. She explains how her own story of artistic self-determination intertwined with those of the three female characters in different moments of her life. Therefore Navales herself becomes another textual element integrating the web of singular voices and spaces which both invites us to explore female subjectivity and the social problematic of the female artist and adds a further twist to the merging of fiction and reality. In

---

1 In this respect it could also be said that Marcus's (1988) call for a new biography of Woolf has been stretched to the limits of reality to enter the fictional arena, thus underlining the mere textuality of the enterprise. According to Marcus, the biographer 'should perhaps be an artist in her own right, considering the problems of female artists on their own ground. And it ought to be a critical biography, so that life and works are one' (Marcus 1988, 159).

2 'La dama escritora' was included in the volume *Zacarías, rey* (Zacarías, King) (Navales 1992) and the character of Julieta was the protagonist of *El regreso de Julieta Always* (The Return of Julieta Always) (Navales 1981).

this respect, the book's cover design, in which the title and the author's name appear as numerator and denominator respectively, can be read as the symbol of an imaginary fraction whose result has to be extracted by the reader. In Navales's case, she admits having a secret and private relationship with Virginia Woolf that one cannot have with men; from María del Pilar Sinués she extracts the latter's rebellious spirit, and with Julieta Aguilar, it is the painter's madness that interests the author. Fictional recreation and real life experiences are thus located on the same level of textuality as if following Virginia's own idea of 'making literature work in and out of daily life' (*ROO*, 6) or maybe making daily life work in and out of literature.

The literary re-creation of different female characters (Virginia Woolf, María del Pilar Sinués and Julieta Aguilar) highlights the textual character of the heritage from artistic foremothers in women's development within society and language. It epitomizes the contemporary quest for female predecessors, which echoes Woolf's famous maxim that 'we think back through our mothers if we are women' (*ROO*, 79). This idea has been read by feminist critics such as Gilbert and Gubar (1979) as a statement of the need to recuperate artistic foremothers for the self-determination of women artists: writers, painters, film directors etc. In Jacobus's words: 'thinking back through the mother becomes a gesture at once of recuperation and revision' (Jacobus 1986, 39). In this sense, the volume emphasizes the significance of re-appropriating and re-writing the role of symbolic/mythical mothers for women's literature in Spain. Therefore, three apparently literary portraits become essays (in the most literal sense of the word) about the female subject. This subject appears trespassed upon by different gazes and divided, narratively and symbolically, into various linguistic voices which plunge into an exploration of creative women's experiences from their respective fissured positions.

Tres mujeres attempts to recuperate through fiction not only female figures 'forgotten' by the establishment, like María del Pilar Sinués or Julieta Aguilar, but also to examine the most problematic aspects of a woman's success, such as Woolf's. This undertaking is not restricted to looking back to the past, for the narrative introduces us to other more contemporary characters who, on the trail of their predecessors, continue to search and to struggle to find their own voices. In this sense, the book mirrors Zavala's argument about the importance of thinking backwards to move forward, dis-placing and reinventing the images and symbols imposed on the subject of History (Zavala 1990, 4). This project could be said to be working, then, both intra- and extradiegetically as Navales not only recuperates historical figures, but her characters also resurrect aspects of past female experiences in order to throw light upon their own personal experiences. The recuperating/resurrecting/revisiting movement acts both ways empowering both the female predecessor and the modern artist in what we will call a movement of 'pendular dynamics' to which we will return later.

From a Spanish perspective, the book echoes, although with a different trajectory, the fictional work of Carmen Martín Gaite and Esther Tusquets in dealing with women's relation to language and writing within the specific historical framework of Spain. Martín Gaite in her *El cuarto de atrás* (The Back

Room) (1978) addresses the social constraints that women encountered during the Francoist dictatorship when faced with the official discourses originating from the national-socialist establishment, from romantic-popular literature for women and from the Church. In *Nubosidad variable* (Variable Cloud) (1996), almost twenty years later, Gaite attempts to rewrite that apparently mutilating past by recuperating a vision of Spain in which women are not silenced by hegemonic discourses but instead use them creatively to negotiate empowering positions which will be left for generations of women in a democratic future. Tusquets in her *El mismo mar de todos los veranos* (The Same Sea as Every Summer) (1978) shares Martín Gaite's and Woolf's view of the reductive power of patriarchal Western female mythology which conceptualizes women in terms of sacrificial mothers, evil stepmothers, chaste daughters, sinful Medusas, etc.[3]

Between Tusquets and Woolf there are other elements of common interest as is evident in the continuous use of sea-symbolism in Tusquets's work.[4] Woolf is further present in Tusquets's novels through direct quotations such as: 'Woolf would recognize in her diaries that once you were over fifty there was no point in lying to yourself' (Tusquets 1985, 43–44).[5] The theme of the passing of time takes us, on the other hand, to the words of other Catalan-born writers such as Montserrat Roig, who in her *L'hora violeta* (The Violet Hour) (1980b), the first work of a trilogy dealing with recent Spanish history viewed through the looking-glass of three generations of Catalan women,[6] says: 'Norma used to think about time and Woolf while listening to the *Jupiter* symphony. As if only time could change the persistent fidelity of the years. *The weather, perpetually changing*, says Woolf' (Roig 1980b, 177).[7] Likewise, Rosa Montero in her *Te trataré como a una reina* (1983) turns again to Woolf to reflect on time but in order to treat issues of staticity or dynamism associated with gender roles: 'She was like a lighthouse, like a lighthouse gripping a rock. And she used to watch men passing her by like waves always going somewhere, always leaving' (Montero 1983, 18).[8]

There are many further intertextual links between Woolf and modern Spanish women writers, and this chapter does not intend to present an exhaustive account of them. It should be mentioned, nevertheless, that Manuela Palacios in her contribution to this volume acknowledges Woolf's influence upon some Galician writers such as Pilar Pallarés and Ana Romaní.

---

3 This is not the only point of conjunction, though, between these authors, as we will see later.

4 This can, on the other hand, give rise to intertextual cultural readings given the Catalan origin of the writer.

5 'la Woolf reconocía en su diario que, pasados los cincuenta, no quedaba ya pretexto alguno para engañarse a sí mismo'. Unless otherwise indicated, all translations are my own.

6 For a comprehensive study of Roig see Davies 1994.

7 'La Norma pensava en el temps i en la Woolf mentre escoltava la Júpiter. Com si només el temps canviés l'obstinada fidelitat dels anys.'

8 'Ella era como un faro, un faro agarrado a una roca, y veía pasar a los hombres, como las olas, siempre hacia alguna parte, siempre yéndose.'

The latter, in particular, shares with Woolf and Tusquets an attraction for the sea, an element that, due to their geographic origins, could also give rise to an engaging cross-cultural reading if combined with issues of gender and autonomous national constructions.[9]

Reinforcing the Woolfian influences we encounter in modern Spanish fiction by women it is worth mentioning some contributions from the scholarly field. In a collection of interviews with Catalan-born women writers (Nichols 1989), Tusquets, Ana María Moix, Roig and Carme Riera acknowledge the influence of Woolf on their work. In particular, it should be noted that Roig and Riera are the two authors who most emphasize the importance of Woolf's ideas on their writings (Nichols 1989, 148 and 203). This is especially interesting given the fact that these two women write in Catalan and talk about Woolf in terms of gender and national identity. They admit to having identified more with Woolf's writings than with those of other Spanish female predecessors,[10] a subject to which we will return later. Both of them have also reflected in academic publications on women and writing, acknowledging again the pioneering importance of Woolf's ideas on this question (Riera 1989; Roig 1980a).

Furthermore, as mentioned above, Martín Gaite (1992) turns to Woolf in her academic reflections about women and writing. Martín Gaite is one of the main translators of Woolf into Spanish as well as one of the most important Spanish female authors engaged in questions of women and language in her fiction. She admits that *ROO* was the text that first sparked her interest in those questions and offers, as in Navales's case, an account of how her own personal story as a woman writer crossed paths with Woolf's. However, in the tone that characterizes most female writers in Spain due to the radical negative connotations associated with feminism during the Spanish dictatorship, she is dismissive of the appropriation of Woolf by feminist scholarship and tries to set Woolf apart from the 'boring feminism' of English female authors (Martín Gaite 1992, 29); this is contrary to Navales's aim of recreating the most challenging facets of a female artist's struggle against the patriarchal establishment.

Finally, it can be said that *Tres mujeres* coincides with the recuperation of past female historical figures carried out fictionally by authors such as Lourdes Ortiz, who in her novel *Urraca* (1982) recuperates through a subversive reading a twelfth-century Spanish queen. Nevertheless, Navales's originality lies in her comparative approach, gathering together female experiences originating in different historical and geographical contexts, and in the meta-textual character of her project.

Tres mujeres opens with a short story entitled 'Regreso a Monk's House' (Return to Monk's House) which first appeared in *Cuentos de Bloomsbury*. The latter is a collection of twelve short stories based on the lives of the

---

9 For references to Woolf's influence on Spanish women poets see Benegas and Munárriz (1997, 186 and 189).

10 Davies (1994, 25) also mentions Woolf as a model to which Roig turned in her writings.

Bloomsbury group. Through the different texts, Navales constructs a homage to the representatives of an intense moment of creative endeavour, especially Virginia Woolf, whose influence runs through the whole book and who is the protagonist of some of the stories. In 'Regreso' the narrator's voice is that of Virginia, who, adopting the first-person pronoun, takes the reader on a trip back to the past in search of an image of herself lost for ever, since it is only as a ghost that she revisits Monk's House. Woolf's writings are, of course, considered one of the main examples of English modernism (Minow-Pinkney 1987; Scott 1995, 1–70); her concern for the oppression of women and women's relationship with representation has also been extensively studied. Nevertheless, Navales's story opens new possibilities of interacting with this figure: in revisiting fictionally some problematic facets of Virginia's life and work Navales highlights her textual/mythical status within women's studies and converts this mythical figure into a textual entry through which to revise the relationship between women and language from a comparatively and culturally informed perspective.

Virginia's introspective journey to her past uncovers the difficulties involved in negotiating between the reflections that the outside sends back to her and her own self-image. Her character exposes the mixture of pleasure and desperation that a successful career inflicts upon her. Her continuous search for an identity revises the different images that family, friends and strangers offer her. Thus, adopting Virginia's voice, the narrative travels through various spaces and subjectivities that, although *other*, contribute to building her identity and frequently force her to accept an image that she never feels to be her own.

The narration starts with Virginia's arrival in Rodmell, the place where she had been living with her husband Leonardo. Throughout her recollections, she appears to be a woman unable to fit into the fashion conventions of her period.[11] She resents the imposition of the rules concerning clothing etiquette: 'What a torture always having to appear elegant, knowing that any piece of cloth suffices to cover the body!' (Navales 1995, 19).[12] This complaint is paradigmatic of her inability to learn and assume the appropriate behaviour that is expected from a woman of her class and position. This incapacity to follow a set of codified prevailing rules is a feature that is also characteristic of the protagonists in 'La dama escritora' and 'Julieta de los espíritus'. In the case of Julieta, for example, she complains that she never listened to what a woman was supposed to do regarding love matters:

---

11 As we have already observed, this aspect of the character's life, along with many others we will encounter later, echoes aspects of Virginia Woolf's life that are known and have been well documented (Poole 1995, 150; Luckhurst 1998, 3). There are also aspects that have worked in and out of literature as is the case with fashion in *O*: 'She was becoming a little more modest, as women are, of her person . . .. The change of clothes had, some philosophers will say, much to do with it. Vain trifles as they seem, clothes have, they say, more important offices than merely to keep us warm. They change our view of the world and the world's view of us' (*O*, 132).

12 '¡Qué martirio tener que aparecer siempre elegante, cuando cualquier tejido vale para cubrir el cuerpo!' All translations from Navales are my own; I would like to

> I made a mistake, I always make a mistake. You have to stay put, love comes slowly, but to save it time I throw myself onto it as it approaches. (98)[13]

Virginia's social inabilities are magnified by her fragile physical nature, both of which are interpreted by the people surrounding her as deficiencies that make her the object of attention and care from others. This image of being unable to take control of her own life sets the tone that marks her everyday experience, even her relation to her writing:[14]

> I was forced to be like an elm, with its branches reaching up to the sky to caress it. Something big, really out there! Who started this madness? Half eleven at my writing-table was the time that split my day, as the clock struck the hour with its menacing bell, my husband smiling beneath the stern face. (17–18)[15]

Although one cannot say that Leonardo is represented as an oppressive figure, he symbolizes the power of established rules, discreet norms, sound judgement in the face of excesses. He cannot understand Virginia's level of madness and sensitive excess:

> Sounds, streaks of light, colours unfelt by people around me. The world emanated life through all its pores. Even the tapping of a bird's beak against the bedroom window looking to the garden would be enough for me to plunge full speed into my veins. Then, ideas would rise up from their ruins and a palace would be erected in their place, the key to which only I had .... Leonardo never saw this palace. (21)[16]

The possibility of identification with such an intense experience is articulated in the text through the image of the palace that Leonardo does not share in seeing. The palace constitutes a place where Virginia can channel her creativity and is particularly relevant in relation to her female subjectivity. This palace is inhabited by 'swans' ('cisnes') whose identity she reveals some lines later by saying that her mother, Vanessa, Violet and Vita are the 'swans' that shared the palace with her. This affirmation highlights both the importance of matrilineage for female creativity and the common linguistic spaces women share in relation to representation and canonical writing.

---

thank Dinos Xenopoulos, though, for his invaluable input.

13 'Me equivoqué, siempre me equivoco, hay que quedarse quieta, el amor llega con pausa, pero cuando va a acercarse, le ahorro el camino y me lanzo'.

14 This is obviously a theme permeating Virginia's Woolf writings both in her fiction (*O*, 190; *BTA*, 46) and her diaries (*D* 1: 9). According to Rose: 'writing was an act that unsexed her, made her an unnatural woman' (paraphrased in Showalter 1977, 270).

15 'me obligaron a ser el olmo que tiende sus ramas al cielo y lo acaricia, algo grande, arriba, arriba, ¿quién empezó esa locura?, y la mañana se me rompía en dos sobre la tabla de mi escritorio cuando el reloj daba su campanada amenazante, las once y media, mi marido, su sonrisa o gesto torvo'.

16 'Sonidos, luces y colores que nadie percibía a mi lado. El mundo estaba vivo en todos sus poros. Y bastaba el tintineo de un pájaro en la ventana de mi cuarto, que daba al jardín, para que a todo vapor navegase yo por mis venas. Entonces, las ideas se alzaban de sus ruinas, y en su lugar se eregía un palacio del que sólo yo tenía la llave .... Leonardo nunca veía ese palacio'.

Virginia's perception of her husband's lack of understanding and the tension it provokes in her can also be read as paradigmatic of the process which, according to Cixous (1981), any woman attempting to be heard goes through:

> Every woman has known the torment of getting up to speak. Her heart racing, at times entirely lost for words, ground and language slipping away .... A double distress, for even if she transgresses, her words fall almost always upon the deaf male ear, which hears in languages only that which speaks in the masculine. (251)

Thus even if Leonardo is not necessarily portrayed as a castrating figure, he is, none the less, the voice that assures the value of Virginia's writing. Leonardo's position is not that of the 'swans' but is, rather, emblematic of the patriarchal system of language through which Virginia strives to find her own voice. The struggle originates in the existence of literary historical norms which dictate what is supposed to be a woman's writing and a man's, both definitions emanating from a phallic system. As Gauthier (1981) notes in his discussion of the definition of women's writing as different:

> In the first case [conceiving feminine literature as different], certain qualities are attributed to women, and are seen as particularly 'feminine' (intuition, sensitivity, etc.); but it is men who render these judgements. Therefore the writing of 'woman' will respond to their expectations and will reassure them. This is a masculine point of view. In the second case [denying the difference between the sexes], the woman (though slightly retarded) is considered to be 'like' a man or is in-the-process of becoming a man. This point of view is equally masculine and reassuring – it is one that can emanate only from a phallic system – and many women give in without any problem at all. (Gauthier 1981, 162)

In 'La dama escritora' we find precisely the labelling of a woman's writing in masculine terms in María del Pilar Sinués's husband's perception of her writing. He is horrified when his wife, fed up with writing 'feminine' novels which portrayed the model of the 'angel in the house', writes a story in which virtue has no reward. Her rejection of the literary patterns expected to be used by women ostracizes her. It has to be said, though, that the canon can also be used by women to stretch and abuse the limits of the patriarchal norms of language as Virginia's character does in relation to the heterosexual literary models that have been placed before women for decades. She talks about her love for Vita, assuming herself the identity of Cinderella (*Tres mujeres*, 34) with no Prince Charming needed.

In *Tres mujeres* Virginia's insecurity emerging from not being able to find her own place within the established patterns makes her go to Leonardo for continuous reassurance as to the value of her texts and contributes to her constructing a powerless image of herself as:

> a scared sparrow pecking over and over on the typewriter, a mole doomed to bite the dirt, digging day after day until I find some light in the pages I write, until I see *that words are mine and nobody else's*. (19–20)[17]

---

[17] 'un gorrión asustado picoteando una y otra vez en la máquina de escribir, un topo

The battle to recognize as her own the words she writes recalls another deeper conflict to reconcile in an image all the different fragments of her personality, that is, the different images of herself that objects and people offer back to her. The character of Virginia is frequently described as split between her self and the image of herself that mirrors, photographs, family and friends reflect. This feeds the female writer's terror of *otherness*.

> I have always lived with the fear that another woman just like me was walking along with me, stuck to my body or invading it .... That woman and I were occasionally two perfectly matching halves. One of them mute, only capable of sketching words ... would hunt for sentences .... The existence of the other would terrify me. (25)[18]

That other woman, the uncontrollable one, is the 'owner of the images preceding the words' (25–26)[19] and the one who, in the brief moments of merging with Virginia, enables literary creation to take place. The duality in her subjectivity is projected upon the vision she has of her body:

> My mind was free, separated from the fragile, sickly nature of a body I detested, a ballast, a dead weight that I necessarily had to drag along. (35)[20]

Virginia is portrayed by Navales as a woman who cannot reconcile herself with the alterity of her personality, not even with Vita, her great love. She projects upon her lover precisely the vitality, elegance and aristocratic talent that she considers lacking in herself. The narrator cannot respond to the relationship with the same overwhelming passion as Vita, but only with

> [a] childish love made up of smiles and caresses, of beach games, so far away from passionate storms because of her fear of drowning in them. (32)[21]

In *Tres mujeres* this fear of drowning in the unknown runs parallel to her fear of otherness, of losing one's identity in another, as the love relationship epitomizes the vulnerability of the self before the other.[22] Inability to relate in love matters leads Virginia to find refuge in other female laps in search of a maternal image that will protect her from her ghosts, without realizing that the

---

cont.
predestinado a morder el barro, excavando día a día hasta encontrar la luz en lás páginas que escribo, hasta ver *que son mías y de nadie más las palabras* [my italics]'.

18 'Siempre he vivido con el temor de que otra mujer igual a mí misma, pegada a mi cuerpo o invadiéndolo, caminaba conmigo .... Esa mujer y yo, a veces dos mitades exactamente coincidentes, una de ellas muda, sólo hábil para dibujar palabras ... cazaba frases .... La existencia de la otra me espantaba.'

19 'dueña de las imágenes que preceden a las palabras'.

20 'La mente libre, separada de mi naturaleza frágil, enfermiza, del cuerpo que detestaba, un lastre, un peso, algo que necesariamente debía arrastrar'.

21 '[su] amor infantil, de sonrisas y caricias, de juegos en la playa, lejos de las tormentas pasionales por miedo a perecer ahogada'.

22 This is a topic that also permeates Virgina Woolf's own writing as Rigney (1978, 40–63) notes in relation to the characters of Septimus and Clarissa in *MD*.

figure of the mother is the first other that creates an illusory unified image of the self. The importance of the figure of the mother in Virginia Woolf has already received attention from the academic community as one of the main drives of her life and work.[23] The studies carried out emphasize the tremendous importance of Virginia's mother in her conception of a woman's role at the turn of the century, as reflected in her novels. They also point to Virginia's frequent turning to other female figures such as Vanessa Bell, Janet Case (her Greek teacher), Vita Sackville-West, Violet Trefusis, etc., who frequently played the role of surrogate mothers. Nevertheless, we should highlight the relevance of the maternal in Navales's recreation of the writer not only because it forms the backbone of the whole writerly project but also because of its very significance in the constitution of the female artist. Let us remember the problematic role of the mother as the first symbolic other against which the female subject has to negotiate her own position within language and society and the scarcity of empowering female models provided by culture.

The kind of struggle between artist and creation that the short stories enact concerning the fictional female characters' relations with their own work is paradigmatic of the 'pendular dynamics' that we mentioned earlier in connection with the reciprocal empowerment implied in the recuperation of female predecessors. Both are based on a dialectical cycle of separation versus union that has been theorized by feminism as underlining the mother/daughter dyad. Kristeva (1986, 38) uses the term 'permanent alternation' to refer to a critical strategy against patriarchal positioning based on the idea of both mother and daughter assuming and criticizing each other's role within society. In these short stories female characters both assume and, with the linguistic tools adopted in the assumption of female positionings, criticize the artistic canon. The distance provided by the inscription of the female subject in the symbolic, aesthetic order of culture and society enables them to negotiate a place from which to exercise power and criticize it, for criticism is required in order to overcome the paralysis of a rigid identity. As Kristeva suggests, what is needed is a process of 'permanent alternation: never the one without the other' (Kristeva 1986, 38) through which 'each must exercise *and* criticize the power; each must be both mother and daughter' (Gallop 1982, 121).

Navales herself reinvents images of mythical foremothers that have contributed to her self-determination as a woman writer in order to appropriate them for her own textual enterprise. In turn, the protagonists of the three narratives themselves go back to their own pasts or those of their own predecessors (as it is the case with María Sinués and her grandmother María del Pilar Sinués) to revise the positions both of them inhabited and recycle them to create new empowering ones. In this sense, the texts give voice to subjectivities that otherwise would remain silent. The narrator in 'Julieta de los espíritus' puts it in the following terms:

---

[23] For a study of the important role of Virginia Woolf's mother and other surrogate mothers in her work and real life see Rosenman (1995).

> You must forgive me, Julieta, you must forgive the lie behind this story that names you. A story growing out of your enigma, caught in the smile from your photograph that is urging me to invent you in an absurd attempt to draw myself near your life, to draw you near life in some way. (85)[24]

Or:

> your life has become a story-telling and picture-painting plot. Not your life but the one we made up for you. (110)[25]

The exploration of the complexities of the female artist's subjectivity does not stop in the narrative time of the protagonists. In Virginia's short story it finds its actualization in the brief but significant entries of another female experience in the narrative. She seems to be one of the new inhabitants of Monk's House. Through various dialogues we encounter a variant of the female problematic that Virginia recalls in her past:

> – You are too naïve, like this you'll get nowhere. The bad thing is that by the time life teaches you that, it is already too late.
> Voices from the other side of the wall, from people that I have never met, living in my own house. (31)[26]
>
> – Come inside. What are you doing under the apple tree like an idiot? – *Are the voices from inside or outside?* (38)[27]
>
> – The roast-beef was inedible, the vegetables were cold, the lemon pudding too sour – [said] a masculine, strong, harsh voice on the other side of the wall. It is lunch time and, probably, a couple is sitting at the table. The woman is silent. (40–41)[28]

These paragraphs stage fragments of another female life lived in silence as a wife, for the only voice appearing in the text is a masculine one. It is especially interesting that sometimes Virginia cannot distinguish whether the voices belong to the memories of her past or to the present of the new inhabitants

---

24 'Debes perdonarme, Julieta, la mentira de esta historia que te nombra, que crece de tu enigma, contagiada por esa sonrisa que ahora me llega desde tu fotografía y que me obliga a inventarte en este absurdo empeño de acercarme a tu vida, de acercarte a la vida de algun modo'.

25 'tu vida ha pasado a ser materia de relatos y de cuadros. Tu vida, no. La que te inventamos.'

26 '– Eres demasiado ingenua, así no llegarás a ninguna parte. Lo malo es que, cuando la vida enseña, ya es tarde. Voces al otro lado del tabique, de personas que nunca he conocido, habitando mi propia casa.'

27 '– Entra en casa. ¿Qué haces ahí, debajo del manzano, como una idiota? – *¿Son voces de dentro o de fuera?* [my italics]'.

28 '– El roast-beef estaba incomible, las legumbres frías, el pudding de limón demasiado ácido. – Una voz masculina, fuerte y desabrida, al otro lado del tabique. Es la hora del almuerzo y, probablemente, una pareja está sentada a la mesa. La mujer permanece en silencio.'

('inside or outside?' she wonders). The excerpts underline the negation of the female voice before the 'strong, harsh' masculine voice which erects itself as the judge of the woman's personality and work. They also highlight the need for continuous re-conceptualization of women's situation in a contemporary historical context that takes for granted the emancipation of women.

As has been noted, there are certain elements of Virginia's experience that reverberate in the other two short stories in *Tres mujeres* although in a different cultural context.[29] By placing 'Regreso' alongside 'La dama escritora' and 'Julieta de los espíritus', Navales is not only thinking back and recuperating symbolic mothers but also emphasizing the need to think sideways through other 'sisters', as if following Virginia Woolf's very steps. As Marcus points out:

> As a literary critic and novelist, Virginia Woolf thought not only back through her mothers but also sideways through her sisters. It was a collective historical effort of committed socialist feminism. (Marcus 1981b, xiv)

Despite the empowering potential of Navales's project, it could be argued that looking for female models outside Spanish frontiers may not always translate well into indigenous experiences. It can sometimes produce a forced reading following the imported conceptual frame. The use of Woolf as a symbol of a successful artistic foremother as against her less successful Spanish counterparts may be considered in terms of what Ilie labels as 'the spectre of the superior European other' (Ilie 1995, 34):[30] a post-Francoist reaction based on the idea that anything from abroad is progressive and liberating, especially if it comes from Anglo-Saxon or French traditions. In this context, it is not surprising, as Labanyi (1995) points out, to find in the first years of democracy a substitution of social realism by modernism and an upsurge of new translations and editions of modernist authors.[31]

Indeed, the two Spanish characters in the remaining short stories do not represent models which were recognized by artistic circles, but I would argue that that is precisely the point in Navales's fiction: to show how success or failure is very much determined by the patriarchal attitudes of the cultural establishment and how the latter shapes and feeds the sense of fissure in the

---

29 In *Cuentos de Bloomsbury* Virginia's experience is set against that of other female characters belonging to her same cultural context.

30 'el espectro del Otro europeo superior'.

31 Laura Lojo Rodríguez, in her contribution to this volume, also points out a similar process, but in a different historical and geographical context, with regard to the relationship between the Argentinian Victoria Ocampo and Virginia Woolf. According to Lojo, Ocampo's admiration for Woolf can be read as part of the Argentinian turning towards Europe at the beginning of the twentieth century in order to build a sense of spiritual independence from the too painful or remote past or from the cultural inferiority of Argentina by comparison with Europe. This perception of cultural inferiority, however, is a subject that could be further explored by questioning the cultural origin of the conceptual frame applied to the judgement of a nation's cultural inferiority or superiority.

experience of the female artist whichever cultural process she may be inscribed in. From a Spanish perspective Navales's strategy can be understood if one considers the need of female writers after the return to democracy to break from the Francoist past and find a renewed voice. It is well known that for almost forty years the dictatorship tried to silence women's voices socially, politically and artistically, leaving future female generations apparently lacking in a tradition of their own. This also contributed to spreading the general simplistic feeling that Spain, as with many other things, had arrived late at feminism. It is not surprising, then, as Ordóñez (1988, 6) observes, to find a compilation of women's narratives in the 1980s which claims to owe more to the Anglo-American tradition of women's writing than to their Spanish counterparts,[32] as is the case with other writers from the 1980s as Basanta (1990, 72) notes. It is especially striking in the case of Roig and Riera, two Catalan-language authors who, because of the political and linguistic repression that their language suffered during the dictatorship, seem to find more common ground with literature in English (Virginia Woolf in particular) than in Spanish as far as gender and national identity are concerned.

We could further translate the symbolic process of separation versus union that we mentioned with regard to the mother/daughter relationship into a comparative framework to explain the process that motivates an initial approach to foreign female writers. The dictatorial heritage with its oppressive over-investment in the maternal as the symbol of a new unified Francoist Spain, along with the paternalistic attitude that anything foreign was damaging and an equally paternalistic attitude towards literature by women in general, was not a particularly good breeding ground for encouraging interest in recuperating Spanish foremothers. A certain distance provided by a progressive 'consolidation' of democracy would be necessary in order to turn the gaze to other things Spanish, to find an empowering voice from apparently silent figures from the past. Or as Marcus (1981a, 21) puts it, there is an initial need to 'murder' our personal/historical mothers as they seem to represent moments of female silence. Stimpson situates this reflection in the context of Virginia Woolf's own writings and feminism by saying that:

> Woolf's mothers seem to be Aphra Behn and Jane Austen rather than Julia Duckworth Stephen. However, feminist critics have responded to the entirety of *A Room of One's Own*. They have also swung along with the return to the figure of the mother that feminist theory made in the mid-1970s. (Stimpson 1992, 174)

Indeed, in recent years several publications by women both in the creative (Benegas and Munárriz 1997; Freixas 1996; Ortiz 1982) and in the critical fields (Brown 1991; Nichols 1989; Ordóñez 1991; Servodidio 1987) stress precisely the need both to revise the established Spanish literary canon in order to recuperate neglected female figures and to strive for the reinvention of different linguistic voices which would express *other* visions of the past, present

---

32 Ordóñez refers to Navajo (1982).

and future. It is in this area that Navales's work stands out by placing the recreation of Woolf alongside that of Sinués and Aguilar.

If with 'Regreso' Navales attempts to revise the most subjective aspects of a successful woman writer's everyday struggle to find her own voice, with 'La dama escritora' and 'Julieta de los espíritus' the author recuperates two female personalities ostracized by the establishment in Spain and offers an alternative reading of their work. In 'La dama escritora' we encounter a character who has already appeared in a previous volume of Navales entitled *Zacarías, rey* (Zacarías, King). The lady writer refers to María del Pilar Sinués, a nineteenth-century Aragonese writer of romantic novels which portrayed women following the model of the 'angel in the house'. The narrator is her granddaughter, María Sinués, who delves into her ancestor's past to discover a life which demythologizes any similarities between her grandmother and the stories she wrote. From the distance of a third-person pronoun the reader is offered the possibility of glancing at a subjective landscape destined otherwise for oblivion, as the established nineteenth-century literary canon intended with the work of the real writer and of other contemporaries as Bieder (1992) observes. The distance is therefore doubled, since the reader accesses the subjectivity of the nineteenth-century writer through the granddaughter's vision, which, in turn, is mediated through the separation permitted by the third-person narration. The reader trespasses upon María's vision of María del Pilar and realizes that the former's experience is closer to the latter's than she desires.

There is a third layer, though, in this kaleidoscopical text: the character of Gálvez, her grandmother's maid and only inhabitant of the palace. She acts as the mediator through which all the memories of the past are articulated and later passed on to the granddaughter. The oral dimension of her personality is very much emphasized throughout the text as María complains of Gálvez's never-ending monologues in which she recalls stories of María's female ancestors. She is, therefore, the oral guarantor of the grandmother's memories and the one who enables María Sinués to access them. It is worth mentioning too that Gálvez is also the motor of the text María finally writes about her grandmother. Thus, through Gálvez's character the narrative offers the possibility of reflecting upon the importance of an apparently silent lower class (silent because it leaves no written trace) that nevertheless embodies an oral tradition in need of being recuperated in women's writing. On the other hand, through Gálvez, Navales incorporates the figure of the maid as an embodiment of the silent workforce which enables the literary recreation by 'ladies' and, therefore, acknowledges 'the women of another class whose labour we rely on so we can write' (Gallop 1986, 146).

María Sinués, after having been left by her husband returns, like the protagonist in 'Regreso', to the house that constituted an important part of her past. She attempts to find and rebuild a renewed image of herself which would help her to face her future life. In this process the house acquires important symbolical connotations, not only because of memories, but also because it is associated with a matrilineal space: women in her family, from her great-grandmother to her mother, lived in that house. They spent their time on needlework, crocheting or writing, like her grandmother. María, like Virginia, in her subjective exploration tries to establish connections with other female maternal figures. María Sinués ends up leaving her own heritage in the form of what looks like a demystifying account of María del Pilar Sinués's life.

The tradition that María del Pilar Sinués embodies proves eventually to be non-paralysing thanks to the granddaughter's revisionary search and the demystifying accounts offered by Gálvez. As Rosenman (1995) argues conclusively:

> Tradition itself is not the problem, however; it is the patriarchal nature of tradition. Tradition can in fact be enabling in several ways. It can show the woman writer that her conflicts about writing are not a purely personal problem but have been shared by many women as a function of patriarchal ideology. It can also provide useful models and examples and can authorize a woman's ambition by showing her that other women have written as well. (Rosenman 1995, 70)

'Julieta de los espíritus' is the last story of the trilogy.[33] The narrative voice addresses Julieta using the second-person pronoun. The character behind the fictional Julieta is that of Juliana Aguilar Coscojuela, a little-known Aragonese painter who, after her mother's death from Alzheimer's disease, went to France between the two World Wars in search of an adventurous life and worked as a music-hall artist. She returned to Spain in her old age to achieve success by mere coincidence a year before her death in 1979.[34] Her figure had already appeared in Navales's writings in *El regreso de Julieta Always* (The Return of Julieta Always). The trigger of the short story in *Tres mujeres* seems to be the non-identified narrator's desire to search for an image of Julieta which would enable the narrator to understand him/herself, although without succeeding in finding any unified answers.

The relationship between the narrator and Julieta is unexplained. There seems to be a strong link and in-depth knowledge of Julieta's life which emerges throughout the whole narrative via references ranging from the smallest detail of her life to accounts of her perceptions and feelings. Moreover, there are some fragments which point to a possible past relationship between the two identities and contribute further to the ambiguity created between narrator and addressee by the confusion of voices at some stages.

One of the keys to accessing the confusion of voices is the assumption of Julieta's madness as a narrative structuring device, permitting one to interpret the text as a composition of different instances originating from the same hallucinated identity. Thus the narrative can be said to construct the problematic of a female subjectivity split between the symbolic conventions of artistic codification and the search for her own position in terms of linguistic madness. The fissure of a female identity that we encountered in the preceding stories reaches its maximum expression in a split narrative of insanity. It makes

---

33 There are obvious parallels between the title of this short story and Fellini's film *Giulietta degli spiriti* (*Juliet of the Spirits*) but the analysis of their intertextual crossing goes beyond the scope of this paper.

34 I would like to thank Ana María Navales for her kind help in providing information on the real Julieta Aguilar.

a clear-cut recognition of the narrator and the addressee impossible. Julieta's alienation places her on the other side of the established symbolic patriarchal order. The text can be read as the means of enabling a dialogue between two interlocuting halves, of exchanging voices and spaces, heard and seen from different sides of the linguistic/symbolic looking-glass:

> You start to look at yourself, you watch over yourself. Splitting into two and not finding inside yourself the one you are looking for frightens you. (98)[35]

> And it seems to her that it is another person the one laughing and speaking, because she remains on this side of the looking-glass, different and distant, estranged from the smiles and words of the other Julieta, the one who becomes detached from her, that someone else who is sitting at the table and occupying a different place from hers. (111)[36]

The text succeeds in constructing an identity alienated between reality and discourse, attempting to find her own subjective space among the scissions of text and imagery available and trying to reconcile into a serene semblance the varied facets of a restless fissured identity. It could be said that Navales's recreation of the blurred boundaries between sanity and insanity mirrors that of Virginia Woolf in *MD*, but instead of choosing two different characters like Clarissa and Septimus to articulate different sides of a problematic subjectivity Navales chooses to explore the theme of madness associated with female gender conditionings. For Julieta is 'mad' insofar as she does not conform to the social expectations for a woman who is supposed to wait for things to come. She cannot imitate the prevailing feminine behaviour the text occasionally echoes:

> *Courage*, you have to know how to move your eyes, do not forget the man-killing smile, but without overdoing it, it is all part of the game. (98)[37]

Throughout our study we have seen how the various portrayals of women's subjectivities in Navales's work explore from different directions the experience of women artists. The texts re-enact a recuperation of the protagonists' self-images or those of their predecessors, as is the case in 'La dama escritora'. All the characters turn their gaze to their past in an attempt to explore the many layers of their specific positionings. This is made possible by Navales's writerly enterprise. Her own voice, appearing in the introductions, forms part of the narrative proposal that attempts to subvert the frustration,

---

35 'Empiezas a verte, te vigilas, te asusta desdoblarte y no encontrar en ti a la que buscas.'

36 'Y le parece que es otra persona la que ríe y habla, porque ella se queda a este lado del espejo, diferente y lejana, extraña a las sonrisas y palabras de la otra Julieta que se despega de sí misma, ese alguien más sentado a la mesa y que ocupa un lugar distinto al suyo.'

37 'Courage, hay que saber mover los ojos, no lo olvides, la risa conquistadora, sin excederse, todo forma parte del juego.'

failure and madness of the female characters and to convert them into empowering texts of artistic female self-determination, thereby questioning the models that the patriarchal canon projects on women. The detailed recreation of these foremothers' feelings and experiences recuperates them in a movement of 'pendular dynamics' for a renewed space in which they are not alone, but intertwined with other textual subjectivities past and present. Navales, in her personal/textual dialogue with those *other* female/maternal texts, tries to highlight the intertextuality of Virginia Woolf's persona and to retrieve the seemingly castrated position of the Spanish female characters by creating a space in which future readers can share and be reflected in a never-ending spiral of kaleidoscopic looking-glasses. The apparently literary sketches of the artists' lives become, then, essays on women's subjectivities. These are influenced by different patriarchal gazes and divided, both literarily and symbolically, into diverse linguistic voices which explore, from their split instances, their unbridgeable experiences. In this sense the author enacts Cixous' idea that:

> Woman must write her self: must write about women and bring women to writing, from which they have been driven away as violently as from their bodies – for the same reasons, by the same law, with the same fatal goal. Woman must put herself into the text – as into the world and into history – by her own movement. (Cixous 1981, 245)

It could be argued, though, that the texts do not question the commonly visited mythical topos of presenting the female writer/artist trapped within an oppressive framework. This strategy is most empowering within feminist discourse as it acknowledges possibilities for resistance by unprivileged or oppressed groups (Janeway 1980), but it could become reductive if it does not account for *other* scenarios from which to resist and to explore women's relationship with representation. This critical argument, however, does not invalidate Navales's project. The narrative approach of the tales echoes questions of great relevance in the feminist debate about women's relation to representation and to fiction in Spanish history.

Navales offers a view of Woolf different from those provided by other female Spanish writers who have turned to Woolf in search of a literary mother apparently lacking in Spain. Navales looks back through Virginia Woolf as a text to uncover different layers of her myth and to open a sideways dialogue with other texts on Spanish women artists. This sideways thinking uncovers, on the one hand, the historical and geographical diversity of women's oppression and, on the other, enables a contemporary re-reading of their experiences in the light of feminist studies in this area which point out the common struggle to resist their specific alienations. It, therefore, avoids the risk of universalizing women's relationship to representation and enables the reader to adopt a critical standpoint with regard to the different cultural parameters to be taken into account (geographical origin, historical period, social class, etc.) when dealing with the constitution of female desire through language. For, despite the obvious empowering effects of re-appropriating Woolf's figure within Spanish female-authored fiction, one could fall into the trap of obscuring specific cultural frameworks and being seduced by the mythical aura of the 'superior European other'. Navales, on the contrary, offers the possibility of adopting a distance from which to exercise the power and criticize it, from which to identify with the mythical mother but critically revisit the specific materiality of her figure in comparison with other Spanish counterparts.

15 'A fastness of their own': The Galician Reception of Virginia Woolf

Manuela Palacios

In her essay 'On Not Knowing Greek' (1925) Virginia Woolf remarks that the Greeks remain in a fastness of their own as she comments on the wide cultural chasm that separates them from the English (*CR 1* 1984, 23). In this discussion of classical Greek literature Woolf acknowledges the irreducible otherness of the Greek language and culture, but she also provides plenty of evidence about the possible ties that allow us to recognize ourselves in the other. It is this tension between otherness and sameness that proves to be especially fruitful in reception studies like the present one. In Galicia, an Atlantic region in the Northwest of Spain, we have made Woolf a writer of our own, but a fastness has been needed because Woolf's work has had to struggle against the most hostile political and social circumstances. Galician is a minority language with a long history of repression, in spite of which feminist activists, creative writers, translators and scholars have been 'intent on verbal victory' (*CR 1* 1984, 25).

The celebration of the silenced word

In this postmodern age in which the possibility of access to the real world has been renounced even by the progressive factions of post-structuralist thought, it is important to remark that the reception of Virginia Woolf in Galicia owes its main momentum to the British writer's stress on the material conditions of production of art. Reality shapes the writer's chances of writing, publishing and reaching an audience. Besides, we perceive in the text the power relations that shape our life. The book by Virginia Woolf that has had the most durable impact on a large part of the Galician audience has been *ROO*, and it is precisely the way in which this fundamental essay in feminist literary theory unrelentingly roots literature in the social and economic circumstances which produce it that has drawn our attention to Woolf.

Outside the academic world, it has been the Galician feminist movement that has done the most to promote, study and discuss the writings of Virginia Woolf. There are two Galician feminist periodicals that have engaged in a dialogue with Woolf: *Festa da palabra silenciada*, which could be translated as 'Celebration of the Silenced Word', and *Andaina* ('Long/Laborious Passage'). The former first came out in Vigo in 1983 and is a yearly publication written in Galician. It is devoted to women's creativity, with a special emphasis on writing. *Festa*'s coordinator, María Xosé Queizán, herself a well-known writer, chose a quotation from *ROO* for the first issue of this periodical:

> Intellectual freedom depends upon material things. Poetry depends upon intellectual freedom. And women have always been poor, not for two hundred years merely, but from the beginning of time. Women have had less intellectual freedom than the sons of Athenian slaves. Women, then, have not had a dog's chance of writing poetry. (*ROO* 1992, 141)[1]

This passage explicitly connects literature with the material conditions of the real world. The fact that Galician feminist writers of the 1980s and 1990s have repeatedly turned to this particular concern of Woolf's means either that the social and economic context for women writers in Galicia is not very different from that of Britain in the 1920s, or that an acquaintance with postmodern debates about the fictionality of all our apprehensions of reality makes many Galician feminist writers uneasy about the idealism and anti-realism of these theories, or it may mean, as I would like to argue, that both interpretations of this appropriation of Woolf's thinking may be possible at the same time. Galicia was largely a rural and almost pre-capitalist society until the middle of the twentieth century; however, the globalization of culture and the radical transformation undergone in Spain since the 1960s has allowed a large student population with access to a nearly free university education to participate in current philosophical debates. The interest of reception studies like this lies partly in the exposure of different social and cultural tempos in the various countries of the newly born European Union.

María Xosé Queizán's choice, as coordinator of the periodical, of the above quotation from *ROO* can be explained on several grounds. On the one hand, she has a preference for Woolf's essays, for her explicitly ideological commitment rather than for her lyrical elaborations of emotions and feelings. This could be in part the consequence of reading Woolf in translation, where Woolf's language may not be evocatively rendered, and the readers of translations may therefore look more deeply into the ideas than into the style. On the other hand, Queizán accompanies Woolf's quotation with three poems by Galician women writers, Xohana Torres, Luz Pozo Garza and herself, Queizán's poem appropriately inaugurating the project of this first issue of

---

[1] Although the Galician public has had to read *ROO* in its Spanish translation because there is no Galician version of this work, all quotations in *Festa* are translated into our minority language. Thus, part of Woolf's writing has appeared in Galician through the translation of quotations like this. Queizán abreviates the quotation slightly: 'A liberdade intelectual depende das cousas materiais. A poesía depende da liberdade intelectual – E as mulleres foron pobres dende sempre. Foron menos libres que os fillos dos escravos atenienses. As mulleres, daquela non tiveron mais oportunidade que un can para escreber poesía' (Queizán 1983, 20).

Festa with a celebration of those earlier Galician women poets whose work was silenced, who had less than a dog's chance of writing poetry:

> We shall finally speak, my friends,
> give me your voice and the lilies of your hands
> let us recover with our hands and our words
> the history of the spread of joy. (1983, 21)[2]

Finally, a third reason for Queizán's preference for Woolf's essays may well be a desire to open new paths for Galician poetry, which has traditionally been lyrical and particularly so in the case of women poets. Without neglecting the importance of those lyrical personae who explore their own feelings, Queizán opts for the challenge of a politically engaged literature that is concerned with the transformation of society.

The same first issue of *Festa* includes an article by María Camino Noia, 'Literatura galega de mulleres' (Galician Literature by Women Writers) which again refers to Virginia Woolf and her notion of a room of one's own. The author claims that very few Galician women writers have enjoyed the privacy of a room of their own: 'But Galician women sleep with their sisters, their aunts, their grandmothers or their little brothers, before they sleep with their husbands' (Noia 1983, 7).[3] Economically dependent on their fathers or their husbands, these women can hardly achieve any intellectual freedom. We only know of five women poets in Galician literature before the twentieth century and all belong to the upper middle class. The twentieth century begins with a literary Renaissance that is mainly a male province. After the Spanish Civil War (1936–39) there is no literary production in the Galician language until 1950. The liberties and rights for which Woolf's nephew Julian Bell died in Spain, together with other courageous and generous members of the International Brigades, were trampled on by Fascist boots. Julian Bell and many others died to defend the right of many Spaniards to speak their minority languages.

The second issue of *Festa* (1985) features an important article by Carmen Blanco, probably the Galician scholar who has done most to promote Woolf's work in the areas of Galician literary criticism, feminist activism and the media, where she compares a significant essay by the most famous Galician writer, Rosalía de Castro (1837–85) with *ROO*. Again, what triggers the comparison is Woolf's concern with the material and psychological grounds that condition women's writing. If in her essay Woolf explores the possibilities of a new sentence that suits women's experience, Carmen Blanco (1985) maintains that Rosalía de Castro, in 'Las literatas: carta a Eduarda' (Literary Women: Letter to Eduarda) (1866), makes use of stylistic devices that are characteristic of marginal writers: irony, ambiguity and playful contradictions.

---

2 'Falaremos por fin, amigas,/dade-me a voz e as vosas mans de lírios/recuperemos coas mans e coas palabras/a história de avanzar felicidade' ('Sen que as visagras ...' (Lest the hinges ...)).

3 'Pero as mulleres galegas durmen coas irmás, as tías, aboas ou irmáns pequenos, antes de dormir cos maridos.'

Galicia has had an outstanding lyrical tradition that can be traced back to the Middle Ages with the poetry written in 'Galaico-Portuguese'. Narrative, however, has played a secondary role, the first Galician novel not being written until 1880. The first novel written by a woman in Galician, *Néveda* (Catmint) by Francisca Herrera, only appeared in 1920 and the light at the end of the tunnel of Franco's dictatorship only glowed in 1965 with a second novel by another woman writer: *A orella no buraco* (Ear to the Hole) by María Xosé Queizán. The reason for this unfortunate absence of women from the literary world is further explained by Isabel Mouriz (1986, 14) with a reference to Woolf's stress on the decisive importance of historical and cultural circumstances as well as of the material conditions in which art is produced.

Another quotation from *ROO* helps María Pilar J. Aleixandre to illustrate the continuing validity of Woolf's words. In her review of María Xosé Queizán's book of essays *Evidencias* (Proofs) (1989), Aleixandre (1990) justifies the appearance of yet another book on feminism by quoting the following:

> What had our mothers been doing then that they had no wealth to leave us? . . . If she had left two or three hundred thousand pounds to Fernham, we could have been sitting at our ease tonight and the subject of our talk might have been archaeology, botany, anthropology, physics, the nature of the atom, mathematics, astronomy, relativity, geography. If only Mrs Seton and her mother and her mother before her had learnt the great art of making money and had left their money, like their fathers and their grandfathers before them, to found fellowships and lectureships and prizes and scholarships appropriated to the use of their own sex. (*ROO* 1992a, 26–27)[4]

Aleixandre regrets that the time has not yet come for women to sit at leisure and speak about astronomy. Philosophical discussions must still prove their relevance and application to the improvement of women's lives. Thus, for instance, Queizán's essay in *Evidencias*, 'Feminismo e epicureísmo', studies how two apparently different discourses like Feminism and Epicureanism share rejection of the determinism of nature, how both attempt to demolish stereotypes and privilege personal relations, the body and the sensorial experience over Platonism.

Other important references to Woolf in *Festa* are Kathleen March's allusion to *ROO* as the most important essay in feminist literary criticism (1994, 71),

---

4 '¿Que fixeron entón as nosas nais, que non puideron deixarnos unha fortuna en herdanza? . . .. Se chegan deixar dúas ou tres mil libras, poderiamos, esta noite, estar comodamente sentadas, e o suxeito da nosa conversa podería ser arqueoloxía, botánica, antropoloxía, física, a natureza do átomo, matemáticas, astronomía, relatividade ou xeografía. Se tan só a señora Seton e a súa nai, e a nai da súa nai aprenderan o grande arte de facer cartos, e tivesen deixado os seus cartos como os seus pais, e os seus avós, para fornecer axudas e bolsas e premios e investigacións apropiadas para o uso de seu propio sexo' (Aleixandre 1990, 136 [quoting from *ROO*]). María Xosé Agra (1996, 64) finds a similarity between Woolf's O and the Spanish philosopher María Zambrano's *Filosofía y poesía* (Philosophy and Poetry) (1939) in that both women question the scission between philosophy and life and consider the unfortunate consequences of the Platonic condemnation of poetry.

Pilar Martín Casalderrey's review of *Tres mujeres*, by Ana María Navales (1996), where the first story 'Regreso a Monk's House' (Return to Monk's House) features Virginia Woolf as the protagonist, and where the language is pregnant with symbols and poetic images.[5] Woolf's room of one's own is even alluded to in number 14 of *Festa* (1998), a monograph on architecture and town planning, where María Xosé Queizán refers to patriarchy as an ascription of spaces, showing how spatial segregation between the two genders has run parallel to women's social position, and how architects have favoured the sexual division of labour in the family through the design and layout of homes.

However prominent, *ROO* is not the only work by Woolf analysed in *Festa*. *BTA* also receives careful consideration in Luz Valencia's article on the concept of time and change that it reveals (1991). Valencia's references to Woolf's essay on Montaigne illustrate the writer's certainty that life is a continuous flux, rigidity and conformity are death. 'The Narrow Bridge of Art' also provides Valencia with the theoretical background for what Woolf was attempting to achieve in *BTA*: to forge a new voice that would enrich prose with the figurative density of poetry and the iconicity of drama. It is because Luz Valencia believes that Woolf found this voice in her last novel that she dismisses the hypothesis that the English writer might have committed suicide for fear of losing her creative powers.

The long and laborious passage

1983 witnessed the launching of another journal, *Andaina*, which was then the flagship publication of the feminist movement and is now subtitled 'Revista galega do pensamento feminista' (Galician Journal of Feminist Thought). Published three times a year, *Andaina* has also provided a forum for the discussion of Woolf's work and ideas. One frequent contributor, Carme Corbalán, has taken issue with Woolf's very influential essay 'Women Novelists' (1918) whose essentialist assertions about the nature of women's writing the Galician critic calls into question. Corbalán quotes Woolf's polemical affirmation: 'Each sex describes itself. The first words in which either a man or a woman is described are generally enough to determine the sex of the writer'[6] (*CW* 1976, 26). Though Corbalán (1988) accepts that one's life experience will affect one's literary output, she rejects the equivalence of sex, gender and way of writing. Rather than a difference in the style of male and female writers, she opts for a difference along the lines of empowering and disempowering positions. From its start, feminism has fought the determinism of sex and the fact that biological features should determine our opportunities in life. However, in my opinion, what remains at issue is the extent to which

---

5 For further information on Ana María Navales see the chapter by María José Gámez Fuentes in this volume.

6 The source most often mentioned by Galician critics when referring to 'Women Novelists' is *W&W*, translated as *Las mujeres y la literatura* (1981b) with a much-quoted introduction by Michèle Barret.

we can disengage the woman's body from the cultural meanings with which it has been invested.

On the fiftieth aniversary of Woolf's death, Corbalán (1991a) wrote another article in which she discusses Woolf's important contribution to feminist literary criticism and where she claims that Woolf's essays are more accessible than her fiction, something which may have contributed to their popularity among feminists. Although Corbalán praises Woolf's commitment to freedom of expression – and she refers to the writer's support for the publication of *The Well of Loneliness* – she is also critical of other aspects of her thought: 'Artistic integrity, according to V. Woolf's theoretical propositions, excludes the possibility of the explicit handling of political issues, including women's issues. There was a time when ideas like this contributed to the dismissal of Woolf's work in feminist circles' (1991a, 46).[7] Corbalán refers here to the 'flaw in the centre' which Woolf identifies in those women writers' work where anger and indignation come up to the surface, an idea that she discusses in *ROO* (1992a, 96). Although this proposition interestingly develops into Woolf's advocacy of the artist's androgynous mind, it is in itself a controversial issue that has provoked, and will continue to provoke, many heated arguments.

Both *ROO* and 'Women Novelists' are the starting point for another interesting article by Corbalán on feminism and the feminine novel (1996). The coordinates that Woolf identified as necessary for creative writing (i.e. space and time of one's own, as well as economic independence) had also been noted by the Galician writer Emilia Pardo Bazán (1851–1921) who, in her book *La cuestión palpitante* (The Burning Question) (1883), devoted a chapter to the English novel where she highlighted the large number of 'institutrices e pedagogas' (governesses and pedagogues) (quoted in Corbalán, 1996, 19) among the British women novelists of the late eighteenth and early nineteenth centuries. But the main body of Corbalán's article is concerned with Woolf's assertion that from the difference between man's and woman's perspective 'spring not only marked differences of plot and incident, but infinite differences in selection, method and style' (*CW* 1976, 27). The Galician critic regrets Woolf's elusiveness when tackling this thorny issue, so she turns to Biruté Ciplijauskaité (1988) to complement Woolf's propositions. The predominant use of the first person and interior monologue, as well as the challenge to linear time, stylistic experimentation and lyricism are some of the formal devices identified by Ciplijauskaité. As for the subject matter in novels by women, she mentions, among others, emancipation, education, motherhood, the vindication of eroticism and the psychoanalytic split of the 'I'.

'Tempo de silencio' (Time of Silence) by Sabela Álvarez Núñez begins with

---

[7] 'A integridade artística, nos plantexamentos teóricos de V. Woolf, exclúe a posibilidade dun tratamento explícito de cuestións políticas, mesmo a da situación da muller. Estes elementos contribuíron, no seu momento, a que se rexeitara desde círculos feministas a valía da súa obra'. In an analysis of the Victorian ghosts in Woolf's work, María V. Rodríguez García claims that this British writer could not be corrosive in her critique of Victorian society because she was attached to a past that she needed to preserve (1992, 20).

a couplet from a poem by Xohana Torres: 'My mother's eyes ... without them/my history has no eyes' (1999, 45) and is a detailed analysis of *ROO*.[8] In it the critic gives some dates which provide a timeline for women's access to higher education in Spain and which can be fruitfully compared with those mentioned in *ROO*. If Woolf affirms that 'there have been at least two colleges for women in existence in England since the year 1866' (*ROO* 1992, 147), in Spain the official date for women's access to the university is 1910. In Galicia the first two women to obtain a university degree graduate in 1919 and it is not until 1924 that the first female lecturer joins the University of Santiago de Compostela.

The topic of chastity and its imprint on women's literature is explored by Carmen Blanco in her comparison of *ROO* and Rosalía de Castro's prologue to *La hija del mar* (*Daughter of the Sea*) from 1859. If Woolf denounces the perverse reasons for the invention of the fetish of chastity, Rosalía de Castro playfully identifies with a fallen woman who cannot control her lust for publishing a new book: 'Once the first step is taken, the next are born from it, because this road to ruin is covered all too quickly.'[9]

The impact of Virginia Woolf on Galician feminism can be best illustrated by Carmen Blanco's book *Literatura galega da muller* (Galician Women's Literature) (1991) where Woolf's name appears in the back cover blurb, in the prologue, in epigraphs for several chapters and throughout the introduction, which pays homage to 'Woolf's intellectual and vital attitude'.[10] Blanco is a lecturer in Galician language and literature at the University of Santiago de Compostela in the city of Lugo. She is a leading participant in the Galician feminist movement and has helped promote women's cultural journals such as *Festa da palabra silenciada*. Her book analyses the literary production of Galician women writers in the nineteenth and twentieth centuries and makes use of the tools provided by gynocriticism and feminist literary criticism. The main sources for her references to Woolf are Spanish translations of *WD* (*Diario de una escritora*) (1981a), *O* (*Orlando*) (1977), *W&W* (*Las mujeres y la literatura*) (1981b), and *ROO* (*Una habitación propia*) (1980) as well as a study that has been very influential in Spanish translation: Herbert Marder's *Feminism and Art* (*Feminismo y arte: un estudio sobre Virginia Woolf*) (trans. 1979), probably the first book about Woolf that many of us read in Spain.

The introduction presents a summary of some of Woolf's main concerns: the multiplicity of identity and the dialectic synthesis of opposites (the material

---

8 'Ollos da miña nai ... sen eles,/a miña historia non ten ollos'.

9 'Dado el primer paso, los demás son hijos de él, porque esta senda de perdición se recorre muy pronto' (quoted in Blanco 1990, 30).

10 This book was reviewed by Carme Corbalán, who argues that one must view Woolf's ideas about the feminine sentence in the context of a whole generation of both male and female writers who were experimenting with language (1991b, 50). Xosé M. Salgado (1993) also reviewed this book and remarked on the recurrent references to Woolf, allusions that he considers necessary and illuminating given that Blanco's research aims to provide the sociological context explaining the marginalization of texts by Galician women writers.

and the spiritual, the rational and the intuitive, the analytical and the poetical, the masculine and the feminine). Woolf's experimentation with time is seen to be at the heart of many of her innovative narrative devices. Woolf's feminism is described as having a philosophical rather than a political basis. *ROO* and *W&W* are recurrently quoted when discussing the search for a feminine language and the need to break with the masculine sentence – a language made and moulded by a masculine cultural tradition. The difference between male and female writers is not seen as lying in their respective choice of subject matter but in their attitude towards what is considered serious or trivial. Future women novelists might do well to implement a carnivalesque reversal of these conventional hierarchies. This subversion, however, may run the risk of releasing too much anger, or, on the contrary, the writer may opt to enter the public world of literature wearing a mask of modesty and docility.

But the construction of a feminine language, though a necessary step, is not the ultimate goal for Woolf, and it is for this reason that, according to Blanco:

> [Woolf] goes further, moving beyond materialist arguments towards speculative and utopian ones. Thus, she sees it as imperative to overcome the limitations of one's sex ... in order to implement a really free type of writing, writing that flows naturally from one's own self, without self-repression in its adjustment to masculine culture, but also without resentment or excessive compensatory self-assertion. For Virginia, non-sexist writing has to free itself from sex without denying it. (1991, 22–23)[11]

It is within the context of the rise of feminism, pacifism and anti-Fascism between the two World Wars that Blanco places Woolf's *TG* in her next book *O contradiscurso das mulleres: historia do feminismo* (Women's Counter-discourse: History of Feminism) (1994). Only through the cross-fertilization of these three discourses can one oppose the institutional domination of the 'warrior' model which structures both public and private worlds and which brings about the oppression of women.[12] Blanco highlights Woolf's integrating and connective vision, which has proved inspirational for more recent literary critics such as Teresa de Lauretis, Nancy Armstrong and Susan Kirkpatrick, who openly acknowledge their debt to Virginia Woolf: 'Undoubtedly, she was the mother of us all. Even though many of her daughters denied her later' (Blanco 1994, 205).[13]

---

11 '[Woolf] vai máis alá, dando un salto das argumentacións de tipo materialista ás de tipo especulativo e utópico. Así, postula o imperativo da superación dos condicionantes do propio sexo ... en condicións de exercer a auténtica escritura en liberdade, a escritura que parte con naturalidade do propio eu, sen autorepresión asimilativa á cultura masculina, máis tamén sen resentimento e sen unha excesiva autoafirmación compensatoria. Para Virginia, a escritura non sexista ten que liberarse do sexo, pero sen negalo.'

12 This book was reviewed by María Xosé Agra (1995), who stressed Blanco's debt to Virginia Woolf.

13 'Sen dúbida, ela foi a nai de todas. Aínda que logo moitas das súas fillas a negasen.'

Lady Woolf in Compostela

Every Woolf scholar knows that she first came to Spain in 1905 and then again on her honeymoon, when she visited Catalonia, Aragón and Castile.[14] Later, in 1923, she also travelled to South-eastern Spain on her visit to Gerald Brenan. In fiction, however, she also stayed in Santiago de Compostela and during her visit wrote, in Galician, the short story 'Os amantes de Sant Iago' (The Lovers of Saint James). This story was published as part of a novel by Ramón Otero Pedrayo and, if it is a good example of the embedded structure of fiction within fiction, the same fictionality applies to its author, 'Lady Woolf', a British writer who comes to Santiago de Compostela in search of inspiration.

Ramón Otero Pedrayo was a member of the *Xeración Nós* (Generation 'Ourselves'), a name that alludes to the Irish Sinn Féin ('Ourselves alone'). This group of Galician writers, between the years 1920 and 1936, attempted to renovate Galician literature by studying the high points of its tradition together with contemporary European literary movements. They published a journal, *A Revista Nós* (The 'Ourselves' Review), which, in the section dealing with international literature, reviewed work by Proust, Gide, Conrad, Rilke, Malraux, Joyce, Faulkner, Bergson, Baudelaire, et al. Nationalism was an important concern for these Galician writers, who often turned to Irish literature in their search for common Celtic roots as well as in their identification with the Irish struggle to create a nation-state.

Otero Pedrayo's *Devalar* (Flowing) was published by Editorial Nós in 1935 at the height of the movement for Galician nationalism, a process that would be dramatically brought to an end by the outbreak of the Spanish Civil War in 1936. The novel describes the intellectual atmosphere of the period and also illustrates the close identification of the Galician people with their landscape through the passing of the four seasons which structures the text. The title of the novel already suggests a similarity in subject matter between Otero Pedrayo and Woolf: the continuous flux of time, the course of history, together with the capture and transfixion of the moment.[15]

The first group of chapters, set in the autumn of 1934, begins with a story involving an elderly woman's memories and anxieties: 'If we knew how to shape her dreams we would complete the book', wrote Otero Pedrayo elsewhere in another parallel with Woolf's association of fiction writing with

---

14 For further information on Woolf's travels in Spain see the chapters by Alberto Lázaro and Laura Lojo in this volume.

15 In María do Carme Ríos Panisse's introduction to the 1992 reprint of Otero Pedrayo's novel, she refers to his interest in Bergson's philosophy of temporal flux and repudiation of comparisons between past, present and future (10). In the appendix (312), Ríos Panisse reveals that Otero Pedrayo had, in his library, two texts by Woolf published in French before 1935: *La Promenade au phare* (*TL*) (1929), and *Orlando* (1931). She therefore argues that he was acquainted with contemporary British fiction through French translations.

the imaginative recreation of an unknown woman's interior life.[16] This set of chapters ends with 'Orballeira na rúa' (Drizzle in the Street), a section where the city plays a similar role to that of Dublin in *Ulysses* or London in *MD*, i.e. highlighting the collective protagonism of city dwellers. The city in *Devalar* is Santiago de Compostela and one of its streets, Rúa Nova (New Street), brings together characters from all social classes: young maidservants, a bartender, a clergyman, the Galician nobility, a carpenter, etc., as well as two other characters who appear again later in the novel: Martiño Dumbría, who could be interestingly compared and contrasted with Stephen Dedalus, and Lady Woolf, a British writer who comes to Santiago aware of the city's cultural weight within Europe. The British writer is described in terms that make her recognizable as a fictional recreation of Virginia Woolf: 'In the middle of the group Lady Woolf, a white and vigorous woman: summers in the Hebrides . . . is embarked on the ship of the hour. It awakens long echoes in her soul calling her down the intense avenues of her inner garden' (Otero Pedrayo 1992, 115–16).[17] Apart from the reference to *TL*, there seems to be no doubt that Otero Pedrayo was acquainted with Woolf's hour imagery as well as with her interest in portraying the workings of the mind. There is also an overt allusion to Woolf's biography and her fictional explorations of the sudden and unexpected truncation of any promising life in the comment 'the company of Death is to her the melancholy call of Life' (Otero Pedrayo 1992, 118).[18]

As she travels in Galicia, Lady Woolf writes about it as the Atlantic Celtic Arcadia that Otero Pedrayo himself contributed towards constructing in his writings. In her notes she likes to include quotations in Greek, while she contrasts the melodious, reflective and creative Galician language with uncouth and harsh Castilian Spanish (Otero Pedrayo 1992, 119–20). She succeeds in identifying the key to Galician history, which she intends to present as intuitive history in an alternative genre to that of erudite research. But this is a book that she will carefully elaborate in the refuge of her home 'in the fog of millions of lives and fumes in enormous London' (121).[19] Nevertheless, as we learn in a later chapter, Miss Woolf apparently spends that winter writing a 'psychoanalytical' novel, the tediousness of which Otero Pedrayo describes by means of the moth imagery that is so recurrent in Woolf's writing: 'she flitted on the frozen typography like a moth on the marble argument of a mausoleum' (187).[20] Annoyed with herself for wasting her time

---

16 'Se souberamos dar forma ós seus soños teriamos feito o libro' (quoted in Ríos Panisse 1992, 12).

17 'No centro do grupo Lady Woolf, branca e rexa dona: veráns nas Hébridas . . . camiña embarcada na nau da hora. Na súa alma resoa longamente chamándoa para as intensas avenidas do xardín interior.'

18 'A compaña da Morte é para ela saudoso chamamento de Vida.'

19 'na néboa de millóns de vidas e fumes, do Londres enorme.'

20 'Choutaba na xeada tipografía como unha voíña no argumento marmóreo dun mausoleo.' Otero Pedrayo now refers not to Lady Woolf but to Miss Woolf. Ríos Panisse explains that the chapter 'Orballeira na rúa' where Woolf is first mentioned was written in 1933 and was later added to the novel, so he may have changed her title inadvertently (1992, 186). As for the 'psychoanalytical' novel that Miss Woolf

– and she is thirty-eight already – she rushes out into the streets of London and finally enters Westminster Abbey: 'Why does it always seem that it is autumn in churches? And she was reminded of another autumn and of another shadow. How would it flow, the sound from the high tower in Sant Iago?'(188).[21] As in Woolf's narrative, the flow of consciousness from one thought, time and space to another parallels the dissolution of the sound waves after the clock strikes the hour. It is this memory of Santiago de Compostela that stirs her creative imagination finally to write her story about Galicia.

The following chapter in *Devalar* is 'Os Amantes de Sant Iago, novela por Miss Agnés Woolf' (The Lovers of Saint James: A Novel by Miss Agnes Woolf).[22] The story is not easily recognizable as one by Virginia Woolf, except for the love plot with a tragic end and the demise of the female protagonist, who has come to Santiago on her voyage out from the United States. Otero Pedrayo's style has some affinities with Virginia Woolf's: both have been characterized as impressionistic and I would also stress the overt metafictionality, the challenge to the convention of the authorial narrator who guides the reader, as well as the juxtaposition of situations, speeches, times and spaces which breaks the linear narrative. Ríos Panisse identifies in this story a certain element of parody through which Otero Pedrayo regards his own writing and ideals from a critical distance (1992, 57-59), a type of parody not unlike that found in *O* (207).[23] It is vital to highlight that the Galician writer is not ridiculing Woolf's style or ideology, but interrogating his own romantic idealism, the forms and contents of romantic aesthetics. The author splits his personality in a way that resembles James Joyce's strategy with Stephen Dedalus, the main difference being that Otero Pedrayo constructs a feminine double, which, in my opinion, makes the parodic intention more problematic.

---

cont.
is writing, there may be a reference here either to passages in Virginia Woolf's novels like the beginning of *TL*, where James's feelings towards his father enact the Oedipus conflict, or to the psychological novel in general in which both Woolf and Otero Pedrayo read widely. Micaela Misiego identifies both Bergson and William James as the 'creators of the intellectual atmosphere which produced the subjective novel' ('os creadores da atmósfera inteleitual que produciu a novela subxetiva') (1969, 264). In this article, Misiego is also at pains to dispel the confusion around the term 'stream of consciousness' which, unlike 'interior monologue', she does not consider to be a technique. It is precisely Woolf's apt combination of both direct and indirect interior monologue which, for Misiego, identifies her as a writer of 'psychological novels'.

21 '¿Por que sempre figura ser outono nas eirexas? E lembrouse doutro outono e doutra sombra. ¿Como devalaría o son da torre grande de Sant Iago?'

22 There also seems to be a certain fluidity in this British writer's identity; her name acquires more associations as the novel advances. The much discussed tension between first and last name in Virginia Woolf is made ironically explicit in the lamb (Agnes)-Woolf oxymoron. As for the genre of this narrative, Miss Woolf's story is certainly a very short one, so the term 'novel' can only be understood as 'novella'.

23 Ríos Panisse also makes a very important contribution to Woolf studies in her comparison of many of Virginia Woolf's motifs with those used by Lucile and François de Chateaubriand as well as by Goethe (1992, 191–92, 196).

As for references to Woolf in contemporary creative writing, it is worth mentioning some Galician women writers of the 1980s and 1990s. Pilar Pallarés (1984) accompanies her poems with quotations from Woolf's texts. Her introspection and validation of ordinary experience reveal her links with a long feminine literary tradition. Another writer, Ana Romaní, acknowledges in an interview that 'Simone de Beauvoir and Virginia Woolf are indispensable references in my literary training and in my intellectual orientation' (quoted in Rodríguez and Seara 1997, 25). Like Woolf, Romaní exploits the ambivalent symbol of the sea, which is a source of life and permanence, but may also engulf us and reveal that death awaits us. Both find in the work of art the only hope for transcendence, for victory over the fragility and transitoriness of life. Both question language, the paradigm and patriarchal poetics. Both vindicate lyrical expression as a mark of gender, 'a dialogue with another feminine poetics in search of that hidden countenance of history' (quoted in Rodríguez and Seara 1997, 25).[24]

But it is not only in literature that one can trace Virginia Woolf's presence. Galician painting features one polyptych by Dolores Padín (1946–) with the title *Vida, Muerte y Resurrección de Virginia Woolf* (Life, Death and Resurrection of Virginia Woolf), on which the painter worked during her stay in Rome in the years 1978–79. The polyptych has ten panels of different size in which Padín interprets the myth of the British writer in small sequences around the central panel, 'the most significant in this work, showing the moment in which the writer is about to drown in the river waters in her search for the lost light of reason, only to emerge later all radiant and luminous' (Sobrino Manzanares, 1974).[25] Rich gradations of colour, veils and transparencies produce a dreamlike effect perfectly suited to this recreation of Woolf's life.

The Lighthouse in *finis terrae*

So far, only one of Woolf's books, *TL* (1993), has been translated into Galician.[26] Although the Galician language is nowadays spoken by approximately three million people and is regularly used by 67 per cent of the population, the literary market for translations is difficult. The fact that a very large proportion of the population of the region were unable to learn Galician at school, because this only became common practice after the implementation of the democratic Spanish Constitution of 1978, makes it easier for many people to read translations into Spanish. Galician publishers therefore opt for translating texts that may be of interest to younger people either because they are part of their secondary school courses or because they are the kind of

---

24 'o diálogo con outras poéticas de mulleres na procura dese rostro oculto da historia.'

25 I would like to thank Helena González Fernández for drawing my attention to this painting.

26 Virginia Woolf's story 'Kew Gardens' has also been translated into Galician, quite recently, by Ana Belén López Pérez as part of a collection of stories by women writers in English (Woolf 1999, 29–37).

popular fiction that attracts most young people, i.e. adventure, thrillers and science fiction. Publishers may also fear that a contemporary audience will not sympathize with, or even understand, British modernist experimentation from the 1920s.

Despite the above-mentioned difficulties, my colleague Xavier Castro and I approached several publishers with the idea of translating a work by Virginia Woolf into Galician. Most expressed interest, but regretted that it was too great an economic risk. Only Sotelo Blanco accepted the challenge and, although we had had Woolf's short narrative in mind, we were asked to translate *TL* instead. The importance and popularity of this novel were no doubt the main bait for the publishers, even though there was also one cause for concern: the novel had already been translated into Spanish by, among others, the well known woman writer, Carmen Martín Gaite, and the popularity of both the writer and her translation might direct many Galician readers to the Spanish version.

My colleague and I opted for fidelity to modernist experimentation with style and narrative devices for the following three reasons:

1. The reader of the translation should go through a decoding process as similar as possible to that undergone by the reader of the original.
2. Woolf's transgressions of standard literary style contribute to the 'literariness' of her narrative. Correcting her deviations undermines the 'literariness' of the text.
3. Modernist transgressions often call our attention to the text's artificiality and break the naturalistic illusion; in other words, the conventional relationship between language and reality is challenged. Modifying transgressions contravenes the modernist claim to expose such arbitrariness in representation.

Thus, there are two main temptations that the translator should resist: 'explaining', rather than translating, the transgressions and 'correcting' those deviations that may look or sound odd.

There are four main levels of discourse where Woolf's deviations may lure the translator away from the original: register, syntax, lexicon and punctuation. I would like to discuss the last, at first sight the most inoffensive level. There are in *TL* occasional examples of free direct discourse in which the character's words are not introduced with a reporting clause (she wondered, he exclaimed, etc.) and are not marked by inverted commas, but only by a capital letter. In this way, the narrator's and the character's words are intermingled and the narrative achieves a polyphonic effect that privileges no voice in particular. If the translator opens a new paragraph and uses the dashes that are normally employed in Galician texts to mark the characters' direct discourse, we eliminate one obstacle to the reader's decoding process, but we also do away with the theoretical point that such ambiguous polyphony wants to make.[27]

---

27 The following passage might exemplify this question: 'They needed his protection;

If Galician readers turn to the Spanish translation of *TL* by the writer Carmen Martín Gaite, they will find an exceedingly well-written book. Her translation may be more flexible than ours with regard to the modernist experimentation mentioned above, but what is lost in fidelity is more than gained in the authenticity of its Spanish style: *TL* is not merely translated but recreated. One device that contributes to the authenticity of idiom is the frequent use of pleonasm (i.e. redundancy), which, though it adds unnecessary information, well suits an everyday Spanish register. In this way, 'when it was ever so much nicer to be alone' (*TL* 1992, 10) is translated into 'spoiling their pleasure in being alone *and at peace*' (my translation and emphasis) (*Al faro* (*TL*) 1978, 12).[28] The use of this type of pleonasm is especially apt in passages that convey the characters' conversational tone.

I would like to complete my overview of the reception of Virginia Woolf's work in Galicia with some references to academic research. Much of this research, although published in Galicia, was written in Spanish, and some was written in Galician or in English depending on publishers' linguistic policies. The first doctoral dissertation on Virginia Woolf written in Spain was actually read at the University of Santiago in 1974 by Manuel Míguez Ben, now a lecturer in English literature at this same university. His thesis, which analyses the structure of *MD*, *TL* and *TW* and establishes rather elaborate patterns

---

cont.

he gave it them. But after Q? What comes next? After Q there are a number of letters the last of which is scarcely visible to mortal eyes, but glimmers red in the distance' (*TL* 1992b, 47). Our translation maintains the free direct discourse of the above passage by not supplying the reporting clause or the quotation marks, and by keeping the present tense: 'Precisaban da súa protección; el dáballela. Pero ¿e despóis do Q? ¿Que vén? Despóis do Q hai unha serie de letras, a última delas a penas visible ós ollos dos mortais, pero que brilla vermella ó lonxe' (*Cara ó faro* (*TL*) 1993, 43). For further examples of both theoretical and practical issues raised by our translation see Palacios González 1996a and 1999a. For a detailed analysis of the first two pages of an unpublished draft of our text see Francisco Xabier Fernández Polo's translation of Peter Newmark's *A Textbook of Translation*, where Fernández Polo uses our text in order to illustrate Newmark's methodology (Newmark 1993, 384–387). Our translation of *TL* was also chosen for the corpus and database used in Alberto Álvarez Lugrís's doctoral dissertation (supervised by Senior Lecturer María Dolores Gómez Penas) on comparative stylistics as a tool for descriptive translation studies (1999). *Cara ó faro* was also positively reviewed in two cultural journals (Álvarez Lugrís 1994, Gómez Clemente 1994).

28 'estropeándoles el placer de estar solos y en paz' (*Al faro* (*TL*) 1978, 12). Other examples of pleonasm are: 'which an old woman could take from a young man without loss of dignity' (*TL* 1992, 11) which Martín Gaite translates into 'que *viniendo como venía* de chicos jóvenes, una mujer de cierta edad podía aceptar sin *el menor* desdoro de su dignidad' [my italics] (*Al faro* (*TL*) 1978, 13) ('which coming as it came [i.e. did] from young men, a woman of a certain age could accept without the slightest loss of dignity') or also 'a mute questioning of deference and chivalry' (*TL* 1992b, 11) which is in Spanish 'un sordo recelo hacia *todo lo que tuviera que ver con* la caballerosidad, la deferencia' [my italics] (*Al faro* (*TL*) 1978, 13) ('a mute resentment towards anything to do with chivalry, deference').

regarding themes, characters, plot and point of view, is representative of the structuralist concerns of English studies in this period.[29] Míguez Ben also supervised my doctoral dissertation on the visual imagery in Virginia Woolf's narrative, where I analyse how her acquaintance with contemporary debates in the visual arts influenced her perception of earlier periods, styles and artistic movements. Her own position as an outsider in the field of art criticism, however, gave her some autonomy to explore the ideological and narrative concerns that were excluded from the predominantly formalist criticism of her time (Palacios González 1992).[30]

I have attempted to cross the chasm between two cultures. Galicia's cultural capital has been augmented by Virginia Woolf's writings, which in turn have gained by their integration into one of the cradles of European lyrical literature. In this appropriation of Woolf's work some distortion may have been inevitable. In Auden's words, 'The words of a dead man/Are modified in the guts of the living' (1966, 141).[31] But the process through which new meanings may be acquired by means of this type of *translatio* lies, after all, at the heart of Virginia Woolf's project.

---

29 A good example of the structuralist approach followed in this dissertation is the following commentary:

> The cohesion of the different levels in the stratification of both importance and extension regarding the presentation of the central character in *MD* is less clear and less successful in *TL*, where Mr Ramsay seems to be the protagonist of the novel if we consider both intention and end of the novel, but he is not the protagonist throughout the novel, since the other two members of the central triad are superimposed by Virginia Woolf and end up blurring the philosopher's protagonist role in the readers' minds' ('la cohesión de los diferentes niveles de estratificación de importancia y extensión de la presentación del personaje central de *MD* es menos clara y está menos conseguida en *TL*, en donde Mr Ramsay parece ser el protagonista de la novela por la intención y final de ésta, pero no a lo largo de su desarrollo, ya que los otros dos miembros de la tríada central son superpuestos por Virginia Woolf y acaban oscureciendo el papel del filósofo de protagonista de la novela cara al lector') (Míguez Ben, 1974, 18).

30 Other publications in Galicia where I further explore the topic of Woolf's pictorial allusions are Palacios González, 1990, 1996b and 1999b. For a feminist analysis of female characters in Woolf's narrative see Barbeito, Blanco and Palacios 1996, and Barbeito 1999.

Manuel Míguez Ben also supervised my MA dissertation (Palacios González 1982) and Laura Lojo's doctoral dissertation on Virginia Woolf's short stories. Besides this and her MA dissertation (Lojo 1997c), Lojo has also published on Woolf in Galicia (see 1997a, 1997b, 1997d, 1998a, 1998b).

31 From 'In Memory of W.B. Yeats'. I would like to thank Carmen Ríos for her help with the documentation for this chapter and the Galician government for their help in funding my research.

16 Modernism, Nationalism and Feminism: Representations of Virginia Woolf in Catalonia

Jacqueline A. Hurtley

Virginia Woolf's writing has occupied no mean place within the cultural production of Catalonia over the last seventy years. It began with Cèsar-August Jordana's translation of *MD* in 1930 and continued into the year 2000 with an exhibition devoted to the writer and her work at the Centre de Cultura Contemporània in Barcelona.[1]

Woolf's writing has signified both appeal and desire. In the period between the Wars,[2] there was, on the one hand, the attraction of the distinguished avant-garde practitioner and, on the other, the will to appropriate both the novelty and distinction for the vernacular struggling to come into its own.[3] In this connection, moreover, Woolf might be seen as one among other contemporary British novelists of repute whose texts were translated or referred to at the time with a view to modernizing and internationalizing Catalan culture.[4] Cases in point were Aldous Huxley, Margaret Kennedy, D.H. Lawrence, Rosamond Lehmann, Mary Webb and H.G. Wells. More recently, translations of Woolf's work and the critical consideration of it have been filtered through a feminist lens, positioned by Catalan women writers, though Woolf's aesthetic contribution within the group identity of Bloomsbury has also been explored.

---

1 The exhibition was held from 18 April until 28 May 2000.

2 I am, of course, referring to the two World Wars.

3 Catalan orthography underwent modernization under the auspices of the Institut d'Estudis Catalans (Institute of Catalan Studies) headed by Pompeu Fabra [i Poch] (1868–1948). The *Normes ortogràfiques* were published in 1913. The development of the language was interrupted by censorship imposed in the wake of General Primo de Rivera's coup in 1923. His dictatorship lasted until 1930.

4 See Fuster 1980.

The arrival of *Mrs Dalloway*: Badalona 1930

MD did not arrive unaccompanied or simply by accident. Woolf's fourth novel was brought into Catalonia as part of a publishing project undertaken by Marcel lí Antich [i Camprubí] (1895–1968) and Josep Queralt [i Clapés] (1896–1965), that is, Edicions Proa,[5] which was based in Queralt's hometown, Badalona, today part of post-Olympic Barcelona. Proa (Prow) was designed to promote a rise of the novel in Catalan following its low ebb during the Noucentista period when the novel was frowned upon.[6] At the height of Noucentisme, there was what the Catalan critic Albert Manent has referred to as: 'a really odd bias against the novel'; the genre was considered 'clumsy, underdeveloped, unsatisfactory' (1984, 184);[7] the British Hispanist Alan Yates has also analysed the roots of the rejection, claiming: 'The novel became a symbol of the values which had been rejected by the Noucentista movement: spontaneity and sincerity, energy, humour in contrast to irony, an interest in the human' (1984, 148).[8] As the Noucentista movement declined, then, the novel rose and Proa was a product, in 1928, of the new surge of interest in the novel on the part of writers and readers. Proa took on the publication of Catalan authors, both canonical and emerging, as well as the translation of established nineteenth-century foreign classics, such as Balzac, Dickens, Dostoievsky and Tolstoy, alongside the contemporary: André Gide, Aldous Huxley, Margaret Kennedy and Virginia Woolf. Hence, as the Valencian critic Joan Fuster remarked: 'With Edicions Proa the Catalan novel market began to be consolidated' (1980, 245).[9]

In an interesting volume of comment and criticism published in 1936, *Lectures europées* (European Readings), the Catalan critic Ramon Esquerra [i Clivillés] (1909–38) referred to English literature as producing the most interesting new authors.[10] Already in 1934, the Catalan translator of *MD*, Cèsar-August Jordana, had revealed his knowledge of, and particular interest in, English literature with his *Resum de literatura anglesa* (A Summary of English Literature).[11] In the same year Catalan poet and translator Marià Manent would publish his *Notes sobre*

---

5 From now on Proa.

6 The Noucentista period was between 1911 and 1925. Its leading ideologue was Eugeni D'Ors i Rovira, also known as Xènius, a journalist and novelist. Aesthetically, the movement revived classical forms and saw the city as encompassing culture. For more information on D'Ors and Noucentisme, see Jardí 1967.

7 'una veritable i curiosa prevenció contra la novel.la'; 'matusser, poc elaborat, insatisfactori'.

8 'El gènere novel.lesc esdevé un símbol dels valors rebutjats pel Noucentisme: espontaneïtat i sinceritat, vigor, humor en oposició a la ironia, interés per l'humà.'

9 'Amb Edicions Proa el mercat català de la novel.la començava a consolidar-se.'

10 'De totes les literatures contemporànies, la més rica en novel.listes interessants és l'anglesa' (Esquerra 1936, 111). Esquerra was a well-informed critic; he died in the Ebro Battle during the Spanish Civil War in 1938.

11 Jordana's summary did not carry any reference to contemporary writing except to G. B. Shaw, given the reputation he had acquired with his plays (Jordana 1934, 123–24).

literatura estrangera (Notes on Foreign Literature) where he would mention a number of new writers – Winifred Holtby, Rosamond Lehmann and Mary Webb – who would be first translated into Castilian Spanish after the Civil War (1936–39) by the pioneer publisher in postwar Spain the Catalan Josep Janés [i Olivé] (transformed into José Janés with a view to adapting his identity to the post-Civil War regime imposed by General Franco).[12] Cèsar-August Jordana [i Mayans] (Barcelona 1893- Buenos Aires 1958), who would become the Argentinian translator of Aldous Huxley during his lifelong exile following the Civil War, had published six novels in Catalan when his rendering of *MD* into the language was brought out in 1930. He was an engineer by profession but came to devote his energies to journalism, the correcting of Catalan texts for the Generalitat de Catalunya (the autonomous Catalan government), translating from English into Catalan, and his own creative writing.[13] Moreover, the influence of contemporary authors writing in English has been detected by critics in two of his works: that of D. H. Lawrence in *Una mena d'amor* (1931) (A Kind of Love)[14] and James Joyce in *El món de Joan Ferrer* (posthumously published in 1971) (The World of John Ferrer). Defined by Alan Yates as a 'young disciple of Noucentisme' (1984, 174),[15] it is relevant to note here that Jordana had lamented over the poor quality of the novel in Catalan.[16] Translating could be a means, therefore, of contributing to raising local standards, of informing, and being informed, with regards to means and mode.

Jordana's translation of *MD* has been labelled 'a model' ('modèlica') by the Catalan writer and critic Marta Pessarrodona (1982, 37) and 'splendid' ('esplèndida') by the Catalan lawyer, critic and biographer Enric Jardí (1986). It may be said to produce a certain degree of accuracy and the text may read well in Catalan but I do not think the translation merits the very positive assessment it has been awarded. Comparison with the original reveals some negligence, some insensitivity to Woolf's method as well as a failure to find appropriate stylistic equivalence. In order to illustrate my point and for the sake of concision, I shall, in all but one case, limit my examples to the first two blocks of narrative in *MD*, which take fifty-two-year-old Clarissa Dalloway out into the London streets and home again on that Wednesday morning in June 1923.

Translating is always a challenging task and particularly so if the original text is subverting established boundaries. A modernist novel presents particular difficulties given the interiorization inherent to stream of consciousness technique, and it will become inevitably more so if the technique is unfamiliar.

---

12 *José* is the Castilian Spanish of the Catalan forename *Josep*. For more information on the publisher Janés, see Hurtley 1983, 1986 and 1992.

13 For more information on Jordana, see the publication brought out on the occasion of the centenary of his birth: *Centenari C.A. Jordana (1893–1993)*.

14 In connection with Lawrence, see Campillo 1977, 107–09.

15 'jove deixeble del Noucentisme.'

16 In this connection, Yates refers to Jordana's article 'Excursió de plaer pels camins de la prosa' (A Pleasurable Outing along the Paths of Prose) published in *La Revista* in 1925 (Yates 1984, 174–75 and 244).

In correspondence with the painter Jacques Raverat towards the end of writing *MD*, Woolf claimed that it was: 'the task of the writer to go beyond the "formal railway line of sentence"' and to show how people 'feel or think or dream ... all over the place' (quoted in Lee 1977, 93). Jordana does tend to take the reader back to the nineteenth-century railway line; he makes Woolf's text conform to established narrative modes, apparently not alive to what the writer is about. Thus, in the interior monologue contained in the first long paragraph of the text, Clarissa muses on Peter Walsh's return from India: 'He would be back one of *these* days' (*MD* 1987, 5). The free indirect speech is made closer to indirect speech by Jordana, who translates: 'Tornaria un d'*aquells* [those] dies' (*Mrs Dalloway* (*MD*) 1930, 5). Similarly, a little later in the text: '*this* moment of June' (6) becomes: '*aquell* [that] moment de juny' (7) and 'on a morning like *this*' (8) is rendered: 'un matí com *aquell* [that]' (10). This would seem to illustrate Jordana's obliviousness to what Woolf is attempting to do, that is, to reproduce the intimacy and immediacy of the character's thought process. Furthermore, an instance of free direct speech is transformed into more direct speech through the introduction of punctuation and capitalization, destroying the flowing representation of thought achieved in the original. '[B]ut suddenly it would come over *her*, if he were *with me* now what would he say?' (8) is reproduced as: 'però de sobte s'acudia a *Clarissa*: Si ell fos ací, ara, què diria?' (10). The reader will notice in the earlier example which begins: '[B]ut suddenly' that Jordana has also omitted 'with me' and replaced the object pronoun 'her' by the proper name 'Clarissa'. The substitution of the pronoun form employed by Woolf in reproducing the flow of thought in her main character's mind by 'Clarissa' is ubiquitous in the Catalan translation. Thus, the translator takes on the role of guide, apparently anxious that the reader should not confuse identities or feel disconcerted.[17] In the paragraph just quoted from, Clarissa Dalloway is recalling memories of Peter Walsh, and Peter is named three times in the paragraph. Jordana will add two more mentions by name: 'It was the state of the world that interested *him*; ... she had the makings of the perfect hostess, *he* said' (8–9) become: 'El que interessava a *Pere* [Peter] era l'estat del món ... tenia vocació d'hostessa perfecta, deia *Pere* [Peter]' (10–11). Another striking example of Jordana's concern to lead the reader lest he/she stumble in the modernist maze can be found in a twenty-line sentence included in the paragraph: 'For it was the middle of June' (6). Jordana has added: 'pensava Clarissa' (Clarissa thought) (8) in line 18 of the twenty-six-line translated version, whereas the original carries no such indication.

The first Catalan translation of *MD* (the only published one to date in Catalan and still on the market in reprint) suffers a number of losses with

---

[17] Note in this connection R. Esquerra's comment on Woolf's novels: 'The first thing one experiences on reading one of her novels is a sense of helplessness. The reader feels lost in the midst of the work. It is difficult for him to situate himself' ('La primera cosa que hom experimenta en llegir una novel.la seva és una sensació de desempar. El lector es troba perdut enmig de l'obra. Li costa de situar-se') (Esquerra 1936, 112).

regard to the English text beyond the deployment of discourse which I have been referring to. A major loss is that of poetic intensity, so integral a part of the texture of Woolf's narrative. This may be seen in Jordana's failure to respond to the author's peculiar use of syntax together with stress in order to create a given sound effect, as in the description of Big Ben striking: '*Out* it boomed' (6), which, in spite of the onomatopoeic 'boom', is conveyed relatively insipidly as: 'Ja engegava el seu bum' (It let out its boom) (6). Again, Jordana makes no attempt to reproduce Woolf's use of alliteration in 'd', together with stress and punctuation, to portray the aeroplane's swooping movement. For the sentence which begins: '*Dropping down dead*, the aeroplane' (20), the Catalan reads, prosaically indeed: '*L'avió es va deixar anar desplomat* [sic]' (The plane let itself fall) (27).[18] On another occasion, alliterative effect will be lost through omission as will the sense of the feather-light flight of the birds, achieved through the interplay of alliteration in 'f' with strong and weak stress patterns. Thus: 'sparrows *fountains fluttering for crumbs*' (25) is reproduced as: '*vols de* pardals *cercant* motlles' (flights of sparrows looking for crumbs) (35). Then, the paused effect created through repetition, working together with strong stresses, introduced by Woolf to contribute to conveying Clarissa Dalloway's dwelling on her past: 'She could remember *scene after scene* at Bourton' (8) is sacrificed by Jordana and a comma introduced by him, which interrupts the flow of memory; the reader will also notice that here again the proper name replaces the pronoun: '*Clarissa* recordava *un seguit d'escenes* [a number of scenes], a Bourton' (9). Furthermore, Woolf's use of imagery is not always respected. As Clarissa Dalloway reflects on her correspondence with Peter Walsh, we are informed: 'she never wrote a letter and his were *dry sticks*' (8), while in Catalan a simile substitutes the metaphor, blander and more clumsy than the original: 'ella no escrivia mai cartes i les d'ell eren *eixarreïdes com un tronc mort* [dry like a dead trunk]' (10). Subsequently, a metaphor will be totally forfeited, one which is of importance in contributing to conveying the elegiac sense in the novel, that is, in the description of the trail of smoke being left behind by the aeroplane advertising in the sky: 'a thick ruffled bar of white smoke ... curled and *wreathed* upon the sky in letters' (20). It stands in Catalan as: 'una tija focosa de fum blanc es torcia i *cargolava* (moved like a snail/snailed its way) al cel en lletres' (20). Jordana also omits a simile from Woolf's description of the nursemaid's voice as heard by Septimus Warren Smith (the comparison with a grasshopper's), as well as failing, in this same instance, to make corresponding sense in the Catalan text with regard to sound. The nursemaid starts to spell out the toffee being advertised in the sky, 'Kreemo': '"K ... R ..." said the nursemaid, and Septimus heard her say "*Kay Arr*" close to his ear, deeply, softly, *like a mellow organ*, but with a roughness in her voice *like a grasshopper's*, which rasped his spine deliciously' (21) and this is rendered in Catalan: '"K ... R ..." va dir la mainadera, i Sèptim li va sentir dir "*Ka Erra*" ben a prop de l'orella, profundament, dolçament, *com un orgue suau*, però amb una aspror que li esgarrinxà l'espinada

[18] The [*sic*] in the Catalan text refers to the mistake in the printed text: the past participle 'desplomat' has been used instead of the present participle 'desplomant'.

deliciosament' (29–30). The Catalan pronunciation of the phonemes 'k' and 'r' does not convey the sound of a 'mellow organ', achieved by the lingering, falling diphthong in 'k' /ei/ and long vowel sound in the English 'r' /a:/. Jordana should have changed the letters or the simile. In this same paragraph, he will distort Septimus's fevered vision of the elm trees: 'the excitement of the elm trees rising and falling, *rising* and *falling* with all the leaves alight and the colour *thinning* and *thickening* from blue to the green of a *hollow* wave,' (21) by omission (the 'hollow' quality of the wave is passed over, thus diminishing the haunting quality of the original) and the failure to find an adequately charged equivalent in Catalan for the hypnotic quality created by the English gerund in the context: 'l'excitació produïda pels oms *que puxaven* [which rose] i *baixaven* [fell], *puxaven* [rose] i *baixaven* [fell] amb totes les fulles enceses i el color *que s'aclaria* [which became lighter] i *enfosquia* [became darker] de blau a verd d'onada' (30).

The reader of Jordana's *MD* must acquire a different impression of certain characters to that which is conveyed in the original text. Characterization too, then, is affected by the translator's failure to respond to Woolf's construction. Clarissa Dalloway herself is a victim of such distortion. What I see to be a note of alienation registered in the female protagonist's reflection on her subjectivity is played down in the Catalan text on a number of counts. Consider the following:

> But often now *this* body she *wore* . . ., *this* body with all its capacities, seemed *nothing* – nothing *at all*. She had the oddest sense of being herself invisible; unseen; *unknown*; *there being* no more marrying, no more having of children now, but only *this* astonishing and rather solemn progress with the rest of them, up Bond Street, *this being* Mrs Richard Dalloway. (11)

Jordana characteristically substitutes the free indirect demonstratives by the indirect. He dilutes Clarissa Dalloway's nihilistic sense with regard to her body and modifies it '[seeming] nothing' by the addition of 'as if it were'. He also imposes a patriarchal logic on the character's thought process by transforming the non-finite 'there being' into a clause of reason: 'as there was' and reveals a lack of sensitivity in not providing an apt equivalence to express the repetition of 'being' in the original, which conveys an existentialist preoccupation. In the climactic part of the second sentence (also the end of a paragraph), it seems to me that Woolf wished to convey the loss of authenticity experienced by Clarissa as a consequence of her married status; 'this being Mrs Richard Dalloway' expresses a sense of acquired, sham identity, also expressed at the beginning of the description through the use of 'wore' in relation to Clarissa's body. In the Catalan version we simply have 'Mrs Ricard Dalloway', which becomes meaningless in Catalan as the married woman does not take on her husband's forename as indicative of her married status. Here, then, is Jordana's version:

> Però ara *aquell* cos que *duia* [she carried] . . ., *aquell* cos amb totes les seves facultats, semblava *que no fos* res – ben bé res. Tenia l'estranya sensació d'ésser invisible; no vista; *no sabuda* [*sic*]; *com que* ja no hi havia casament a fer, ni infants a tenir, aleshores, sinó *aquell* avenç sorprenent i més aviat solemne amb tota la resta, Bond Street

amunt, i ella era Mrs Dalloway [and she was Mrs Dalloway]; ni tan sols ja Clarissa [not even Clarissa anymore]; Mrs Ricard Dalloway. (15)[19]

The final note, the 'up-beat', as David Lodge has qualified it (1977, 180), on which the novel ends: 'For there she was' (172), which captures Clarissa Dalloway's charisma, the spell she casts about her, is totally forfeited in the Catalan to evoke Peter's possession of her, reified through his gaze: 'Perquè allí la tenia' ('For there he had her in front of him') (257).

Further examples of distortion in characterization may be detected through the failure to reproduce particular idiolect or dialect. The characters of Scrope Purvis, Edgar J. Watkiss and Mrs Dempster illustrate my point. Purvis contemplates Clarissa Dalloway as she waits to cross the road: 'A charming woman, Scrope Purvis thought her (knowing her as one does know people who live next door to *one* in Westminster)' (5). The class register evoked through the use of the pronoun 'one' is forfeited in Jordana's version by the mixing of the second person pronoun with the third. The emphatic use of 'does', echoing the colloquial middle-class register is also overlooked. The commas introduced by Jordana around the adverbial 'in Westminster' attribute a meaning on the part of the speaker, moreover, which the original does not contain. As the Catalan is expressed, the reader is given to understand that Scrope Purvis is highlighting Westminster as a special case whereas in the original no such significance is suggested: 'Una dona encisera, pensava Scrope Purvis (que la coneixia com un coneix, a Westminster, la gent que *us* viu al costat de casa)' (6). Edgar J. Watkiss's dialectal pronunciation: 'The *Proime* Minister's *kyar*' (15) and Mrs Dempster's ungrammatical speech: 'That girl … *don't* know a thing yet' (25–26) are translated with no indication that the original contained variations on the standard tongue: 'El cotxe del primer ministre' (20) and 'Aquella noia … és una infeliç [is an unhappy specimen]' (36).

Lastly, some of Woolf's satire and criticism are lost in the translation. Clarissa Dalloway's childhood friend Hugh Whitbread is described as having a 'perfectly *upholstered* body' (7), which is simply rendered as: 'el seu cos molt ben *cobert* [covered]' (9). In the English text, the ritualism of dress is suggested, the façade value of clothes within a particular social class – Hugh holds a 'little job at Court' (7). The passing criticism of the apparatus of ruling-class appearances is absent, then, in the Catalan. The tall men in the bow window at White's are described as having their hair '*raked* back' (18). The metaphor is sacrificed in the translation and the caricature of the public school drill in consequence: 'llurs cabells pentinats [combed] endarrera' (25). And Sir John Buckhurst, the old judge, is described in English as having 'laid down the law for years' (17) whereas in Catalan the reader may acquire a misleading idea with regard to Sir John's activity since creativity can be understood: 'havia fet la

---

19 I have translated pieces in this quote which are additions by Jordana. The [*sic*] which follows 'no sabuda' indicates the misuse of the verb in Catalan. Jordana has translated 'unknown' with the verb used in the context of knowing facts (saber) rather than people (conèixer), which is the context here.

llei durant anys' (he had made the law for years) (23). The pun is lost as well as the criticism of the patriarchal structure.

Examination of the translated text, indeed, only a part of it, reveals that *MD* arrived in Badalona in 1930 somewhat harassed; splendidly attired,[20] but less modernist, less poetic, less critical of the British establishment, less an evocation of London too[21] – a lesser product as text. Woolf herself said of the novel: 'I have almost too many ideas' (quoted in Lee 1977, 93). There are certainly fewer in the 1930 Catalan translation. Thus, in the hands of C. A. Jordana, 'educated in the *Noucentista* school' (Yates 1984, 201),[22] *MD* became a victim of the 'fear of the novel' syndrome, still in the air on her arrival.[23]

Jordana's translation was published the year after the French translation of *MD* (also titled *Mrs Dalloway*) appeared in Paris. The title page of the Catalan novel, as well as the dustcover, announce that the translation by Jordana is from the English. However, the paragraph of potted plot, taken from the preface to the French translation and reproduced on the Catalan dustcover, would suggest that Jordana was aware of the existence of the French edition. In his *Lectures europées* (European Readings) (1936), Ramon Esquerra recorded that the French translation of Woolf's *Flush* appeared around the time that the film starring Charles Laughton, *The Barretts of Wimpole Street*, was showing in Barcelona (Esquerra 1936, 115). Therefore, the translation by Roser Cardús [i Malarriaga] (Barcelona 1920–74), a University of Barcelona graduate in pharmacy who became a writer of short stories and children's literature,[24] of the playful biography of Elizabeth Barrett Browning's dog, published in war-stricken Barcelona in 1938, might evoke more peaceful times. There is no comparison between the choice Proa edition of *MD* and the simple paperback copy of *FB*, brought out in the Edicions de la Rosa dels Vents (Compass Editions) series, created by the enterprising young publisher, poet and journalist Josep Janés [i Olivé] (1913–59) as a continuation of his Quaderns Literaris (Literary Notebooks) series, begun in 1934 and finally brought to a close in this year before the end of the Civil War.[25]

---

20 The print and binding of the hardback, which also carried a dustcover with the title in large silver letters against a green background, are of high quality. The dustcover also carries an eleven-line summary of the novel extrapolated from André Maurois's preface to the 1929 French edition.

21 See the reference to Regent's Park tube station in *MD* 1987, 25. The name of the tube station is omitted in the Catalan *Mrs Dalloway (MD)* 1930, 34.

22 'format a l'escola Noucentista.'

23 'por a la novel.la.' See Josep M. de Sagarra, 'La por a la novel.la', *La Publicitat*, 26 April 1925. Cited by Yates 1984, 201.

24 For more information on Cardús, see the entry in McNerney and Enríquez de Salamanca 1994, 102–03.

25 A number of Anglophone writers were published in the Quaderns Literaris: Oscar Wilde, Maurice Baring, H. G. Wells, Aldous Huxley, among others. Janés would resuscitate these writers in post-war Spain, perforce in Castilian translation.

Fetching *Flush*

TL was published in French in the same year as *MD* (see *La Promenade au phare (TL)* 1929), but, had it been considered, the novel would have been too ambitious a text for publication in the Quaderns Literaris, and especially in a city well-nigh under siege. Woolf's parodic piece was an appropriate text, then, both in terms of length (some one hundred pages) and together with the fact that a French translation existed. As Ramon Esquerra observed, for the Catalans French was the customary channel for acquiring knowledge about English literature.[26] Cardús's translation is a fair rendering of the original, carefully reproducing the six chapters of Woolf's text as well as the substantial notes, including the long disquisition on Lily Wilson, and list of 'Authorities'. The ironic narrative voice of the original is successfully achieved in Catalan, though intertextual gems such as the opening of the text: 'It is universally admitted', playfully evocative of the gambit employed by Jane Austen in the first chapter of *Pride and Prejudice*, would be lost on the common reader in Catalonia through Cardús's 'Per consentiment universal' ('By universal consent'). The problem is not, of course, so much a matter of textual translation as the canonical cultural absence in Catalonia. Within the same opening paragraph, Cardús has recourse to a footnote (the only one in the whole translated text) aimed at explaining the impossibility of providing an equivalence for the punning on spaniel/span/Spain constructed by Woolf in her parodic scholarship. Woolf's, again, playful reference to a 'school of thought' (*FB* 1978, 7) which connects Hispania with 'the Basque word *españa*, signifying an edge or boundary' (7) is rendered by Cardús as '*espana*' (*Flush* (*FB*) 1938, 5), as little Basque as '*españa*'!

Cardús's translation of *Flush* would be the last translation of any of Woolf's texts to be published in Catalan until the 1970s. The publisher Janés, anxious to produce books in post-Civil War Spain with a view to continuing a cultural project initiated in pre-Civil War Barcelona, would struggle with the limitations imposed by the regime's Vice-Secretary's Office for General Education (La Vice-Secretaría de Educación Popular) under Patricio G. de Canales.[27] In a letter to the Catalan poet Carles Riba, in exile in Montpellier in 1942, Janés lamented the fact that Woolf couldn't be published in Spain at that time, even in Castilian: 'Unfortunately Virginia Woolf cannot be published in Spain today.'[28] However, Janés did manage to publish further novels by Woolf

---

[26] '[L]a traducció francesa – camí normal, a casa nostra, del coneixement de la literatura anglesa' ('French translation – the normal path/channel in our culture for obtaining knowledge about English literature') (Esquerra 1936, 115).

[27] See my unpublished PhD thesis *La literatura inglesa del siglo XX en la España de la postguerra: la aportación de José Janés* (Hurtley 1983), vol. 2, chapter 2.4 on censorship, and Appendix D, which carries some correspondence from Janés to P.G. de Canales as well as censors' reports and scored-out texts.

[28] 'Malheureusement Virginia Woolf n'est pas publiable aujourd'hui en Espagne.' Letter from Josep Janés i Olivé to Carles Riba, 18 September 1942, in the Carles Riba correspondence held by his daughter Eulàlia Riba i Arderiu in Barcelona.

in the wake of the Allied victory in 1945. Thus, *TY* and *JR* appeared in 1946 and were followed by *ND* in 1947.[29] These translations were, perforce, in Castilian. Contemporary Catalan writing or translations into Catalan of contemporary novelists would not be re-established to a degree comparable with the pre-war period until the 1970s.[30] Therefore, it was not until 1973 that Woolf would reappear in Catalan with a translation of *TY*, which begins an identification with Woolf on the part of Catalan women writers interested in women's rights, an identification which coloured the perception of Woolf in Catalonia over the last quarter of the twentieth century.

Forging a room of one's own

> If we want to meditate on women's condition, [Woolf] must be read, and even more so with a view to understanding what it means to be a woman and a writer. (Pessarrodona 1982, 39)[31]

Writer and translator Marta Pessarrodona's claim, in an article published on the occasion of the centenary of Woolf's birth, is representative of a dominant critical discourse on Woolf in Catalonia over the 1970s and into the 1980s, which must be assessed within the context of the growing struggle for women's rights in Spain in the wake of May 1968 and the death of General Franco in November of 1975.[32] A fundamental figure in renewing the translation of Woolf into Catalan is the novelist, playwright, essayist and cultural activist Maria-Aurèlia Capmany [i Farnés] (1918–91).

From the 1960s and into the 1970s, Capmany was in charge of the J.M. series produced by the Nova Terra (New Land) publishing house in Barcelona. The series was so called in order to evoke Joanot Martorell, the author of the Catalan epic *Tirant lo Blanc*, and was geared towards publishing both classical and contemporary writing in Catalan together with foreign authors 'who ought to be read'.[33] The only other foreign authors published before Woolf's *TY* were Panaït Istrati and Honoré de Balzac. For the Woolf translation, Capmany, who had herself been publishing as a creative writer in

---

29 See *Los años* (*TY*), trans. P. Fraga de Porto (1946); *El cuarto de Jacobo* (*JR*), trans. S. Santainés (1946); *Noche y día* (*ND*), trans. E. de Guzmán (1947). Both Fraga de Porto and Guzmán were political prisoners, translating as a means of survival in post-war Spain. Santainés had done some translating for Janés in the Quaderns Literaris into Catalan and was employed by him in the post-war period, like other out-of-work Catalan writers or supporters of the Republic. For more information on the translators, see Hurtley 1983, 1986 and 1992.

30 See Vallverdú 1988 and Gallofré i Virgili 1991.

31 'Si volem meditar sobre la condició de la dona, cal llegir-la, i més encara per entendre el que significa ésser dona i escriptora.'

32 For more information on the contemporary women's movement in Spain, see Threlfall 1996.

33 'que cal llegir'. The text is taken from the description of the series at the end of the 1973 Catalan translation of *TY* (*Els anys*).

Catalan since the 1950s, produced an essay, 'Virginia Woolf o la nova realitat' (Virginia Woolf or a New Reality) (1973b), which was appended as an epilogue to the translation by the Mallorcan writer and translator Maria Antònia Oliver [i Cabrer] (1946–). In the same year that Nova Terra brought out the translation in question, Capmany published a text on feminism in Catalonia (1973a); however, her projection of Woolf in her epilogue to *Els anys* (*TY*) does not highlight a feminist Woolf (there is an isolated reference to *ROO* as Woolf's contribution to feminist vindication (1973b, 388)) so much as the avant-garde writer. The blurb on the back cover of the paperback edition also concentrates on the formal aspect of the text, thus: 'Without a doubt, *The Years* is Woolf's most dense book. It is also her most ambitious .... It constitutes a passionate pilgrimage through time.'[34] Capmany's own novel *Quim/Quima* (1971), published just two years before the translation of *TY*, introduces the time-travelling technique exploited by Woolf in *O*. The novel begins in the year 1000 and takes us up to the period of the Spanish Civil War. Like Orlando, the protagonist Quim/Quima experiences an androgynous identity. Indeed, in a prologue to the novel in the form of a letter to Woolf, Capmany acknowledged the influence of Woolf's text.[35]

The generation of women writers following Capmany's have expressed admiration for, acknowledged a debt to, or recognized the influence of Virginia Woolf on their work. Their parents had already had access to Virginia Woolf's writings in Castilian translation from editions published in South America and to those made accessible by Barcelona publishing houses, principally Janés's, following the Allied victory and in the early 1950s.[36] The Barcelona publishing house Seix Barral published *Una habitación propia* (*ROO*) in Castilian in 1967,[37] and over the 1970s another Barcelona-based publisher, Lumen, would bring out a number of Woolf titles in Castilian.[38] The 1967 Castilian translation of *ROO* appeared when the Catalan writer born and bred in Barcelona, Montserrat Roig [i Fransitorra] (1946–92), was studying at the University of Barcelona. Whether it was the impact of that text in translation, Roig's access to her father's library (his creative work was published by Janés in the Quaderns Literaris, like Cardús's translation of *FB*) or her direct access to writers in English between 1973 and 1974 when she was a language assistant in Spanish at the University of Bristol, she would declare in the 1980s that 'to read *A Room of One's Own* ... was a major revelation for me' (quoted in Nichols 1989, 148).[39] Woolf's impact as a creative writer on Roig can be perceived in what has become the latter's most widely known novel, *L'hora*

---

34 '*Els anys* és, sense dubte, el seu llibre més dens. També la seva novel.la més ambiciosa, ... És una peregrinació apassionada a través del temps.'

35 See Soler i Marcet 1994, 95 and Pérez 1993, 96–97 and 99.

36 See, in connection with the Latin American translations, the essay in this volume by Laura Maria Lojo Rodríguez.

37 In a new translation by Laura Pujol.

38 See *La Señora Dalloway* (*MD*) (1975); *La torre inclinada y otros ensayos* ('The Leaning Tower' and Other Essays) (1977); *La casa encantada y otros cuentos* (*HH*) (1979).

39 'leer *Una habitación propia*... fue toda una revelación para mí'.

violeta (The Violet Hour) (1980), both in the concern with expressing time passing and in the (re-)writing of women's lives.[40]

Roig is one of a number of Catalan women who have read Woolf, translated her or re-written her in their own work. Helena Valentí [i Petit] (1941–91), Maria-Antònia Oliver [i Cabrer] (1946–) and Marta Pessarrodona [i Artigues] (1941–) are cases in point. It was while Roig was in charge of the series 'Plec de Setze' (Quire of Sixteen) at the Barcelona publishing house Grijalbo that she included Valentí's translation of *ROO* in 1985.[41] Valentí was very well equipped to translate Woolf, having been resident in England for twelve years after graduating in Romance Languages from the University of Barcelona. She completed her PhD at Cambridge and lectured in Catalan at Cambridge and Durham before returning to Barcelona in the 1970s, where she published her first creative work (see Valentí 1977). She translated into both Castilian and Catalan, producing a version of I. A. Richards's *Practical Criticism* in 1967. Her translation, again into Castilian, of Doris Lessing's *The Golden Notebook* appeared in 1978, before she turned to Woolf in the 1980s when she translated *TL* (*Al far*) (1984) for the Barcelona publishing house responsible for bringing out *MD* in 1930, that is, Proa, and *ROO*, mentioned above.

Writing on the occasion of the centenary of Virginia Woolf's birth in 1982, Pessarrodona observed that translations of Woolf's work into Catalan had not increased as much as would have been desirable.[42] However, before the decade came to an end, Valentí's translation of *TL* would have appeared as well as translations of *O* and *TW* by the 1970s translator of *TY*, Maria-Antònia Oliver.

The Catalan poet Francesc Parcerisas was responsible for the setting up of the series 'Clàssics Moderns' (Modern Classics) at the Barcelona publishing house Edhasa, where he worked from 1985 until 1992.[43] Edhasa had already republished Antonio Marichalar's 1938 Castilian translation of *TL* (1981) and Jorge Luis Borges's 1945 version of *O* (1980) - both of which originally appeared in Buenos Aires – therefore the acquisition of rights over texts by Woolf was facilitated. Oliver would take on the translating of *O* and *TW* as a challenge as well as a pleasure.[44] She saw her translating of Woolf within the context of the struggle for women's rights but now argues that the language question (great efforts were being made in the 1980s to 'normalize' Catalan following its deprived status under General Franco's regime) and her commitment to Catalonia were more important to her.[45] Oliver's translation of *O* (1985) appeared almost twenty years after Edhasa's success with

---

40 See my introduction to the Castilian translation of *L'hora violeta (La hora violeta)* (Hurtley 2000).

41 See R.B. 1991.

42 'La bibliografia en llengua catalana de l'autora no [ha] augmentat tan sensiblement com seria de desitjar' (Pessarrodona 1982, 37).

43 Telephone interview with F. Parcerisas, 28 April 2000.

44 Interview with Maria-Antònia Oliver, 18 January 2000.

45 Interview with Maria-Antònia Oliver, 18 January 2000.

Borges's,[46] and appears to have followed Borges's text on occasion. Thus, when Orlando becomes a woman in chapter 3 and the narrator '[takes] advantage of this pause in the narrative to make certain statements' (*O* 1998, 81), Borges passes over the play of singular and plural, masculine and feminine, wrought by Woolf. The subject pronoun may be omitted in both Castilian and Catalan and the possessive adjective stands in agreement with what is possessed rather than with the possessor so whether it is a masculine or feminine possessor may become ambiguous. However, the plural is modified in a manner not consistent with Woolf's text. The text in question reads as follows in the original:[47]

> Orlando had become a woman – there is no denying it. But in every other respect, Orlando remained precisely as *he* had been. The change of sex, though it altered *their* future did nothing whatever to alter *their* identity. *Their* faces remained, as their portraits prove, practically the same. *His* memory – *but in future we must, for convention's sake, say 'her' for 'his', and 'she' for 'he'* – *her* memory, then, went back through all the events of *her* past life without encountering any obstacle. (*O* 1998, 81)

Borges's rendering reads as follows:

> Orlando se había transformado en una mujer – inútil negarlo. Pero, en todo lo demás, Orlando era el mismo. El cambio de sexo modificaba *su* porvenir, no *su* identidad. Su cara, como lo pueden demostrar sus retratos, era *la misma*. *Su* memoria podía remontar sin obstáculos el curso de *su* vida pasada. (*Orlando (O)* 1980, 90–91)

Oliver's translation also distorts Woolf's text and follows Borges's omission of the narrator's parenthetic statement in connection with convention:

> Orlando s'havia convertit en dona . . . no es pot negar. Però en tots els altres aspectes, Orlando continuava sent exactament el que havia estat fins ara. El canvi de sexe, malgrat que alterava *el seu futur*, no tenia per què alterar *la seva identitat*. Els seus rostres, com demostren els retrats, varen continuar sent pràcticament els mateixos. *Els seus records*, en retrocedir a través de tots els esdeveniments de la vida passada, no trobaren cap obstacle. (*Orlando (O)* 1985, 107)

The Edhasa-cum-Proa[48] texts are fine objects. *Orlando* carries a reproduction of Dante Gabriel Rossetti's *Daydream* on the front cover while *Les ones (TW)* carries a fragment of Pierre Bonnard's *La promenade en mer*.

Without a doubt, the 1980s was a decade of Woolfian intensity in relation to the incorporating of Woolf's texts into Catalan and the projection of her work both in her own right and as part of the Bloomsbury Group. This was largely due to the energy and dedication of Marta Pessarrodona who, like

---

46 For example, there were reprints every year between 1977 and 1980.

47 I have italicized the pronouns and possessive adjectives which are modified in the Castilian or Catalan text as well as what is omitted.

48 Proa took on the Edhasa texts.

Roig, was in England in the 1970s and became an assistant in the Department of Spanish at Nottingham University.[49] She had originally arrived in England on 17 July 1972 and heard Quentin Bell being interviewed on the radio in connection with the publication of his two-volume biography of his aunt. It was, according to Pessarrodona, Esther Tusquets of the Lumen publishing house, a Woolf reader herself (Nichols 1989, 73) and a good friend of Pessarrodona's, who persuaded the latter to translate Bell's 'fascinating, beautifully composed study of Woolf's life' (Marcus 1997, 186–87). Volume 1 of Bell's biography was published by Lumen, in Castilian, in 1979; Volume 2 in 1980. In June 1983, the major Catalan Savings Bank, La Caixa de Pensions, would bring out Pessarrodona's 'Reading Guide' ('Guia de Lectura') on Woolf in its series of guides on major authors, both of Catalan and non-Catalan origin. The guide provides basic biographical data, outlines Woolf's contribution as a novelist and essayist, pointing out that *ROO* signalled her political capacity as well as the beginnings of feminist literary criticism. Quentin Bell and his wife Anne Olivier were interested in meeting Pessarrodona and out of her contact with them, together with the collaboration of Maria Rossinés Bayó, Head of Coordination in the Arts Section of La Caixa, a course and a splendid exhibition on the Bloomsbury Group were held in Barcelona between 17 September and 31 October 1986. Visitors to the exhibition were able to feast on Vanessa Bell, Roger Fry and Duncan Grant paintings from the Tate, Courtauld Institute Galleries and the Anthony d'Offay Gallery in London as well as on furniture designed by Fry, Grant and Joseph Kallenborn from the Victoria and Albert Museum and Anthony d'Offay Gallery. In the month of October, there were talks by local scholars, such as Sam Abrams, Fabià Estapé, José María Valverde and Pessarrodona herself; leading contibutors from England were Noël Annan, Quentin Bell, Lyndall Gordon and Robert Skidelsky. A selection of the contributions were reproduced in the exhibition catalogue. The exhibition drew on a number of individuals and institutions, among them the British Council.[50] Another Catalan writer of Pessarrodona's generation, the Mallorcan Carme Riera [i Guilera] (1948–), who has also spoken of her reading of Woolf (see Nichols 1989, 190–92) would write somewhat sceptically about the exhibition in the Barcelona arts magazine *Quimera*, but recognized that it contained 'un gran interés didáctico' ('a great didactic interest') (Riera 1986, 13).

The impact of Woolf on the cultural life of Barcelona would also be felt in 1984 when the Tarragona writer Olga Xirinacs [i Díaz] (1936–) was awarded the Sant Jordi (St George) Prize for her novel *Al meu cap una llosa* (A Gravestone at My Head).[51] Xirinac's novel deals with Woolf as a haunting presence: 'nameless, simply memory' (1985, 232),[52] over the period between

---

49 Interview with Marta Pessarrodona, 18 January 2000.

50 See the exhibition catalogue: *El grup de Bloomsbury* (1986).

51 The title comes from the Catalan writer Marià Manent's rendering of a William Cowper poem.

52 'sense nom, tota memòria.'

her suicide and the discovery of her body and within the context of the Second World War, expressed through reports as relayed over the BBC and the registering of events in relation to local people's lives in East Sussex. Woolf's own perceptions are documented at the end of each chapter. In the 1980s too, Maria-Antònia Oliver would publish a revised version of her 1973 translation of *TY* (*Els anys*) (1988) and her own *Punt d'arròs* (Knit-purl) would carry as epigraph a quote from Virginia Woolf's *BTA*.[53] The translated version of this posthumously published novel would begin another decade of Woolf's presence in Catalonia, which has continued.

From *Between the Acts* to women and literature

In 1989, the Barcelona publishing house Edicions 62, in conjunction with La Caixa, would publish the translation by Marta Pera [i Cucurell] (1959–) of *BTA* (*Entre els actes*) in the series Les millors obres de la literatura universal/segle vint (The Best Works of World Literature/Twentieth Century). The series began with Huxley's *Point Counter Point* (Contrapunt) (1986) and published texts by E. M. Forster, D. H. Lawrence, Malcolm Lowry and G. B. Shaw before Woolf's appeared. The aim of the series was to introduce the most important twentieth-century authors in translations of a high standard. The Woolf translation carries an essay by Marta Pessarrodona, 'Virginia Woolf: l'últim acte' (Virginia Woolf: The Last Act), before the translation proper, which focuses on Woolf's life and work. Marta Pera is a graduate (1985) in English Language and Literature from the University of Barcelona and is indicative of a change in the translating field in Barcelona, increasingly noticeable over the last decade. Although translation may still be practised by contemporary writers in Catalan, there are a number of graduates who are earning their living through translation, engaged by publishing houses as Marta Pera was.

In 1992, Woolf was woven into Maria-Antònia Oliver's novel *Joana E* (Joanna E.). She appears as a presence, like Charlotte Brontë and the Catalan writer Caterina Albert i Paradís (1869–1966) (who wrote under the male pseudonym Víctor Català) that the reader may be unaware of, as Oliver points out in a note to the reader (1992, 9–10), but which, she insists, can be found throughout.

In 1994, Oliver's translation of *O* was reprinted and in 1996, a small publishing concern in Barcelona, Deriva (Drift), republished Valentí's translation of *ROO* (*Una cambra pròpia*). In the final year of the 1990s, a volume composed of essays by Woolf on literary criticism appeared under the title *Dones i literatura* (Women and Literature). The essays were selected by the Professor of Literary Theory at the Universiy of Barcelona Jordi Llovet, who supervises the series Biblioteca d'Idees Literaris (The Library of Literary Ideas)

---

53 'I l'aire, al seu voltant, es va teixir de sensacions' (The air around her was full of sensation.) (Oliver 1985). *Knit-Purl* is the translation of Oliver's novel *Punt d'arròs* supplied in the entry on Oliver in McEnerney and Enríquez de Salamanca 1994.

produced by the Barcelona publishing house Columna. The translation and notes are the work of another graduate (1990) in English Language and Literature from the University of Barcelona, Jordi Ainaud [i Escudero] (1967–) and the volume carries a prologue by the Catalan writer from Alcoi in the province of Alacant, Isabel-Clara Simó [i Monllor] (1943–). In 1978, Simó collaborated with Maria-Aurèlia Capmany and three other women professionals in producing *Dona i societat a la Catalunya actual* (Women and Society in Catalonia Today).[54] However, her approach to Woolf in the prologue seeks to restore a canonical Woolf, the 'great writer' ('gran escriptora') (Simó 1999, 23). She recognizes that 'the feminist theme ... is a subject that [Woolf] frequently refers to and always in a sharply intelligent way' (9–10),[55] but, Simó insists: 'the writer's real [*sic*] aims were always exclusively literary' (10).[56]

The lighthouse: Barcelona 2000

Springtime in Barcelona in the year 2000 brought a representation of Woolf in the series of exhibitions at the Centre de Cultura Contemporània 'Fars del segle XX' (Lighthouses of the Twentieth Century). The exhibition was fashioned by the Argentinian Nora Catelli, who has lived in Barcelona since 1976 and currently teaches Literary Theory and Comparative Literature at the University of Barcelona, and the Barcelona artist Eugènia Balcells. They produced an audio-visual exhibition, composed of selections from Woolf's writings, reproduced on vertically hanging banners which formed a circle; a cone-like formation occupied the central space within this circle, made of a transparent fabric which enabled visitors to walk in and out of it at will. A video, produced for the exhibition, showed a woman's body moving on the shore and through the sea, a movement which, a text explained, had no beginning or end, like the sound effects, inspired by the rhythms of the sea.

On the evening of the opening of the exhibition, the Danish film *The War Within: A Portrait of Virginia Woolf* was shown. The Director of the Centre, Josep Ramoneda, introduced Nora Catelli and Eugènia Balcells, who spoke briefly of their exhibition. The auditorium was full, suggesting that Barcelona does not tire of Woolf; her appeal continues. These seventy years may be just the beginning, the desire appears not to be on the wane.

---

54 Cited by McEnerney and Enríquez de Salamanca 1991 in the entry on I. C. Simó.

55 'el tema feminista ... és un tema a què fa referència sovint i sempre amb la intel.ligència esmolada.'

56 'els veritables [*sic*] objectius de l'escriptora van ser sempre exclusivament literaris.'

17 The Portuguese Reception of Virginia Woolf

Graça Abranches

In his contribution to the Portuguese edition of A. C. Ward's *História da literatura inglesa* (History of English Literature), Jorge de Sena started by remarking how the fortune of English literature in Portugal, though varied, had always been intermittent, partial and ephemeral, never approaching the relevance, both positive and negative, that political and economic ties had had, for many centuries, in the history of both countries (1959–60, 9–10).[1]

In fact, until well into this century, English literature was mostly known in Portugal, as had been the case for other European countries culturally or ideologically close to France,[2] as France had read and translated it. Shakespeare, Byron and Dickens were usually quoted in French by nineteenth-century Portuguese writers. And the success of the sporadic cultural approaches tried through the century by a few individuals had been, as Sena reminds us, 'poisoned by patriotic tempests in a colonial teacup' (1959–60, 10)[3] – namely the social and political unrest marked by strong anti-British feelings that followed the English Ultimatum of 1890, which put an end to Portugal's claim to rule the territories between Angola and Mozambique and opened the crisis that would lead to the establishment of the Republican regime in 1910. Thus, in the early decades of the twentieth century, ideas and forms for Portuguese modernists would continue to come from Paris, in spite of the importance of English culture as a reference for Fernando Pessoa or the fortuitous connections, in the late 1930s, of a few poets with England, or with English (as was the case of Tomás Kim, Rui Cinatti, Jorge de Sena, José Blanc de

---

[1] Political and diplomatic relations between Portugal and England date from 1294, when the first commercial treaty was signed. A treaty of perpetual alliance (Treaty of Windsor), renewed several times in the last six centuries, was signed in 1386 by Richard II and D. João I. Jorge de Sena (1919–78), poet, critic, essayist, novelist, scholar and literary translator is one of the major names in twentieth-century culture. He played an unquestioned role in bridging the gap that isolated Portugal from other cultures and he never ceased trying to make English literature known and read in Portugal.

[2] This was also the case in Spain (see the chapter by Alberto Lázaro in this volume).

[3] 'envenenada ... pelas tempestades patrióticas em copo de água colonial'.

Portugal). The first real challenge to the cultural supremacy of France in Portugal was to happen during the Second World War. The fall of France, in 1940, affected negatively, for a few years, the diffusion of French books in Portugal and gave rise, among Portuguese publishers, keen to explore a market under the influence of anti-French tendencies from various sources, to an industrious commissioning of translations from English (Sena 1992, 81). The 1940s saw an unprecedented number of English books translated into Portuguese. And if publishers, as was to be expected, showed a preference for authors no longer protected by copyright (a preference that allowed George Eliot, for example, to enjoy a great popularity at the time), thanks to the good offices of some of their literary advisors (such as João Gaspar Simões and Adolfo Casais Monteiro, who were themselves writers), some twentieth-century fiction in English then became available for the first time in Portuguese.[4] Again, the interest some of these authors had sparked in France – the cases of Charles Morgan, Aldous Huxley, Joseph Conrad, Katherine Mansfield and Rosamond Lehman come to mind – no doubt contributed to, if not determined, their being chosen to be translated into Portuguese. But, whatever the role played by events in France in this process, a change was taking place in the Portuguese cultural scene of the late 1950s, as Jorge de Sena was one of the first to detect, with literature in English starting to gain some significance in terms of readership, both in the original and in translation.[5] It should be added, though, that in spite of this new situation of having to share the market with other literatures in translation, French literature easily regained, at the end of the war, much of its former prestige, and France, as a cultural power, would continue to maintain in Portugal, for a few decades still, its status as a privileged cultural referent and its function of mediator of other cultures – a role sustained by an educational system which, until the 1970s, gave absolute priority to French.

Ten years after the 1974 Revolution that put an end to half a century of dictatorship, the philosopher and critic Eduardo Lourenço (1984), in an important essay in which he charts Portugal's growing detachment from France as the irresistible and indispensable cultural referent, linked the long-lasting role of French literature as 'an inspiration' for Portuguese culture with

---

4 For example, D. H. Lawrence had six books translated in the 1940s, Aldous Huxley two books in the early 1940s and six other titles in the 1950s, Joseph Conrad nine titles published between 1941 and 1945, Charles Morgan two titles in the 1940s, and James Joyce had a selection of his short stories published in 1946; among women writers, Katherine Mansfield had four titles published between 1943 and 1951 and Rosamond Lehmann had *A Note in Music* translated in 1944.

5 Sena further added that (typically) 'the most powerful noise in English' ('o mais poderoso ruído em Inglês') then heard in Portugal was coming from North America (1959–60, 10). In an earlier text (a talk given in 1952 at the British Council in Porto) Sena had harshly judged this cultural change as merely apparent, so far as the critics were concerned. In his opinion, English authors were being quoted and written about, but the tone of the references was one of 'dishonest flippancy' ('leviandade desonesta'); knowledge and understanding of English literature remained as occasional and hasty as before (1986, 14).

its paradigmatic character of *littérature-pensée* – thus suggesting that its function had been, to a great extent, that of allowing us to think what was not yet explicitly thinkable in our own national context. And Lourenço, interestingly, further related the decline of that French 'inspiration' to the progressive 'ascendancy' of Portuguese women writers in the final period of the crisis of Salazar's regime. For him, the real benchmark of Portugal's literary autonomy from France lies in the emergence of what he called *le double regard* in Portuguese literature, a 'double look' brought about by the development of women's perspective in fiction. Lourenço saw the culmination of this process in the final re-appropriation of the Portuguese nun Mariana – the supposed author of the *Lettres portugaises* (Portuguese Letters) (1669) – as accomplished in *Novas cartas portuguesas* (the Three Marias' New Portuguese Letters, published in 1972).[6]

These two points made by Lourenço in *Envoi et adieu à Madeleine* (Envoy and Adieu to Madeleine) are to my mind crucial if we are to understand the double role Virginia Woolf has played in Portuguese culture: through her poetics, her contribution to the development of what Lourenço named *le double regard* in Portuguese literature; through her politics, in helping Portuguese women, if not to think the unthinkable, at least to say the unsayable in their own political and cultural context. Given the role played by translations from English in the cultural shift of the 1950s in Portugal, and the fact that the early translations of Woolf epitomize some of the most noteworthy aspects of her reception, I will develop my argument by using a chronological overview of the translations of her work as the background against which to try to gain some insights into the trends, both poetical and political, of her literary reception.

6 '[C]e livre réecrit, cette fois sérieusement, l'aventure de Mariana Alcoforado, que la France nous a fabriquée. Nos comptes avec Madeleine sont soldés.' ('[T]his book rewrites, this time seriously, the adventure of Mariana Alcoforado which France fabricated for us. Our accounts with Madeleine are thus settled.') (Lourenço 1984, 247). The *Lettres portugaises* (Portuguese Letters) were published anonymously in France in 1669 and consisted of five love letters supposedly written by a Portuguese nun, Mariana Alcoforado, from her convent in Beja, to her former lover, a French cavalier, the Marquis de Chamilly, who had seduced and abandoned her. The book was at the centre of a long international scholarly debate over biography, authorship and authenticity. In *Novas cartas portuguesas* (New Portuguese Letters), Maria Isabel Barreno, Maria Teresa Horta and Maria Velho da Costa make the nun their point of departure for a series of anonymous letters, essays and verses to one another, written as if from Mariana, her lover and a host of invented characters: relations, descendants and contemporary Portuguese Marias, Anas, Marias Anas, Mainas and Marianas. The book came out in 1972, to be immediately banned by the fascist regime on charges of offending public decency and to become the object of a famous trial. The trio of authors became collectively known as the Three Marias during the international feminist solidarity campaign for their acquittal. They were finally acquitted in 1974, a few days after the Revolution that put a end to the dictatorship.

II

The first translation of Virginia Woolf to be published in Portugal came out in 1951, in Coimbra, the tenth volume of a collection named 'Anthology of the Modern Short Story' (Antologia do Conto Moderno).[7] The selection of texts, translation and preface were the responsibility of Manuela Porto, herself a novelist, engaged citizen and cultural activist, whose poetry recitals had first revealed Fernando Pessoa to a wider audience. Manuela Porto, who died before the book was published (she committed suicide in 1950, at the age of 42),[8] dated her preface to the translation April 1947, scarcely three months after she had lectured on Virginia Woolf at the Sociedade Nacional de Belas Artes (National Society of Fine Arts), in Lisbon, thus suggesting that her translations were, in some way, a further outcome of that occasion. Her talk on Woolf at SNBA was one of the events around the international 'Exposição de Livros escritos por Mulheres' (Exhibition of Books Written by Women), organized by the Conselho Nacional das Mulheres Portuguesas (National Council of Portuguese Women) in January 1947.[9] The Council, founded in 1914, had been the only feminist organization of the First Republic (1910–26) to survive in Salazar's dictatorship, ignored or tolerated because it was practically inactive after the early 1930s. It had been reactivated after the Second World War, with strong links to the political opposition to the regime (a considerable number of its members, among them Manuela Porto herself, had signed the lists to found MUD Juvenil – the youth branch of the United Democratic Movement – in 1945). The tremendous public impact of the

---

7 The previous volumes in the collection had been dedicated to Steinbeck, Dorothy Parker, Ignazio Silone, Caldwell, Elsa Triolet, Saroyan, Unamuno, Somerset Maugham and Faulkner. The anthology of Woolf's stories – not included in Kirkpatrick's bibliography (1997) – was published in Coimbra by Atlântida and is entitled *Virginia Woolf*. It includes 'O Legado', 'A Casa Assombrada', 'O Vestido Novo', 'Lapin e Lapinova', 'A Marca na Parede', 'Três Quadros', 'A Velha Mrs Grey' and a 75-page extract from *MD* 'A História de Septimus Warren Smith' ('The Legacy', 'A Haunted House', 'The New Dress', 'Lappin and Lappinova', 'The Mark on the Wall', 'Three Pictures', 'Old Mrs Grey' and 'The Story of Septimus Warren Smith').

8 It is interesting to note – and most revealing of the practically unchanged dominant critical stance towards women writers – that Porto's entry in a recent Dictionary of Portuguese Authors insinuates that her 'familiarity' with Woolf's work was the 'most influential cause of her premature death' ('a mais influente causa da sua prematura morte') (Rocha 1998, 368). The personal and political difficulties of her life at that time, as well as her publications on Woolf, go unmentioned – one cannot miss the warning as to the dangers of becoming too familiar with Woolf's writings.

9 The exhibition comprised nearly 3000 books, by 1500 women writers from 28 countries. France, England and Portugal (with 288, 249 and 240 books respectively) were the three best represented countries. Portraits of women writers, scientists and politicians drawn by Portuguese women artists and art students were also exhibited, and during the nine days the exhibition lasted there were talks on famous women, and films based on books written by women were shown to a vast and enthusiastic audience (for further details, see Fiadeiro 1999).

international exhibition on women writers would finally move the authorities into action: the Council's office was sealed off by the police and the organization was declared extinguished by the government in June 1947. No other independent women's organization would be allowed to exist for the nearly three decades that the regime was still to last.

Manuela Porto's lecture, given on 7 January 1947, was entitled 'Virginia Woolf: o problema da mulher nas letras' (VW: The Problem of Women in Literature) and would be published the same year in the biography series of 'Cadernos da *Seara Nova*', a collection of booklets published by the militant cultural journal *Seara Nova* (The New Harvest).[10] The essay starts with the account of Porto's own relationship with Woolf's work (her enthusiastic reading of *MD*, *TW*, *TL*, *TY* and *O*), interspersed with acute comments on the revolutionary character of Woolf's poetics and vision,[11] and develops into a passionate paraphrase, translation and appropriation of *ROO*. Porto borrows Woolf's words explicitly to dis-locate her analysis of the material conditions of the production of art and to denounce the situation of 'the disinherited – women and the so-called poor –' (44)[12] in the political and cultural claustrophobia of Salazar's time. She is careful to remind her audience: 'I'm keeping as close as possible to Virginia Woolf's text, but you may *translate* and all those statements will remain true [my italics]' (1947, 42).[13] And she further re-stages Woolf's address to Oxbridge students in her final incitement to the women in her audience: substituting Woolf for Shakespeare's sister, she urges them to fight and work, 'for it is indispensable that when the great artist

---

10 *Seara Nova: revista de doutrina e crítica* (The New Harvest: A Journal of Doctrine and Critique) was a very prestigious journal with clear pedagogical and political aims, concerned with the social dimension of literature. It was first published in the 1920s and managed to survive during Salazar's regime, counting among its regular collaborators most of the leading intellectuals of the time. Manuela Porto had close political affinities with the *Seara* group, who would publish her short novel *Uma ingénua: a história de Beatriz* (An Ingénue: The Story of Beatriz) in 1948. It is very likely that she herself suggested that they publish her essay on Woolf.

11 Porto tells us how she had been discouraged from reading Woolf by being told she was 'an odd artist, inaccessible, extremely intellectual, inhuman, not to say barren or artificial' ('artista curiosa, pouco acessível, intelectual em extremo, desumana, para não chamar-lhe árida ou artificial') (1947, 9) and uses her comments on the novels to try and prove the sheer beauty of Woolf's power of expression, command of language and original technique used at the service of a new vision. She explains how, by reading the novels, she had reached the conclusion that in Woolf's spirit there was a curious *pli* (in French in the original) that made her look at things from a different perspective. And how, though the limits of her own perception had expanded after reading Woolf's fiction, there was still something lacking in her understanding. It is the 'key' to a fuller understanding of Woolf's poetics and vision that Porto purports to have found in *ROO* (1947, 13–16).

12 'os . . . deserdados – as mulheres e os chamados pobres'.

13 'para me manter o mais possível perto do texto de Virginia Woolf, mas podeis *traduzir* que as afirmações se mantêm de pé' [my italics].

[Virginia Woolf] is born again she may write her work to the last line, bequeathing us her secret – whole' (1947, 47).[14]

The two texts – Porto's essay on Woolf/*ROO*, and her subsequent preface to and translation of Woolf's stories – offer us one of the most telling examples of a metatextual strategy frequently employed by women to codify their own poetics of marginalization, and whose relevance for Portuguese writers of that period has yet to be systematically studied. I mean the conscious use of translation and preface writing as writing activities allowing them to say by proxy that which was forbidden in their social context, that which they were not allowed to say in an autonomous text. If translation always is, in the words of Pessoa, 'only a plagiarism in the author's name' – or 'a serious parody', since it implies 'an adaptation to the spirit of the author for a purpose which the author did not have' (1993, 220)[15] – some of the most serious parodies in fascist Portugal were precisely those that allowed people to voice their muteness; and women writers, doubly silenced, would often seize this chance of 'speaking culturally from the margins' (Díaz-Diocaretz 1993, 105).[16]

Only two other translations of Virginia Woolf would be published in Portugal before the 1974 Revolution: *MD*, in 1954 (with a second edition in 1970), and *O* in 1962 (with a second edition in 1969). Both were published by Livros do Brasil, a publishing house that played a crucial role in the diffusion of contemporary foreign literature in Portugal. It should be noted that since the early 1940s there had flourished in Brazil an immense translating activity, in which many poets and novelists participated, often offering us some exemplary Portuguese versions of modern classics of world literature. *MD* came out in a correct and sensitive translation by Mário Quintana (a Brazilian poet and professional translator – he also first translated Proust into Portuguese) and *O* in the magnificent 1948 version of Cecília Meireles, the great Brazilian poet who also translated Rilke, Rabindranath Tagore and Lorca. The free translation by Meireles – for many Portuguese readers of the 1960s the first approach to Woolf's work – remains to this day, in my opinion, the best Portuguese version of Woolf's prose (the text was unfortunately out of print in Portugal for several years and, though reprinted in 1988, is now almost forgotten amidst the babble of better distributed and advertised second- or third-rate versions). Cecília Meireles's preface to her translation shares with Porto's an empathetic exaltation of Virginia Woolf's innovative poetics, and both comment on the risks of translating Woolf into another language.

---

14 'porque é indispensável que, quando a grande artista [Virginia Woolf] volte a nascer, possa escrever a sua obra até à última linha, legando-nos o seu segredo todo inteiro.'

15 This fragment was written in English by Pessoa.

16 'habla[r] culturalmente desde el margen'. The number of twentieth-century Portuguese women writers who published before 1974 and who at one time or other dedicated themselves to translation is extremely high (as is the number of those holding arts degrees, particularly in modern languages and literatures). This familiarity with 'foreign' voices was no doubt relevant to the particular capacity to refract the voice of the other(s) that has been detected in the best contemporary poetry and fiction written by Portuguese women.

Meireles invites her readers to take her as a guide and follow the same route she travelled in reading/translating Woolf, highlighting that the hardships of the journey lie in the complexity of the poetics and the originality of the vision, thus implying that travellers would not have an easier time by reading Woolf in Portuguese. Because Woolf requires attentive readers, 'meditating carefully on each sentence . . . for each sentence prepares a certain repercussion, and the most apparently disdainful is indispensable and irreplaceable' (Meireles 1962, 7–8).[17] A similar point, in a more modest register concerning her own ability to render Woolf in another language, is made by Manuela Porto (1951). Porto, arguing that perhaps in other readers are as unprepared as the Portuguese to read Woolf (having been trained into lazy reading and taught to enjoy the plain and obvious), invites her readers to approach Woolf's stories as she did, when translating them: that is to say, as poems,[18] and to consider the effort of the search, of the re-writing to which the reader will inevitably be challenged, as the gateway to reading Woolf later in the original. She insists on that point: her 'modest translation' is offered as a mere 'preamble' for 'attentive readers' who will then undoubtedly proceed to try and read Woolf's essays and fiction in English (Porto 1951, 15).[19] One cannot but wonder if Manuela Porto did not also have in mind, when chastising Portuguese readers for their attitude and taste and trying to 'educate' them, through her rendering of Woolf's prose, into careful and demanding readers, the fate of Irene Lisboa (1892–1959), the Portuguese modernist whose radically marginal aesthetic – in some ways similar to Woolf's[20] – found no readers among the wider public in her time.

It should be stressed that Porto's and Meireles's prefaces remain the only instances where Woolf's translators into Portuguese address the question of the difficulties of Woolf's prose by considering her language as an integral part of her poetics and her vision. The few prefaces to more recent translations (very rarely written by the translators themselves) tend to concentrate on Woolf's

---

17 'Meditando bem sobre cada frase . . . cada frase prepara uma certa repercussão, e o mais aparentemente desdenhável é indispensável e insubstituível'.

18 For when reading Woolf 'it is common to find ourselves before a page where we know all the words, where we clearly surmise a sense and that, nevertheless, becomes absolutely impossible to translate' ('é comum encontrarmo-nos diante de uma página de que conhecemos todos os vocábulos, da qual pressentimos claramente o sentido e que, no entanto, se torna absolutamente impossível de traduzir') (Porto 1951, 10).

19 'tradução modesta'; 'preâmbulo', 'o leitor atento'.

20 Although parallels between Irene Lisboa and Katherine Mansfield were drawn by several critics (probably due to Mansfield's popularity in Portugal), in an article first published in 1964 in a Brazilian newspaper (and later reprinted in Portugal), certain affinities between Woolf's and Lisboa's styles were remarked upon (Cunha 1965). But a better sense of what Lisboa's and Woolf's poetics may have had in common can be gained by looking at Maria Irene Ramalho de Sousa Santos's perceptive reading of Lisboa's poetry in 'Re-inventing Orpheus: Women and Poetry Today' (Santos 1998). See also the comparisons established by Maria Velho da Costa (Costa 2000a and 2000c).

biography, often used as the key to her work,[21] and scarcely make any comment on the problems encountered, even less on the methodology used by the translator. And when they do, as is the case of Michael Gordon Lloyd, in the short concluding lines of his preface to Mário Cláudio's translation of *TL*, it is to refer to the difficulties of facing a prose 'not infrequently *unconnected*, not infrequently *disorganized* in its structure' or the same 'various *problems of vocabulary* that we know that the French translation, made while the writer was still alive, had to deal with' (my italics) (Lloyd 1985, 13).[22] We could not be further from the stance – and the tone – adopted by Meireles and Porto (and – inevitably? – that would show in the later translations themselves).

The three Portuguese translations of Woolf that circulated in Portugal before 1974 were in a sense, as we have seen, fortuitous: Porto and Meireles had translated Woolf as the expression of a personal aesthetic encounter, in Porto's case also as a militant political and cultural gesture; Meireles' and Quintana's translations were 'imported' from Brazil in a collection of mainly Brazilian translations of old and modern classics.[23] If we turn to the academic circles, we find a similar contingency. Two scholars of distinction had written on Woolf in that period – Paulo Quintela and Jorge de Sena. But both Jorge de Sena's excellent chapter on Woolf in Ward's *História da literatura inglesa* (*History of English Literature*) (see above) and Paulo Quintela's splendid review of *TY* in 1938 seem to have gone unnoticed and met with no response from the publishing quarters.[24] In his reading of the novel – the first extended reference to Woolf's writings, beyond passing mentions, to come out in Portugal – Quintela made use of cinematic and musical parallels to analyse and comment

---

21 Other times it is her fiction that is used as 'the key' to her life – and to her death (as in Vale 1984, 93). The approach and the tone of the more recent interest in Woolf's biography doesn't often go beyond idle talk about her 'madness' and suicide or a voyeuristic curiosity about her sexuality (largely supported by or at the root of the popularity of Sally Potter's *O* and Nigel Nicolson's *Portrait of a Marriage* (see below)). The case of Manuela Porto's (1947) and Maria Ondina Braga's (1980; 1982) feminist interest in Woolf's biography was, on the other hand, of a different order – Woolf's life was 'read' by those writers as that of a modern(ist) Judith Shakespeare and as a supreme 'lesson' in the connections of politics and poetics.

22 'uma prosa ... não raro desconexa, não raro desorganizada em sua estrutura'; 'diversos problemas de vocabulário, que sabemos haverem-se colocado à tradução francesa, realizada ainda em vida da escritora'.

23 This does not mean that there were no other translations of Woolf's books in Brazil: *TW* had been translated by Sylvia Valladão Azevedo and published by Livraria do Globo in S. Paulo in 1946, but the book did not circulate in Portugal.

24 Paulo Quintela (1905–87), professor of English and German literature at the University of Coimbra, essayist, critic, eminent translator, theatre director and engaged citizen, played a very important role in Portuguese culture, and was particularly noteworthy for his lifelong fight against cultural and political parochial closure and oppression. He published his review of *TY* (Quintela 1996, 462–64) in 1938, in the prestigious literary journal *Revista de Portugal* (Porto, 1937–40), edited by Vitorino Nemésio, to which he contributed several pieces on contemporary English literature.

on Woolf's 'supreme technique of selection and condensation of an extremely rich fictional material' and to argue the complexity and final unity achieved by the 'masterly orchestration' of the novel.[25] His emphasis throughout on the 'fluency', 'unartfulness' and 'spontaneity' achieved by Woolf's 'superior narrative technique' seems at times to be an indirect answer to Edwin Muir's negative review of *TY* in *The Listener*, published in March 1937, which he may have read.[26] Also significant – of the times and of Quintela's own position – is his stress on how Woolf had managed to convey the 'historical forces that supported' Colonel Pargiter's family history, or the 'deep imprints' left on her characters by the 'blind forces that sculpt societies and men' (1996, 462–63).[27] A regular reader of *Scrutiny*, Paulo Quintela was no doubt also refuting here its 'case' against Virginia Woolf.

Given the quality of those few essays and translations published before the 1960s and their unreserved praise of Woolf's art, one cannot but wonder whether her poetics or her politics weighed more heavily in shaping the lack of interest of Portuguese publishers (who are probably cautious at best), particularly at a time when, for instance, Katherine Mansfield received much wider attention.[28] The fact remains that Paulo Quintela, Jorge de Sena and Manuela Porto were all political outsiders to the regime – and that it would be among the members of an 'Outsiders' Society' of sorts, the 'daughters of educated men' that were finally finding a voice in Portuguese literature, that Woolf's poetics would find the most attentive readers.

The common reader – and we must remember that readers were still not very common in Portugal then, and particularly women readers (in 1900, 85 per cent of Portuguese women were illiterate and we would have to wait until the 1950s to see the illiteracy rate among women fall slightly below 50 per

---

25 'técnica exemplar na capacidade de selecção e condensação do essencial da massa romanesca riquíssima' 'orquestração magistral'.

26 'tudo isto, repito, sem crispação nem entorse – espontâneo, fluente, nítido'.

27 'as forças históricas que a suportam' 'as dedadas fundas' 'forças cegas que esculpem as sociedades e os homens'.

28 No doubt the popularity of Katherine Mansfield in Portugal in the 1940s owes much to the writer and critic João Gaspar Simões (who translated and prefaced *The Garden Party* in 1940). Simões, who also acted as literary advisor to publishers, is no doubt responsible, in that capacity, for the subsequent publishing by Portugália of Manuela Porto's translation of the complete edition of Mansfield's *Letters*, which he prefaced. Simões frequently refers to Mansfield in his literary reviews – he also occasionally mentions Woolf when reviewing women's fiction (for instance, in a 1962 review, when establishing the 'affiliation' of Maria Judite de Carvalho's *Palavras Poupadas* (Spared Words), he mentions both *MD* and *TW* (1981, 282)). Interestingly enough, he keeps comparing Mansfield to Woolf, always to Woolf's advantage – for instance, in the preface to his translation of *The Garden Party*, he refers to Mansfield's 'art' ('arte') as 'less powerful' ('menos poderosa') than Woolf's (1940, 18). Why he never translated Woolf himself or advised others to do so remains an open question.

cent) – undoubtedly read Woolf in translation.[29] I cannot ascertain at this point how many Portuguese women writers discovered Woolf in translation (I presume some did), though I know of a few who read her in English in the 1950s and 1960s (Maria Velho da Costa, Maria Teresa Horta, Maria Isabel Barreno, Maria Ondina Braga). But I would be prepared to argue that Woolf played a significant role in the forging of that particular ability shown by Portuguese women writers of the 1950s and 1960s to 'unread' Portuguese isolation and describe that 'great absence of us to ourselves' that Lourenço detected in the *double regard* that affirmed itself in that period (1993, 257).[30] Without a national tradition of women's writing (middle-class Portuguese women began to write very late in the nineteenth century), and in a cultural context strongly under the dominance of a masculine and monologic social text, the thinking in common that lies behind the multiple and fractured single voices that emerged in the polyphony of Portuguese women's writing in the 1960s would owe more to the contribution of the modernist 'outsider from the centre' Virginia Woolf than to the modernist 'outsider from our margins' Irene Lisboa, ignored by the literary market.

It is no doubt an instance of feminist 'poetic justice' that *Novas Cartas Portuguesas* (New Portuguese Letters) – that final charter of our cultural autonomy – invites comparison with Woolf's work on several counts. In my reading of *ROO* those affinities were only hinted at by my use of references to the Three Marias (Abranches 1980). But Hilary Owen has since fully developed the parallels between the texts, highlighting both their use of the fragmentation of voice and the interplay between subject and object positions to deal with the relationships between gender and writing, and the political function they performed in the development of women's writing in their respective national traditions (Owen 1995). In the words of Maria de Lurdes Pintasilgo, in *Novas Cartas,* 'each one is who she is and many others too' ('cada uma é quem é e muitas outras') (1980, 15) – in the new letters Portuguese women were writing

---

29 Besides the three titles in Portuguese, French translations of Woolf were available in bookshops, as were a few English copies of her novels and essays. Local public libraries did not even have copies of the Portuguese versions (though both the Biblioteca Nacional (National Library) in Lisbon and the Biblioteca Geral (General Library) of the University of Coimbra, and, I presume, a couple of other large libraries also under the regime of 'legal deposit' of all books published in Portugal, had received from the publishers copies of Porto's, Quintana's and Meireles's translations). As for university libraries, the library of the English Institute of the Arts Faculty of the University of Coimbra, founded in 1932, and the first English library in a Portuguese university, acquired *TW* and *TL* in 1935, *CR 1-2* in 1936, *ROO* in 1938 (other copies of *ROO* entered in 1946, 1963 and 1975) and *BTA* in 1943. Not until three decades later, in December 1977, would other books by Virginia Woolf be bought (twelve titles in 1977, three in 1978, one in 1980 and eleven in 1981). A copy of *O* was finally donated to the library in 1986.

30 'essa grande ausência de nós a nós mesmos'.

in the 1960s and 1970s, Woolf gained her place among those others that '*they were*', by having helped them find their voice.[31]

III

After Meireles's *O*, first published in Portugal in 1962, we would have to wait another fifteen years for another translation from Woolf to come out. But in the last twenty years, twenty-five translations have been added to the three published before the 1974 Revolution, corresponding to thirteen new titles and thirty-three paperback editions. If we look into this renewed interest in translating Virginia Woolf's work, three different phases can be perceived, corresponding to different attitudes on the part of publishers, translators and the market.

A first phase is marked by the publishing of the translation of *ROO* and *TG*, in the aftermath of the revolution. *Um quarto que seja seu* (*ROO*) opened a new collection, called 'Fecunditas', that was to be dedicated to feminist texts, and *Os três guinéus* (*TG*) soon followed in the same series (the books were published in March and June 1978). This context may appear to repeat, forty years later, that of Manuela Porto's presentation of Virginia Woolf to Portuguese readers: again militant women are responsible for the initiative of (re)discovering Woolf and having her translated. Also, corresponding to Porto's preface (and to her reading of *ROO* in her 1947 lecture), we now have the text of *Um quarto que seja seu* preceded by an essay by one of the Three Marias, Maria Isabel Barreno. Barreno, who, like Porto, adopted a localized political perspective, approached Woolf from a more sociological and critically distanced stance than Porto (whom, by the way, she does not mention in her essay),[32] emphasizing the relevance of reading Woolf, while remarking on the historical limitations of her ideology – 'the book lacks a conclusion on the causes of the [social and political] asymmetry [between men and women], or even a decisive pointing out of that asymmetry' (1978, 10).[33] For Barreno,

---

[31] Reviewers have occasionally pointed to Woolfian characteristics in Portuguese women writers – Maria Judite de Carvalho and Irene Lisboa, for example (see notes *H* 20, 28), or Teolinda Gersão (Owen 1995, 186-7). Maria Ondina Braga would be another case in point. Quotations from Woolf have also occasionally been used as epigraphs (see Costa 1969, 163 and 1973, 77, in both instances from *TW*). But the affinities I am suggesting are more general and of a more diffuse order; they have to do with the 'new' characteristics that were detected in Portuguese women's writing after the 1950s (their use of free indirect speech, multiple voice, or 'fragmentary' discourse, for example) and imply, more than a case of 'direct influence' or quotation, closely related stylistic and poetical strategies.

[32] Porto's essay and her translation of Woolf's stories had the same fate as her fiction – they were never reprinted. And her manuscripts (among which there was very probably more work on Woolf) disappeared soon after her death (Rodrigues 1998, 329).

[33] 'o que falta neste livro: a conclusão relativa às causas da assimetria, ou mesmo o decisivo apontar dessa assimetria'.

Woolf 'seems to accept' a model of complementarity that leaves unquestioned the asymmetrical character of gendered social functions in the 'real' world, and in this ideal of 'complementarity' lies the flaw in Woolf's argument (11). If women have to enter 'the economic realm' to be able to find and affirm their own voice in literature, Barreno goes on to ask, how will they be able 'to continue to express the vision of a world of their own, a world where the structure of relations remains fundamentally linked to the ideological, a world which is exterior to the possibility and to the very necessity of earning money?' (12).[34] Barreno would more than once stress the historical impossibility of having Woolf write what she herself was able to argue in a different context[35] – but her reading of the ideology and politics of the text did not go beyond the more 'immediate' considerations (their value for Portuguese women of the post-revolutionary period); there is not one comment on the 'political' dimensions of Woolf's literary strategies (though she praises Woolf's 'clear argument' and 'innovative' style (8)).[36] She also makes no reference in her preface to the Portuguese translation that follows it, which she definitely did not read. For it is an unreadable text – without question the most incompetent, gross and arrogantly dishonest version of Woolf's work that has been published in Portugal.[37] Some excuse may be sought in the

---

34 'continuar a exprimir a visão de um mundo só delas, onde a estrutura de relações se mantém fundamentalmente ligada ao ideológico, um mundo que é exterior à possibilidade e à necessidade de ganhar dinheiro'.

35 Barreno was at the time about to publish a major text on which she had been working for about ten years: *A morte da mãe* (The Death of the Mother) (1979), a long poetical philosophical essay where, in a long 'dialogue' with Marx and Freud, she deconstructs the political and cultural history as written by Western patriarchy. The preface she wrote to *ROO* is indicative of her own concerns at the time.

36 'a sua clareza' 'inovador'.

37 My harsh review of the translation (Abranches 1980, 154–56) had, as might be expected, no effect as regards subsequent editions or reviews of the text. Both translations (*ROO* and *TG*) were made by Maria Emília Ferros Moura, a very prolific professional translator (nearly 200 titles since the early 1970s, ranging from erotic literature to popular bestsellers and mainstream texts, translated from English, French and German). Besides a total deafness to tone and register and such a bad command of Portuguese that some sentences and expressions are utterly incomprehensible, we can count among the operations performed on Woolf's text the amputation of whole 'difficult' paragraphs, the 'undoing' of metaphors and analogies and gross translation mistakes – all 'compensated for' by bold attempts to 'enrich' and 'improve on' Woolf's style. Adjectives and figures of speech are added, the vocabulary is 'raised' to what is no doubt considered a more dignified register (of irresistible comic effect) and 'variety' is offered to break the 'monotony' of repetition – one of the most telling examples of this last strategy can be found in the first two pages of the version of *ROO*, where four completely different translations are offered as the equivalent to 'a room of one's own'; and, by mischance, not one of them is right. Had I not had direct testimony of people inspired into thought and action by reading those texts I would not have considered it possible to go beyond the first page of either book. It is no doubt a measure of the strength of Woolf's ideas and prose that some of their power managed to survive the treatment to which her language was subjected.

revolutionary context, which asked for a reading of Woolf's essays as political tracts. And that is what *Um quarto que seja seu* and *Os três guinéus* became then, integrated within the large corpus of engaged literature, eagerly and urgently translated and read in a country finally freed from censorship. When, a few years later, *Um quarto que seja seu* was first reprinted, it would be the turn of another of the Three Marias, Maria Teresa Horta, to write an enthusiastic review of the book in the feminist magazine *Mulheres* (Women) – as a sign of the times, the long extracts she quotes from Barreno's preface do not include Barreno's ideological reservations; Horta simply urges women to make the book their 'bedside' text, to read and meditate on, 'pausing to look at the portrait of the other and of ourselves' (Horta 1985).[38] The hot days of the revolution were over, and with them 'material' historical 'difference' seemed to have been replaced by 'idealist' psychological 'identification'.

By then a second stage had been reached with regard to translations of Woolf into Portuguese, no doubt more in the wake of the international impact of the centenary of Woolf's birth, rather than as a reflection of Woolf's timid entrance into university curricula in the late 1970s or of a couple of essays on Woolf that came out in 1980.[39] In 1982, the Portuguese press published a number of articles on Woolf – for the most part imported from international news agencies – and national TV showed a BBC documentary on her life and work. Maria Ondina Braga's 'Evocação de Manuela Porto: no centenário de Virginia Woolf' (An Evocation of Manuela Porto: On Virginia Woolf's Centenary) (1982) is a remarkable exception both to the dominant acritical repetition of biographical chatter and, because of her timely evocation of Porto, to the capacity for non-inscription that seems so characteristic of Portuguese culture. In the following years, a number of respectable publishers were to bring out nine new titles by Virginia Woolf, for the most part in careful, and often scrupulous, translations.[40] A selection of Woolf's essays on the Art of Fiction *O momento total* (edited and translated by an academic and published by a commercial publishing house in a collection addressed to university students) would also be published in 1985. The number of publishers and translators (no translator translated more than one book) appears to indicate an overall response to Woolf's international reputation more than a particular strategy of a particular publisher. In some cases, the initiative came from the translators themselves, as happened with *Rumo ao Farol*

---

38 'determo-nos – a olharmos o retrato da outra e de nós mesmas'.

39 Abranches 1980 and Braga 1980. Since 1977, texts by Woolf have been taught in Portuguese universities (usually *MD* or *TL*, in modern English Literature courses) with some regularity. Very few new academic essays and no full-length studies have been published on Woolf in Portugal. The most interesting recent readings and references seem to be those of scholars familiar with Woolf's work, but not Woolf 'specialists' themselves, often writing from abroad or for foreign audiences.

40 Ulisseia (*MD*, 1982); Moraes (*TY*, 1983); Bertrand (*D*, 1-5, 1985-87); Afrontamento (*TL*, 1985, reprinted three times between 1985 and 1998; and *FB*, 1987); Cotovia (*JR*, 1989, *MDP*, 1990 and *BTA*, 1991); Relógio d'Água (*HH* and *TW*, 1988; they reprinted *TY* in 1992 and published a new translation of *O* in 1994).

(*TL*), proposed by the writer Mário Cláudio to his usual publishers. The fact remains that the translators chosen – writers, academics, literary critics and some respected literary translators[41] – seem to bear witness to a new concern for the quality of the Portuguese texts, absent both in the case of the two translations published in the 1970s (*ROO* and *TG*) and in the new paperback versions of the novels that were to proliferate in the 1990s.

In fact, after 1991, a new stage was reached with the end of copyright protection and with Woolf's rising popularity in Portugal after Sally Potter's film *Orlando* (1992) came out.[42] The moment was exploited by a commercial publisher (Europa-América) to launch eight new versions of previously translated novels (and a new title, *VO*) in paperback format. As might be expected (one title at the end of 1991 and four others in 1992, all by the same prolific translator who was responsible for a few other translations in the same period),[43] these are careless, often grossly incorrect versions (the number and the type of errors belied my initial suspicion of plagiarism of previous versions). Unfortunately, though some of the translations of the 1980s have been reprinted in the 1990s, a few went out of print and most are more difficult to find (both in bookshops and public libraries) than the cheap, better distributed but blatantly defective new translations. One cannot underestimate the negative effect of this situation for Woolf's reception in a country where even university students in Modern Language and Literature programmes often read the assigned books in translation. Even the more respectable translations of the 1980s have left Woolf 'reft of her coat and manners', beyond the inevitable in 'a railway accident' (Woolf, 'The Russian Point of View', *CE* 1: 240). Manuela Porto hit the mark when she chastised her readers for their love of the plain and obvious, though she might as well have been addressing future Portuguese translators of Woolf. Few (if any) have since resisted the need to

---

41 Mário Cláudio, writer (*TL*), Ricardo Alberty, writer and translator (*MD*), Miguel Serras Pereira, literary translator and academic (*HH*), Mário Avelar, academic (*MDP*), Francisco Vale, literary critic and writer (*TW*), and also Pedro Elston (*TY*), Isabel de Freitas Lopes (*BTA*), Maria José Jorge (*D*), Maria Teresa Guerreiro (*JR*) and Maria de Lourdes Guimarães (*FB*).

42 Potter's film has since been shown several times on national TV. The launching of the film in Portugal was used by 'Círculo de Leitores' (a book club whose books have the highest circulation among all publishers in Portugal) to issue a much advertised new translation of Nicolson's *Portrait of a Marriage* (the first translation had been brought out by other publishers in 1976). On a different level, the performance of Darryl Pinckney and Bob Wilson's *Orlando*, with Isabelle Huppert, at Culturgest in Lisbon (17–19 February 1995) motivated a number of lengthy reviews in the press, thanks mainly to Wilson's trendy popularity in Lisbon's intellectual circles. Those events may have helped the popularity of Woolf's *O* (the latest translation of the book, published in 1994, had received considerable attention from reviewers) – though the coffee-table 1992 edition of *Retrato de um casamento* (Portrait of a marriage) sold much more and no doubt had many more readers.

43 Lucília Rodrigues (*O* in 1991, *JR*, *TL*, *TW* and *BTA* in 1992, *VO* and *HH* in 1995, all for Europa-América).

'fill in' what they perceive as Woolf's 'blanks' or answer the questions she 'left in mid air' (substituting nouns for pronouns is the milder manifestation of this rage to improve on and clarify a prose that must presumably be made to conform to the supposedly atavistic laziness of Portuguese readers).[44] But at times, unexpectedly, Portuguese common readers have been able to 'fly off at a tangent close to the truth' (*CE* 1: 246); though rarely again so close as when taken into flight by the language of Cecília Meireles's *O*.

Or by Maria Velho da Costa. In her latest novel, *Irene ou o contrato social* (Irene, or The Social Contract), Maria Velho da Costa – the third Maria – creates 'the ultimate diatopic character' ('a personagem diatópica por excelência') (Santos, in print) and names him Orlando.[45] Orlando is 'the great mystery on earth': of 'unclear origins', he is a mixed-'race' black young man that 'inhabits two absolute privileges: extreme intelligence and extreme wealth' (Costa, 2000a, 2).[46] Handsome, politically aware and sensitive, multicultural, multilingual and multidimensional, he moves at ease in worlds as different as the international upper class set to which his stepfather – a Jewish

---

44 Pronouns are a problem when translating into Portuguese, for in Portuguese they are frequently omitted in the subject position – but to substitute them, almost systematically, for their referents, is no 'solution' to the problem, and it is a particularly awkward strategy when used within an interior monologue (see, to give an example of a careful translation, its repeated use in Cláudio's *Rumo ao Farol* (*TL*)).

45 Maria Velho da Costa, not for the first time, 'borrows' names from Woolf in her characteristically brilliant use of parodic allusion and (mis)quotation – with 'Orlando' though, the parody is more 'serious' and sustained than with 'Flush', Sara's dog in *Missa in Albis* (1988), one of the many intertextual Woolfian 'winks' in Velho da Costa's fiction (the case of Raquel/Rachel in *Irene ou o contrato social* would also be worth pursuing). In a recent interview (2000a, 2), she acknowledged that Orlando in *Irene ou o contrato social* was a 'reference to Woolf, to *Orlando Furioso* and also to a writer, [her] friend Orlando da Costa' ('uma referência à Virginia Woolf, ao "Orlando Furioso" e também a um escritor, um amigo . . ., que é o Orlando da Costa'); but that 'nothing in the character is androgynous' ('nada na personagem é andrógino') – the 'only thing' ('a única coisa') she took from Woolf's *Orlando*, Velho da Costa said, was a joke where she has Orlando say 'when the journey is over I'll be a boy and a girl too' ('quando acabar a viagem sou menino e menina também'). (Velho da Costa is referring to the passage where Orlando recalls the Nursery Rhymes/'Hystery rhymes' that Frau Hannah, his governess, used to teach him (2000b, 45–46) – Frau Hannah owes her name, of course, to Hannah Arendt.) If we remember that Ariosto's Orlando was the perfect knight fighting the Saracens and that the writer Orlando da Costa is a politically engaged citizen, born in Goa, of Portuguese-Indian descent, we may have a glimpse of the (iconoclastic) *métissage* in the genealogy of 'literary' allusions of Velho da Costa's Orlando – and of her superb re-writing of the 'inter-identitary' androgyny of Woolf's hero/ine. Significant also is the fact that, in the interviews she gave when the novel came out, Velho da Costa makes several references to Woolf and stresses the affinities between Irene Lisboa (to whom she is explicitly 'paying homage' in the novel) and Virginia Woolf (2000a, 2000c).

46 'um grande mistério ao cimo da terra' 'a sua filiação não é clara' 'habitante de dois privilégios absolutos, a extrema inteligência e a riqueza'.

diplomat – belongs, the black youth subcultures of Lisbon, or the working-class society where he serves his one year of 'wandering' as an apprentice mason. 'If he has any ethical virtue, it is just because he wants to' (Costa, 2000a, 2):[47] postcolonial 'Caliban reinvented as Ariel' (Santos, in print),[48] Orlando will enter into a 'contract' with Irene (the elderly poet from Lisbon who in the novel 'authors' Irene Lisboa's lines) to 'take care' of her own death, by killing her under bond of euthanasia. In the complex inter-textual and inter-identitary journey that the novel so powerfully performs, Shakespeare, Irene Lisboa and Woolf thus become passengers in transit in postcolonial Lisbon – and Orlando, the *mestizo* who 'will be a boy and a girl too', stands, in a superb homage to Virginia Woolf, as the metaphor for the future of Europe (Costa, 2000c, 22).

---

47 'E se alguma virtude ética tem é porque a quer ter.'
48 'Caliban-reinventado-Ariel.' *The Tempest* is actually staged in the novel.

18 The European Dimensions of the Hogarth Press

Laura Marcus

Discussion of the Hogarth Press, the publishing house started by Leonard and Virginia Woolf in 1917, may seem tangential to the topic of the reception of Virginia Woolf in Europe. Yet the Hogarth Press not only played a key role in British modernist cultural production; it was also an important site and conduit for the European and internationalist dimensions of modernist culture. The topic is a broad one, and not all of its aspects and ramifications can be explored in detail here. The areas I have touched on include the Hogarth Press's negotiations with European publishers and translators, particularly over Virginia Woolf's writings; its translations of European texts, most extensively of Russian literature and the poetry of Rilke; and the complex history of its publication of the International Psycho-Analytical Library, the English branch of the Internationaler Psychoanalytischer Verlag, founded in Vienna in 1919. My focus is primarily on the history of the Press in the 1920s and 1930s.[1]

In recent years interest has grown in the 'institutions of modernism', including the 'little magazines' and the small presses of the early decades of the twentieth century, and publishing history is being reintegrated into cultural history. The history of the Hogarth Press is particularly intriguing, not least because it survived when so many other small presses established at around the same time failed to do so, retaining total autonomy until the merger with Chatto and Windus in 1946. The Woolfs began their Press as a hobby, with printing rather than publishing as their goal. They hand-printed some thirty-five books between 1917 and 1932, including Katherine Mansfield's short story 'Prelude', T. S. Eliot's *Poems* (1919) and *The Waste Land*, and Nancy Cunard's *Parallax* (1925), as well as their own *Two Stories* (1917), Virginia's 'Kew Gardens' and 'On Being Ill', and Leonard's 'Stories of the East'. (During the same period, 315 books in total were published by the Press.) To some extent the list of hand-printed books corresponded to Virginia Woolf's first imaginings for the Press, described in a letter of 1916: 'We are thinking of starting a printing press, for all our friends' stories' (*L* 2: 120). By 1920,

1 The fullest history of the Hogarth Press is given in Willis 1992. See also Marcus 1996.

however, the Woolfs were turning to a commercial printer (Francis Meynell's Pelican Press) for the entire production of a book: S. S. Koteliansky's and Leonard Woolf's translation of Maxim Gorky's *Reminiscences of Tolstoi*, whose success, Leonard Woolf later wrote, 'was really the turning point for the future of the Press and for our future' (L. Woolf 1980, 254). He also locates the success of Virginia Woolf's 'Kew Gardens' as 'the first of many unforeseen happenings which led us, unintentionally and often reluctantly, to turn the Hogarth Press into a commercial publishing house', as well as a turning-point in her own development as a writer: 'Kew Gardens' was 'a microcosm of all her then unwritten novels' (1980, 228–29).

This account suggests some of the most interesting dimensions of the Press: the interdependency of the Press's expansion and of Virginia Woolf's development as a writer, and the importance of the Press's translations from the Russian. S. S. Koteliansky is a figure to whom I will return; for the moment I will simply note that his name first appears in one of Virginia Woolf's early discussions of the Press. She wrote to David Garnett, after he had admired her short story 'The Mark on the Wall' (first published, as the Press's first publication, alongside Leonard Woolf's 'Three Jews' in *Two Stories*):

> I'm very glad you liked the story. In a way its easier to do a short thing, all in one flight than a novel. Novels are frightfully clumsy and overpowering of course; still if one could only get hold of them it would be superb. I daresay one ought to invent a completely new form. Anyhow it's very amusing to try with these short things, and the greatest mercy to be able to do what one likes – no editors, or publishers, and only people to read who more or less like that sort of thing. We've been seeing a Russian named Koteliansky who says that to write for a small public is damnation. However, I dont like writing for my half brother George [Gerald Duckworth]. (*L* 2: 167–68)

Emphasizing the importance of experiment, of freedom and of a sympathetic readership – the keys to the meaning of the Hogarth Press for her – Virginia Woolf also evinces a desire to cut out the literary 'middleman'. In writing for the Hogarth Press, she suggests here and elsewhere, her work will no longer be mediated by editors and publishers, nor received by an indiscriminate public. After 1919, all Virginia Woolf's novels and many of her other writings were published by the Woolfs' own press. Thus various forms of mediation were eliminated.

Yet, from another perspective – the perspective of this essay – others open up. As the publishers and the distributors of their own writings, the Woolfs as authors were more than usually closely involved in negotiation with translators and foreign publishers. As the publisher of other writers (and here Leonard Woolf played a far more active role than Virginia), the Press had two particularly significant European dimensions: the translation and publication of Freud's and other psychoanalytic texts, and translations from Russian literature. Both developments helped turn the Hogarth Press into a substantial publishing house. Both raise crucial questions of translation and mediation, linguistic and cultural. In addition, the Press's publication of European writers – including Cavafy, Svevo, Hölderlin and, most extensively, Rilke – played a decisive role in the ways in which these writers were translated into English and received in Britain.

Virginia Woolf is more obviously present in some of the aspects of the Hogarth Press I explore than in others. Yet even where her involvement was slight or unrecorded, as with the Press's Rilke translations, the history of cultural mediation and dissemination makes its contribution to the more particular story of the European connections of Virginia Woolf and her milieu. Her engagement and concern with the translation process, as in her work with and on Russian literature, suggests that, despite her seeming indifference to foreign-language versions of her own texts, she was fascinated by the historical, philosophical, cultural and literary questions raised by translation.

Virginia Woolf in translation

In the early to mid-1920s, the Woolfs were prepared to consider requests from freelance translators eager to translate Virginia's writings. By the late 1920s, would-be translators were informed that the Press would deal only with publishers, and not with agents or freelancers. The Press was clearly keen to develop formal and consistent relationships with foreign publishers, and in the late 1920s these were to some extent established with Insel-Verlag and Éditions Stock in Germany and France respectively.

The translation and publication of Virginia Woolf's work was earliest in France; letters in the Hogarth Press archives date from 1926,[2] with a proposal from Mlle Lichnerowicz – apparently supported by Valéry Larbaud, the novelist and translator of James Joyce – for the publication of sections of *JR* (*La Chambre de Jacob*) in an anthology of modern foreign authors (26.3.26, HP). Translations into French have been of particular interest not only because of these early beginnings, but because of the literary status of the translators, who included Charles Mauron and Marguerite Yourcenar. Mauron, the translator of *O* and *FB*, also translated the 'Time Passes' section of *TL*, which was published in advance of the book in *Commerce*, Paris, winter 1926. Its first appearance was thus in French, a situation referred to by Woolf in a letter to Edward Sackville-West: 'I'm glad, but surprised, that you like Time Passes. I thought that between The Princesse Bassiano [the publisher of *Commerce*] and the translator it had got into a hopeless mess, and was too ashamed to read it' (*L* 3: 315–16).

By 1927, the Press was involved in negotiations with the Librairie Stock over the publication of *MD*, translated by Simone David, with a preface by André Maurois, whose literary influence in France was considerable. The following year, *TL* was translated for the same publishers by Maurice Lanoire, from whom a surviving letter, written to Virginia, refers to 'your kind assurance that you would help me through my translation of "To the Lighthouse", which is nearly completed'. The translator asks for clarification of

---

2 The Chatto and Windus–Hogarth Press files are held in the publishers' archives at the University of Reading Library. My thanks to Random House for permission to quote from these records, and to Michael Bott, the archivist at the University of Reading, for his help.

particular lines (' "There was something, of course, that people wanted". What do you mean? The sense must be plain but somehow i[t] baffles me') and refers to the difficulty of translating 'the flow, the admirable flow of your sentences or periods. The French language does not possess the plasticity of the English and its roll cannot always have the same length' (4.7.1928, HP).

Paul Dottin, in an essay on Woolf, published in the *Revue de France* in 1930, asserted that 'All the novels of Mrs Virginia Woolf will soon be available to the French public: Stock have undertaken to publish all of them and have recruited a really excellent team of translators' (Majumdar 1975, 250). The Press archives reveal, however, a more provisional and at times fraught relationship between the Hogarth Press and Éditions Stock over Woolf's writings. Having published *TL* and *MD*, Stock initially turned down *O*:

> We are sure that Mrs Woolf will understand when we say that it is impossible to believe, or even to hope, that a very large public should appreciate it here. It is not only that the work is, in itself, for English readers, extremely puzzling and difficult, but also that for French readers, quite apart from the difficulty of translation, there is a real enigma in this book for which the public will not have the key, and one cannot expect success from a book which is not understood. (17.1.1929, HP)[3]

Although Stock did finally agree to publish *O*, it is noticeable that they gave similar reasons for rejecting first *ROO* and later *TG*. It would seem that Woolf's most overtly feminist texts were received by Stock as untranslatable in cultural terms, their topics and its treatment specific to England. Thus the subject of *ROO* is held to be 'too special and too exclusively related to problems of English life to be published with any success in French' (28.5.1930, HP).[4] A letter from a French translator (Mme M. T. Gueritte) who had learned that Stock was not planning to publish *ROO* comes straight to the point:

> I have repeatedly stressed to them the interest of this volume, but the interest of women is the last concern of men over here, and I did not succeed. But this book really must be published in French. All the women in France who write need it, and I am also very keen that you be known here as an essayist as well as a novelist. (7.11.1930, HP)[5]

---

3 'Nous sommes persuadés que Madame Woolf nous comprendra quand nous dirons qu'il est impossible de croire, ou même d'espérer, qu'un très nombreux public, ici, puisse l'apprécier. Non seulement, il y a le fait que l'œuvre est, en soi-même, pour des lecteurs anglais, extrêmement curieuse et difficile, mais encore pour les lecteurs français, mise à part la difficulté de la traduction, il y a dans ce livre une véritable énigme dont le public n'aura pas la clef, et on ne peut pas espérer un succès d'un livre qui n'est pas compris.'

4 'Trop spécial et tient trop exclusivement aux questions de la vie anglaise pour pouvoir être publié avec succès en français.'

5 'J'ai insisté plusieurs fois près d'eux en leur montrant l'intérêt de ce volume; mais l'intérêt des femmes est le dernier souci des hommes de chez nous, et je n'ai pas réussi. Mais il faut absolument que ce livre soit publié en français. Toutes les

This letter, addressed to Virginia Woolf and written in the spirit of *ROO* against the professional belittlers of women, received the standard response that the Press did not grant translation rights directly to translators.

While the Hogarth Press was from its inception, as I have suggested, conceived as a means to cut out the middlemen of publishing, the literary agent Curtis Brown was employed from the mid-1920s to negotiate foreign rights. There is no very substantial evidence of Woolf's interest in the translations of her work, though she did write to Roger Fry in 1928, after he had praised *O*: 'I'm vaguely in treaty with a French professor who wants to translate it, but Mauron would be much better of course' (*L* 3: 562). Mauron's translation of *O* was published in 1931. As a close friend of Roger Fry's, Mauron was the translator with whom Virginia Woolf had most contact and connection; the Hogarth Press published his *Aesthetics and Psychology* (translated by Roger Fry and Katherine John) in 1935, and he contributed to the Press's memorial volume for Virginia Woolf's nephew Julian Bell, who was killed in Spain in 1937.

Woolf's diaries and letters also evidence her meeting with Marguerite Yourcenar, whose translation of *TW* was published as *Les Vagues* in 1937. Woolf protests in her diary and in a letter to Ethel Smyth about the interruption to her work and her evening – 'That extraordinary scribble means, I suppose, the translator coming. Madame or Mlle Youniac (?) Not her name. And I had so much to write about Julian' – but ends by expressing some interest in Yourcenar:

> I've no time or room to describe the translator, save that she wore some nice gold leaves on her black dress; is a woman I suppose with a past; amorous; intellectual; lives half the year in Athens; is in with Jaloux &c, red lipped, strenuous; a working Fchwoman; friend of the Margeries; matter of fact; intellectual; we went through The Waves. What does 'See here he comes?' mean & so on. (*D* 5: 60–61)

Woolf appears far more interested in Yourcenar as a 'type' than in her work on *TW*. In fact, Mary Ann Caws and Sarah Bird Wright, in their recent book on *Bloomsbury in France*, suggest that Woolf's novel was not well served by Yourcenar: her translation was 'a surprisingly literal rendering' and her language was heavy, 'unsuited to Woolf's subtlety' (Caws and Wright 2000, 355). *TW* was subsequently re-translated by Cécile Wajsbrot.

The Hogarth Press archives reveal the Woolfs' – more particularly Leonard's – hostility towards the practice in France of allowing translators to arrange publication of extracts from the translated work in journals prior to book publication, the translator receiving part or all of the fee. An indignant letter was written in response to Stock's explanation that the practice of pre-publishing 'bonnes feuilles' served not only as publicity for the translated work in its entirety, but was a way of helping translators: 'We publishers often leave

---

cont.

femmes qui écrivent, en France, en ont besoin, et puis je désire vivement qu'on vous connaisse chez nous comme essayiste aussi bien que comme romancière.'

these small profits from the publication of 'bonnes feuilles' to the translators, who are often poor' (4.2.1931, HP). The exchange arises in the context of the Hogarth Press's assertion in 1931 that 'there is no point in having Mrs Woolf's books in future published in France' and that payments in the United States, Sweden, Germany, Czechoslovakia and Italy were considerably higher (30.1.1931, HP). Librairie Stock's response – at this point and in later correspondence – was to point out that their particular contribution to the European dissemination of Woolf's work had been to cultivate a critical climate for the appreciation of her work as well as a reading public: 'We obtained this result by the care we took over our translations and the literary reputation of our output which have contributed to the great value of books accessible only to the elite' (27.5.1938, HP).[6]

Although relations with Librairie Stock were, as I have suggested, not always smooth, the Hogarth Press did establish a more consistent pattern of translation and publication in France than in Germany in the pre-war period. In the middle years of the 1920s the Press, and on occasion Virginia Woolf herself, were in discussion with freelance translators. In the autumn of 1927, however, Curtis Brown succeeded in interesting Insel-Verlag in *MD*, with an option on *TL*, and, as in France, independent translators were informed that the Press dealt only with publishers. Such arrangements were, of course, very much to the disadvantage of translators, who could not secure the work, as they might well have done if allowed to approach a publisher themselves. The Press files contain numerous letters from disgruntled translators, whose idiosyncratic English calls to mind a scene in Dorothy Sayers's *Gaudy Night*: 'Imbecile, writing very bad English, was eager to translate Miss Vane's works into Italian. Could Miss Vane inform the writer of what books she had composed? Translators were all like that – no English, no sense, no backing' (Sayers 1988, 203). The files also contain extensive correspondence over 'pirated' versions of Woolf's essays, sold by unauthorized translators to journals.

Insel-Verlag contracted to publish the German translation of *O*, but with *FB* German rights were given to S. Fischer-Verlag. (The number of requests from would-be translators enquiring about *FB* is striking; *FB* was clearly an attractively translatable text, linguistically and culturally.) In 1936 Fischer-Verlag refused *TW*, however, on the grounds that it would appeal to too small a circle of readers. The German translator of *FB* for Fischer-Verlag (Herberth Herlitschka), writing in 1936, suggested that Virginia Woolf had been ill-served by her first translators in Germany – 'Mrs Dalloway came out in a translation which is an abomination' – and that 'German readers were frightened off and never asked for a book of yours again .... After that the Insel-Verlag lost courage ... you have as yet no public over here.' The writer also noted the uncertain situation with S. Fischer-Verlag: 'The firm is bound to split. The Berlin part will go Nazi and the real owner is trying to set up a new firm at Zurich, but has not yet quite succeeded in doing so' (10.3.36, HP).

---

[6] 'Nous avons obtenu ce résultat par le soin donné à nos traductions et la renommée littéraire de nos productions qui ont soutenu la grande valeur de livres d'accès réservé à l'élite.'

In the following year – 1937 – a letter from a German literary agent writing from New York expressed interest in placing German rights on *TY*, providing 'that the author is not jewish' (17.7.37, HP). There are few subsequent letters in the files, though from those that exist it is clear that German publishers experienced increasing difficulty in making payments, and that Swiss publishers were taking over a substantial amount of publishing activity, including the printing of German translations of books banned in Germany.

Translating Rilke

J. H. Willis, in his invaluable history of the Hogarth Press, writes that: 'Whatever else may be said about the achievement or influence of the Hogarth Press between the wars, its preeminence is unchallenged in the field of Rilke translations' (Willis 1992, 344). With their first two publications of Rilke translations, both of which appeared in 1931, the Hogarth Press played a relatively limited role. It acted as English publisher for the American Norton edition of *The Notebook of Malte Laurids Brigge*, translated by John Linton, and as distributor for the Cranach Presse's limited edition of *Duineser Elegien: Elegies from the Castle of Duino*, translated by Vita Sackville-West and her cousin Edward Sackville-West. The *Duineser Elegien*, of which 238 copies were printed, was expensively designed and produced for Count Harry Kessler of the Cranach Presse, in specially cut type on hand-made paper, and represents one of the very few Hogarth Press involvements with the 'fine printing' typifying those small presses which extended late nineteenth-century arts and crafts publishing into the twentieth century and which, for the most part, lasted only a few years.

Although Leonard Woolf expressed disappointment in the results of the Sackville-West translation of Rilke – only seventy copies were sold in the first year – he remained interested in the possibilities of publishing Rilke translations in England. Between 1930 and 1934, the Insel-Verlag published the six-volume *Collected Poetry* of Rilke. Given the Hogarth Press's existing connections with Rilke translation and publishing, Leonard Woolf was favourably disposed towards extending this aspect of the list; Rilke was, moreover, one of his favourite poets. In 1933 he was approached by J. B. Leishman, a Germanist and Rilke scholar at University College Southampton, about the publication of a selection of Rilke's poems; as Willis notes, Leonard Woolf agreed to publish them after Leishman had obtained publishing rights from the Insel-Verlag (Willis 1992, 269), and the Press acquired sole English rights for Rilke's poems, with the exception, at this stage, of the *Duino Elegies*.

Nonetheless, Leonard Woolf's letters of 1933 show his concern over the political situation in Germany and his profound reservations over dealings with German companies. In a letter to Leishman (27 August 1933), he asks to be released from 'negotiations with you and the Insel Verlag ... if you see your way to releasing me from it, I should be greatly obliged. In that case I shall write to Insel-Verlag and say that I cannot sign an agreement with them as long as the present conditions exist in Germany' (Spotts 1989, 316). Leishman replied at length from Germany, where he was staying, giving his own perceptions of the situation: the thrust of his argument is that Rilke belongs to Europe rather than to Germany alone, and that internationalism must be kept open at all costs as a counter to dangerous nationalisms (31.8.1933, HP 387). Woolf's response was that while he was not really convinced of such arguments:

> I have decided to sign the agreement with the Insel-Verlag and I have now done so. I have discussed the matter with various people here and I find that few share my view. I am afraid that I still maintain it, but I do not think that in a case like this I should act upon it, particularly where I have already gone so far both with you and the Insel-Verlag. The chance of doing any good and the good that one might do are so small; the possibility of forming a sound or unprejudiced opinion is so doubtful that I do not think that I should be justified in going back on what amounts to an undertaking. (Spotts 1989, 319)

The Press in fact maintained relatively untroubled relations with Insel-Verlag, and the most fraught correspondence over the Rilke translations arose in two rather different contexts. The first was Leishman's collaboration with Stephen Spender in a new translation of the *Duino Elegies*. The second, related context was Leonard Woolf's determination to retain the Hogarth Press's monopoly as Rilke's English publisher. Both raise questions about modes of translation, a topic on which Spender and Leishman disagreed radically.

In November 1933, Leishman called the Press's attention to a translation of Rilke's 'Orpheus, Eurydice, Hermes' by Stephen Spender in the journal *New Verse*, an infringement of copyright which the Press investigated. Spender apologized to the Woolfs – whom he knew personally – for the infringement, pleading ignorance of the Hogarth Press's purchase of the option. Nonetheless, he argues, he would find it hard to believe that any publisher could object to the publication of 'a single very beautiful poem by Rilke, accurately translated' (HP 387); he had, moreover, hoped to continue with his Rilke translations, and to produce a complete volume. Leonard Woolf responded by alerting Spender to the Press's agreements with the Insel-Verlag and with Leishman as translator, and, noting the small public for Rilke's poetry in England, insists that 'there is no possible place for two translations' (24.11.33, HP 387). Spender's response points up the difference between the aesthetic considerations of the writer and the commercial considerations of the publisher: 'Not being a business man I still have a feeling that translation is almost as wide a field as original work, and that two translations of the same work would be complementary to each other and not competing' (4.12.33, HP 387).

This correspondence is indicative of Leonard Woolf's determination to maintain the Hogarth Press's position as the English publisher of Rilke, and to keep other translators – Robert (R. F. C.) Hull being the most persistent applicant for permission – out of the field. Leonard Woolf was also increasingly committed to translating and publishing complete works or volumes by Rilke, as they appeared in German, rather than selections from the works, not only because he felt Rilke should be represented in full rather than in part, but as a way of retaining and extending the Hogarth Press's position as publishers of Rilke in English.

It was Leishman's suggestion that he collaborate with Stephen Spender on a new translation of the *Duino Elegies*. Whatever Leishman's motives for this – perhaps the feeling that a Rilke scholar and a practising poet might together do justice to the work – he clearly began to regret the proposal from an early stage. It was one which Leonard Woolf had been very keen to encourage, and on the strength of the proposed collaboration with Spender, the Hogarth Press was able to interest W. W. Norton in acting as co-publishers in America. Norton rejected other translations of Rilke by Leishman, which failed to impress Mrs Herter Norton, herself a Rilke scholar and translator, who later produced a translation of *The Notebooks of Malte Laurids Brigge*.

In the early stages of the collaboration, which began in 1937, Leishman began to express concern that Spender was insufficiently committed to the project, and became increasingly vexed at his 'off-hand manner'. As Spender pointed out to Leonard Woolf, 'he [Leishman] objects to my having anything else to do except Rilke during these few months. In that case, I had better say frankly that it is impossible for me to put everything else aside, that I am preoccupied by such things as work for Spain, and that for the next six months, for financial reasons, I shall have to earn my own income. Therefore I can't guarantee that I won't be behind with work' (1.12.37, HP 380). The tension grew a good deal greater when the two men realized their very different approaches to the work itself. Whereas Leishman insisted on the importance of maintaining the metre of the *Elegies*, but believed that the translator should aim for an equivalent rather than a literal translation of Rilke's imagery, Spender wanted to use an irregular metre – 'because it seems to me that the hexameter is boring and monotonous in English and also demands too many sacrifices in the way of distortion, verboseness and paraphrase from the translator: too much is sacrificed to the metre' (8.12.37, HP 380). In a later letter to Leonard Woolf, Spender wrote that 'my objection to writing in hexameters is fundamental – it is an objection that any English poet, of the past or present, would uphold' (14.12.37, HP 380). Spender committed himself to the 'exact imagery which Rilke uses', whereas Leishman, as he wrote to Spender, felt that: 'it is as necessary to preserve Rilke's metre, or the nearest possible equivalent of his metre, as to preserve his imagery'. Moreover, 'it is impossible to preserve the "exact imagery", because the appeal is to the *ear* as well as to the *eye*'. Your 'numerous inversions', Leishman adds, 'make Rilke appear like a savage in a top hat' (11.12.37, HP 380).

Leishman's solution to their failure to agree on fundamental principles of translation was to suggest that both their versions be published in the same volume, 'perhaps with letters to each other, expressing our disagreement' (11.12.37, HP 380). Not surprisingly, Leonard Woolf rejected this suggestion summarily, and, in response to Leishman's numerous attempts to detach Spender from the project, informed him with increasing frankness that 'it was Spender's name which induced Norton to make the agreement ... if there is any question of publishing a translation by only one translator, it is more probable that I should choose Spender than you' (15.12.37, HP 380).

The translation of the *Duino Elegies* was completed in early 1939, though enmities continued even in the final stages over the translators' note, with Leishman claiming the greater part of the credit for the translations, and, in

W. W. Norton's reading, seeking to repudiate Spender's collaboration. The note was changed on Norton's insistence, and with Leonard Woolf's approval, to represent the translation as a full collaboration between Leishman and Spender and for many years the Leishman–Spender translation of the *Duino Elegies* remained the classic English version of the text, despite the chequered history of its creation and production.

Leishman continued to translate Rilke for Hogarth Press publications. In 1949, when it became permissible to negotiate contracts directly with German publishers, Leonard Woolf reopened relations with Insel-Verlag. He also wrote to Leishman: 'In looking through the *Ausgewählte Werke* and comparing it to our scattered publications, I feel very strongly that Rilke's stature demands now a complete English translation of the collected works as in this volume .... Would you consider undertaking such a translation if the Insel-Verlag agree?' (18.5.49, HP 606). Woolf's correspondence at this time – with Insel-Verlag and with Leishman – suggest the extent of the Hogarth Press's commitment to Rilke's writings and to their accessibility to an English-speaking readership. As with the publication of Freud's writings, Leonard Woolf was also committed to the representation of Rilke in translation by the fullest possible versions of his œuvre.

The International Psycho-Analytical Library

In June 1914, the *New Weekly* published the first review of Freud's work to appear in a non-medical English journal – Leonard Woolf's review of *The Psychopathology of Everyday Life* (translated by A. A. Brill, who had also translated *The Interpretation of Dreams*). Ten years later, in 1924, the Hogarth Press became the English-language publishers of Freud's work, and other psychoanalytic writings, taking over the publications of the International Psycho-Analytical Library, which from 1924 onwards were produced under the auspices of the newly created Institute of Psycho-Analysis. In the same year, *The Nation*, the journal for which Leonard Woolf was literary editor, published a series of essays on Freud, opening with Clive Bell's 'Dr Freud and Art', and the Hogarth Press published Roger Fry's *The Artist and Psycho-Analysis*. 1924–25 were also the years of Alix Strachey's analysis with Karl Abraham in Berlin, during which time she formed friendships with a number of analysts, including Melanie Klein; Alix, with her husband James Strachey, who had been analysed by Freud in Vienna, had already embarked upon their lifelong task of translating Freud into English.[7] Virginia Woolf's brother, Adrian Stephen, and his wife Karin (Costello) Stephen, had already trained as doctors and psychoanalysts.

Nineteen twenty-four, then, was a key year for 'Bloomsbury Freud', and the decade preceding it one in which Bloomsbury interest in psychoanalysis, cultural and professional, had steadily grown. The Hogarth Press was thus an appropriate choice when Ernest Jones was seeking a publisher to take over the

---

[7] See Strachey and Strachey 1985.

business of publishing the works of the International Psycho-Analytical Press, founded in London under the aegis of the London Institute of Psycho-Analysis (reformed as the British Psycho-Analytical Society in 1919), to produce a periodical and English translations of the works published in Vienna by the Internationaler Psychoanalytischer Verlag, founded in January 1919. The London Institute had begun, as Leonard Woolf notes in his autobiography (L. Woolf 1980, 308), by acting as their own publisher, printing and binding their books in Vienna, and having them distributed by a London publishing firm. This had proven an unsatisfactory arrangement, and they decided to hand over to a publisher the entire business of publishing the International Psycho-Analytical Library in which they hoped regularly to publish a considerable number of important books by Freud and other analysts.

Ernest Jones's letters to Freud reveal that the International Psycho-Analytical Press was in a parlous situation by the time that the Hogarth Press agreed to take over its publications, and that the sticking-point in negotiations with other publishers prior to the Hogarth Press agreement had been the question of American rights. This remained a point of contention between Freud and those involved in producing English translations of his works. For Freud the issue was almost entirely a financial one, for his attitude towards America was dismissive and mercenary; the independent sale of rights to American presses would, he believed, bring in more money for the Verlag without compromising the interests of his English publishers. For Jones, in particular, the issues were in part financial but predominantly institutional and political. The retention of sole rights over the English-language versions of Freud's texts – with the sale of the English translation to selected American presses – meant control over the ways in which Freud, and psychoanalysis more generally, was represented and disseminated. Freud capitulated to Jones (although the question was periodically revisited, along with Freud's complaints about the slowness of his English translators, James Strachey included) and his agreement to grant sole English language rights to the Hogarth Press was clearly central to the success of negotiations between Jones and Leonard Woolf.

Leonard Woolf writes in some detail about the agreement the Hogarth Press came to with the Institute: this entailed the Press's purchase of the six books already published, and the publication of all future books in the International Psycho-Analytical Library. 'For a fledgling inexperienced publisher', Woolf writes, 'this was a bold undertaking' (L. Woolf 1980, 308). It also proved to be a financially astute one: Freud's *Collected Papers* 'was from the start one of the most successful of our publications .... The sale of these four fat volumes (we added a fifth later) has gone on steadily for over forty years' (L. Woolf 1980, 309). The Hogarth Press bought the rights in the four volumes from the Institute for £200, though they began to pay a royalty to Freud when the books showed a profit.

In correspondence of 1924 Freud and Ernest Jones discuss these negotiations, though Freud was clearly bemused by Jones's explanations about the American rights for the Hogarth Press publications: 'I can make neither head nor tail of your earlier letter about the American rights. I am glad that the matter remains between you and [Otto] Rank' (Paskauskas 1993, 550).

Freud's rather cavalier attitude towards translations of his work created a good deal of confusion over the years, as Ernest Jones noted in a letter to Leonard Woolf: 'I will write to Freud about the English rights [of *An Autobiographical Study*], including the translation and have no doubt at all he will agree. He always agrees to every request of this kind, but the trouble is he is indifferent to the question whether he accords the same rights to different people and I am sure he would be quite vague about whether these American publishers have the English rights as well or not' (21.6.35, HP 112). A letter from Jones to Leonard Woolf raises similar questions, while elaborating on their context:

> I have been in correspondence with Freud about his new book. He is rather difficult in the matter, owing to a bee in his bonnet about publishing a translation simultaneously in England and America. The motives for this are (1) Pressure from the Americans, who feel that his works are not sufficiently accessible in America, (2) A desire to get as much money as possible; he devotes this to the Verlag in Vienna which at present is in a parlous financial situation, (3) a feeling, I fear partly justified, that he has behaved over-generously in the past and that we have taken undue advantage of it. (4.10.32, HP 113)

In a subsequent letter Jones reassured Leonard Woolf that the advantage-taking 'we' referred to the analysts in England, the Institute, and not the Hogarth Press (8.10.32, HP 113). Freud's son Martin took over as managing director of the Verlag in 1931, and extensive business correspondence in the Hogarth Press archives reveals his eagerness to increase royalty payments on his father's books (which Freud used to finance the Verlag) and growing anxieties over the currency situation in Austria.

The period of the Verlag's founding, in 1919, was, as Murray G. Hall notes, a flourishing one for Austrian publishing, following the proclamation of the First Republic in November 1918. Despite their very different contexts and histories, there are some striking similarities between the Verlag and the Hogarth Press. Both were created to bring into being a supportive, relatively unmediated space for the publication of the works of their founders and their close circle. Both survived on extremely low overheads, and long outlived many other presses founded at the same time. As Hall notes of the Verlag: 'Most of the firms which – some with almost no capital at all, other with a great deal of it – set out to repatriate Austrian literature, or at least to reap the benefits of relatively low domestic production and labour costs compared with neighbouring Germany, were gone again by the mid-1920s at the latest. The Verlag itself at times only eked out an existence' (Timms and Segal 1988, 91). Peter Gay details the amount of personal money Freud gave to the Verlag, writing that 'Freud called the Verlag his child, and did not wish to survive it' (Gay 1988, 561). Ernest Jones, in his biography of Freud, emphasizes the significance of the Verlag for Freud in ways that again resonate strikingly with the Woolfs' accounts of the meanings of the Hogarth Press for them:

> Freud's interest in the fortunes of the Verlag was mainly an expression of his strong desire for independence. The idea of being completely free of the conditions imposed by publishers, which had always irked him, and of being able to publish just what he liked and when he liked, made a forcible appeal to this side of his nature.

> Then, with his own Verlag the continued existence of the psychoanalytical periodicals, which had been gravely threatened during the war, should be more secure. Lastly, penurious authors could be sure of having a good work published which commercial publishers might not accept. From the point of view of the outside public there would be some guarantee that books published by such a Verlag, although inevitably varying in value, belonged to the corpus of psychoanalytical literature, and could thus be distinguished from many other publications masquerading under that name. (Jones 1957, 32)

The emphasis here on freedom from publishers and on the production of non-commercial works closely echoes the values of the Hogarth Press. The major, obvious difference between the two enterprises (apart from the relative financial security enjoyed by the Hogarth Press) was that the Verlag was devoted to psychoanalytic texts, while the keynote of the Hogarth Press was its heterogeneity, with psychoanalysis representing one area of interest, albeit a very important one, among many others.

In fact, as Hall notes, the Verlag was restricted, by the terms of its legal registration, to the publication of psychoanalytic works alone. In 1937, Martin Freud attempted to save the press – which had suffered not only extreme financial difficulties but persecution under the Nazis in its outpost in Leipzig – by adding to the Verlag's list a limited number of books of general interest. The plan could not be effected before the Nazi occupation of Austria in 1938. The history of the press at this point is contested: it would seem that the Nazi Security Service ordered the immediate liquidation of the Verlag and the banning of further book sales, but that the company did not legally cease to exist until the spring of 1941. The fate of the Verlag's stocks is also unclear. Martin Freud's account in his autobiography, *Glory Reflected*, suggests widescale destruction: 'the Nazis were not satisfied to destroy the books remaining in Vienna; they arranged to have returned a much larger number which I had sent to Switzerland for safe keeping. The Nazi official who organized this business showed a strange sense of humour when he debited father's account with the quite considerable cost of the books' transportation to their funeral pyre in Vienna' (M. Freud 1957, 214).

Martin Freud's letters to Leonard Woolf at the Hogarth Press indicate the growing crisis by an increasing concern over royalty payments and finances in general, rather than by any direct reference to the political situation. Prior to Martin Freud's management of the Verlag, negotiations over translations and finances were largely mediated through Ernest Jones, with Sigmund Freud and Jones in regular correspondence, and Jones purveying information to Leonard Woolf. The most direct contact between Woolf and Freud arose with the translation and publication of Freud's last work *Moses and Monotheism*, when Freud and his family were resident in London after their forced departure from Vienna in 1938. A letter from Leonard Woolf to Freud expresses concern over the title of the work. Woolf wished it to be simply called *Moses*: 'From the publishing point of view it is, I am sure, a great mistake to have the long title, for in England many people will be frightened by the word monotheism' (Spotts 1989, 337). Freud did not agree to the use of the shorter title.

Leonard and Virginia Woolf met Freud only once, visiting him at his home in Maresfield Gardens in January 1939, some eight months before his death from the cancer from which he had long suffered. Leonard Woolf describes the occasion in his autobiography:

> It was not an easy interview. He was extraordinarily courteous in a formal, old-fashioned way – for instance, almost ceremoniously he presented Virginia with a flower. There was something about him as of a half-extinct volcano, something sombre, suppressed, reserved. He gave me the feeling which only a very few people whom I have ever met gave me, a feeling of great gentleness, but behind the gentleness, great strength. The room in which he sat seemed very light, shining, clean, with a pleasant, open view, through the windows into a garden. His study was almost a museum, for there were all around him a number of Egyptian antiquities which he had collected. He spoke about the Nazis. When Virginia said that we felt some guilt, that perhaps if we had not won the 1914 war there would have been no Nazis and no Hitler, he said, no, that was wrong; Hitler and the Nazis would have come and would have been much worse if Germany had won the war.
>
> A few days before we visited him I had read the report of a case in which a man had been charged with stealing books from Foyle's shop, and among them one of Freud's; the magistrate fined him and said that he wished he could sentence him to read all Freud's work as a punishment. I told Freud about this and he was amused and, in a queer way, also deprecatory about it. His books, he said, had made him infamous, not famous. A formidable man. (L. Woolf 1980, 311–12)

Virginia Woolf's diary fleshes out the uneasy atmosphere of the 'interview', and has a harsher response to the Freud family:

> Dr Freud gave me a narcissus. Was sitting in a great library with little statues at a large scrupulously tidy shiny table. We like patients on chairs. A screwed up shrunk very old man: with a monkeys light eyes, paralysed spasmodic movements, inarticulate: but alert. On Hitler. Generation before the poison will be worked out. About his books. Fame? I was infamous rather than famous. Didnt make £50 by his first book. Difficult talk. An interview. Daughter & Martin helped. Immense potential, I mean an old fire now flickering. When we left he took up the stand What are you going to do? The English – war .... A certain strain: all refugees are like gulls with their beaks out for possible crumbs. Martin & his novel; she [Anna Freud] on her book. The strain on us too of being benefactors. (*D* 5: 202)

Written in long retrospect, Leonard Woolf's account has smoothed away the rough edges of the encounter, and presents Freud outside the particularities and exigencies of the moment. Virginia Woolf's more immediate and unnerving response connects the 'interview' with the events closest to it in time: a fancy-dress party given by her brother Adrian Stephen; Hitler on the radio; 'thought of the refugees from Barcelona walking 40 miles, one with a baby in a parcel' (*D* 5: 203). Her attitude to the Freuds combines pity and anger.

Three months after Freud's death, Virginia Woolf's diary records her 'gulping up Freud' (D 5, 249). The Freudian term which particularly struck her was 'ambivalence', a new term in the language. 'Freud is upsetting', Woolf wrote:

> reducing one to whirlpool; & I daresay truly. If we're all instinct, the unconscious, whats all this about civilisation, the whole man, freedom &c? His savagery against

> God good. The falseness of loving one's neighbour. The conscience as censor. Hate .... But I'm too mixed. (*D* 5: 250)

The last phrase ostensibly refers to Woolf's 'thinking of a dozen things as usual', but is in fact a definition and an enactment of 'ambivalence': 'Hate .... But I'm too mixed'. The co-existence of 'love' and 'hate' runs throughout Woolf's last novel, *BTA*, which she was writing in 1939, and 'ambivalence' is reframed in the context of war, as it is in a number of the psychoanalytic works published by the Hogarth Press in the 1930s, including Joan Riviere's and Melanie Klein's *Love, Hate and Reparation* and Freud's *Civilization, War and Death*. Virginia Woolf was almost certainly reading *Moses and Monotheism* in 1939 (in a letter to John Lehmann she states 'Moses had a very good show – I'm reading it' (*L* 6: 346)) and, as Elizabeth Abel suggests, she borrowed directly from the text in *BTA* (Abel 1989, 110). 1939 was also the year in which Virginia Woolf began to explore her personal history and memories in her autobiographical work 'A Sketch of the Past' including her 'ambivalence' towards her father.

It remains one of the puzzles of modern literary and cultural history that Virginia Woolf was surrounded, metaphorically and literally, by the works of Freud and other psychoanalytic writings (she wrote much of her work in the basement of the house in Tavistock Square which was the Hogarth Press's premises from 1924 and in which stock was stored) but claims not to have read Freud until the end of his life and near the end of hers. It would indeed seem that she turned to psychology and psychoanalysis at times of public rather than personal crisis, and that her concern lay with group or mass rather than individual psychology. During the First World War she read Wilfred Trotter's *Instincts of the Herd in Peace and War* (1916) as she read Freud's cultural texts at the onset of the Second World War.

For the most part, however, and as Elizabeth Abel notes, 'she consistently represents [Freud's books] as objects to be handled rather than as texts' (Abel 1989, 14). Woolf wrote to Marjorie Joad in 1924, on the occasion of the Hogarth Press's adoption of the International Psycho-Analytical Library: 'all the psycho-analyst books have been dumped in a fortress the size of Windsor castle in ruins on the floor' (*L* 3: 119). It is as if the role of the publisher – not always one she adopted in full – legitimized an absence of engagement with the content of the psychoanalytic books she packaged, sat on, and skirted around in the room that served as her study and the Press's store. It may well be that Virginia Woolf needed to retain such a distance: Lisa Appignanesi and John Forrester write that Alix Strachey is said to have approved Woolf's unwillingness to undertake analysis, 'noting, as Lou Andreas-Salomé had of Rilke, that her artistic imagination was so enmeshed with her madness that stopping the latter could well endanger the former' (Appignanesi and Forrester 1992, 370).

Nonetheless, and as critics such as Elizabeth Abel and Mary Jacobus have argued,[8] Virginia Woolf's fiction engaged in extremely complex ways with

---

[8] See Jacobus 1986.

psychoanalytic thought from an early stage of her writing career. Using the work of Melanie Klein as well as Freud, Abel explores the 'narrative project' which conjoins Woolf's writing and psychoanalysis in the 1920s and 1930s, while reading Woolf's fictions as a critique of Freudian versions of the 'family romance'. For Abel, Klein is as significant a figure for Woolf as Freud – an equally structuring absence – though in the literary and historical narrative Abel constructs there is a turn away from Klein and towards Freud in the late 1930s. Abel's emphasis on the centrality of questions of femininity to psychoanalytic thought also usefully points up the exceptional role played by women analysts and translators in the dissemination of psychoanalysis in Britain.

In historical and biographical terms, Klein had significant connections with 'Bloomsbury'. As I have noted, she and Alix Strachey became friends in Berlin in the early 1920s. In 1925 Klein came to London to give a series of lectures, which were delivered in Karin and Adrian Stephen's drawing-room at 50 Gordon Square. In attendance were the Stracheys and other central figures of the British Psycho-Analytic Society – John Rickman, Ella Freeman Sharpe, Joan Riviere, Sylvia Payne – all of whom were to be centrally involved in the writing, translating and editing of the psychoanalytic works produced by the Hogarth Press.

Translation is again the key term here. This is not the place to detail the history of the English translation of Freud, from the Stracheys' translations of the *Collected Papers* (edited by Ernest Jones) in the 1920s to their *Standard Edition* of Freud's work, the twenty-four volumes of which appeared between 1953 and 1974, and fulfilled the dream of an English Freud long held by Jones. Leonard Woolf was also extremely active as a publisher in bringing the *Standard Edition* to fruition, and held fiercely to the Hogarth Press's prerogative, against competition from a number of other publishers.

With Freud's recent release from copyright, new translations and editions are appearing which eschew the very concept of standardization, including such apparatus as the 'Glossary Committee', established by the British Society to determine the ways in which technical terms should be translated, and the meticulous and detailed Indexes to the whole. The aim is largely to reject what is seen as a false model of scientificity. We could question, however, whether scientificity was the only aim of the original translators and editors of Freud in English. An early review of James Strachey's translation of Freud's *Group Psychology and the Ego* (1923) by Joan Riviere, one of the finest translators of German psychoanalytic works into English and Translation Editor of the *International Journal of Psycho-Analysis* from 1922 to 1937, raises fascinating issues about the difficulties of translating 'new conceptions' which, she suggests, combine the scientific and the affective in an entirely novel way:

> To begin with, this new science was entirely without a terminology in our language. The long literary traditions of English have so hardened and stereotyped the meaning of such numbers of our words, so many others have become degraded and colloquialized till they are unfit for use in any impersonal document, that we cannot fall back, to anything like the degree that is possible in German, on our ordinary speech for rendering these new conceptions. Our English shyness in matters of sex, our extreme sensitiveness in matters of 'taste', results in an almost insuperable

> difficulty in expressing ourselves at all, outside poetry, on anything relating to the emotions. Psycho-analysts have to grow accustomed to mentioning love, but even they cannot find an English word for *Verliebtheit*, the state of being in love. All these things increase the difficulties of the translator. (Riviere 1991, 61)

Regrettably, she argues, beauty of language 'can only be a secondary consideration', but there is a beauty in 'a rendering of the language that furnishes the reader with a complete and clear expression of the writer's thought, in the spirit of his own language and undisturbed by any reminiscence of the original wording'. This 'Mr Strachey has achieved most remarkably'.

Riviere's brief review helps open up some of the ways, linguistic and cultural, in which the Hogarth Press editions represented and disseminated Freud, and other psychoanalytic works, in English. James Strachey stated that he took as his goal in the *Standard Edition* the task of transforming Freud into 'an English man of science of wide education born in the middle of the nineteenth century'. Yet English-language Freud was, in Appignanesi and Forrester's words, 'part and parcel of a very different hothouse of the avant-garde: Bloomsbury. The rapid dissemination of Freud's ideas in the English-speaking world after the First World War, the depth with which they took hold, owed much to the manner in which Freud was reimagined in English' (Appignanesi and Forrester 1992, 352). The forms of this re-imagining, in which the Hogarth Press played such a central role, still bear further investigation, as does the modernity which embraces both the mid-nineteenth-century man of science and the modernism to which his ideas were so central.

Russian literature

Between 1912 and 1925 Virginia Woolf wrote a dozen essays and reviews on Russian literature, and in further essays used Russian fiction as a standard against which to measure English writers – as in her essay 'On Rereading Meredith' – or, more broadly, to explore a modern aesthetic – as in 'Modern Fiction'. These are also the years of widespread and intense interest in Russian literature and culture – fuelled in part by Constance Garnett's translations of Russian novels.[9] It is also the period of the Hogarth Press's most active publishing of translations of Russian writers (taken up again, though less intensively, in the 1930s). The broader question of Russian culture as spectacle of modernity – in which Diaghilev's *Ballets Russes* of the 1910s is central – is outside the parameters of this essay, though we might note in passing its relationship to the decorative art projects of Roger Fry and the Omega Workshop and, in biographical terms, the entry of one of Diaghilev's dancers

---

9 Constance Garnett, née Black (1861–1946), studied Classics at Newnham College, Cambridge. She began to learn Russian in about 1890, inspired by friendship with the political exile Felix Volkhovsky, and became the foremost translator of Russian literature – particularly Turgenev, Tolstoy, Dostoyevsky, Chekhov and Gogol – into English. See the biography by Richard Garnett (1991).

into the Bloomsbury orbit, with the marriage of Lydia Lopokova to Maynard Keynes.

In looking at the relationships of Woolf and the Hogarth Press to Russian literature, I want to open up two areas for discussion. First, some of the circumstances underlying the Hogarth Press's extensive translation and publication of Russian writing. Secondly. Woolf's own relationship to Russian fiction, as explored in her essays and fictional writings.

In looking at the first question, the Hogarth Press and Russian literature, the name of one individual becomes central. It is a name likely to be familiar to those who work on D. H. Lawrence, Dorothy Richardson, Katherine Mansfield or the painter Mark Gertler – that of Samuel Solomonovich Koteliansky, or 'Kot' as he was known, whom the Woolfs first met around 1917 through Katherine Mansfield and John Middleton Murry.

Kot – a Russian Jew born in Ostropol, Ukraine in 1880 – arrived in England in 1911, possibly escaping from police surveillance resulting from his revolutionary affiliations, if not activities. When Lawrence first met him, in 1914, Kot was working in London at a small office, the Russian Law Bureau, as a secretary and translator. Lawrence's hundreds of letters to Kot, left to the British Museum as part of the extensive Koteliansky archive, were published in the 1970s, and give a fascinating account of a friendship, a literary partnership and a segment of history. Lawrence, like many other of their friends and acquaintances, moved across and between countries and continents. Kot, the Ukrainian, remained a constant presence in London, in the house he briefly shared with Katherine Mansfield (for whom he nursed a painful passion), John Middleton Murry and Mark Gertler in 1915, and which he occupied until his death in 1955: 5 Acacia Road, St John's Wood. Kot gave up work at the Law Bureau after a couple of years, and thereafter seems to have subsisted on the very small amounts he made as a translator. Letters to Leonard Woolf up to the early 1950s reveal him continually seeking to place his translations of the 1920s and 1930s with various publishers in reprints of Russian literature.

Koteliansky, now largely forgotten, played a key role in the networks of friendship, enmity and influence of literary London in the first decades of the twentieth century. Not himself a writer, he played an important part as a translator and mediator between two cultures – Russia and England. His letters suggest the extent to which he maintained connections with Russian letters and politics; the nature of his contact with Maxim Gorky is not altogether clear, but Kot was extremely active in 1917 in soliciting support from British writers, politicians and intellectuals on the Left for Gorky's paper (*Novaya Zhizn*) (New Life). He also appears to have been directly in contact with Gorky over the translation and publication of his works in Britain. Leonard Woolf refers in his autobiography to an early encounter with Koteliansky:

> In 1919 he came to us with a copy of the Reminiscences [of Leo Nicolayevitch Tolstoy] which Gorky had sent to him, giving him the English translation rights. Kot suggested that he and I should translate it and the Hogarth Press publish it. We agreed to do this and thus began a collaboration between Kot and Virginia and me in translating Russian books. (L. Woolf 1980, 179)

Koteliansky acted not only as a cultural mediator but as a conduit between those who did not know or, more frequently, had ceased to wish to know each other; Lawrence and Middleton Murry, for example, in the early years. He also became involved in a number of the publishing projects of his friends, including Lawrence's short-lived journal *Signature* (for which he acted as 'business manager'): its three issues (all in 1915) were written almost entirely by Lawrence, Murry and Mansfield. He subsequently became business manager, a little less briefly but far more catastrophically for their friendship, of Murry's *Adelphi*. Prior to their business relationship, Kot and Murry had co-translated stories by Chekhov, as well as Dostoyevsky's *Pages from the Journal of an Author* (1916). It would also be interesting to know how many of Kot's ideas entered into Murry's *Fyodor Dostoevsky: A Critical Study* (1916), Murry's first, and very successful, work of literary criticism.

In the context of the Hogarth Press, Koteliansky's name appears as one of a duo or trio of translators. The translation of Ivan Bunin's *The Gentleman from San Francisco* and other stories, published in 1922, was shared between Lawrence, Koteliansky and Leonard Woolf, with Lawrence and Kot credited as translating the title story, Kot and Leonard Woolf the remaining three. In 1934, the Hogarth Press published Gorky's *Reminiscences of Tolstoy, Chekhov and Andreev* – 'translated from the Russian' by Katherine Mansfield, S. S. Koteliansky and Leonard Woolf. More usually, Kot co-translated with one or other of the Woolfs. As George Zytaruk, editor of D. H. Lawrence's letters to Koteliansky, notes, 'Koteliansky was instrumental in placing before the English reading public no fewer than thirty-three works by Russian writers' (Zytaruk 1970, xxvii).

For Lawrence Russia was at times the Promised Land, as in this letter written to Kot in May 1917:

> I got your telegram yesterday about Gorky's paper. Write and tell me what it means exactly – I shall be only too glad to contribute anything I can.
>
> I feel that our chiefest hope for the future is Russia. When I think of the new young country there, I love it inordinately. It is the place of hope. We must go, sooner or (a little) later. But let us go gently. I feel a violent change would be the death of me. *Toujours doucement*, as the nuns say. I am working in the garden. We will go to Russia. Send me a Berlitz grammar book, I will begin to learn the language – religiously. And when Farbman comes back, we will scheme – and perhaps you will come down here for a few weeks. *Nuova speranza - la Russia* – Please send me a grammar book. (Zytaruk 1970, 117)

Lawrence did not advance far with his Russian, though he made a second attempt in 1926: Frieda Lawrence wrote at the time that 'He learnt quite a lot and sat in the evening making Russian noises' (Hyde 1981, 16). Russian noises aside, the impact of Russian literature, especially the work of Dostoyevsky and Shestov, on Lawrence's work and thought was profound.

Leonard and Virginia Woolf were somewhat more successful in learning Russian, to the point where Leonard, at least, was able to read the work of Sergei Aksakov in the original (L. Woolf 1980, 179): Kot was their teacher. Virginia Woolf's diaries record her attempts to learn the language, as the writing of *JR* was drawing to a close. On 31 January 1921, she asks: 'And now, am I to learn Russian with him [Leonard] & Kot? If he can read it & solace his age with it I shall be furious' (*D* 2: 88). On 5 February she writes that: 'Jealousy or ambition has won the day & I've just had my first Russian lesson & mortgaged my time to the extent of doing three lessons weekly. L. is mumbling Russian as I write' (*D* 2: 89). On 16 February 1921, she wrote:

> Russian is snatching all the time spared for this book. I can only keep up with L. by running as hard as I can. Everyone prophesies an early end. But I feel myself attached to an express train. With Kot & Leonard dragging me, I must be pulled through somehow. Six months continued at this rate – Russian from 12.15 to 12.45 & from 5.30 to 6. from 9.30 to 10, & on the way to Waterloo & back again must have some result. So far the chief one is as I say that I don't write here. (*D* 2: 90)

The Hogarth Press translations from the Russian included Gorky's *Reminiscences of Tolstoy* (1920), translated by Kot and Leonard Woolf, which for Leonard, as I have noted, marked the moment at which the Press became a small publishing house: 'The success of Gorky's book was really the turning point for the future of the Press and for our future' (L. Woolf 1980, 234). Subsequently, the Press published Gorky's *The Note-Books of Anton Tchehov* (Kot and Leonard Woolf); Leonid Andreev's *The Dark* (1923); Bunin's *The Gentleman from San Francisco and Other Stories* (Lawrence, Kot and Leonard Woolf); Dostoyevsky's *Stavrogin's Confessions* (Kot and Virginia Woolf, 1922); Countess Sophie Tolstoy's *Autobiography* (1922); Goldenveizer's *Talks with Tolstoi* (Kot and Virginia Woolf, 1923); *Tolstoi's Love Letters with a Study of the Autobiographical Elements in Tolstoi's Work* by Paul Biryukov (Kot and Virginia Woolf, 1923). Later came Bunin's *The Well of Days* (1933); Gorky's *Reminiscences of Tolstoy, Chehov and Andreev* (1934); Bunin's *Grammar of Love* (translated by John Cournos) (1935); Tolstoy's *On Socialism* (1936).

Neither of the Woolfs say very much about the work of translation from the Russian itself, though Leonard wrote in his autobiography of his work with Kot on Gorky's *Reminiscences of Tolstoy*: 'I do not think that I have ever got more aesthetic pleasure from anything than from doing that translation'. He describes the work in its two stages:

> Our actual procedure in translating was that Kot did the first draft in handwriting, with generous space between the lines, and we then turned his extremely queer version into English. In order to make this easier and more accurate, we started to learn Russian and at one moment I had learned enough to be able to stumble through a newspaper or even Aksakof. (L. Woolf 1980, 179)

Both the Woolfs seem to have seen their work as 'translating' rather than editing or correcting: Virginia Woolf wrote to Dorothy Brett on 5 March 1923: 'I'm being driven by Kotsky to translate Russian, and have no time to write' (*L* 3: 18). The works in question were *Tolstoi's Love Letters* and *Talks with Tolstoi* by A. B. Goldenveizer, of which Virginia Woolf wrote to Kot on 9 March 1923: 'I'm greatly interested in the Tolstoi – almost the best we've done, I think' (*L* 3: 19).

Clearly, the early 1920s were the most intensive period of the translations, the Woolfs sharing in the widespread fascination with Russian literature and culture of the 1910s and 1920s in Britain. The Hogarth Press publicity statement of 1922 made translations from Russian literature central to the Press's aims:

> It is our intention to proceed more boldly in the future, and to publish a greater number of books and books of greater length. But we do not mean to depart in any other respect from the principles which guided us in the beginning. We shall continue to give particular attention to the work of young and unknown writers. We shall proceed with our translation from the Russian. We intend to issue reproductions from the works of living painters. On the other hand, it is none of our purpose to reprint the classics; nor shall we sacrifice time or money to embellish our books beyond what is necessary for ease of reading and decency of appearance.

The fact that eight out of twenty-seven of the Hogarth Press publications in its first years (up to 1923) were Russian translations also renders the Press, as Willis notes, an important publisher of Russian literature and letters in the post-war, post-Revolutionary period (Willis 1992, 101).

One obvious aspect of the Russian translations was that the Hogarth Press were not publishing large novels (such as those translated by Constance Garnett), but the apparatus of memoirs, letters, diaries and commentaries surrounding them, which became available rather later and to which Kot was presumably alerted by his literary contacts in Russia. The function of such publications, it could be argued, was to reinforce the cult of personality surrounding Dostoyevsky, Tolstoy and others. T. S. Eliot, in the early days of *The Criterion*, was extremely eager to publish Russian literature in the journal, and letters from Eliot in the early 1920s shows him expressing interest in the publication of material by Dostoyevsky, Tolstoy and Andreev. The Dostoyevsky contribution was, Eliot wrote to Kot, 'the most important thing in no. 1 [of *The Criterion*]' (11.1 23, BL 9). Eliot was referring to the Koteliansky- Virginia Woolf translation 'Plan of the novel "The Life of a Great Sinner"', which appeared in *The Criterion* alongside *The Waste Land* and Valéry-Nicolas Larbaud's interpretation of Joyce's *Ulysses*. The translation was published by the Hogarth Press in 1922. The material had been discovered the year previously in Russia, along with chapters from *The Possessed* (which Dostoevsky had been persuaded by his publisher to omit) recounting Stavrogin's rape of a young girl and her subsequent suicide.

By 1927, it should be said, Eliot appears to have become less welcoming of the amount of Dostoyevsky material Kot was sending to the journal, and encouraging him to 'make a book of the whole. May I suggest such a book to my firm? [Faber]'. Neither this book, nor the history of Russian art discussed at one point between Kot and Roger Fry, ever materialized. Eliot's tactful hint that *The Criterion* had published enough of Kot's Dostoyevsky translations may say something about the decline of interest in Dostoyevsky, which became more marked in the 1930s. On 23 August 1933, Kot wrote the following letter to Virginia Woolf:

> My dear Virginia
>
> Your letter and the Dostoevsky MS. came this morning. I feel a certain disappointment that the 'Scenes of the Devils' won't have an introduction by you. I

can't think (nor do I want to) of any other writer here, who could write of D. as freely and personally as you. But, as you say, to those who are interested in D. the MS by itself ought to be sufficient, and with this I fully agree. The difficulty is in finding a publisher, who would regard it in the same way. Yet one day I hope to have a MS published.

My desire to have an introduction by you was on the surface, – as nearly all practical ideas are, – an attempt to win a publisher's consideration of the MS more easily. Your name would certainly make the MS more attractive to a publisher. But, unconsciously, that desire must have been an imitation of the Jewish belief & practice of adding a new name to a person, who happens to be dangerously ill. Whether this means the desire to circumvent the powers of evil, used to a familiar name, by suddenly giving a person a perfectly new name; or [whether] it has a greater esoteric significance, I do not know. (MHP)

The letter is interesting both because it suggests that cultural interest in Dostoyevsky had largely died away, and because it alludes to Woolf's characteristic reluctance to 'preface' books. The letter of Woolf's to which Kot refers (a response to his request (10 July 1933) that she write a preface to his translation of a Dostoyevsky story) also indicates her reluctance to turn her attention fully to Dostoyevsky at this time:

I do not think I can write an introduction, because in order to say anything of interest about these notes one would have to go rather deeply into the whole question of Dostoevsky's psychology as a writer. I do not feel that I know enough about him. He is such an extraordinary case as a writer that I should feel it silly to hazard guesses about him; I should want to think a great deal about it. And I feel I should say nothing interesting in the end and because the problems it raises are very difficult ones. (21.8. 1933, BL 9)

This might not have been Virginia Woolf's response ten years earlier, when Russian 'strangeness', and the strangeness of Dostoyevsky in particular, was its fascination rather than a barrier to engagement. I want to move now, therefore, to some suggestions about the impact of translation, and of Russian literature more generally, on Virginia Woolf's work. During the period of the Hogarth Press's 'Russian translations', Woolf was also writing a number of reviews and essays on Russian literature, and her thinking about this writing clearly informed her thoughts about literature in general, and about her own writing. She reviewed works by Dostoyevsky, Tolstoy, Aksakov, Turgenev and Chekhov, but, as Andrew McNeillie states, she was also interested in less canonical Russian writers.

McNeillie notes that a citation in Woolf's review of Aksakov's *A Russian Schoolboy* (*Times Literary Supplement*, 8 November 1917), a comparison between Aksakov and Gilbert White, shows that she had been reading Peter Kropotkin's *Russian Literature*, published by Duckworth in 1905, in preparing her review (*E* 2: xvi). A diary entry of 26 November 1921 also reveals the extent to which Koteliansky was working as the Woolfs' literary, as well as linguistic, guide in Russian:

Kot just gone after hearing Leonard his Russian; & so I have an odd half hour to fill up, & reach for this book. I have been cross examining Kot upon the quarrel

> between Dostoevsky & Turgenev, & find him stuffed with facts, & of course passionate severe & uncompromising. For once in a way I shall have some truth to put in my article. (*D* 2: 145)

In one of her earliest reviews of Russian literature, a review of Constance Garnett's translation of *The Eternal Husband and Other Stories* (*Times Literary Supplement*, 22 February 1917), titled 'More Dostoevsky', Woolf wrote:

> Again and again we are thrown off the scent in following Dostoevsky's psychology; we constantly find ourselves wondering whether we recognize the feeling that he shows us, and we realise constantly and with a start of surprise that we have met it before in ourselves, or in some moment of intuition have suspected it in others. But we have never spoken of it, and that is why we are surprised. (*E* 2: 86)

The question of Dostoyevsky's 'strangeness' – the term Woolf uses in 'More Dostoevsky' – is raised in similar terms by a number of critics at this time. Arthur Clutton-Brock described Dostoyevsky as a reminder 'of what we had forgotten about ourselves', rather than as a purveyor of an unknown world (Muchnic 1969, 99). This recalls the structure of Freud's 'uncanny' – as 'something we had known before' (Freud 1919h) – and resonates with the close of Woolf's 'The Art of Biography': 'For how often, when a biography is read and tossed aside, some scene remains bright, some figure lives on in the depths of the mind, and causes us, when we read a poem or a novel, to feel a start of recognition, as if we remembered something we had known before' (*CE* 4: 228).

The echo of Freud is telling, for 'Freud and the Russians' became a habitual pairing. As D. S. Mirsky wrote: 'together with Freud, Dostoevsky was the most powerful single influence to give the death-blow to the Victorian mental order' (Mirsky 1930, 8), although he took a critical distance from this, and from the 'Russopaths of the War generation' (9). For Virginia Woolf, as for many of her contemporaries, including Lawrence, Russian literature came to represent the spheres of the psychological and of unconscious life more generally. It was a psychoanalytically informed model which enabled Woolf to engage with, and seek to represent, unconscious processes long before she acknowledged any real familiarity with Freud's work. As I discussed above, Woolf was particularly captured by the concept of 'ambivalence' (as the admixture of 'love and hate') when she came to read Freud, and it is the co-existence of 'affection and hatred ... attraction and repulsion' on which she comments in 'More Dostoevsky' some two decades earlier. Woolf's turn to 'ambivalence' is also a reworking of the structures of vacillation and of oscillation which run throughout her work, and which lead us back to her fascination with Russian literature. It may also be that 'ambivalence' best describes her attitude towards Dostoyevsky himself. In 'More Dostoevsky' (1917) she writes of 'this great genius who is beginning to permeate our lives so curiously', but a diary entry of 1922 records her agreement with T. S. Eliot's 'Dostoevsky – the ruin of English literature' (*D* 2: 203).

In 'More Dostoevsky', Woolf also wrote:

> if we try to construct our mental processes later, we find that the links between one thought and another are submerged. The chain is sunk out of sight and only the

> leading points emerge to mark the course. Alone among writers Dostoevsky has the power of reconstructing the whole train of thought in all its speed, now as it flashes into light, now as it lapses into darkness; for he is able to follow not only the vivid streak of achieved thought, but to suggest the dim and populous underworld of the mind's consciousness where desires and impulses are moving blindly beneath the sod.
>
> This is the exact opposite of the method adopted, perforce, by most of our novelists. They reproduce all the external appearances – tricks of the manner, landscape, dress, and the effect of the hero upon his friends – but very rarely, and only for an instant, penetrate to the tumult of thought which rages within his own mind. (*E* 2: 85)

Such comparisons between Russian and English novelists inform, explicitly and implicitly, her best-known essays on fiction, including 'Mr Bennett and Mrs Brown' and 'Modern Fiction'. 'Mr Bennett and Mrs Brown' is of particular significance here, for it not only contains a critique of the English naturalist novelists – Wells, Bennett and Galsworthy – in terms very similar to those applied to 'our novelists' in 'More Dostoevsky', but sets its scene on a train, as 'More Dostoevsky' turns the metaphor of 'train of thought' into a train journey itself. In 'A Minor Dostoevsky' (*Times Literary Supplement*, 11 October 1917), a review of Garnett's translation of *The Gambler and Other Stories*, Woolf writes that Russian literature represents 'the psychology of souls flying at full speed' (*E* 2: 166). The train imagery echoes Woolf's comments on learning Russian – 'I feel myself attached to an express train' (and she was partly learning her Russian on the commuter train from Richmond to Waterloo). It again resonates with the model of literary history, more particularly the transition from nineteenth-century realism/naturalism to modernism, dramatized in 'Mr Bennett and Mrs Brown' – 'And so the smashing and the crashing began' – suggesting the extent to which the image of modernism as cultural and historical rupture is linked with that of revolutionary forces.

If Russian literature represents 'speed' for Woolf, it also opens up the depths: 'the net drags the floor of the sea and encloses stranger monsters than have ever been brought to the light of day before', she writes in 'More Dostoevsky' (*E* 2: 84). Such terms become increasingly present in Woolf's accounts of her novel-writing in the 1920s: 'I have netted that fin', she wrote on completing *TW*. It was the writing of *TW*, too, that concentrated her habitual preoccupation with the relationship between speed and surface, on the one hand, and depth and immutability on the other: 'Now is life very solid, or very shifting?', she wrote in her diary in early 1929: 'I am haunted by the two contradictions. This has gone on for ever: will last for ever; goes down to the bottom of the world – this moment I stand on. Also it is transitory, flying, diaphanous. I shall pass like a cloud on the waves' (*D* 3: 218). This contradiction – to which, in different guises, Woolf alludes in much of her writing on Russian literature – echoes Charles Baudelaire's formulation of the paradox of modernity itself, which is 'the ephemeral, the fugitive, the contingent, the half of art whose other half is the eternal and the immutable' (Baudelaire 1964, 13).

The contradiction, or paradox, is also realized in the shift from *JR* (1922) to

MD (1925); the 'gleams & lights', 'something turning away, always in movement', of the one, and the desire to give depth to 'character' of the second, 'how I dig out beautiful caves behind my characters' (*D* 2: 263), the 'tunnelling process' she describes strongly reminiscent of her account of Dostoyevsky. The years of Woolf's fullest engagement with Russian literature, as a 'translator' and reviewer, are also those in which her experimental aesthetics were being forged, from the early short stories – 'Mark on the Wall', 'Kew Gardens', 'An Unwritten Novel', the first two of which were also among the first Hogarth Press publications – through to *JR* and *MD*. Her essay 'Modern Fiction', first published in 1919 (as 'Modern Novels') and then in a revised version in 1925, makes the Russian novelist the epitome of the modern novelist: 'The tendency of the moderns and part of their perplexity is no doubt that they find their interest more and more in [the] dark region of psychology .... No one but a modern, perhaps no one but a Russian, would have felt the interest of the situation which Tchehov has made into the short story which he calls "Gusev". (*E* 4: 162)

Extrapolating from the Chekhov story, Woolf writes of 'the inconclusiveness of the Russian mind. It is the sense that there is no answer, that if honestly examined life presents question after question which must be left to sound on and on after the story is over' (*E* 4: 163). In 'Modern Novels' Woolf counterpoises the more robust English national character, as realized in its fiction, with the 'despair' of the Russian. Yet she is drawn again and again in her reviews of Russian literature to the power of its 'inconclusiveness'. 'Nothing is finished; nothing is tied up; life merely goes on', she writes in a review of Tolstoy's *The Classics* (1917), and in 'Tchehov's Questions', a 1918 review of a collection of Chekhov's short stories, 'There we hang asking questions in mid-air' (*E* 2: 245). In *JR* she adopted the device of closing with a question (that of Betty Flanders after her son's death: 'What am I to do with these, Mr Bonamy? She held out a pair of Jacob's old shoes') and an entire aesthetic of 'inconclusiveness'. *TY*, a novel of the 1930s which embodies incompletions of many kinds, ends with Eleanor's unanswered question 'And now?' In the first section of *O*, Woolf's most playful novel, Russia and Russianness make their impact (Orlando has fallen in love with a Russian princess) in the terms of sexual ambiguity, passion, secrecy, 'violent see-saws from life to death', linguistic ornamentation, and 'sentences often left unfinished from doubt as to how best to end them ...'.

'The Russian Point of View', Woolf's fullest discussion of Russian literature, synthesizes a number of these issues: Russian inconclusiveness; ambivalence; soul as a communality of experience. 'The soul is not restrained by barriers. It overflows, it floods, it mingles with the souls of others'. The soul for Dostoyevsky is, Woolf writes, like the tea in the samovar – 'Out it tumbles upon us, hot, scalding, mixed, marvellous, terrible, oppressive – the human soul' (*E* 4: 187). The communality of the samovar is contrasted with the bourgeois, familial, differentiated sphere of the teapot. New resonance is added to the image of the fusion of souls that Woolf proposes in novels such as *MD* and *TL*. Dostoyevsky's representation of the interrelationships between subjects, a topic brought out by Mikhail Bakhtin in his study of Dostoyevsky's work, is also echoed in Woolf's models of 'intersubjectivity', through which she moves in and out of 'consciousnesses' and emphasizes the relationship between them, and points up the permeable boundaries between selves.

'The Russian Point of View' is first and foremost an essay about translation and, like Woolf's 'On Not Knowing Greek', also published in *CR 1* in 1925, it is a meditation on the impossibility of 'knowing' other cultures and historical epochs: 'But the mind takes its bias from the place of his birth, and no doubt, when it strikes upon a literature so alien as the Russian, flies off at a tangent far from the truth' (*E* 4: 189). This claim closes 'The Russian Point of View', thus putting into doubt the assertions about Russian literature that have led up to it. Uncertainty also governs the question of language. Does Russian literature appear to us stark and simple because it has been 'stripped of its style', as 'in some terrible catastrophe', by translation, or is this effect due 'to some more profound cause'? When the English respond, with fanatical admiration, to the translations of Russian literature, inadequate as all translations are inadequate, what in fact are they responding to? Woolf's essay uses Russian literature, and the response to two decades of its translation into English, to make literary judgement, understanding and knowledge relative, uncertain and inconclusive.

We might also note that the 'strangeness' of Russian literature seems to be becoming a barrier, rather than the draw to engagement that it had been for Woolf. An unpublished note on 'Reading' has Woolf asking 'whether the D.[ostoevskyan] psychology can be understood by English: whether the effect on Eng lit (at any rate now) has not been bad. Also we know the Russians in Mrs Garnett. Therefore we only get the broad outline' (*MHP* B2q, 66). The essay 'Phases of Fiction' (1929) takes Dostoevsky as one of its central examples, situating him with James and Proust as one of 'The Psychologists', and focusing on *The Possessed* and its 'strange emotional effect'. Woolf is undoubtedly taking a greater distance from Dostoevsky than she did when she first read *Crime and Punishment* on her honeymoon in 1912, when she wrote to Lytton Strachey:

> It is directly obvious that he [Dostoevsky] is the greatest writer ever born: and if he chooses to become horrible what will happen to us? Honeymoon completely dashed. If he says it – human hope – had better end, what will be left but suicide in the Grand Canal. (*L* 2: 5)

Reading Dostoevsky, as so many of her contemporaries did, as a writer in whom intense emotion pours itself onto the page, she undoubtedly underestimated his art and his irony. Her essays from the mid and late 1920s express a degree of ambivalence about the overflow of emotion and feeling that she found in his fiction which recalls her habitually expressed unease with 'excess', whether of subjectivity, of feeling, or of anger. The problem of excess is also raised as an image of translation:

> For without any disrespect to the translator we have grown intolerably weary in reading Dostoevsky, as if we were reading with the wrong spectacles or as if a mist had formed between us and the page. We come to feel that every idea is slipping about in a suit badly cut and many sizes too large for it. For a translation makes us understand more clearly than the lectures of any professor the difference between raw words and written words; the nature and importance of what we call style. Even

> an inferior writer, using his own tongue upon his own ideas, works a change at once which is agreeable and remarkable. Under his pen the sentence shrinks and wraps itself firmly round the meaning, if it be but a little one. The loose, the baggy, shrivels up. (*CE* 2, 89)

Her metaphors find their echoes in Walter Benjamin's 'The Task of the Translator': 'While content and language form a certain unity in the original, like a fruit and its skin, the language of the translation envelops its content like a royal robe with ample folds', Benjamin wrote (Benjamin 1969, 75). Benjamin's paradoxical argument is that translation makes language more rather than less pure, bringing it closer to a universal linguistic realm and 'expressing the central reciprocal relationship between languages'; excess is here valued in very different terms by Woolf and Benjamin.

'Phases of Fiction', in its linking of, or slippages between Dostoevsky, excess, misprision, misreading, is at one level a retreat from the uncertainties of the foreign to the safety of home. It recalls other instances in Woolf's writing in which transgressive energies are said to require containment through art, and in which it is suggested that excess in the system is potentially corrupting and distorting. The question, which I must leave open, is whether Woolf is in fact holding to the image of Dostoevsky's writing as the outpouring of an uncontained and uncontainable self, or whether her unease with 'excess' hints at a more complex understanding of the role of duplicity, parody and authorial unreliability in his work – at a different version, that is, of his modernity. Is there too little irony, in other words, or too much?

Dostoevsky, Woolf wrote, became unreadable, or un-rereadable for her in the 1930s. In 1933, she turned to Turgenev, who, her reading notes and diary entries suggest, enabled her to think through the problems of 'form' troubling her in the writing of the early versions of *TY*. Yet *BTA* seems to echo throughout with the remarks in 'Phases of Fiction': violence is simple, Woolf states of Dostoevsky's fiction, but 'also lays bare regions deep down in the mind where contradiction prevails', where 'all is chaos and complication'. Cruelty, violence, monstrosity and, as I have suggested, ambivalence, are more emphatically present in Woolf's last novel than in any of her earlier works, and the inseparability of 'inner life' and 'instinctual life' creates a new sense of the imbrications of desires and drives. Dostoevsky remained, I would argue, a powerful force in Woolf's writing, even or especially when she had most fully sought to distance herself from his work.

I want to draw this section to a close with another, but related, perspective on the question of the Russian language. Delivering the second Jane Harrison Memorial Lecture in 1930, D. S. Mirsky took as his topic 'Jane Ellen Harrison and Russia'. The classical scholar and anthropologist Harrison had become absorbed by Russian language and culture in her final years, in the early 1920s, leaving Cambridge, where she had studied and taught classical civilization for most of her adult life, for Paris and the study of Russian. The Hogarth Press published the translation she and Hope Mirrlees made of *The Life of the Archpriest Arvakum* in 1924, followed a year later by Harrison's memoir, *Reminiscences of a Student's Life* (1925). (One of the first Hogarth Press books, hand-printed by the Woolfs, was the modernist poem *Paris* written by Harrison's companion Hope Mirrlees.)

As D. S. Mirsky notes, Harrison's fascination with Russia was revealed as early as 1915, with her *Russia and the Russian Verb: A Contribution to the Psychology of the Russian People*. It grew directly out of her anthropological studies, in that she was interested, in Mirsky's words, in the 'direct and recognizable survivals of the oldest cults' in the Russian Orthodox Church, and, more idiosyncratically, by the Totem of the bear. (Harrison and Mirrlees also translated a collection of Russian folk stories which was titled *The Book of the Bear*.)

Harrison was most absorbed, however, by the Russian language and in her representations we find a telling view of Russia as both archaic and (proto-) modern. In her lecture/pamphlet on *Russia and the Russian Verb*, Harrison pointed to the dominance of 'aspect' over tense and 'imperfective' over 'perfective': 'The imperfective has internal time but no time order; it may be past, present or future .... The perfective is of the accomplished act ... standing on its apex or vertex; the imperfective is of non-accomplishment, of process .... Immediately what we get from Russia, is the impulse to live in the living fact rather than outside it, to look to process, durée, rather than to achievement.' As Mirsky notes, Harrison thus links the Russian imperfective with the Bergsonian idea of *durée*; Bergson's *L'Évolution créatrice* (Creative Evolution) was, Harrison notes in her *Reminiscences of a Student's Life*, one of the three most significant texts in her development, the other two being Aristotle's *Ethics* and Freud's *Totem and Taboo* (Harrison 1925, 80–82). Harrison's Russian civilization is, in Mirsky's words, 'the civilization of nineteenth-century Russia minus Tsarism' (Mirsky 1930, 14). Her Bergsonism, however, and the relationships she implies between the forms of the Russian language (understood as a manifestation of culture and national psychology) and concepts of time and duration, suggest that 'Russia' comes to represent the movement – conceived as both transition and relation – between the old order and the new.

Harrison's remarks resonate suggestively with the Bergsonism underlying so much modernist fiction, conceptually simplified into 'stream of consciousness' techniques. Writing to a researcher in 1968, Leonard Woolf rejected the suggestion that Woolf had read Bergson, while in the same letter insisting on her early interest in Russian literature (Spotts 1989, 571). Lines of influence are clearly neither simple nor singular, so that the 'Bergsonism' of Woolf's novels, including their striking emphases on process, incompleteness and duration, may well have been mediated through her understanding of the techniques of Russian fiction. In Harrison's words: '[t]he Russian stands for the complexity and concreteness of life-felt-whole, unanalysed, unjudged, lived into'. The description resonates strongly with Woolf's fictional experiments and with her aesthetics. It is worth remark, at least, that in a brief note Woolf sent to Koteliansky in the early days of their acquaintance, when she and Leonard were beginning to learn Russian, she writes that 'The aspects [in Russian] seem to me very interesting – that is not to say that I understand them at all' (*BL*).

Russian literature and language were both equated with a modernist or proto-modernist aesthetic by Woolf and her contemporaries, and seen to stand outside its terms. With some exceptions – Bunin being one – it was primarily nineteenth-century Russian literature that was translated. D. S. Mirsky's 1930 history of Russian literature includes some discussion of Russian futurism and the rest of the Russian avant-garde, but there is no reference to this new work in Woolf's writings, nor, I believe, in that of Lawrence, though at one point he contrasts Russian literature unfavourably, as the old, with the work of the Italian futurists. This topic merits discussion, which it cannot receive here. I have also had to pass over the highly complex relationship between images of Russia and images of the Soviet Union, the old Russia and the new.

It may, however, be the concept of 'strangeness', to which Woolf was so drawn, that allows us some little way into the difficulty. For the 'strangeness' of nineteenth-century Russia, situated at a different stage of 'modernization', to the Western eye or the Western reader, may be linked to the 'making strange' – *ostranenie* – that became central to the theories of Russian modernism and avant-gardism. There are interesting similarities between the influential essay of the leading theorist of Russian Formalism, Victor Shklovsky, 'Art as Technique' (1917) and Woolf's thoughts on Russian literature, particularly in Shklovsky's comments on Tolstoy: 'Tolstoy makes the familiar seem strange by not naming the familiar object. He describes an object as if he were seeing it for the first time, an event as if it were happening for the first time' (Lemon and Reis 1965). Thus the great nineteenth-century realist also becomes the exemplar of modernist 'defamiliarization'. 'Defamiliarization', I would argue, is the technique informing Woolf's most experimental novel, *JR*. It may also be the term, though Woolf is unlikely to have recognized it or to have known of Shklovsky and his circle, that makes her Russian reading (predominantly nineteenth century) more than just a document of an irrecoverable past.

Bibliography

Introduction

Amrain, Susanne (1999) 'Virginia Woolf 1882–1941', in Duda, Sibylle and Luise F. Pusch (eds) *Wielkie Szalone*, trans. Aleksandra Górska, Warsaw Sic!, pp. 125–74. Translation of 'Virginia Woolf (1882–1941): "Gleichmut - üben Sie sich in Gleichmut, Mrs Woolf", in Duda, Sibylle and Luise F. Pusch (eds), *Wahnsinns-Frauen*, Frankfurt: Suhrkamp, 1992, pp. 174–224.

Bell, Quentin (1972) *Virginia Woolf: A Biography*, London: Hogarth Press, 1972.

Blanche, Jacques-Émile (1927) 'Entretien avec Virginia Woolf', *Les Nouvelles littéraires*, 13 August 1927, 1–2.

Caws, Mary Ann and Sarah Bird Wright (2000) *Bloomsbury and France: Art and Friends*, Oxford: Oxford University Press.

Cixous, Hélène (1981) 'The Laugh of the Medusa', in Marks, Elaine and Isabelle de Courtivron (eds) *New French Feminisms: An Anthology*, New York: Harvester, pp. 245–64.

Crick, Joyce (1999) 'The German Reception of Virginia Woolf' (unpublished MS).

de Beauvoir, Simone (1965) Introduction to *James Joyce in Paris: His Final Years*, New York: Harcourt Brace, pp. vii–ix.

Friedman, Susan Stanford (1996) 'Uncommon readings: Seeking the Geopolitical Woolf', *South Carolina Review*, 29.1: 24–44.

Labanyi, Jo (1995) 'Postmodernism and the Problem of Cultural Identity', in Graham, Helen and Jo Labanyi (eds) *Spanish Cultural Studies: An Introduction*, Oxford: Oxford University Press, pp. 396–406.

Lee, Hermione (1996) *Virginia Woolf*, London: Chatto & Windus.

Luckhurst, Nicola and Martine Ravache (2000) *Virginia Woolf in Camera*, London: Cecil Woolf.

Ocampo, Victoria (1946) *Testimonios*, vol. 3, Buenos Aires: Sudamericana.

Silver, Brenda (1999) *Virginia Woolf, Icon*, Chicago: University of Chicago Press.

Staveley, Alice (2000) 'Reconfiguring "Kew Gardens": Virginia Woolf's *Monday or Tuesday* Years', unpublished doctoral thesis, University of Oxford.

Woolf, Leonard (1988) *Mein Leben mit Virginia: Erinnerungen*, ed. and German trans. Friederike Groth, Frankfurt am Main: Frankfurter Verlagsanstalt.

Woolf, Leonard (1989) *La mia vita con Virginia*, ed. Friederike Groth, foreword by Marisa Bulgheroni, Italian trans. Ilide Carmignani, Milan: Serra e Riva.

Woolf, Leonard (1991) *Virginia: Erindringer*, ed. and preface Friederike Groth, Danish trans. Nina Lautrup-Larsen, Copenhagen: Rosinante.

Woolf, Virginia (1938) *Three Guineas*, London: Hogarth Press.

Woolf, Virginia (1947) 'The Leaning Tower', in *The Moment and Other Essays*, London: Hogarth Press.

Woolf, Virginia (1975–80) *The Letters of Virginia Woolf*, eds Nigel, Nicolson and Joanne Trautmann, 6 vols, London: Hogarth Press; New York: Harcourt Brace.

Woolf, Virginia (1977–84) *The Diary of Virginia Woolf*, ed. Anne Olivier Bell, 5 vols, London: Hogarth Press.

Chapter 1

VIRGINIA WOOLF IN FRANCE (1926–60)

Blanche, Jacques-Émile (1927) 'Entretien avec Virginia Woolf', *Nouvelles littéraires* [Paris], 252: 1–2.

Blanche, Jacques-Émile (1929) 'Un nouveau roman de Virginia Woolf', *Nouvelles littéraires* [Paris], 16 February, 9.

Blot, Jean (1992) *Bloomsbury: histoire d'une sensibilité artistique et politique anglaise*, Paris: Balland.

Cazamian, Louis (1952) 'La Philosophie de Virginia Woolf', *Études anglaises* [Paris], 4: 343–435.

Chastaing, Maxime (1951) *La Philosophie de Virginia Woolf*, Paris: Presses Universitaires de France.

Collet, Georges-Paul (1965) 'Jacques-Émile Blanche and Virginia Woolf', *Comparative Literature*, 27.1: 73–81.

Delattre, Floris (1931) 'La Durée bergsonienne dans le roman de Virginia Woolf', *Revue anglo-américaine*, 9: 97–108.

Delattre, Floris (1932) *Le Roman psychologique de Virginia Woolf*, Paris: Librairie Philosophique J. Vrin.

Delattre, Floris (1937) 'Le Nouveau Roman de Virginia Woolf', *Études anglaises* [Paris], 3: 289–96.

Delattre, Floris (1938) '*Les Vagues*', *Études anglaises* [Paris], 2: 201–02.

Delattre, Floris (1939) '*Three Guineas*', *Études anglaises* [Paris], 2: 177–78.

Delattre, Floris (1950) 'Virginia Woolf et le monologue intérieur', in *Feux d'automne*, Paris: Didier, pp. 225–47.

Delattre, Floris (1994) *The Psychological Novel of Virginia Woolf*, trans. Constance Hunting, Toronto: Puckerbrush Press.

Eliot, T. S. (1927) 'Les Lettres anglaises: le roman anglais contemporain', *Nouvelle Revue Française* [Paris], 669–75.

Gillet, Louis (1929) '*L'Orlando* de Mme Virginia Woolf', *Revue des deux mondes* [Paris], 53: 218-30.

Gillet, Louis (1930) *Esquisses anglaises*, Paris: Firmin Didot.

Gillet, Louis (1935) 'Virginia Woolf et le conte philosophique', *Nouvelles littéraires*, 26 January.

Jaloux, Edmond (1946) 'Mort de Virginia Woolf', in *D'Eschyle à Giraudoux*, Fribourg: Egloff.

Maurois, André (1927) 'Première rencontre avec Virginia Woolf', *Nouvelles littéraires* [Paris], 13 August, 1.

Mayoux, Jean-Jacques (1928) 'Sur un livre de Virginia Woolf', *Revue anglo-américaine* [Paris], 5: 424–38.

Mayoux, Jean-Jacques (1930a) À propos d'*Orlando* de Virginia Woolf', *Europe* [Paris], 22 (15 January): 117–22.

Mayoux, Jean-Jacques (1930b) 'Le Roman de l'espace et du temps: Virginia Woolf', *Revue anglo-américaine* [Paris], 7 April, 312–26.
Mayoux, Jean-Jacques (1960) *Vivants Piliers: le roman anglo-saxon et les symboles*, Paris: Julliard.
Nathan, Monique (1956) *Virginia Woolf*, Paris: Seuil.
Steel, David (1989) 'Les Strachey, Bloomsbury, Gide et le groupe de *La Nouvelle Revue Française', Bulletin des Amis d'André Gide* [Nancy], 22.84: 401–29.
Woolf, Virginia (1926) 'Le Temps passe', trans. Charles Mauron, *Commerce* [Paris], Winter: 91–133. [Translation of 'Time Passes' from *TL*]
Woolf, Virginia (1929) 'On Not Knowing French', *New Republic*, 348–49.
Woolf, Virginia (1937) *Les Vagues* (*TW*), trans. Marguerite Yourcenar, Paris: Le Livre de Poche.
Woolf, Virginia (1980) *The Letters of Virginia Woolf*, ed. Nigel Nicolson and Joanne Trautmann, vol. 6, London: Hogarth Press.
Woolf, Virginia (1985) *The Diary of Virginia Woolf*, ed. Ann Olivier Bell, vol. 5, Harmondsworth; New York: Penguin Books.

SIMONE DE BEAUVOIR

Bair, Deirdre (1990) *Simone de Beauvoir: A Biography*, New York: Touchstone.
de Beauvoir, Simone (1943) *L'Invitée*, Paris: NRF/Gallimard.
de Beauvoir, Simone (1949) *She Came to Stay*, trans. Yvonne Moyse and Roger Senhouse, London: Secker & Warburg.
de Beauvoir, Simone (1946) *Tous les hommes sont mortels*. Paris: Gallimard.
de Beauvoir, Simone (1955) *All Men Are Mortal*, trans. Leonard M. Friedman, New York: World.
de Beauvoir, Simone (1953) *The Second Sex*, trans. and ed. H. M. Parshley, London: Jonathan Cape.
de Beauvoir, Simone (1963) *La Force des choses*, 2 vols, Paris: Gallimard.
de Beauvoir, Simone (1964) *Force of Circumstance*, trans. Richard Howard, New York: G. P. Putnam's Sons.
de Beauvoir, Simone (1972) *Tout compte fait*, Paris: Gallimard.
de Beauvoir, Simone (1974a) *All Said and Done*, trans. Patrick O'Brian, New York: G.P. Putnam's Sons.
de Beauvoir, Simone (1947) *Pour une morale de l'ambiguité*, Paris: Gallimard.
de Beauvoir, Simone (1948) *The Ethics of Ambiguity*, trans. Bernard Frechtman, New York: Philosophical Library.
de Beauvoir, Simone (1976) *Le Deuxième Sexe*, 2 vols, Paris: Gallimard.
de Beauvoir, Simone (1979) *Les Écrits de Simone de Beauvoir*, ed. Claude Francis and Fernande Gonthier, Paris: Gallimard.
Dayan, Josée and Malka Ribowska (1979) *Simone de Beauvoir: un film*, Paris: Gallimard.
Francis, Claude (1978) *Simone de Beauvoir et le cours du monde*, Paris: Klincksieck.
Moi, Toril (1990) *Feminist Theory and Simone de Beauvoir*, Oxford: Blackwell.
Moi, Toril (1994) *Simone de Beauvoir: The Making of an Intellectual Woman*, Oxford: Blackwell.
Scharzer, Alice (1984) *After The Second Sex: Conversation with Simone de Beauvoir*, New York: Random House.
Woolf, Virginia (1986) *Three Guineas*, introd. Hermione Lee, London: Hogarth Press.

NATHALIE SARRAUTE

Allemand, André (1980) *L'Œuvre romanesque de Nathalie Sarraute*, Neuchâtel: À la Baconnière.
Asso, Françoise (1995) *Nathalie Sarraute: une écriture de l'effraction*, Paris: Presses Universitaires de France.
Barbour, Sarah (1993) *Nathalie Sarraute and the Feminist Reader: Identities in Process*, London: Bucknell University Press.
Benmussa, Simone (1987) *Nathalie Sarraute: qui êtes-vous?* Lyon: La Manufacture.
Clayton, Alan (1989) *Nathalie Sarraute ou le tremblement de l'écriture*, Paris: Lettres Modernes.
Cohn, Ruby (1964) 'Nathalie Sarraute et Virginia Woolf: "sisters under the skin" ', in Matthews, J. H. (ed.), *Un Nouveau Roman? critique et tradition*, Paris: Lettres Modernes, pp. 167–80.
Cornwell, Ethel F. (1977) 'Virginia Woolf, Nathalie Sarraute and Mary McCarthy: Three Approaches to Character in Modern Fiction', *International Fiction Review*, 4: 3–10.
Minogue, Valérie (1987) 'Ironie et réalité dans les romans de Nathalie Sarraute', in Duchatelet (ed.), *Trois Femmes romancières: M. Duras, N. Sarraute, M. Yourcenar*, Brest: Cahier du CERF, pp. 7–22.
Noël, Roger (1970) 'Nathalie Sarraute's Criticism of Virginia Woolf', *Revue des langues vivantes* [Liège, Belgium], 36: 266–71.
Sarraute, Nathalie (1953) *Martereau*, Paris: Gallimard.
Sarraute, Nathalie (1964) *Martereau: A Novel*, trans. Maria Jolas, London: John Calder.
Sarraute, Nathalie (1956) *L'Ère du soupçon*, Paris: Gallimard.
Sarraute, Nathalie (1963a) *The Age of Suspicion*, New York: Georges Braziller.
Sarraute, Nathalie (1957) *Tropismes*, Paris: Minuit.
Sarraute, Nathalie (1963) *Tropisms and The Age of Suspicion*, trans. Maria Jolas, London: John Calder.
Sarraute, Nathalie (1959) *Le Planétarium*, Paris: Gallimard.
Sarraute, Nathalie (1961a) *The Planetarium*, trans. Maria Jolas, London: John Calder.
Sarraute, Nathalie (1961b) 'Virginia Woolf ou la visionnaire du "maintenant" ', *Lettres françaises* [Paris], 882: 1–5.
Sarraute, Nathalie (1963b) *Les Fruits d'or*, Paris: Gallimard.
Sarraute, Nathalie (1965) *The Golden Fruits*, trans. Maria Jolas, London: John Calder.
Sarraute, Nathalie (1968) *Entre la vie et la mort*, Paris: Gallimard.
Sarraute, Nathalie (1970) *Between Life and Death*, trans. Maria Jolas, London: Calder & Boyars.
Sarraute, Nathalie (1976) *'Disent les imbéciles'*, Paris: Gallimard.
Sarraute, Nathalie (1977) *Fools Say: A Novel*, trans. Maria Jolas, London: John Calder.
Sarraute, Nathalie (1978) *Théâtre*, Paris: Gallimard.
Sarraute, Nathalie (1980) *Collected Plays*, trans. Maria Jolas and Barbara Wright, London: John Calder.
Sarraute, Nathalie (1980) *L'Usage de la parole*, Paris: Gallimard.
Sarraute, Nathalie (1982a) *The Use of Speech*, trans. Barbara Wright, London: John Calder.
Sarraute, Nathalie (1982b) *Pour un oui ou pour un non*, Paris: Gallimard.
Sarraute, Nathalie (1983a) *Enfance*, Paris: Gallimard.
Sarraute, Nathalie (1983b) *Childhood*, trans. Barbara Wright, London: John Calder.
Sarraute, Nathalie (1986) *Paul Valéry et l'enfant d'éléphant et Flaubert le précurseur*, Paris: Gallimard.
Tison Braun, Micheline (1971) *Nathalie Sarraute ou la recherche de l'authenticité*, Paris: Gallimard.

MAURICE BLANCHOT

Blanchot, Maurice (1943) 'Le Temps et le roman', in *Faux Pas*, Paris: Gallimard, pp. 282-86.
Blanchot, Maurice (1955) *L'Espace littéraire*, Paris: Gallimard.
Blanchot, Maurice (1959) *Le Livre à venir*, Paris: Gallimard.
Blanchot, Maurice (1969) *L'Entretien infini*, Paris: Gallimard.
Blanchot, Maurice (1982) 'Outwitting the Demon: A Vocation', in *The Siren's Song: Selected Essays*, ed. and introd. Gabriel Josipovici, trans. Sacha Rabinovitch, Brighton: Harvester, pp. 87–93.
Blanchot, Maurice (1982) *The Space of Literature*, trans. and introd. Ann Smock, Lincoln: University of Nebraska Press.
Blanchot, Maurice (1983) *La Communauté inavouable*, Paris: Minuit.
Blanchot, Maurice (1986) *Michel Foucault tel que je l'imagine*, Montpellier: fata morgana. Translated in Foucault and Blanchot (1987).
Blanchot, Maurice (1988) *The Unavowable Community*, trans. Pierre Joris, Barrytown, N.Y: Station Hill Press.
Blanchot, Maurice (1993) *The Infinite Conversation*, trans. and introd. Susan Hanson, Minneapolis: University of Minnesota Press.
Bruns, Gerald L. (1997) *Maurice Blanchot: The Refusal of Philosophy*, Baltimore: Johns Hopkins University Press.
Collin, Françoise (1986) *Maurice Blanchot et la question de l'écriture*, Paris: Gallimard.
Foucault, Michel (1994) 'La Pensée du dehors', in *Dits et Écrits*, Paris: Gallimard, 1: 518–39. First published in *Critique* [Paris], 229 (1966): 523–46.
Foucault, Michel and Maurice Blanchot (1987) *Foucault, Blanchot: 'Maurice Blanchot: The Thought from Outside'; 'Michel Foucault as I Imagine Him'*, trans. Brian Massumi and Jeffrey Mehlman, New York: Zone Books.
Hill, Leslie (1997) *Blanchot: Extreme Contemporary*, London: Routledge.
Laporte, Roger (1987) *Maurice Blanchot: l'ancien, l'effroyable ancien*, Montpellier: fata morgana.

OTHER WORKS CITED

Aubert, Jacques and Fritz Senn (eds) (1985) *James Joyce*, Cahiers de l'Herne, no. 50, Paris: Éditions de l'Herne, 1985.
Auden, W.H. (1995) *'In Solitude for Company': W.H. Auden after 1940*, ed. Katherine Bucknell and Nicholas Jenkins, Oxford: Clarendon Press.
Beer, Gillian (1996) '*Between the Acts:* Reading the End', in *Virginia Woolf: The Common Ground: Essays*, Edinburgh: Edinburgh University Press, pp. 125–48.
Lenne, Francine (1985) 'James Joyce et Louis Gillet', in Aubert and Senn, pp. 151–75.
Ricardou, Jean (1978) *Le Nouveau Roman*, Paris: Seuil.
Spender, Stephen (1951) *World within World*, London: Faber and Faber.
Villeneuve, Pierre-Éric (1996) 'Virginia Woolf and the French Reader: An Overview', *South Carolina Review*, 29.1: 109–21.
Wilson, Angus (1994) 'The Always Changing Impact of Virginia Woolf', in McNees, Elinor (ed.), *Virginia Woolf: Critical Assessments*, London: Helm 1: 153–61.
Woolf, Virginia (1993a) 'Modern Fiction', in *The Crowded Dance of Modern Life*, ed., introd. and notes by Rachel Bowlby, London: Penguin, pp. 5-12.
Woolf, Virginia (1993b) *Les Vagues* (*TW*), trans. Cécile Wajsbrot, Paris: Calmann-Lévy.
Woolf, Virginia (1994) *Mrs Dalloway*, trans. Marie-Claire Pasquier, Paris: Gallimard.

Woolf, Virginia (1996) *Vers le phare (TL)*, trans. Françoise Pellan, Paris: Gallimard.
Yourcenar, Marguerite (1989) *En pélerin, en étranger*, Paris: Gallimard.

Chapter 2

BOOKS AND ARTICLES

Bakhtin, M. (1987) *Le Marxisme et la philosophie du langage: essai d'application de la méthode sociologique en linguistique*, trans. from Russian by Marina Yaguello, introd. Roman Jakobson, Paris: Éditions de Minuit. Translated into English as *Marxism and the Philosophy of Language*, trans. Ladislav Matejka and I. R. Titunik, Cambridge, MA: Harvard University Press, 1986.

Barthes, Roland (1973) *Le Plaisir du texte*, Paris: Gallimard. Translated as *The Pleasure of the Text*, trans. Richard Miller, Oxford: Basil Blackwell, 1990.

Bernard, Catherine (1996) '*To the Lighthouse* et *The Waves:* la fiction comme entrelacs phénoménologique', *Les Cahiers FORELL* [Poitiers], 6: 201–18.

Bernard, Catherine (1997) '*The Waves:* vers une poétique de la sensation', *Écriture poétique moderne* [Nantes], 131–62.

Bernard, Catherine (1999) 'Capricious Friendships with the Unknown and the Vanished: A Reading of Some of Virginia Woolf's Essays', *Études britanniques contemporaines* [Montpellier], Special Issue for the Société d'Études Woolfiennes, 123–35.

Bernard, Catherine and Christine Reynier (eds) (1995) '*The Waves' by Virginia Woolf*, Paris: Didier-érudition–CNED.

Blanchot, Maurice (1955) *L'Espace littéraire*, Paris: Gallimard. Translated as *The Space of Literature*, trans. Ann Smock, Lincoln, NE; London: University of Nebraska Press, 1982.

Blanchot, Maurice (1959) 'L'Échec du démon: la vocation' in *Le Livre à venir*, Paris: Gallimard, pp. 120-28. Translated as 'Outwitting the Demon: A Vocation' in *The Siren's Song: Selected Essays*, ed. and introd. Gabriel Josipovici, trans. Sacha Rabinovitch, Brighton: Harvester, 1982, pp. 87–93.

Blot, Jean (1992) *Bloomsbury: histoire d'une sensibilité historique et politique anglaise*, Paris: Balland.

Bragance, Anne (1984) *Virginia Woolf, ou, la dame sur le piédestal*, Paris: Édition des Femmes.

Cohn, Ruby (1964) 'Nathalie Sarraute et Virginia Woolf', *Revue des lettres modernes* [Paris], 94–99.

Cotte, Pierre (1996) *L'Explication grammaticale des textes anglais*, Paris: Presses Universitaires de France.

de Beauvoir, Simone (1949) *Le Deuxième Sexe*, Paris: Gallimard. Translated as *The Second Sex*, trans. and ed. H. M. Parshley, London: Cape, 1953.

Defromont, Françoise (1985) *Virginia Woolf: vers la maison de lumière*, Paris: Édition des Femmes.

Deleuze, Gilles (1997) *Dialogues*, Paris: Flammarion. Translated as *Dialogues*, trans. Hugh Tomlinson and Barbara Habberjam, London: Athlone, 1987.

Deleuze, Gilles and Félix Guattari (1980) *Mille Plateaux: capitalisme et schizophrénie*, Paris: Minuit. Translated as *A Thousand Plateaus: Capitalism and Schizophrenia*, trans. and introd. Brian Massumi, London: Athlone, 1988.

Delourme, Chantal (1996a) '*To the Lighthouse:* Virginia Woolf, diamantaire du visible', *Les Cahiers FORELL* [Poitiers], 5: 11–28.

Delourme, Chantal (1996b) 'De l'espace au phrasé: "Exquisite shapes" dans *To the Lighthouse*', *TLE (Théorie Littérature Enseignement)* [Vincennes], 14: 151–69.

Delourme, Chantal (1997) 'La Figure, la Nuit dans "Time passes" ', *Études britanniques contemporaines* [Montpellier], Special Issue for the Société d'Études Woolfiennes, 119–34.

Derrida, Jacques (1967) *L'Écriture et la différence*, Paris: Seuil. Translated as *Writing and Difference*, trans. Alan Bass, London: Routledge & Kegan Paul, 1978.

Derrida, Jacques (1972) *Marges de la philosophie*, Paris: Minuit. Translated as *Margins of Philosophy*, trans. Alan Bass, Brighton: Harvester Press, 1982.

Didier, Béatrice (1981) *L'Écriture-femme*, Paris: Presses Universitaires de France.

Durand, Gilbert (1969) *Les Structures anthropologiques de l'imaginaire: introduction à l'archétypologie générale*, Paris: Bordas. Translated as *The Anthropological Structures of the Imaginary*, trans. Margaret Sankey and Judith Hatten, Mount Nebo, Jordan: Bombana Press, 1999.

Ferrer, Daniel (1984) '*To the Lighthouse*', in Ellmann, Maud (ed.), *Psychoanalytic Literary Criticism*, London: Longman, pp. 143–70.

Ferrer, Daniel (1985a) 'Au bord des vagues: l'ouverture du champ de l'écriture dans un fragment manuscrit de Virginia Woolf', in Grésillon, Almuth and Michael Werner (eds), *Leçons d'écriture, ce que disent les manuscrits*, Paris: Lettres Modernes, pp. 187–93.

Ferrer, Daniel (1985b) 'Sister Art and Victorian Parents: Virginia Woolf et la peinture', in Hamard, M. C (ed.), *Home Sweet Home or Bleak House*, Paris: Les Belles Lettres, pp. 51–56.

Ferrer, Daniel (1987a) 'Écritures de la folie: Joyce, Virginia Woolf, W. Faulkner' (unpublished doctoral thesis, University of Paris VIII).

Ferrer, Daniel (1987b) 'Fantasmes de l'écriture: James Joyce, Virginia Woolf', *Tropismes* [Nanterre], 3.

Ferrer, Daniel (1987c) '*Between the Acts*, la représentation et ses doubles', in Ferrer, Daniel and C. Petrault (eds), *Les Forteresses vides de l'oncle Toby: études sur la représentation dans les pays anglo-saxons*, Paris: Les Belles Lettres.

Ferrer, Daniel (1990) *V. Woolf and the Madness of Language*, trans. G. Bennington and R. Bowlby, London: Routledge.

Ferrer, Daniel (1997) 'Récit, métamorphose du récit, récit de métamorphose du récit: quelques éléments programmatiques de génétique woolfienne', *Études britanniques contemporaines* [Montpellier], Special Issue for the Société d'Études Woolfiennes, 3–15.

Ferrer, Daniel and M. Contat (eds) (1998) *Pourquoi la critique génétique?: méthodes, théories*, Paris: CNRS.

Forrester, Viviane (1973) *Virginia Woolf*, Paris: Les Éditions de l'Équinoxe.

Gallix, François (1995) *Le Roman britannique du XXème siècle: modernistes et postmodernes*, Paris: Masson.

Genette, Gérard (1966–72) *Figures*, 3 vols, Paris: Seuil. Translated as *Figures of Literary Discourse*, trans. Alan Sheridan, introd. Marie-Rose Logan, Oxford: Blackwell, 1982.

Ginfray, Denise (1994) 'V. Woolf: de l'écriture-défi à l'expérience des limites', in Béranger, Élisabeth and Ginette Castro (eds), *Le Genre et la loi, 2*, Proceedings of the ERCIF Symposium, Talence: Éditions de la Maison des sciences de l'homme d'Aquitaine, pp. 121–28.

Ginfray, Denise (1995a) 'Identité et Création: le Masculin et le Féminin dans l'œuvre de V. Woolf' (unpublished doctoral thesis, University of Bordeaux III).

Ginfray, Denise (1995b) 'Le Désordre ordonné de V. Woolf', *Idéologies dans le monde anglo-saxon* [Grenoble], 8: 123–34.

Ginfray, Denise (1997) 'Entre Nature et Culture, féminin et masculin: la problématique du sujet dans l'œuvre fictionnelle de V. Woolf', in Béranger, Élisabeth, Ginette Castro and Marie-Lise Paoli (eds), *Femme et nature, I*, Proceedings of the ERCIF Symposium, Talence: Éditions de la Maison des sciences de l'homme d'Aquitaine, pp. 143–49.

Ginfray, Denise (1999) 'Modernité et esthétique: l'exemple de Virginia Woolf', *Études anglaises* [Paris], 1: 28–39.
Guiguet, Jean (1962) *Virginia Woolf et son œuvre: l'art la quête du réel*, Paris: Didier. Translated as *Virginia Woolf and Her Work*, trans. Jean Stewart, London: Hogarth Press, 1965.
Guiguet, Jean (1973) 'La Biographie de Virginia Woolf', *Études anglaises* [Paris], 26: 331–37.
Guiguet, Jean (1974) 'V. Woolf et James Joyce: un problème de dates et de tempéraments', in Bonnerot, Louis, Jean Jacquot and Claude Jacquet (eds) *'Ulysse': cinquante ans après*, Paris: Didier, pp. 23–31.
Guiguet, Jean (ed.) (1977) *Virginia Woolf et le groupe de Bloomsbury*, Paris: Union Générale d'Éditions.
Heath, Stephen (1972) *Le Nouveau Roman: A Study in the Practice of Writing*, London: Elek Books.
Jondot, Jacqueline (1996) '"A voice answering a voice": *Orlando* à *The Waves*', *Les Cahiers FORELL* [Poitiers], 5: 43–58.
Jordis, Christine (1999) *Gens de la Tamise: le roman anglais au XXème siècle*, Paris: Seuil.
Joubert, Claire (1999a), 'The Point of Pins: le détail et l'érotique de la lettre dans les nouvelles de Dorothy Richardson, Katherine Mansfield et V. Woolf', *La Licorne* [Poitiers], Special Issue, Maison des Sciences de l'Homme et de la Société.
Joubert, Claire (1999b) 'The Feminine: A Critical Angle for Poetics', *European English Messenger*, 8.1: 24–28.
Joubert, Claire (1999c) 'From the real thing to character: V. Woolf's poetics of life', *Études britanniques contemporaines* [Montpellier], Special Issue for the Société d'Études Woolfiennes, 137–49.
Kristeva, Julia (1974) *La Révolution du langage poétique: l'avant-garde à la fin du XIXe siècle*, Paris: Seuil. Translated as *Revolution in Poetic Language*, trans. Margaret Waller, introd. Leon S. Roudiez, New York: Columbia University Press, 1984.
Lacan, Jacques (1957) *Écrits*, Paris: Seuil.
Lanone, Catherine (1996) 'Fenêtres vers la mère: *To the Lighthouse*', *Les Cahiers FORELL* [Poitiers], 5: 29–42.
Lanone, Catherine (1997) 'Métaphore et métamorphose dans *To the Lighthouse*', *Études britanniques contemporaines* [Montpellier], Special Issue for the Société d'Études Woolfiennes, 135–48.
Lanone, Catherine (1999) 'Abject Objects in JR', *Études britanniques contemporaines* [Montpellier], Special Issue for the Société d'Études Woolfiennes, 79–90.
Lecercle, Jean-Jacques (1997) 'L'Écriture féminine selon Virginia Woolf', *Études britanniques contemporaines* [Montpellier], Special Issue for the Société d'Études Woolfiennes, 16–29.
Lemaire, Gérard-Georges (1990) *Un thé au Bloomsbury: l'art autour de Virginia Woolf*, Paris: Henri Veyrier.
Lipovetski, Gilles (1983) *L'Ère du vide: essais sur l'individualisme contemporain*, Paris: Gallimard.
Louvel, Liliane (1996) 'V. Woolf. *The Waves*: "une histoire, un soupir, une vague", questions de réflexion', *Les Cahiers FORELL* [Poitiers], 5: 73–94.
Louvel, Liliane (1997) 'Virginia Woolf: "The Lady in the Looking Glass": portrait(s) de dame(s) avec miroir', *Études britanniques contemporaines* [Montpellier], Special Issue for the Société d'Études Woolfiennes, 70–86.
Louvel, Liliane (1999) 'Love with a Dish-Fruit/Nature morte avec l'amour en plâtre: An Instance of Pictorial Eroticism', *Études britanniques contemporaines* [Montpellier], Special Issue for the Société d'Études Woolfiennes, 29–43.
Lyotard, Jean-François (1971) *Discours, Figure*, Paris: Klincksieck.
Mannoni, Maud (1998) *Elles ne savent pas ce qu'elles disent*, Paris: Denoël.

Mayoux, Jean-Jacques (1960) *Vivants Piliers: le roman anglo-saxon et les symboles*, Paris: Maurice Nadeau.

Mayoux, Jean-Jacques (1981) *Sous de vastes portiques: études de littérature et d'art anglais*, Paris: Nadeau et Papyrus.

Merleau-Ponty, Maurice (1955) *Phénoménologie de la perception*, Paris: Gallimard. Translated as *Phenomenology of Perception*, trans. Colin Smith, London: Routledge & Kegan Paul; New York: Humanities Press, 1962.

Merleau-Ponty, Maurice (1964) *Le Visible et l'invisible*, Paris: Gallimard. Translated as *The Visible and the Invisible*, trans. Alphonso Lingis, Evanston, IL: Northwestern University Press, 1968.

Monneyron, Frédéric (1995) *Le Mythe de l'androgyne*, Grenoble: Ellug.

Noël, Roger (1970) 'Nathalie Sarraute's Criticism of Virginia Woolf', *Revue des langues vivantes* [Liège, Belgium], 36: 266–71.

Paccaud-Huguet, Josiane (1999) 'The Jarring Rebus of Subjectivity', *Études britanniques contemporaines* [Montpellier], Special Issue for the Société d'Études Woolfiennes, 45–60.

Pellan, Françoise (1994) *L'Ancrage et le voyage*, Presses Universitaires de Lyon.

Pillière, Linda (1997) 'Quelques aspects du style de V. Woolf' (unpublished doctoral thesis, University of Paris-Sorbonne).

Quéré, Henri (1984) 'Problèmes et techniques de la narration chez quelques grands romanciers anglais du XXème siècle: E. M. Forster, V. Woolf, D. H. Lawrence', Lille: ANRT (microfiches).

Quéré, Henri (1985) 'D'une énonciation singulière: le cas des *Vagues*', in Parret, H. and H. Ruprecht (eds), *Aims and Prospects of Semiotics/Exigences et perspectives de la sémiotique*, Amsterdam: John Benjamins, pp. 791–99.

Quéré, Henri (1994) *Récit. Fictions. Écritures. Méthodologie de l'analyse littéraire: œuvres et écrivains de langue anglaise*, Paris: Presses Universitaires de France.

Regard, Frédéric (1997) 'Clapham Junction 1910: éthique et esthétique de "Mr Bennett and Mrs Brown"', *Études britanniques contemporaines* [Montpellier], Special Issue for the Société d'Études Woolfiennes, 30–57.

Regard, Frédéric (1999) 'Things and the Signature of the Feminine in *TG*', *Études britanniques contemporaines* [Montpellier], Special Issue for the Société d'Études Woolfiennes, 107–22.

Reynier, Christine (1988) 'La Technique romanesque de V. Woolf: aspects de la mise en relation' (unpublished doctoral thesis, University of Paris VII).

Reynier, Christine (1993) '"The Lady in the Looking-glass": réflexions sur un miroir', *Cahiers Victoriens et Édouardiens* [Montpellier], 37: 121–28.

Reynier, Christine (1994) 'Writing in the Making in Virginia Woolf's Short Stories', *Journal of the Short Story in English*, 23: 77–88.

Reynier, Christine (1995a) 'L'un et l'autre: regards croisés dans trois nouvelles de V. Woolf: "The New Dress", "The Introduction" et "The Lady in the Looking-Glass"', *Études britanniques contemporaines* [Montpellier], 7: 97–108.

Reynier, Christine (1995b) 'Le Corps révélateur dans les nouvelles de Virginia Woolf', *Le Corps dans tous ses états* [Bordeaux], 245–54.

Reynier, Christine (1996a) 'Les Nouvelles de Virginia Woolf et l'art pictural', *Cahiers Victoriens et Édouardiens* [Montpellier], 44: 147–66.

Reynier, Christine (1996b) 'La Clôture différée dans *The Waves*'. *Les Cahiers FORELL* [Poitiers], 5: 127–38.

Reynier, Christine (1997) 'Récit de métamorphoses, métamorphoses du récit dans "The Shooting Party"', *Études britanniques contemporaines* [Montpellier], Special Issue for the Société d'Études Woolfiennes, 87–100.

Richard, Jean-Pierre (1996) *Terrains de lecture*, Paris: Gallimard.

Ricoeur, Paul (1975) *La Métaphore vive*, Paris: Seuil. Translated as *The Rule of Metaphor:*

Multi-Disciplinary Studies of the Creation of Meaning in Language, trans. Robert Czerny, Kathleen McLaughlin and John Costello, London: Routledge & Kegan Paul, 1978.

Ricoeur, Paul (1984) 'Entre le temps mortel et le temps monumental: *Mrs Dalloway*', in *Temps et récit*, Paris: Seuil, 2: 152–67. Translated as 'Between Mortal Time and Monumental Time: *Mrs Dalloway*', in *Time and Narrative*, trans. Kathleen McLaughlin and David Pellauer, Chicago, IL; London: University of Chicago Press, 1985, 2: 101–12.

Rivoire, Michèle (1996) '*The Waves:* le spectre de la Chose', *Les Cahiers FORELL* [Poitiers], 5: 113–26.

Rivoire, Michèle (1997a) 'Célavie ou une cause qui démange: "An Unwritten Novel" de V. Woolf', in Haberer, Adolphe and Josiane Paccaud-Huguet (eds) *De la littérature à la lettre: poésie, fiction, arts: domaine anglophone*, Lyon: Presses Universitaires de Lyon.

Rivoire, Michèle (1997b) 'Pour l'amour de Mrs Brown', *Études britanniques contemporaines* [Montpellier], Special Issue for the Société d'Études Woolfiennes, 58–69.

Rodier, Carole (1994) 'La Dynamique des âges de la vie dans *Les Vagues* de V. Woolf', *Iris* [Grenoble], 14: 83–98.

Rodier, Carole (1995) 'Vision mythique et transfiguration poétique de la ville chez V. Woolf: Londres dans *La Chambre de Jacob* et *Mrs Dalloway*', *Albion* [Grenoble], 1: 131–50.

Rodier, Carole (1996) 'De la perception à la vision: la conversion du regard chez V. Woolf', *Iris* [Grenoble], 16: 107–25.

Rodier, Carole (1997a) 'Espace, dialectique, résolution: une étude des relations entre les personnages dans *Night and Day* de V. Woolf', *Albion* [Grenoble], 2: 31–49.

Rodier, Carole (1997b) 'De "sword" à "words" ou la métamorphose de la quête de Perceval dans *The Waves*', *Études britanniques contemporaines*, Special Issue for the Société d'Études Woolfiennes, 149–64.

Rodier, Carole (1998) 'L'Imaginaire Woolfien' (doctoral thesis, University Stendhal-Grenoble III), published by Editions du Temps, Paris, 2001.

Rodier, Carole (1999a) 'Golden Light and Substance: "the prose of the world" in Virginia Woolf's Novels', *Virginia Woolf Bulletin*, 1: 22–24.

Rodier, Carole (1999b) 'Apprehending the World: Surface, Substance and the True Experience of Things in Woolf's Novels', *Études britanniques contemporaines* [Montpellier], Special Issue for the Société d'Études Woolfiennes, 19–27.

Rosolato, Guy (1969) *Essais sur le symbolique*, Paris: Gallimard.

Rosolato, Guy (1978) *La Relation d'inconnu*, Paris: Gallimard.

Roth-Sonton, Danièle (2001) *Bloomsbury côté cuisine*, Paris: Harmattan.

Sagalovitsch, Laurent (1998) *La Canne de Virginia Woolf*, Arles: Actes Sud.

Sarraute, Nathalie (1956) 'Conversation et sous-conversation', in *L'Ère du soupçon*, Paris: Gallimard. Translated as 'Conversation and Sub-Conversation', in *Tropisms and The Age of Suspicion*, trans. Maria Jolas, London: John Calder, 1963, pp. 97–120.

Sarraute, Nathalie (1961) 'Virginia Woolf ou la visionnaire du "maintenant"', *Lettres françaises* [Paris], 882 (29 June).

Teyssandier, Hubert (1988) 'La Guerre dans *To the Lighthouse* (1927), de Virginia Woolf', in *Guerre et littérature dans le monde anglophone*, Proceedings of the Conference organized by the Groupe de recherches en Études anglophones du Mans, Université du Maine, November 1988, Le Mans: Publication de l'Université du Maine, pp. 266–79.

Teyssandier, Hubert (1997) 'L'Ondulation dans *The Waves*', *Études britanniques contemporaines* [Montpellier], Special Issue for the Société d'Études Woolfiennes, 181–95.

Topia, André (1995) '*The Waves:* l'œil et le monde', *Études anglaises* [Paris], 48: 430–41.

Topia, André (1997) 'Intensité(s): de l'utilisation de la couleur chez Virginia Woolf', *Études britanniques contemporaines* [Montpellier], Special Issue for the Société d'Études Woolfiennes, 165–80.

Vigne, Marie-Paule (1980) *Le Thème de l'eau dans l'œuvre de Virginia Woolf*, Bordeaux: Presses universitaires de Bordeaux.
Vigne, Marie-Paule (1985) 'Les Lieux de la parole dans *The Years*', *Études anglaises* [Paris], 38: 49–59.
Wajsbrot, Cécile (1982) *Une vie à soi*, Paris: Mercure de France.
Zéraffa, Michel (1969) *La Révolution romanesque*, Paris: Klincksieck.
Zéraffa, Michel (1978) 'Conscience et fiction', *Journal de psychologie* [Boulogne-sur-Seine], 1: 115–31.

SPECIAL ISSUES OF JOURNALS DEVOTED TO VIRGINIA WOOLF

Les Cahiers FORELL [Poitiers], 5 (1996) ('Autour de Virginia Woolf').
Études britanniques contemporaines [Montpellier] (1997) Special Issue for the Société d'Études Woolfiennes ('Métamorphose et récit dans l'œuvre de Virginia Woolf').
Études britanniques contemporaines [Montpellier] (1999) Special Issue for the Société d'Études.
Europe [Paris], 676–77 (1985) ('Virginia Woolf/Gertrude Stein')
Magazine Littéraire, 275 (March 1990), 16–57.

In September 1997 a TV programme 'A Life of One's Own' was broadcast on the educational channel 'Arte'. One should also mention a radio programme 'Une vie, une œuvre' on 'France Culture' in 1998. In this programme Lise Andries interviewed Frances Partridge and other female critics, including the writer A. S. Byatt.

Chapter 3

FRENCH TRANSLATIONS

Novels (including extracts)

BTA

(1945) *Entre les actes*, trans. Yvonne Genova, Paris: Charlot.
(1947) *Entre les actes*, trans. Charles Cestre, Paris: Stock.

Collected novels

(1973–79) *L'Œuvre romanesque*, trans. Jean Talva and others, 2 vols, Paris: Stock. (Contains: *JR*, trans. Jean Talva; *MD*, trans. Simone David; *TL*, trans. Maurice Lanoire; *O*, trans. Charles Mauron; *TW*, trans. Marguerite Yourcenar; *BTA*, trans. Charles Cestre; *FB*, trans. Charles Mauron; *TY*, trans. Germaine Delamain; *MB*, trans. Colette-Marie Huet.)

Extracts from fictional works

(1926) 'Le Temps passe', trans. Charles Mauron, *Commerce* [Paris], Winter, 91–133. [Translation of 'Time Passes' from *TL*]
(1927) 'La Chambre de Jacob', trans. Claude Daravaine and Marie Kieffer, *La Revue nouvelle* [Paris], 28: 27–37. [Extracts from *JR*]

FB

(1935) *Flush*, trans. Charles Mauron, Paris: Stock.

JR
(1942) *La Chambre de Jacob*, trans. Jean Talva, Paris: Stock.
(1993) *La Chambre de Jacob*, trans. Magali Merle, Paris: Le Livre de Poche.

MD
(1929) *Mrs Dalloway*, trans. Simone David, Paris: Stock.
(1993) *Mrs Dalloway*, trans. Pascale Michon, Paris: Le Livre de Poche.
(1994) *Mrs Dalloway*, trans. Marie-Claire Pasquier, Paris: Gallimard.

ND
(1933) *Nuit et jour*, trans. Maurice Bec, Paris: Editions du Siècle.
(1985) *Nuit et jour*, trans. Catherine Naveau, Paris: Flammarion.

O
(1931) *Orlando*, trans. Charles Mauron, Paris: Stock.
(1993) *Orlando*, trans. Catherine Pappo-Musard, Paris: Le Livre de Poche.

Selected fictional works
(1993) *Romans et nouvelles: 1917–1941*, trans. Magali Merle and others, Paris: Librairie Générale Française. (Contains: *JR* and *TL*, trans. Magali Merle; *MD* and 7 short stories, trans. Pascale Michon; *O*, trans. Catherine Pappo-Musard; *TW*, trans. Marguerite Yourcenar; twelve short stories, trans. Pierre Nordon.)

TL
(1929) *La Promenade au Phare*, trans. Maurice Lanoire, Paris: Stock.
(1993) *Voyage au Phare*, trans. Magali Merle, Paris: Le Livre de Poche.
(1996) *Vers le Phare*, trans. Françoise Pellan, Paris: Gallimard.

TP
(1985) *Le Livre san nom: Les Pargiter: roman-essai à l'origine d'Années'*, trans. Sylvie Durastanti, Paris: Des Femmes.

TW
(1937) *Les Vagues*, trans. Marguerite Yourcenar, Paris: Stock.
(1993) *Les Vagues*, trans. Cécile Wajsbrot, Paris: Calmann-Lévy.

TY
(1938) *Années*, trans. Germaine Delamain, Paris: Stock.

VO
(1948) *La Traversée des apparences*, trans. Ludmila Savitsky, Paris: Le Cahier Gris.
(1952) *Croisière*, trans. Armel Guerne, Paris: Robert Marin.

Short stories

'Kew Gardens'
(1927) 'Jardins de Kew', trans. Georgette Camille, *Nouvelles littéraires* [Paris], 13 August, 4.

'The String Quartet'
(1928) 'Le Quatuor à cordes', trans. Georgette Camille, *Revue nouvelle* [Paris], October, 41–45.

'The Mark on the Wall'
(1929) 'Le Signe sur le mur', trans. Yves de Longevialle, *Revue européenne* [Paris], 1 December, 505–14.

'Slater's Pins have No Points'
(1929) 'Les Épingles de chez Slater ne piquent pas', trans. Georgette Camille, *Échanges* [Paris], December, 38–44.

'The Lady in the Looking-Glass: A Reflection'
(1932) 'La Dame dans le miroir', trans. Simone David, *Nouvelles littéraires* [Paris], 8 October, 4.

'Street Haunting: A London Adventure'
(1944) 'Vagabondage: une aventure londonienne', trans. J. M. Rivet and M. P. Foucher, *Fontaine*, Algiers, 37–40: 234–46.

'The New Dress'
(1945) 'La Robe neuve', trans. Hélène Bokanowski, *L'Arche* [Paris], September, 9, 44–53.

'The Moment: Summer's Night'
(1960) 'Le Moment: soir d'été', trans. Roger Giroux, *Tel Quel* [Paris], 1: 44–48.

Selected Short Stories
(1990) *La Fascination de l'étang: proses*, ed. Susan Dick, trans. Josée Kamoun, Paris: Seuil. [25 short stories from *CSF*]

'An Unwritten Novel'
(1995) *Le Faux Roman*, trans. Guillaume Villeneuve, Paris: Editions Mille et Une Nuits.

Biographies

RF
(1999) *La Vie de Roger Fry*, trans. Jean Pavans, Paris: Payot.

Pamphlets

ROO
(1951) *Une chambre à soi*, trans. Clara Malraux, Paris: Robert Marin.

TG
(1977) *Trois Guinées*, trans. Viviane Forrester, Paris: Des Femmes.

Essays

'On Not Knowing French'
(1929) 'Quand on ne sait pas le français', trans. unknown, *Figaro* [Paris], 10 February, 1–2.

'Dr Burney's Evening Party'
(1929) 'La Soirée du docteur Burney', trans. J. Fournier-Pargoire, *Figaro* [Paris], 19–23 August, 4.

'Cowper and Lady Austen'
(1929) 'Cowper et Lady Austen', trans. J. Fournier-Pargoire, *Figaro* [Paris], 22–23 September, 4.

'Beau Brummel'
(1929) 'Le Beau Brummel', trans. J. Fournier-Pargoire, *Figaro* [Paris], 14–15 October, 4.

'Dorothy Wordsworth'
(1930) 'Dorothy Wordsworth', trans. J. Fournier-Pargoire, *Figaro* [Paris], 5–6 May, and 10 May.

'Augustine Birrell'
(1930) 'Les Essais d'Augustin Birrell', trans. J. Fournier-Pargoire, *Figaro* [Paris], 28–29 August, 5.

'Fanny Burney's Half-Sister'
(1931) 'La Demi-sœur de Fanny Burney', trans. J. Fournier-Pargoire, *Figaro* [Paris], 16 February, 6, 17 February, 10, 18 February, 7.

'Edmund Gosse'
(1931) 'Edmond Gosse', trans. J. Fournier-Pargoire, *Figaro* [Paris], 5 August, 5.

Aurora Leigh
(1932) 'Un Roman-poème: *Aurora Leigh*', trans. J. Fournier-Pargoire, *Figaro* [Paris], 5 January, 7, 6 January, 8, 7 January, 4.

'The Novels of Turgenev'
(1935) 'Une opinion: les romans de Tourguénieff', trans. unknown, *Le Mois* [Paris], 51: 153–62.

'Middlebrow'
(1948) 'Le Demi-intellectuel: voilà le fléau', trans. unknown, *La Bataille* [Paris], 6 October, 5.

W & W
(1983) *Les Fruits étranges et brillants de l'art*, ed. Michèle Barrett, trans. Sylvie Durastanti, Paris: Des Femmes.

LS
(1984) *La Scène londonienne*, trans. Pierre Alien, Paris: C. Bourgois. [Also includes a translation of 'Portrait of a Londoner']

LYP
(1996) *Lettre à un jeune poète*, trans. Jacqueline Délia, introd. Viviane Forrester, Paris: Arléa.
(1998) *A John Lehmann, lettre à un jeune poète*, trans. Guillaume Villeneuve, Paris: Éditions Mille et une Nuits.

Selected essays
(1963) *L'Art du roman*, trans. Rose Celli, Paris: Seuil. [10 essays]
(1976) *Essais*, trans. Claudine Jardin et Florence Herbulot, Paris: Seghers. [25 essays]
(1985) *Beau Brummel et autres essais*, trans. Guillaume Villeneuve, Paris: Obsidiane. [6 essays from *CR 2*]
(1989) *De la lecture et de la critique*, selected, ed. and trans. Sylvie Durastanti, Paris: Des Femmes. (Translations of 'Reading' and *Reviewing*]
(1990) *Entre les livres: essais sur les littératures russe et anglo-américaine*, trans. Jean Pavans, Paris: Éditions La Différence. [34 essays]

Memoirs, Diaries and Letters

WD
(1958) *Journal d'un écrivain*, trans. Germaine Beaumont, Monaco: Éditions du Rocher.

MB
(1977) *Instants de vie*, trans. Colette-Marie Huet, Paris: Stock.

'Old Bloomsbury'
(1977) 'Du côté de Bloomsbury', trans. Colette-Marie Huet, *Les Nouvelles littéraires* [Paris], 30 June–7 July, 7.

D
(1981–90) Journal, trans. Colette-Marie Huet and Marie-Ange Dutartre, 8 vols, Paris: Stock.

PA
(1993) *Journal d'adolescence*, trans. Marie-Ange Dutartre, Paris: Stock.

Selected correspondence
(1985) 'Lettres', trans. Nelly Stéphane, *Europe*, August-September, 53–63. [5 letters]
(1985) Woolf, Virginia and Vita Sackville-West, *Correspondance*, ed. Louise DeSalvo and Mitchell A. Leaska, trans. Raymond Las Vergnas, Paris: Stock. [Translation of *The Letters of Vita Sackville-West to Virginia Woolf* and selections from *L* 3–6]
(1992) *Lettres illustrées*, ed. Frances Spalding, trans. Thérésa and Christine de Cherisey, Paris: Herscher. [Translation of *Paper Darts*, London: Collins & Brown, 1991]
(1993) *Lettres*, ed. Nigel Nicolson, trans. Claude Demanuelli, Paris: Le Seuil (selections from *L* and *Congenial Spirits: The Selected Letters of Virginia Woolf*, ed. Joanne Trautmann Banks, London: Hogarth, 1989]
(1995) *Quatre Lettres cachées*, trans. Jean Guiloineau, Paris: C. Bourgois. [Translation of 'Four Hidden Letters']

Drama

FC
(1981) *Freshwater*, ed. Lucio P. Ruotolo, trans. Elisabeth Janvier, Paris: Des Femmes.

Children's stories

Nurse Lugton's Golden Thimble
(1983) *Le Dé en or*, trans. Frédéric Armel, Luçon: F. Nathan.

Miscellaneous selections

(1956) *Virginia Woolf par elle-même*, Paris: Seuil. [Selections from: *O* and *TL*, trans. Charles Mauron; *TW*, trans. Marguerite Yourcenar; *HH*, trans. Hélène Bokanowski, and *L* and *WD*, trans. Monique Nathan]
(1968) *La Mort de la phalène: nouvelles*, trans. Hélène Bokanowski, Paris: Seuil. [21 short stories and 9 essays]

Other works cited

Woolf, Virginia (1966) *Collected Essays*, vol. 1, London: Hogarth Press.
Woolf, Virginia (1972) *The Waves*, London: Hogarth Press.
Woolf, Virginia (1974) *To the Lighthouse*, London: Hogarth Press.
Woolf, Virginia (1980) *The Letters of Virginia Woolf*, ed. Nigel Nicolson and Joanne Trautmann, vol. 6, London: Hogarth Press.
Woolf, Virginia (1984) *The Diary of Virginia Woolf*, ed. Anne Olivier Bell with Andrew McNeillie, vol. 5, London: Hogarth Press.
Yourcenar, Marguerite (ed. and trans.) (1979) *La Couronne et la lyre*, Paris: Gallimard.

Chapter 4

Bell, Quentin (1973–74) *Virginia Woolf: biographie*, trans. Francis Ledoux, 2 vols, Paris: Stock. Translation of *Virginia Woolf: A Biography*, 2 vols, London: Hogarth Press, 1972.
Caws, Mary Ann and Sarah Bird Wright (eds) (1999) *Bloomsbury and France: Arts and Friends*, Oxford: Oxford University Press.
Études britanniques contemporaines [Montpellier] (1999) Special Issue for the Société d'Études.
Fawcett, Peter (1977) 'Bloomsbury et la France', in Guiguet 1977, pp. 57–72.
Forrester, Viviane (1973) *Virginia Woolf*, Paris: Les éditions de l'Équinoxe.
Guiguet, Jean (1962) *Virginia Woolf et son œuvre: l'art la quête du réel*, Paris: Didier. Translated as *Virginia Woolf and Her Work*, trans. Jean Stewart, London: Hogarth Press, 1965.
Guiguet, Jean (1973) 'Virginia Woolf devant la critique', *Études anglaises* [Paris], 26: 338–45.
Guiguet, Jean (ed.) (1977a) *Virginia Woolf et le groupe de Bloomsbury*, Paris: Union Générale d'Éditions.

Guiguet, Jean (1977b) 'Introduction', in Guiguet 1977a, pp. 9–20.
Inglis, Anthony (1977) 'Virginia Woolf et la critique', in Guiguet 1977a, pp. 219–54.
King, Francis (1978) *E. M. Forster and His World*, New York: Charles Scribner's Sons.
Mallarmé, Stéphane (1936) *Poems*, eds. Charles Mauron and Julian Bell, trans. Roger Fry, London: Chatto & Windus.
Merle, Gabriel (1977) 'Virginia Woolf et Lytton Strachey', in Guiguet 1977a, pp. 139–64.
Nathan, Monique (ed.) (1989) *Virginia Woolf*, Paris: Seuil.
Nordon, Pierre (1993) Introduction and Notes to Woolf, Virginia, *Kew Gardens and Other Short Stories*, Les langues modernes-bilingue: Série anglaise, Paris: Librairie générale française.
Vigne, Marie-Paule (1977) 'Reflections autour d'un thème: Virginia Woolf et l'eau', in Guiguet 1977a, 179–206.
Woolf, Virginia (1926) 'Le Temps passe', trans. Charles Mauron, *Commerce* [Paris], Winter 1926, 91–133. [Translation of 'Time Passes' from *TL*]
Woolf, Virginia (1956) *Orlando*, New York: Harcourt Brace.
Woolf, Virginia (1974) *Orlando*, trans. Charles Mauron, in *Œuvres romanesques*, vol. 2, Paris: Stock.
Woolf, Virginia (1993) *Orlando*, trans. Catherine Pappo-Musard, Paris: Le Livre de Poche.

Chapter 5

(compiled by Carola Surkamp)

Where authors' summaries of their books and dissertations are available in English, the entries are supplemented with the abbreviation *EASG* (plus year and page numbers). The reference is to the series *English and American Studies in German (EASG): Summaries of Theses and Monographs: A Supplement to Anglia*, 1968– , established by Werner Habicht, ed. Horst Weinstock (Tübingen: Niemeyer, 1969–)

Adorno, Theodor Wiesengrund (1958) 'Standort des Erzählers im zeitgenössischen Roman', in *Noten zur Literatur*, Frankfurt a. M.: Suhrkamp, 1: 61–72. Translated as 'The Position of the Narrator in the Contemporary Novel', in *Notes to Literature*, ed. Rolf Tiedemann, trans. Shierry Weber Nicholsen, New York: Columbia University Press.
Amrain, Susanne (1992) 'Virginia Woolf (1882–1941): "Gleichmut – üben Sie sich in Gleichmut, Mrs Woolf!"', in Duda, Sibylle and Luise F. Pusch (eds) *Wahnsinns-Frauen*, Frankfurt a. M.: Suhrkamp, pp. 174–224.
Amrain, Susanne (1994) *So geheim und vertraut: Virginia Woolf und Vita Sackville-West*, Frankfurt a. M.: Suhrkamp.
Antor, Heinz (1986) *The Bloomsbury Group: Its Philosophy, Aesthetics and Literary Achievement*, Forum Anglistik, Heidelberg: Winter. [Abstract in *EASG* (1986): 94–95]
Antor, Heinz (1998) '(Post-)Moderne Historiographie und Biographie im englischen Roman des 20. Jahrhunderts: Virginia Woolf und Julian Barnes', in Ahrens, Rüdiger, and Fritz-Wilhelm Naumann (eds) *Fiktion und Geschichte in der anglo-amerikanischen Literatur: Festschrift für Hans-Joachim Müllenbrock zum 60. Geburtstag*, Anglistische Forschungen, vol. 256, Heidelberg: Winter, pp. 415–30.
Antor, Heinz (2000) 'Woolf, Virginia Stephen', in Ansgar, Nünning (ed.) *Metzler Lexikon Literatur- und Kulturtheorie: Ansätze – Personen – Grundbegriffe*, 2nd rev. edn, Stuttgart; Weimar: Metzler, pp. 684–5.
Apelt, Walter (1952) 'Das romantische Element in den Werken Virginia Woolfs' (unpublished doctoral thesis, University of Halle).
Arnheim, Else (1930–31) 'Die eigenen vier Wände', *Die Frau: Monatsschrift für das*

gesamte Frauenleben unserer Zeit: Organ des Bundes deutscher Frauenvereine [Berlin], 38: pp. 167–69.

Auerbach, Erich (1946) 'Der braune Strumpf', in *Mimesis: Dargestellte Wirklichkeit in der abendländischen Literatur*, Bern: A. Francke, pp. 488–514. Translated as 'The Brown Stocking', in *Mimesis: The Representation of Reality in Western Literature*, trans. William Trask, Princeton: Princeton University Press, 1953, pp. 525–53.

Badenhausen, Ingeborg (1932) *Die Sprache Virginia Woolfs: Ein Beitrag zur Stilistik des modernen englischen Romans*, Marburg: Ebel.

Bartschi, Helen (1991) 'Die Last des Seins oder die verlorene Kunst der Virginia Woolf: *Between the Acts*', in Lavizzari (1991a), pp. 162–75.

Beck, Andrea (1988) *Konstitution von ästhetischen Sinnsystemen in sieben Hauptwerken Virginia Woolfs*, Aspekte der englischen Geistes- und Kulturgeschichte, vol. 14, Frankfurt a. M.; Bern; New York: Lang.

Bell, Quentin (1977) *Virginia Woolf: eine Biographie*, trans. Arnold Fernberg, Frankfurt: Insel. Translation of *Virginia Woolf: A Biography*, 2 vols, London: Hogarth Press, 1972.

Bettinger, Elfi (1993) *Das umkämpfte Bild: Zur Metapher bei Virginia Woolf*, Ergebnisse der Frauenforschung, vol. 34, Stuttgart; Weimar: Metzler. [Abstract in *EASG* (1993): 99–101]

Bettinger, Elfi (1995) 'Virginia Woolf in Spanien', *Tranvia* [Berlin], 37: 10–13.

Bettinger, Elfi (1998a) ' "Chloe liked Olivia": Ein Literaturbericht zu Virginia Woolf', in Eickenrodt, Sabine and Cettina Rapisarda (eds) *Querelles* [Stuttgart; Weimar] 3: 326–33.

Bettinger, Elfi (1998b) 'Virginia Woolf', in Hechtfischer, Ute and others (eds) *Metzler Autorinnen Lexikon*, Stuttgart; Weimar: Metzler, pp. 566–68.

Bisanz, Adam John (1981) 'Virginia Woolfs Literaturkritiker Nicholas Greene auf dem Hintergrund der geschichtsphilosophischen Kulturzyklen-Theorie', in Erlebach, Peter and Wolfgang G. Müller (eds) *Geschichtlichkeit und Neuanfang im sprachlichen Kunstwerk: Studien zur englischen Philologie zu Ehren von Fritz W. Schulze*, Tübingen: Narr, pp. 239–47.

Blöcker, Günter (1966) 'Virginia Woolf: *Zwischen den Akten*', in *Literatur als Teilhabe: Kritische Orientierungen zur literarischen Gegenwart*, Berlin: Argon, pp. 327–30.

Boekhorst, Peter te (1987) *Das literarische Leitmotiv und seine Funktionen in Romanen von Aldous Huxley, Virginia Woolf und James Joyce*, Europäische Hochschulschriften XIV: Angelsächsische Sprache und Literatur, vol. 176, Frankfurt a. M.; Bern: Lang, pp. 98–172. [Abstract in *EASG* (1988): 83–85]

Bondy, François (1989) *Harenbergs Lexikon der Weltliteratur: Autoren, Werke, Begriffe*, 5 vols, Dortmund: Harenberg Lexikonverlag.

Borgers, Wilhelm (1953) '*The Waves* von Virginia Woolf: Die Untersuchung eines literarischen Experiments' (unpublished doctoral thesis, University of Hamburg).

Borinski, Ludwig (1963) 'Die Vollendung der radikalen Stilformen und Virginia Woolf', in Borinski, Ludwig (ed.) *Meister des modernen englischen Romans*, Heidelberg: Quelle & Meyer, pp. 158–202.

Bovenschen, Silvia (1979) *Die imaginierte Weiblichkeit: Exemplarische Untersuchungen zu kulturgeschichtlichen und literarischen Präsentationsformen des Weiblichen*, Frankfurt a. M.: Suhrkamp.

Brandt, Magdalene (1968) *Realismus und Realität im modernen Roman: Methodologische Untersuchungen zu Virginia Woolfs 'The Waves'*, Linguistica et litteraria, vol. 2, Bad Homburg: Gehlen.

Brunkhorst, Martin (1993) 'Virginia Woolf und die Restaurationskomödie', *Sprachkunst* [Vienna], 24.1: 73–86.

Bußmann, Hadumod and Renate Hof (eds) (1995) *Genus: Zur Geschlechterdifferenz in den Kulturwissenschaften*, Stuttgart: Kröner.

Crick, Joyce (1999) 'The German Reception of Virginia Woolf' (unpublished MS).

Deistler, Petra (1999) *Tradition und Transformation – der fiktionale Dialog mit dem viktorianischen Zeitalter im (post)modernen historischen Roman in Großbritannien*, Neue Studien zur Anglistik und Amerikanistik, vol. 77, Frankfurt a. M.; Bern: Lang, pp. 55–70.

DeSalvo, Louise (1990) *Virginia Woolf: Die Auswirkungen sexuellen Mißbrauchs auf ihr Leben und Werk*, trans. Elfi Hartenstein, Munich: Kunstmann. Translation of *Virginia Woolf: The Impact of Childhood Sexual Abuse on Her Life and Work*, London: Women's Press, 1989.

Dittmar, Wilfried (1992) '*Jacob's Room*', in Jens, Walter (ed.) *Kindlers Neues Literatur Lexikon*, Munich: Kindler, 17: 825–26.

Dölle, Erika (1971) *Experiment und Tradition in der Prosa Virginia Woolfs*, Zur Erkenntnis der Dichtung, vol. 8, Munich: Fink. [Abstract in *EASG* (1972): 97–99]

Drescher, Horst W. (1979) 'James Joyce und Virginia Woolf: Ästhetik, Funktion und Form des modernen Romans', in Ahrens, Rüdiger and Erwin Wolff (eds) *Englische und amerikanische Literaturtheorie*, Heidelberg: Winter, 2: 344–61.

Egloff, Gerd (1978) 'Die Rezeption der Romane Virginia Woolfs in den zwanziger Jahren', in *Soziale Norm und literarische Form: Gesellschaftliche Bedingungen der Romanrezeption in England in den Jahren 1918–1930*, Meisenheim am Glan: Hain, pp. 125–42.

Engler, Bernd (1987) 'Virginia Woolfs "An Unwritten Novel": Realistische Erzählkonventionen und innovative Ästhetik', *Anglia* [Tübingen], 105: 390–413.

Engler, Bernd (1993) 'Imagining Her-Story: Virginia Woolf's "The Journal of Mistress Joan Martyn" as Historiographical Metafiction', *Journal of the Short Story in English* [Angers], 20: 9–25.

Engler, Bernd (1995) 'Virginia Woolf, "Modern Fiction"', in Renner, Rolf Günter and Engelbert Habekost (eds) *Lexikon literaturtheoretischer Werke*, Stuttgart: Kröner, pp. 241–42.

Erhart, Walter and Britta Herrmann (1996) 'Feministische Zugänge – "Gender Studies"', in Arnold, Heinz Ludwig and Heinrich Detering (eds) *Grundzüge der Literaturwissenschaft*, Munich: Deutscher Taschenbuchverlag, pp. 498–515.

Erzgräber, Willi (1965) 'Virginia Woolf: *Mrs Dalloway*', in Oppel Horst (ed.) *Der moderne englische Roman: Interpretationen*, Berlin: Erich Schmidt, pp. 160–200. Reprint, 1971.

Erzgräber, Willi (1973) 'Virginia Woolf: "The Shooting Party"', in Göller, Karl-Heinz and Gerhard Hoffmann (eds) *Die englische Kurzgeschichte*, Düsseldorf: Bagel, pp. 182–92.

Erzgräber, Willi (1974) 'Nachimpressionistische Anschauungen über Kompositionstechnik und Farbsymbolik in Virginia Woolfs Roman *To the Lighthouse*', in Schuhmann, Kuno, Armin Paul Frank and Wilhelm Hortmann (eds) *Miscellanea Anglo-Americana: Festschrift für Helmut Viebrock*, Munich: Pressler, pp. 148–83.

Erzgräber, Willi (1980) '"The Moment of Vision" im modernen englischen Roman', *Literaturwissenschaftliches Jahrbuch im Auftrage der Görres-Gesellschaft* [Berlin], n.s. 21: 283–301.

Erzgräber, Willi (1981) 'Zur Ästhetik des Augenblicks bei Virginia Woolf', in Grabes, Herbert (ed.) *Anglistentag 1980 Gießen: Tagungsbeiträge und Berichte*, Großen-Linden: Hoffmann, pp. 241–61. Reprint, *Germanisch-Romanische Monatsschrift* [Heidelberg], 34 (1984): 133–48]

Erzgräber, Willi (1982a) *Virginia Woolf: Eine Einführung*, Munich; Zurich: Artemis. Reprint, 1993. [Abstract in *EASG* (1982): 81–82]

Erzgräber, Willi (1982b) '"Who is Afraid of Virginia Woolf?" (zur Behandlung moderner Literatur in Leistungskursen des Gymnasiums)', in Hunfeld, Hans (ed.) *Literaturwissenschaft – Literaturdidaktik – Literaturunterricht: Englisch: II. Eichstätter Kolloquium zum Fremdsprachenunterricht*, Königstein: Scriptor, pp. 140–48. [Abstract in *EASG* (1982): 146]

Erzgräber, Willi (1984a) 'Function and Form of Virginia Woolf's Novels' in Broich, Ulrich Theo, Stemmler and Gerd Stratmann (eds) *Functions of Literature: Essays Presented to Erwin Wolff on His Sixtieth Birthday*, Tübingen: Niemeyer, pp. 285–303. [Abstract in *EASG* (1984): 36–39]

Erzgräber, Willi (1984b) ' "The Moment of Vision" im modernen englischen Roman', in Thomsen, Christian W. and Hans Holländer (eds) *Augenblick und Zeitpunkt: Studien zur Zeitstruktur und Zeitmetaphorik in Kunst und Wissenschaften*, Darmstadt: Wissenschaftliche Buchgesellschaft, pp. 361–87.

Erzgräber, Willi (1991a) 'Feminismus und Androgynie bei Virginia Woolf', in Fischer-Seidel, Therese (ed.) *Frauen und Frauendarstellung in der englischen und amerikanischen Literatur*, Tübingen: Narr, pp. 115–41.

Erzgräber, Willi (1991b) '*The Waves:* Die Struktur des Romans und ihre Beziehung zur Thematik', in Lavizzari (1991a), pp. 138–62.

Erzgräber, Willi (1991c) 'Virginia Woolf', in Fabian, Bernhard (ed.) *Die englische Literatur*, vol. 2, *Autoren*, Munich: Deutscher Taschenbuchverlag, pp. 435–38. Reprints, 1994, 1997.

Erzgräber, Willi (1995) *Von Thomas Hardy bis Ted Hughes: Studien zur modernen englischen und anglo-irischen Literatur*, Freiburg i.B.: Rombach.

Erzgräber, Willi (1999) 'Virginia Woolf – der Roman als Instrument der Wirklichkeitsentdeckung', in *Der englische Roman von Joseph Conrad bis Graham Greene: Studien zur Wirklichkeitsauffassung und Wirklichkeitsdarstellung in der englischen Erzählkunst der ersten Hälfte des 20. Jahrhunderts*, Tübingen: Francke, pp. 125–72.

Fabian, Bernhard (ed.) (1991) *Die englische Literatur*, 2 vols, Munich: Deutscher Taschenbuchverlag. Reprints, 1994, 1997.

Fietz, Lothar (1994) 'Die Erfahrung von Vereinzelung und Fragmentarität und die Fiktion von der Ganzheit im Werke von Virginia Woolf', in *Fragmentarisches Existieren: Wandlungen des Mythos von der verlorenen Ganzheit in der Geschichte philosophischer, theologischer und literarischer Menschenbilder*, Tübingen: Niemeyer. [Abstract in *EASG* (1994): 35–37]

Fischer, Hermann (1971) 'Virginia Woolf', in Sühnel, Rudolf and Dieter Riesner (eds) *Englische Dichter der Moderne*, Berlin: Erich Schmidt, pp. 299–316.

Fludernik, Monika (1993) *The Fictions of Language and the Languages of Fiction: The Linguistic Representation of Speech and Consciousness*, London; New York: Routledge.

Fludernik, Monika (1996) *Towards a 'Natural' Narratology*, London; New York: Routledge, pp. 410–83.

Freund, J. Hellmut (1980) 'Spiel um Tante Julia: Zwischennotiz', *Neue Rundschau* [Berlin], 91.1: 193–96.

Fricker, Robert (1966) 'Virginia Woolf', in *Der moderne englische Roman*, 2nd edn, Göttingen: Vandenhoeck & Ruprecht, pp. 128–44.

Füger, Wilhelm (1980) *Eine 'Extravagante Engländerin': Untersuchungen zur deutschen Frührezeption von Virginia Woolf*, Anglistische Forschungen, vol. 146, Heidelberg: Winter. [Abstract in *EASG* (1980): 94]

Geraths, Armin (1999) 'Virginia Woolf: "The New Dress" ', in Borgmeier, Raimund (ed.) *Englische Short Stories von Thomas Hardy bis Graham Swift*, Stuttgart: Reclam, pp. 115–27.

Glaser, Brigitte (1998a) ' "A Short Space in the Hollow of the Wave": zur Darstellung des lebendigen Totseins in Virginia Woolfs Romanen', in Blaicher, Günther (ed.) *'Death-in-Life': Studien zur historischen Entfaltung der Paradoxie der Entfremdung in der englischen Literatur*, Literatur – Imagination – Realität: Anglistische, germanistische, romanistische Studien, vol. 16, Trier: Wissenschaftlicher Verlag Trier, pp. 243–60.

Glaser, Brigitte (1998b) 'The Role of Memory in the Works of Virginia Woolf and James Joyce', in *Memory, History and Critique: European Identity at the Millennium: Proceedings of the Fifth Conference of the International Society for the Study of European Ideas*, CD-ROM, Utrecht: MIT Press.

Gohrbandt, Detlev (1975) 'Aspekte der Heldenfunktion in den Romanen von George Eliot, Henry James und Virginia Woolf' (unpublished doctoral thesis, University of Saarbrücken), pp. 410–83. [Abstract in *EASG* (1975): 113]

Gohrbandt, Detlev (1998) *Textanlässe, Lesetätigkeiten: Poetik und Rhetorik der Unabgeschlossenheit*, Tübingen: Narr, pp. 73–76. [Abstract in *EASG* (1998): 43–44]

Gordon, Lyndall (1987) *Virginia Woolf: das Leben einer Schriftstellerin*, trans. Tommy Jacobsen, Frankfurt: S. Fischer. Translation of *Virginia Woolf: A Writer's Life*, Oxford: Oxford University Press, 1984.

Gruber, Ruth (1935) *Virginia Woolf: A Study*, Leipzig: Tauchnitz.

Grünewald-Huber, Elisabeth (1979) *Virginia Woolf: 'The Waves': Eine textorientierte psychoanalytische Interpretation*, Schweizer Anglistische Arbeiten, vol. 99, Bern: A. Francke. [Abstract in *EASG* (1980): 95–97]

Hackenberg, Heide (1957) 'Das Wirklichkeitserlebnis in den Werken Virginia Woolfs' (unpublished doctoral thesis, University of Freiburg i.B.).

Haefner, Gerhard (1990) *Klassiker des englischen Romans im 20. Jahrhundert: Joseph Conrad, D.H. Lawrence, James Joyce, Virginia Woolf, Samuel Beckett: Begründung der Moderne und Abrechnung mit der Moderne*, Anglistische Forschungen, vol. 209, Heidelberg: Winter, pp. 292–409. [Abstract in *EASG* (1992): 79]

Hamburger, Käte (1976) '*Mrs Dalloway*', in Borman, Alexander von (ed.) *Wissen aus Erfahrungen: Werkbegriff und Interpretationen heute: Festschrift für Herman Meyer zum 65. Geburtstag*, Tübingen: Niemeyer, pp. 712–23.

Hartung, Rudolf (1982) 'Centenarium Virginia Woolf', *Neue Deutsche Hefte* [Berlin], 29.1: 124–28.

Hasler, Jörg (1982) 'Virginia Woolf and the Chimes of Big Ben,' *English Studies* [Amsterdam], 63: 145–58.

Häußler, Karl-J. (1982) 'Das beispielhafte Experiment: Virginia Woolfs "Kew Gardens"', *Literatur in Wissenschaft und Unterricht* [Würzburg], 15.3: 241–67.

Hesse, Eva, Michael Knight and Manfred Pfister (1984) *Der Aufstand der Musen: Die 'Neue Frau' in der englischen Moderne*, Passau: Haller. [Abstract in *EASG* (1984): 108]

Hillgärtner, Rüdiger (1988) *Von den Schwierigkeiten der Modernität: Aporetische Aspekte in frühen poetologischen Ansätzen von Joyce, Woolf, Pound und Eliot*, Oldenburger Universitätsreden, vol. 24, Oldenburg: Bibliotheks- und Informationssystem der Universität Oldenburg, pp. 3–39.

Hof, Renate (1991) 'Virginia Woolf als Essayistin', in Lavizzari (1991a), pp. 201–11.

Hotho-Jackson, Sabine (1990) *Zwischen Tradition und Moderne: Geschichte bei Virginia Woolf*, Heidelberg: Winter.

Hotho-Jackson, Sabine (1998) '"Überhaupt tendiert alles auf das Fassen von Geschichte hin" – Varianten der Geschichtsaneignung bei Virginia Woolf und Ingeborg Bachmann', in Ahrens, Rüdiger and Fritz-Wilhelm Naumann (eds) *Fiktion und Geschichte in der anglo-amerikanischen Literatur: Festschrift für Hans-Joachim Müllenbrock zum 60. Geburtstag*, Heidelberg: Winter, pp. 395–414.

Hüllen, Werner (1966) 'Virginia Woolf, *Mrs Dalloway*', in Hüllen, Werner, Horst Meller and H. Nyszkiewicz (eds) *Zeitgenössische englische Dichtung: Einführung in die englische Literaturbetrachtung mit Interpretationen*, vol. 2, *Prosa*, Frankfurt a. M.: Hirschgraben, pp. 53–66. Reprint, 1971.

Isenberg, Aloysia (1952) 'Studien zur Erzählkunst Virginia Woolfs' (unpublished doctoral thesis, University of Mainz).

Jackson, Gertrude (1973) 'Bemerkungen zur Kritik des Woolfschen Realitätsbegriffs', *Sprachkunst – Beiträge zur Literaturwissenschaft* [Vienna], 4: 296–313.

Jäger, Dietrich (1998) *Erzählte Räume: Studien zur Phänomenologie der epischen Geschehensumwelt*, Kieler Beiträge zur Anglistik und Amerikanistik, n.s. 14, Würzburg: Königshausen & Neumann.

Jahn, Manfred (1996) 'Der englische Roman in der ersten Hälfte des 20. Jahrhunderts:

eine narratologische Gattungsgeschichte mit Schwerpunkt Modernismus', in Nünning, Ansgar (ed.) *Eine andere Geschichte der englischen Literatur: Epochen, Gattungen und Teilgebiete im Überblick*, WVT-Handbücher zum literaturwissenschaftlichen Studium, vol. 2, Trier: Wissenschaftlicher Verlag Trier, pp. 171–93.

Klein, Jürgen (1984) *Virginia Woolf: Genie – Tragik – Emanzipation*, Munich: Heyne. [Abstract in *EASG* (1985): 94–95]

Klein, Jürgen (1985) 'Virginia Woolfs Idee des neuen Romans', *Neue Rundschau* [Berlin], 96.1: 143–53.

Klein, Jürgen (1995) 'Gesellschaftskritik und Sinnsuche in Virginia Woolfs Roman *To the Lighthouse*', *Anglistik* [Heidelberg], 6: 52–64.

Klein, Jürgen and Karin van Behr (1986) 'Das Landleben der Virginia Woolf', *Architektur & Wohnen* [Hamburg], 2: 173–76.

Klinner, Birgit (1995) *Androgynie bei Manuel Puig ('El beso de la mujer arana') und bei Virginia Woolf ('Orlando'): Mit einem Exkurs über Schlegels 'Lucinde'*, Edition Wissenschaft, vol. 1, 2 microfiches, Marburg: Tectum.

Kluge, Walter (1992a) '*Orlando: A Biography*', in Jens, Walter (ed.) *Kindlers Neues Literatur Lexikon*, Munich: Kindler, 17: 828–29.

Kluge, Walter (1992b) '*To the Lighthouse*', in Jens, Walter (ed.) *Kindlers Neues Literatur Lexikon*, Munich: Kindler, 17: 832–33.

Kluge, Walter (1992c) '*The Waves*', in Jens, Walter (ed.) *Kindlers Neues Literatur Lexikon*, Munich: Kindler, 17: 834–36.

Kohl, Stephan (1998) 'Die Zeitkonzeption der Literatur', in Bode, Christoph and Ulrich Broich (eds) *Die Zwanziger Jahre in Großbritannien: Literatur und Gesellschaft einer spannungsreichen Dekade*, Tübingen: Narr, pp. 157–75.

Kohlhagen, Norgard (1983) 'Virginia Woolf (1882–1941)', in '*Sie schreiben wie ein Mann, Madame!*': *Von der schweigenden Frau zur schreibenden Frau*, Frankfurt: Fischer, pp. 111–17.

Kowalkowskij-Petzold, Ellen (1996) *Das Leben wie es ist, das Umsonst oder das Wunderbare: Philosophische Strukturen in Virginia Woolfs Romanen*, Vienna: Passagen Verlag.

Kröger, Helmut (1955) 'Die Essays Virginia Woolfs' (unpublished doctoral thesis, University of Kiel).

Kross, Meike (1998) 'Eine postimpressionistische Romanästhetik – Virginia Woolfs literarisches Schaffen zwischen Bloomsbury und Charleston, Pont-Aven und der Provence' (unpublished MA thesis, University of Gießen).

Lavizzari, Alexandra (ed.) (1991a) *Virginia Woolf*, suhrkamp taschenbuch materialien, Frankfurt a. M.: Suhrkamp.

Lavizzari, Alexandra (1991b) 'Vorwort', in Lavizzari (1991a), pp. 7–15.

Lavizzari, Alexandra (1991c) 'Von "The Mark on the Wall" (1917) zu *Jacob's Room* (1922): Virginia Woolfs Aufbruch in die Moderne', in Lavizzari (1991a), pp. 40–60.

Lavizzari, Alexandra (1991d) '"The Mind Receives a Myriad Impressions": Ein Beispiel für Virginia Woolfs formalen Kompromiß mit dem *stream of consciousness*', in Lavizzari (1991a), pp. 88–97.

Lindhoff, Lena (1995) 'Virginia Woolf und die Frage nach einer weiblichen Tradition', in *Einführung in die feministische Literaturtheorie*, Stuttgart; Weimar: Metzler, pp. 30–39.

Lohmüller, Gertrud (1937) *Die Frau im Werk von Virginia Woolf: Ein Beitrag zur psychologischen und stilistischen Untersuchung des neuesten englischen Frauenromans*, Leipzig: Universitätsverlag Robert Noske.

Loster-Schneider, Gudrun (1999) '"Wer hat Angst vor Virginia Woolf?": Genderwissenschaftliche Paradigmen in den historischen Kulturwissenschaften', in Loster-Schneider, Gudrun (ed.) *Geschlecht – Literatur – Geschichte*, St Ingbert: Röhrig, pp. 9–32.

Maack, Annegret (1977) 'Das Simultanerlebnis der Wirklichkeit: Zur Struktur von Virginia Woolfs Roman *Jacob's Room', Literatur in Wissenschaft und Unterricht* [Würzburg], 10: 88–103.

Maack, Annegret (1978) 'Aspekte der Woolf-Kritik', *Literatur in Wissenschaft und Unterricht* [Würzburg], 11: 230–58.

Maassen, Irmgard (1987) 'Die Überwindung der Geschichte in der Kunst: Virginia Woolfs historischer Roman *Between the Acts*', in Bettinger, Elfi and Thomas Meier-Fohrbeck (eds) *Von Shakespeare bis Chomsky: Arbeiten zur Englischen Philologie an der FU Berlin*, Frankfurt a. M.; Bern; New York: Lang, pp. 69–93. [Abstract in *EASG* (1987): 45–48]

Maassen, Irmgard (1990) 'Virginia Woolf (1882–1941)', in Lange, Bernd Peter (ed.) *Classics in Cultural Criticism*, vol. 1, *Britain*, Frankfurt; Bern; New York: Lang. 245–80. [Abstract in *EASG* (1991): 88–89]

Maassen, Irmgard (1991) 'Kunst, Tradition und Modernität in *To the Lighthouse*', in Lavizzari (1991a), pp. 116–34.

Maassen, Irmgard (1992) 'Virginia Woolf's *To the Lighthouse*: A Portrait of the Artist as a Romantic', in Blaicher, Günther and Michael Gassenmeier (eds) *Romantic Continuities: The Eichstätt Symposium, Proceedings of the Symposium of the 'Gesellschaft für Englische Romantik', Catholic University of Eichstätt, 3–6 October 1990*, Studien zur Englischen Romantik, vol. 4, Essen: Die Blaue Eule, pp. 105–18. [Abstract in *EASG* (1992): 21–23]

Marek, Heidi (1990) 'Die Rezeption von Virginia Woolfs *Mrs Dalloway* in Elio Vittorinis *Piccola Borghesia*', *Arcadia* [Berlin], 25.3: 287–303.

Mengel, Ewald (1986) *Geschichtsbild und Romankonzeption: Drei Typen des Geschichtsverstehens im Reflex der Form des englischen historischen Romans*, Heidelberg: Winter. [Abstract in *EASG* (1984): 90]

Moi, Toril (1989) 'Wer hat Angst vor Virginia Woolf?', in *Sexus, Text, Herrschaft: feministische Literaturtheorie*, Bremen: Zeichen & Spuren, pp. 11–32. Translation of 'Introduction: Who is Afraid of Virginia Woolf?' in *Sexual/Textual Politics: Feminist Literary Theory*, London; New York: Methuen, 1985, pp. 1–18.

Moser, Christian (1990) 'Der Blick der Künstlerin: Zur Revision ästhetischer Wahrnehmungsformen in Virginia Woolfs *To the Lighthouse*', *Poetica* [Munich], 22: 384–412.

Mosthaf, Franziska (2000) *Metaphorische Intermedialität: Formen und Funktionen der Verarbeitung von Malerei im Roman: Theorie und Praxis in der englischsprachigen Erzählkunst des 19. und 20. Jahrhunderts*, Horizonte: Studien zu Texten und Ideen der europäischen Moderne, vol. 25, Trier: Wissenschaftlicher Verlag Trier, pp. 138–69.

Müller, Marlene (1985) 'Das Begehren der Sprache oder Virginia Woolfs Kampf mit den Symbolen gegen das System', in Berger, Renate (ed.) *Frauen – Weiblichkeit – Schrift, Das Argument: Argument-Sonderband* [Berlin], 134 (*Literatur im historischen Prozeß*, n.s. 14): 68–78.

Müller, Marlene (1993) *Woolf mit Lacan: Der Signifikant in den Wellen*, Bielefeld: Aisthesis.

Nestvold-Mack, Ruth (1990) 'Geschlechtertausch und Gesellschaftskritik: Virginia Woolf's Orlando', in *Grenzüberschreitungen: Die fiktionale weibliche Perspektive in der Literatur*, Erlanger Studien, vol. 93, Erlangen: Palm & Enke, pp. 235–38. [Abstract in *EASG* (1990): 64–65]

Neubert, Albrecht (1957) *Die Stilformen der 'Erlebten Rede' im neueren englischen Roman*, Halle: Niemeyer.

Neukirchen, Gunilla (1999) *Aktive Spiegelungen: die Konstituierung des Subjekts im Werk Virginia Woolfs*, Neue Studien zur Anglistik und Amerikanistik, vol. 79, Frankfurt a. M.; Bern: Lang.

Neumann, Fritz-Wilhelm (1993) *Der englische historische Roman im 20. Jahrhundert: Gattungsgeschichte als Diskurskritik*, Forum Anglistik, n.s. 13, Heidelberg: Winter.

Nink, Rudolf (1993) *Literatur und Typographie: Wort-Bild-Synthesen in der englischen Prosa des 16. bis 20. Jahrhunderts*, Buchwissenschaftliche Beiträge aus dem Deutschen Bucharchiv München, vol. 45, Wiesbaden: Harrassowitz.

Nünning, Ansgar (1991) 'Tradition und Transformation: Virginia Woolf und das viktorianische Erbe' in Lavizzari (1991a), pp. 19–40.

Nünning, Ansgar (1992a) '*Between the Acts*', in Jens, Walter (ed.) *Kindlers Neues Literatur Lexikon*, Munich: Kindler, 17: 822–24.

Nünning, Ansgar (1992b) '*Three Guineas*' in Jens, Walter (ed.) *Kindlers Neues Literatur Lexikon*, Munich: Kindler, 17: 831–32.

Nünning, Ansgar (1992c) '*The Years*', in Jens, Walter (ed.) *Kindlers Neues Literatur Lexikon*, Munich: Kindler, 17: 836–37.

Nünning, Ansgar (1998) *Der englische Roman des 20. Jahrhunderts*, Uni-Wissen Anglistik/ Amerikanistik, Stuttgart; Düsseldorf; Leipzig: Klett, pp. 40–68.

Nünning, Ansgar (1999) '*Her*story als History: Bausteine für eine (noch zu schreibende) Geschichte des historischen Frauenromans', in Gutenberg, Andrea and Ralf Schneider (eds) *Gender – Culture – Poetics: Zur Geschlechterforschung in der Literatur- und Kulturwissenschaft: Festschrift für Natascha Würzbach*, Trier: Wissenschaftlicher Verlag Trier, pp. 277–312.

Nünning, Vera (1988) 'Voraussetzungssystem und Produktionshandlungen Virginia Woolfs am Beispiel von *Orlando*', *Spiel* [Siegen], 7: 347–72.

Nünning, Vera (1990) *Die Ästhetik Virginia Woolfs: eine Rekonstruktion ihrer philosophischen und ästhetischen Grundanschauungen auf der Basis ihrer nichtfiktionalen Schriften*, Neue Studien zur Anglistik und Amerikanistik, vol. 49, Frankfurt a. M.; Bern; New York: Lang. [Abstract in *EASG* (1990): 90–92]

Nünning, Vera (1991) 'Virginia Woolf als Literaturkritikerin', in Lavizzari (1991a), pp. 179–201.

Nünning, Vera (1992a) '*The Common Reader*', in Jens, Walter (ed.) *Kindlers Neues Literatur Lexikon*, Munich: Kindler, 17: 824–25.

Nünning, Vera and Ansgar Nünning (1992b) '*A Room of One's Own*', in Jens, Walter (ed.) *Kindlers Neues Literatur Lexikon*, Munich: Kindler, 17: 829–30.

Nünning, Vera and Ansgar Nünning (1992c) '*The Voyage Out*', in Jens, Walter (ed.) *Kindlers Neues Literatur Lexikon*, Munich: Kindler, 17: 833–34.

Nünning, Vera and Ansgar Nünning (1991a) *Virginia Woolf zur Einführung*, Hamburg: Junius. [Abstract in *EASG* (1991): 100–03]

Nünning, Vera and Ansgar Nünning (1991b) ' "Fifty pairs of eyes were not enough to get round that one woman with . . .": A Survey of Recent Developments in Virginia Woolf Criticism', *Literatur in Wissenschaft und Unterricht* [Würzburg], 24: 41–65.

Nünning, Vera and Ansgar Nünning (1996) 'From Thematics and Formalism to Aesthetics and History: Phases and Trends of Virginia Woolf Criticism in Germany, 1946–1996', *South Carolina Review*, 29.1: 90–108.

Olejniczak, Verena (1983) 'Virginia Woolfs *Mrs Dalloway*: Die prekäre Balance des Selbst', in Glage, Liselotte and Jörg Rublack (eds) *Wahn in literarischen Texten*, Vortragsreihe des englischen Seminars der Universität Hannover, Frankfurt a. M.: R.G. Fischer, pp. 108–25.

Olejniczak, Verena (1985) 'Virginia Woolfs *Mrs Dalloway* – psychologische Norm und Leseerfahrung', *English and American Studies*, 4: 711–25.

Olejniczak, Verena (1987) *Wirkungsstrukturen in ausgewählten Texten T.S. Eliots und Virginia Woolfs: Eine Untersuchung zur Lesewirkung moderner englischer Literatur*, Hildesheim: Olms. [Abstract in *EASG* (1993): 101]

Olejniczak, Verena (1994) 'Die Prosa Virginia Woolfs: Konzentration und Entgrenzung', in Piechotta, Hans Joachim, Ralph-Rainer Wuthenow and Sabine

Rothmann (eds) *Die literarische Moderne in Europa*, vol. 1, *Erscheinungsformen literarischer Prosa um die Jahrhundertwende*, Opladen: Westdeutscher Verlag, pp. 219–42.

Otten, Kurt (1986) 'Der Roman der Bewußtseinskunst: Virginia Woolf', in *Der englische Roman vom Naturalismus zur Bewußtseinskunst*, Grundlagen der Anglistik und Amerikanistik, vol. 15, Berlin: Schmidt, pp. 142–53. [Abstract in *EASG* (1986): 84–85]

Pasternak, Gerhard (1962) 'Aspekte des Komischen bei Virginia Woolf' (unpublished doctoral thesis, University of Cologne).

Quadflieg, Helga (1991) ' "The Values of a Woman Are Not the Values of a Man": Die Feministin Virginia Woolf', in Lavizzari (1991a), pp. 211–34.

Richter, Martin (1996) *Past and Present: Geschichtserfahrung und Geschichtsdeutung im englischen Essayismus und Roman des 20. Jahrhunderts*, Frankfurt a. M.; Bern; New York: Lang, pp. 87–94.

Riedl, Thomas (1986) *Emanzipation bei Virginia Woolf: Eine Studie zu ihrer nichtfiktionalen Prosa*, Kultur – Literatur – Kunst, vol. 5, Essen: Die Blaue Eule.

Riley, Helene M. Kastinger (1983) *Virginia Woolf*, Köpfe des 20. Jahrhunderts, vol. 99, Berlin: Colloquium.

Rogge-Wiest, Gudrun (1999) *Wahrnehmung und Perspektivik in ausgewählten Romanen Virginia Woolfs*, Neue Studien zur Anglistik und Amerikanistik, vol. 75, Frankfurt a. M.; Bern; New York: Lang.

Roughley, Neil (1994) ' "A Sort of Death? A New Assembly of Elements?": Zum "Tod des Subjects", in Virginia Woolfs *The Waves*', *Anglia* [Tübingen], 112: 364–89.

Schabert, Ina (1981) *Der historische Roman in England und Amerika*, Darmstadt: Wissenschaftliche Buchgesellschaft.

Schabert, Ina (1990) *In Quest of the Other Person: Fiction as Biography*, Tübingen: Francke, pp. 66–84.

Schabert, Ina (1997) *Englische Literaturgeschichte: Eine neue Darstellung aus der Sicht der Geschlechterforschung*, Stuttgart: Kröner.

Schabouk, Werner (1990) 'Relativismus und Perspektivismus: Zum Standort des Erzählers bei Pirandello, Kafka und V. Woolf', in Rössner, Michael and Frank-Rutger Hausmann (eds) *Pirandello und die europäische Erzählliteratur des 19. und 20. Jahrhunderts, Proceedings of the 4th Pirandello Colloquium, Aachen, 7–9 October 1988*, Bonn: Romanistischer Verlag, pp. 119–40.

Schneider, Ulrich (1993) 'Virginia Woolf (1882–1941)', in Lembach, Joachim and Kurt Reichenbach (eds) *Autoren der zwanziger Jahre*, Kassel: Reichenberger, pp. 163–68.

Schoeller, Wilfried E. (1992) '*Mrs Dalloway*', in Jens, Walter (ed.) *Kindlers Neues Literatur Lexikon*, vol. 17, Munich: Kindler, pp. 826–28.

Schöneich, Christoph (1989) *Virginia Woolf*, Erträge der Forschung, vol. 266, Darmstadt: Wissenschaftliche Buchgesellschaft. [Abstract in *EASG* (1989): 101–02]

Schwab, Gabriele (1981) 'Das augenlose Schweigen: Zur Subjektivität in Virginia Woolfs *The Waves*', in Cremerius, Johannes and others (eds) *Freiburger literaturpsychologische Gespräche*, vol. 1, Frankfurt a. M.; Bern; New York: Lang, pp. 283–97.

Schwab, Gabriele (1984) 'Selbstzerstörerische Bewahrung des Selbst bei den Frauenfiguren in Virginia Woolfs Romanen', in Opitz, Claudia (ed.) *Weiblichkeit oder Feminismus? Beiträge zur Interdisziplinären Frauentagung Konstanz 1983*, Weingarten: Drumlin, pp. 195–212.

Schwab, Gabriele (1987) *Entgrenzungen und Entgrenzungsmythen: Zur Subjektivität im modernen Roman: Daniel Defoe, Herman Melville, Virginia Woolf, James Joyce, Samuel Beckett, Thomas Pynchon*, Stuttgart: Steiner.

Schwank, Klaus (1975) *Bildstruktur und Romanstruktur bei Virginia Woolf: Untersuchungen zum Problem der Symbolkonstitution in 'Jacob's Room', 'Mrs Dalloway' und 'To the Lighthouse'*, *Anglistische Forschungen*, vol. 107, Heidelberg: Winter.

Schwank, Klaus (1984) '"Granite and rainbow": Virginia Woolfs *Orlando* (1928) zwischen Historiographie und Fiktion', in Borgmeier, Raimund and Bernhard Reitz (eds) *Der historische Roman, Anglistik & Englischunterricht* [Trier], 24: 7–21.

Seeber, Hans Ulrich (ed.) (1999) *Englische Literaturgeschichte*, 3rd edn, Stuttgart; Weimar: Metzler, pp. 343–45.

Seiler-Franklin, Andreas (1991) '"Ein Dichter ist Ozean und Löwe in einem": Ein fiktiver Dialog zur Entstehungsgeschichte von *Orlando*', in Lavizzari (1991a), pp. 134–38.

Simonis, Annette and Linda Simonis (2000) '"An immortal ode to Time?": Zeitkonzeptionen und Zeitdarstellung im modernistischen Roman', in Nünning, Ansgar and Vera Nünning (eds) *Klassiker und Strömungen des englischen Romans im 20. Jahrhundert: Festschrift zum 65. Geburtstag von Gerhard Haefner*, Trier: Wissenschaftlicher Verlag Trier, pp. 65–85.

Smuda, Manfred (1981) '*Stream of consciousness* und *durée:* Das Problem ihrer Realisation und Wirkung im modernen englischen Roman', *Poetica* [Munich], 133: 309–26.

Spater, George and Ian Parsons (1980) *Porträt einer ungewöhnlichen Ehe: Virginia und Leonard Woolf*, trans. Barbara Scriba-Sethe, Frankfurt a. M.: Fischer Taschenbuchverlag. Translation of *A Marriage of True Minds: An Intimate Portrait of Leonard and Virginia Woolf*, London: Cape/Hogarth Press, 1977.

Spiel, Hilde (1953) 'Virginia Woolf: Bildnis einer genialen Frau', in *Der Park und die Wildnis: Zur Situation der neueren englischen Literatur*, Munich: Beck, pp. 13–33. Reprint, as Introduction to Woolf, Virginia (1981) *Augenblicke: Skizzierte Erinnerungen*, trans. Elizabeth Gilbert, Stuttgart: Deutsche Verlagsanstalt, 1981, 15–39.

Stadtfeld, Frieder (1973) 'Virginia Woolfs letzter Roman: "more quintessential than the others"', *Anglia* [Tübingen], 91: 56–67.

Stanzel, Franz (1954) 'Die Erzählsituation in Virginia Woolfs *Jacob's Room, Mrs Dalloway* und *To the Lighthouse*', *Germanisch-Romanische Monatsschrift* [Heidelberg], 35: 196–213.

Stanzel, Franz (1955) *Die typischen Erzählsituationen im Roman: Dargestellt an 'Tom Jones', 'Moby Dick', 'The Ambassadors', 'Ulysses' u.a.*, Wiener Beiträge zur Englischen Philologie, vol. 63, Vienna: Braumüller. Reprints, 1963, 1965, 1969. Translated as *Narrative Situations in the Novel: Tom Jones, Moby Dick, The Ambassadors, Ulysses*, trans. James P. Pusack, Bloomington: Indiana University Press, 1971.

Stegmaier, Edmund (1970) 'Die Auflösung der Szene im Übergang vom traditionellen zum modernen englischen Roman: Dargestellt an Hauptwerken Jane Austens, Joseph Conrads und Virginia Woolfs' (unpublished doctoral thesis, University of Tübingen) [Abstract in *EASG* (1971): 62]

Steiger, Klaus Peter (1973) 'Der Romananfang von Virginia Woolfs *To the Lighthouse*', *Germanisch-Romanische Monatsschrift* [Heidelberg], 54, n.s. 23: 105–15.

Steinmann, Theo (1970) 'Virginia Woolf: *To the Lighthouse* – die doppelte Funktion der Malerin', *Die Neueren Sprachen* [Frankfurt a. M.; Berlin; Bonn], n.s. 19: 537–47.

Stürzl, Erwin A. (1956) 'Virginia Woolfs Romankunst im Lichte ihres Tagebuchs', *Die Neueren Sprachen* [Frankfurt a. M.; Berlin; Bonn], n.s. 2: 201–11.

Thume, Ralf (1997) *Quantenlogische Aspekte von Virginia Woolfs 'The Years'*, Edition Wissenschaft, vol. 21, 3 microfiches, Marburg: Tectum.

Villgradter, Rudolf (1966) 'Die Konzeption der Wirklichkeit als Strukturelement der Erzählungen Virginia Woolfs', *Germanisch-Romanische Monatsschrift* [Heidelberg], 48, n.s. 16: 283–97.

Volk-Birke, Sabine (1993) '"Nothing is simply one thing": Das Problem der Wahrnehmung in Virginia Woolfs Roman *To the Lighthouse*', *Literaturwissenschaftliches Jahrbuch* [Berlin], 34: 115–30.

Waldmann, Werner (1983) *Virginia Woolf in Selbstzeugnissen und Bilddokumenten*, rowohlts monographien, vol. 323, Reinbek: Rowohlt.

Walter, Margot (1952) 'Strukturanalysen von Romanen Virginia Woolfs' (unpublished doctoral thesis, University of Bonn).

Webel, Susanne (1999) ' "I am so sex-obsessive *I must know*": Literarische Strategien zur Dekonstruktion des biologischen Geschlechts', in Gutenberg, Andrea and Ralf Schneider (eds) *Gender – Culture – Poetics: Zur Geschlechterforschung in der Literatur- und Kulturwissenschaft: Festschrift für Natascha Würzbach*, Trier: Wissenschaftlicher Verlag Trier, pp. 387–400.

Weber-Brandies, Ingeborg (1974) *Virginia Woolf – 'The Waves': Emanzipation als Möglichkeit des Bewußtseinsromans*, Neue Studien zur Anglistik und Amerikanistik, vol. 1. Frankfurt a. M.; Bern; New York: Lang. [Abstract in *EASG* (1974): 121–23]

Weber, Ingeborg (1986) 'Die Sprache des Schweigens in Virginia Woolfs Roman *Between the Acts*', in Herget, Winfried, Klaus Peter Jochum and Ingeborg Weber (eds) *Theorie und Praxis im Erzählen des 19. und 20. Jahrhunderts: Studien zur englischen und amerikanischen Literatur zu Ehren von Willi Erzgräber*, Tübingen: Narr, pp. 141–52. [Abstract in *EASG* (1986): 40–42]

Weber, Ingeborg (1994) 'Ein Porträt der Künstlerin als junge Frau: Virginia Woolfs Kurzgeschichte "The Introduction" ', in Weber, Ingeborg (ed.) *Weiblichkeit und weibliches Schreiben: Poststrukturalismus – Weibliche Ästhetik – Kulturelles Selbstverständnis*, Darmstadt: Wissenschaftliche Buchgesellschaft, pp. 87–96. [Abstract in *EASG* (1994): 104–05]

Weber, Robert W. (1965) 'Die Glocken von Big Ben: zur Strukturfunktion der Uhrzeit in *Mrs Dalloway*', *Deutsche Vierteljahrsschrift* [Stuttgart], 39: 246–58.

Weber, Robert W. (1981) *Der moderne Roman: Proust, Joyce, Belyj, Woolf und Faulkner*, Abhandlungen zur Kunst-, Musik- und Literaturwissenschaft, vol. 317, Bonn: Bouvier, pp. 207–24.

Weidner, Eva (1934) 'Impressionismus und Expressionismus in den Romanen Virginia Woolfs' (unpublished doctoral thesis, University of Greifswald).

Wende, Waltraud (1999) 'Ästhetische Innovation: zur Dekonstruktion etablierter Erzählstrukturen am Beispiel von Virginia Woolf, Nathalie Sarraute und Ingeborg Bachmann', in Gnüg, Hiltrud and Renate Möhrmann (eds) *Frauen – Literatur – Geschichte: Schreibende Frauen vom Mittelalter bis zur Gegenwart*, 2nd, completely revised and enlarged edn, Stuttgart; Weimar: Metzler, pp. 533–47.

Wenner, Claudia (1998) *Moments of Being: Zur Psychologie des Augenblicks bei Virginia Woolf*, Leipziger Schriften zur Kultur-, Literatur-, Sprach- und Übersetzungswissenschaft, vol. 6, Frankfurt a. M.: Vervuert.

Wicht, Wolfgang (1978) 'The Fact and the Vision: Virginia Woolfs Auffassungen von Wesen und Funktion der Literatur', *Zeitschrift für Anglistik und Amerikanistik* [Tübingen], 26: 5–27.

Wicht, Wolfgang (1980) 'Wandlungen im Funktionsverständnis: Virginia Woolf', in Klotz, Günther (ed.) *Romane im 20. Jahrhundert: USA, England, Frankreich, BRD*, Berlin: Akademie, pp. 36–45.

Wicht, Wolfgang (1981) *Virginia Woolf, James Joyce, T. S. Eliot: Kunstkonzeptionen und Künstlergestalten*, Berlin: Akademie.

Wicht, Wolfgang (1985a) 'Die Ermordung des Hausengelchens', *Sinn und Form* [Berlin], 37.1: 188–99.

Wicht, Wolfgang (1985b) 'Joyce and Woolf: The Deprivation of the Narrator', in Hawthorn, Jeremy (ed.) *Narrative: From Malory to Motion Pictures*, London: Edward Arnold, pp. 133–44.

Wiget, Erik (1949) *Virginia Woolf und die Konzeption der Zeit in ihren Werken*, Zurich: Juris.

Wiggershaus, Renate (1987) *Virginia Woolf: Leben und Werk in Texten und Bildern*, Frankfurt a. M.: Insel.

Wilpert, Gero von, (ed.) (1968) *Lexikon der Weltliteratur*, Stuttgart: Kröner [2nd. edn 1980, 3rd edn 1993].

Winnett, Susan and Bernd Witte (1985) 'Ästhetische Innovationen', in Gnüg, Hiltrud and Renate Möhrmann (eds) *Frauen – Literatur – Geschichte: Schreibende Frauen vom Mittelalter bis zur Gegenwart*, Stuttgart: Metzler, pp. 318–37.

Winter, Günter (1977) 'Die Deutung von Virginia Woolfs Romanen (*Mrs Dalloway*, *To the Lighthouse* und *The Waves*) im Lichte der Zeitigung' (unpublished doctoral thesis, Aachen University of Technology).

Winter, Helmut (1999) *Virginia und Leonard Woolf*, Berlin: Rowohlt.

Wolf, Werner (1996) 'Intermedialität als neues Paradigma der Literaturwissenschaft? Plädoyer für eine literaturzentrierte Erforschung der Grenzüberschreitungen zwischen Wortkunst und anderen Medien am Beispiel von Virginia Woolfs "The String Quartet"', *Arbeiten aus Anglistik und Amerikanistik* [Tübingen], 21: 85–116.

Wolf, Werner (1999) *The Musicalization of Fiction: A Study in the Theory and History of Intermediality*, Internationale Forschungen zur allgemeinen und vergleichenden Literaturwissenschaft, vol. 35, Amsterdam: Rodopi.

Woolf, Leonard (1988) *Mein Leben mit Virginia: Erinnerungen*, ed. and trans. Friederike Groth, Frankfurt a. M.: Frankfurter Verlagsanstalt.

Woolf, Virginia (1978a) *Drei Guineen*, trans. Anta Eichholz, Munich: Verlag Frauenoffensive.

Woolf, Virginia (1978b) *Ein Zimmer für sich allein*, trans. Renate Gerhardt, Berlin: Gerhardt.

Woolf, Virginia (1981) *Augenblicke: Skizzierte Erinnerungen*, trans. Elizabeth Gilbert, Stuttgart: Deutsche Verlagsanstalt.

Würzbach, Natascha (1996) 'Der englische Frauenroman vom Modernismus bis zur Gegenwart (1890–1990): Kanonrevision, Gattungsmodifikationen, Blickfelderweiterung', in Nünning, Ansgar (ed.) *Eine andere Geschichte der englischen Literatur: Epochen, Gattungen und Teilgebiete im Überblick*, WVT-Handbücher zum literaturwissenschaftlichen Studium, vol. 2, Trier: Wissenschaftlicher Verlag Trier, pp. 195–211.

Würzbach, Natascha (1998) 'Virginia Woolfs feministische Literaturtheorie im Wandel kultureller Kommunikation. Bestandsaufnahme, Re-Interpretation und Rezeption', *Anglia:* [Tübingen], 116: 1–29.

Wysocki, Gisela von (1982) *Weiblichkeit und Modernität: Über Virginia Woolf*. Frankfurt a. M.: Paris: Qumran.

Chapter 6

GERMAN TRANSLATIONS

BTA

(1963) *Zwischen den Akten*, trans. Herberth and Marlys Herlitschka, Frankfurt: S. Fischer.

CR 1

(1989) *Der gewöhnliche Leser. Band 1*, ed. Klaus Reichert, trans. Hannelore Faden and Helmut Viebrock, Frankfurt: S. Fischer.

CR 2

(1990) *Der gewöhnliche Leser. Band 2*, ed. Klaus Reichert, trans. Hannelore Faden and Helmut Viebrock, Frankfurt: S. Fischer.

CSF
(1989) *Das Mal an der Wand: Gesammelte Kurzprosa*, ed. Klaus Reichert, trans. Marianne Frisch, Frankfurt: S. Fischer.

FB
(1934) *Flush: Die Geschichte eines berühmten Hundes*, trans. Herberth and Marlys Herlitschka, Berlin: S. Fischer. Reprint, 1957; Marburg: Dt. Blindenstudienanst., 1986 (braille ed.).

GR
(1960) *Granit und Regenbogen*, trans. Herberth Herlitschka, Berlin; Frankfurt: Suhrkamp.

JR
(1981) *Jacobs Raum*, trans. Gustav K. Kemperdick, Frankfurt: S. Fischer.

MB
(1981) *Augenblicke: Skizzierte Erinnerungen*, trans. Elizabeth Gilbert, with an essay by Hilde Spiel, Stuttgart: Deutsche Verlags-Anstalt.

MD
(1928) *Eine Frau von fünfzig Jahren: Mrs Dalloway: Ein Roman*, trans. Therese [Thesi] Mutzenbecher, Leipzig: Insel-Verlag.
(1955) *Mrs Dalloway*, trans. Herberth and Marlys Herlitschka, Frankfurt: S. Fischer.
(1978) *Mrs Dalloway*, trans. Therese [Thesi] Mutzenbecher, editor's essay and notes by Wolfgang Wicht, Leipzig: Insel-Verlag.

ND
(1983) *Nacht und Tag*, trans. Michael Walter and Walter Hartmann, Frankfurt: S. Fischer.

O
(1929) *Orlando: Geschichte eines Lebens*, trans. Karl Lerbs, Leipzig: Insel-Verlag.
(1961) *Orlando: Eine Biographie*, trans. Herberth and Marlys Herlitschka, Frankfurt: S. Fischer.
(1983) *Orlando: Eine Biographie*, trans. Karl Lerbs, rev. Heide Steiner, editor's essay and notes by Wolfgang Wicht, Leipzig: Insel-Verlag.

ROO
(1978) *Ein Zimmer für sich allein*, trans. Renate Gerhardt, Berlin: Gerhardt. Reprint, Fischer-Taschenbuch-Verlag, 1981.
(1989) *Ein eigenes Zimmer-Drei Guineen*, trans. Susanne Thurm, with an essay 'Die Ermordung des Hausengelchens' by Wolfgang Wicht, Leipzig: Verlag Philipp Reclam jun.

Selected essays
(1957) *Der schiefe Turm: 5 Essays*, trans. Herberth and Marlys Herlitschka, Munich: Verlag Langen-Müller.
(1986) *Die schmale Brücke der Kunst: Ausgewählte Essays*, ed. Wolfgang Wicht, trans. Barbara Cramer-Neuhaus, Bernhard Scheller and Sigrid Wicht, Leipzig: Insel-Verlag.
(1994) *Die schmale Brücke der Kunst*, trans. and ed. Kyra Stromberg, Berlin: Verlag Klaus Wagenbach.

Selected stories
(1960) *Die Dame im Spiegel: 5 Erzählungen*, trans. Herberth and Marlys Herlitschka, Frankfurt: S. Fischer.
(1965) *Die Erzählungen und Flush*, trans. Herberth and Marlys Herlitschka, Frankfurt: S. Fischer.

TG
(1978) *Drei Guineen*, trans. Anita Eichholz, Munich: Frauenoffensive.
(1989) *Ein eigenes Zimmer-Drei Guineen*, trans. Susanne Thurm, with an essay 'Die Ermordung des Hausengelchens' by Wolfgang Wicht, Leipzig: Verlag Philipp Reclam jun.

TL
(1931) *Die Fahrt zum Leuchtturm*, trans. Karl Lerbs, Leipzig: Insel-Verlag.
(1956) *Die Fahrt zum Leuchtturm*, trans. Herberth and Marlys Herlitschka, Frankfurt: S. Fischer.
(1979) *Die Fahrt zum Leuchtturm*, trans. Karl Lerbs, editor's essay and notes by Wolfgang Wicht, Leipzig: Insel-Verlag. Reprint, Berlin; Weimar: Aufbau-Verlag, 1987.

TW
(1959) *Die Wellen*, trans. Herberth and Marlys Herlitschka, Frankfurt: S. Fischer. Reprint, Darmstadt: Moderner Buch-Club, 1961; Frankfurt: Suhrkamp, 1964.
(1988) *Die Wellen*, trans. Herberth and Marlys Herlitschka, editor's essay and notes by Wolfgang Wicht, Leipzig: Insel-Verlag.

TY
(1954) *Die Jahre*, trans. Herberth and Marlys Herlitschka, Frankfurt: S. Fischer.

VO
(1989) *Die Fahrt hinaus*, trans. Karin Kersten, Frankfurt: S. Fischer.

W & W
(1989) *Frauen und Literatur: Essays*, ed. Klaus Reichert, trans. Hannelore Faden and Helmut Viebrock, Frankfurt: S. Fischer.

OTHER WORKS CITED

Auerbach, Erich (1946) 'Der braune Strumpf', in *Mimesis: Dargestellte Wirklichkeit in der abendländischen Literatur*, Bern; Munich: A. Francke Verlag, pp. 467–93. Translated as 'The Brown Stocking', in *Mimesis: The Representation of Reality in Western Literature*, trans. William Trask, Princeton, NJ: Princeton University Press, 1953, pp. 525–53.
Bell, Quentin (1972) *Virginia Woolf: A Biography*, 2 vols, London: Hogarth Press.
Black, Naomi (1983) 'Virginia Woolf: The Life of Natural Happiness', in Spender, Dale (ed.) *Feminist Theories: Three Centuries of Women's Intellectual Traditions*, London: The Women's Press, pp. 296–313.
Blackstone, Bernard (1949) *Virginia Woolf: A Commentary*, London: Hogarth Press.
Crick, Joyce (1998) 'The German Reception of Virginia Woolf' (unpublished manuscript).
Derrida, Jacques (1977) *Of Grammatology*, trans. Gayatri Chakravorty Spivak, Baltimore: Johns Hopkins University Press.

Eliot, T. S. (1975) *Selected Prose of T. S. Eliot*, ed. Frank Kermode, London: Faber.
Füger, Wilhelm (1980) *Eine 'Extravagante Engländerin': Untersuchungen zur deutschen Frührezeption von Virginia Woolf*, Heidelberg: Carl Winter Universitätsverlag.
Geisthardt, Hans-Jürgen (1979) 'Festhalten flüchtiger seelischer Vorgänge', *Neues Deutschland* [Berlin], 22–23 September, 14.
Guntner, J. Lawrence and Andrew M. McLean (eds) (1998) *Redefining Shakespeare: Literary Theory and Theater Practice in the German Democratic Republic*, Newark, DE: University of Delaware Press.
Klotz, Günther (1980) 'Literatur kapitalistischer Länder im revolutionären Weltprozeß: Eine Einleitung', in Klotz, Günther (ed.) *Romane im 20. Jahrhundert: USA, England, Frankreich, BRD*, Berlin: Akademie-Verlag, pp. 7–17.
Lenin, W. I. (1970) 'Erfolge und Schwierigkeiten der Sowjetmacht', in *Werke*, Berlin: Dietz Verlag, 29: 39–72.
Maar, Michael (1994) 'Nächtliches Beben: Virginia Woolf verewigt den Schmetterling', *Frankfurter Allgemeine Zeitung*, 13 August.
Magister, Karl-Heinz (1989) ' "Ich bin viele ..." ', *Sonntag*, no. 42, 15 October, 12.
Marcus, Jane (ed.) (1981) *New Feminist Essays on Virginia Woolf*, Lincoln, NE: University of Nebraska Press.
Marcus, Jane (ed.) (1983) *Virginia Woolf: A Feminist Slant*, Lincoln: University of Nebraska Press.
Modern Fiction Studies, 18.3 (1972).
Naumann, Manfred and others (1973) *Gesellschaft Literatur Lesen: Literaturrezeption in theoretischer Sicht*, Berlin; Weimar: Aufbau-Verlag.
Neissner, Guido (1983) 'Mann und Frau: Furioser Ritt durch vier Jahrhunderte Geschichte und Kultur', *Junge Welt* [Berlin], 6 September, 8.
Nünning, Vera and Ansgar Nünning (1991) ' "Fifty pairs of eyes were not enough to get round that one woman with ...": A Survey of Recent Developments in Virginia Woolf Criticism', *Literatur in Wissenschaft und Unterricht* [Würzburg], 24.1: 41–64.
Nünning, Vera and Ansgar Nünning (1996) 'From Thematics and Formalism to Aesthetics and History: Phases and Trends of Virginia Woolf Criticism in Germany, 1946–1996', *South Carolina Review*, 29.1: 91–108.
Reynolds, Mary (1982) Review of Wicht 1981, *Modern Fiction Studies*, 28: 634–35.
Riese, Utz (1983) Review of Wicht 1981, *Weimarer Beiträge* [Berlin], 29: 759–64.
Riese, Utz (1999) 'Über den Umgang mit dem Diskurs von Poststrukturalismus und Postmoderne in der DDR', in Schnoor 1999, pp. 189–210.
Sander, Hans-Jochen (1983) Review of Wicht 1981, *Zeitschrift für Anglistik und Amerikanistik* [Berlin], 31: 69–72.
Schneider, Ulrich (1991) 'The Reception of Joyce in a Divided Germany', in Flood, John L. (ed.) *Common Currency?: Aspects of Anglo-German Literary Relations Since 1945*, Stuttgart: Verlag Hans Dieter Heinz, pp. 133–50. Reprinted in Schneider, Ulrich, *James Joyce: Studien zu 'Dubliners' and 'Ulysses'*, ed. Eberhard Kreutzer, Arno Löffler and Dieter Petzold, Erlangen: Universitätsverbund Erlangen-Nürnberg, 1997, pp. 304–25.
Schnoor, Rainer (ed.) (1999) *Amerikanistik in der DDR: Geschichte-Analysen-Zeitzeugenberichte*, Berlin: trafo verlag.
Skotnicki, Irene (1987) 'Scharfsinnige Gedanken über Kunst und Leben', *Neues Deutschland* [Berlin], 30–31 May, 14.
Skotnicki, Irene (1989) '3 Frauen und 3 Männer reflektieren ihr Leben', *Neues Deutschland* [Berlin], 28–29 October, 14.
Teissler, Annett (1977) 'Eine Frau von fünfzig Jahren', *Junge Welt* [Berlin], 6 September, 8.
Thierse, Wolfgang and Kliche, Dieter (1985) 'DDR-Literaturwissenschaft in den siebziger Jahren', *Weimarer Beiträge* [Berlin], 31: 267–308.

Ulbricht, Walter (1961) *Der XXII. Parteitag der KPdSU und die Aufgaben in der Deutschen Demokratischen Republik*, Berlin: Dietz Verlag.

Weimann, Robert (1980) 'Literaturwissenschaft und historisch-materialistische Theorie', *Zeitschrift für Anglistik und Amerikanistik* [Berlin], 28: 12–31.

Weimann, Robert (1988a) *Shakespeare und die Macht der Mimesis: Autorität und Repräsentation im elisabethanischen Theater*, Berlin; Weimar: Aufbau-Verlag.

Weimann, Robert (1988b) 'Mimesis zwischen Zeichen und Macht: Neue Perspektiven in Literaturtheorie und -geschichte (am Beispiel Shakespeare)', *Zeitschrift für Germanistik* [Berlin], 9.2: 133–55.

Weimann, Robert (1998) 'Shakespeare Redefined: A Personal Retrospect', in Guntner and McLean 1998, pp. 120–40.

Weimann, Robert (1999a) 'Shakespeare im anderen Deutschland: Weimar als grenzüberschreitender Ort der Literaturgeschichte', in Fürbeth, Frank and others (eds) *Zur Geschichte und Problematik der Nationalphilologien in Europa*, Tübingen: Max Niemeyer Verlag, pp. 953–62.

Weimann, Robert (1999b) 'Westöstliche *engagements*: Eine bi(bli)ographische Reminiszenz', in Schnoor 1999, pp. 173–88.

Wicht, Wolfgang (1978a) 'The Fact and the Vision: Virginia Woolfs Auffassungen von Wesen und Funktion der Literatur', *Zeitschrift für Anglistik und Amerikanistik* [Berlin], 26: 5–27.

Wicht, Wolfgang (1978b) 'Nachwort', in Woolf, Virginia, *Mrs Dalloway*, trans. Therese [Thesi] Mutzenbecher, Leipzig: Insel-Verlag.

Wicht, Wolfgang (1979) 'Nachwort', in Woolf, Virginia, *Die Fahrt zum Leuchtturm*, trans. Karl Lerbs, Leipzig: Insel-Verlag.

Wicht, Wolfgang (1980) 'Wandlungen im Funktionsverständnis: Virginia Woolf', in Klotz, Günther (ed.) *Romane im 20. Jahrhundert: USA, England, Frankreich, BRD*, Berlin: Aufbau-Verlag, pp. 36–45.

Wicht, Wolfgang (1981) *Virginia Woolf, James Joyce, T. S. Eliot: Kunstkonzeptionen und Künstlergestalten*, Berlin: Akademie-Verlag.

Wicht, Wolfgang (1985a) 'Joyce and Woolf: The Deprivation of the Narrator', in Hawthorn, Jeremy (ed.) *Narrative: From Malory to Motion Pictures*, London: Edward Arnold, pp. 133–44.

Wicht, Wolfgang (1985b) 'Die Ermordung des Hausengelchens', *Sinn und Form* [Berlin], 37.1: 188–99. Reprinted as Wicht 1989.

Wicht, WolfgangWeimann, Robert (1988) 'Nachwort', in Woolf, Virginia, *Die Wellen*, trans. Herberth and Marlys Herlitschka, Leipzig: Insel-Verlag.

Wicht, Wolfgang (1989) 'Die Ermordung des Hausengelchens', in Woolf, Virginia, *Ein eigenes Zimmer-Drei Guineen*, Leipzig: Reclam-Verlag, pp. 282–97. First published as Wicht 1985b.

Wicht, Wolfgang (1991) 'Entwicklung und Stand der anglistischen Literaturwissenschaft in der DDR', in Drews, Jörg and Christian Lehmann (eds) *Dialog ohne Grenzen*, Bielefeld: Aisthesis Verlag, pp. 90–105.

Woolf, Virginia (1950) *The Captain's Death Bed, and Other Essays*, London: Hogarth Press.

Woolf, Virginia (1975) 'Notes on an Elizabethan Play', in *The Common Reader. First Series*, London: Hogarth Press.

Chapter 7

POLISH TRANSLATIONS

'A Sketch of the Past'
(1999) 'Szkic przeszłości' [fragment], trans. Katarzyna Bratkowska, *Kresy* [Lublin], 35: 127–29.

D [Selections]
(1958) 'Z dziennika', trans. Helena Błaszkiewicz, *Kierunki* [Warsaw], 45: 6–7.
(1999) 'Dzienniki: Rok 1927', trans. Agnieszka Graff, *Kresy* [Lublin], 35: 119–26.

FB
(1994) *Flush*, trans. Maria Ryć, Warsaw: Alkazar.

'Joseph Conrad'
(1958) 'Joseph Conrad', trans. Antoni Dębnicki, *Przegląd Humanistyczny*, 1: 139–44

'Madame de Sévigné'
(1963) 'Madame de Sévigné', trans. Anna Iwaszkiewicz, *Twórczość*, 4: 26–29.

'Modern Fiction'
(1963) 'Dwa szkice o powieści', trans. Ignacy Sieradzki, *Przegląd Humanistyczny*, 3: 121–31.
(1969) 'Literatura współczesna', trans. T. Rybkowski, *Odra* [Wrocław], 5: 39–43.

MD
(1961) *Pani Dalloway*, trans. Krystyna Tarkowska, Warsaw: PIW.
(1997) *Pani Dalloway*, trans. Krystyna Tarkowska, Warsaw: PIW.

O
(1994a) *Orlando*, trans.Tomasz Bieroń, Poznań: Zysk i s-ka.
(1994b) *Orlando*, trans. Władysław Wójcik, Warsaw: Sic!

ROO
(1997) *Własny pokój*, trans. Agnieszka Graff, Warsaw: Sic!

Selected essays
(1977) *Pochyła Wieża*, ed. Aleksandra Ambros, trans. Aleksandra Ambros and Ewa Życieńska, Warsaw: Czytelnik.

'The Art of Biography'
(1963) 'Sztuka biografii', trans. Anna Iwaszkiewicz, *Twórczość*, 4: 29–34.

'The Death of the Moth'
(1963) 'Zgon Ćmy', trans. Anna Iwaszkiewicz, *Twórczość*, 4: 24–26.

'The Introduction'
(1973) 'Prezentacja', trans. Jacek Hołówka, *Literatura* [Warsaw], 18: 11.

'The Lady in the Looking Glass: A Reflection'
(1959) 'Pani w zwierciadle', trans. Jerzy Prokopiuk, *Życie i Myśl*, 11–12: 57–61.

'The Russian Point of View'
(1963) 'Dwa szkice o powieści', trans. Ignacy Sieradzki, *Przegląd Humanistyczny*, 3: 121–31.

TL
(1962) *Do latarni morskiej*, trans. K. Klinger, Warsaw: Czytelnik.

TW
(1983) *Fale*, trans. Lech Czyżewski, Cracow: Wydawnictwo Literackie.
(1998) *Fale*, trans. Lech Czyżewski, Wrocław: Wydawnictwo Wacław Bagiński.

TY
(1958) *Lata*, trans. Małgorzata Szercha, Warsaw: Czytelnik.

'Women and Fiction'
(1974) 'Kobiety i powieść', trans. Urszula Niklas, *Literatura* [Warsaw], 35: 11.

OTHER WORKS CITED

Abrahamowicz, Marianna (1960) 'Virginia Woolf as a Short Story Writer', *Rocznik Humanistyczny* [Lublin], 9.3: 37–45.
Amrain, Susanne (1999) 'Virginia Woolf 1882–1941', in Duda, Sibylle and Luise F. Pusch (eds), *Wielkie Szalone*, trans. Aleksandra Górska, Warsaw: Sic!, pp. 125–74. Translation of 'Virginia Woolf (1882–1941): Gleichmut - üben Sie sich in Gleichmut, Mrs Woolf', in Duda, Sibylle and Luise F. Pusch (eds), *Wahnsinns-Frauen*, Frankfurt: Suhrkamp, 1992, pp.174–224.
Auerbach, Erich (1968) *Mimesis: rzeczywistość przedstawiona w literaturze Zachodu*, Warsaw: PIW. Translation of *Mimesis: dargestellte Wirklichkeit in der abendländischen Literatur*, Bern: A. Francke AG, 1946.
Bałutowa, Bronisława (1987) *Historia literatury angielskiej dwudziestego wieku*, Warsaw: PWN, pp. 68–77.
Baranowska, Agnieszka (1988) 'Sekretna wiadomość', *Kultura* [Warsaw], 51: 11.
Bereza, Henryk (1961) 'Virginia Woolf', *Nowe Książki* [Warsaw], 15: 912–14.
Beszczyńska, Zofia (1997) 'Siostra Szekspira', *Nowe Książki* [Warsaw], 9: 43.
Borkowska, Grażyna (1996) *Cudzoziemki*, Warsaw: Instytut Badań Literackich.
Brucz, Stanisław (1939) 'Virginia Woolf', *Wiadomości Literackie* [Warsaw], 23: 9.
Burek, Tomasz (1961) 'Elegia pośród wrzawy ulicznej', *Twórczość* [Warsaw], 10: 124–27.
Carter, Ron (2001) 'Studies in Postwar Poland, 1945–1999' (awaiting publication).
Czerwiński, Marcin (1962) 'Monadologia znakomitej pani Woolf', *Przegląd Kulturalny* [Warsaw], 44: 5.
Ćwiąkała-Piątkowska, Jadwiga (1972) 'The Feminist Pamphlets of Virginia Woolf', *Kwartalnik Neofilologiczny* [Warsaw], 3: 271–79.
Daiches, David (1976) *Krytyk i jego światy: szkice literackie*, Warsaw: PIW. Translation of *The Novel and the Modern World*, Chicago: University of Chicago Press, 1939.
Dolecki, Zbigniew (1958) 'Kronika wielkiego przemijania', *Kierunki* [Warsaw], 41: 7.
Dunin, Kinga (1999) 'Do czego służą wodospady', *Wysokie obcasy*, Saturday supplement to *Gazeta Wyborcza*, 17 July.

Dyboski, Roman (1939) 'O powojennej literaturze angielskiej', *Przegląd Współczesny* [Cracow], 4: 3–25.
Elektorowicz, Leszek (1963) 'Joyce – pisarz nieznany', *Życie Literackie* [Cracow], 8: 7.
Filipiak, Izabela (1997) 'Własny pokój, własna twórczość', in Virginia Woolf, *Własny pokój*, Warsaw: Sic!, pp.5–18.
Filipiak, Izabela (1998) 'Virginia Woolf, *Orlando*, i stare Bloomsbury', *Kresy* [Lublin], 35: 106–16.
Górnicka-Boratyńska, Aneta (1997) 'Siostry Szekspira', *ResPublika Nowa* [Warsaw], 6: 71–73.
Graff, Agnieszka (1997) 'W poszukiwaniu integralności *Własnego pokoju*', *Literatura na świecie* [Warsaw], 3: 299–312.
Grochowski, Grzegorz (1997) 'Feminizm w stylu retro', *Literatura na świecie* [Warsaw], 6: 305–17.
Gruszecka, Aniela (1933) 'Stare i nowe w powieści współczesnej', *Przegląd Współczesny* [Cracow], 132: 68–78.
Janion, Maria (1996) *Kobiety i duch inności*, Warsaw: Sic!
Jarniewicz, Jerzy (1996) 'Orlando, Orlanda i to trzecie', *Literatura na świecie* [Warsaw], 4: 323–33.
Juszczak, Zbigniew (1981) *Zasłona w rajskie ptaki*, Warsaw: PIW.
Kasiński, Władysław Jerzy (1962) 'Mikrokosmos Pani Ramsay', *Kierunki* [Warsaw], 41: 8.
Kędzielska, Alicja 'Recepcja literatury angielskiej w latach 1945–65' (unpublished manuscript).
Klimowicz, Adam (1962) 'Czas niepowstrzymany', *Nowe Książki* [Warsaw], 17: 2+.
Kołyszko, Anna (1983) 'Szprycha w wielkim kole', *Nowe Książki* [Warsaw], 11: 35–36.
Korotyńska, Katarzyna (1975) 'Renesans Virginii Woolf we Francji', *Literatura na świecie* [Warsaw], 1: 28–31.
Kostkowska, Justyna (1992) '*Jacob's Room* and *The Waves:* Virginia Woolf's Pursuit of Mrs Brown or Life Itself', *Zagadnienia Rodzajów Literackich* [Łódź], 35: 51–59.
Krzeczkowski, Henryk (1958) 'Eksperyment sprzed lat trzydziestu', *Nowa Kultura* [Warsaw], 24: 2.
Księżyk, Rafał (1994) 'Psi węch Virginii Woolf', *Wiadomości Kulturalne* [Warsaw], 14: 21.
Kurowska, Elżbieta (1987) *Recepcja literatury angielskiej w Polsce 1932–1939*, Wrocław; Warsaw; Cracow: Zakład Narodowy im.Ossolińskich.
Lam, Andrzej (1962) 'Tęsknota do latarni', *Widnokręgi*, 12: 59–60.
Lehmann, John (1975) 'Wspomnienia o Virginii Woolf', trans. S. Gajewski, *Literatura na świecie* [Warsaw], 1: 8–27.
Łapiński, Zdzisław (1958) 'Ach, szczęśliwe gałęzie, szczęśliwe', *Tygodnik Powszechny* [Cracow], 36: 6.
Mroczkowski, Przemysław (1981) *Historia literatury angielskiej*, Wrocław: Zakład Narodowy im. Ossolińskich.
Niemojewska, Maria (1985) 'Nie bój się więcej . . .', *Twórczość*, 5: 75–99.
Popiel, Jacek (1979) 'Architektonika pochyłej wieży', *Twórczość*, 4: 148–50.
Promiński, Marian (1957) 'W stronę Virginii Woolf', *Życie Literackie* [Cracow], 22: 4–5.
Quidam (Wiktor Weintraub) (1937a) 'Nowa powieść Virginii Woolf', *Wiadomości Literackie* [Warsaw], 23: 5.
Quidam (Wiktor Weintraub) (1937b) '*Lata* Virginii Woolf', *Wiadomości Literackie* [Warsaw], 44: 5.
Quidam (Wiktor Weintraub) (1938) 'Szkoła z Bloomsbury', *Wiadomości Literackie* [Warsaw], 17: 21.
Ratajczak, Mirosław (1978) 'Dla kogo pisać', *Odra* [Wrocław], 7–8: 130–32.

Sadkowski, Wacław (1997) 'Lęki i wdzięki Virginii Woolf', *Wiadomości Kulturalne* [Warsaw], 33: 10.
Stamirowska, Krystyna (1975) 'Virginia Woolf's Concept of Reality and Some Theories of Her Time', *Kwartalnik Neofilologiczny* [Warsaw], 2: 207–17.
Stawiński, Julian (1958) 'Nieodwracalny nurt czasu', *Nowe Książki* [Warsaw], 16: 981–83.
Świątek, Tadeusz (1936) 'Nowe formy romansu', *Kurier Literacko Naukow* [Cracow], 6: 8–9.
Terentowicz, Urszula (1995) 'The World and the Word in *The Waves* by Virginia Woolf', *Lubelskie Materiały Neofilologiczne* [Lublin], 19: 49–64.
Terentowicz, Urszula (1996) 'Triptych of Non-Verbal Search for Reality: The Female Mind in *The Waves* by Virginia Woolf', in Kolek, Leszek (ed.), *Approaches to Fiction*, Lublin: Wydawnictwo Forum, pp. 197–213.
Terentowicz, Urszula (1998a) 'Virginia Woolf: biograficzna fikcja czy fikcyjna biografia', in Blaim, Artur and Zbigniew Maciejewski (eds), *Literatura i komunikacja: od listu do powieści autobiograficznej*, Lublin: Wydawnictwo UMCS, pp. 359–68.
Terentowicz, Urszula (1998b) 'Centre and Periphery in *To the Lighthouse* by Virginia Woolf' in Gussman, Edmund and Bogdan Szymanek (eds), *PASE Papers in Literature, Language and Culture*, Lublin: The University Press of the Catholic University of Lublin, pp. 369–76.
Ulicka, Danuta (1984) 'Złudzenia', *Miesięcznik Literacki* [Warsaw], 10: 146–49.
Walas, Teresa (1978) 'Rozmowa piękna i mądra', *Nowe Książki* [Warsaw], 18: 35–37.
Wiśniewski, Bronisław (1956) 'O powieści subiektywistycznej', *Twórczość*, 9: 202–07.

Chapter 8

SWEDISH TRANSLATIONS

BTA

(1993) *Mellanspel*, trans. Ingegerd Wiking, Lund: Umbra Solis & Wistrand.

CSF

(1990) *Virginia Woolfs samlade noveller och prosaskisser*, trans. Margareta Ekström, Stockhom: Forum.

FB

(1982) *Flush*, trans. with a preface by Margareta Ekström, Stockholm: Trevi.

JR

(1927) *Jacobs Rum*, trans. Siri Thorngren Ohlin, Stockholm: Geber.

MB

(1977) *Ögonblick av Liv*, trans. Harriet Alfons, Stockholm: Bokförlaget Alba.

MD

(1977) *Mrs Dalloway*, trans. Else Lundgren, Stockholm: Forum.

O
(1982) *Orlando*, trans. with a postscript by Margareta Ekström, Stockholm: Norstedts.

'Professions for Women'
(1988) 'Kvinnor och yrkesliv', trans. Brita Enoksson, *Allt om Böcker* [Stockholm], 4: 25–27.

ROO
(1958) *Ett eget rum och andra essäer*, trans. Jane Lundblad, Stockholm: Tidens Klassiker.

Selected essays
(1952) *Det lutande tornet: tre essäer*, trans. Per Erik Wahland, Stockholm: Wahlström.

TG
(1984) *Tre Guineas*, trans. Margareta Ekström, Stockholm: Författarförlaget.

TL
(1953) *Mot Fyren*, trans. Ingalisa Munck and Sonja Bergvall, introd. Anders Österling, Stockholm: Albert Bonniers. Reprint, 1999.

TW
(1980) *Vågorna*, trans. with a postscript by Jane Lundblad, Södertälje: Trevi.

TY
(1942) *Åren*, trans. Ingalisa Munck, Stockholm: Tiden.

OTHER WORKS CITED

Abenius, Margit (1939) 'Sex visa, mer och mindre', *Bonniers litterära magasin* [Stockholm], 8: 41–51.

Algulin, Ingemar (1989) *A History of Swedish Literature*, Stockholm: The Swedish Institute.

Allen, Walter (1970) *The English Novel*, Harmondsworth: Penguin.

Ärvström, Annelie (1998) 'Performance as Narrative and Narrative as Performance in Virginia Woolf's *Between the Acts*' (unpublished research paper, University of Stockholm).

Bell, Quentin (1991) *Virginia Woolf: ett diktarliv*, trans. Margaretha Ekström, Stockholm: Forum. Translation of *Virginia Woolf: A Biography*, 2 vols, London: Hogarth Press, 1972.

Björk, Nina (1996) 'En dans på feminismens spända lina', in *Under det rosa täcket: om kvinnlighetens vara och feministiska strategier*, Stockholm: Wahlström & Widstand, pp. 115–26.

Brugge, Anne (1995) 'Alla dog ifrån Virginia Woolf', *Arbetarbladet* [Helsingfors], 18 July, 4.

Burgess, Anthony (1958) *English Literature*, London: Longman. Reprint, 1974. (First edn published under the name John Burgess Wilson.)

Danius, Sara (1992) 'Virginia Woolfs ensamhet', *Dagens Nyheter* [Stockholm], 6 April, 4.

Eduards, Maud (1992) 'Den feministiska utmaningen: om kvinnors kollektiva handlandet', in Hirdman, Yvonne and Gertrud Åström (eds) *Kontrakt i Kris*, Stockholm: Carlssons, pp. 237–69.

Ekbom, Torsten (1988) Postscript to Virginia Woolf, *Jacob's rum*, trans. Siri Thorngren-Olin, Stockholm: Författarförlaget, pp. 233–36.

Ekström, Margareta (1981) 'De minsta byggstenarna', *Sydsvenska Dagbladet* [Malmö], 18 February, 3.

Ekström, Margareta (1982) Postscript to Virginia Woolf, *Orlando*, trans. Margareta Ekström, Stockholm: Norstedts, pp. 219–21.

Elert, Kerstin (1979) *Portraits of Women in Selected Novels by Virginia Woolf and E.M. Forster*, Umeå Studies in the Humanities, 29, Umeå: Umeå univ. bibl.

Enoksson, Brita (1988) 'Virginia Woolf: lustläsare, autodidakt, essayist', *Allt om böcker* [Stockholm], 4: 20–24.

Frostin, Greta (1980) 'Kvinnokämpe av klass', *Skånska Dagbladet* [Malmö], 17 October, 2.

Goring, Rosemary (ed.) (1998) *Vem är vem i världslitteraturen: författarlexikon från A till Ö* (1998), trans. and adapt. Marianne Levander, ed. and additions Hans Levander, Stockholm: Raben & Sjögren. Translation and adaptation of Rosemary Goring (ed.) *Larousse Dictionary of Writers*, Edinburgh: Larousse, 1994, pp. 170, 343.

Göransson, Sverker (1972) 'Virginia Woolf', in Lennart Breitholtz (ed.) *Epochs and Writers*, Stockholm: Almquist & Wiksell, p. 363.

Halldén, Ruth (1999) 'En bok i fickan, ett fyrtorn som magnet: Ruth Halldén läser om Virginia Woolf', *Dagens Nyheter* [Stockholm], 16 March, B3.

Holm, Birgitta (1981) *Frederika Bremer och den borgerliga romanens födelse*, Stockholm: Norstedts, pp. 11–13, 63–65.

Kane, Annnika (1977) 'Orlando through the Centuries: She Was a Man, He Was a Woman' (unpublished research paper, Uppsala University).

Kållestål, Carina (1989) 'Ett kvinnligt bidrag till modernismens genombrott', *Västerbottens-kuriren* [Umeå], 17 February, 3.

Lagerkrantz, Olof (1979) *August Strindberg*, Stockholm: Wahlström & Widstrand.

Laurence, Patricia (1991) *The Reading of Silence: Virginia Woolf in the English Tradition*, Stanford: Stanford University Press.

Levander, Hans and Kerstin Annergren (1971) *Litteraturhandboken*, Stockholm: Forum, p. 197.

Lindberger, Örjan (1939) 'Låta bli att skriva som en man', *Hertha* [Stockholm], 26.2 (February): 42–43.

Lundblad, Jane (1958) Introduction to Woolf, Virginia, *Ett eget rum (ROO)*, trans. Jane Lundblad, Stockholm: Tidens engelska klassiker, pp. 5–7.

Lundquist, Arthur (1933) 'Virginia Woolf,' *Bonniers Litterära Magasin* [Stockholm], 1.4: 44–47.

Lundquist, Arthur (1980) 'Självanalys i stämmor,' *Arbetet* [Malmö], 6 October, 3.

Lutherson, Peter (1988) 'En milstolpe i romanens utveckling', *Sydsvenska Dagbladet* [Malmö], 3 October, 5

Malmberg, Carl-Johan (1994) 'Sjukdom gav nytt sätt att se', *Sydsvenska Dagbladet* [Stockholm], 18 July, 24.

Martin, Jane Roland (1994) 'Bildade kvinnor – motsägelse och utmaningar', *Kvinnovetenskaplig Tidskrift* [Umeå], 4: 3–17.

Martin, Jane Roland (1998) *Medieurvalsprinciper för Jämtlands Läns Bibliotek*, Östersund: Jämtlands Läns Bibliotek.

Moi, Toril (1985) *Sexual/Textual Politics*, London: Methuen, pp. 1–18.

Nordberg, Carl-Eric (1992) 'En sällsam eldfågel: stor biografi om Virginia Woolf', *Arbetet* [Malmö], 4 March, 4.

Nordberg, Carl-Eric (1993) 'Det förfinade Bloomsbury: Virginia Woolfs liv i brev och bilder', *Arbetet* [Malmö], 19 October, 5.

Öhtan, Annelie Brännström (1995) 'Introduktion till *Ett eget rum*', *Kvinnovetenskaplig Tidskrift* [Umeå], 2–3: 9–11.

Österling, Anders (1953) Introduction to Virginia Woolf, *Mot Fyren* (*TL*), trans.

Ingalisa Munck and Sonja Bergvall, Stockholm: Bonniers, pp. 5–6.

Petersson, Margareta (1991) '"Tändstickor som oväntat flammar om natten": ögonblick och oändlighet i *Mot Fyren*', *Tidskrift för litteraturvetenskap* [Gothenburg], 4: 21–35.

Posti, Piia (1997) 'Woolf' (unpublished research paper, Department of English, Stockholm University).

Ritamäki, Tapani (1991) 'Rösterna och rummen,' *Nya Argus* [Stockholm], 8: 246–47.

Sandbach-Dahlström, Catherine (1986) 'The Moth and the Fish: Images of Creativity in the Writings of Virginia Woolf', in *Proceedings from the Third Nordic Conference of English Studies*, Stockholm: Acta Universitatis Stockholmiensis, pp. 761–71.

Sandbach-Dahlström, Catherine (1996) 'Razgovor o dosluhu: *Tri Gvineje* virdzinije vulf' trans. Dragana Starćević, in *Pro Femina*, Belgrade: Radio B 92, pp. 145–53. Translation of 'Conversing about Collusion'.

Sandquist, Mona (1991) 'Att säga det osägbara: om tystnadens politik i Virginia Woolfs *To the Lighthouse*', *Tidskrift för litteraturvetenskap* [Gothenburg], 4: 36–55.

Shima, Alan (1993) *Skirting the Subject: Pursuing Language in the Works of Adrienne Rich, Susan Griffin and Beverly Dahlen*, Uppsala: Acta Universitatis Uppsaliensis.

Sjöblad, Cristina (1992) 'Liv stå still här! Tid och tavlor i Virginia Woolfs roman *Mot Fyren*', *Moderna Klassiker: Absolon* (Stockholm), 1: 97–115.

Spalding, Frances (ed.) (1992) *Din tillgivna Virginia: Virginia Woolfs liv i brev och bilder*, trans. Margareta Ekström, Stockholm: Forum. Translation of Spalding, Frances (ed) *Paper Darts: The Letters of Virginia Woolf*, London: Collins & Brown, 1991.

Svanberg, Birgitta (1989) *Sanningen om kvinnorna: En läsning av Agnes von Krusenstjernas romanserie Fröknarna von Pahlen*, Stockholm: Gidlunds.

Svanberg, Helena (1998) 'Multiple Voices: The Relationship between Discourse and Consciousness in Virginia Woolf's *Mrs Dalloway*' (unpublished research paper, University of Gothenburg).

Svenneros, Linda (1999) 'Identity in Virginia Woolf's *Orlando*: Gender – Intrinsically Connected with Sex or Not?' (unpublished research paper, University of Gothenburg).

Söderberg, Boel (1991) 'Hänförande minnen av vännen Virginia', *Nerikes Allehanda* [Örebro]. 20 November, 4.

Söderberg, Boel (1993) 'Lysande brevskriverska med allvaret under ytan', *Nerikes Allehanda* [Örebro], 18 August, 4.

Tavares, Maura (1996) 'Virginia Woolf Paints with Words: Pictorial Qualities in *Jacob's Room* and *Orlando*' (unpublished research paper, Department of English, Stockholm University).

Troy, Mark (1988) 'A Wedge-Shaped Core of Darkness', in *Papers in Language and Literature, Presented to Alvar Ellegård and Erik Frykman*, Gothenburg: Acta Universitatis Göteborgiensis, pp. 362–72.

Troy, Mark (1998) '"BBBBBLLLLBLBLBLABSCHBL"', in Clive Hart *et al.* (eds) *Images of Joyce. 1*, Gerrards Cross: Colin Smythe, pp. 310–14.

Velicu, Adrian (1985) *Unifying Strategies in Virginia Woolf's Experimental Fiction*, Uppsala: Acta Universitatis Uppsaliensis.

Wahlund, Per Erik (1952) Introduction to Virginia Woolf, *Det lutande tornet*, trans. Per Erik Wahlund, Stockholm: Wahlström & Widstands Kulturbibliotek, pp. 5–8.

Westerlund, Gabriella (1998) 'Killing the Angel in the House: Women's Roles in Virginia Woolf's *To the Lighthouse*' (unpublished research paper, University of Uppsala).

Westholm, Carl Axel (1986) 'Klingemann och Woolf: klassiker i ny utgåvor', *Uppsala Nya Tidning*, 6 March, 16.

Westholm, Carl Axel (1991) 'Novelisten Virginia Woolf', *Uppsala Nya Tidning*, 5 October, 3, review of *Virginia Woolfs samlade noveller och prosaskisser* (*CSF*).

Wiking, Ingegerd (1993) 'Efterskrift' in *Mellanspel* (*BTA*), Lund: Umbra Solis, 1993, pp. 139–41.

Woolf, Virginia (1939) *Reviewing: With a Note by Leonard Woolf*, London: Hogarth Press.

Woolf, Virginia (1977) *To the Lighthouse*, London: Granada

Woolf, Virginia (1982) *Three Guineas*, Harmondsworth: Penguin.

Woolf, Virginia (1992) *The Waves*, Harmondsworth: Penguin.

Woolf, Virginia (1992) 'The Leaning Tower' in *A Woman's Essays*, ed. Rachel Bowlby, Harmondsworth: Penguin, pp. 159–78.

Chapter 9

DANISH TRANSLATIONS

FB

(1953) *Flush: historien om en Cocker Spaniel*, trans. Mogens Boisen, Copenhagen: Aschehoug Dansk Forlag, reprint, Charlottenlund: Rosinante, 1983, 1991.

LYP

(1949) *Brev til en ung digter*, trans. Martin Melsted, Copenhagen: Borgens Forlag.

MD

(1945) *Mrs Dalloway*, trans. Aage Brusendorff, Copenhagen: Gyldendal.

(1984) *Mrs Dalloway*, trans. Jørgen Christian Hansen, Charlottenlund: Rosinante, reprint 1990, 1998.

O

(1962) *Orlando: en biografi*, trans. Jørgen Årup Hansen, Copenhagen: Gyldendal, reprint, Charlottenlund: Rosinante, 1983, 1992, 1999.

ROO

(1973) *Eget værelse*, trans. Elsa Gress and David Gress-Wright, Copenhagen: Samlerens Piccolobøger, reprint, Copenhagen: Munksgaard/Rosinante, 1978, 1994.

Selected essays

(1953) *Et London-Eventyr og andre Essays*, trans. Niels Lyhne Jensen, Copenhagen: Steen Hasselbalchs Forlag.

TG

(1983) *Tre Guineas*, trans. Inger Christensen, Charlottenlund: Rosinante.

TL

(1982) *Til fyret*, trans. Merete Ries, Charlottenlund: Rosinante, reprint 1991, 1999.

TW

(1994) *Bølgerne*, trans. Anne Marie Bjerg, Copenhagen: Munksgaard/Rosinante. Reprint, Copenhagen: Samlerens Bogklub 1997, reprint, Copenhagen: Rosinante, 1997.

TY

(1941) *Aarene gaar*, trans. Paula Biehe, Copenhagen: Hagerup.

OTHER WORKS CITED

Borum, Poul (1994) 'Som bølger i havet', *Ekstra Bladet* [Copenhagen], 14 December.
Brøgger, Suzanne (1997) 'Jeg vil skrive om døden, men livet brød ind som sædvanlig', *Weekendavisen* [Copenhagen], 12 September.
Buhl, Dorte, Birgitte Fogh and Regitze Petri (1984) 'Ikke kun det skønne billede: et kaleidoskopisk blik på et portræfotografi af Virginia Woolf', *Litteratur og samfund* [Copenhagen], 37: 9–24.
Erichsen, Svend (1941) 'Virginia Woolf paa Dansk', *Socialdemokraten* [Copenhagen], 16 December.
Grønfeldt, Vibeke (1982) 'Kinesiske æsker: en parafrase', *Luftskibet* [Copenhagen], 3: 75–82.
Hansen, Jørgen Christian (1989) *Den skrigende Buddha*, Copenhagen: Centrum.
Kristensen, Tom (1945) 'London set gennem bølgende vand', *Politiken* [Copenhagen], 6 March.
Kruuse, Jens (1945) 'En poetisk roman', *Jyllandsposten* [Viby], 16 March.
Kaas Johansen, Niels (1953) 'Bloomsburys første lady', *Information* [Copenhagen], 15 April.
Levy, Jette Lundbo (1987) 'Den store vægring ved historien og politikken', in *Modstandens figurer: fiktion, historie og køn*, Charlottenlund: Rosinante, pp. 11–22.
Levy, Jette Lundbo (1994) 'Det flygtiges former', *Information* [Copenhagen], 14 December.
Lyhne Jensen, Niels (1953) Introduction to Virginia Woolf, *Et London-Eventyr og andre Essays*, trans. Niels Lyhne Jensen, Copenhagen: Steen Hasselbalchs Forlag.
McLaurin, Allen (1984) 'Consciousness and Group Consciousness', in Warner, Eric (ed.), *Virginia Woolf: A Centenary Perspective*, London: Macmillan, pp. 28–40.
Mørk, Ebbe (1982) 'Myten Virginia Woolf', *Politiken* [Copenhagen], 11 September.
Politiken [Copenhagen], Millennium Issue, 1999.
Sauerberg, Lars Ole (1994) 'Hypnotisk læsning', *Jyllandsposten* [Viby], 14 December.
Schack, May (1982) 'Den sandhed som øjeblikket skaber', *Politiken* [Copenhagen], 13 October.
Schack, May (1983) 'Forsørgelse er afhængighed', *Politiken* [Copenhagen], 23 November.
Schack, May (1994) 'Øjeblikkets skildrer', *Politiken* [Copenhagen], 14 December.
Thrane, Lotte (1982) 'Den knivskarpe ligevægt: introduktion til Virginia Woolf', *Hug!* [Copenhagen], 7.3: 25–31.
Woolf, Leonard (1991) *Virginia: erindringer*, trans. Nina Lautrup-Larsen, Copenhagen: Rosinante.
Woolf, Virginia (1925) *Mrs Dalloway*, London: Hogarth Press.
Woolf, Virginia (1968) *Flush: A Biography*, London: Hogarth Press.
Woolf, Virginia (1972a) 'The Leaning Tower', in *CE*, 2: 162–81.
Woolf, Virginia (1972b) *A Writer's Diary*, London: Hogarth Press.
Ørum, Tania (1982) 'Men bemærkede han blomsterne?', *Information* [Copenhagen], 20.
Ørum, Tania (1985) *Pamelas døtre*, Copenhagen: Tiderne Skifter.
Ørum, Tania (1995) 'Lange bølger', *Kristeligt Dagblad* [Copenhagen], 14 July.

Chapter 10

GREEK TRANSLATIONS

Books

BP (selections)

(1988) *Ginekia portreta: dokimia kai kritiki*, trans. Dimitris Kostelenos, Athens: Glaros.

FB
(1992) *Flush: Mia viographia*, trans. E. I. Varsos, Athens: Gnosi.

HH
(1987) *Ena stihiomeno spiti kai alla diigimata*, trans. Despina Kerevanti and Yiannis Vallourdos, Athens: Grammata.
(1996) *Ena stihiomeno spiti kai alla diigimata*, trans. Alexandra Panagi, Athens: Patakis.

JR
(1987) *To domatio tou Jacob*, trans. Errikos Bellies, Athens: Odysseas.
(1988) *To domatio tou Iakovou*, trans. Despina Kerevanti and Yiannis Vallourdos, Athens: Grammata.

LYP
(1997) *Gramma s'ena neo piiti*, trans. Aris Berlis, Athens: Agra.

MD
(1967) *I kiria Dalloway*, trans. Kostoula Mitropoulou, Athens: Galaxias. Reprint, Athens: Ermias, 1987, 1992.
(1973) *Mia imera tis kirias Dalloway*, trans. Vas. L. Kalantzi, Athens: Papiros Press.
(1990) *I kiria Dalloway*, trans. Despina Kerevanti and Yiannis Vallourdos, Athens: Grammata.

O
(1984) *Orlando*, trans. Anastasia Linardaki, Athens: Astarti. Reprint, 1993.

'On Not Knowing Greek'
(1998) *Gia tin agnia ton arheon Ellinikon*, trans. Vaios Liapis, Athens: Stigmi.

ROO
(1980) *Ena diko sou domatio*, trans. Mina Dalamanga, Athens: Odysseas. Reprint, 1993.

Selected essays
(1998) *Skotonondas ton angelo tou spitiou*, trans. Tatiana Konstandinidou, Athens: Kastaniotis. ['Killing the Angel in the House' and Other Essays]
(1999) *Dokimia*, trans. Argiro Mantoglou, ed. Spiros Tsaknias, Athens: Scripta.

Selected short stories
(1996) *Leshi ginekon kai alla diigimata*, trans. Maria Apostoli, ed. Katerina Shina, Athens: Nefeli. ['A Society' and Other Short Stories]

Selections
(1987) *Ellada kai Mais mazi*, trans. Maria Tsatsou, ed. Aris Berlis, Athens: Kristallo. Reprint, Athens: Ipsilon, 1996. [A selection of letters and diary entries during Woolf's visit to Greece in 1932]

TG
(1982) *Tris ginees*, trans. Mirto Anagnostopoulou-Pissalidou, Thessaloniki: Barbounakis.

TL

(1981) *Mehri to faro*, trans. Elli Marmara, Athens: Odysseas. Reprint, 1982.

(1982) *Sto faro*, trans. Aris Berlis, Athens: Kristallo. Reprint, 1985; Athens: Ipsilon, 1995.

TW

(1945) 'Ta kimata', trans. Dimitris Stavrou, *Nea Estia* [Athens], 43 (February): 224–32. [Excerpts]

(1984) *Ta kimata*, trans. Rita Kolaiti, Athens: Nefeli.

(1984) *Ta kimata*, trans. Mina Dalamanga, Athens: Odysseas.

(1986) *Ta kimata*, trans. Aris Berlis, Athens: Kristallo. Reprint, Athens: Ipsilon, 1994.

TY

(1991) *Ta hronia*, trans. Soti Triandafillou, Athens: Sinhroni Epohi.

Short Stories and Essays by Woolf

'Moments of Being: Slater's Pins Have No Points'

(1936) 'Stigmes zois: *I karfitses tis Slater then tripoun*', trans. Yiorgos Delios, *Makedonikes Imeres* [Thessaloniki], 8 (September): 263–71.

'The Haunted House'

(1946) 'To stihiomeno spiti', trans. Sofia Papasinesiou, *Nea Estia* [Athens], 39 (January): 22–23.

'The Legacy'

(1946) 'I klironomia' (no translator given), *Angloelliniki Epitheorisi* [Athens], 2 (August): 182–84.

'An Unwritten Novel'

(1948) 'To mithistorima pou then graftike', trans. Sofia Papasinesiou and Errikos Hatzianestis, *Alexandrini Logotehnia*, 30–40.

'Three Pictures'

(1949) 'Ikones tris', trans. Yiorgos Delios, *Nea Estia* [Athens], 45 (January): 78–82.

(1956) 'Ikones tris', trans. Yiorgos Delios, *Eklogi* [Athens], IB' 130 (August).

(1999) 'Ikones tris', trans. Yiorgos Delios, *Diavazo* [Athens], 399 (September): 93–96.

'The Lady in the Looking Glass'

(1950) 'I kiria kai o kathreftis', trans. Sofia Papasinesiou and Errikos Hatzianestis, *Nea Estia* [Athens], 47 (March): 310–12.

D (selections)

(1955a) 'Virginia Woolf: Apo to Imerologio [1940–41]', trans. Yiorgos Delios, *Nea Estia* [Athens], 57 (January): 117–18. [Excerpts from *D*, 1940–41]

(1955b) 'Virginia Woolf: Apo to Imerologio [1940–41]', trans. Yiorgos Delios, *Nea Estia* [Athens], 57 (February): 179–81. [Excerpts from *D*, 1940–41]

Selections

(1979) 'Adeline Virginia Woolf: Apospasmata apo to aftoviografiko kimeno "Mia skiagrafia tou parelthontos", "I ginekes kai to mithistorima" apo to "A Room of One's Own", apo to Imerologio, kai apo to "Tris ginees"', trans. Fani Ziozia, Mariana Kondili, Georgia Papageorgiou, Marina Papagiannaki and Angelika Psarra, *Skoupa* [Athens], 3: 78–92. ['A Sketch of the Past', 'Women and Fiction' from *ROO*, selections from *D* and from *TG*]

'How Does One Read a Book'
(1980) 'Pos diavazoume ena vivlio', trans. Zinovia Drakopoulou, *Epoptia* [Athens], 52 (December): 971–76. Reprint, in Drakopoulos, P. (ed.) *Theoria logotehnias* [Theory of literature], Athens: Imago, pp. 7–23.

'The Mark on the Wall'
(1983) 'To simadi ston tiho', trans. and commentary Efi Lambadaridou, *Lexi* [Athens] 22 (February): 100–107.

'The Sentimental Journey'
(1994) 'Mia isagogi sto *Sinesthimatiko taxidi*', trans. Dimitris Naziris, *Endefktirio* [Thessaloniki], (Spring): 85–89.

'A Society'
(1995) 'I eteria', in *Apohrosis: Virginia Woolf, Djuna Barnes, Gertrude Stein*, trans. Giorgos Depastas, Athens: Olkos, pp. 18–44.

Letter to Vanessa Bell, 2 May 1932
(1996) 'Gramma apo tous Delfous', trans. Persa Apostoli, *Dendro* [Athens], Summer: 21–23.

'Professions for Women'
(1998) 'Epangelmata ginekon', trans. and notes Irini A. Vris, *Odos Panos* [Athens], (January–February): 2–10.

CRITICISM

Books, dissertations and journal articles

Anastasopoulou, Maria T. (1986) 'To liriko mithistorima kai i Virginia Woolf', *Diavazo* [Athens], 153 (October): 21–27.

Behlikoudi, Dimitra G. (1999) 'To neoelliniko mithistorima tou mesopolemou kai i Virginia Woolf: Mia singritiki prosengisi' (unpublished doctoral thesis, University of Ioannina).

Berlis, Aris (1982) 'I Virginia Woolf kai to mithistorima', *Diavazo* [Athens], 56 (September–October): 76–80.

Bowen, Elizabeth (1946) 'To angliko mithistorima sto diastima tou mesopolemou', *Angloelliniki Epitheorisi* [Athens], 2 (May): 68–72. Translation of 'English Fiction at Mid-Century', *New Republic*, 129 (1953): 15–16.

Delios, Yiorgos (1938a) 'Apopsis gia to angliko mithistorima', *Makedonikes Imeres* [Thessaloniki], 8–9 (August–September): 212–24.

Delios, Yiorgos (1938) 'Virginia Woolf', *Makedonikes Imeres* [Thessaloniki], 10–12 (October–November–December): 245–47.

Delios, Yiorgos (1939) *To sinhrono mithistorima*, Thessaloniki: n.p.

Delios, Yiorgos (1963) *Dio Anglides pezografi: Virginia Woolf and Katherine Mansfield: Dokimia kai metafrasis*, Athens: Fexi.

Faulkner, Peter (1982) 'Kritika dokimia tis Virginia Woolf', in *Modernismos*, trans. Ioulietta Ralli and Kaitie Hatzidimou, Athens: Ermis, pp. 58–73. Translation of 'Virginia Woolf's Critical Essays' in *Modernism*, London: Methuen, 1977.

Himonas, Yiorgos (1995) 'Pion fovate i Virginia Woolf?', in *Pion fovate i Virginia Woolf?*, Athens: Kastaniotis, pp. 14–17.

Karagiorga, Olympia (1981) *Virginia Woolf: mia megali agnosti*, Athens: Epikerotita.

Karagiorga, Olympia (1986) 'O erotas sto ergo tis Virginia Woolf', *Diavazo* [Athens], 153 (October): 50–51.

Kazakou, Sofia I. (1986) 'I feministiki apopsi tis Woolf mesa apo dio dokimia tis', Diavazo [Athens], 153 (October): 52–54.

Kitsi-Mitakou, Katerina K. (1991–92) ' "Which Is the Greater Ecstasy?": Desiring the Body's Text and Writing the Body's Desire in Virginia Woolf's *Orlando*', *Yearbook of English Studies* [Aristotle University of Thessaloniki], 3: 215–52.

Kitsi-Mitakou, Katerina K. (1993) 'Clarissa Dalloway's Body: Transformations of Christian Concepts of Femininity and Maternity in Virginia Woolf's *Mrs Dalloway*', *Gramma* [Thessaloniki], 1: 86-104.

Kitsi-Mitakou, Katerina K. (1994) 'Living in a Human Oxymoron: Rachel's Anorexic Body in Virginia Woolf's *The Voyage Out*', in Douka-Kabitaglou, E. (ed.), *Logomachia: Forms of Opposition in English Language/Literature*, Thessaloniki: [Hellenic Association for the Study of English], pp. 159–70.

Kitsi-Mitakou, Katerina K. (1997) *Feminist Readings of the Body in Virginia Woolf's Novels*, Thessaloniki: Giahoudi-Giapouli Press.

Koutsoudaki, Maria (1986) 'Pia ine i kiria Dalloway', *Diavazo* [Athens], 153 (October): 28–30.

Koutsoudaki, Maria (1986) 'O "Ellinas" Iakovos: I Ellada sto *Domatio tou Iakovou*', *Diavazo* [Athens], 153 (October): 42–49.

Lambadaridou, Efi (1986) 'Diania kai fantasia ston *Orlando* tis Virginia Woolf', *Diavazo* [Athens], 153 (October): 34–38.

Lehmann, John (1946) 'Virginia Woolf', *Angloelliniki Epitheorisi* [Athens], 2 (August): 178–82.

Mantoglou, Argiro (1999) 'I papagali tis grafis', *Diavazo* [Athens], 401 (November): 112–17.

Nathan, Monique (1986) *Virginia Woolf*, trans. Katerina Marinaki, Athens: Themelio. Translation of *Virginia Woolf par elle-même*, Paris: Seuil, 1956.

Ntokos, Thanasis (1997) *Hristiki isagogi sto mithistorima*, Athens: Kastaniotis. [References to Virginia Woolf in the section on the 'stream of consciousness' technique]

Panagi, Afroditi M. (1986) 'To thema tou kallitehni sto *Pros to faro* tis Virginia Woolf', *Diavazo* [Athens], 153 (October): 31–33.

Reed, Henry (1950) 'To angliko mithistorima apo to 1939', *Angloelliniki Epitheorisi* [Athens], 5 (November–December): 48–57. Translation of excerpts from 'The Novel since 1939', *The Arts in Britain. 4*, British Council Series, London: Longman, 1946.

Sakelliou-Schultz, Liana (1986) '*Ta kimata* kai i "ipogia" metaphora tous', *Diavazo* [Athens], 153 (October): 39–41.

Tsatsou, Maria (1986) 'Ena gramma tis Virginia Woolf gia tin Ellada', *Diavazo* [Athens], 153 (October): 55–57.

Xefloudas, Stelios (1935) 'Sholia', *Makedonikes Imeres* [Thessaloniki], 4 (May): 159–63.

Newspaper articles

Aragis, Y. (1999) 'Katastrofikes shesis', *To Vima* [Athens], 3 October.
Athanasopoulos, Vangelis (1999) 'O kathreftis tis istorias: To mithisthorima tis Argiro Mantoglou *Virginia Woolf*', *Kathimerini* [Athens], 12 October.
Boukalas, Pandelis (1999) 'Boroume arage na gnorisoume tous arheous?', *Kathimerini* [Athens], 9 March.
Faraklas, Yiorgos (1999) 'Then xeroume ellinika', *Avgi* [Athens], 17 June.
Georgakopoulou, Vena (1996) 'Nai stin ithopio, ohi sto skinotheti', *Eleftherotypia* [Athens], 22 August.
Georgakopoulou, Vena (1999a) 'Apogiosi me ton (kai tin) *Orlando*', *Eleftherotypia* [Athens], 15 March.
Georgakopoulou, Vena (1999b) 'I Virginia Woolf tou Paradisou kai tis Kolasis', *Eleftherotypia* [Athens], 5 August. [Review of P. Dally's *Virginia Woolf: The Marriage of Heaven and Hell*]
Georgousopoulos, Kostas (1999) 'Foni horis soma, soma horis foni', *Ta Nea* [Athens], 26 April.
Hartoulari, Mikela (1998) 'Apo ton Lord Byron eos ton Koundera: Dio erevnes gia ti metaphrasi sta ellinika xenon vivlion kai ellinikon se xenes glosses', *Ta Nea* [Athens], 15 January.
Hatziandoniou, Natali (2000) 'Otan kati mas aresi poli, kapia stigmi to synandame', *Eleftherotypia* [Athens], 12 February.
Hatziioannou, Elena D. (1999) 'Then ime moni ston monologo', *Ta Nea* [Athens], 24 March.
Hatzivasiliou, Vangelis (1999) 'Magiki metamorphosi', *Eleftherotypia* [Athens], 24 September.
Kapsalis, Dionisis (1997) 'I anagnostria', *Avgi* [Athens], 20 April.
Katsoularis, Kostas (2000) 'Michael Cunningham: Ti fovate i Virginia Woolf?', *To Vima* [Athens], 14 May.
Loizou, Stella (1999) 'Engefaliki temahismi', *To Vima* [Athens], 28 March.
Loverdou, Mirto (1999) 'Monologos gia to taxidi tis zois', *To Vima* [Athens], 28 February.
Mantoglou, Argiro (1999) 'Dimiourgi pou simadepsan ton eona: Virginia Woolf', *Eleftherotypia* [Athens], 26 November.
Mantoglou, Argiro (2000a) 'Ginekia apotypomata sta tihi tis hartinis polis', *Eleftherotypia* [Athens], 5 March.
Mantoglou, Argiro (2000b) '*I kiria Dalloway* tis Woolf "stihioni" s' ena sinhrono mithistorima', *Eleftherotypia* [Athens], 26 May.
Mantoglou, Argiro (2000c) 'Mia gineka pou tin elegan Virginia', *To Vima* [Athens], 9 January.
Mikelidis, Ninos Fenek (2000) 'I Dimitra os Virginia', *Eleftherotypia* [Athens], 12 March.
Papageorgiou, Kostas G. (1999) 'To pehnidi tis afigisis', *Eleftherotypia* [Athens], 20 August.
Papaspyrou, Stavroula (2000) 'Pios then fovate tin Virginia Woolf', *Eleftherotypia* [Athens], 7 May.
Roumboula, Dimitra (1999) 'I alli Virginia Woolf', *Ethnos* [Athens], 16 January.
Rouvalis, Vasilis (1998) 'Ena gramma panda epikero', *Eleftherotypia* [Athens], 8 February.
Sakelliou-Schultz, Liana (1998) 'Lernees idres', *To Vima* [Athens], 17 May.
Shina, Katerina (1999) 'I drimitita tis ironias kai i lampsi tis prototipias', *Eleftherotypia* [Athens], 27 August.
Spinou, P (1999) 'Pios diavazi ti Virginia Woolf?', *Eleftherotypia* [Athens], 11 July.
Toulatou, Isma M. (2000) 'Se proto prosopo Dimitra hatoupi: Ego i Virginia Woolf', *To Vima* [Athens], 30 January.
Tsirimokou, Lisy (1999) 'Amethodi methodos', *To Vima* [Athens], 14 August.
Vatopoulos, Nikos (1999) 'I Vita kai i Virginia', *To Vima* [Athens], 21 March.

OTHER WORKS CITED

Christianopoulos, Dinos (1958) 'Yiorgos Delios: *Ikogenia*', *Diagonios* [Thessaloniki], 1: 13–15.

Cixous, Hélène (1981) 'The Laugh of the Medusa', in Marks, Elaine and Isobelle de Courtivron (eds) *New French Feminisms*, Brighton: Harvester, pp. 245–64.

Conrad, Joseph (1993) *The Heart of Darkness*, in Abrams, M. H. (ed.) *The Norton Anthology of English Literature*, 6th edn, New York: W. W. Norton, 2: 1759–1817.

Cunningham, Michael (2000) *I ores*, trans. Leo Kalovirnas, Athens: Nea Sinora, Livani. Translation of *The Hours*.

Dally, Peter (1999) *Virginia Woolf: The Marriage of Heaven and Hell*, New York: St Martin's Press.

Delios, Yiorgos (1937) 'To mithistorima', *Makedonikes Imeres* [Thessaloniki], 5–6 (May–June): 135–41.

Gana, Mike, Mary Gana and Lena Gana (1987) 'Esoterikos monologos', *Filologos* [Thessaloniki], 48: 136–60.

Kitsopoulos, Yiorgos (1962) 'Paradosi esoterikotitas: I pezografi tis Thessalonikis', *Nea Estia* [Athens], 72 (December): 1782–85.

Lacan, Jacques (1987) 'God and the *Jouissance* of the Woman: A Love Letter' in Mitchell, Juliet and Jacqueline Rose (eds) *Feminine Sexuality: Jacques Lacan and the école freudienne*, trans. Jacqueline Rose, London: Macmillan. Reprint, pp. 137–61.

Lehmann, Rosamond (1947) 'To mellon tou mithistorimatos', *Angloelliniki Epitheorisi* [Athens], 3 (May): 14–16.

Mantoglou, Argiro (1999) *Virginia Woolf Café*, Athens: Apopira.

Mourelos, Yiorgos (1966) 'O hronos tou mithistorimatos', *Nea Poria* [Thessaloniki], 12 (January–February): 140–47.

Moullas, Pan. (1993) 'Isagogi', in Karvelis, Takis and others (eds) *I mesopolemiki logotehnia (1914–1939)*, Athens: Sokoli, 1: 17–170.

Parashos, Kleon (1947) 'I "ananeosis" sto neotero mithistorima', *Nea Estia* [Athens], 41: 158–60.

Piniatoglou, L. (1932) 'Merikes apopsis giro sto elliniko mithistorima', *Makedonikes Imeres* [Thessaloniki], 12 (December): 391–97.

Spandonidis, Petros S. (1932) 'Kathreftismata', *Makedonikes Imeres* [Thessaloniki], 1 (January): 29–31.

Spandonidis, Petros S. (1934) 'I pezografia ton neon (1929–1933)', *Makedonikes Imeres* [Thessaloniki], 1 (January): 22–28.

Steryiopoulos, Kostas (1996) 'Yiorgos Delios', in Karvelis, Takis and others (eds) *I mesopolemiki logotehnia (1914–1939)*, Athens: Sokoli, 3: 278–321.

Vafopoulos, G. T. (1962) 'I palia froura', *Nea Estia* [Athens], 72 (December): 1714–17.

Vitti, Mario (1987) *Istoria tis Neoellinikis logotehnias*, trans. Mirsini Zorba, Athens: Odisseas. Translation of *Storia della letteratura neogreca*, Turin, ERI, 1971.

Vitti, Mario (1995) *I genia tou trianda*, Athens: Ermis.

Wilson, Robert and Daryl Pinckney (adapt.) (1999) *Orlando*, trans. Thanasis Hatzopoulos, Athens: Kedros.

Woolf, Virginia (1982) *The Letters of Virginia Woolf*, Vol. 5: 1932–1935, ed. Nigel Nicolson, London: Chatto & Windus.

Woolf, Virginia (1983) *The Diary of Virginia Woolf*, Vol. 4, ed. Anne Olivier Bell, Harmondsworth: Penguin.

Woolf, Virginia (1993) 'Modern Fiction', in Abrams, M. H. (ed.) *The Norton Anthology of English Literature*, 6th edn, New York: W. W. Norton, 2: 1921–26.

Woolf, Virginia (1998a) *To the Lighthouse*, Oxford: Oxford University Press.

Woolf, Virginia (1998b) *The Waves*, Oxford: Oxford University Press.

Xefloudas, Stelios (1955) *To sinhrono mithistorima*, Athens: Ikaros.

Chapter 11

ITALIAN TRANSLATIONS

Individual works

BTA

(1978) *Tra un atto e l'altro*, trans. Francesca Wagner and Franco Cordelli, introd. Franco Cordelli, Milan: Guanda. Reprint, Milan: Feltrinelli, 1981.

CR 1–2

(1995–96) *Il lettore comune*, ed. Daniela Guglielmino, trans. Vittoria Sanna and D. Guglielmino, 2 vols, Genova, il melangolo.

CSF

(1980) *Lunedì o maortedì: tutti i racconti*, trans. F. Duranti, Milan: La Tartaruga. Enlarged edition, 1988.

D

(1991) 'Dal *Diario* degli anni di guerra', trans. and note by Rossana Bonaolei, *Il piccolo Hans*, 72, pp. 177–82.

FB

(1946) *Flush, vita di un cane*, trans. A. Scalero, Milan: Mondadori, 1946. Reprint as *Flush: una biografia*, Milan: La Tartaruga, 1979; Milan: Bruno Mondadori, 1992.

FC

(1983) *Freshwater*, trans. L. P. Ruotolo and M.V. Malvano, introd. Barbara Lanati, Turin: La Rosa.

(1992) *Freshwater*, trans. S. Bartoli and A. Tesauro, Salerno: Ripostes.

HH

(1950) *La casa degli spiriti*, trans. Desideria Pasolini, Milan: Mondadori.

JR

(1950) *La camera di Giacobbe*, trans. Anna Banti, Milan: Mondadori. Reprint, 1983.

(1994) *La stanza di Jacob*, trans. and introd. Mirella Billi, Venice: Marsilio, 1994 (bilingual edition).

LS

(1982) *Scene di Londra*, ed. with an afterword by Grazia Livi, Milan: Mondadori.

MB

(1977) *Momenti di essere* trans. A. Bottini, introd. J Schulkind, Milan: La Tartaruga. Enlarged edition, Milan: La Tartaruga, 1993.

(1995) *Momenti di essere*, trans. Marcella Dallatorre, Milan: Rizzoli.

MD

(1946) *La Signora Dalloway*, trans. Alessandra Scalero, Milan: Mondadori, 1946. Reprint, 1979 (introd. Sergio Perosa), 1989.

(1992a) *La Signora Dalloway*, trans. Pier Francesco Paolini, introd. Armanda Guiducci, Rome: Newton Compton.
(1992b) *La Signora Dalloway*, trans. Laura Ricci Doni, Milan: SE.
(1993) *La Signora Dalloway*, trans. and introd. Nadia Fusini, Milan: Feltrinelli.

ND
(1957) *Notte e giorno*, trans. Luisa Quintavalle Theodoli, Milan: E. L. I. Reprint, 1987.
(1982) *Notte e giorno*, trans. Maria Vittoria Malvano, with a note by N. Fusini, Turin: La Rosa. Reprint, Turin: Einaudi, 1987.
(1996) *Notte e giorno*, trans. Pietro Meneghelli, introd. Armanda Guiducci, Rome: Newton Compton.

O
(1933) *Orlando*, trans. Alessandra Scalero, Milan: Mondadori. Reprint, Milan: Garzanti, 1978 (introd. Attilio Bertolucci), 1986.
(1993) *Orlando*, trans. A. Rossotti, introd. Viola Papetti, Milan: Rizzoli.
(1994) *Orlando*, trans. M. Del Serra, introd. Armanda Guiducci, Rome: Newton Compton.

ROO
(1974) *Una stanza tutta per sé*, trans. L. Bacchi Wilcock and J. R. Wilcock, in *Per le strade di Londra*, Milan: Garzanti. Reprint, Milan: Il Sappiatore, 1980. (introd. Marisa Bulgheroni); Milan: SE, 1993.
(1993) *Una stanza tutta per sé*, trans. M. Del Serra, introd. Armanda Guiducci, Rome: Newton Compton.
(1995) *Una stanza tutta per sé*, trans. Graziella Mistrali, Torriana: Orsa Maggiore.
(1995) *Una stanza tutta per sé*, trans. Maria Antonietta Saracino, Turin: Einaudi (bilingual edition).

TG
(1975) *Le tre ghinee*, trans. Adriana Bottini, Milan: La Tartaruga. Reprint, Milan: Feltrinelli, 1979 (introd. L. Muraro), 1990, 1992.

TL
(1934) *Gita al faro*, trans. Giulia Celenza, pref. Emilio Cecchi, Milan: Treves. Reprint, 1948; Milan: Garzanti, 1954, 1974 (introd. Attilio Bertolucci); Milan: Mondadori, 1989.
(1992a) *Al faro*, trans. and introd. Nadia Fusini, Milan: Feltrinelli.
(1992b) *Gita al faro*, trans. A. L. Malagò, Rome: Newton Compton, 1992 (introd. Armanda Guiducci).
(1995) trans. Luciana Bianciardi, Introd. V. Papetti, Milan: Rizzoli.

TP
(1981) *La famiglia Pargiter*, trans. and introd. Alide Cagidemetrio, Milan: La Rosa.

TW
(1956) *Le onde*, trans. Giulio De Angelis, Milan: Mondadori. Reprint, Milan: Rizzoli, 1979 (introd. Stephen Spender, ed. Franco Marucci).
(1992) *Le onde*, trans. M. Del Serra, Rome: Newton Compton (introd. Armanda Guiducci).
(1995) *Le onde*, trans. N. Fusini, Turin: Einaudi.

TY
(1955) *Gli anni*, trans. Giulio De Angelis, Milan: Mondadori. Reprint, Milan: Garzanti, 1981 (introd. E. Groppali).
(1994) *Gli anni*, trans. Paola Faini, Rome: Newton Compton.

VO
(1951) *Il lungo viaggio (VO)*, trans. Giorgia Valensin, Milan: Longanesi.
(1956) *La crociera*, trans. Oriana Previtali, Milan: Rizzoli. Reprint, 1972 (introd. Giuseppe Gadda Conti), 1994.
(1994), trans. Luciana Bianciardi, Rome: Newton-Compton.

WD
(1959) *Diario di una scrittrice*, trans. Giuliana De Carlo and V. Guerrini, Milan: Mondadori.
(1979) *Diario di una scrittrice*, trans. G. De Carlo, Milan: Mondadori.

W & W
(1981) *Le donne e la scrittura*, trans. A. Bottini, Milan: La Tartaruga. Reprint, 1990.

Selected novels

(1998) *Romanzi*, ed. Nadia Fusini, Milan: Mondadori, 1998 (*JR*, trans. A. Banti; *MD*, *TL*, *TW*, trans. N. Fusini; *O*, trans. A. Scalero; *BTA*, trans. F. Wagner and F. Cordelli).

Selected essays

(1946) 'Gli spilli di Slater non pungono', trans. Marise Ferro, *La lettura*, 27 July.
(1963) *Per le strade di Londra*, trans. L. Bacchi Wilcock and J. R. Wilcock, introd. Attilio Bertolucci, Milan: Il Saggiatore. Reprint (with *Una stanza tutta per sé* (*ROO*) and without introd.), Milan: Garzanti, 1974.
(1979) *La signora dell'angolo di fronte*, trans. Masolino D'Amico, introd. Ginevra Bompiani, Milan: Il Saggiatore, 1979.
(1980) *Lettera a Margaret Llewellyn Davies*, Introduction to Margaret Llewellyn Davies (ed.) *La vita come noi l'abbiamo conosciuta: autobiografie di donne proletarie inglesi*, trans. A. Rossi-Doria, with a note by N. Fusini, Rome: Savelli. (Translation of *Life as We Have Known It: By Cooperative Working Women*, London: Virginia & Leonard Woolf, 1931).
(1981) *Le donne e la scritttura*, trans. A. Bottini, Milan: La Tartaruga. Reprint 1990.
(1990) *Leggere, recensire*, trans. A. Bottini, Milan: Marcos y Marcos.
(1991) *Ore in biblioteca e altri saggi*, ed. Paola Splendore, trans. Daniela Daniele, Milan: La Tartaruga.
(1992) *Volare su Londra*, trans. E. Pea, foreword by Grazia Livi, Milan: Marcos y Marcos.
(1994) *Libri e scrittori*, Catanzaro: Abrams.
(1995) *Ritratti di scrittori*, ed. and trans. Mirella Billi, Parma: Pratiche.
(1996) *'Come si leppe un libro?' e altri saggi*, Milan: La Tartaruga.

Miscellaneous selections

(1978) *Romanzi e altro*, ed. Sergio Perosa, Milan: Mondadori. (*MD*, trans. A. Scalero;

TL, trans. G. Celenza; *O*, trans. A. Scalero; *ROO* and selected essays, trans. L. Bacchi Wilcock and J. R.Wilcock; selected letters, trans. Alide Cagidemetrio; selections from *DW*, trans. G. De Carlo.)
(1983) *Itinerario con immagini*, ed. A. Tesauro, Salerno: Ripostes (with a note by Edith Sitwell).
(1994) *Romanzi e racconti*, ed. A. L. Zazo, Oscar, Milan: Mondadori. (*JR*, trans. A. Banti; *MD*, trans. A. Scalero; *TW*, trans. G. De Angelis; *TL* and selected short stories, trans. A. L. Zazo.)
(1998) *Saggi, prose, racconti*, ed. Nadia Fusini, Milan: Mondadori. (Selected short stories, trans. F. Duranti and N. Fusini; selected essays, trans. L. B. Wilcock and J. R. Wilcock; *ROO*, trans. M. A. Saracino; *FB*, trans. A. Scalero; *RF*, trans. N. Fusini; *MB*, trans. A. Bottini; selected letters, trans. A. Cane, N. Fusini, S. Gariglio, S. Gianetti and C. Pennati.)

Letters

(1980) *Il volo della mente: lettere 1888–1912* (*L*, 1). Trans. A. Cane, Turin: Einaudi.
(1980) *Le cose che accadono: lettere 1912–1922* (*L*, 2), trans. S. Gianetti, Turin: Einaudi.
(1983) *Cambiamento di prospettiva: lettere 1923–1928* (*L*, 3), trans. S. Gariglio, Turin: Einaudi.
(1985) *Un riflesso dell'altro: lettere 1929–1931* (*L*, 4), trans. C. Pennati, Turin: Einaudi.
(1993) *Cara Virginia: le lettere di Vita Sackville-West a Virginia Woolf*, trans. Fiorello Cagnoni and Sylvie Coyaud, Milan: La Tartaruga.
(1996) *Quattro lettere nascoste*, trans. Francesco Bruno, Milan: Archinto (afterword by Joanne Trautmann).

SECONDARY CRITICISM

Articles: unsigned or anonymous

'Il Gran Gelo' (1933), *La fiera letteraria* [Rome], 20 August.
'V. Woolf: rassegna della stampa straniera' (1933), *Occidente* [Rome], 2.3.
'Turgheniev e la Woolf' (1935), *L'Italia letteraria* [Rome], 20 April.
'La fata della letteratura inglese' (1935), *L'Italia letteraria* [Rome], 4 May.
'Virginia Woolf – romanziera inglese di grande originalità' (1946), *Pensiero femminile* [Milan], 2.6.
'Virginia Woolf scrittrice: profilo' (1947), *Pensiero femminile* [Milan], January–February.
'Virginia, il genio e il sesso' (1974), *Il Mondo* [Rome], 5 September.

Signed articles, books and monographs

Aleramo, Sibilla (1931), 'Orlando inglese', *L'Italia letteraria*, 18 October. Reprinted in *Anolando e stando*, Milan: Feltrinelli, 1997.
Amoruso, Vito (1968) *Virginia Woolf*, Bari: Adriatica.
Angioletti, G.B. (1958) 'Virginia Woolf nella gloria', *La nuova Stampa* [Turin], 28 September. Reprinted in *I grandi ospiti*, Florence: Vallecchi, 1960.
Antonini, Giacomo (1954a) 'Diario di Virginia Woolf', *La Nazione Italiana* [Florence], 10 January.
Antonini, Giacomo (1954b) 'V. Woolf: per la creazione della sua opera', *La fiera letteraria* [Rome], 17 January.

Apollonio, Carla (1989) *L'enigma del tempo*, Milan: Guerini.
Astaldi, Maria Luisa (1953) *Letture inglesi*, Venice: Neri Pozza.
Astaldi, Maria Luisa (1954a) 'Diario postumo di Virginia Woolf', *Il Giornale d'Italia* [Rome], 31 January.
Astaldi, Maria Luisa (1954b) 'Diario di Virginia Woolf', *Ulisse*, Spring. Reprinted in *Nuove letture inglesi*, Florence: Sansoni, 1958.
Astaldi, Maria Luisa, G. Bompiani and N. Fusini (1981) *Virginia Woolf: lettere*, ed. P. Candinas, Rome: Edizioni Centro Culturale Virginia Woolf.
Auerbach, Erich (1956) 'Il calzerotto marrone', in *Mimesis: il realismo nella letteratura occidentale*, trans. A. Romagnoli and A. Hinterhauser, introd. Aurelio Roncaglia, Turin: Einaudi. Translation of 'Der braune Strumpf', in *Mimesis: dargestellte Wirklichkeit in der abendländischen Literatur*, Bern: A. Francke AG, 1946, pp. 467–93.
Banti, Anna (1952) 'Umanità della Woolf', *Paragone* [Florence], 3. Reprint in *Opinioni*, Milan: Il Saggiatore, 1961.
Banti, Anna (1963) 'Il testamento di Virginia Woolf', *Paragone* [Florence], December.
Barucca, Primo (1961) 'Intellettualismo e lirismo nell'opera di Virginia Woolf', *La fiera letteraria* [Rome], 8 October.
Beach, J.W. (1948) *La tecnica del romanzo novecentesco*, Milan: Bompiani. Translation of *The Twentieth Century Novel: Studies in Technique*, New York: Century, 1932.
Bell, Quentin (1974) *Virginia Woolf*, trans. Marco Papi, Milan: Garzanti. Translation of *Virginia Woolf: A Biography*, London: Hogarth Press, 1972.
Bellonci, Maria (1960) 'Il Diario di Virginia Woolf', *Il Punto*, 20 February.
Bernabò, Antonella (1993) 'Virginia Woolf e la biografia', *Stultifera navis* [Pisa], 215–36.
Bertea, C. and others (eds) (1985) *Progetto Virginia Woolf. Parole. Immagini*, Rome: Quaderni del centro DWF.
Bertinetti, R. (1985) *Virginia Woolf: l'avventura della conoscenza*, Milan: Jaca Book.
Bianchini, Angela (1963) 'Forster e la Woolf', *Il Mondo* [Rome], 19 February.
Bianchini, Angela (1965) 'I signori Woolf', *Il Mondo* [Rome], 16 March.
Billi, Mirella (1975) *Virginia Woolf*, Florence: La Nuova Italia. Reprint (expanded edition), 1981.
Billi, Mirella (1983) 'Struttura ritmica e significato in *The Waves*', *Filologia moderna* [Pisa], 5.
Billi, Mirella (1993) 'Orlando', in *Il testo riflesso: la parodia nel romanzo inglese*, Naples: Liguori.
Billi, Mirella (1994) Introduction to *La stanza di Jacob* (*JR*), Venice: Marsilio, pp. 9–26.
Billi, Mirella (1995) Introduction to Virginia Woolf, *Ritratti di scrittori*, Parma, Pratiche.
Billi, Mirella (1999) '*Jacob's Room:* elegia e riscatto di una terra desolata', in Palusci, Oriana (ed.) *La tipografia nel salotto: saggi su V. Woolf*, Turin: Tirrenia Stampatori.
Biovi, Maria Grazia (1960) 'La muta e la lepre – ovvero il Diario di Virginia Woolf', *Paragone* [Florence], August.
Blackstone, Bernard (1965) *Virginia Woolf*, trans. G. Bernardi, Milan: Mursia. Translation of *Virginia Woolf: A Commentary*, London: Hogarth Press, 1949.
Blanchot, Maurice (1969) *Il libro a venire*, trans. G. Ceronetti and G. Neri, Turin: Einaudi. Translation of *Le Livre à venir*, Paris: Gallimard, 1959.
Bohl, Anna (1933) 'Virginia Woolf', *Occidente* [Rome], 2.
Bonadei, Rossana (1993) 'Virginia Woolf nella stanza di Freud: costruzione biografica e verità narrativa', in A. M. Accerboni (ed.), *Le frontiere della psicanalisi: storie-narrazioni, biografie-costruzioni*, Lavarone: Edizioni Centro Studi Gradiva, pp. 37–58.
Brawer, Anna (1987) *Ritratto come autoritratto: 'Al Faro' di Virginia Woolf*, Turin: Tirrenia Stampatori.
Bulgheroni, Maria Luisa (1960) 'La scrittrice e il tempo', *Il Mondo* [Rome], 17 May.
Bulgheroni, Maria Luisa (1980) Introduction to *Una stanza tutta per sé* (*ROO*), Milan: Il Saggiatore, 1980. Reprint as Afterword to *Una stanza tutta per sé* (*ROO*), Milan: SE, 1993.

Bulgheroni, Maria Luisa (1989) Introduction to L. Woolf.
Cagidemetrio, Alide (1982) Introduction to *La famiglia Pargiter* (*TP*), Turin: La Rosa.
Caliumi, Grazia (1956) 'Il diario di Virginia Woolf', *Letterature moderne* [Milan], July.
Camerino, Aldo (1933), 'Biografia di un cane', *Gazzettino di Venezia*. Reprinted in *Scrittori di lingua inglese*, Naples: Ricciardi, 1968.
Camerino, Aldo (1958) 'Virginia Woolf inattesa', *La fiera letteraria* [Rome], 12 October.
Camarino, Aldo (1963) 'Saggi critici della Woolf', *La Nazione* [Florence], 22 October.
Camerino, Aldo (1968) 'Virginia Woolf', in *Scrittori di lingua inglese*, Milan; Naples: Ricciardi, pp. 158–75.
Campesan, Sara (1987) *Virginia Woolf: itinerario (bio)grafico*, Venice: Eidos.
Cecchi, Emilio (1930), 'Altori prosatori', *L'Italia lettereria*, 20 April.
Cecchi, Emilio (1964) 'La *Gita al faro* tradotta' (1934); 'La morte della tignuola' (1945); ' "Serata in casa del Dott. Burney" di V. Woolf' (1945); '*Gita al faro* di V. Woolf' (1946); 'La Woolf e il "personaggio" ' (1950), in *Scrittori inglesi e americani*, vol. 2, 4th edn, Milan: Il Saggiatore.
Cecchi, Emilio (1945) 'Lettera a un giovane poetà', *Poesia* [Rome], 2.
Cecchi, Emilio (1946) 'Commemorazione di un capolavoro', *La fiera letteraria* [Rome], 18 April.
Chiesura, Giorgio (1946) 'A proposito di *Mrs Dalloway*', *Letteratura* [Florence], 8.4.
Colaiacomo, Paola (1993) 'Il silenzio del greco antico' (1984), 'Il punto di vista di Flush' (1986), 'Something unvisual beneath' (1984), in *La prova: saggi da Shakespeare a Beckett*. Rome: Editori Riuniti.
Cordelli, Franco (1978) Introduction to *Tra un atto e l'altro* (*BTA*), Parma, Guanda. Reprint, Milan: Feltrinelli, 1981.
Corsini, Gianfranco (1974) 'Virginia Woolf e Joyce', *L'Ora*, 12 April.
Crisafulli Jones, Lilla (1988) 'V. Woolf: per un'estetica della crisi', in Fortunati, Vita and Lilla Crisafulli Jones (eds), *Ritratto dell'artista come donna*, Urbino, QuattroVenti.
Daiches, David (1945) 'Virginia Woolf scrittrice', *Aretusa* [Naples], December.
Debenedetti, Antonio (1963) 'Strade dell'intelligenza', *Corriere della sera* [Milan], 24 November.
Debenedetti, Antonio (1971) *Il romanzo del '900*, Milan: Garzanti.
De Feo, Sandro (1954) 'Il diario di Virginia Woolf è il suo libro più disperato', *L'Europeo* [Milan], 7 March.
De Feo, Sandro (1966) *Qualcosa di certo*, Florence: Vallecchi.
Del Sapio Garbero, Maria (1992) 'Il flusso e l'ingorgo: percorsi della frase femminile nel romanzo modernista', in Oriana Palusci (ed.), *La città delle donne: immaginario urbano e letteratura del Novecento*, Turin: Tirrenia Stampatori, pp. 4–29.
Del Sasso, Rino (1963) 'Per le strade di Londra', *L'Unità*, 13 October.
De Rigo, Giorgio (1962) '*The Waves* di Virginia Woolf', *Letterature moderne* [Milan], March-June.
De Robertis, D. (1951) 'Virginia Woolf', in *Paragone* [Florence], February.
Dettore, Ugo (1937) 'Virginia Woolf e il tempo', in *Meridiano di Roma* [Rome], 20 June.
Di Piazza, Elio (1975) *Virginia Woolf nella critica italiana (1927–74)*, Palermo: Facoltà di Lettere, 3.
Donahue, Delia (1977) *The Novels of Virginia Woolf*, Rome: Bulzoni.
Drago, Antonietta (1955) 'La follia fu il suo segreto', *Il Tempo* [Rome], 20 January.
Dunn, Jane (1995) *Sorelle e complici: Vanessa Bell e Virginia Woolf*, trans. Luciana Verga, Turin: Bollati Boringhieri. Translation of *A Very Close Conspiracy: Vanessa Bell and Virginia Woolf*, London: Cape, 1990.
Eco, Umberto (1962) 'Una chiave per comprendere l'universo della Woolf', *Il Giorno* [Milan], 31 October.
Ferrata, Giansiro (1963) 'Una stanza tutta per sé', *Rinascita*, 9 November.

Fidanza, Daniela (1999) 'Giuseppe Tomasi di Lampedusa e Virginia Woolf', in Orlando, Francesco (ed.) *Giuseppe Tomasi di Lampedusa: cento anni dalla nascita, quaranta dal 'Gattopardo': Atti del Convegno 12–14 dicembre 1996*, Palermo: Asessorato alla cultura, pp. 235–57.

Fortunati, Vita (1988) 'Parodia e ironia in *Orlando*' in Fortunati,Vita and Lilla Crisafulli Jones, (eds), *Ritratto dell'artista come donna*, Urbino: QuattroVenti.

Fusini, Nadia (1977) 'Sulle donne e il loro poetare', *Nuova DWF* [Rome], 5 (October–December).

Fusini, Nadia (1982) 'Nota', in *Notte e giorno* (*ND*), Turin: Einaudi.

Fusini, Nadia (1992a) 'Virginia Woolf o del tremore', in *Nomi: il suono della vita*, Milan: Feltrinelli.

Fusini, Nadia (1992b) Introduction to *Al Faro*, Milan: Feltrinelli.

Fusini, Nadia (1993) Introduction to *La signora Dalloway* (*MD*), Milan: Feltrinelli.

Fusini, Nadia (1995) 'Nota del traduttore', *Le onde* (*TW*), Turin: Einaudi.

Fusini, Nadia (1998a) Introduction to Virginia Woolf, *Romanzi*, Milan: Mondadori.

Fusini, Nadia (1998b) Introduction to Virginia Woolf, *Saggi, prose, racconti*, Milan: Mondadori.

G. B. (1963) 'La Woolf ci insegna a leggere', *La Stampa* [Turin], 5–6 December.

G. P. (1955) 'Virginia Woolf', *Rivista di letterature moderne* [Asti], January–March.

Guidi, Augusto (1945) 'Appunti da una lettura di Virginia Woolf', *Mercurio* [Rome], 2.9 (May).

Guidi, Augusto (1951) 'Spender, Praz e V. Woolf', *Letteratura e arte contemporanea* [Florence], 2.

Guiducci, Armanda (1991) *Virginia e l'Angelo*, Milan: Longanesi.

Guiducci, Armanda (1992) 'Il percorso creativo di V. Woolf', in *La signora Dalloway* (*MD*), Rome: Newton-Compton. Reprint, in *Le onde* (*TW*), Rome: Newton-Compton, 1992, *Gita al faro* (*TL*), Rome: Newton-Compton, 1992, *Una stanza tutta per sé* (*ROO*), Rome: Newton-Compton, 1993, *Orlando* (*O*), Rome: Newton-Compton, 1994, *Notte e giorno* (*ND*), Rome: Newton-Compton, 1996.

Izzo, Carlo (1961) 'Testimonianze sul Bloomsbury Group', in *Studi in onore di Vittorio Lugli e Diego Valeri*, Venice: Neri Pozza.

Izzo, Carlo (1970), 'La torre d'avorio di V. Woolf', in *Civiltà britannica*, Rome: Edizioni di storia e letteratura, vol. 2, pp. 332–63.

Kotnik, Dara (1999), *Virginia Woolf: La Minerva di Bloomsbury*, Milan: Rusconi.

Lanati, Barbara (1983) Introduction to *Freshwater*, Turin: La Rosa.

Lanzetta Gnoli, Ines (1957) 'Virginia Woolf', *L'educatore italiano* [Milan], April.

Lehmann, John (1977) *Virginia Woolf: una biografia con immagini*, trans. M. Pizzorno, Milan: La Tartaruga. Reprint, 1983. Translation of *Virginia Woolf and Her World*, London: Thames and Hudson, 1975.

Linati, Carlo (1927) 'Virginia Woolf', *Corriere della sera* [Milan], 24 January. Reprint in *Scrittor anglo-americani d'oggi*, Milan: Corticelli, 1932.

Linati, Carlo (1935) 'Virginia Woolf', *Emporium* [Bergamo], January.

Livi, Grazia (1980) 'Disgregazione e fusione in Virginia Woolf', *Paragone* [Florence], June, 15–40.

Livi, Grazia (1982a) Introduction to *Orlando* (*O*), Milan: Mondadori, pp. 5–15.

Livi, Grazia (1982b) Afterword to *Scene di Londra* (*LS*), Milan: Mondadori.

Livi, Grazia (1984) 'V. Woolf: stanza tutta per sé con poltrona', in *Da una stanza all'altra*, Milan: La Tartaruga.

Livi, Grazia (1991) 'Virginia Woolf: il grembo', in *Le lettere del mio nome*, Milan: La Tartaruga.

Livi, Grazia (1992) Introduction to Virginia Woolf, *Volare su Londra*, Milan: Marcos y Marcos.

Locatelli, Carla (1992) 'Rappresentazione e referenza autobiografica in *Moments of*

Being', in Agazzi, Elena and Angelo Canavesi (eds), *Il segno dell' io: romanzo e autobiografia nella traduzione moderna*, Udine: Camparotto.

Locatelli, Carla (1980) 'Autore Empirico ed Autore Modello: un confronto su *Mrs Dalloway*', *Annali della Facoltà di Lingue e Letterature Straniere* [Ravenna], 5.

Lombardi, Olga (1951) 'V. Woolf, la signora nello specchio', *La fiera letteraria* [Rome], 11 February.

Lombardo, Agostino (1955) 'Il diario di V. Woolf', *Convivium* [Turin], 2 (March–April). Reprint, in *Ritratto di Enobarbo: saggi sulla letteratura inglese*, Pisa, Nistri Lischi, 1971.

L. P. (1963) 'Per le strade di Londra', *La Stampa* [Turin], 9 October.

Luciani, Giovanni (1994) *La polvere della lettura: la critica letteraria di Virginia Woolf*, Bari, Adriatica.

Manzini, Gianna (1947) 'La lezione della Woolf', in *Forte come un leone*, Milan: Mondadori, pp. 76–96.

Melchiori, Giorgio (1951) 'L'attimo come unità di tempo nella narrativa', *Lo spettatore italiano* [Rome].

Melchiori, Giorgio (1954) 'Il diario di Virginia Woolf', *Lo spettatore italiano* [Rome], 7.2 (February).

Melchiori, Giorgio (1963) 'L'attimo come unità di tempo nella narrativa contemporanea' (1951), in *I Funamboli: il manierismo nella letteratura inglese contemporanea*, trans. Ruggero Bianchi, Turin: Einaudi, pp. 199–211. Translation of 'The Moment as a Time Unit in Fiction', in *The Tightrope Walkers: Studies of Mannerism in Modern English Literature*, London: Routledge & Kegan Paul, 1956.

Merlini, Madeline (1991) *Invito alla lettura di Virginia Woolf*, Milan: Mursia.

Merope [Chieti] (1992) 6.6 (June) (special number on Virginia Woolf).

Mizzau, Marina (1965) *Tecniche narrative e romanzo contemporaneo*, Milan: Mursia.

Morra, Umberto (1928) 'Virginia Woolf', *Il Baretti* [Turin], 6 (27 May).

Morra, Umberto (1929), 'Orlando – A Biography', in *Solaria*, 5: 51–6.

Morra, Umberto (1931) 'Il nuovo romanzo inglese: Virginia Woolf', *La cultura* [Florence], January.

Morra, Umberto (1932) 'Virginia Woolf: *The Waves*', *Pegaso* [Florence], March.

Morra, Umberto (1937), 'The Years di Virginia Woolf', in *Letteratura* (July–September): 172–4.

Morra, Umberto (1946) 'Omaggio alla Woolf', *La Nuova Europa* [Rome], 10 March.

Nathan, Monique (1962) *Virginia Woolf*, trans. Pietro Lazzaro, Milan: Mondadori. Translation of *Virginia Woolf par elle-même*, Bourges: Seuil, 1956.

Nathan, Monique (1963) 'La casa di Virginia Woolf', *La Stampa* [Turin], 13 April.

Palusci, Oriana (1996) *Le dimore del tempo: Mrs Dalloway, Orlando, Mrs Woolf*, Turin: Tirrenia Stampatori.

Palusci, Oriana (ed.) (1999), *La tipografia nel salotto: saggi su Virginia Woolf*, Turin: Tirrenia Stampatori.

Pardi, F. (1960) 'Il Diario di Virginia Woolf', *Nuova Antologia* [Rome], 478, January–April.

Pasolini, Desideria (1950) Introduction to *La casa degli spiriti* (*HH*), trans. Desideria Pasolini, Milan: Mondadori.

Pavolini, Corrado (1933) 'Casi di Coscienza', *Occidente* [Rome], July–September.

Perosa, Sergio (1978a) Introduction to Virginia Woolf, *Romanzi e altro*, Milan: Mondadori.

Perosa, Sergio (1978b) 'Scopriamo il mondo di V. Woolf', *Epoca* [Milan], 25 November.

Perosa, Sergio (1979) Introduction to *La Signora Dalloway* (*MD*), Milan: Mondadori. Reprint as 'V. Woolf e la dissoluzione narrativa', in *Il precario equilibrio*, Turin: Stampatori, 1980, pp. 264–305.

Perosa, Sergio (1987) in *Le isole Aran*, Venice: Marsilio, pp. 147–60.

Perosa, Sergio (1995) 'L'ordinaria esaltazione: V. Woolf', *EtruriaOggi* [Arezzo], September.

Praz, Mario (1930) 'Una camera propria', *La Stampa* [Turin], 14 January. Reprint in *Cronache letterarie anglo-sassoni*, Rome: Edizioni di Storia e Letteratura, 1950.

Praz, Mario (1931) '*Le onde*', *La Stampa* [Turin], 5 November. Reprint in *Cronache letterarie anglo-sassoni*, Rome: Edizioni di Storia e Letteratura, 1950.

Praz, Mario (1933) 'Il cane di Mrs Browning', *La Stampa* [Turin], 11 October. Reprint in *Cronache letterarie anglo-sassoni*, Rome: Edizioni di Storia e Letteratura, 1950.

Praz, Mario (1946) *Prospettiva della letteratura inglese da Chaucer alla Woolf*, Florence: Bompiani.

Praz, Mario (1960) *Storia della letteratura inglese*, 5th edn, Florence: Sansoni.

Praz, Mario (1983) 'Cinquant'anni fa nasceva il travestito in letteratura' (1978), in *Studi e svaghi inglesi*, vol. 2, Milan: Garzanti.

Raboni, Giorgio (1960), 'Diario di una scrittrice', *Aut Aut*, May.

Rasy, Elisabetta (1984) *Le donne e la letteratura*, Rome: Editori Riuniti.

Rebora, Pietro (1938) 'Virginia Woolf', *Le lingue estere* [Milan], 1 December.

Rebora, Pietro (1950) *Letteratura inglese del '900*, Florence: Edizioni lingue estere.

Rebora, Roberto (1964), 'V. Woolf o la consacrezione', *Questo e altro*, 7–8: 79–81.

Riccio, Attilio (1933), 'Flush: vita d'un cane', *Occidente*, 2,4.

Riem, Antonella (1990) 'Orlando: A Biography', in *Il seme e l'urna: il 'doppio' nella letteratura inglese*, pref. Mario Domenichelli, Ravenna, Longo.

Romano, Lalla (1974) 'Presentazione di V. Woolf alla trasmissione televisiva', *Settimo giorno* [Milan], 25 August.

Rosati, Salvatore (1933) 'Letteratura inglese: V. Woolf', *Nuova Antologia* [Rome], 1482 (16 December).

Rosati, Salvatore (1945) 'Virginia Woolf postuma', *La Nuova Europa* [Rome], 11 February.

Rosati, Salvatore (1950) 'Virginia Woolf', *English Miscellany* [Rome], 1.

Rosati, Salvatore (1953) 'Virginia Woolf e il suo diario', *Il Mondo* [Rome], 15 December.

Rose, Phyllis (1980) *Virginia Woolf*, trans. Cristina Bertea, Rome: Editori Riuniti. Translation of *Woman of Letters: A Life of Virginia Woolf*, London: Routledge & Kegan Paul,1978.

Runcini, Romolo (1968) *Illusione e paura nel mondo borghese da Dickens a Orwell*, Bari: Laterza.

Sanna, Vittoria (1951) *Il romanzo di Virginia Woolf: ispirazione e motivi fondamentali*, Florence: Marzocco.

Siciliani, Erina (1984) *Tele con strani disegni: un viaggio verso il faro (V. Woolf: 1917–1927)*, Bari: Adriatica.

Siciliano, Enzo (1962) '"Sento che sto per diventare pazza: sento delle voci ..."', *L'Unità*, 30 September.

Siciliano, Enzo (1963) 'La stanza di Virginia Woolf', *Il Mondo* [Rome], 22 October.

Sommavilla, Guido (1957) 'Il testamento di V. Woolf', *Letture* [Milan], 3.

Spender, Stephen (1954) *Un mondo nel mondo*, Milan: Bompiani. Translation of *World within World*, London: Hamish Hamilton, 1951.

Spina, Giorgio (1980) *Il Romanzo psicologico di Virginia Woolf*, Genoa: Opera Universitaria.

Splendore, Paola (1991) Introduction to Virginia Woolf, *Ore in biblioteca e altri saggi*. Milan: La Tartaruga.

Stampa Barracco, M. (1978) *Virginia Woolf: l'immagine dialettica*, Naples: Liguori.

Tassi, Roberto (1965) 'Nota su un saggio di Virginia Woolf', *L'approdo letterario* [Turin], April–June.

Tomasi di Lampedusa, Giuseppe (1978) 'Virginia Woolf', *Corriere della sera* [Milan], 19 February.

Troy, William (1954) 'Virginia Woolf e il romanzo della sensibilità', *Prospetti*, 6. Translation of 'Virginia Woolf and the Novel of Sensibility', *Perspectives*, 16 (1954).
Vanessa Bell and Virginia Woolf: 'Disegnore la vita' (essays by various authors) (1996), Ferrara: SATE.
Woolf, Leonard (1989) *La mia vita con Virginia*, trans. Ilide Carmignani, introd. Marisa Bulgheroni, Milan: Serra e Riva. Translation of extracts from Leonard Woolf's Autobiography based on the German edition *Mein Leben mit Virginia: Errinerungen*, ed. and trans. Friederike Groth, Frankfurt: Frankfurter Verl.-Anst., 1988.
Yourcenar, Marguerite (1937) 'Una donna sfavillante e timida', in *Pellegrina e Straniera*, trans. Elena Giovanelli, Turin: Einaudi, 1990. Translation of 'Une femme étincelante et timide', in *En pélerin, en étranger*, Paris: Gallimard, 1989, pp. 107–20.
Zaccaria, Paola (1980) *Virginia Woolf: trama e ordito di una scrittura*, Bari: Dedalo.
Zaccaria, Paola (1981) *Virginia Woolf*, Bari: Dedalo Libri.
Zaccaria, Paola (1988) 'V. Woolf: corpo violentato, parola innamorata', *Il confronto letterario* [Fasano], 10, November.
Zampa, Giorgio (1960) 'La tragedia di una nobile vita nel diario', *Corriere della sera* [Milan], 17 March.
Zazo, A. L. (1994) Introduction to Virginia Woolf, *Romanzi e racconti*, Milan: Mondadori.

Chapter 12

SPANISH AND CATALAN TRANSLATIONS

FB (Catalan)
(1938) *Flush*, trans. Roser Cardús, *Quaderns literaris* [Barcelona], 211–12.

JR (Spanish)
(1946) *El cuarto de Jacob*, trans. J. Santainés, Barcelona: Lauro.

MD (Catalan)
(1930) *Mrs Dalloway*, trans. César August Jordana, Barcelona: Proa.

MD (Spanish)
(1939) *La señora Dalloway*, trans. Ernesto Palacio, Buenos Aires: Sudamericana.

ND (Spanish)
(1947) *Noche y día*, trans. E. Guzmán, Barcelona: Lauro.

O (Spanish)
(1937) *Orlando: Una biografía*, trans. Jorge Luis Borges, Buenos Aires: Sur. Reprints, Buenos Aires: Sudamericana, 1945; Barcelona: Edhasa, 1977.

ROO (Spanish)
(1935–36). '*Un cuarto propio*', trans. Jorge Luis Borges, *Sur* [Buenos Aires], 15 (1935): 8–29; 16 (1936): 26–58; 17 (1936): 41–61; 18 (1936): 46–81. Reprint in book form, Buenos Aires: Sur, 1936.
(1967) *Una habitación propia*, trans. Laura Pujol, Barcelona: Seix-Barral.

Selected novels (Spanish)
(1956) *Obras completas*, trans. P. Fraga de Porto and others, Barcelona: Janés.

'Thoughts on Peace in an Air Raid'
(1947) 'Reflexiones sobre la paz durante una incursión aérea', trans. B. R. Hopenhaym, *Sur* [Buenos Aires], 153–56: 66–72.

TG (Spanish)
(1941) *Tres guineas*, trans. Román Jiménez, Buenos Aires: Sudamericana.

TL (Spanish)
(1938) *Al faro*, trans. Antonio Marichalar, Buenos Aires: *Sur*. Reprints, Buenos Aires: Sudamericana, 1946; Barcelona: Edhasa, 1979; Barcelona: Seix-Barral, 1984.
(1938) 'Pasa el tiempo', trans. Antonio Marichalar, *Sur* [Buenos Aires], 43: 7–30. Translation of 'Time Passes' section of *TL*.
(1978) *Al faro*, trans. Carmen Martín Gaite, Barcelona: Edhasa.

TW (Catalan)
(1989) *Les ones*, trans. María Antònia Oliver, Barcelona: Edhasa.

TY (Catalan)
(1988) *Els Anys*, trans. María Antònia Oliver, Barcelona: Edhasa.

TY (Spanish)
(1946) *Los años*, trans. P. Fraga de Porto, Barcelona: Lauro.

WD (Spanish)
(1954) *Diario de una escritora*, trans. José M. Coco Ferraris, Buenos Aires: Sur.

OTHER WORKS CITED

Abella, Encarna (1996) 'Victoria Ocampo: historia de una vocación literaria: éxitos y retos', in Hernández de López, Ana María (ed.) *Narrativa hispanoamericana contemporánea*, Madrid: Pliegos, pp. 17–29.

Anderson Imbert, Enrique (1962) *Testimonios sobre Victoria Ocampo*, Buenos Aires: La Comisión.

Ayerza del Castillo, Laura and Odile Felgine (1991) *Victoria Ocampo*, Barcelona: Circe.

Baquero Goyanes, Mariano (1955) 'La trayectoria de la novela actual', *Ínsula* [Madrid], 117: 5.

Barral, Carlos (1978) *Los años sin excusa*, Barcelona: Seix-Barral.

Beer, Gillian (1996) 'Virginia Woolf and Prehistory,' in *Virginia Woolf: The Common Ground*, Edinburgh: Edinburgh University Press, pp. 6–28.

Borges, Jorge Luis (1965) *Introducción a la literatura inglesa*, Madrid: Alianza, 1999.

Borges, Jorge Luis (1977) *Prólogos*, Buenos Aires: Torres Agero.

Borges, Jorge Luis (1989) 'El escritor argentino y la tradición,' in *Obras completas*, ed. Carlos V. Frías, Barcelona: Emecé, 1: 267–74.

Borges, Jorge Luis (2000) 'The Argentine Writer and Tradition', trans. Esther Allen, in *The Total Library: Non-Fiction 1922–1986*, ed. Eliot Weinberger, trans. Esther Allen, Suzanne Jill Levine and Eliot Weinberger, London: Allen Lane: The Penguin Press, pp. 420–27.

Borges, Jorge Luis and María Esther Vázquez (1974) *An Introduction to English Literature*, ed. and trans. L. Clark Keating and Robert O. Evans, London: Robson Books; Lexington: University Press of Kentucky.
Botana, Natalio R. and Ezequiel Gallo (1984) 'La política argentina entre las dos guerras mundiales', *Revista de Occidente* [Madrid], 37: 45–58.
Canito, Enrique (1949) 'Victoria Sackville-West', *Ínsula* [Madrid], 40: 2, 6.
Ferrari, Osvaldo and Jorge Luis Borges (1982) *Diálogos*, Barcelona: Seix-Barral.
García Lora, José (1957) 'Virginia Woolf y Azorín: encuentro alrededor del tiempo', *Ínsula* [Madrid], 131: 9, 12.
García Pinto, Roberto (1984) 'Los pasos de Ortega en la Argentina', *Revista de Occidente* [Madrid], 37: 74–98.
Gargatagli, Ana (1993) *Jorge Luis Borges y la traducción*, Barcelona: Servicio de Publicaciones e Intercambio Científico.
Garrido, Julio (1949) 'La institución cultural española de Buenos Aires y las relaciones intelectuales hispano-argentinas', *Ínsula* [Madrid], 48: 6.
Gracia, Jordi (1995) *Estado y cultura: el despertar de una conciencia crítica bajo el franquismo*, Toulouse: Presses Universitaires du Mirail.
Hausman, Bernice L. (1990) 'Words Between Women: Victoria Ocampo and Virginia Woolf', in Valis, Noel and Carol Maier (eds) *In the Feminine Mode: Essays on Hispanic Women Writers*, Lewisburg: Bucknell University Press, pp. 204–26.
Hermes Villordo, Oscar (1993) *El grupo Sur: una biografía colectiva*, Buenos Aires: Planeta.
Howell, Christina (1975) *In Vogue: Six Decades of Fashion*, London: Condé Nast Publications.
Hurtley, Jacqueline (1984) *La literatura inglesa del siglo XX en la España de postguerra: la aportación de Josep Janés*, Barcelona: Edicions Universitat de Barcelona.
Hurtley, Jacqueline (1985) 'La obra editorial de Josep Janés: 1940–1959', *Anuario de Filología* [Barcelona], 11: 293–329.
Hurtley, Jacqueline (1986) *Josep Janés: el combat per la cultura*, Barcelona: Curial.
Hurtley, Jacqueline (1991) 'On the Arrival of *Mrs Dalloway*', *Catalan Review* [Barcelona], 1.5: 121–32.
Jarnés, Benjamín (1984) 'Sur', *Revista de Occidente* [Madrid], 37 (June 1984): 25–29. First published in *Revista de Occidente*, 96 (1931).
Kaminsky, Amy Katz (1980) 'Women and Feminism in Victoria Ocampo's *Testimonios*', in Cruz de Mendizábal, Juan (ed.) *Proceedings of the Sixth Annual Hispanic Literatures Conference*, Philadelphia: University of Pennsylvania Press, pp. 69–85.
Laurence, Pat (1999) 'Virginia Woolf in/on Translation', *Virginia Woolf Miscellany*, 54: 1–2.
Mainer, José-Carlos (1998) 'El lento regreso: textos y contextos de la colección "El Puente" ', in Aznar Solel, Manuel (ed.) *El exilio literario español de 1939: actas del primer congreso internacional*, Barcelona: Gexel, pp. 395–415.
Matamoro, Blas (1975) *Oligarquía y literatura*, Buenos Aires: Ediciones del Sol.
Meyer, Doris (1979) *Victoria Ocampo*, Austin: University of Texas Press.
Meyer, Doris (1990) 'Virginia Woolf y la literatura femenina: escribir como una mujer', *Suplemento Literario La Nación*, 2 (December):1.
Nicholson, Norman (1947) 'Panorama de la literatura inglesa contemporánea', *Ínsula* [Madrid], 17: 2.
Ocampo, Victoria (1934) 'Carta a Virginia Woolf', *Revista de Occidente* [Madrid], 46: 170–77.
Ocampo, Victoria (1935) *Testimonios*, vol. 1, Madrid: Revista de Occidente.
Ocampo, Victoria (1938) *Virginia Woolf, Orlando y cía*, Buenos Aires: Ediciones Sur.
Ocampo, Victoria (1941) *Testimonios*, vol. 2, Buenos Aires: Ediciones Sur.
Ocampo, Victoria (1946) *Testimonios*, vol. 3, Buenos Aires: Sudamericana.
Ocampo, Victoria (1954a) *Virginia Woolf en su diario*, Buenos Aires: Ediciones Sur.

Ocampo, Victoria (1954b) 'Una nueva ley', *Sur* [Buenos Aires], 231 (November–December).
Ocampo, Victoria (1963) 'Releer, reincidir, regraciar', *Revista de Occidente* [Madrid], 1: 72–79.
Ocampo, Victoria (1981) *Autobiografía*, III, *La rama de Salzburgo*, Buenos Aires: Sur.
Ocampo, Victoria (1991) *Victoria Ocampo: autobiografía*, ed. Francisco Ayala, Madrid: Alianza.
Ortega y Gasset, José (1948) *The Dehumanization of Art, and, Notes on the Novel*, trans. Helen Weyl, Princeton, NJ: Princeton University Press.
Ortega y Gasset, José (1964) 'Ideas sobre la novela', in *Meditaciones sobre El Quijote/Ideas sobre la novela*, Madrid: Espasa–Calpe, 1964.
Ortega, Soledad (1984) 'Victoria Ocampo al trasluz de una doble amistad', *Revista de Occidente* [Madrid], 37: 7–23.
Sebreli, Juan José (1993) 'Defensa de Victoria Ocampo', *Quimera* [Barcelona], 121: 28–33.
Torre, Guillermo de (1951) 'Victoria Ocampo y el Conde de Keyserling', *Ínsula* [Madrid], 71: 2.
Torre, Guillermo de (1962) 'Charlas en *Ínsula*: Guillermo de Torre', *Ínsula* [Madrid], 193: 3. *Virginia Woolf Miscellany*, 54 (1999).
Waissbein, Daniel V. (1984) 'Cosmopolitismo e irreverencia: la tradición argentina según Borges', *Revista de Occidente* [Madrid], 37: 59–73.
Woolf, Virginia (1905a) 'Journeys in Spain', in *The Complete Essays of Virginia Woolf*, ed. Andrew McNeillie, London: Hogarth Press, 1986, 1: 44–46.
Woolf, Virginia (1905b) 'An Andalusian Inn', in *The Complete Essays of Virginia Woolf*, 1: 49–52.

Chapter 13

SPANISH TRANSLATIONS

FB

(1944) *Flush*, trans. Rafael Vazquez Zamora, Barcelona: Ediciones Destino.

JR

(1946) *El cuarto de Jacob*, trans. Simón Santainés, Barcelona: Ediciones Lauro.

MD

(1939) *La señora Dalloway*, trans. Ernesto Palacio, Buenos Aires: Editorial Sudamericana.
(1993) *La señora Dalloway*, ed. María Lozano, trans. Mariano Baselga, Madrid: Cátedra.

ND

(1947) *Noche y día*, trans. Eduardo de Guzmán, Barcelona: José Janés.

O

(1937) *Orlando*, trans. Jorge Luis Borges, Buenos Aires: Editorial Sur.

ROO

(1936) *Un cuarto propio*, trans. Jorge Luis Borges, Buenos Aires: Editorial Sur.
(1967) *Una habitación propia*, trans. Laura Pujol, Barcelona: Seix-Barral.

TL
(1931) 'El tiempo pasa', *Revista de Occidente* [Madrid], 31.93 (March): 283–97. [Translation of 'Time Passes']
(1938) 'Pasa el tiempo', trans. Antonio Marichalar, *Sur* [Buenos Aires], 43 (April): 7–30. [Translation of *Time Passes*].
(1938) *Al faro*, trans. Antonio Marichalar, Buenos Aires: Editorial Sur.
(1999) *Al faro*, ed. and trans. Dámaso López, Madrid: Cátedra.

TW
(1940) *Las olas*, trans. Lenka Franulic, Santiago de Chile: Ediciones Ercilla.
(1972) *Las olas*, trans. Andrés Bosch, Barcelona: Lumen.
(1994) *Las olas*, ed. María Lozano, trans. Dámaso López, Madrid: Cátedra.

TY
(1946) *Los años*, trans. Pedro Fraga de Porto, Barcelona: Ediciones Lauro.

VO
(1946) *Fin de viaje*, trans. Guillermo Gossi, Barcelona: Luis de Caralt.

OTHER WORKS CITED

Abellán, Manuel L. (1980) *Censura y creación literaria en España (1939–1976)*, Barcelona: Ediciones Península.
Alexander, Sally (1998) 'Una habitación propia: las utopías de las mujeres en los años 20 en Gran Bretaña', *Arenal* [Granada], 5.1: 131–50.
Álvarez, María Antonia (1997) 'Estrategias narrativas del poema en prosa "Kew Gardens", de Virginia Woolf', in Guardia, P. and J. Stone (eds) *Proceedings of the 20th International AEDEAN Conference*, Barcelona: Universitat de Barcelona, pp. 353–57.
Anievas Gamallo, Isabel Carmen (1992) 'Virginia Woolf's *Mrs Dalloway:* A Journey into the Inner Mind', *Estudios humanísticos, Filología* [León], 14: 157–69.
Aranguren, José Luis L. (1974a) 'Virginia Woolf y su época', *Triunfo* [Madrid], 9 February, 41.
Aranguren, José Luis L. (1974b) 'Las novelas de Virginia Woolf, hoy', *Triunfo* [Madrid], 23 February, 41.
Armstrong, Isobel (1992) 'Virginia Woolf: Founding Feminist or Anxious Influence?', in Bengoechea 1992, pp. 3–25.
Baquero Goyanes, Mariano (1948) 'Tiempo y "tempo" en la novela', *Arbor* [Madrid], 11.33–34 (September–October): 85–94.
Baquero Goyanes, Mariano (1949) 'Sobre la novela y sus límites', *Arbor: revista general de investigación y cultura* [Madrid], 13.42 (June): 271–83.
Baquero Goyanes, Mariano (1954) 'Novela autobiográfica y monólogo interior', *Ateneo* [Madrid], 15 January 1954, 10.
Bengoechea, Mercedes (ed.) (1992) *La huella de Virginia Woolf*, Alcalá de Henares: Servicio de Publicaciones, Universidad de Alcalá.
Bozal, Valeriano (1969) 'La edición en España: notas para su historia', *Cuadernos para el diálogo* [Madrid], 14 (May): 85–93.
Brass, Denis (1945) 'Algunos aspectos de la crítica moderna inglesa', *Escorial* [Madrid], 17.52: 319–45.
Campbell, Roy (1949) 'Tendencias de la literatura inglesa contemporánea', *Escorial* [Madrid], 20 (August): 1021–37.

Campoy, Adolfo (1993) '*Auction:* Emily Dickinson, Virginia Woolf y el discurso *borderline*', *Asparkía* [Castelló], 2: 75–91.
Castroviejo, Concha (1968) 'Virginia Woolf, la mujer y la novela', *Ínsula* [Madrid], 257: 4–5.
Díaz López, J. A. (1982) 'Los Woolfs en España', *Estudios de filología moderna* [Granada], 10: 15–27.
Galán Moya, Rafael (1996) ' "El hecho fértil": *Orlando*, de Virginia Woolf', in García-Doncel, María del Rosario (ed.) *La mujer en la literatura de habla inglesa*, Cádiz: Servicio de Publicaciones, Universidad de Cádiz, pp. 123–41.
Gallego Méndez, María Teresa (1983) *Mujer, Falange y franquismo*, Madrid: Taurus.
García Lora, José (1957) 'Virginia Woolf y Azorín: encuentro alrededor del tiempo', *Ínsula* [Madrid], 131: 9+.
García Santa Cecilía, Carlos G. (1997) *La recepción de James Joyce en la prensa española, 1921–1976*, Seville: Universidad de Sevilla, Secretariado de Publicaciones.
Gee, Maggie (1992) 'Male and Female in the Woman Who Writes', in Bengoechea 1992, pp. 29–43.
Gullón, Ricardo (1945) 'Virginia Woolf o la novela en crisis', in *Novelistas ingleses contemporáneos: cinco damas y nueve caballeros*, Saragossa: Ediciones Cronos, pp. 157–69.
Gullón, Ricardo (1984) *La novela lírica*, Madrid: Cátedra.
Guzmán, Flora (1982) 'Los dos lenguajes de Virginia Woolf,' *Cuadernos hispano-americanos* [Madrid], 389 (November): 347–60.
Herrero Quirós, Carlos (1992) 'Virginia Woolf y la pasión de escribir', *Brispania* [Valladolid], 1: 221–40.
Herrero Quirós, Carlos (1996a) 'Virginia Woolf, el panorama contemporáneo y el relevo de las generaciones', in Abad, Pilar, José M. Barrio and José M. Ruiz (eds) *Estudios de literatura en lengua inglesa del siglo XX*, Valladolid: Servicio de Apoyo a la Enseñanza, Universidad de Valladolid, 3: 221–25.
Herrero Quirós, Carlos (1996b) *Virginia Woolf: proceso creativo y evolución literaria*, Valladolid: Secretariado de Publicaciones e Intercambio Científico, Universidad de Valladolid.
Hidalgo, Pilar (1980) 'Virginia Woolf: el contexto inglés', *Arbor* [Madrid], 107.417–18 (September–October): 85–91.
Kirkpatrick, B. J. and Stuart N. Clarke (1997) *A Bibliography of Virginia Woolf*, 4th edn, Oxford: Clarendon Press.
Lojo, Laura (1997) 'O camiño cara a unha biografia definitiva: *Virginia Woolf: A Biography*, de Hermione Lee', *Boletin galego de literatura* [Santiago de Compostela], 17: 89–97.
Lojo, Laura (1999) 'Interweaving Patterns in Virginia Woolf's Writing, 1917–1924: *Monday or Tuesday* (unpublished doctoral thesis, University of Santiago de Compostela).
López García, Dámaso (1980) 'Las novelas de Virginia Woolf desde su *Diario*', *Arbor* [Madrid], 105.409 (January): 77–86.
López García, Dámaso (1993) 'Virginia Woolf', in *La crítica literaria del grupo de Bloomsbury*, Madrid: Universidad Complutense, pp. 169–200.
Lozano Mantecón, María (1977) 'Estructuras narrativas en la novela de Virginia Woolf' (unpublished doctoral thesis, University of Saragossa).
Majumdar, Robin (1976) *Virginia Woolf: An Annotated Bibliography of Criticism 1915–1974*, New York: Garland.
Manent, María (1946) 'Crónica de libros ingleses', *Ínsula* [Madrid], 6: 4.
Marichalar, Antonio (1928) 'Las "vidas" y Lytton Strachey', *Revista de Occidente* [Madrid], 19.57 (March): 343–58.
Marichalar, Antonio (1929) 'Nueva dimensión', *Revista de Occidente* [Madrid], 24.72 (June): 380–83.
Marichalar, Antonio (1931) 'Último grito', *Revista de Occidente* [Madrid], 31.91 (January): 101–07.

Meouchi, Edmundo (1953) 'La novela "yanqui" en España', *Correo literario* [Madrid], 15 November, 12.

Míguez Ben, Manuel (1974) *Análisis y estructura de 'Mrs Dalloway', 'To the Lighthouse' y 'The Waves' de Virginia Woolf*, Santiago de Compostela: Servicio de Publicaciones de la Universidad.

Montes, Catalina (1980) *En torno a 'Mrs Dalloway' de Virginia Woolf*, Madrid: Rubicam Ediciones Universitarias.

Montes, Catalina (1982) 'Voces de T. S. Eliot en *Mrs Dalloway*, de Virginia Woolf', *Studia Zamorensia* [Zamora], 3: 527–38.

Montes, Catalina (1983) 'Algunas consideraciones sobre Doris Kilman, en *Mrs Dalloway*, de Virginia Woolf', in Asociación Española de Estudios Anglo-Norteamericanos (ed.) *Héroe y antihéroe en la literatura inglesa: Actas del V Congreso AEDEAN*, Madrid: Alhambra, pp. 423–27.

Montes, Catalina (1984) 'Locura y muerte de Septimus Warren Smith en *Mrs Dalloway* de Virginia Woolf', in Asociación Española de Estudios Anglo-Norteamericanos (ed.) *Actas del IV Congreso de la Asociación Española de Estudios Anglo-Norteamericanos*, Salamanca: Ediciones Universidad de Salamanca, pp. 289–98.

Montes, Catalina (1990) 'Una replica a *The Waste Land: Mrs Dalloway*', *Bells (Barcelona English Language and Literature Studies)* [Barcelona], 1: 125–38.

Montes, Catalina (1991) '*To the Lighthouse*, un viaje en el espacio de la imaginación', in González y Fernández-Corugedo, Santiago and others (eds) *Studia Patriciae Shaw oblata*, Oviedo: Universidad de Oviedo, Servicio de Publicaciones, 2: 134–46.

Morales, Marisol (1999) *Breve introducción a la literatura comparada*, Alcalá de Henares: Servicio de Publicaciones de la Universidad de Alcalá de Henares.

Navales, Ana María (1992) 'Dos mujeres, una pasión y un paisaje (*Cuentos de Bloomsbury*)', in Bengoechea 1992, pp. 45–52.

Nicholson, Norman (1947) 'Panorama de la literatura inglesa contemporánea', *Ínsula* [Madrid], 17: 2.

Ocampo, Victoria (1934) 'Carta a Virginia Woolf', *Revista de Occidente* [Madrid], 46.137 (November): 170–7.

Ocampo, Victoria (1935) *Testimonios*, Madrid: Revista de Occidente.

Palacios González, Manuela (1990) 'Virginia Woolf: a teima da aveleira', *Grial* [Vigo], 28.108 (October–December): 499–505.

Palacios González, Manuela (1992) *Virginia Woolf y la pintura*, Santiago de Compostela: Servicio de Publicaciones e Intercamio Científico.

Palancar, Alberto (1944) 'Música, pintura y arquitectura (Sobre la novela contemporánea)', *Escorial* [Madrid], 14.41 (March): 138–45.

Pérez Gállego, Cándido (1966–67) '*To the Lighthouse* y la estructura de las novelas de Virginia Woolf', *Filología moderna* [Madrid], 6.25–26 (October–January): 115–31.

Pérez Gállego, Cándido (1982) 'Quién teme leer a Virginia Woolf?', *Ínsula* [Madrid], 424: 11.

Pérez Minik, Domingo (1968) *Introducción a la novela inglesa actual*, Madrid: Ediciones Guadarrama.

Pérez Minik, Domingo (1973) *La novela extranjera en España*, Madrid: Taller de Ediciones Josefina Betancor.

Pérez Minik, Domingo (1980) '*Entre Actos*, de Virginia Woolf', *Ínsula* [Madrid], 407: 7+.

Perojo Arronte, María Eugenia (1993) '"That fluidity out there": el tiempo como factor estructural y temático en *To the Lighthouse*', *Brispania* [Valladolid], 2: 243–71.

Pessarrodona, Marta (1976) 'Mrs Dalloway and Mrs Woolf', *Camp de l'arpa* [Barcelona], 28 (January): 12–16.

Pessarrodona, Marta (1978) 'Virginia Woolf y el libro azul', *Camp de l'arpa* [Barcelona], 52 (June): 21–25.

Pessarrodona, Marta (1982a) 'El grup de Bloomsbury: una aproximació,' *L'Avenç* [Barcelona], 46: 20–22.
Pessarrodona, Marta (1982b) 'La literatura al grup de Bloomsbury', *L'Avenç* [Barcelona], 46: 26–29.
Pessarrodona, Marta (1987) 'The Bloomsbury Group Exhibition', *Catalònia* [Barcelona], 1: 46–47.
Plomer, William (1946) 'Virginia Woolf', *Ínsula* [Madrid], 9: 3.
Riera, Carme (1986) 'Una tarde en Bloomsbury', *Quimera* [Barcelona], 57: 13–21.
Rodríguez Palomero, Luisa-Fernanda (1997) 'Virginia Woolf y su traducción: los diarios', *Livius* [León], 10: 165–81.
Rodríguez Palomero, Luisa-Fernanda (1998) 'Diarios de artista: Virginia Woolf', in Abad García, Pilar, José Manuel Barrio Marco and José María Ruiz Ruiz (eds) *Estudios de literatura en lengua inglesa del siglo XX*, Valladolid: Servicio de Apoyo a la Enseñanza, Universidad de Valladolid, 4: 253–64.
Sábato, Ernesto (1964) 'Realidad y realismo en la literatura de nuestro tiempo', *Cuadernos hispanoamericanos* [Madrid], 178 (October): 5–20.
Sánchez-Pardo González, Esther (1996) 'Las madres de Virginia Woolf', in Turbet, Silvia (ed.) *Figuras de la madre*, Madrid: Ediciones Cátedra, pp. 189–221.
Sanz Mateo, Oscar (1988) 'The Handkerchief as Suggested Symbol in Virginia Woolf's *The Waves*', *Miscelánea* [Saragossa], 9: 95–109.
Seixo, María Alzira (1994) 'L'Imagination du voyage: Woolf, Michaux, Saramago: enquêtes périodologiques', in Blesa, Túa and others (eds) *Actas del IX Simposio de la Sociedad Española de Literatura General y Comparada: La parodia y el viaje imaginario*, Saragossa: Universidad de Zaragoza, 2: 519–29.
Sosa López, Emilio (1968) 'Visión y técnica novelísticas de Virginia Woolf', in *La novela y el hombre*, Madrid: Editorial Gredos, pp. 45–60.
Usandizaga, Aránzazu (1993) *Amor y literatura: la búsqueda literaria de la identidad femenina*, Barcelona: PPU.
Varela, M. E. (1993) 'La narración lírica en Binyamin Tammuz y en Virginia Woolf: un estudio comparativo', *Miscelánea de estudios árabes y hebraicos* [Granada], 42.2: 143–57.
Vargas Llosa, Mario (1989) 'Prólogo: la vida intensa y suntuosa de lo vanal', in *La señora Dalloway* (*MD*), trans. Andrés Bosch, Barcelona: Círculo de Lectores.
Woolf, Virginia (1967) 'The Art of Biography', in *Collected Essays*, London: The Hogarth Press, 4: 221–28.
Zamorano Rueda, Ana I. (1997) 'The Carnivalesque Body of the Hermaphrodite: A Reading of Woolf's *Orlando*', in Guardia, P. and J. Stone (eds) *Proceedings of the 20th International AEDEAN Conference*, Barcelona: Universitat de Barcelona, pp. 647–52.

Chapter 14

Basanta, Angel (1990) *La novela española de nuestra época*, Madrid: Anaya.
Benegas, Noni and Jesús Munárriz (eds) (1997) *Ellas tienen la palabra: dos décadas de poesía española*, Madrid: Hiperión.
Bieder, Maryeelen (1992) 'Woman and the Twentieth Century Spanish Literary Canon. The Lady Vanishes', *Anales de la literatura española contemporánea (ALEC)* [University of Colorado, Boulder, CO], 17.3: 301–24.
Bowlby, Rachel (ed.) (1992) *Virginia Woolf*, New York: Longman.
Bowlby, Rachel (1997) *Feminist Destinations and Further Essays on Virginia Woolf*, Edinburgh: Edinburgh University Press.
Brown, Joan L. (ed.) (1991) *Feminine Concerns in Contemporary Spanish Fiction by Women: Women Writers of Contemporary Spain: Exiles in the Homeland*, Newark: University of Delaware Press.

Caws, Mary Ann (1990) *Women of Bloomsbury: Virginia, Vanessa and Carrington*, New York: Routledge.
Cixous, Hélène (1981) 'The Laugh of the Medusa', in Marks, Elaine and Isabelle de Courtivron (eds), *New French Feminisms: An Anthology*, London: Harvester, pp. 245–64.
Davies, Catherine (1994) *Contemporary Feminist Fiction in Spain: The Work of Montserrat Roig and Rosa Montero*, Oxford: Berg.
Encinar Félix, Angeles (1996) '*Cuentos de Bloomsbury*: entre la realidad y la ficción', in *Mundos de ficción, I: Actas del VI Congreso Internacional de Semiótica*, Murcia: Universidad de Murcia.
Freixas, Laura (ed.) (1996) *Madres e hijas*, Barcelona: Anagrama.
Gallop, Jane (1982) *Feminism and Psychoanalysis: The Daughter's Seduction*, London: Macmillan.
Gallop, Jane (1986) 'Annie Leclerc Writing a Letter with Vermeer', in Miller, Nancy K. (ed.), *The Poetics of Gender*, New York: Columbia University Press, pp. 137–56.
Gauthier, Xavière (1981) 'Is There Such a Thing As a Woman's Writing?', in Marks, Elaine and Isabelle de Courtivron (eds), *New French Feminisms: An Anthology*, London: Harvester, pp. 161–64.
Gilbert, Sandra M. and Susan Gubar (1979) *The Madwoman in the Attic: The Woman Writer and the Nineteenth-Century Literary Imagination*, New Haven: Yale University Press.
Hawkes, Ellen (1981) 'Woolf's "Magical Garden of Women"', in Marcus 1981b, pp. 31–60.
Ilie, Paul (1995) 'La cultura posfranquista, 1975–1990: La continuidad dentro de la discontinuidad', in Monleón, José B. (ed.), *Del franquismo a la posmodernidad*, Madrid: Akal, pp. 21–40.
Jacobus, Mary (ed.) (1986) *Reading Woman: Essays in Feminist Criticism*, New York: Columbia University Press.
Janeway, Elizabeth (1980) *Powers of the Weak*, New York: Knopf.
Kristeva, Julia (1986) 'Stabat Mater', in *The Kristeva Reader*, ed. Toril Moi, New York: Columbia University Press, pp. 160–86.
Labanyi, Jo (1995) 'Postmodernism and the Problem of Cultural Identity', in Helen Graham and Jo Labanyi (eds), *Spanish Cultural Studies: An Introduction*, Oxford: Oxford University Press, pp. 396–406.
Luckhurst, Nicola (1998) *Bloomsbury in Vogue*, London: Cecil Woolf.
Marcus, Jane (1981a) 'Thinking Back through Our Mothers', in Marcus 1981b, pp. 1–30.
Marcus, Jane (ed.) (1981b) *New Feminist Essays on Virginia Woolf*, Lincoln: University of Nebraska Press.
Marcus, Jane (1987) *Virginia Woolf and Bloomsbury*, London: Macmillan
Marcus, Jane (1988) *Art and Anger: Reading Like a Woman*, Columbus: Ohio State University Press.
Martín Gaite, Carmen (1978) *El cuarto de atrás*, Barcelona: Destino. Translated by Helen R. Lane as *The Back Room*, New York: Columbia University Press, 1983.
Martín Gaite, Carmen (1992) *Desde la ventana*, Madrid: Espasa-Calpe.
Martín Gaite, Carmen (1996) *Nubosidad variable*, Barcelona: Anagrama. Translated by Margaret Jull Costa as *Variable Cloud*, London: Harvill, 1996.
Minow-Pinkney, Makiko (1987) *Virginia Woolf and the Problem of the Subject*, New Brunswick, NJ: Rutgers University Press.
Montero, Rosa (1983) *Te trataré como a una reina*, Barcelona: Seix Barral.
Navajo, Imelda (ed.) (1982) *Doce relatos de mujeres*, Madrid: Alianza Editorial.
Navales, Ana María (1981) *El regreso de Julieta Always*, Barcelona: Bruguera.
Navales, Ana María (1991) *Cuentos de Bloomsbury*, Barcelona: Edhasa.

Navales, Ana María (1992) *Zacarías, rey*, Huelva: El fantasma de la glorieta.
Navales, Ana María (1993) 'Los diarios de Virginia Woolf', *Turia* [Teruel], 26: 33–42.
Navales, Ana María (1995) *Tres mujeres*, Madrid: Huerga y Fierro.
Navales, Ana María (1996a) 'Strachey y Carrington', *Turia* [Teruel], 35–36: 39–45.
Navales, Ana María (1996b) 'Una mirada sobre Virginia Woolf', *Taller de Literatura A. C. E.* [Madrid], 3: 1–7.
Navales, Ana María (1999) 'Las cartas de Virginia Woolf', *Turia* [Teruel], 47–48.
Navales, Ana María (2000) *La lady y su abanico: acercamiento a la literatura femenina del S. XX (De Virginia Woolf a Mary McCarthy)*, Madrid: Sial Ediciones.
Nichols, Geraldine (1989) *Escribir espacio propio: Laforet, Matute, Moix, Tusquets, Riera y Roig por si mismas*, Minneapolis, MN: Institute for the Study of Ideologies and Literature.
Ordóñez, Elizabeth J. (1988) 'Rewriting Myth and History: Three Recent Novels by Women', in Roberto C. Manteiga *et al.* (eds), *Feminine Concerns in Contemporary Spanish Fiction by Women*, Potomac, MD: Scripta Humanística, pp. 6–28.
Ordóñez, Elizabeth J. (1991) *Voices of Their Own: Contemporary Spanish Narrative by Women*, Toronto: Associated University Presses.
Ortiz, Lourdes (1982) *Urraca*, Barcelona: Puntual.
Poole, Roger (1995) *The Unknown Virginia Woolf*, Cambridge: Cambridge University Press.
Riera, Carme (1989) 'Femenino singular: Literatura de mujer', in López, Aurora and María Angeles Pastor (eds), *Crítica y ficción literarias: mujeres españolas contemporáneas*, Granada: Universidad de Granada, Servicio de publicaciones, pp. 25–38.
Rigney, Barbara Hill (1978) *Madness and Sexual Politics in the Feminist Novel*, Madison: University of Wisconsin Press.
Roig, Montserrat (1980a) *¿Tiempo de mujer?*, Barcelona: Plaza y Janés.
Roig, Montserrat (1980b) *L'hora violeta*, Barcelona: edicions 62.
Rosenman, Ellen Bayuk (1986) *The Invisible Presence: Virginia Woolf and the Mother–Daughter Relationship*, Baton Rouge, LA and London: Louisiana State University Press.
Rosenman, Ellen Bayuk (1995) *A Room of One's Own: Women Writers and the Politics of Creativity*, New York: Twayne Publishers.
Scott, Bonnie Kime (1995) *Refiguring Modernism*, Vol. 2, *Postmodern Feminist Readings of Woolf, West and Barnes*, Bloomington: Indiana University Press.
Servodidio, Mirella (ed.) (1987) *Reading for Difference: Feminist Perspectives on Women Novelists of Contemporary Spain. Anales de la Literatura Española Contemporánea (ALEC)* [University of Colorado, Boulder], special issue, 12.1–2.
Showalter, Elaine (1977) *A Literature of Their Own: British Women Novelists from Brontë to Lessing*, Princeton: Princeton University Press.
Stimpson, Catherine R. (1992) 'Woolf's Room, Our Project: The Building of Feminist Criticism', in Bowlby 1992, pp. 162–79.
Tusquets, Esther (1978) *El mismo mar de todos los veranos*, Barcelona: Lumen. Translated by Margaret E. W. Jones as *The Same Sea As Every Summer*, Lincoln: University of Nebraska Press, 1990.
Tusquets, Esther (1985) *Para no volver*, Barcelona: Lumen.
Valls, Fernando (1989) 'La literatura femenina en España: 1975–1989', *Ínsula* [Madrid], 13: 512–13.
Woolf, Virginia (1929) *A Room of One's Own*, London: Hogarth Press.
Woolf, Virginia (1925) *Mrs Dalloway*, London: Hogarth Press.
Woolf, Virginia (1928) *Orlando*, London: Hogarth Press.
Woolf, Virginia (1941) *Between the Acts*, London: Hogarth Press.
Woolf, Virginia (1977) *The Diary of Virginia Woolf*, vol. 1, London: Hogarth Press.
Zavala, Iris M. (1990) *Nocturna mas no funesta*, Madrid: Ateneo Cultural Primero de Mayo.

Chapter 15

Agra, María Xosé (1995) Review of Carmen Blanco, *O contradiscurso das mulleres*, *Anuario de estudios galegos* [Vigo], 193–95.
Agra, María Xosé (1996) 'O pensamento afundiu a súa cana no río: sobre *Orlando* de V. Woolf', *Olisbos* [Santiago de Compostela], 18: 63–66.
Aleixandre, María Pilar (1990) Review of María Xosé Queizán, *Evidencias*, *Festa da palabra silenciada* [Vigo], 7: 136.
Álvarez Lugrís, Alberto (1994) Review of Virginia Woolf, *Cara ó faro (TL)*, *Grial* [Vigo], 121: 118–19.
Álvarez Lugrís, Alberto (1999) 'A traducción do inglés ó galego: proposta de Estilística Comparada' (unpublished doctoral thesis, University of Vigo).
Álvarez Núñez, Sabela (1999) 'Tempo de silencio', *Andaina* [Santiago de Compostela], 23: 45–48.
Auden, W.H. (1966) 'In Memory of W.B. Yeats', in *Collected Shorter Poems, 1925–1957*, London: Faber, pp. 141–43.
Barbeito, Manuel (1999), 'O silencio de Mrs Ramsay: unha nota da subxectividade feminina', in Couceiro, Xosé Luís and others (eds) *Homenaxe ó profesor Camilo Flores*, Santiago de Compostela: Servicio de Publicacións da Universidade de Santiago de Compostela, pp. 33–45.
Barbeito, Manuel, Cristina Blanco and Manuela Palacios (1996) 'El problema del sujeto femenino en *Mrs Dalloway* and *To the Lighthouse*', in Javier Pérez Guerra (ed.) *Proceedings of the XIXth International Conference of AEDEAN*, Vigo: Servicio de Publicacións da Universidade de Vigo, pp. 613–14.
Blanco, Carmen (1985) 'Las literatas', *Festa da palabra silenciada* [Vigo], 2: 13–18.
Blanco, Carmen (1990) 'Sobre o feminismo literario de Rosalía de Castro', *Andaina* [Santiago de Compostela], 20: 27–30.
Blanco, Carmen (1991) *Literatura galega da muller*, Vigo: Xerais.
Blanco, Carmen (1994) *O contradiscurso das mulleres: historia do feminismo*, Vigo: Nigra Ensaio.
Castro, Rosalía de (1859) *La hija del mar*, Vigo: Imprenta de Juan Compañel.
Castro, Rosalía de (1944) 'Las literatas: carta a Eduarda', *Cuadernos de estudios gallegos* [Santiago de Compostela] 1: 127–31.
Castro, Rosalía de (1995) *Daughter of the Sea*, trans. Kathleen March, New York: P. Lang, 1995.
Ciplijauskaité, Biruté (1988) *La novela femenina contemporánea (1970–1985)*, Barcelona: Anthropos.
Corbalán, Carme (1988) 'Das novelas femininas, de mulleres, para mulleres ...', *Andaina* [Santiago de Compostela], 16: 16–17.
Corbalán, Carme (1991a) 'Presencia de Virginia Woolf (no cincuentenário do seu pasamento)', *Andaina* [Santiago de Compostela], 1: 45–46.
Corbalán, Carme (1991b) Review of Carmen Blanco, *Literatura galega da muller*, *Andaina* [Santiago de Compostela], 1: 50–51.
Corbalán, Carme (1996) 'Feminismo e novela feminina', *Andaina* [Santiago de Compostela], 15: 18–22.
Gómez Clemente, Xosé María (1994) Review of Virginia Woolf, *Cara ó faro (TL)*, *Anuario de estudios literarios galegos* [Vigo], 179.
Herrera Garrido, Francisca (1920) *Néveda*, La Coruña: Lit. e Imp. Roel.
Lojo, Laura (1997a) 'O camiño cara a unha biografía definitiva: *Virginia Woolf. A Biography* de Hermione Lee', *Boletín galego de literatura* [Santiago de Compostela], 17: 89–97.
Lojo, Laura (1997b) Review of Gillian Beer, *Virginia Woolf: The Common Ground*, *Boletín galego de literatura* [Santiago de Compostela], 18: 159–62.

Lojo, Laura (1997c) 'Three Stories by Virginia Woolf: An Approach' (unpublished MA dissertation, University of Santiago de Compostela).

Lojo, Laura (1997d) 'Virginia Woolf's "Monday or Tuesday": An Approach', *Babel: AFIAL* [Vigo], 6: 107–22.

Lojo, Laura (1998a) Review of J. Kirkpatrick and Stuart N. Clarke, *A Bibliography of Virginia Woolf, Boletín galego de literatura* [Santiago de Compostela], 20: 116–19.

Lojo, Laura (1998b) Review of Peter Stansky, *On or about December 1910: Early Bloomsbury and Its Intimate World, Boletín galego de literatura* [Santiago de Compostela], 20: 129–33.

March, Kathleen (1994) '¿Que é a crítica literaria feminista? Unha perspectiva norteamericana', *Festa da palabra silenciada* [Vigo], 10: 71–75.

Marder, Herbert (1979) *Feminismo y arte: un estudio sobre Virginia Woolf*, trans. Rosa Aguilar, Madrid; Bogotá: Debate-Pluma. Translation of *Feminism and Art: A Study of Virginia Woolf*, Chicago, IL; London: University of Chicago Press, 1968.

Martín Casalderrey, Pilar (1996) Review of Ana María Navales, *Tres mujeres: cuentos, Festa da palabra silenciada* [Vigo], 12: 107.

Míguez Ben, Manuel (1974) 'Análisis de la estructura de *Mrs Dalloway, To the Lighthouse* y *The Waves* de Virginia Woolf' (unpublished doctoral thesis, University of Santiago de Compostela).

Misiego, Micaela (1969) 'Encol da moderna novela psicolóxica', *Grial* [Vigo], 7: 261–78.

Mouriz, Isabel (1986) 'As narradoras galegas', *Festa da palabra silenciada* [Vigo], 3: 14–16.

Navales, Ana María (1995) *Tres mujeres: cuentos*, Madrid: Huerga & Fierro Editores.

Newmark, Peter (1993) *Manual de traducción*, trans. Francisco Xabier Fernández Polo, Santiago de Compostela: Servicio de Publicacións da Universidade de Santiago de Compostela. Translation of *A Textbook of Translation*, Hemel Hempstead: Prentice Hall International, 1987.

Noia, María Camino (1983) 'Literatura galega de mulleres', *Festa da palabra silenciada* [Vigo], 1: 7–9.

Otero Pedrayo, Ramón (1992) *Devalar*, ed. María do Carme Ríos Panisse, Vigo: Galaxia. First published, Santiago de Compostela: Editorial Nós, 1935.

Palacios González, Manuela (1982) 'Short Narrative by Virginia Woolf' (unpublished MA dissertation, University of Santiago de Compostela).

Palacios González, Manuela (1990) 'Virginia Woolf: a teima da aveleira', *Grial* [Vigo], 108: 499–505.

Palacios González, Manuela (1992) *Virginia Woolf y la pintura*, Santiago de Compostela: Servicio de Publicacións da Universidade de Santiago.

Palacios González, Manuela (1996a) 'Some Considerations on the Translation of Virginia Woolf's *To the Lighthouse* into Galician', in Fernández-Corugedo, S.G. (ed.) *Some Sundry Wits Gathered Together*, La Coruña: Servicio de Publicacións da Universidade da Coruña, pp. 177–81.

Palacios González, Manuela (1996b) 'V. Woolf's *To the Lighthouse*: A Portrait of the Artist as a Young Woman', *Babel: AFIAL* [Vigo], 3–4–5: 47–56.

Palacios González, Manuela (1999a) 'The Linguistic Politics of Translation: Translating Woolf into Galician', *Virginia Woolf Miscellany*, 54: 8–9.

Palacios González, Manuela (1999b) '*Ut Pictura Poesis*: impresionismo y postimpresionismo en *The Waves*, de Virginia Woolf', in Couceiro, Xosé Luís and others (eds) *Homenaxe ó profesor Camilo Flores*, Santiago de Compostela: Servicio de Publicacións da Universidade de Santiago de Compostela, pp. 569–77.

Pallarés, Pilar (1984) *Sétima Soidade*, Ferrol: Sociedad de cultura Valle-Inclán.

Queizán, María Xosé (1965) *A orella no buraco*, Vigo: Galaxia.

Queizán, María Xosé (1983) 'Sen que as visagras', *Festa da palabra silenciada* [Vigo], 1: 20–21.

Queizán, María Xosé (1989) 'Feminismo y epicureísmo' in *Evidencias*, Vigo: Xerais, pp. 171–87.
Queizán, María Xosé (1998) '¿Por qué un monográfico sobre arquitectura e urbanismo?' *Festa da palabra silenciada* [Vigo], 14: 8–10.
Ríos Panisse, María do Carme (1992) Introduction, Notes and Appendix to Ramón Otero Pedrayo, *Devalar*, Vigo: Galaxia, pp. 7–76, 81–247, 249–313.
Rodríguez, Luciano and Teresa Seara (eds) (1997) *Para saír do século: nova proposta poética*, Vigo: Xerais.
Rodríguez García, María V. (1992) 'El fantasma victoriano en la obra de Virginia Woolf', in *Xornadas de psiquiatría, psicoanálise e literatura*, Ourense: Asociación Galega de Saúde Mental, pp. 17–26.
Salgado, Xosé M. (1993) Review of Carmen Blanco, *Literatura Galega da Muller, Boletín galego de literatura* [Santiago de Compostela], 10: 107–08.
Sobrino Manzanares, María Luisa (1974) 'Dolores Padín', in *Gran enciclopedia gallega*, vol. 23, Santiago de Compostela; Gijón: Silverio Cañada.
Valencia, Luz (1991) 'O concepto do tempo e o cambio en *Entreactos* de Virginia Woolf', *Festa da palabra silenciada* [Vigo], 8: 89–91.
Woolf, Virginia (1929) *La Promenade au phare* (*TL*), trans. Maurice Lanoire, Paris: Stock.
Woolf, Virginia (1931) *Orlando*, trans. Charles Mauron, Paris: Stock.
Woolf, Virginia (1938) *Three Guineas*, London: Hogarth Press.
Woolf, Virginia (1966) 'The Narrow Bridge of Art', in *Collected Essays*, ed. Leonard Woolf, London: Hogarth Press, 1966, 2: 218–29.
Woolf, Virginia (1976) 'Women Novelists', in *Contemporary Writers*, New York; London: Harcourt Brace Jovanovich, pp. 24–27.
Woolf, Virginia (1977) *Orlando*, trans. Jorge Luis Borges, Barcelona: Edhasa.
Woolf, Virginia (1978) *Al Faro* (*TL*), trans. Carmen Martín Gaite, Barcelona: Edhasa.
Woolf, Virginia (1980) *Una habitación propia* (*ROO*), trans. Laura Pujol, Barcelona: Seix Barral.
Woolf, Virginia (1981a) *Diario de una escritora* (*WD*), trans. Andrés Bosch, Barcelona: Lumen.
Woolf, Virginia (1981b) *Las mujeres y la literatura* (*W&W*), trans. Andrés Bosch, introd. Michèle Barret, Barcelona: Lumen.
Woolf, Virginia (1984a) 'Montaigne', in *The Common Reader: First Series*, ed. Andrew McNeillie, London: Hogarth Press, pp. 58–68.
Woolf, Virginia (1984b) 'On Not Knowing Greek', in *The Common Reader: First Series*, pp. 23–38.
Woolf, Virginia (1992a) *A Room of One's Own*, ed. Morag Schiach, Oxford: Oxford University Press.
Woolf, Virginia (1992b) *To the Lighthouse*, ed. Margaret Drabble, Oxford: Oxford University Press.
Woolf, Virginia (1993) *Cara ó faro* (*TL*), trans., introd. and notes by Manuela Palacios and Xavier Castro, Santiago de Compostela: Sotelo Blanco.
Woolf, Virginia (1999) 'Kew Gardens', trans. Ana Belén López Pérez, in Blanco Outón, Cristina (ed.) *Mulleres fronte ó século XX*, Santiago de Compostela: Editorial Compostela, pp. 29–37.
Zambrano, María (1939) *Filosofía y poesía*, Morelia: Publicaciones de la Universidad.

Chapter 16

CATALAN TRANSLATIONS

BTA
(1989) *Entre els actes,* trans. M. Pera, Barcelona: Edicions 62 & La Caixa.

FB
(1938) *Flush*, trans. R. Cardús, Barcelona: Edicions de la Rosa dels Vents.

MD
(1930) *Mrs Dalloway*, trans. C.-A. Jordana, Badalona: Edicions Proa.

O
(1985) *Orlando*, trans. M.-A. Oliver, Barcelona: Edhasa. Reprint, 1994.

ROO
(1985) *Una cambra propia*, trans. H. Valentí, Barcelona: Grijalbo. Reprint, Barcelona: Deriva, 1996.

Selected essays
(1999) *Dones i literatura*, trans. J. Ainaud, introd. I.-C. Simó. Barcelona: Columna.

TL
(1984) *Al far*, trans. H. Valentí, Barcelona: Edicions Proa.

TW
(1989) *Les ones*, trans. M.-A. Oliver, Barcelona: Edhasa.

TY
(1988) *Els anys*, trans. M.-A. Oliver, Barcelona: Edhasa.

OTHER WOOLF PUBLICATIONS (INCLUDING TRANSLATIONS INTO CASTILIAN AND FRENCH)

(1929a) *Mrs Dalloway* (*TL*), trans. S. David, introd. A. Maurois, Paris: Librairie Stock.
(1929b) *La Promenade au phare* (*TL*), trans. M. Lanoire, Paris: Librairie Stock.
(1946a) *Los años* (*TY*), trans. Pedro Fraga de Porto, Barcelona: Ediciones Lauro.
(1946b) *El cuarto de Jacob* (*JR*), trans. S. Santainés, Barcelona: Ediciones Lauro.
(1947) *Noche y día* (*ND*), trans. Eduardo de Guzmán, Barcelona: Ediciones Lauro.
(1967) *Una habitación propia* (*ROO*), trans. Laura Pujol, Barcelona: Seix Barral
(1968) *The Years*, Harmondsworth: Penguin.
(1973) *To the Lighthouse*, Harmondsworth: Penguin.
(1975) *La señora Dalloway* (*MD*), trans. Andrés Bosch, Barcelona: Lumen.
(1976) *Between the Acts*, London: Hogarth Press.
(1977) *La torre inclinada y otros ensayos* ('The Leaning Tower' and Other Essays), trans. A. Bosch, Barcelona: Lumen.
(1978) *Flush*, Harmondsworth: Penguin.
(1979) *La casa encantada y otros cuentos* (*HH*), trans. A. Bosch, Barcelona: Lumen.

(1980) *Orlando* (*O*), trans. J. L. Borges, Barcelona: Edhasa.
(1981a) *Al faro* (*TL*), trans. A. Marichalar, Barcelona: Edhasa.
(1981b) *The Waves*, London: Granada.
(1987) *Mrs Dalloway*, London: Grafton.
(1995) *A Room of One's Own*, Cambridge: Cambridge University Press.
(1998) *Orlando*, ed. J. H. Stape, Oxford: Blackwell for The Shakespeare Head.

OTHER WORKS CITED

Bell, Quentin (1972) *Virginia Woolf: A Biography*, 2 vols, London: Hogarth Press.
Bell, Quentin (1979, 1980) *Virginia Woolf*, trans. [into Castilian] Marta Pessarrodona, Barcelona: Lumen.
Campillo, Maria (1977) 'Situació i sentit d'*Una mena d'amor* de C.A. Jordana', *Els Marges* [Barcelona], 11 (September), 101–09.
Capmany, Maria-Aurèlia (1971) *Quim/Quima*, Barcelona: Laia.
Capmany, Maria-Aurèlia (1973a) *El feminisme a Catalunya*, Barcelona: Nova Terra.
Capmany, Maria-Aurèlia (1973b) 'Virginia Woolf o la nova realitat', in Virginia Woolf, *Els anys* (*TY*), trans. M.-A. Oliver, Barcelona: Nova Terra, 381–92.
Capmany, Maria-Aurèlia and others (1978) *Dona i societat a la Catalunya actual*, Barcelona: Edicions 62.
Centenari C.A. Jordana 1893–1993 (1993) Barcelona: Generalitat de Catalunya, Departament de Cultura; Institució de les Lletres Catalanes.
El Grup de Bloomsbury (1986) Barcelona: Fundació Caixa de Pensions.
Esquerra, Ramon (1936) *Lectures europees*, Barcelona: Publicacions de La Revista.
Fuster, Joan (1980) *Literatura catalana contemporània*, Barcelona: Edicions Curial. First publ. 1971.
Gallofré i Virgili, Maria Josepa (1991) *L'edició catalana i la censura franquista (1939–1951)*, Barcelona: Publicacions de l'Abadia de Montserrat.
Hurtley, Jacqueline Anne (1983) *La literatura inglesa del siglo XX en la España de la postguerra: la aportación de José Janés* (unpublished PhD thesis, University of Barcelona).
Hurtley, Jacqueline Anne (1986) *Josep Janés: el combat per la cultura*, Barcelona: Edicions Curial.
Hurtley, Jacqueline Anne (1992) *José Janés: editor de literatura inglesa*, Barcelona: Publicaciones y Promociones Universitarias, SA.
Hurtley, Jacqueline Anne (2000) Introduction and notes to Montserrat Roig, *La hora violeta*, Madrid: Castalia.
Jardí, Enric (1967) *Eugeni D'Ors: vida i obra. Barcelona: Aymà SA Editora.*
Jardí, Enric (1986) 'Els de Bloomsbury,' *Avui*, 5 November.
Jordana, Cèsar-August (1925) 'Excursió de plaer pels camins de la prosa', *La Revista* [Barcelona].
Jordana, Cèsar-August (1931) *Una mena d'amor*, Barcelona: Edicions Proa.
Jordana, Cèsar-August (1934) *Resum de literatura anglesa*, Barcelona: Editorial Barcino.
Jordana, Cèsar-August (1971) *El món de Joan Ferrer*, Barcelona: Edicions Proa.
Lee, Hermione (1977) *The Novels of Virginia Woolf*, London: Methuen.
Lessing, Doris (1978) *El cuaderno dorado*, trans. Helen Valentí, Barcelona: Noguer. Castilian translation of *The Golden Notebook*, London: Michael Joseph; New York: Simon & Schuster, 1962.
Lodge, David (1977) *The Modes of Modern Writing*, London: Edward Arnold.
McNerney, Kathleen and Cristina Enríquez de Salamanca (eds) (1994) *Double Minorities of Spain*, New York: MLA.
Manent, Albert (1984) *Escriptors i editors del Nou-cents*, Barcelona: Edicions Curial.

Manent, Marià (1934) *Notes sobre literatura estrangera*, Barcelona: Edicions de La Revista.
Marcus, Laura (1997) *Virginia Woolf*, Plymouth: Northcote House in association with The British Council.
Nichols, Geraldine C. (1989) *Escribir, espacio propio: Laforet, Matute, Moix, Tusquets, Riera y Roig por si mismas*, Minneapolis, MN: Institute for the Study of Ideologies and Literature.
Oliver, Maria-Antònia (1985) *Punt d'arròs*, Barcelona: Kapel.
Oliver, Maria-Antònia (1992) *Joana E*, Barcelona: Edicions 62.
Pérez, Janet (1993) 'Maria-Aurèlia Capmany's *Quim/Quima*: Apocalyptic and Millenial Context, Text and Subtext', in Martí-Olivella, J. (ed.) 'Women, History and Nation in the Works of Montserrat Roig and Maria-Aurèlia Capmany,' *Catalan Review* [Barcelona], 7.2, 91–103.
Pessarrodona, Marta (1982) 'En el centenari de Virginia Woolf: un comentari', *Serra D'Or* [Barcelona], 268, 37–39.
Pessarrodona, Marta (1983) 'Virginia Woolf', *Guies de lectura* [Barcelona], 2 (June).
Pessarrodona, Marta (1989) 'Virginia Woolf: últim acte', in Virginia Woolf, *Entre els actes*, trans. Marta Pera, Barcelona: Edicions 62; La Caixa.
R. B. (1991) 'Traduccions a la postguerra', *El País*: *Quadern* [Barcelona] [Thursday Supplement in Catalan], 28 March, 8.
Richards, I.A. (1964) *Lectura y crítica*, by H. Valentí, Barcelona: Seix Barral. Castilian translation of *Practical Criticism: A Study of Literary Judgment*, London: Kegan Paul, 1929.
Riera, C. (1986) 'Una tarde en Bloomsbury,' *Quimera*, 57, 12–21.
Sagarra, Josep M. (1925) 'La por a la novel.la', *La Publicitat* [Barcelona], 26 April.
Simó, Isabel-Clara (1999) Introduction to Virginia Woolf, *Dones i literatura*, trans. J. Ainaud, Barcelona: Columna.
Threlfall, M. (1996) 'Feminist Politics and Social Change in Spain', in *Mapping the Women's Movement*, London; New York: Verso in association with New Left Books, 115–51.
Valentí, Helena (1977) *L'amor adult*, Barcelona: Edicions 62.
Vallverdú, Francesc (1988) 'Els problemes de la traducció', in Arnau, C. and others, *Una aproximació a la literatura catalana universal*, Barcelona: Fundació Caixa de Pensions, 1988.
Xirinacs, Olga (1985) *Al meu cap una llosa*, Barcelona: Edicions Proa.
Yates, Alan (1984) *Una generació sense novel.la?* Barcelona: Edicions 62, first pub. 1975.

Chapter 17

PORTUGUESE TRANSLATIONS

BTA

(1991) *Entre os actos: romance*, trans. Isabel de Freitas Lopes, Lisbon: Cotovia.
(1992) *Entre os actos*, trans. Lucília Rodrigues, Mem Martins: Europa-América.

D

(1985–87) *Diário: 1927–1941*, selected and trans. Maria José Jorge, 2 vols, Lisbon: Bertrand.

FB

(1987) *Flush: uma biografia*, trans. Maria de Lourdes Guimarães, introd. Fernando Guimarães, Porto: Afrontamento.

HH
(1988) *A casa assombrada*, trans. Miguel Serras Pereira, Lisbon: Relógio d'Água.
(1995) *A casa assombrada e outros contos*, trans. Lucília Rodrigues, Mem Martins: Europa-América.

JR
(1989) *O quarto de Jacob: romance*, trans. Maria Teresa Guerreiro, Lisbon: Cotovia.
(1992) *O quarto de Jacob*, trans. Lucília Rodrigues, Mem Martins: Europa-América.

MD
(1954) *Mrs Dalloway*, trans. Mário Quintana, Lisbon: Livros do Brasil. Reprinted, Amadora: Ibis, 1970; Lisbon: Livros do Brasil, 1992.
(1982) *Mrs Dalloway*, trans. Ricardo Alberty, Lisbon: Ulisseia.
(1996) *Mrs Dalloway*, trans. Lucília Rodrigues, Mem Martins: Europa-América.

MDP
(1990) *A festa de Mrs Dalloway: uma sequência de contos*, ed. and introd. Stella McNichol, trans. Mário Avelar, Lisbon: Cotovia.

O
(1962) *Orlando*, trans. Cecília Meireles, Lisbon: Livros do Brasil. Reprinted, Rio de Janeiro: Bruguera, 1969; Lisbon: Livros do Brasil, 1988.
(1991) *Orlando*, trans. Lucília Rodrigues, Mem Martins: Europa-América.
(1994) *Orlando: uma biografia*, trans. Ana Luísa Faria, Lisbon: Relógio d'Água.

ROO
(1978) *Um quarto que seja seu*, introd. Maria Isabel Barreno, trans. Maria Emília Ferros Moura, Lisbon: Vega.

Selected essays
(1985) *O momento total: ensaios*, introd. and trans. Luísa Maria Rodrigues Flora, Lisbon: Ulmeiro.

Selected letters
(1994) *Cartas íntimas a Vita Sackville-West*, trans. Ana Fontes, Sintra: Colares Editora.

Selected short stories
(1951) *Antologia do conto moderno*, selected, trans. and introd. Manuela Porto, Coimbra: Atlântida.
(1996) *O vestido novo*, trans. Lucília Rodrigues, Mem Martins: Europa-América.

TG
(1978) *Os três guinéus*, trans. Maria Emília Ferros Moura, Lisbon: Vega.

TL
(1985) *Rumo ao farol*, trans. Mário Claúdio, Porto: Afrontamento.
(1992) *Rumo ao farol*, trans. Lucília Rodrigues, Mem Martins: Europa-América.

TW
(1988) *As ondas*, trans. Francisco Vale, Lisbon: Relógio d'Água.
(1992) *As ondas*, trans. Lucília Rodrigues, Mem Martins: Europa-América.

TY

(1983) *Os anos: a história de uma família*, trans. Pedro Elston, Lisbon: Moraes. Reprinted, Lisbon: Relógio d'Água, 1992.

VO

(1995) *A viagem*, trans. Lucília Rodrigues, Mem Martins: Europa-América.

OTHER WORKS CITED

Abranches, Graça (1980) 'Re-lendo *A Room of One's Own*: onde se conta de mudas que ouvem, surdos que falam e mudas que aprenderam a falar', *Revista crítica de ciências sociais* [Coimbra], 4–5, 128–56.

Barreno, Maria Isabel, Maria Teresa Horta and Maria Velho da Costa (1972) *Novas Cartas Portuguesas*, Lisbon: Estúdios Cor. Translated as *New Portuguese Letters*, trans. Helen R. Lane, Faith Gillespie and Suzette Macedo, London: Gollancz, 1975.

Barreno, Maria Isabel (1978) 'Prefácio', in Virginia Woolf, *Um quarto que seja seu* (*ROO*), trans. Maria Emília Ferros Moura, Lisbon: Vega, pp. 7–13.

Barreno, Maria Isabel (1979) *A morte da mãe*, Lisbon: Moraes.

Braga, Maria Ondina (1980) 'Virginia Woolf', in *Mulheres escritoras*, Lisbon: Bertrand, pp. 201–17.

Braga, Maria Ondina (1982) 'Evocação de Manuela Porto – no centenário de Virginia Woolf', *Diário de notícias* [Lisbon], 24 June.

Costa, Maria Velho (1969) *Maina Mendes*, Lisbon: Moraes.

Costa, Maria Velho (1973) *desescrita*, Porto: Afrontamento.

Costa, Maria Velho (1998) *Missa in Albis*, Lisbon: Dom Quixote.

Costa, Maria Velho (2000a) ' "A Arte é a Vida": entrevista de Alexandra Lucas Coelho', in *Público Leituras* [Lisbon], 1 July, 1–3.

Costa, Maria Velho (2000b) *Irene ou o contrato social*, Lisbon: Dom Quixote.

Costa, Maria Velho (2000c) 'Esta cidade!' (interview by Rodrigues da Silva), in *Jornal de Letras* [Coimbra], 31 May, 22–23.

Cunha, Maria Helena Ribeiro da (1965) 'Woolf, Mansfield e Irene Lisboa', *Diário de Lisboa* [Lisbon], 18 February.

Díaz-Diocaretz, Myriam (1993) ' "La palavra no olvida de dónde vino": para una poética dialógica de la diferencia', in Díaz-Diocaretz, Myriam and Iris M. Zavala (eds) *Breve historia feminista de la literatura española (en lengua castellana)*, vol. 1, *Teoría feminista: discursos y diferencia*, Madrid: Anthropos, pp. 77–124.

Fiadeiro, Maria Antónia (1999) 'A exposição de livros escritos por mulheres na Sociedade Nacional de Belas Artes, Lisboa, 1947', in Cova, Anne and Maria Beatriz Nizza da Silva (eds), *As mulheres e o Estado*, Lisbon: Universidade Aberta, pp. 91–134.

Horta, Maria Teresa (1985) 'Livro do mês: *Um quarto que seja seu* de Virginia Woolf', *Mulheres* [Lisbon], 89: 66.

Kirkpatrick, B. J and Stuart N. Clarke (1997) *A Bibliography of Virginia Woolf*, 4th edn, Oxford: Clarendon Press.

Lloyd, Michael Gordon (1985) 'As origens de um romance', in Virginia Woolf, *Rumo ao Farol* (*TL*), trans. Mário Cláudio, Porto: Afrontamento, pp. 7–13.

Lourenço, Eduardo (1984) *Envoi et adieu à Madeleine: divagation autour d'un amour rêvé*, Paris: Fondation Calouste Gulbenkian: Centre Culturel Portugais.

Lourenço, Eduardo (1993) *O canto do signo: existência e literatura (1957–1993)*, Lisbon: Presença.

Meireles, Cecília (1962) Preface, in Virginia Woolf, *Orlando*, Lisbon: Livros do Brasil, pp. 5–9.

Muir, Edwin (1937) Review of *TY*, *The Listener*, 31 March, 622.
Nicolson, Nigel (1992) *Retrato de um casamento*, trans. Maria Eduarda Correia, Lisbon: Círculo de Leitores. Translation of *Portrait of a Marriage*, London: Weidenfeld & Nicolson, 1973.
Owen, Hilary (1995) '*Um quarto que seja seu*: The Quest for Camões's Sister', *Portuguese Studies* [London], 11: 179–91.
Pessoa, Fernando (1993) '[Para uma teoria da tradução – 2]', in Lopes, Teresa Rita (ed.) *Pessoa inédito*, Lisbon: Livros Horizonte, pp. 220–21.
Pintasilgo, Maria de Lurdes (1980) 'Pré-Prefácio' and 'Prefácio', in Barreno, Maria Isabel, Maria Teresa Horta and Maria Velho da Costa, *Novas Cartas Portuguesas*, 3rd edn, Lisbon: Moraes Editores, pp. 7–28.
Porto, Manuela (1947) *Virginia Woolf: o problema da mulher nas letras*, Lisbon: Cadernos da *Seara Nova*.
Porto, Manuela (1951) 'Prefácio', in *Virginia Woolf*, ed. and trans. Manuela Porto, Coimbra: Atlântida, pp. 7–15.
Quintela, Paulo (1996), *Obras Completas*, vol. 1, *Hölderlin e outros estudos*, Lisbon: Fundação Calouste Gulbenkian.
Rocha, Ilídio (ed.) (1998) *Dicionário cronológico de autores portugueses*, vol. 4, Lisbon: Publicações Europa-América.
Rodrigues, Armindo (1998) *Um poeta recorda-se: memórias de uma Vida*, Lisbon: Cosmos.
Santos, Maria Irene Ramalho de Sousa (1998) 'Re-inventing Orpheus: Women and Poetry Today', *Portuguese Studies* [London], 14: 122–37.
Santos, Maria Irene Ramalho de Sousa (2001) 'A sogra de Rute ou intersexualidades', in Santos, Boaventura de Sousa (ed.), *Globalização: Fatalidade ou Utopia?*, Porto: Afrontamento, pp. 525–55.
Sena, Jorge de (1959–60) 'Prefácio e Notas' and chapters in 'O Período 1900–1960', in Ward, A. C. (ed.), *História da Literatura Inglesa*, Lisbon: Estúdios Cor.
Sena, Jorge de (1986) *Inglaterra revisitada*, Lisbon: Edições 70.
Sena, Jorge de (1992) 'Anglicismo' 1971, in *Amor e outros verbetes*, Lisbon: Edições 70, pp. 74–88.
Simões, João Gaspar (1981) *Crítica IV: Contistas, novelistas e outros prosadores contemporâneos 1942–1979*, Lisbon: Imprensa Nacional/Casa da Moeda.
Vale, Fernando (1984) 'Virginia Woolf: viajante solitária de regiões desconhecidas', in Virginia Woolf, *A casa assombrada e outros contos* (*HH*), trans. Miguel Serras Pereira, Lisbon: Relógio d'Agua, pp. 91–100.
Woolf, Virginia (1968) 'The Russian Point of View', in *Collected Essays*, London: Hogarth Press, 1: 238–46.

Chapter 18

The Hogarth Press

ARCHIVAL SOURCES

BL: Koteliansky Papers, British Library
HP: Hogarth Press files, University of Reading Library
MHP: Monks House Papers, University of Sussex Library

BOOKS

Abel, Elizabeth (1989) *Virginia Woolf and the Fictions of Psychoanalysis*, Chicago: University of Chicago Press.

Appignanesi, Lisa and John Forrester (1992) *Freud's Women*, London: Weidenfeld and Nicolson.

Baudelaire, Charles (1964) *The Painter of Modern Life and Other Essays*, trans. and ed. Jonathan Mayne, London: Phaidon.

Benjamin, Walter (1969) 'The Task of the Translator', in his *Illuminations*, trans. Harry Zohn, New York: Schocken.

Caws, Mary Ann and Sarah Bird Wright (2000) *Bloomsbury and France: Art and Friends*, Oxford: Oxford University Press.

Freud, Martin (1957) *Glory Reflected*, London: Angus & Robertson.

Freud, Sigmund (1919h) 'The Uncanny', in *The Standard Edition of the Complete Psychological Works of Sigmund Freud* (trans. and ed. James Strachey), vol. 17, London: Hogarth Press and the Institute of Psychoanalysis.

Garnett, Richard (1991) *Constance Garnett: A Heroic Life*, London: Sinclair-Stevenson.

Gay, Peter (1988) *Freud: A Life for Our Time*, London: J. M. Dent.

Hall, Murray G. (1988) 'The Fate of the Internationaler Psychoanalytischer Verlag', in Timms, Edward and Naomi Segal (eds) *Freud in Exile: Psychoanalysis and Its Vicissitudes*, New Haven: Yale University Press, pp. 90–108.

Harrison, Jane Ellen (1925) *Reminiscences of a Student's Life*, London: Hogarth Press.

Hyde, G. M. (1981) *D. H. Lawrence and the Art of Translation*, London: Macmillan.

Jacobus, Mary (1986) *Reading Woman: Essays in Feminist Criticism*, London: Methuen.

Jones, Ernest (1957) *Sigmund Freud: Life and Work*, vol. 3, London: Hogarth Press.

Lemon, Lee T. and Marion J. Reis (1965) *Russian Formalist Criticism: Four Essays*, Lincoln: University of Nebraska Press.

Majumdar, Robin and Allen McLaurin (1975) *Virginia Woolf: The Critical Heritage*, London: Routledge & Kegan Paul.

Marcus, Laura (1996) 'Virginia Woolf and the Hogarth Press', in Willison, Ian, Warwick Gould and Warren Chernaik, *Modernist Writers in the Marketplace*, London: Macmillan, pp. 124–50.

Mirsky, D. S. (1930) *Jane Ellen Harrison and Russia*, Cambridge: Heffer.

Muchnic, Helen (1969) *Dostoevsky's English Reputation, 1881–1936*, New York: Octagon.

Paskauskas, R. Andrew (ed.) (1993) *The Complete Correspondence of Sigmund Freud and Ernest Jones 1908–1939*, Cambridge: Harvard University Press.

Riviere, Joan (1991) *The Inner World and Joan Riviere*, ed. Athol Hughes, London: Karnac.

Sayers, Dorothy (1988) *Gaudy Night*, Sevenoaks: Hodder & Stoughton.

Spotts, Frederic (ed.) (1989) *Letters of Leonard Woolf*, London: Bloomsbury.

Strachey, James and Alix Strachey (1985) *Bloomsbury/Freud: The Letters of James and Alix Strachey*, ed. Perry Meisel and Walter Kendrick, New York: Basic Books.

Timms, Edward and Naomi Segal (eds) (1988) *Freud in Exile: Psychoanalysis and Its Vicissitudes*, New Haven: Yale University Press.

Willis, J. H. (1992) *Leonard and Virginia Woolf as Publishers: The Hogarth Press 1917–41*, Charlottesville: University Press of Virginia.

Woolf, Leonard (1980) *An Autobiography*, vol. 2, *1911–1969*, Oxford: Oxford University Press.

Zytaruk, George (ed.) (1970) *The Quest for Rananim: D. H. Lawrence's Letters to S. S. Koteliansky, 1914–1930*, Montreal: McGill-Queen's University Press.

Index

Note: There is no entry for Virginia Woolf herself in the index. Specific aspects of her life and work appear as separate entries, as do the titles of her works. The titles are identified by her name in parentheses; the entries also include the abbreviations used throughout the text and listed on p. xxxvii. See also the entries under 'essays' and 'short stories'.